American
Political Leaders

American
Political Leaders

RICHARD L. WILSON

☑® Facts On File, Inc.

American Political Leaders

Copyright © 2002 by Richard L. Wilson

Facts On File, Inc.
132 West 31st Street
New York NY 10001

Library of Congress Cataloging-in-Publication Data

Wilson, Richard L., 1944-
    American political leaders / by Richard L. Wilson.
        p. cm.—(American biographies)
Summary: Profiles of major figures in American politics, from Bella Abzug through Woodrow Wilson, arranged alphabetically, by area of activity, and by year of birth. Includes bibliographical references (p.) and index.
    ISBN 0-8160-4536-4
    1. Politicians—United States—Biography. 2. Statesmen—United States—Biography. 3. United States—Biography. 4. United States—Politics and government. [1. Politicians. 2. Statesmen. 3. United States—Biography. 4. United States—Politics and government.] I. Title. II. Series.
    E176 .W75 2002
    973'.09'9—dc21   2002001293

You can find Facts On File on the World Wide Web at http://www.factsonfile.com

Text design by Joan M. Toro
Cover design by Cathy Rincon

Printed in the United States of America

VB Hermitage 10 9 8 7 6 5 4 3 2 1

This book is printed on acid-free paper.

To my mother

CONTENTS

Note on Photos

Many of the illustrations and photographs used in this book are old, historical images. The quality of the prints is not always up to modern standards, as in some cases the originals are from glass negatives or are damaged. The content of the illustrations, however, made their inclusion important despite problems in reproduction.

LIST OF ENTRIES

AUTHOR'S NOTE

This reference work aims to provide students and general readers with a concise, readable guide to present and past leaders in U.S. politics. Those included in these profiles are presidents, vice presidents, major party candidates for president, significant third party presidential candidates, Supreme Court justices, Speakers of the U.S. House of Representatives, Senators, Representatives, cabinet officers, significant agency heads, and diplomats. A number of colonial and Revolutionary War figures—and the most significant representatives of the Confederate States of America—are also included. The most important of the women who have served the nation as first ladies are included if their service has had a significant political component.

The people selected to have their profiles included were chosen based on a review of the most important political leaders mentioned in secondary and college textbooks in U.S. history and political science. For contemporary leaders not yet widely mentioned in such textbooks, a review of newspaper and media files was used to determine the names of those political leaders who are most widely mentioned.

The headnote for each profile contains the individual's name, the birth and death dates, and the most important political offices that he or she held (or aspired to in the case of unsuccessful candidates). Based on the appropriate authoritative sources consulted, each entry aims to provide concise, accurate data about the person's life. Although brief biographical sketches cannot be comprehensive biographies, I have included colorful facts or personal information to add some human depth to the study of each person wherever possible. Since the entries are intended as starting points for further study, I have included an extensive further reading list for each entry. Wherever possible, reliable Internet sources are also provided, but only if the Internet source is truly authoritative.

A simple cross-referencing system is used whereby SMALL CAPITALS designate a person mentioned in a profile who has been given a separate entry.

Black and white portraits or photographs have been included for almost 60 of the more than 250 individuals profiled in this work.

The people profiled are indexed by various categories of the offices they held and by the decade in which they were born. Those indexes are found at the back of the book.

The author is grateful for the excellent assistance and guidance of Nicole Bowen as the project editor for this work. Her patience with frustrating computer failures is truly appreciated.

ACKNOWLEDGMENTS

The author gratefully acknowledges the assistance of the staff of the Library of Congress, the University of Tennessee at Chattanooga, and the Nobles County (Minnesota) Public Library and Information Center.

INTRODUCTION

American Political Leaders includes more than 250 profiles of men and women in the United States who have demonstrated their political leadership primarily by being elected, nominated, or appointed to significant—primarily national—governmental offices in the United States, or what is now the United States.

Included here are the profiles of all presidents. Not all presidents are equally great political leaders, but all of them would be included in any list of 250 political leaders simply because of the leadership required to gain election (or appointment in the case of GERALD RUDOLPH FORD) to that office. In some cases, such as that of WILLIAM HENRY HARRISON, who served so briefly before his death 30 days into his term, his prior record of public service justifies his inclusion. This is even truer for the immensely talented JAMES ABRAM GARFIELD, who served only a few short months before an assassin killed him; he accomplished much during the first few months in office and had a distinguished career before he was elected as president.

Since all who have held the office of president are included, those vice presidents who were elevated to the presidency upon the death or resignation of a president are also included. Several additional vice presidents are included if their service before or after election to the vice presidency was especially significant. If their vice presidency was marked by some special circumstance, they were also included. JOHN CALDWELL CALHOUN was included because of his long distinguished Senate career and experience as a cabinet officer. Calhoun was one of only two vice presidents who served

under two different presidents and was also one of only two vice presidents to resign. While Calhoun resigned because of his principled differences with President ANDREW JACKSON, the second vice president to resign, SPIRO THEODORE AGNEW, did so because he was about to be indicted for criminal activity. Some vice presidents passed their tenure unremarkably, and they are not included. This office alone was deemed not sufficiently important to merit inclusion of all its occupants.

The most significant unsuccessful major party candidates for president are also included, as well as significant third party presidential candidates, but the evaluation of their contribution is necessarily subjective. WILLIAM JENNINGS BRYAN and BARRY MORRIS GOLDWATER each ran unsuccessfully for the presidency as his party's nominee, but both were voices for significant political movements whose objectives were not realized immediately, but whose presence was felt far beyond the season in which they were candidates.

Bryan served only two short terms in the House of Representatives, and then late in life, a brief period as THOMAS WOODROW WILSON's secretary of state. However, the intensity of Bryan's 1896 campaign, the fact that his devoted Democratic rank-and-file followers nominated him for president three times (Bryan was the only loser thrice nominated), and the impact of his political agenda on the decades to come all are clear indications of his political leadership. Goldwater served a much longer time in the U.S. Congress, where he was elected to five full terms. His loss in 1964 was much greater than any of Bryan's three losses, but Goldwater similarly had a political impact on the Republican Party and its national agenda for decades after his race.

HENRY CLAY, STEPHEN ARNOLD DOUGLAS, ADLAI EWING STEVENSON, and DANIEL WEBSTER had significant political careers beyond their races for president, but they also had an impact on the national political agenda beyond the brief periods in which they ran. Many unsuccessful candidates for president were also political leaders during their service in the U.S. Congress.

Many important U.S. political leaders held a seat in either the House of Representatives or the Senate as their only political base. Several Speakers of the U.S. House of Representatives are included, particularly if they led movements to reform the House or defended its traditions against insurgents. Only one Speaker, JAMES KNOX POLK, has ever been elected president, but several others have been significant political leaders either over their long tenure in the office (SAMUEL TALIAFERRO RAYBURN) or because of the intensity of their leadership over a much shorter period of time (NEWTON LEROY GINGRICH).

The Senate lacks any figure with the status of Speaker since its presiding officer is the vice president, but the majority party in the Senate does elect its Senate majority leader. Several of these have been genuine political leaders (e.g., MICHAEL JOSEPH MANSFIELD) and one significant Senate majority leader (LYNDON BAINES JOHNSON) became president. Because the Senate has a higher public profile and a longer term, it has been the home to several significant leaders whose only national office was a seat in the Senate.

One does not have to be, or seek to be, elected to a governmental office to be a significant political leader. The increasing importance of the Supreme Court, not just as the final arbiter of political issues that take the form of legal questions but also as the creator of the national political agenda, shows the impact of several leaders who never ran for any office. They nonetheless had the ear of the nation as the result of their appointment to the Supreme Court. For this reason, the most significant of all the justices on the Supreme Court are included. The list is perhaps top-heavy with those who served as chief justice. Although the

chief justice of the Supreme Court (whose official constitutional title is chief justice of the United States) has no greater vote than that of any associate justice, tradition has given the position a more significant voice. Some chief justices have used it effectively, while others have not. By the same token, some associate justices have risen to a level of influence by the force of their contributions to equal or exceed some chief justices. Whatever their rank, if their contribution is especially noteworthy, they have been included.

Other appointees who qualify as political leaders are officers in the president's cabinet, a few significant agency heads, and a few diplomats. The overlap between these appointees and the other elected offices is often great (JOHN CALDWELL CALHOUN, WILLIAM HENRY SEWARD, and CORDELL HULL), but a few cabinet officers (ELIHU ROOT, HENRY LEWIS STIMSON, and ROBERT STRANGE MCNAMARA) were never elected to any office.

For some other appointees, it was for their diplomatic service that they should be best remembered. CHARLES FRANCIS ADAMS is included because of his service as the U.S. ambassador to the Court of Saint James (Great Britain), because without his skill in keeping the British from granting diplomatic recognition to the Confederacy, the outcome of the Civil War might have been very different.

The most significant representatives of the Confederate States of America are included, because they were clearly representatives of a substantial portion of what was—and is now once again—a part of the United States, even though they sought for four brief years to try to leave the country.

Similarly, it would be wrong to exclude those political leaders who served the citizens of the United States before the nation existed. A number of colonial and Revolutionary War figures are also included. In these cases, the question of whether the person was elected or appointed is less important during the colonial period.

Among nonelected political leaders, the category of first lady requires special comment. If a first lady qualifies as a political leader, it is nearly always because her spouse has, in one sense or another, "appointed" her to fill that role. The most important of the women who have served the nation as first lady are included if their service has had an especially significant political component beyond the norm for their historical period.

Dolley Madison, Sarah Polk, and Lucy Hayes were significant 19th-century first ladies, but they cannot be said to have changed the overall characteristics of the position, although they were perhaps the best of the traditional first ladies. All first ladies since Jackie Kennedy have played a larger media role than almost any of their predecessors in the 19th and 20th centuries. The media expectations are so much higher now that they are fulfilling an enhanced role, not creating a new one.

ANNA ELEANOR ROOSEVELT is, of course, special. She did change the nature of the role of first lady. Eleanor Roosevelt and Senator HILLARY RODHAM CLINTON are the only two first ladies who held political or governmental office. Senator Clinton is the only first lady to be elected to public office. EDITH GALT WILSON is a special case because of the extraordinary circumstances that surrounded her political role during the incapacity of President THOMAS WOODROW WILSON. After all, offering high-level government appointments to Wilson loyalists over tea at the White House, while the president is incapacitated, is an extraordinary exercise of political power not usually associated with taking tea at 1600 Pennsylvania Avenue.

Since much of U.S. political leadership involves the representation of successive waves of new groups within the U.S. political system, special care has been taken to include the contributions of women, Native Americans, African Americans, Hispanic Americans, whether Cuban, Mexican, or of other national origins, a wide variety of Asian Americans, and representatives of earlier waves of German, Italian, and Irish immigrants to the United States.

Leaders of political groups, organizations, and movements are included if they had a significant political, as opposed to a merely social or religious, component. Some of these political groups, organizations, and movements are no longer important in the current political system but played a major role in the past. Some of those included were leaders of "lost causes." Even if their cause was not successful and their contribution is not readily apparent, the U.S. political system is not a blank slate, and the cumulative impact of the various "lost causes" may still be felt even if it is not quantifiable. Thus, significant socialist and/or communist leaders are included.

Some of those included in *American Political Leaders* may not be remembered in a positive light by history. They began, of course, as legitimate political leaders and only later tarnished their reputations. Spiro Agnew was a 20th-century case. Before his downfall, he had a legitimate political following in the United States. Other leaders, including presidents whose behavior was subject to question, were—for better or worse—important to U.S. history. Learning about all the major historical figures is important, among other reasons, to help citizens recognize questionable behavior in current or future leaders. To paraphrase ABRAHAM LINCOLN, one can fool all of the people some of the time or some of the people all of the time, but one cannot fool all of the people all of the time.

As these profiles of 250-plus important political leaders show, there is great variation. Whether a particular person was significant enough for inclusion became more difficult as one got closer to the least significant of the 250. At that point, who constitutes a political leader, or what constitutes political leadership, is difficult to define objectively. This introduction has tried to demonstrate with concrete examples why various categories of leaders are included.

This work does not contain profiles of those U.S. leaders who should be considered primarily as social, religious, business, educational, scientific, artistic, or literary leaders. Some prominent U.S. leaders, such as Benjamin Franklin or Martin Luther King, Jr., are political leaders in a sense, but their political leadership did not take the form of seeking to hold governmental office (although Franklin did serve in colonial or Revolutionary War legislative bodies and was a diplomat for the fledgling republic). In Franklin's case, his contributions were in so many fields that it is hard to say that the majority of his contribution was political. The best that can be done is to take the stance that THOMAS JEFFERSON did when he arrived in Paris as the American minister to follow Franklin. When Jefferson was asked if he came to Paris to replace Franklin, he responded that no one could replace Franklin, and that he (Jefferson) could only succeed him. Franklin may be too large to categorize. Similarly, Martin Luther King may well be too large to categorize and may be diminished by being considered merely a political leader.

The basic decision rule for inclusion in *American Political Leaders* was whether the person included sought to bring about change principally by seeking to hold, through election or appointment, governmental office.

A

Abzug, Bella Savitsky
(1920–1998) *representative, women's rights leader, author*

Bella Abzug was the first Jewish woman ever elected to the U.S. House of Representatives, the founder of a number of organizations for the advancement of women, and a prominent leader of liberal causes. By the 1970s, she was a household word as a champion of a variety of important political issues.

Born Bella Savitsky on July 24, 1920, in the Bronx, New York, as the daughter of Jewish immigrants from Russia, she graduated from Hunter College in 1942. While in Columbia University Law School, she majored in labor law and was selected as the editor of the *Columbia Law Review*. She graduated from Columbia in 1945 and was admitted to the New York bar in 1947. She married Maurice M. Abzug in 1944, and the couple had two daughters, born in 1949 and 1952.

From 1947 to 1970, Bella Abzug gained a considerable national reputation both as an attorney and as a champion of various liberal causes. Working mainly on a pro bono basis for the American Civil Liberties Union and the Civil Rights Congress, she defended some individuals with liberal political viewpoints in the early 1950s when they were attacked for being Communists by Senator JOSEPH RAYMOND McCARTHY during his anti-Communist crusade against Americans accused of sympathy toward the Soviet Union.

In 1961, Abzug was one of the founders of the Women Strike for Peace, a national organization opposed to U.S. military and foreign policies. She chaired the group from 1961 to 1970, working on disarmament and peace issues. As the United States became more involved in the war in Vietnam in the late 1960s, she led the public protest and supported a variety of antiwar candidates, most notably Senator EUGENE JOSEPH McCARTHY's effort against Democratic incumbent President LYNDON BAINES JOHNSON in the 1968 presidential campaign.

In 1970, she became a candidate herself for the Reform Democratic Party and unseated the Democratic incumbent in the primary for New York City's 19th District. She was elected to the first of three consecutive terms in the U.S. House of Representatives (1971–1977).

Abzug opened her career in Congress with a strong attack on the seniority system that allowed newcomers to advance only very slowly to prestigious committee assignments. She was defeated in her attempt to be named to the powerful House Armed Services Committee and was relegated to the less powerful Government Operations and Public Works Committees. Her protests helped other women, such as SHIRLEY ANITA ST. HILL CHISHOLM, secure better committee assignments and led to a few reforms, but these were not enough to satisfy her and other congressional insurgents.

As a founder and chair of several of the leading U.S. liberal political organizations for women, Abzug supported the Equal Rights Amendment, abortion rights, a woman's right to establish credit, and children's day-care legislation. In 1971, with

Gloria Steinem and Shirley Chisholm, Bella Abzug cofounded the National Women's Political Caucus, which sought to increase the influence and participation of women in government.

Conservative political forces in the New York state legislature sought to defeat her by redrawing her congressional district, but she confounded them by winning reelection from the 20th District in 1972 and 1974. She gave up her seat in the U.S. House of Representatives to run against DANIEL PATRICK MOYNIHAN for the Senate in 1976, but she failed in the primary. In 1977, she lost the primary election for mayor of New York City. In the following year, she was defeated for a vacant congressional seat in a special election.

In 1977, Abzug was prominent in the National Women's Conference at Houston, and President JAMES EARL CARTER appointed her the cochairperson of the National Advisory Committee on Women, but later, in January 1979, Carter dismissed her for her highly publicized criticism of him.

In 1980, she returned to private law practice and continued her political crusade. She led Women USA, a grassroots political action group, contributed to Ms. magazine, and served as a news commentator for the Cable News Network. She was a 1994 inductee to the National Women's Hall of Fame. In 1997, she attended the United Nations Conference on Women in Beijing.

In the 1970s, she was so well known that simply stating her first name, Bella, left no doubt about her identity. She was known by friends and critics alike by such nicknames as "Battling Bella," "Hurricane Bella," and others. A critical part of her prominent political identity was her fondness for wearing large, floppy hats. Anyone who thought this was a sign of frivolity quickly learned of her steely determination—a decisive personal characteristic that highlighted her career.

Abzug died after heart surgery in New York City on March 31, 1998.

Further Reading

Abzug, Bella. Bella! Ms. Abzug Goes to Washington. New York: Saturday Review Press, 1972.

———, and Mim Kelber. Gender Gap: Bella Abzug's Guide to Political Power for American Women. Boston: Houghton Mifflin, 1984.

Faber, Doris. Bella Abzug. New York: Lothrop, Lee & Shepard, 1976.

Witt, Linda, Karen M. Paget, and Glenda Matthews. Running as a Woman: Gender and Power in American Politics. New York: Free Press, 1993.

Acheson, Dean Gooderham
(1893–1971) secretary of state, author

As secretary of state from 1949 to 1953, Dean Acheson was, as the title of his Pulitzer Prize–winning memoirs indicates, Present at the Creation of the U.S. foreign policy of containment against the expansionistic policies of the Soviet Union. He assisted in the creation of the North Atlantic Treaty Organization (NATO) and the 1951 Japanese Peace Treaty, and the prosecution of the Korean War.

Born on April 11, 1893, in Middleton, Connecticut, Dean Gooderham Acheson was educated at Groton and graduated from Yale University in 1915. During World War I, he served in the U.S. Navy briefly. After the war, he returned to Harvard Law School, from which he graduated in 1918. His early prestige is indicated by his service as Associate Supreme Court Justice LOUIS DEMBITZ BRANDEIS's private secretary from 1919 to 1921. Although mainly involved in the practice of corporate and international law from then until 1941, he did work briefly in 1933 as President FRANKLIN DELANO ROOSEVELT's undersecretary of the treasury.

Acheson returned to Washington as assistant secretary of state in 1941 where he lobbied Congress successfully for the Lend-Lease Act, which gave armaments to the British (already at war with Germany). This enactment was a major accomplishment for him because many in the United States were still "isolationists," strongly opposed to giving war materials to the British for fear of involving the United States in the war. After Pearl Harbor was bombed on December 7, 1941, Acheson's actions seemed especially farsighted. His second major wartime success came in 1944 when he helped secure congressional passage of the Bretton Woods Monetary Agreement, the product of an international conference to revalue postwar European currencies and create international bank funds.

Elevated to undersecretary of state in 1945, Acheson was more than merely "present at the creation" of the Truman Doctrine, the most fundamental U.S. foreign policy doctrine from 1945 to 1990; he largely conceived and actively promoted it. He assisted Secretary of State George Catlett Marshall in the development of the major economic assistance program known as the Marshall Plan, which aided in the recovery of European economies as a bulwark against the Communists' appeal.

For these successes, President HARRY S. TRUMAN named Acheson secretary of state in 1949. His greatest achievement as secretary of state was to persuade 10 (later increased to 14) European nations to join Canada and the United States in the North Atlantic Treaty Organization. Initially intended merely to prevent the expansion of the Soviet Union, NATO succeeded so well that it arguably contributed to the demise of the Soviet empire in 1990 and became the premier regional security organization in the aftermath of the cold war.

Acheson was generally less successful in Asia, although he concluded the 1951 Japanese Peace Treaty. The treaty was different from the surrender agreement signed at the end of the war in 1945, for it officially ended World War II in the Far East and allowed Japan to reenter the world community on an equal footing with other nations. Such a treaty might have taken even longer to negotiate, but Acheson was anxious to restore normality to U.S. relations with Japan in an effort to help resist communist expansion by Russia and China in Asia, especially important after the outbreak of the Korean War in 1950.

However well he may have understood Asia, he was unable to persuade either the United States or some major Asian countries to pursue genuine peaceful policies. Despite the visit of the new Indian Prime Minister Jawaharlal Nehru to the United States soon after independence in 1949, the U.S. relationship with India, the world's largest democracy, began poorly. Even worse, although probably no outside force could have prevented Mao Ze-dong's Communists from coming to power in China in 1949, Acheson failed to provide a more cooperative diplomatic attitude to mitigate the growing hostility toward the People's Republic of China.

In 1950, North Korean military forces, instigated by the Russians (but not the Chinese), attacked South Korea across a temporary demarcation line running through the middle of the Korean peninsula. The North Koreans soon clashed with the U.S. military forces stationed there, and the Korean War began. This frustrating war dogged Acheson's tenure as secretary of state. Many of his domestic political opponents blamed him for misleading potential adversaries of the United States as to U.S. determination on Korea. In a speech outlining the U.S. interests in Asia, Acheson omitted any reference to South Korea, thereby implying that the United States would not defend the area and, his critics charged, inviting the Soviet Union to use North Korean proxy forces to take over the South. Whether or not this was truly Acheson's mistake, 1950 marked the beginning of a costly four-year struggle on the Korean peninsula. With the tragic U.S. advance to the Yalu River, the Chinese Communists entered the war and the United States stiffened its Asian policy by taking on the defense commitment of the island of Taiwan.

In retrospect, it is easy to see that Dean Acheson was one of the most important secretaries of state in U.S. history, for he was critical to the development of the U.S. policy of containment of the Soviet Union—the policy in place from 1945 until the collapse of the Soviet empire in the early 1990s.

At the time he held office, he was very controversial. With Acheson's eastern background, immaculate dress, and patrician style, he was a prime target for conservative Republican Party politicians. Some of these, notably Senator JOSEPH RAYMOND McCARTHY, had already started their attacks on purported communist infiltrators in the government for whose continued presence they sought to blame Democrats, such as Truman and Acheson. Acheson was hurt by his stalwart defense of Alger Hiss, whom Republicans accused of being a communist spy in the State Department and who was convicted of perjury for purportedly lying about his spying. Because Senator McCarthy's attacks on the Truman and Eisenhower administrations also included attacks on General George Catlett Marshall, an undoubted hero of World War II and well known for his conservative views, there may have been no way to prevent the rancorous political debate over foreign policy in the late 1940s and early 1950s.

As much a member of an old establishment family as President Franklin Roosevelt, Acheson seemed to epitomize elitism, pro-European internationalism, and Rooseveltian liberalism. Curiously, Acheson candidly admitted that he was not close (personally or politically) to Roosevelt but had great respect for the Midwesterner Truman.

Upon leaving office at the end of the Truman administration in 1953, Acheson returned to the private practice of law, but unofficially he continued to advise presidents and write books until his death on October 12, 1971.

Further Reading

Acheson, Dean Gooderham. *A Democrat Looks at His Party.* Westport, Conn.: Greenwood Press, 1977.
———. *Pattern of Responsibility.* New York: Kelley, 1972.
———. *Present at the Creation: My Years at the State Department.* New York: Norton, 1970.
Brinkley, Douglas. *Dean Acheson: The Cold War Years.* Hartford, Conn.: Yale University Press, 1994.
———. *Dean Acheson and the Making of U.S. Foreign Policy.* New York: St. Martin, 1993.
Harper, John L. *American Visions of Europe: Franklin D. Roosevelt, George F. Kennan, and Dean G. Acheson.* Cambridge, Mass.: Cambridge University Press, 1994.

Adams, Charles Francis
(1807–1886) *diplomat, representative, author*

Charles Francis Adams followed his father, JOHN QUINCY ADAMS, in service in the U.S. House of Representatives, but he earned his highest honor as U.S. ambassador to Great Britain during the Civil War. In line with his position as scion of one of this nation's most distinguished political families, he made his great contribution to the United States by persuading the British not to grant diplomatic recognition to the Confederacy. This was a superb achievement given the long-standing British hostility to the United States, the Confederate courtship of Great Britain, and the fact that British industry was starved for southern cotton as the result of the northern blockade of southern ports.

Born in Boston on August 18, 1807, Charles Francis Adams was the grandson of a president (JOHN ADAMS) and the son of a man who would be president (John Quincy Adams). Because his father was in Europe on diplomatic service during his formative years, Adams was educated abroad by his family until he was 10. He graduated from Harvard in 1825 and "read in the law" in the law office of DANIEL WEBSTER until admitted to the bar in 1829, the same year he married. His father-in-law was a millionaire several times over, and this provided a basis for his career as a writer and politician.

Adams began by serving in the Massachusetts legislature from 1840 to 1845. Beginning as a Whig abolitionist, he became the vice presidential running mate of MARTIN VAN BUREN on the Free-Soil ticket in 1848. Becoming a Republican, he was elected to two terms in Congress in 1858 and 1860. In 1861, President ABRAHAM LINCOLN appointed Adams the ambassador to the Court of Saint James.

Britain's natural inclination was to aid the South in the Civil War because British mills were dependent on the U.S. cotton bottled up in southern ports by the northern naval blockade. The essence of the Adams mission was to keep the British from intervening diplomatically on the side of the South. Having lived in Britain while his father, John Quincy Adams, was a diplomat, he knew the British well and acted in a British manner. His superb diplomacy in this most difficult of posts earned him his greatest accolades.

His first major challenge arose when a Union gunboat stopped the British ship *Trent* and removed two Confederate commissioners on their way to London. British opinion was inflamed, but war was avoided when Adams helped gain the release of the two men.

The more enduring challenge was to limit the building of Confederate warships in British shipyards, which the United States regarded as a violation of international law governing neutrality. Adams was not able to stop all such efforts, but in 1863, he did succeed in blocking the departure of two ironclad vessels that stood a good chance of breaking the northern blockade.

One ship that the British allowed to reach the South was the notorious Confederate raider the *Alabama,* which heavily damaged Union shipping during the war. Although Adams had left his diplomatic post in 1868, he was called back to serve as U.S. commissioner to the international tribunal arbitrating the U.S. claims. Adams won a great diplomatic victory in securing a complete recovery of all direct war claims from the British. Adams's success was especially important since he had to resist more radical claims from some U.S. citizens for all indirect damages caused by the raiders. His skill in focusing on the essential issues and avoiding distracting side skirmishes was critical to his success in one of the most important diplomatic efforts in U.S. history.

Adams spent his career after 1872 writing history books; serving in several civic organizations; editing the papers of his father, grandfather, and grandmother; and writing a biography of his grandfather. He died on November 1, 1886.

Further Reading

Adams, Charles Francis *Diary.* Cambridge, Mass.: Harvard University Press, 1964.

———, ed. *Familiar Letters of John Adams and His Wife, Abigail Adams, During the Revolution.* Boston: Houghton Mifflin, 1898.

———, *Life of John Adams.* New York: Chelsea House, 1980.

———, ed. *Memoirs of John Quincy Adams,* 1874. Reprint, Freeport, N.Y.: Books for Libraries Press, 1969.

———, ed. *The Works of John Adams, Second President of the United States.* Boston: Little, Brown, 1856.

Duberman, Martin B. *Charles Frances Adams, 1807–1886.* Boston: Houghton Mifflin, 1961.

McCulloch, David, *John Adams.* New York: Simon & Schuster, 2001.

Nagel, Paul C. *John Quincy Adams: A Public Life, A Private Life.* New York: Knopf, 1997.

Parsons, Lynn H. *John Quincy Adams.* Madison, Wis.: Madison House, 1998.

———. *John Quincy Adams: A Bibliography.* Westport, Conn.: Greenwood Press, 1993.

Adams, John
(1735–1826) *president, vice president, diplomat, Revolutionary leader, author*

John Adams served the United States as diplomat, first vice president, and second president. Known

John Adams, the second U.S. president and first U.S. vice president, was called the "Atlas of Independence" for his Revolutionary War efforts. *(Library of Congress)*

as the "Atlas of Independence," Adams was a critically important Revolutionary War leader and diplomat. His career was the basis for creating one of the United States's greatest political dynasties; he was the first president to see his son, JOHN QUINCY ADAMS, inaugurated president. Yet his reputation has generally not matched his contributions because he served in the shadow cast by the first president, GEORGE WASHINGTON, and was upstaged by the more charismatic third president, THOMAS JEFFERSON.

Adams was born on October 19, 1735, in Braintree (now Quincy), Massachusetts. Descended from Pilgrims John and Priscilla Alden and other early Massachusetts settlers, he graduated from Harvard in 1755, read law privately, and was admitted to the bar in 1758. He soon established a successful practice in Boston. A conservative upholder of the law, he was not naturally a revolutionary, but the British Stamp Act of 1765 provoked him to draft protest resolutions against this tax on legal documents and newspapers because the colonies had not consented to the tax.

Committed to principle even if unpopular, he agreed to defend the British soldiers accused of killing five Americans in the Boston Massacre. Ironically, his cousin, SAMUEL ADAMS, had instigated these events. Despite the popular outcry over the martyrdom of these five colonists, John Adams successfully defended the soldiers without destroying his own political future. Although a reluctant revolutionary, once convinced that principle dictated independence, Adams was tireless in the cause. Elected to the First and Second Continental Congresses, he served on many important committees. He seconded the motion of RICHARD HENRY LEE to declare independence from Britain.

Although often criticized as vain and ambitious, such judgments must be balanced by his self-effacing actions on many occasions. Appointed to the committee to draft the Declaration of Independence, he generously gave the opportunity to draft this famous document to Thomas Jefferson. In this, he was guided by the notion that the good of the American Revolution depended on having a Virginian write the document since Virginia was the largest colony and in a critical geographic position in the colonies. The same kind of consideration led, in part, to John Adams pressing the Second Continental Congress to appoint George Washington as the commander in chief. Although Adams was sometimes accused of having a difficult personality, this judgment is hard to square with his success as a diplomat in persuading the Dutch to recognize the fledgling republic and grant the former colonies badly needed loans. With Benjamin Franklin and JOHN JAY, Adams also negotiated the favorable terms of the Treaty of Paris that ended the Revolutionary War.

As the U.S. minister, he remained in Britain until 1788 and did not participate in the controversial drafting of the Constitution. Having avoided alienating either one side or the other in the ratification controversy, he was an acceptable candidate for the first vice presidency. He was close to Washington and his Federalist views, but he was not directly in the line of fire during the growing controversies between Thomas Jefferson,

the first secretary of state, and ALEXANDER HAMILTON, the first secretary of the treasury.

In brief, the Jeffersonians, called the Democratic Republicans, were more fearful of the growth of the national government at the expense of the states. In foreign policy, the Jeffersonians supported the French Revolution after 1789 and the French struggles with the European monarchies, including Britain. They had a sentimental attachment to the French as supporters of the American Revolution and had sympathy for the revolutionary cause. The Hamiltonians, called Federalists, favored a strong national government and were fearful enough of the excesses of the French Revolution—the so-called Reign of Terror after 1789—to side with Britain against the French. The Hamiltonians also believed they had more to gain economically by doing business with the British rather than the French.

While Washington deplored factionalism and claimed to be above it, his views were closer to the ideas of the emerging Federalist Party. Adams adhered closely to Washington's ideas. This would seem to put Adams on the side of Hamilton, but there was deep antagonism between the two. At the end of the first term, Hamilton tried and failed to block Adam's second term as vice president and also his candidacy to be Washington's successor as president.

The political divisions between the two groups were so great that even Washington came under serious criticism, the tenor of which may have contributed to his desire to retire after his second term. Washington was convinced that the United States was too small and weak to become embroiled in the conflict between Britain and France and wisely adopted a neutrality policy. As president, Adams attempted to follow this policy, but events made this very difficult. France, regarding the United States as ungrateful for not coming to their aid against Britain, began attacking U.S. shipping in the late 1790s. Adams sent emissaries to France to resolve the conflict, but the French refused to meet them unless the United States agreed to loan France $10 million and pay a $250,000 bribe before negotiations could begin. Adams claimed that the United States had been insulted. When the Democratic Republicans demanded proof, Adams supplied documentation in which he blacked out the names of the French agents and substituted the letters "XYZ"—thereby supplying the name by which the affair became known.

Adams's popularity soared as the result of the XYZ affair and his prompt efforts to strengthen national defense. For the last two years of the 18th century, the United States and France were in an undeclared naval war. After Napoleon came to power in 1800, he sought peace with the United States so he could concentrate on his other conflicts. Still favoring neutrality and aware that Britain still abused the United States as well, Adams negotiated peace with France. As wise as it was for the United States, this peace angered Hamilton and his Federalists, leaving Adams without significant political support.

The Federalists in Congress further damaged Adams by enacting (as a wartime measure) the Alien and Sedition Acts, making criticism of the president, cabinet officers, or other U.S. officials criminal libel. These acts have long been regarded as a serious infringement on free speech. They were also regarded as a brazen partisan vendetta since they exempted the office of vice president (occupied by Thomas Jefferson) from the purview of the law. This meant one could legally criticize Jefferson but could go to jail for criticizing Adams. Adams neither vetoed the act nor enforced it vigorously, thereby pleasing no one. Adams believed the Alien and Sedition Acts were constitutional since they did not represent a prior restraint on speech and press, but the Jeffersonians still saw the criminal penalties as a threat to the First Amendment.

Despite Adams's wise attempt to follow Washington's middle course, he lacked Washington's prestige and he lost the 1800 election to Jefferson. Upon losing, Adams tried to perpetuate Federalist control by packing the judiciary. These so-called midnight appointments were only partially successful, but his last-minute appointment of JOHN MARSHALL as chief justice of the United States left an impact on the judiciary for more than three decades.

Adams has often been criticized for excessive ambition and poor judgment. However, four times in his lifetime, he acted *against* his own ambition by making decisions that have stood the test of time as profoundly correct for the good of the nation. First, as a member of the committee to draft the Declaration of Independence, he pushed for Thomas Jefferson to draft the essential language. Second, he acted against the sectional interest of his native Massachusetts by urging the selection of the Virginian, George Washington, to be the commander in chief of the American Revolutionary War armies. Third, to the satisfaction of neither the Federalists nor the Democratic Republicans and the detriment of his own political future, Adams kept the United States out of a war with either or both France or England—a war that could easily have led to the destruction of the newly founded republic. Finally, Adams selected John Marshall (another Virginian) as chief justice of the United States, thereby allowing Marshall to shape the U.S. Supreme Court and the federal judiciary in ways that no one before or since has done.

In 1801, Adams returned to Massachusetts and spent his last 25 years writing about his experiences and corresponding with friends. Fortunately, Adams and Jefferson were reconciled as friends. In one of the great coincidences in U.S. history, these two long-term friends died on the same day—the 50th anniversary of the signing of the Declaration of Independence—July 4, 1826.

Further Reading

Adams, Charles Francis, ed. *Familiar Letters of John Adams and His Wife, Abigail Adams, During the Revolution.* Boston: Houghton, Mifflin, 1898.

———, ed. *The Works of John Adams, Second President of the United States.* Boston: Little, Brown, 1856.

Adams, James Truslow. *The Adams Family.* New York: Blue Ribbon Books, 1933.

"Adams, John," Available on–line. URL: http://www. whitehouse.gov/history/presidents/ja2.html. Downloaded on October 20, 2001.

Bowen, Catherine Drinker. *John Adams and the American Revolution.* Boston: Little, Brown, 1950.

Burleigh, Ann Husted. *John Adams.* New Rochelle, N.Y.: Arlington House, 1969.

Chinard, Gilbert. *Honest John Adams.* Boston: Little, Brown, 1933.

Ellis, Joseph J. *Passionate Sage: The Character and Legacy of John Adams.* New York: Norton. 1993.

Falkner, Leonard. *John Adams: Reluctant Patriot of the Revolution.* Englewood Cliffs, N.J.: Prentice-Hall, 1969.

Ferling, John E. *John Adams: A Life.* Knoxville: University of Tennessee Press, 1995.

McCulloch, David. *John Adams.* New York: Simon & Schuster, 2001.

Shaw, Peter. *The Character of John Adams.* Chapel Hill: University of North Carolina Press, 1999.

Shepard, Jack. *The Adams Chronicles: Four Generations of Greatness.* Boston: Little, Brown, 1975.

Adams, John Quincy

(1767–1848) *president, secretary of state, diplomat, representative, author*

John Quincy Adams stands as an exemplar of a former president for his distinguished post-presidential service as a 16-year veteran of the House of Representatives. His earlier career as a diplomat and secretary of state indicated considerable promise as a president—an expectation that

John Quincy Adams, the first president whose father was president, was the only former president to serve in the House of Representatives. *(Library of Congress)*

could not be fulfilled because of the political divisions of the age. Still he advanced his family's prestige as one of the United States's greatest political dynasties. Until GEORGE WALKER BUSH in 2001, he was the only president whose father previously served as president.

Born on July 11, 1767, in Braintree (now Quincy), Massachusetts, Adams received a remarkable education as he traveled through various European capitols while his father was the U.S. minister abroad. Upon his return, he graduated from Harvard in 1787, was admitted to the bar in 1790, and opened a practice in Boston. He anonymously published a set of articles in response to THOMAS PAINE's *Rights of Man*, which were so well reasoned they were mistakenly attributed to his father, JOHN ADAMS.

His experience in Europe was so valuable that GEORGE WASHINGTON appointed him minister to the Dutch government in 1794 when Adams was only 27 and later named Adams minister to Prussia. When his father became president, the public criticism of his son still serving the government was quashed by none other than Washington himself, who praised John Quincy Adams as "the most valuable public character we have abroad."

John Quincy Adams was principled even if the cause was unpopular—just as his father had been. Returning to the United States in 1801, Adams was elected to the Massachusetts state senate in April 1802, but his political opponents defeated him in his race for Congress later that year as being "too unmanageable." Elected by the legislature to the U.S. Senate in 1803, he was still "unmanageable." Adams supported THOMAS JEFFERSON's Louisiana Purchase, his handling of the impressments of sailors, or forcing seamen on American ships to join the British navy, and his embargo despite the severe economic consequences to New England. So far did he act contrary to his party's wishes that the Federalist legislature elected his successor a full two years before the end of his term. Recognizing this intense hostility, Adams resigned his term and declined to run even from the opposite party, the Democratic Republicans.

Although often criticized for having an aloof and forbidding personality, he was an exceptional diplomat. He served both presidents Thomas Jefferson and JAMES MADISON ably as minister to Russia and even negotiated the Treaty of Ghent, which ended the War of 1812 on very favorable terms to the United States. Despite criticism at the time, the terms were very beneficial to the United States and were far more generous than the mediocre U.S. military accomplishments justified. This was accomplished before ANDREW JACKSON's great New Orleans victory, which came after the treaty was signed.

When Adams was named JAMES MONROE's secretary of state in 1817, he had established a diplomatic record unequaled by any previous secretary of state, and he accomplished much in that turbulent period. He reached an agreement with Britain over the joint occupation of the Oregon territory, maintained the U.S. neutrality during the wars for independence of the Spanish colonies in South America, and even negotiated the cession of Florida from Spain. These accomplishments paved the way for the Monroe Doctrine—which Adams was most responsible for drafting—asserting that the United States would regard European encroachments in this hemisphere as direct threats to the United States.

Since the three preceding secretaries of state went on to be president, Adams was naturally a presidential contender in 1824. The Federalists had abandoned the field, but there were three other Democratic candidates: HENRY CLAY, William Crawford, and Andrew Jackson. Jackson received the highest number of popular votes but not the required majority of electoral college votes. Constitutionally, this required throwing the election into the House of Representatives where the absolute discretion of the body was recognized. Since Clay could not win and recognized Adams as being closest to his views, he threw the critical votes to Adams, which gave him the presidency. When Adams subsequently appointed Clay secretary of state, Jackson's followers charged a corrupt bargain. Jackson began the United States's first four-year campaign for president and, coupled with other sectional and political conflicts, this blocked any significant legislative progress. Congress would not let Adams have money for internal improvements, negotiate effectively with Latin America, or

fashion a genuine compromise on the Tariff of 1828. Jackson decisively defeated Adams in the 1828 presidential contest.

Adams intended, as his father had, to retire to Massachusetts, but this was not to be. Ironically, the Massachusetts voters who rejected his service in the early 1800s now elected him to the House of Representatives even though he had not entered his name in the campaign. He decided to serve, and over the next 17 years, he compiled one of the most distinguished records of any former president for his public service at the end of his presidency. While famous for his defense before the U.S. Supreme Court of the African slaves aboard the Amistad, his lengthy, ultimately successful struggle against the southern House members' long-standing practice of imposing a gag rule on antislavery petitions was probably more significant. Called "Old Man Eloquent" for his defense of the First Amendment, he went too far in one respect. Adams introduced the practice of allowing House members to be present but refuse to vote on measures on the floor. Although not recognized at the time, this practice had to be forcefully abandoned by House Speaker "Czar Reed" (THOMAS BRACKETT REED) in the late 1800s or the House would have fallen into complete inefficiency.

During a strenuous debate on February 21, 1848, Adams suffered a stroke and died two days later in the Speaker's office without recovering consciousness. The Adams family suffered much. John Quincy Adams's brother and two of his sons all died essentially of alcoholism. Still, as John Quincy Adams died, his last son, CHARLES FRANCIS ADAMS, was beginning his career. At the end of Charles Francis Adams's career, the three generations of Adams had cumulatively represented the United States diplomatically and in other public service for more than a hundred years. This remains a record unequaled in U.S. history.

Further Reading
Adams, Charles Francis, ed. Memoirs of John Quincy Adams. Freeport, N.Y.: Books for Libraries Press, 1969.
"Adams, John Quincy." Available online: URL: http://www.whitehouse.gov/history/presidents/ja6.html. Download on October 20, 2001.

Bemis, Samuel Flagg. *John Quincy Adams and the Foundations of American Foreign Policy.* Norwalk, Conn.: Easton Press, 1987.

———. *John Quincy Adams and the Union.* Norwalk, Conn.: Easton Press, 1987.

Falkner, Leonard. *The President Who Wouldn't Retire.* New York: Coward-McCann, 1967.

Hargreaves, Mary W. M. *The Presidency of John Quincy Adams.* Lawrence: University Press of Kansas, 1985.

McCulloch, David. *John Adams.* New York: Simon & Schuster, 2001.

Nagel, Paul C. *John Quincy Adams: A Public Life, A Private Life.* New York: Knopf, 1997.

Parsons, Lynn H. *John Quincy Adams.* Madison, Wis.: Madison House, 1998.

———. *John Quincy Adams: A Bibliography.* Westport, Conn.: Greenwood Press, 1993.

Richards, Leonard L. *The Life and Times of Congressman John Quincy Adams.* New York: Oxford University Press, 1986.

Shepard, Jack. *The Adams Chronicles: Four Generations of Greatness.* Boston: Little, Brown, 1975.

———. *Cannibals of the Heart: A Personal Biography of Louise Catherine and John Quincy Adams.* New York: McGraw-Hill, 1980.

Adams, Samuel

(1722–1803) *Revolutionary War leader, governor*

Samuel Adams, the American revolutionary leader most identified with inciting the Boston Massacre and planning the Boston Tea Party, was a cousin of President JOHN ADAMS. These two men both played critical roles for U.S. independence in the Revolutionary War, but they represented dramatically different approaches to politics and philosophy.

Samuel Adams was born in Boston on September 27, 1722, some 13 years before his cousin, John Adams. Both cousins attended Harvard; Samuel graduated in 1740 and obtained a master's degree in 1743. Samuel Adams gave up on the study of law, tried a number of businesses, and failed at all of them. For most of his life, he was dependent on the help of friends to take care of himself and his family.

As early as 1747, he was writing articles on public affairs for local newspapers as a way of gaining political influence. With the British imposition of the Stamp Act requiring a tax on newspapers and legal documents, Adams acquired his clearest target. His vocal opposition to the tax was his first important claim to fame. Adams gained sufficient support to be asked to write the instructions for Boston's elected representatives in the assembly from 1764 to 1765. The British repealed the Stamp Act but replaced it with the Townshend Acts. The British thought these would be more acceptable because they did not use the same legal theory of the tax as the Stamp Act, but the Townshend Acts were revenue measures and still drew the wrath of Samuel Adams and the other radical colonists committed to separation from England.

In the fall of 1765, Adams was elected to the lower house of the colonial legislature where he was active in promoting the seating of other radicals and expanding revolutionary contacts with other colonial legislatures. Adams never openly advocated violence, but his opposition to the British was so strong that many others became violent. His writings are generally credited with creating a climate in which the Boston Massacre occurred. Beset by a mob of colonials, exasperated British soldiers fired into the mob, killing five individuals.

To placate the colonials, the British actually indicted their own soldiers for murder in the incident. In one of the most interesting situations of the pre-Revolutionary War period, the future U.S. president John Adams—a Massachusetts attorney and a cousin of Samuel Adams—agreed to defend the soldiers against the murder charge. Although John and Samuel Adams were on the same side in defending colonial rights against the British, they approached these issues differently. John Adams succeeded in saving the British soldiers from the gallows by arguing self-defense. Despite the rancor against the British, John Adams also preserved his reputation as a patriot.

The British repealed the Townshend Acts in 1772, and the spirited opposition to the Crown diminished. Samuel Adams was by now convinced that a break with England was inevitable and kept up his writing. He also persuaded the Boston town meeting to institute "Committees of Correspondence" with the other colonies. As a further aggravation to the British, Samuel Adams organized the opposition to the 1773 Tea Act and was behind the Boston Tea Party. When the British responded with the Coercive Acts, Adams again led the resistance.

Through the Committees of Correspondence, he urged the other colonies to join Massachusetts in resisting Britain by refusing to trade with it. When Adams found the other colonies were not responding, he proposed formation of a congress among all the colonies. Upon gaining some acceptance, Samuel Adams and four others were named to the First Continental Congress scheduled to meet in Philadelphia. Before going to Philadelphia, Adams instigated the convention that passed the Suffolk Resolves that effectively placed Massachusetts at war with the Crown.

In 1775, Samuel Adams was elected to the Second Continental Congress, where he recommended immediate independence from England. He was naturally one of the signers of the Declaration of Independence in 1776. He continued to serve in the Continental Congress until 1781 when he returned to Massachusetts to serve in the convention that adopted the new state constitution. Under this new state government, he served as a senator and member of the leadership council.

He supported the proposed new federal constitution in 1787 with the provision that a Bill of Rights would be added. Although he was not elected to the first Congress in the 1788 elections, he was elected lieutenant governor in 1789 and later governor in 1794. After three years as governor, he retired from public life and died on October 2, 1803.

Further Reading

Beach, Stewart. *Samuel Adams: The Fateful Years, 1764–1776.* New York: Dodd, Mead, 1965.

Fowler, William M. *Samuel Adams: Radical Puritan.* New York: Longman, 1997.

Galvin, John R. *Three Men of Boston.* Washington, D.C.: Brassey's, 1997.

Hosmer, James Kendall. *Samuel Adams.* New York: Chelsea House, 1980.

Lewis, Paul. *The Grand Incendiary: A Biography of Samuel Adams.* New York: Dial Press, 1973.

Miller, John Chester. *San Adams: Pioneer In Propaganda.* Stanford, Calif.: Stanford University Press, 1966.

Adams, Sherman

(1899–1986) *governor, representative, White House chief of staff*

Sherman Adams made his most important contribution to American history by helping create the prototype for the White House chief of staff that was developed in President DWIGHT DAVID EISENHOWER's administration and has continued largely unchanged since that time.

Sherman Adams was born in East Dover, Vermont, on January 8, 1899, but grew up in Providence, Rhode Island. After high school he entered the U.S. Marine Corps during World War I. After the war he attended and graduated from Dartmouth College. He settled in New Hampshire and worked as an executive in the lumber business.

Adams began his political career by being elected to the New Hampshire House of Representatives in 1940. Reelected in 1942, he served as Speaker in 1943 and 1944. Adams served one term in the U.S. House of Representatives from 1945 to 1947. He served two terms as governor from 1949 to 1953.

Adams recognized the extraordinary potential of a Republican nomination for Eisenhower and backed him very early in this effort. He played a key role in Eisenhower's Republican National Convention victory and went on to direct Eisenhower's successful presidential campaign.

After Eisenhower's inauguration, Adams became White House chief of staff. It was in this role that Adams's genius blossomed. He organized Eisenhower's time with such efficiency and controlled access to the president with such hard-nosed determination that it has served as a model for nearly all presidencies since. Occasionally, a president experiments with alternative styles, but they have all returned to something similar to the Adams model before long.

Unfortunately, consequences of Adams's success included increased scrutiny and a much-heightened profile in the press, where he was often referred to as the "assistant president." Adams made a mistake in taking a vicuña coat for his wife and some other gifts from Bernard Goldfine, a businessman who needed federal help. An investigation by a subcommittee of the House of Representatives revealed this fact and led to his resignation in 1958. Adams did not return to public life, and he died on October 27, 1986.

Further Reading

Adams, Sherman. *Firsthand Report: The Story of the Eisenhower Administration.* Westport, Conn.: Greenwood Press, 1974.

———. *The Weeks Act: A 75th Anniversary Appraisal.* New York: Newcomen Society of the United States, 1986.

Kaufman, Burton I. "Dwight D. Eisenhower," in *The American Presidents,* edited by Frank N. Magill, John L. Loos, and Tracy Irons-Georges. Pasadena, Calif.: Salem Press, 2000.

Agnew, Spiro Theodore
(1918–1996) *vice president, governor, county executive*

Spiro Agnew was the first vice president of the United States to resign the office as the result of his conviction of felonious criminal conduct. Had he not resigned, he would surely have been impeached. Agnew was not the only vice president to resign, however; JOHN CALDWELL CALHOUN resigned as vice president under President ANDREW JACKSON as the result of serious political, philosophical, and constitutional differences with Jackson.

Spiro Theodore Agnew was born to Greek immigrant parents (who changed their last name to Agnew) on November 9, 1918, in Baltimore, Maryland. After serving as an army officer in World War II, Agnew earned a law degree from the University of Baltimore in 1947. Along with having a successful law practice, Agnew became active in local Republican politics in the 1950s.

Since he lived in solidly Democratic Baltimore County, it initially appeared that he had no prospect of holding elective public office. However, in 1962, the local Democratic Party became deeply divided as the result of a competitive primary, and Agnew seized the chance to be elected Baltimore County executive. By 1966 the Baltimore County Democrats had patched up their differences and were planning to oust Agnew from office.

Knowing he would be unable to win reelection as county executive, Agnew decided to run for governor. Again, the Democrats were facing a bruising gubernatorial primary. The Democratic vote was due to be split by the campaign of a conservative former Democrat, George P. Mahoney, who ran on the slogan, "Your home is your castle," to symbolize his opposition to open housing laws. In this context, Agnew was able to appear to be a moderate reformer, and he took advantage of the three-way race to win the gubernatorial seat usually reserved for Democrats.

The Democrats again patched up their differences, and Agnew would have faced almost certain defeat in the next Maryland gubernatorial contest in 1970. However, luck, in the form of yet another three-way split, again intervened. In the 1968 presidential contest, the badly divided Democrats nominated Vice President HUBERT HORATIO HUMPHREY as their presidential nominee to replace incumbent President LYNDON BAINES JOHNSON, who had chosen not to run again. Alabama's governor, GEORGE CORLEY WALLACE, had already bolted from the Democratic Party to run for president on the American Independent Party ticket, thereby splitting the potential votes for the Democratic Party.

In these circumstances, RICHARD MILHOUS NIXON decided that Agnew, a border state governor with a reform image, would be an excellent vice presidential running mate. Duly nominated, Agnew proved an able campaigner and the Nixon-Agnew ticket was elected by a narrow margin. As President DWIGHT DAVID EISENHOWER's vice president, Nixon had often played the role of partisan spokesperson so that Eisenhower could appear presidential and above the fray. Nixon now assigned similar duties to Agnew. So popular did Agnew prove as a partisan political speaker that he became the key administrative spokesman in the Nixon administration, especially as the demonstrations over the Vietnam War continued to rile the body politic. Agnew was probably the best-known partisan spokesperson to serve as vice president up to that time in American history. Agnew aided Nixon's landslide victory over the weak Democratic nominee, GEORGE STANLEY MCGOVERN, in 1972.

By 1973, Agnew's luck had run out. In 1970 J. Glenn Beale was a relatively unknown Republican who had defeated the Democratic incumbent in another contest in which the Democrats were badly split and had been elected to the U.S. Senate. Knowing he would have difficulty being reelected when the Democrats reunited again, Beale asked that his brother be appointed the U.S. attorney for Maryland. In this way, Beale hoped he could win reelection on the heels of his brother's vigorous prosecution of corrupt Maryland Democratic politicians. U.S. Attorney Beale had no trouble finding corrupt Democrats to prosecute. Baltimore County was particularly rife with them and Baltimore County Executive Dale Anderson was duly indicted on multiple corruption charges.

This same investigation also discovered that Agnew had been involved in the same kind of corruption as Baltimore County executive and later as Maryland's governor. In fact, he had been owed a final payoff when he left the governor's office in 1969, and that final payment was made to him in his vice presidential office in Washington. The evidence was so overwhelming that the U.S. attorney, though a Republican, had no choice but to prosecute Agnew.

Further complicating the situation was the fact that the Watergate investigation had already suggested the possibility that Nixon might not be able to serve out his full term. Clearly a new vice president was necessary, but impeachment of Agnew would be time consuming. Agnew was forced to cut a deal whereby he would resign as vice president, would not contest one felony charge (of the more than 40 that were arrayed against him), would be forced to pay a fine, but would avoid going to prison. The state of Maryland later forced him to repay $248,000 in bribe money to the state. Agnew retired from public life in 1973. He died of acute leukemia on September 17, 1996.

Further Reading

Agnew, Spiro T. *Go Quietly . . . Or Else.* New York: Morrow, 1980.

Cohen, Richard M. *A Heartbeat Away: The Investigation and Resignation of Vice President Spiro T. Agnew.* New York: Viking Press, 1974.

Coyne, John R. *The Impudent Snobs: Agnew vs. the Intellectual Establishment.* New Rochelle, N.Y.: Arlington House, 1972.

Hernon, Joseph Martin. *Profiles in Character: Hubris and Heroism in the U.S. Senate—1789–1990.* Armonk, N.Y.: M. E. Sharpe, 1997.

Hoff-Wilson, Joan. "Richard M. Nixon" in *The American Presidents,* edited by Frank N. Magill, John L. Loos, and Tracy Irons-Georges. Pasadena, Calif.: Salem Press, 2000.

Peterson, Robert W. *Agnew: The Coining of a Household Word.* New York: Facts On File, 1972.

"Spiro Agnew" in *The Presidency A to Z: Second Edition,* edited by Michael T. Nelson. Washington, D.C.: Congressional Quarterly Press, 1998.

Witcover, Jules. *White Knight: Rise of Spiro Agnew.* New York: Random House, 1972.

Albert, Carl Bert

(1908–2000) *Speaker of the U.S. House of Representatives, representative, author*

Carl Albert is remembered as one of the best Speakers of the House of Representatives in the last third of the 20th century. Although he was Speaker for only six years, his distinguished service capped off his excellent 30-year career in the U.S. House of Representatives.

Born on May 10, 1908, in McAlester, Oklahoma, Carl Bert Albert was the son of a coal miner and a farmer. An excellent student, he was a Rhodes scholar in law at Oxford after graduating with a political science degree from the University of Oklahoma at Norman in 1931. In 1934, he returned to the United States, worked briefly for the Oklahoma branch of the Federal Housing Administration, and was admitted to the bar in 1935. He had a private law practice but was also a corporate lawyer for the Ohio Oil Company until he went into the armed forces in World War II. He served in the Judge Advocate General's Department and as an army air force officer.

Albert was elected to Congress in 1946. As a moderate, border state Democrat he earned a reputation for intelligence, hard work, and loyalty. He supported President HARRY S. TRUMAN's legislative agenda and followed the mainstream Democratic position during the administration of President DWIGHT DAVID EISENHOWER. In 1955 he was rewarded with the position of majority party whip.

After long-term Democratic speaker SAMUEL TALI-AFERRO RAYBURN died in 1962, Democratic Majority Leader JOHN WILLIAM MCCORMACK moved up to speaker and Carl Albert moved up to the position of majority leader. In that capacity, he was very instrumental in helping enact President LYNDON BAINES JOHNSON's "Great Society" program. Albert also strongly supported Johnson's foreign and military policies in Vietnam.

When McCormack left the Speaker's office in 1971, Albert was elevated to the position in which he would earn his greatest recognition. He strongly opposed many of RICHARD MILHOUS NIXON's domestic policies while generally supporting Nixon's efforts to disengage from Vietnam. Albert was credited with distinguished impartial conduct over the House impeachment investigation of Nixon. Albert twice stood next in line to succeed to the presidency. During 1973, the office of vice president was vacant because of the resignation of SPIRO THEODORE AGNEW (before GERALD RUDOLPH FORD was appointed vice president). In 1974, Albert was again next in line to the presidency after President Richard Nixon resigned and Gerald Ford became president, leaving the vice presidency vacant until NELSON ALDRICH ROCKEFELLER was selected as the new appointive vice president. Carl Albert retired from the U.S. House of Representatives in 1971 and died February 2, 2000.

Further Reading

Albert, Carl Bert. *The Office and the Duties of the Speaker of the House of Representatives.* Washington, D.C.: U.S. Government Printing Office, 1976.

Albert, Carl Bert, and Danney Goble. *Little Giant: The Life and Times of Speaker Carl Albert.* Norman: University of Oklahoma Press, 1990.

Albright, Madeleine Korbell

(1937–) *secretary of state, ambassador to the United Nations, author*

Madeleine Albright was the first woman to serve as secretary of state and one of the few women to serve as the U.S. ambassador to the United Nations.

She emerged from a family with a long history of diplomatic service. She was born Madeleine Korbell on May 15, 1937, in Prague, Czechoslovakia. Her father was a diplomat and her mother was the daughter of wealthy parents. Both came from Jewish families. Her parents converted to Catholicism in an effort to avoid persecution, but this was an incomplete defense. Three of her grandparents died in the Holocaust. This fact was kept secret from Albright until she became secretary of state. Her parents went through a long, anxious period after the German Nazis conquered the country in 1937 until they were able to escape to Britain using false papers. Even such an escape left the family vulnerable to the Germans, as they were subject to air raids during the Battle of Britain during World War II.

After the war, her father returned to Czechoslovakia to resume his diplomatic career. Fortunately, he was a Czech representative at the United Nations in New York when the Communists took over the government—again making him unwelcome in his home country. He was granted political asylum in the United States and he took a teaching position in Colorado.

Madeleine Korbell was educated in a private school in Colorado and at Wellesley. After college, she married Joseph Albright, scion of the family that owned the *Chicago Sun-Times.* As the spouse of a journalist, she was prohibited as a practical matter from a career in journalism. Instead she began a lengthy graduate program in international relations and earned her doctorate in 1976. She worked briefly on the Senate staff of Senator EDMUND SIXTUS MUSKIE and transferred to the National Security Council after the election of President JAMES EARL CARTER when her dissertation director, ZBIGNIEW KAZIMIERZ BRZEZINSKI, became Carter's national security adviser.

After RONALD WILSON REAGAN was elected president, Albright returned to the academic world as a researcher at the Center for Strategic and International Studies and the Smithsonian Institution's Woodrow Wilson Center for Scholars. From 1982 to 1993, she was on the faculty of Georgetown University. She was a foreign policy adviser to Walter Mondale and GERALDINE ANNE

FERRARO during their 1984 presidential campaign. She served as the senior foreign policy adviser and speechwriter for Michael Dukakis in 1988.

During the 1992 campaign, Albright wrote position papers for the Democratic presidential nominee, WILLIAM JEFFERSON CLINTON, and she helped write the foreign policy sections of the Democratic Party platform. Based on these experiences, Albright was named the U.S. ambassador to the United Nations in 1993 and became a member of President Clinton's cabinet. She had a successful career as UN ambassador. More important, she became increasingly friendly with HILLARY RODHAM CLINTON and traveled with her on important international tours.

After Clinton's 1996 reelection, it was clear that Secretary of State Warren Christopher would retire. Although several prominent men were considered, Clinton selected Albright in part because she had carefully cultivated conservatives in Congress. She was confirmed in the U.S. Senate by a vote of 99–0.

As secretary of state, she was active in promoting the expansion of the North Atlantic Treaty Organization to include the former Communist-bloc countries of Poland and the Czech Republic. Albright supported aid to the former Soviet Union as well as U.S. involvement in promoting peace and the institution of democracy in the new states arising out of the breakup of the former Yugoslavia. She supported numerous peace efforts in the Middle East. While maintaining the firm policy of restraint on Iraq, she attempted to promote moderation within Iran by trying to improve U.S. relations there. To the extent possible, she worked to improve the status of women around the globe and urged the U.S. Senate to ratify the Convention on the Elimination of All Forms of Discrimination Against Women (CEDAW).

Albright was not only the first woman to serve as secretary of state, but she was one of the very few women to hold high diplomatic posts for the United States. JEANE DUANE JORDAN KIRKPATRICK preceded her as U.S. ambassador to the United Nations, and ANNA ELEANOR ROOSEVELT had served as a delegate to the original United Nations Conference and to the Commission on Human Rights. Madeline Albright certainly advanced the efforts of women to participate in international relations.

Further Reading

Albright, Madeleine Korbell. *Focus on the Issues. Africa.* Washington D.C.: U.S. Department of State, 1999.

———. *Focus on the Issues. The Americas.* Washington D.C.: U.S. Department of State, 2000.

———. *Focus on the Issues. Asia and the Pacific.* Washington D.C.: U.S. Department of State, 1999.

———. *Focus on the Issues: Europe.* Washington D.C.: U.S. Department of State, 1999.

———. *Poland: The Role of the Press in Political Change.* New Yark:Praeger, 1983.

———. *Focus on the Issues. Strengthening Civil Society and the Rule of Law.* Washington, D.C.: U.S. Department of State, 2000.

Blackman, Ann. *Seasons of Her Life: A Biography of Madeleine Korbell Albright.* New York: Scribner's, 1998.

Blood, Thomas. *Madam Secretary: A Biography of Madeleine Albright.* New York: St. Martin's, 1997.

Dobbs, Michael. *Madeleine Albright: A Twentieth-Century Odyssey.* New York: Holt, 1999.

Aldrich, Nelson Wilmarth
(1841–1915) *senator, representative*

Nelson Aldrich was a dominant figure in American national politics for 30 years from 1881 to 1910, and his efforts to create the U.S. Federal Reserve Banking System had particularly long-lasting effects.

Born in Foster, Rhode Island, on November 6, 1841, Nelson Wilmarth Aldrich had a meteoric rise in business and politics. By the time he was 28 years old, Aldrich was already an extremely wealthy man with millions of dollars invested in Rhode Island business ventures. In 1869, he began his political career as Providence, Rhode Island, city councillor. He quickly moved up to the Rhode Island legislature in 1875, to the U.S. House of Representatives in 1879, and to the U.S. Senate in 1881.

It was in the U.S. Senate that Aldrich made his lasting mark on American politics. He was a particularly powerful voice within the Republican Party taking issues popular with Republicans and fortifying them against the attacks of their opponents. The tariff and commerce were important issues among New England conservatives and Republicans throughout the 19th century. Aldrich continued to fight for high tariffs even after segments of his own Republican Party had moved in the direction of lower tariffs as a result of the influence of the Progressive Movement.

On critical commerce questions, Aldrich held the conservative line. He supported THEODORE ROOSEVELT in his first term and up through his 1904 election campaign. However, the two clashed vehemently in 1906 over the Hepburn Rate Act, which was designed to let the Interstate Commerce Commission (ICC) set rates for railroads. Aldrich lost battles but essentially won the war by forcing the acceptance of an amendment allowing the railroads to appeal any commission-mandated rate changes to the courts. In the court system, Aldrich felt he could count on conservative judges to mitigate the controls of the ICC rate makers.

Because he was a staunch conservative eastern businessman, there was never any question of where he stood on the question of hard currency—or a preference for the gold standard over the silver standard. He secured the passage of the Gold Standard Act of 1900.

Unfortunately, the financial panic of 1907 exposed a weakness of the U.S. economic system that high tariffs, unregulated business, and sound money could not cure: It revealed the need for a national bank. So strongly did Aldrich feel about this issue that he resigned his Senate seat to devote full time to the effort. The essence of the system was the use of rediscounting commercial paper (or loans) to create a fund of emergency currency, which could be released in liquidity crises (or times when there was not enough money in circulation). The release of these funds depended on a system of regional branches (Aldrich preferred 15) that were associated together for this purpose.

Aldrich thought his hopes of imposing his own version of this system would be complicated if either WILLIAM HOWARD TAFT or Theodore Roo-

sevelt were elected in 1912 because he had clashed with both men in the past, but he was certain they were doomed if THOMAS WOODROW WILSON won, as happened because of the Republican split between Taft and Roosevelt. Curiously, portions of Aldrich's plan were so sound that Wilson adopted them as a part of his own proposal for the Federal Reserve System. These portions have continued as a part of the Federal Reserve System still in place at the start of the 21st century.

Aldrich's contributions were often long-lasting if unappreciated. Aldrich retired from public life after 1912 and died on April 16, 1915.

Further Reading

"Aldrich, Nelson," in *Congress A to Z: Third Edition,* edited by David R. Tarr and Ann O'Connor. Washington, D.C.: Congressional Quarterly, 1999.

Hernon, Joseph Martin. *Profiles in Character: Hubris and Heroism in the U.S. Senate—1789–1990.* Armonk, N.Y.: M. E. Sharpe, 1997.

Stephenson, Nathaniel Wright. *Nelson W. Aldrich, A Leader in American Politics.* Port Washington, N.Y.: Kennikat Press, 1971.

Anderson, John Bayard
(1922–   ) *candidate for president, representative*

John B. Anderson ran for president as an independent in 1980 hoping that a split would develop between the Republican and Democratic candidates sufficient for him to win. Such a split did not materialize, although he may have drawn more votes away from the Democratic Party's nominee, the incumbent JAMES EARL CARTER, to help the Republican RONALD WILSON REAGAN to win. He contributed one of the most effective phrases in American political history when he described Ronald Reagan's plan to cut taxes while increasing defense spending as being achievable only if Reagan used "Blue Smoke and Mirrors." The phrase has been so memorable that it has been widely used to describe a variety of federal budget proposals.

John Bayard Anderson was born in Rockford, Illinois, on February 15, 1922. He graduated from the University of Illinois in 1942 and then served in the army until 1945. After World War II, he returned to the University of Illinois to finish his law degree, which he received in 1946. He practiced law in Rockford from 1946 to 1952, but he also attended Harvard University during part of that period, earning a master of laws and letters in 1949. He joined the U.S. Foreign Service in 1952 and was stationed in West Berlin until he left the diplomatic service in 1955. He returned to Rockford in 1955 and won election as Winnebago County state's attorney in 1956. In 1960 he was elected to the U.S. House of Representatives where he served until he ran for president in 1980.

While in Congress, his views evolved. He remained a fiscal conservative, yet he became more liberal on a variety of social issues. He supported the Equal Rights Amendment for Women, civil rights legislation, and gun control. As a fiscal conservative, he advocated the end of duplicate defense spending programs. In 1968, Anderson was named the chairman of the influential House Republican Conference.

Anderson abandoned his safe congressional seat to run for president in the Republican primaries in 1980. After losing critical primaries while gaining national recognition, Anderson decided to continue running for president as an independent. He selected a Democrat, former Wisconsin governor Patrick J. Lucey, as his running mate and described his effort as the National Unity Party. His appeal was to liberal Republicans and to moderate Democrats who had become disenchanted with the administration of Jimmy Carter.

President Carter correctly perceived that Anderson's campaign might draw relatively more votes away from him and attempted to avoid giving Anderson any extra publicity. As a part of this effort, Carter refused to participate in any televised debates with Ronald Reagan if John Anderson were included. This proved to be a mistake as a debate between Anderson and Reagan took place without Carter, allowing the voters to infer that Carter was afraid to debate. In the end, Carter agreed to debate Reagan without Anderson in the closing days of the campaign. Reagan was perceived as having done relatively better in that debate than Carter, and the debate occurred so late in the campaign that Carter had no opportunity to recover.

Anderson had polled as high as 15 percent early in the campaign, but his strength faded as voters concluded that voting for Anderson was taking votes away from their second-choice candidate and helping the election of their last choice. Still Anderson did manage to garner about 7 percent of the national vote for president. A disproportionate percent came from potential Carter voters and perhaps aided Reagan's election.

After 1980 Anderson taught at a variety of U.S. colleges and universities and wrote several books.

Further Reading
Anderson, John B. *The American Economy We Need.* New York: Atheneum, 1984.
———. *A Proper Institution: Guaranteeing Televised Presidential Debates.* New York: Priority Press Publications, 1988.
Bisnow, Mark. *Diary of a Dark Horse: The 1980 Anderson Presidential Campaign.* Carbondale: Southern Illinois University Press, 1983.
Brown, Clifford W., Jr., and Robert J. Walker. *A Campaign of Ideas: The 1980 Anderson/ Lucey Platform.* Westport, Conn.: Greenwood Press, 1984.
Golubovskis, George M. *Crazy Dreaming—The Anderson Campaign, 1980.* Flint, Mich.: Talking Seal Press, 1981.
"John B. Anderson" in *The Presidency A to Z: Second Edition,* edited by Michael T. Nelson. Washington, D.C.: Congressional Quarterly Press, 1998.

Arnold, Thurman Wesley
(1891–1969) *federal court of appeals judge, assistant attorney general*

Thurman Arnold is best known for his vigorous prosecution of the trusts and monopolistic corporations as the head of President FRANKLIN DELANO ROOSEVELT's Justice Department Antitrust Division from 1939 to 1943.

Born on June 2, 1891, in Laramie, Wyoming, Thurman Wesley Arnold was an excellent student and made a distinguished academic career in Ivy League schools. Arnold graduated from Princeton in 1911 and earned a law degree at Harvard in 1914. Moving to Chicago, he practiced law there until he enlisted in the army during World War I.

After the war, he returned to Laramie where he practiced law and began a political career as the mayor and a state legislator. He abandoned this career to become the dean of the West Virginia University School of Law in 1927. By 1930, he was offered a law professorship at Yale. Nonetheless, he continued to be active in governmental affairs, serving as legal counsel to the Agricultural Adjustment Administration in 1933 and as a trial examiner for the Securities and Exchange Commission in 1935.

It was his appointment as assistant attorney general for the Antitrust Division of the Department of Justice in 1939 that led to his national reputation. He resisted attempts to pass new antitrust legislation, arguing that the existing legislation needed to be vigorously enforced. He proceeded to file hundreds of lawsuits in industries, which had not seen such prosecutions before.

Arnold was also evenhanded in attacking certain trade associations and labor unions. This aroused the anger of many traditional allies of Roosevelt's administration, but Arnold defended himself by asserting that he was taking a balanced approach against anyone who engaged in a restraint of trade.

A careful reading of Arnold's efforts reveals that he was far less a "trust buster" than he was a "trust regulator." He was not interested in breaking up corporations merely for the sake of breaking them up but simply preferred to restrain them if they engaged in unfair marketing practices. His efforts eventually were curtailed by the difficulty of any sort of prosecution during World War II. In 1943, he was appointed to the U.S. Circuit Court of Appeals, but he resigned after only two years to return to private practice.

He was the author of several books on economics and law especially oriented toward the trust question. His service and his extensive writing made him the generally recognized authority on the questions of trusts. His influence extended throughout the next half century. He died on November 7, 1969.

Further Reading

Arnold, Thurman Wesley. *The Bottlenecks of Business.* New York: Reynal & Hitchcock, 1940.

———. *Cartels or Free Enterprise?* New York: Public Affairs Committee, Inc., 1947.

———. *The Folklore of Capitalism.* Garden City, N.Y.: Blue Ribbon, 1941.

———. *The Future of Democratic Capitalism.* New York: A. S. Barnes, 1961.

Bird, Kai. *The Chairman: John J. McCloy and the Making of the American Establishment.* New York: Simon & Schuster, 1992.

Smith, James A. *The Idea Brokers.* New York: Free Press, 1993.

Wallace, James A. *Overdrive.* New York: John Wiley, 1997.

Arthur, Chester Alan

(1830–1886) *president, vice president, party leader*

Nicknamed the "Gentleman Boss," Chester Arthur was expected to be a loyal Republican Party spoils man, who gave jobs to the party workers who had helped the party win under the custom of the spoils system of public employment of the times. However, his elevation to the presidency in the wake of the assassination of JAMES ABRAM GARFIELD by a disappointed office seeker led to one of the most dramatic political reversals in American history as Arthur turned to civil service reform during his presidency.

The son of a preacher, Chester Alan Arthur was born on October 5, 1830, in Fairfield, Vermont. Bright and diligent, he graduated from Union College in 1848 when he was only 18. He became an idealist lawyer interested in civil rights and a successful member of the bar before the Civil War. During the war, he served as a militia officer and held a variety of administrative posts, such as inspector general, engineer in chief, and quartermaster general.

Instead of returning to Vermont after the war, he settled in New York where he rose quickly in the Republican Party ranks. Because New York was home to some of the most corrupt party politics in America, he had to shed a good deal of his youthful idealism. Apparently, this did not prove difficult as Arthur found he liked money and power. Dressing impeccably, he soon was a favorite of ROSCOE CONKLING, head of the Republican Party's Stalwart faction.

By 1871, President ULYSSES S. GRANT appointed him the customs collector for New York City. At that time, this post was the highest paid civil service federal job in the nation. Almost three-quarters of all U.S. customs receipts came through his office. The nature of the job meant there were dozens of ways to siphon off money. While Arthur was never personally charged with corruption, bribery, or payoffs, he must have known that they went on. The story has been told of a friend who accused him of tolerating corruption in others, to which Arthur replied that his friend was too "goody-goody" and set moral standards too high for people to reach.

Whether or not Grant was aware of the corruption that ran through his administration, the popular perception was that something needed to be done. In 1876, RUTHERFORD BIRCHARD HAYES was elected president with a popular expectation that some sort of civil service reform was necessary. The New York City Custom House was a natural place to begin. Arthur resisted the investigation, and Hayes fired him. This made Arthur a martyr to the spoils men, and Arthur's stock rose in party councils.

By 1880, Hayes had aggravated critical party constituencies to such a degree that he could not be renominated. Roscoe Conkling's Stalwart faction (of which Arthur was a member) tried to renominate Grant for a third term, but the Grant administration's reputation for corruption led the anti-Grant forces (known as the Half-breeds) to defeat Grant with the more moderate James Garfield. As a concession to the Stalwarts, Arthur was nominated for vice president. Since Arthur was regarded as the cleverest political operative in the country, he organized the publicity, raised the cash, and managed the campaign orators.

Arthur's reputation as a crafty manager became a serious liability when Garfield was shot a mere three months into his term. The assassin was a disgruntled office seeker who openly proclaimed that he shot Garfield in order to make Arthur the president. With his reputation as a Stalwart conniver, this was the sort of rumor that could have destroyed Arthur. There was no evidence that Arthur was involved in the assassination plot, but he devotedly prayed for Garfield's recovery and

Chester Arthur became president after James Garfield's assassination by a disappointed office seeker and pushed through the first civil service reform. *(Library of Congress)*

was reported to have been devastated by Garfield's death on September 19, 1881.

Arthur was very mindful of the previous cases in which a vice president took over on the death of a president. He knew in virtually every case that the elevated vice president had failed. The JOHN TYLER, MILLARD FILLMORE, and ANDREW JOHNSON presidencies were all lackluster at best and clear failures at worst. Arthur deeply feared the political situation caused by an assassin killing Garfield and saying that he wanted to make Arthur president.

Probably no vice president elevated by the death of a president more clearly reversed his prior political inclinations than Arthur. He departed from tradition by giving an inaugural speech praising his predecessor and promising he would earnestly pursue the reforms Garfield had planned to make.

If his political cronies thought he was kidding, they were disabused of that notion as Arthur promoted civil service reform. He did not fire Garfield's "Half-breed" appointees and replace them with "Stalwarts" as his Stalwart friends wished. He worked in the context of a Congress almost evenly divided between Republicans and Democrats to pass the 1883 Pendleton Act. This law set up the first bipartisan Civil Service Commission to determine on the basis of merit whether a candidate was qualified for federal appointment. It also forbade federal appointees from making political campaign contributions.

On the level of national policy, Arthur also departed from the long-standing Republican policy on tariffs by recommending lower rates. Arthur was anxious to earn a favorable verdict from history, but it came at a heavy price: He lost so much of his original party support that he could not secure renomination in 1884. The Republicans nominated JAMES GILLESPIE BLAINE, who went down to defeat when faced by another incorruptible New Yorker, STEPHEN GROVER CLEVELAND. While the Republicans might have recognized that their opposition to Arthur's reform contributed to their presidential defeat in 1884, they did not do so and punished Arthur further by denying him a seat in the U.S. Senate when he sought that post in the following year.

Although Arthur very carefully kept his medical problems from public view, he suffered from a kidney problem called Bright's disease. Whether this debilitating disease or the strain of the opposition of his friends while he served as president was responsible, Arthur lived only two years after leaving the presidency. He died on November 18, 1886, at the age of 56.

Further Reading

"Arthur, Chester," Available online. URL: http://www.whitehouse.gov/history/presidents/ca21.html. Downloaded on October 20, 2001.

"Chester Arthur" in *The American President*, by Philip B. Kunhardt, Jr., Philip B. Kunhardt III, and Peter W. Kunhardt. New York: Riverhead Books, 1999.

Doenecke, Justus D. *The Presidencies of James A. Garfield and Chester A. Arthur.* Lawrence: Regents Press of Kansas, 1981.

Hernon, Joseph Martin. *Profiles in Character: Hubris and Heroism in the U.S. Senate—1789–1990.* Armonk, N.Y.: M. E. Sharpe, 1997.

Howe, George F. *Chester A. Arthur: A Quarter-Century of Machine Politics.* New York: F. Ungar Pub. Co., 1957.

Nelson, Michael T. ed. "Chester Arthur" in *The Presidency A to Z: Second Edition.* Washington, D.C.: Congressional Quarterly Press, 1998.

Peskin, Alan. "Chester A. Arthur" in *The American Presidents,* edited by Frank N. Magill, John L. Loos, and Tracy Irons-Georges. Pasadena, Calif.: Salem Press, 2000.

Reeves, Thomas Charles. *Gentleman Boss: The Life of Chester Alan Arthur.* New York: Knopf, 1975.

Atchison, David Rice
(1807–1886) *senator, Confederate leader*

David Rice Atchison was a famous representative of his age, and an important part of his fame extends from his long struggle against his great rival, THOMAS HART BENTON. The city of Atchison, Kansas, is named after him.

Atchison was born on August 11, 1807, in Frogtown, Kentucky. He graduated from Transylvania University, "read" to become a lawyer in Lexington, and was admitted to the bar in Kentucky. Early in his career, he moved to Missouri where his political career took off. By the age of 27 he had been elected to the Missouri state legislature and reelected in 1838. In 1841, he served as Platte County Circuit Court judge until elected to the U.S. Senate in 1843.

Atchison was initially elected by the state legislature to fill the unexpired term of L. F. Finn, who died early in his term, and Atchison succeeded in winning reappointment from the state legislature in 1849.

As a pro-slavery Democrat, he was bound to come into conflict with Missouri's other more senior senator, Thomas Hart Benton, who headed the antislavery forces. Benton had initially supported slavery but gradually came to oppose it. Atchison and Benton fought so vigorously for control of the Missouri Democratic Party that it hurt both of them in the end. Benton was defeated after failing to support southern demands on the Compromise of 1850. Atchison regarded his efforts to secure passage of the Kansas-Nebraska Act as the high point of his career, but it was the kind of extreme policy that caused his opponents to come out in force against him. Atchison was defeated in 1855, effectively ending his political career.

After he was out of office, he led a group of proslavery terrorists who raided antislavery settlements in Kansas in 1855 and 1856. He thus was doubly responsible for creating what became known as "Bleeding Kansas." He moved to Texas from which he supported the Confederacy, but he avoided political life after the Civil War. He died on January 26, 1886.

Further Reading

Hernon, Joseph Martin. *Profiles in Character: Hubris and Heroism in the U.S. Senate—1789–1990.* Armonk, N.Y.: M. E. Sharpe, 1997.

Parrish, William Earl. *David Rice Atchison of Missouri, Border Politician.* Columbia: University of Missouri Press, 1961.

Baker, Howard Henry, Jr.

(1925–) *senator, minority leader, White House chief of staff*

A distinguished three-term senator and Republican Senate minority leader, Howard Baker will probable always be remembered for his service as the leading Republican on the Senate committee investigating the Watergate scandal. His best-known line from that experience was his accurate insistence that the essence of the case against President RICHARD MILHOUS NIXON turned on the answer to the question, "What did the president know and when did he know it?"

Born in Huntsville, Tennessee, on November 15, 1925, Howard Henry Baker, Jr., was the son of an east Tennessee Republican member of the U.S. House of Representatives. He was raised in Washington during the months when his father was in the congressional session. In that capacity, he met Joy Dirksen, daughter of Illinois's famous Republican Senator EVERETT MCKINLEY DIRKSEN, and married her in 1951.

Baker was educated at the McCallie School, a distinguished private high school in Chattanooga, Tennessee. He attended the University of the South (Sewanee), Tulane University, and finally the University of Tennessee, from which he received his law degree in 1949. He practiced law for many years. When his father died, he considered running for the U.S. House of Representatives from his father's district, where he would have been virtually guaranteed election to a very safe

congressional seat held by a Republican almost continuously since the Civil War.

However, Baker perceived the time might be ripe for him to win the first statewide race for the Senate. In 1964, he mounted the first serious Republican race for the U.S. Senate. He was running in the same year that BARRY MORRIS GOLDWATER was the Republican nominee for president. With Goldwater threatening to sell the Tennessee Valley Authority (TVA) to private power companies, Baker had a hard time persuading the state's voters to abandon Tennessee's long-term affection for the federal agency that brought electric power to the state. Although he failed in 1964, the exposure of a statewide race made him a strong contender in the future.

Turmoil in the Tennessee Democratic Party helped as well. In 1964 Ross Bass, a Democratic congressman, had defeated the incumbent governor Frank Clement for the Democratic nomination for the Senate. Bass had then defeated Baker in the race to fill a vacancy created by the death of long-term Democratic senator ESTES COREY KEFAUVER, but his victory was only good for two years. When Bass ran again, he again faced Frank Clement in the Democratic primary. This time Clement had cut a deal with the Republicans. If the Republicans would cross over to vote in the Democratic primary, help him defeat Bass for the Democratic nomination, and help him name his personal choice for speaker of the Tennessee Senate, he would give them control of about a quarter of the election commissions in Tennessee, patronage control over a portion of the Tennessee State Troopers, and a new building for East Tennessee State University. Clement wrongly believed he would be able to take care of himself in the general election.

Although all parties denied the deal had been cut, the terms were so obvious that the denials could not be believed. Bass's supporters were incensed when the East Tennessee Republicans—having only unopposed candidates in their own primary—voted in the Democratic primary to defeat Bass and nominate Clement. Not only was there this vehement split among the Tennessee Democrats, but nationally the Democrats also suffered political reverses on both civil rights and the Vietnam War. By 1966, the political tide had turned sharply against President LYNDON BAINES JOHNSON and the Democratic Party. This time Baker defeated the Democratic nominee, Frank Clement, with ease.

Baker won reelection by a wide margin in 1972. In 1973, he received national recognition for his role as the senior Republican in the Senate's investigation of the Watergate scandal. The committee, chaired by Democratic Senator Sam Irvin of North Carolina, had Baker as the ranking Republican. He managed to portray himself as a moderate with a disinterested passion to learn the truth about the scandal, although his critics maintain he constantly informed the Nixon White House of the Watergate Committee's next move and helped steer the committee whenever he could. Baker's national reputation soared.

In 1977, at the start of the administration of President JAMES EARL CARTER, Baker was named the Republican Senate minority leader. He served until 1981 when he became the first Republican majority leader since the early 1950s. He received high marks for his role as majority leader, but he chose to retire from the Senate by not seeking reelection in 1984.

His retirement was short-lived as he was called upon to serve as President RONALD WILSON REAGAN's White House chief of staff from 1987 until the end of Reagan's term in 1989. Baker retired to private life where he maintained a law practice and authored a number of books. After his first wife died in 1993, Baker married one of his

Senate colleagues, former Senator NANCY LANDON KASSEBAUM, in 1996.

Further Reading
Annis, J. Lee. *Howard Baker: Conciliator in an Age of Crisis.* Lanham, Md.: Madison Books, 1995.

Baker, James Addison III
(1930–) *secretary of state, secretary of the treasury, undersecretary of commerce, White House chief of staff*

With his reemergence as the postelection point man for the GEORGE WALKER BUSH presidential campaign, James Baker stretched to more than a quarter of a century his involvement at the core of Republican presidential campaigns. His official bureaucratic posts pale beside his record for winning or almost winning presidential campaigns for his favorite Republican candidate.

James Addison Baker III was born on April 28, 1930, in Houston, Texas, in a well-to-do family. He graduated from Princeton in 1952, served in the Marine Corps until 1954, and graduated from the University of Texas at Austin Law School in 1957.

After practicing law for 13 years, he entered politics as a campaign manager for his old friend GEORGE HERBERT WALKER BUSH in his failed race for the U.S. Senate in 1970. In 1972, he was the chief fund-raiser for the Texas Republican Party in tandem with President RICHARD MILHOUS NIXON's 1972 reelection campaign. After Nixon's resignation, President GERALD RUDOLPH FORD brought Baker to Washington as undersecretary of commerce.

A year later, Baker resigned to become President Ford's campaign manager in his 1976 primary and general election campaign. Baker was credited with turning aside a spirited and very close challenge by RONALD WILSON REAGAN for the Republican presidential nomination—a contest so close that it was decided by fewer than 200 delegate votes at the Republican convention. Although President Ford was the Republican nominee, he faced an uphill battle against the Democratic presidential nominee, JAMES EARL CARTER, who held a double-digit lead in the polls during the summer of 1976. Baker was credited with having almost pulled the losing campaign to victory since the final vote was very close.

In 1980, Baker was again involved in a presidential campaign as the national campaign director for Bush in his race against Reagan for the presidential nomination. Although Bush lost, Baker was given credit for having made a strong showing against Reagan. When Reagan selected Bush as his running mate, Baker was again catapulted into a major national campaign role. He served so ably that he was selected as Reagan's chief of staff in 1981. Not only did he manage the personal and ideological minefield represented by the rest of Reagan's White House staff but he also aided in the passage of the famous "supply side" tax and budget package of 1981.

By 1985, Baker saw a chance to improve his own personal reputation by serving in the cabinet as U.S. secretary of the treasury. He promoted a plan to help underdeveloped nations stimulate their economies and pay down their debts. This so-called Baker plan failed, but Baker did succeed modestly in lowering the value of the dollar so that the burden was temporarily eased.

In 1988, Baker again left his governmental position to run a national presidential campaign for Vice President George Herbert Walker Bush. He handily outmaneuvered the other Republican hopefuls and then pulled off a come-from-behind victory for Bush over the Democratic nominee, Michael Dukakis.

Baker was rewarded with the post of secretary of state. As with his predecessors in that office, he attempted without success to broker a comprehensive peace agreement in the Middle East. He succeeded in facilitating the creation of the coalition that expelled the Iraqi forces from Kuwait in the Desert Storm campaign. He supported a variety of plans to cope with the collapse of the Soviet Union and its Eastern European communist regimes, the reunification of Germany, and the promotion of democratic reforms in Europe.

By 1992, Baker was again on the campaign trail. Initially, he had not intended to resign as secretary of state to run President Bush's reelection campaign since it was expected that Bush would

win easily. However, as the Bush campaign fell apart, Baker was pressured to take it over. Reluctantly, he accepted the assignment, but his magic did not work this time as WILLIAM JEFFERSON CLINTON won the presidency by a comfortable margin in a close race.

Baker returned to his private law practice and was out of the national spotlight until the day after the 2000 presidential election when he was called in to lead the attempt to win the White House for George W. Bush, the son of George Herbert Walker Bush. The younger Bush had lost a lead in polls before Election Day and had not won a majority of the popular votes. Bush was also behind in the Electoral College vote, but there remained a chance that Bush could still be elected president if he could maintain the popular vote totals in Florida to produce a narrow win. Baker led the effort and succeeded in assisting the election of George W. Bush with a victory in the U.S. Supreme Court. Baker remained in private life in 2001.

Further Reading

Baker, James Addison III. *The Politics of Diplomacy: Revolution, War, and Peace, 1989–1992.* New York: G. P. Putnam's Sons, 1995.

Bush, George H. W. *All the Best, George Bush.* New York: A Lisa Drew Book/Scribner, 1999.

Campbell, Colin, and Bert Rockman. *The Bush Presidency.* Chatham, N.J.: Chatham House Publishers, 1991.

Goldman, Peter, Tom Matthews, and the Newsweek Special Election Team. *The Quest for the Presidency 1988.* New York: Simon & Schuster, 1989.

Graubard, Stephen R. *Mr. Bush's War.* Hill & Wang, 1992.

Baker, Newton Diehl
(1871–1937) *secretary of war*

Newton Baker is credited with having created the essential framework of the federal government's civil service system in his efforts to build up the government's strength during World War I.

Born on December 3, 1871, in Martinsburg, West Virginia, Newton Diehl Baker moved to Maryland and then Virginia to attend school.

Graduating from Johns Hopkins in 1892 and Washington and Lee Law School in 1894, he returned to Martinsburg briefly to practice law. Political connections landed him a brief post as secretary to the U.S. postmaster general in the closing days of STEPHEN GROVER CLEVELAND's administration.

After the end of the Cleveland administration, Baker moved to Cleveland, Ohio. He practiced law but was attracted to the politics of the Progressive movement. At the turn of the century, he was the city solicitor for Cleveland under the Progressive reform administration of Democrat Tom Johnson. Elected mayor in his own right in 1911, he improved the city's hospitals, organized a city orchestra, built a new city-owned electric power plant, and pushed through a new home rule charter.

With this background, he was interested in the candidacy of THOMAS WOODROW WILSON (who shared the Johns Hopkins connection as well). Baker arranged for Wilson to receive all 19 of Ohio's Democratic National Convention delegates, and then he served out his term as Cleveland's mayor. When it was over, Wilson offered Baker the cabinet post of secretary of war. Their mutual quiet, scholarly approach to government made them natural allies.

Baker was a pacifist by background, but he loyally committed himself to the war once it began. He organized the draft and marshaled national economic resources for the war effort. After 1916, the army grew from less than 100,000 to more than 4 million. During the two years of United States participation in World War I, 2 million served in France. These soldiers were Baker's responsibility since the U.S. troops served only under U.S. General Pershing. While he faced some congressional criticism for a lack of preparedness when the war broke out, the real cause of any lack of preparedness predated Baker. History has recorded that he did an outstanding job of efficiently and honestly expanding the U.S. armed forces to an unprecedented degree.

Baker's close association with Wilson continued after the president suffered his incapacitating strokes in 1919. He strongly defended the president's plan for the League of Nations as a part of the Versailles Peace Treaty. After the end of the Wilson administration, he returned to Cleveland

to practice law, but he continued to support U.S. participation in the League. In 1928, he was appointed to the Permanent Court of Arbitration located at The Hague. He supported Democratic candidates for president including FRANKLIN DELANO ROOSEVELT, but he came to oppose portions of the New Deal, such as the Tennessee Valley Authority, as being too close to socialism. He suffered a severe heart attack in July 1937 and died on December 25 of that year.

Further Reading

Ambrosius, Lloyd E. *Wilsonian Statecraft: Theory and Practice of Liberal Internationalism During World War I.* Wilmington, Del.: SR Books, 1991.

Baker, Newton Diehl. *Frontiers of Freedom.* New York: George H. Doran Company, 1918.

———. *Progress and the Constitution.* New York: Scribner's, 1925.

———. *Why We Went to War.* New York: Harper, 1936 (also Freeport, N.Y.: Books for Libraries Press, 1972).

Beaver, Daniel R. *Newton D. Baker and the American War Effort, 1917–1919.* Lincoln: University of Nebraska Press, 1966.

Cramer, Clarence Henley. *Newton D. Baker, A Biography.* Cleveland, Ohio: World Publishing Company, 1961.

Knock, Thomas J. *To End All Wars: Woodrow Wilson and the Quest for a New World Order.* Princeton, N.J.: Princeton University Press, 1995.

Ninkovich, Frank A. *The Wilsonian Century: U.S. Foreign Policy Since 1900.* Chicago: University of Chicago Press, 1999.

Palmer, Frederick. *Newton D. Baker: America At War.* New York: Kraus, 1969.

Thornton, Willis. *Newton D. Baker and His Books.* Cleveland, Ohio: Press of Western Reserve University, 1954.

Ballinger, Richard Achilles
(1858–1922) *secretary of the interior*

Richard Achilles Ballinger was at the center of the first genuine scandal surrounding conservation and the preservation of the environment in the United States. His middle name invited the observation that he was the "Achilles heel" of President

WILLIAM HOWARD TAFT's administration efforts to balance economic development with concerns about conservation.

Born in Boonesboro (now Boone), Iowa, on July 9, 1858, Ballinger attended Williams College, graduated in 1884, read in the law, and was admitted to the bar in 1886. Ballinger moved to Washington shortly before it became a state. By 1894, he was a Jefferson County Superior Court judge. From 1904 to 1906, he was Seattle's mayor. After serving as commissioner of the General Land Office after 1907, Ballinger was appointed secretary of the interior in 1909 by President William Howard Taft.

Ballinger was controversial from the start. L. R. Glavis of the General Land Office charged that Ballinger had stopped an investigation into allegedly false coal claims in Alaska by going over Glavis's head directly to Taft. Taft responded by authorizing Ballinger to fire Glavis. Glavis took his case to the public through an article in Collier's Weekly.

GIFFORD PINCHOT, the most prominent conservationist of the age and the chief of the Bureau of Forestry, took up the Glavis cause. A firestorm of criticism erupted among conservationists and their Progressive allies. President Taft seemed personally out of step with the movement and reluctant to pursue the interests of the Progressives despite policies and actions compatible with conservation and the Progressive movement. Glavis's charges gained traction. That Ballinger was a corporate lawyer made him seem an obvious target.

At best, Ballinger was accused of being slow to defend conservationist principles; at worst, he was accused of being willing to allow all Alaska land claims. Although a congressional hearing eventually exonerated Ballinger of the specific wrongdoing charged, Ballinger realized he had become a problem for the Taft administration and he resigned in March 1911. Taft managed to control enough of the Republican Party apparatus to secure the presidential nomination over former Republican president THEODORE ROOSEVELT, but Roosevelt walked out of the party and secured the Progressive Party nomination. Both the Democratic presidential nominee, THOMAS WOODROW WILSON, and the Progressive Party nominee, Roosevelt, ravished Taft

on the Ballinger issue in the 1912 presidential election. Taft came in third in the election, the only time the Republican Party had come in third in a national election since 1860. These political side issues have overshadowed the fact that Ballinger was never found to have done anything wrong. Pinchot's defense of Glavis's charges was essentially incorrect on the facts.

Ballinger withdrew from public life and died on June 6, 1922.

Further Reading

Hays, Samuel P. Conservation and the Gospel of Efficiency: The Progressive Conservation Movement, 1890–1920. Pittsburgh, Pa.: University of Pittsburgh Press, 1999.

Mason, Alpheus Thomas. Bureaucracy Convicts Itself: The Ballinger-Pinchot Controversy of 1910. New York: Viking, 1941.

McCulloch, Winifred. The Glavis-Ballinger Dispute. Syracuse, N.Y.: Inter-University Case Program, 1952.

Penick, James L. Progressive Politics and Conservation: The Ballinger-Pinchot Affair. Chicago: University of Chicago Press, 1968.

Bankhead, William
(1874–1940) Speaker of the House, representative

Although a lifelong conservative, William Bankhead made his greatest contribution as a loyal Democratic Party leader who supported the New Deal as Speaker of the House of Representatives.

Born in Moscow, Alabama, on April 12, 1874, William Bankhead came from a prominent Alabama political family. Both his father and brother were U.S. senators. Bankhead was an excellent student and graduated from the University of Alabama in 1893. Moving to Washington, D.C., he graduated from Georgetown University in 1895, but he returned to Huntsville, Alabama, to establish a law practice.

Bankhead entered politics in 1900 with a winning race for the state legislature where he served for 14 years. He failed in his first race for Congress in 1914, but he won in 1916 and was reelected continuously until 1940. Bankhead was a loyal

Democrat who overcame his conservative principles to support FRANKLIN DELANO ROOSEVELT's New Deal program in the Congress. While he was pleased with programs such as the Tennessee Valley Authority (TVA), because it aided his home state greatly, he was generally afraid of the growth of the federal government.

His loyalty was rewarded by his being elevated to the House Rules Committee in 1933. Two years later, he moved up to be the Democratic majority leader. Finally, he was elected the Speaker of the U.S. House of Representatives in 1936. Serving as Speaker for four critical years, he repeatedly advanced the cause of New Deal programs in the House.

Bankhead was selected as the keynote speaker for the 1940 Democratic National Convention. Conservative Democrats saw this speech as an opportunity to attempt to block the nomination of Henry A. Wallace as Roosevelt's vice presidential running mate in 1940, and they put forward Bankhead's name for vice president. Surprising pundits by marshaling 329 delegate votes, Bankhead was unable to sustain the effort, and Henry A. Wallace was selected as the vice presidential nominee. Still this was the highest honor of Bankhead's career and came shortly before his death on September 15, 1940.

Further Reading

Davis, Kenneth S. *FDR: Three Volumes.* New York: Random House, 1993.

McJimsey, George T. *The Presidency of Franklin Delano Roosevelt.* Lawrence: University Press of Kansas, 2000.

Morris, Jeffrey. *The FDR Way.* Minneapolis: Lerner Publications, 1996.

Owen, Thomas McAdory. *History of Alabama and Dictionary of Alabama Biography.* Chicago: The S. J. Clarke Publishing Co., 1921.

Banks, Nathaniel Prentiss
(1816–1894) *Speaker of the House, representative*

Nathaniel Banks was one of the most interesting politicians in American history, because he successfully ran for office in three different political parties during the course of his career.

Born on January 30, 1816, in Boston, Massachusetts, Nathaniel Prentiss Banks received little formal schooling because he had to work in his father's cotton mill. This experience led people to refer to him as "Bobbin Boy" when he switched back and forth among three different parties.

Banks's ambition went far beyond the textile business. Admitted to the bar at the age of 23 after having merely "read" in the law, he did not practice law immediately. Rather he served as an inspector in the Boston customs house until he became the proprietor and editor of the daily newspaper.

Banks was determined to win public office. Before he was 33 years old, he had already run seven times unsuccessfully for the Massachusetts House of Representatives. Finally, in 1849, he was elected to the Massachusetts legislature and was successfully elevated to Speaker in 1851. The following year he was elected to the U.S. House of Representatives as a Democrat.

His antislavery views were so strong that he refused to vote for the Kansas Nebraska Act in 1854. This angered his Democratic supporters and they refused to back him for reelection. Banks then switched to the American or Know-Nothing Party to win reelection in that year. Surprisingly, Banks was elected Speaker in 1856. Banks viewed the office of Speaker as an impartial job and he served all sides fairly. He was so impressive that he was offered the presidential nomination of the northern branch of the American Party. Banks declined in order to lead his antislavery supporters into the Republican Party. In 1857 Banks left the House of Representatives to run for governor of Massachusetts where he served for three years as a distinguished progressive governor.

In early 1861, he moved to Chicago to become president of the Illinois Central Railway. With the outbreak of the Civil War, he joined the army as a major general in the militia. His military career was unsuccessful, except for the help he gave to General ULYSSES S. GRANT at Vicksburg. Against his wishes, he was placed in charge of the ill-conceived Red River campaign, which ended in a bloody defeat at Mansfield.

Banks returned to Boston and ran for Congress as a Republican. He was very independent and opposed his party's policy on tight money, but he backed Secretary WILLIAM HENRY SEWARD's purchase of Alaska from the Russians. His reputation for integrity was so great that he was selected for the Committee of Five to investigate the Crédit Mobilier scandal, a financial scandal that occurred during the administration of President Grant.

Dismayed by the conduct of his former army commander, President Grant, Banks supported HORACE GREELEY, the Democratic presidential nominee, over Grant in 1872. This angered Republican friends and he was not reelected. However, he was easily elected to Congress in 1875 as a Democrat. Two years later, he switched back and ran as a Republican. After being out of politics for 10 years he came back to serve one term as a Republican from 1889 to 1891. He died on September 1, 1894.

Further Reading

Harrington, Fred Harvey. *Fighting Politician, Major General N. P. Banks.* Westport, Conn.: Greenwood Press, 1970.

Silbey, Joel H. "Nathaniel P. Banks" in *The Encyclopedia of Third Parties in America,* edited by Immanuel Ness and James Ciment. Armonk, N.Y.: M. E. Sharpe, Inc., 2000.

Barkley, Alben William

(1877–1956) *vice president, senator, representative*

Alben Barkley had a long and distinguished career in Congress and was one of the most popular vice presidents in U.S. history. He was also the oldest person to serve as vice president.

Born on November 24, 1877, in Graves County, Kentucky, Alben William Barkley was the son of a poor tobacco farmer. He attended Marvin College and later studied law at Emory in Georgia and the University of Virginia.

Barkley passed the bar, returned to Kentucky to practice law in 1901, and was a judge in McCraden Court from 1909 to 1913. He was quickly elected to Congress in 1912 and served in the House of Representatives until 1926. Starting in 1926, he served four consecutive Senate terms and became the Democratic Senate majority leader in 1937. He was a strong supporter of both President FRANKLIN DELANO ROOSEVELT's New Deal legislation and President HARRY S. TRUMAN's Fair Deal program.

As a popular border state Democrat, Barkley had been considered as a vice presidential possibility at various times for 20 years before President Truman selected him in 1948. Truman initially thought that the 70-year-old Barkley was too old to run in 1948. Truman had wanted to persuade the associate Supreme Court justice WILLIAM ORVILLE DOUGLAS to step down from the Court to be his running mate, but Douglas decided against the risk. In the end, Barkley surprised everyone by being a very active campaigner. He campaigned more vigorously than many younger individuals might have. His border state popularity no doubt held Truman in the critical middle of the political spectrum. Barkley was a clear success. As vice president, he participated in important meetings and discussed major issues with Truman. Truman decided the vice president should be well informed.

He was so popular that he became a nationally known beloved figure: the "Veep." The very adoption of that appellation reveals the national affection. It was Barkley's grandson who gave him the name. He once referred to Barkley as "Veep," and the moniker stuck.

Although he was considered too old to run for president in 1952, he returned to Kentucky and was elected to the Senate in 1954. Although he did not have the seniority he had earned prior to becoming vice president, he was a much respected and beloved elder statesman of the Senate. He died on April 30, 1956, at the age of 79 while making a speech in Lexington, Virginia.

Further Reading

Barkley, Alben William. *That Reminds Me.* Garden City, N.Y.: Doubleday, 1954.

Barkley, Jane Rucker. *I Married the Veep.* New York: Vanguard Press, 1958.

Davis, Polly Ann. *Alben W. Barkley, Senate Majority Leader and Vice President.* New York: Garland Publishing, 1979.

Hernon, Joseph Martin. *Profiles in Character: Hubris and Heroism in the U.S. Senate—1789–1990.* Armonk, N.Y.: M. E. Sharpe, 1997.

Libbey, James K. *Dear Alben: Mr. Barkley of Kentucky.* Lexington: University Press of Kentucky, 1979.

Belknap, William Worth
(1829–1890) *secretary of war*

William Belknap was the only cabinet officer to be impeached by the U.S. House of Representatives; however, he was not convicted and removed from office because he resigned before the Senate vote was taken.

William Worth Belknap was born in Newburgh, New York, on September 22, 1829. An able student, he attended the College of New Jersey (now called Princeton). After studying law at Georgetown University, he was admitted to the Iowa bar in 1851 and began his law career in Keokuk, Iowa.

Belknap was elected as a Democrat to the Iowa legislature in 1857 and again in 1858. With the coming of the Civil War, he was named a major in the Iowa militia. He fought well at Shiloh and was promoted to general, receiving numerous citations for bravery from General William T. Sherman and General (later President) ULYSSES S. GRANT.

Belknap was a tax collector when he returned Ohio after the Civil War. In 1869 President Grant invited him to be secretary of war. In that job, Belknap was responsible for appointments to military installations. In one case, he was accused of taking a bribe in order to make a favorable choice.

It now seems possible that the real culprit was Belknap's wife, who apparently took the bribe without telling her husband. Based on preliminary evidence, Belknap was impeached by the House of Representatives. However, Grant allowed him to resign and therefore the Senate concluded that they could no longer convict him. Belknap's conviction failed, but his political career was ruined.

For the last 20 years of his life, he practiced law in Philadelphia and Washington, D.C. He died on October 13, 1890.

Further Reading

Hernon, Joseph Martin. *Profiles in Character: Hubris and Heroism in the U.S. Senate—1789–1990.* Armonk, N.Y.: M. E. Sharpe, 1997.

Bell, John
(1797–1869) *secretary of war, candidate for president, senator, representative*

John Bell had a distinguished political career until the Civil War when his career was destroyed by the sectional disunity over slavery. Bell's fate is a classic case of the failure of a moderate politician in times when radicals and political extremists pulled a society apart.

John Bell was born on February 15, 1797, in Nashville, Tennessee, shortly after Tennessee became a state. He was a gifted student who graduated from Cumberland College before the age of 17. He completed his legal studies, was admitted to the bar, served one term as a state senator, established a successful law practice in Franklin, Tennessee, and then celebrated his 21st birthday.

By the time he was 30, he had been elected to the U.S. House of Representatives. As a Tennesseean, he strongly supported the policies of President ANDREW JACKSON for many years. However, he parted with the president over Jackson's war against the Second National Bank. He resisted Jackson's threat to destroy him and went on to build the Whig Party in Tennessee. Under Bell's leadership, the Whig Party dominated Tennessee for almost two decades after the demise of Jackson.

In 1841, WILLIAM HENRY HARRISON selected Bell to be his secretary of war. Six years later, Bell was elected to the Senate where he served until 1859. He had long advocated moderation and he did so on the divisive slavery issue. He believed that Congress could ban slavery in the territories won during the Mexican War, but he never pushed for that position legislatively. He opposed HENRY CLAY over those parts of the Compromise of 1850 that dealt with slavery and the territories, but he supported the law after it was adopted. He differed with his southern friends over the Kansas

Nebraska Act and later opposed the admission of Kansas as a state under the controversial pro-slavery state constitution (as favored by the South). Having earlier lost his friends in the North for not opposing slavery strongly enough, he was now hated in the South.

The Whig Party was torn apart over slavery. Bell and the other former Whigs formed the Constitutional Unity Party in a forlorn attempt to avoid the Civil War. Bell was nominated for president and Edward Everett of Massachusetts was nominated for vice president from that party, but their ticket carried only Tennessee, Kentucky, and Virginia.

Bell opposed secession but also hated ABRAHAM LINCOLN for using force to try to restore the Union. When Union troops entered Tennessee, Bell fled farther south and urged Tennesseans and other Southerners to resist the Union forces at any cost. Having spent most of the war in Georgia, he returned to Tennessee after the war and died on September 10, 1869.

Further Reading

"John Bell" in *The Presidency A to Z: Second Edition,* edited by Michael T. Nelson. Washington, D.C.: Congressional Quarterly Press, 1998.

Parks, Joseph Howard. *John Bell of Tennessee.* Baton Rouge: Louisiana State University Press, 1950.

Parks, Norman Lexington. *The Career of John Bell as Congressman from Tennessee, 1827–1841.* Nashville, Tenn.: Joint University Libraries, 1942.

Benjamin, Judah Philip
(1811–1884) *senator, Confederate leader*

Judah Philip Benjamin held more high-ranking national offices than any other Jewish person in 19th-century America. These offices were mainly held in the Confederate states during the Civil War. Benjamin was regarded as the brightest intellect among the leaders of the Confederacy. While he held an office as senator in the U.S. government, he is best known for having served as JEFFERSON DAVIS's attorney general, secretary of war, and secretary of state during the Civil War.

Benjamin was born on August 6, 1811, to Jewish parents on the island of St. Thomas, then a part of the British West Indies. He immigrated with his family to Charleston, South Carolina. Benjamin was a brilliant student and attended Yale. After Yale, he moved to New Orleans and supported himself as a teacher while reading for the law. He was only 21 years old when he was admitted to the bar in 1832. He quickly established a prosperous legal practice and later gained national recognition for his dissertation on the international and domestic legal consequences of slavery in the *Creole* case.

With his very successful legal practice, Benjamin was able to earn enough money to buy a large sugar plantation. Soon he entered politics as a Whig, running for and winning a seat in the Louisiana state legislature in 1842. Based on his legislative service, he was elected to the U.S. Senate in 1852. Four years later, the Whig Party was torn apart by slavery and Benjamin became a Democrat.

In the U.S. Senate, Benjamin strongly supported slavery and other Southern positions, but he was not blind to national concerns. He supported the creation of the Illinois Central Railroad and other commercial ventures that could have united the nation, had not the growing tension over slavery split it apart. Reelected to the U.S. Senate in 1858, Benjamin concluded that the South could never succeed given the dominance of the Northern states in the union. As soon as President ABRAHAM LINCOLN was elected, Benjamin advocated secession. He resigned from the Senate immediately after Louisiana voted for secession in 1861.

During his Senate career, Benjamin became a close friend and political supporter of Jefferson Davis. When Davis was elected president of the Confederacy, he appointed Benjamin his attorney general. As soon as active fighting began a few months later, Davis appointed Benjamin the secretary of war.

The Confederacy, by its nature, lacked centralized control and Benjamin was unable to persuade the individual states to provide the necessary men and other military resources. Nonetheless, Benjamin was blamed for the South's early failures. After the South lost control of Roanoke Island in 1862, Benjamin's southern enemies tried to have him removed as secretary of war. President Davis reacted to the criticism against Benjamin as an attack on himself. To spite his critics, Davis removed Benjamin as secretary of war and appointed him the Confederacy's secretary of state.

Benjamin's popularity did not increase by this move. Still he did his best to ignore hostile public opinion and continued to work hard to obtain diplomatic recognition for the Confederacy. He was unable to counter the able representation of the Union by CHARLES FRANCIS ADAMS in his capacity as U.S. ambassador to Great Britain. Benjamin had no better success elsewhere in Europe, and the Confederacy remained isolated. In the closing days of the war, Benjamin advocated allowing slaves to enlist in the Confederate Army in return for promising to free them at the end of the war. His view was not adopted.

Benjamin managed to flee to the West Indies and later immigrated to Great Britain. He spent the last two decades of his life in Europe and died on May 6, 1884.

Further Reading

Butler, Pierce. *Judah P. Benjamin.* New York: Chelsea House, 1980.

Evans, Eli N. *Judah P. Benjamin, The Jewish Confederate.* New York: Free Press, 1989.

Goodhart, Arthur Lehman, Sir. *Five Jewish Lawyers of the Common Law.* Freeport, N.Y.: Books for Libraries Press, 1971.

Hagan, Horace H. (Horace Henry). *Eight Great American Lawyers.* Oklahoma City, Okla.: Harlow Publishing Company, 1923.

Meade, Robert Douthat. *Judah P. Benjamin: Confederate Statesman.* New York: Arno Press, 1975.

Neiman, Simon I. *Judah Benjamin.* Indianapolis, Ind.: Bobbs-Merrill, 1963.

Osterweis, Rollin Gustav. *Judah P. Benjamin, Statesman of the Lost Cause.* New York: Putnam, 1933.

Rosen, Robert N. *The Jewish Confederates.* Columbia: University of South Carolina Press, 2000.

Young, Mel. *Where They Lie.* Lanham, Md.: University Press of America, 1991.

Benton, Thomas Hart
(1782–1858) *senator, representative*

Thomas Hart Benton was the first person to serve 30 years (or five full terms) in the U.S. Senate. By looking on the Senate as a long-term career—instead of futilely seeking the presidency as some of his colleagues did—he compiled a historical reputation that exceeds many others who sought the presidency. Identified with American expansion through the doctrine of Manifest Destiny, Benton strongly favored the granting of homesteads to farmers as a method of settling the West. He is perhaps best remembered for his conversion from a supporter of slavery to an ardent opponent of slavery's spread to the territories.

Benton was born on March 14, 1782, in Hillsboro, North Carolina. In 1801, he moved to Ten-

Thomas Hart Benton, the first senator to serve 30 years, evolved into an opponent of slavery. *(Library of Congress)*

nessee to help his widowed mother run her farm, but he returned to North Carolina where he was elected to the state senate in 1809. During his early career, he was involved in land ownership issues and the rights of slaves in capital trials. He "read" in the law and was admitted to the bar in 1811.

He fought in the War of 1812 and then moved to St. Louis, Missouri, where he practiced law and became the editor of the *St. Louis Enquirer*. Benton rose quickly in politics and was elected by the state legislature to the U.S. Senate in 1820. Although he initially favored slavery and opposed restricting its expansion into Missouri, he changed his mind after 1828 and came to favor slavery's gradual abolition. Partly because he was in favor of the United States expanding westward and improving its continental transportation and communication, Benton saw slavery as an obstacle to the further development and settlement of the West.

Benton strongly endorsed President ANDREW JACKSON's policies and became the Senate floor leader during Jackson's war on the Second National Bank. Benton feared that the National Bank would create inequities. He also favored gold coin and the payment for public lands in hard currency. This led him to oppose the Second National Bank's power to issue commercial loans and notes. It was for these views that he was nicknamed "Old Bullion."

In 1831, Benton sponsored legislation to oppose rechartering the National Bank and favored the removal of government receipts from the bank before the expiration of its old charter. More than anyone else, he was responsible for seeing that Jackson's veto of a new charter was sustained. This, in turn, led to making the rechartering of the National Bank the key issue in the 1832 presidential campaign.

Benton initially opposed the annexation of Texas because he saw it as clearly tied to the expansion of slavery, but he later supported the war with Mexico that grew out of the Texas annexation. His views on slavery did not call for complete, immediate abolition but did include his conviction that Congress had the right to prohibit slavery in the territories. As part of his political moderation, he supported states' rights but was not willing to endorse the extreme nullification doctrine. Eventually, he concluded that the southern

support of slavery was a serious threat to the peace and continued existence of the United States.

By 1850, Benton had become so concerned about the spread of slavery to the territories that he opposed the southern position on the Compromise of 1850, even though that compromise was favored in his home state of Missouri. This last fight caused him to lose his Senate seat after five terms and a total of 30 years. Although he had carefully advanced Missouri's interests by supporting the Pony Express, the telegraph, and the transcontinental railroad, his constituents' strong support of slavery overrode their otherwise great appreciation of his accomplishments.

Always a fighter, Benton then ran for and won a seat in the U.S. House of Representatives, where he fought against the repeal of the Missouri Compromise. This angered his constituents still more and he was not reelected. In 1856, he was defeated when he ran for the Missouri governorship. He retired from public life and wrote two books on his congressional career in the next two years. His lifetime record makes him one of the most colorful and controversial figures in 19th-century American politics. He died on April 10, 1858.

Further Reading

Benton, Thomas Hart. *A History of the Working of the American Government for Thirty Years*. New York: D. Appleton, 1854.

"Benton, Thomas Hart" in *Congress A to Z: Third Edition*, edited by David R. Tarr and Ann O'Connor. Washington, D.C.: Congressional Quarterly, 1999.

Chambers, William Nisbet. *Old Bullion Benton; Senator from the New West: Thomas Hart Benton, 1782–1858*. New York: Russell & Russell, 1970.

Hernon, Joseph Martin. *Profiles in Character: Hubris and Heroism in the U.S. Senate—1789–1990*. Armonk, N.Y.: M. E. Sharpe, 1997.

Meigs, William Montgomery. *The Life of Thomas Hart Benton*. New York: Da Capo Press, 1970.

Rogers, Joseph Morgan. *Thomas H. Benton*. Philadelphia: G. W. Jacobs & Company, 1905.

Roosevelt, Theodore. *Thomas H. Benton*. New York: AMS Press, 1972.

Smith, Elbert B. *Magnificent Missourian: The Life of Thomas Hart Benton*. Westport, Conn.: Greenwood Press, 1973.

Berger, Victor Luitpold
(1860–1929) *representative (rare socialist elected official), author*

A leading Progressive thinker, Victor Berger was the first socialist, and one of only a few socialists ever, to be elected to the U.S. House of Representatives.

Born on February 28, 1860, in Austria, Victor Luitpold Berger grew up in nearby Hungary. Before he was 18, he had already attended universities in Vienna and Budapest. In 1878, he immigrated to the United States by way of Bridgeport, Connecticut, where he lived until he moved to Milwaukee, Wisconsin, in 1881. Although he first worked at a wide variety of menial and semiskilled jobs, he became a teacher of German language studies in the public schools in Milwaukee.

Always progressive in his thinking, he was active in several reform movements, trade unions, and local socialist organizations. He strongly favored cooperation among socialist groups and called for gradual reform. In cooperation with Eugene V. Debs, he founded the Social Democratic Party in 1899. Two years later, he transformed the Social Democratic Party into the Socialist Party. Because of his commitment to gradualism, he is generally referred to as a right-wing socialist who was willing to work through the democratic election process, as opposed to a left-wing socialist who advocated the revolutionary overthrow of the government.

Key to Berger's political success was his establishment in 1892 of the Milwaukee *Vorwaerts*, a German-language daily newspaper, which he edited until 1898. From 1901 to 1911 he also edited the weekly *Social Democratic Herald*. Finally he moved on to the editorship of the *Milwaukee Leader*, a position he held until his death. Involved in politics at all levels, he was determined to make Milwaukee an outstanding example of "municipal socialism" by supporting public ownership of basic utilities and transportation systems.

In 1910, Berger won a very close election to Congress as a representative of Milwaukee and its neighboring suburbs. During this brief two-year term, he set the agenda for wide-ranging and long-lasting reforms, such as the eight-hour workday, child labor protection laws, federal aid for farmers, and old age pensions.

A pacifist, Berger also supported international disarmament, but this position led to his defeat in 1912 and 1914. By 1918, however, his pacifist views were more popular and he was elected on a strong antiwar platform. Despite his support in Milwaukee, the Congress as a whole barred him from his seat in November 1919, alleging that he was disloyal to the United States by giving "aid and comfort" to the German enemy during World War I by supporting antiwar efforts.

Berger followed the views of most U.S. socialists in opposing U.S. participation in World War I. This was a popular position among his overwhelmingly German immigrant constituents in Milwaukee. However, Congress had passed the Espionage Act of 1917 and the Sedition Act of 1918, which allowed the federal government to imprison socialists for expressing their opposition to the war. Berger was sentenced to 20 years for sedition, but the U.S. Supreme Court overturned his conviction. In a special election in 1919, Berger was elected to a vacant congressional seat but again was refused admission by the House of Representatives.

Determined to make a comeback, Berger fought for and won three successive terms in Congress starting in 1922. The political climate of the 1920s was not favorable for the socialist movement, so his influence and success in Congress were limited. He left the Congress in 1928; he died less than a year later on August 7, 1929.

Further Reading

Berger, Victor L. *Broadsides: Third Edition*. Milwaukee, Wis.: Social-Democratic Publishing Company, 1913.

Chafee, Zechariah. *Free Speech in the United States*. Cambridge, Mass.: Harvard University Press, 1967.

De Leon, Daniel. *A Socialist in Congress: His Conduct and Responsibilities*. New York: New York Labor News Company, 1963.

Miller, Sally M. *Victor Berger and the Promise of Constructive Socialism, 1910–1920*. Westport, Conn.: Greenwood Press, 1973.

———. "Victor Luitpold Berger" in *The Encyclopedia of Third Parties in America*, edited by Immanuel Ness and James Ciment. Armonk, N.Y.: M. E. Sharpe, Inc., 2000.

Sullivan, David Knowles. *The Exclusion of Victor Berger from Congress*. Chicago.: De Paul University, 1968.

Beveridge, Albert Jeremiah

(1862–1927) *senator, Progressive Party leader*

Both a professional historian and a politician, Albert Jeremiah Beveridge was a leading figure in the Republican Party and the Progressive movement.

Born in Highland County, Ohio, on October 6, 1862, Beveridge and his family moved to Illinois shortly thereafter, and he grew up there on a small farm. In 1885, he graduated from Asbury College in Greencastle, Indiana (now called DePauw University). Two years later, he moved to Indiana where he was admitted to the bar and began a law practice in 1887.

An excellent orator, Beveridge used his skills to advance the cause of many Republican candidates. When a deadlock developed in the Indiana legislature over the naming of a new senator in 1899, Beveridge was selected as the compromise choice and was easily reelected in 1905.

Both Republican and Progressive, Beveridge supported President THEODORE ROOSEVELT's conservation programs, trust regulation reform, and the strengthening of the U.S. Navy. He also introduced one of the first meat inspection laws and worked for the passage of child labor protection acts.

Beveridge's progressive views included opposition to the Payne-Aldrich Tariff Act of 1909 and a variety of business regulation measures. Eventually his advanced views created such opposition among his constituents that he lost his reelection attempt in 1911.

In 1912, Beveridge helped found the Progressive (or Bull Moose) Party and delivered the keynote address at its first national nominating convention. As a Progressive, he lost the gubernatorial election in Indiana that year. In 1914, he ran unsuccessfully for the U.S. Senate as a Progressive. In 1922, he switched back to being a Republican, but he lost a U.S. Senate race again.

After 1922, he retired from politics and became an accomplished historian, winning the Pulitzer Prize for his four-volume biography of JOHN MARSHALL. When he died on April 27, 1927, he had completed two volumes of a still more ambitious multivolume biography of ABRAHAM LINCOLN. The two volumes were published in 1928 after his death.

Further Reading

Beveridge, Albert Jeremiah. *Abraham Lincoln, 1809–1858*. Boston: Houghton Mifflin Company, 1928.

———. *The Life of John Marshall*. Boston: Houghton Mifflin Company, 1919.

———. *The State of the Nation*. Indianapolis, Ind.: Bobbs-Merrill, 1924.

Bowers, Claude Gernade. *Beveridge and the Progressive Era*. Boston: Houghton Mifflin Company, 1932.

Braeman, John. *Albert J. Beveridge: American Nationalist*. Chicago: University of Chicago Press, 1971.

"Beveridge, Albert" in *Congress A to Z: Third Edition*, edited by David R. Tarr and Ann O'Connor. Washington, D.C.: Congressional Quarterly, 1999.

Hernon, Joseph Martin. *Profiles in Character: Hubris and Heroism in the U.S. Senate—1789–1990*. Armonk, N.Y.: M. E. Sharpe, 1997.

Biddle, Nicholas

(1786–1844) *diplomat, president of the Second Bank of the United States*

Nicholas Biddle was a child prodigy whose rapid rise to national prominence was cut short when the Second National Bank, which he headed, was eliminated by the policies of President ANDREW JACKSON.

Biddle was born on January 8, 1786, in Philadelphia, Pennsylvania. When he was only 10, he entered the University of Pennsylvania and graduated at 13. He completed his advanced degree at Princeton University (then called the College of New Jersey) in 1801 at the age of 15. In 1804, when he was 18, he became the secretary to the U.S. minister to France and later to England. At the age of 21, he returned to Philadelphia, "read" for the law, and was admitted to the bar in 1809.

Biddle apparently never intended to practice law but used its study merely as an intellectual exercise. He pursued a cultured life, participated in academic discussions, and wrote literary articles. Early on, he prepared the official account—based on the notes and journals written by the explorers—of Lewis and Clark's expedition to the Pacific Ocean. He served a single term from 1810 to 1811 in the Pennsylvania House of Representatives and served one term in the state senate in 1814.

President JAMES MONROE was authorized to select five of a total of 25 directors of the Second National Bank of the United States. In 1819 he selected the 33-year-old Biddle to be one of them. Biddle quickly advanced as a member of the board and was selected to replace the original president in 1823. While he was president, the bank group increased its public confidence by providing a stable money supply and restraining state chartered banks from engaging in unwise loans and other risky business ventures.

At first, Biddle was determined to keep the bank out of politics. Biddle was naive in thinking that the bank was so necessary to the United States that nothing could cause it to be destroyed. However, Biddle and his friends recognized that the election of Andrew Jackson was a threat to the progress of the bank because Jackson had spoken so strongly against the bank in the campaign of 1828. Still Biddle thought that educating the public about currency, finance, and economics would be sufficient to save the bank.

Biddle launched an aggressive campaign for the bank by writing articles. He also sought political support from politicians by granting them various bank favors. HENRY CLAY and DANIEL WEBSTER, two of the most famous senators of the day, influenced Biddle to seek a new charter in 1832, years before it was due to expire. This mistake allowed President Jackson to veto the bank recharter measure and make the bank the chief issue in the presidential campaign. Missouri Senator THOMAS HART BENTON led the effort in the Congress to sustain the president's veto.

When Jackson won reelection, it was clear that the Second National Bank of the United States was finished. In 1836, it became a state bank and in 1841 went bankrupt. Biddle bailed out of the bank in 1839 and spent the remainder of a short life writing and engaging in academic discussions from his home in Delaware. He died on February 27, 1844.

Further Reading
Govan, Thomas Payne. *Nicholas Biddle: Nationalist and Public Banker, 1786–1844.* Chicago: University of Chicago Press, 1959.
Hernon, Joseph Martin. *Profiles in Character: Hubris and Heroism in the U.S. Senate—1789–1990.* Armonk, N.Y.: M. E. Sharpe, 1997.
McGrane, Reginald Charles. *The Correspondence of Nicholas Biddle Dealing with National Affairs, 1807–1844.* Boston: J. S. Canner, 1966.
———. *The Panic of 1837.* New York: Russell & Russell, 1965.

Birney, James Gillespie
(1792–1857) *state legislator, candidate for president, author*

James Gillespie Birney was a key figure in the pre–Civil War antislavery movement. Having begun life as a slave owner, he evolved from a mild supporter to a militant abolitionist leader, which made him a key figure in the effort of abolitionism despite his failure to win public office.

Birney was born on February 4, 1892, near Danville, Kentucky. At the age of 18, he graduated from Princeton University (then known as the College of New Jersey). Having read in the law, Birney was admitted to the bar in 1814 at the age of 22. He was practicing law in Danville when he was elected to the Kentucky state legislature in 1816.

Birney became a slave owner in his own right—not just the son of a slave owner—when he moved to Madison County, Alabama. Although not elected to the Alabama constitutional convention, Birney nonetheless was instrumental in adding to the new Alabama Constitution certain provisions copied from the Kentucky Constitution, such as permitting the legislature to free slaves and also barring the introduction of slaves into the state for sale. He opposed the election of ANDREW JACKSON, a position that was so unpopular that he was defeated in the next state legislative election.

After a trip to the North in 1829, Birney became convinced that slavery was slowing economic growth in the South. By August 1832, he became a member of the American Colonialization Society, which supported the sending of African Americans back to Africa. In the mid-1830s, he decided that returning slaves to Africa was unjust and he became a strong supporter of the abolitionists. He freed his own slaves in 1834 and, five years later, freed the slaves he had inherited from his father.

Birney started the Kentucky Anti-Slavery Society in 1835 and began publishing a weekly newspaper, *The Philanthropist*, in the following year. His antislavery views created great hostility because he attacked both Democrats and Whigs for their failure to take prompt action against slavery.

In 1837, Birney was named executive secretary of the American Anti-Slavery Society and he moved to New York. His best-known work, *American Churches: Bulwarks of American Slavery*, was published in England in 1840. He was nominated as the Liberty Party candidate for president on an antislavery platform in 1840. Although he polled only a little more than 7,000 votes, he was renominated in 1844 and saw his popularity rise fivefold to more than 60,000 popular votes in that year.

He retired from political life in 1845 and died on November 25, 1857.

Further Reading

Berg, John C. "James Gillespie Birney" in *The Encyclopedia of Third Parties in America*, edited by Immanuel Ness and James Ciment. Armonk, N.Y.: M. E. Sharpe, Inc., 2000.

Birney, William. *James G. Birney and His Times: The Genesis of the Republican Party*. New York: Bergman Publishers, 1969.

Fladeland, Betty. *James Gillespie Birney: Slaveholder to Abolitionist*. New York: Greenwood Press, 1969.

Hernon, Joseph Martin. *Profiles in Character: Hubris and Heroism in the U.S. Senate—1789–1990*. Armonk, N.Y.: M. E. Sharpe, 1997.

Black, Hugo LaFayette

(1886–1971) *associate justice of the Supreme Court, senator*

Hugo Black was one of the longest serving and most significant members of the Supreme Court in history. Often in dissent with Justice WILLIAM ORVILLE DOUGLAS in the early years, Black lived to see his minority views become established constitutional law.

Born on February 27, 1886, in rural Clay County, Alabama, Hugo LaFayette Black was educated at the University of Alabama and held a variety of local governmental posts before his election as a Democrat to the U.S. Senate in 1926. Reelected in 1932, he became a staunch New Dealer. In 1937,

Hugo Black has been consistently ranked as a great Supreme Court justice for his contributions to the constitutional law on civil liberties. *(Library of Congress, by permission from the Maurice Constant Collection)*

President FRANKLIN DELANO ROOSEVELT—whose economic recovery program for ending the Great Depression was stymied by a majority of conservative, older Supreme Court justices—chose Black, one of his most devoted congressional supporters, for his first appointment to the Court.

After Black's prompt Senate confirmation, the newspapers discovered his brief membership in the Ku Klux Klan (KKK), a notoriously antiblack and anti-Jewish organization, and serious criticism erupted. Black defended himself by pointing out that any successful Alabama politician had to be part of the KKK and that his Senate voting record showed he was not subservient to the Klan. Black was faithful to Roosevelt's expectations and helped transform the Court's opposition to New Deal legislation. On civil rights and civil liberties issues, he remained in a minority for many years.

As a member of the Warren Court (1953–69) liberal majority, he voted racial discrimination unconstitutional and "one-person, one-vote" the proper standard for legislative apportionment. A deeply religious man, Black nonetheless wrote the majority opinion declaring officially sponsored public school prayers to be an unconstitutional violation of the First Amendment's establishment clause.

Black was one of the strongest supporters of free expression. He opposed prior restraints on speech believing that the First Amendment's words, "Congress shall make no law . . . abridging freedom of speech or the press. . ." should be taken as an absolute standard for judging whether a law or other government action constituted censorship. Many other justices favored a balancing test to decide whether the free speech was more valuable than government regulations for maintaining public order. Black's position was that the only balancing needed had been done when the First Amendment's framers set the balance in favor of free speech and press. He declined to censor pornography, although he personally was appalled by it. He dissented in the cases upholding the convictions of Communists during the Red Scare and wrote a stirring defense of free press in the Pentagon Papers case, his last opinion before his death.

Despite Black's long support of free speech and press, he did not agree that protections of speech and press automatically extended to actions and, particularly, did not hold that demonstrations were protected as fully as speech and press. Black upheld an absolute right of people to write and speak because he was a literal textualist in interpreting the Constitution. He held that assemblies must be peaceable, because the First Amendment only protects the right "peaceably to assemble." When he voted to oppose convictions of groups violating various laws governing demonstrations, he was being consistent with a larger understanding that the Constitution should be read for the closest possible meaning of its words.

Many constitutional scholars describe Black's method of constitutional interpretation as textualism: The Constitution's words should be followed exactly whenever possible. Black's position on assembly would thus be consistent, because the word *peaceably* appears before the word *assembly* in the First Amendment, allowing prior restraints to be applied to assemblies. Black opposed expanding speech to include actions, such as "symbolic" speech.

Hugo Black's health deteriorated in his later years on the Court and he resigned only a few days before his death on September 19, 1971, in Washington, D. C.

Further Reading

Ball, Howard. *Hugo L. Black: Cold Steel Warrior.* New York: Oxford University Press, 1996.

Dunne, Gerald T. *Hugo Black and the Judicial Revolution.* New York: Irvington, 1977.

Freyer, Tony. *Hugo L. Black and the Dilemma of American Liberalism.* Reading, Mass.: Addison-Wesley, 1989.

Goldstein, Leslie F. *In Defense of the Text: Democracy and Constitutional Theory.* Lanham, Md.: Rowman and Littlefield, 1991.

Newman, Roger K. *Hugo Black: A Biography.* New York: Pantheon, 1994.

Blackmun, Harry Andrew

(1908–1999) *associate justice of the Supreme Court*

Originally named to the Supreme Court as one of the strict constructionists promised by President RICHARD MILHOUS NIXON in the 1968 presidential campaign, Blackmun will be remembered in history primarily for his authorship of the well-known *Roe v. Wade* decision allowing abortion in the United States.

Harry Andrew Blackmun was born on November 12, 1908, in Nashville, Tennessee, but moved as a child to St. Paul, Minnesota, where his father was a storeowner. He majored in mathematics at Harvard but moved over to the law school at Harvard after finishing his undergraduate degree. He continued to have an interest in the scientific and medical area as the legal counsel for the Mayo Clinic.

President DWIGHT DAVID EISENHOWER appointed Blackmun to the Eighth Circuit Court of Appeals in 1959, where he replaced the judge for whom he had clerked when first out of law school.

In 1970, President Nixon sought to redeem a campaign promise he had made to name strict constructionists—particularly a southerner—to the

Supreme Court. Nixon was frustrated because his first nominee, Clement Haynesworth, although a suitable legal scholar, had failed to recuse himself from a case in which he had arguably a financial stake in the outcome. When this came to light, Haynesworth's nomination was doomed.

Nixon reacted in anger and was rumored to have decided that, if the Senate did not like Haynesworth, he would nominate someone worse, challenging them to defeat him twice. Nixon's choice was the undistinguished G. Harold Carswell, who had often been reversed by higher courts on appeal. Despite his weak record, his Senate defenders continued to support him, arguing, as Nebraska's Senator Roman Hruska did, that even mediocre people deserved representation on the high court. However, when it was discovered that Carswell was a member of a white-only country club and had made prosegregation speeches in his earlier career, no defense could save him.

By now, Nixon clearly needed a nominee who could survive Senate scrutiny whether he met his preferred characteristics or not. He apparently turned to Chief Justice WARREN EARL BURGER for advice, for Nixon's next nominee was Blackmun, an old friend of Burger's from Minnesota. Nixon's strategy of naming a southerner to the Supreme Court had now resulted in the naming of two Minnesotans. At least, Nixon calculated, he had named another strict constructionist.

At first, Blackmun followed the script that the political circumstances indicated he should. He voted with Burger so often that the two of them were nicknamed the "Minnesota Twins," a reference not only to their closeness but also to the professional baseball team from the Minneapolis-St. Paul metropolitan area.

Gradually, Blackmun evolved in a different direction from Burger. He became skeptical of the innate goodness of government officials. He moved away from the conservative view on civil liberties questions, often finding himself on the same side as Justices WILLIAM JOSEPH BRENNAN, JR., and THURGOOD MARSHALL. Blackmun was also willing to defend the rights of legal aliens in the United States. He believed that legal aliens were eligible for welfare and could he hired as public employees, although not as police officers.

Blackmun held his conservative views on law enforcement longer than his views on any other conservative position, but gradually he saw a problem of police abuse of criminal defendants. He began to dissent from the conservative majority on search and seizure questions. Still more telling, he came to act on what he said was a long-term childhood belief that there was something seriously amiss in a society that takes the life of a criminal, no matter how serious the crime. In this area, it may be worth noting that Blackmun's home state, Minnesota, was one of the few states that did not provide for the death penalty throughout the 20th century.

On questions of federalism, Blackmun started out more conventionally conservative and moved to the middle during the course of his career. He provided a critical vote on the conservative *National League of Cities v. Usery* (1971) decision, which upheld state exceptions for some of their employees to federal wage and hour regulations. A decade later he was a swing justice on the more nationalistic *Garcia v. San Antonio Metropolitan Transit Authority* (1983), which subjected state and local agencies to federal regulations. Blackmun was supportive of nondiscriminatory, fairly apportioned franchise taxes. He gradually came to defend the right of states, through their state constitutions, to grant their citizens broader rights than the Supreme Court was willing to give on civil liberties.

Despite these accomplishments, Blackmun will always be remembered for his decisions on abortion. At the time of his appointment to the Supreme Court, no one could have predicted that he would have the kind of influence on this question that he did. In *Roe v. Wade* (1971) and its companion case, *Doe v. Bolton* (1971), Blackmun used the U.S. Constitution's Ninth Amendment and its unenumerated rights as interpreted in *Griswold v. Connecticut* (1965) to strike down all criminal penalties for performing abortions. The opinion established the comprehensive trimester scheme now familiar to court decisions over abortion. Supporters see the decision as a logical outgrowth of the earlier *Griswold* decision, while detractors see only an overreaching federal judiciary creating a new piece of judicial legislation out of whole cloth.

Popular reaction has been strong, both affirmative and negative. More than 30 years later, the abortion issue figures in presidential campaigns and Senate confirmation hearings for the Supreme Court. Having written the opinion, Blackmun never wavered in its support. He reacted strongly to the Supreme Court's upholding of the congressional denial of Medicaid funds. His dissent in *Webster v. Reproductive Health Services* (1989) castigated his colleagues on the Court for their dismantling of important parts of the *Roe* decision.

Blackmun retired from the Court on August 3, 1994, and died on March 4, 1999, in Arlington, Virginia.

Further Reading

Brennan, William J., et.al. "A Tribute to Justice Harry Blackmun," *Harvard Law Review* 108, no. 1 (November 1994).

Clark, Clifford E. Jr., ed. *Minnesota in a Century of Change: The State and its People Since 1900.* St. Paul, Minn.: Minnesota Historical Society Press, 1989.

Hair, Penda D. "Justice Blackmun and Racial Justice," *Yale Law Review* 104, no. 1 (October 1994).

Reuben, Richard C. "Justice Defined," *ABA Journal* 80 (July 1994).

Kohlmeier, Louis M., Jr. *God Save This Honorable Court.* New York: Scribner, 1972.

Rosen, Jeffrey. *The New Republic* 210, no. 18 (May 2, 1994).

Blaine, James Gillespie

(1830–1893) *secretary of state, candidate for president, Speaker of the House, senator, representative*

Excellent at public relations, James Gillespie Blaine was called the "Plumed Knight" of the Republican Party because every issue with which he was associated seemed as if it were a righteous cause. This self-righteousness in the face of his own shortcomings did not please everyone: In the 1884 presidential contest against President STEPHEN GROVER CLEVELAND, Blaine was identified in a popular ditty as "the continental liar from the state of Maine." Either way he was a major political figure in the latter half of the 19th century.

Born on January 31, 1830, in West Brownsville, Pennsylvania, Blaine went to school at Washington College in Delaware. After graduation in 1852, he taught for two years at the Pennsylvania School for the Blind in Philadelphia. He moved to Maine in 1854 when he bought a newspaper, *The Kennebec Journal.*

By 1856, Blaine was already heavily involved in Republican politics, having been named a delegate to the first Republican National Convention. Two years later, he was elected to the Maine state legislature and promptly became the Speaker of the lower house. In 1859, he took over the chairmanship of the Maine Republicans and never relinquished the post.

He emerged on the national scene in 1860 and, by age 32, had been elected to the U.S. House of Representatives in 1862. While he did not personally serve in the Civil War, he became famous for his "bloody shirt" speeches lauding the accomplishments of the veterans. For six years, from 1869 to 1875, he served as Speaker of the House. He served a term as one of Maine's senators from 1876 until 1881. In 1876, due to his success as a moderate who supported all the most popular of his party's policies, he was a front-runner for the presidential nomination and would have prevailed except for accusations of having an improper conflict of interest regarding railroad stocks while he was Speaker of the House. RUTHERFORD BIRCHARD HAYES edged him out. He similarly lost to JAMES ABRAM GARFIELD in 1880. Blaine served briefly as Garfield's secretary of state, but CHESTER ALAN ARTHUR removed him after Garfield's assassination, since Arthur and Blaine were clearly from different Republican Party factions.

By 1884, Blaine had lived down most of his problems over the railroad stock as far as the Republicans were concerned, and they nominated him for president. However, the taint of the scandal was still a drag on his national candidacy. The elections of 1884, 1888, and 1892 were very evenly divided. In 1888, the shift of a few thousand votes elected BENJAMIN HARRISON since this is the number of votes by which he carried the key state of New York. By winning New York and a few other heavily populated states narrowly, Harrison won the presidency even though Cleveland received more popular votes.

Blaine could have been as lucky as Benjamin Harrison but for an incident late in the campaign. Blaine attended a rally in New York City and sat through a speech in which a rabid Protestant Christian minister condemned the Democrats as the party of "Rum, Romanism, and Rebellion." When Blaine did not denounce the speaker, or even distinguish his own position from that of the speaker, the remark was used against him, and he lost the Catholic vote, and thereby New York state, by about 5,000 votes.

In 1888, Blaine helped Benjamin Harrison win the Republican nomination and the election. In return, Blaine was made secretary of state. He did much to articulate a coherent U.S. foreign policy, especially aimed at improving relations in Latin America. He resigned his post to be free to campaign against Harrison for the presidential nomination, but he was badly beaten.

After that, his health suffered and he died just shy of his 63rd birthday on January 27, 1893.

Further Reading

Crapol, Edward P. *James G. Blaine: Architect of Empire.* Wilmington, Del.: SR Books, 2000.

Muzzey, David S. *James G. Blaine.* Port Washington, N.Y.: Kennikat Press, 1963.

Stanwood, Edward. *James Gillespie Blaine.* New York: AMS Press, 1972.

Tutorow, Norman Eugene. *James Gillespie Blaine and the Presidency.* New York: P. Lang, 1989.

Tyler, Alice Felt. *The Foreign Policy of James G. Blaine.* Hamden, Conn.: Archon Books, 1965.

Bland, Richard Parks

(1835–1899) *representative, candidate for president*

Known widely in his day as "Silver Dick" Bland because of his long-term fight for the silver interests, Richard Parks Bland played a key role in the contentious fight over U.S. monetary policy in the late 19th century.

Born near Hartford, Kentucky on August 19, 1835, Bland attended Hartford Academy. He worked for more than 10 years in the silver mines in the western states of California, Nevada, and Colorado. His career began with the opening of a law practice in Lebanon, Missouri, in 1869.

Bland was elected as a Democratic member of the U.S. House of Representatives in 1872. Except for the brief two-year period from 1895 to 1897, he served in Congress continuously until he died in 1899. He was nicknamed "Silver Dick" because of his support for the proposition that silver dollars should be minted as long as the supply of silver allowed. The owners and employees of silver mines naturally supported the idea to maintain their incomes. This idea also appealed to farmers and others who found that the extra silver in circulation increased economic activity, allowed the repayment of debts in cheaper dollars, and made credit easier to obtain.

His greatest legislative success came when he engineered the override of President RUTHERFORD BIRCHARD HAYES's veto of the Bland Allison Act of 1878, which mandated government purchase of $2 million of silver monthly. He defended the act against repeal in 1886, but he failed to obtain his dream of the unlimited coinage of silver. On August 11, 1893, he finally announced in his "Parting of the Ways" speech that he would put the silver issue over his basic party loyalty. He was defeated for reelection in 1894 by a slender margin but fought his way back into Congress in 1896. He ran for the Democratic presidential nomination in 1896, but he was defeated by much younger, charismatic WILLIAM JENNINGS BRYAN. While he declined to be Bryan's vice presidential running mate, he did work hard for Bryan's election.

Bland was still serving in Congress when he died on June 15, 1899.

Further Reading

Byars, William Vincent. *An American Commoner: The Life and Times of Richard Parks Bland.* St. Louis, Mo.: V. Bland, 1900.

Hollister, Wilfred R. *Five Famous Missourians: Authentic Biographical Sketches of Richard P. Bland, et al.* Kansas City, Mo.: Hudson-Kimberly Publishing Company, 1900.

Hoogenbloom, Ari. *Rutherford B. Hayes: Warrior and President.* Lawrence: University Press of Kansas, 1995.

Borah, William Edgar
(1865–1940) *senator*

Both an isolationist and a Progressive, William Borah left his mark on American politics in the first half of the 20th century. His earliest contributions were in urging the creation of the U.S. Department of Labor and the direct election of U.S. senators. His most memorable legacy in his later career came from his deep and unyielding opposition to the creation of the League of Nations as a part of the Versailles Peace Treaty that ended World War I.

Born in Jasper County, Illinois, on June 29, 1865, William Edgar Borah went to the University of Kansas. Admitted to the Kansas bar in 1887, he relocated to Boise, Idaho, where he began his law practice.

In 1907, he was elected to the Senate as a Republican and he continuously represented Idaho in the Senate until his death. His national reputation began with his failed attempt to convict William Haywood, founder of the Industrial Workers of the World, of the murder of Idaho Governor Frank Steunenberg.

A staunch supporter of a wide range of progressive proposals, he was often referred to as the "great opposer" for fighting so many of his own party's proposals. He supported THEODORE ROOSEVELT against incumbent President WILLIAM HOWARD TAFT in 1912, but he did not quit the Republican Party to support Roosevelt as the Progressive (or Bull Moose) Party candidate in the general election.

The Republican Party was generally skeptical of his strong progressive views (which the Democratic Party would have better appreciated), but his foreign policy views were strictly isolationist and fully in line with the basic tenets of many Republicans. He strongly opposed President THOMAS WOODROW WILSON's League of Nations treaty and campaigned against it in a national speaking tour. After the defeat of the League treaty, his political position improved, particularly since the Republicans controlled the Congress in the 1920s. Borah became chairman of the prestigious Senate Foreign Relations Committee. His isolationism was rooted in pacifism and opposition to war, even if his proposals for avoiding war were not always well founded. He

supported the misguided Washington Disarmament Conference of 1922 and the unenforceable Kellogg-Briand Pact of 1928 (which outlawed war as an instrument of national policy). He sponsored the Neutrality Act of 1935 and fought for strict neutrality after the war broke out in Europe in 1939. Despite his domestic progressive views, he criticized President FRANKLIN DELANO ROOSEVELT's New Deal programs as being unconstitutional, but he was most bitterly remembered by Roosevelt's supporters as an unreasoning and immovable opponent of many practical steps necessary to prepare the United States for war against Germany and Japan.

He did not live to see the United States enter that war, for he died on January 19, 1940.

Further Reading

Ashby, Darrel LeRoy. *The Spearless Leader: Senator Borah and the Progressive Movement in the 1920's.* Urbana: University of Illinois Press, 1972.

"Borah, William E" in *Congress A to Z: Third Edition,* edited by David R. Tarr and Ann O'Connor. Washington, D.C.: Congressional Quarterly, 1999.

Hernon, Joseph Martin. *Profiles in Character: Hubris and Heroism in the U.S. Senate—1789–1990.* Armonk, N.Y.: M. E. Sharpe, 1997.

Johnson, Claudius Osborne. *Borah of Idaho.* Seattle: University of Washington Press, 1967.

Maddox, Robert James. *William E. Borah and American Foreign Policy.* Baton Rouge: Louisiana State University Press, 1970.

McKenna, Marian C. *Borah.* Ann Arbor: University of Michigan Press, 1961.

Vinson, John Chalmers. *William E. Borah and the Outlawry of War.* Athens: University of Georgia Press, 1957.

Bradford, William
(1590–1657) *colonial leader, author*

William Bradford was the most important figure in the successful founding of the Plymouth Colony (or Plimoth Plantation), the first permanent English settlement in New England. He served almost continuously for more than 30 years as its governor.

Bradford was born in Austerfield, Yorkshire, England, on or about March 29, 1590. As a teenager, he joined the strict Protestant sect known as the Separatists, a reform group that split off from the Episcopal Church (or Anglican Church, the official church of England). To avoid continued persecution by British authorities, he left England for Holland about three years later. In Holland, he became a cloth maker and continued his religious studies. While Holland, the European country most tolerant to religious diversity, provided a safe haven, the Separatists wished to raise their families on English territory. By 1617, Bradford was among those pressing for creation of a colony of their very own. Granted permission to settle in the Virginia colony by London authorities, Bradford set sail with about 100 other Separatists on the ship the *Mayflower.*

Blown off course, they landed on the coast of what is now Massachusetts on December 21, 1620, just as the harsh New England winter was setting in. Since they were far from the jurisdiction of Virginia, they drafted the Mayflower Compact, which was designed to establish a government to settle any disputes that might arise among them. This brief document of little more than a paragraph was the first written constitution in the New World.

The Pilgrims, as these Separatists were called in America, were ill prepared for the inhospitable winters in New England, and half of the group died before spring, including the original governor, John Carver. To save the colony from abandonment, the survivors elected Bradford as governor. He instituted food rationing and started successful fishing, farming, and basic trades. He then negotiated peaceful relations with the Narragansett Indians, paid off the debt to the London creditors, resisted encroachment by the larger Massachusetts Bay Colony, and staved off resistance to continued Pilgrim domination of the settlement. He was rewarded by being named the governor from 1621 to 1656, except for the years of 1633–36, 1638, and 1644 when he was the assistant to the governor.

While he was not as tolerant as the settlers of the nearby Rhode Island colony, he was more tolerant of diversity than some of the other Pilgrims. At the end of his life, he was pleased with the economic success of the colony, but he worried that the colony was not quite the religious paradise he hoped it would be. William Bradford died on May 9, 1657.

Further Reading

Bradford, William. *Of Plymouth Plantation.* New York: Random House, 1952.

Delbanco, Andrew. *The Real American Dream.* Cambridge, Mass.: Harvard University Press, 1999.

Wakefield, Robert S. *Mayflower Families in Progress: William Bradford in Four Generations.* Plymouth, Mass.: General Society of Mayflower Descendants, 1994.

Brandeis, Louis Dembitz
(1856–1941) *associate justice of the Supreme Court, presidential adviser*

Louis Brandeis has had more biographies and legal analysis books written about him than nearly any other Supreme Court associate justice. While it is tempting to categorize Brandeis for his long association with the famous Supreme Court Justice OLIVER WENDELL HOLMES, JR., such a summary overlooks the breadth of Brandeis's powerful and inquisitive mind. While Brandeis will long be remembered for joining Holmes in famous dissenting opinions that advanced civil liberties and other liberal causes, a fully balanced profile should include the complexity of his long involvement in a variety of political causes.

Born in Louisville, Kentucky, on November 13, 1856, of Bohemian Jewish parents who immigrated to the United States after the Revolution of 1848, Louis Dembitz Brandeis was always a precociously brilliant student. He studied in Dresden, Germany, at the Annen-Realschule and then at Harvard University from which he graduated in 1877 at the age of 21. With Samuel Warren, he established a successful law practice in Boston in 1879.

Brandeis was committed from the beginning to revising the law to make it more compatible with human experience, and he insisted on including statistical evidence from economics, sociology, and other social sciences instead of simply using legal categories in his briefs. These briefs became known as Brandeis briefs, and they are now widely used in the law.

This effort was part of a broader attempt to reform society, often turning on the improvement of working conditions for ordinary people. Brandeis frequently took cases for ordinary citizens without a fee, and he was given the nickname, "the people's advocate." Brandeis also sought to limit monopolies, such as the railroads, by encouraging the use of the Interstate Commerce Commission to limit railroad rate increases. He further sought negotiations to end labor disputes, most notably the garment workers' strike in New York City in 1910.

President THOMAS WOODROW WILSON nominated Brandeis to the U.S. Supreme Court in 1916. Because Brandeis was Jewish and had supported so many liberal causes, his confirmation process was the most contentious and long lasting in American history. While Brandeis was confirmed in a straight party line vote, it signaled the depth of opposition to his ideas.

Brandeis was committed to judicial reform and judicial activism throughout his 23 years on the bench. While he did not write as many dissents as Justice Oliver Wendell Holmes (whom he often joined in dissent), he was an influential dissenter who found his dissents frequently being adopted by a Supreme Court majority at a later date. Brandeis also influenced such important younger justices as FELIX FRANKFURTER and BENJAMIN NATHAN CARDOZO.

He was convinced of the need to create a Jewish homeland in Palestine and committed himself to Zionism after he retired from the U.S. Supreme Court in 1939. He died on October 5, 1941.

Further Reading

Baker, Leonard. *Brandeis and Frankfurter.* New York: New York University Press, 1986.

Dawson, Nelson L. *Louis D. Brandeis, Felix Frankfurter, and the New Deal.* Hamden, Conn.: Archon Books, 1980.

Gal, Allon. *Brandeis of Boston.* Cambridge, Mass.: Harvard University Press, 1980.

Halpern, Ben. *A Clash of Heroes—Brandeis, Weizmann, and American Zionism.* New York: Oxford University Press, 1987.

Konefsky, Samuel J. *The Legacy of Holmes and Brandeis.* New York: Da Capo Press, 1974.

Mason, Alpheus T. *Brandeis, Lawyer and Judge in the Modern State.* Princeton, N.J.: Princeton University Press, 1933.

Noble, Iris. *Firebrand for Justice: A Biography of Louis Dembitz Brandeis.* Philadelphia, Pa.: Westminster Press, 1969.

Peare, Catherine Owens. *The Louis D. Brandeis Story.* New York: Crowell, 1970

Strum, Philippa. *Brandeis: Beyond Progressivism.* Lawrence: University Press of Kansas, 1993.

Todd, Alden. *Justice on Trial: The Case of Louis D. Brandeis.* Chicago: University of Chicago Press, 1968.

Urofsky, Melvin I. *Louis D. Brandeis and the Progressive Tradition.* Boston: Little, Brown, 1981.

Breckinridge, John Cabell
(1821–1875) *vice president, candidate for president, senator*

Suffering from the dubious distinction of being the only vice president (other than AARON BURR) to be accused of treason, John Breckinridge's long and distinguished career was affected by the difficult decisions he made in response to the wrenching dislocation of the Civil War.

John Cabell Breckinridge was born on January 15, 1821, near Lexington, Kentucky. He attended Princeton University (then known as the College of New Jersey) only briefly before transferring to Transylvania College where he studied law. He established his law practice in Lexington, Kentucky, in 1841.

Although he did not favor the Mexican War initially, Breckinridge eventually headed a unit of Kentucky volunteers in the war. He began his career as a pro-slavery Democrat in the Kentucky legislature in 1849. In 1851, he ran in what was thought to be a strongly Whig district and won. After being reelected as a Democrat in a Whig district, he was perceived as being very popular. As a border state Democrat, he was an ideal choice for vice president, running on a ticket with President JAMES BUCHANAN. Breckinridge was so popular in Kentucky that the legislature elected him to the U.S. Senate before the end of his term as vice president (even though he could not take office until his vice presidential term ended).

In the 1860 campaign, the Democrats split. Although Breckinridge did not campaign for the nomination, the Southern group nominated him and he accepted. His position on slavery and dis-union was a careful position on the very knife-edge of the issues. Breckinridge supported the federal system, but he believed the Congress could not block slavery in the territories. While he thought states could secede, he believed that se-cession was unnecessary at that time. If secession came, the Union could not use force to keep a state in the United States. Under the circum-stances, his position was closest to that of most southerners. The only Electoral College votes he received were from the South.

As a U.S. senator in 1861, he opposed Lincoln on his attempt to call up troops. When the Union forces pushed the Confederate army out of Ken-tucky, Breckinridge went South, joined the Con-federate Army, and fought with distinction at Cold Harbor, Shiloh, Chickamauga, and Vicksburg. Un-like other southerners, Breckinridge was from a state that had not seceded. As a former vice presi-dent, he was extremely high profile. It was then not unexpected when the Union indicted Breckin-ridge for treason. At the end of the war, Breckin-ridge faced capture and execution, so he fled to Cuba, Europe, and then Canada. Former southern plantation owners and other Confederate sympa-thizers abroad maintained him.

Having survived impeachment and faced with the closing days of his unsuccessful administration, President ANDREW JOHNSON granted a broad amnesty to Confederates on Christmas Day in 1868. Although the indictment against Breckin-ridge was still pending (and was not actually dis-missed for another 90 years until 1958), he was allowed to return home. In Kentucky, he received a tumultuous welcome.

Breckinridge never again sought public office. He had some success as a corporate officer in the Elizabethtown, Lexington, and Big Sandy railroad by building new railroads in the central part of the United States. He died on May 17, 1875.

Further Reading

Davis, William C. *Breckinridge: Statesman, Soldier, Symbol.* Baton Rouge: Louisiana State University Press, 1974.
Harrison, Lowell Hayes. *John Breckinridge: Jeffersonian Republican.* Louisville, Ky.: Filson Club, 1969.
Nelson, Michael T., ed. "John Breckenridge" in *The Presidency A to Z: Second Edition.* Washington, D.C.: Congressional Quarterly Press, 1998.
Stillwell, Lucille. *John Cabell Breckinridge.* Caldwell, Idaho: The Caxton Printers, Ltd, 1936.

Brennan, William Joseph, Jr.
(1906–1997) *associate justice of the Supreme Court, state judge*

William Brennan was central figure in the majority that supported Chief Justice EARL WARREN, WILLIAM ORVILLE DOUGLAS, HUGO LAFAYETTE BLACK, and THURGOOD MARSHALL in their trans-formation of U.S. constitutional law.

Brennan was born on April 25, 1906, in Newark, New Jersey, in a family headed by an Irish immigrant who worked as a coal shoveler in a local brewery. An Irish Catholic Republican, he was ap-pointed to the high court by President DWIGHT DAVID EISENHOWER during his 1956 reelection campaign when Eisenhower wished to appear to be a nonpartisan political figure above the partisan fray. Although Eisenhower subsequently came to declare he made a mistake in his appointment, there is al-ways some reason to doubt that Eisenhower was en-tirely candid on this. After all, Eisenhower had ample evidence of Brennan's overall philosophy be-fore appointing him to the high court.

Brennan was educated at the Wharton School of the University of Pennsylvania and received high marks at the Harvard Law School. He joined a prominent New Jersey law firm in the 1930s.

After Warren, Black, Douglas, and Marshall had either died or resigned, Brennan remained the leader of the liberal wing of the court, defending the achievements of the Warren Court against their determined assault by the more conservative justices appointed subsequently.

When Chief Justice Earl Warren led the Supreme Court, Brennan was most often found at the middle of the Court. Regarded as one of the five members of the liberal block, he nonetheless was the pivotal figure in deciding what could and could not be adopted. Therefore, he had more in-fluence than almost any other member of the Court. Although he was often in the minority during the years when the Court was under the leadership of Chief Justices WARREN EARL BURGER and WILLIAM HUBBS REHNQUIST, he wrote relatively few dissents. He was a conciliator, not a dissenter.

As an example of his influence on the Warren Court, Brennan introduced a concept of "actual malice" into the determination of the point at which a public official could sue a newspaper for libel. Newspapers were free to make statements about public figures as long as they did not engage in "actual malice" or a "reckless disregard for the truth." Had Brennan followed the lead of the more outspoken members of the liberal wing, such as Hugo Black or William O. Douglas, he would perhaps have adopted their notion that there were never occasions on which public figures could sue newspapers for libel, thereby granting the media an unrestrained license to destroy reputations. Brennan chose a more moderate approach.

Brennan's moderation can also be seen in the Court cases dealing with obscenity. When Brennan was named to court, he was almost immediately handed one of the most difficult problems with which the 20th century Supreme Court would grapple. In 1957, Brennan was asked to write a majority opinion that would define obscenity for the modern age. Before then, the United States had essentially judged pornography and obscenity according to a standard devised by the British courts in the middle of the 19th century. This British standard, known as the Hicklin Rule, banned any publication if any portion of that publication—no matter how small—might lead to harmful thoughts on the part of any individual. As one lower court judge had commented, under the Hicklin Rule, a seed catalog could be banned because it might lead an idiot to a sexual thought.

The Hicklin Rule was clearly outdated but finding a replacement was difficult. The more liberal justices, such as Black and Douglas, believed there was no basis on which the United States could censor any publication because of the First Amendment's promise of free speech. The conservatives wanted only small changes in the Hicklin Rule. The moderate Brennan attempted to find a middle ground in *Roth v. United States* (1957). Misunderstood by many, *Roth* continued to be used as a definition for a decade despite its failure to sat-

isfy either liberals or conservatives. Liberals thought *Roth* provided an excessive amount of censorship, while conservatives felt *Roth* failed to provide a basis for needed regulation of obscenity.

Brennan attempted a refined definition in the case *Memoirs vs. Massachusetts* (1966), but again the same division persisted. By the 1970s, the Court was under the leadership of Chief Justice Burger and his more conservative colleagues who attempted to fashion their own definition in the case of *Miller vs. California* (1973). None of the standards set out in any of these cases satisfied everyone, and Brennan ultimately decided that Douglas and Black were correct that no rule could be devised that would not represent unacceptable censorship, except for the ban on child pornography. He also thought, however, that it was probably vital to attempt to fashion a rule before the idea of rejecting such a rule was put forward.

Brennan was one of the few justices who concluded that U.S. society had evolved to such a degree that capital punishment was no longer a valid punishment for crimes under the U.S. Constitution. Since capital punishment is mentioned explicitly in the Constitution, Brennan found it necessary to use an evolving standard of judicial interpretation in order to reach the conclusion that capital punishment is unconstitutional. For using an evolving standard, Brennan was accused of excessive judicial activism by many conservatives.

As the Supreme Court became increasingly conservative over the years, Brennan found himself in the minority, but he was still able to defend the legacy of the Warren Court against its critics and even to advance the Warren agenda somewhat. For example, on the flag-burning cases, Brennan was a critical figure in persuading two of the more conservative justices to join the liberal block in determining that flag burning was a permissible form of free speech.

Brennan was one of the leaders in establishing the issue of gender equality under the law. He openly advocated the adoption of the new constitutional amendment advancing the rights of women. It is unusual for Supreme Court justices to recommend the adoption of constitutional amendments, but Brennan did not shrink from recommending the adoption of the Equal Rights Amendment.

Brennan was widely praised for his accomplishments. Former Chief Justice Earl Warren said that he relied on Brennan, more than any other justice, to create coalitions behind various decisions. In fact, Warren met with Brennan prior to the Supreme Court conferences precisely to go over the agenda and work out strategies for resolving many cases. Even conservative Justice Byron White said Brennan was one of the greatest justices in the history of the Court.

William Brennan retired in July 1990 and died on July 24, 1997, in Arlington, Virginia.

Further Reading

Eisler, Kim Isaac. *A Justice for All: William J. Brennan, Jr., and the Decisions That Transformed America*. New York: Simon & Schuster, 1993.

Goldman, Roger L. *Justice William J. Brennan, Jr.: Freedom First*. New York: Carroll & Graf Publishers, 1994.

Hopkins, W. Wat. *Mr. Justice Brennan and Freedom of Expression*. New York: Praeger, 1991.

Irons, Peter H. *Brennan vs. Rehnquist: The Battle for the Constitution*. New York: Knopf, 1994.

Michelman, Frank I. *Brennan and Democracy*. Princeton, N.J.: Princeton University Press, 1999.

Brooke, Edward William
(1919–) *senator*

Edward Brooke was the first African American to be popularly elected to the U.S. Senate (a few African Americans were appointed to the Senate by Reconstruction-era state legislatures). No other African American was elected to the U.S. Senate until nearly the end of the 20th century.

Born on October 26, 1919, in Washington, D.C., Edward William Brooke attended Howard University and graduated in 1941. One of the few African Americans to be an officer in the U.S. armed forces, he served in the infantry in Italy during World War II. After the war, he attended law school at Boston University, receiving a law degree in 1948 and a graduate law degree in 1949.

Brooke ran for the Massachusetts legislature as a Republican in 1950 and 1952, but he was de-

feated in both elections. Withdrawing from politics for a time to build up his legal practice, Brooke reentered politics but lost a very close race for Massachusetts secretary of state in 1960. Brooke was appointed chairman of the Boston Finance Commission, a position in which he uncovered improper dealings by several city officials. His public relations skills were extraordinary, and he gained broad, positive news coverage, although he had only been on the job for about a year.

The nature of Brooke's favorable publicity made him the perfect candidate for state attorney general, and he handily won the race for that Massachusetts office in 1962. Again, Brooke vigorously investigated corruption cases of many government officials. He won reelection by the largest margin of any Republican in Massachusetts's history.

Brooke became an extremely popular Massachusetts figure, received the Republican nomination for the U.S. Senate, and won a general election victory in 1966. Brooke compiled a moderate voting record in the Senate and was easily reelected in 1972. Unfortunately, as he began his race for reelection in 1978, his daughter charged that Brooke had engaged in financial misdealing, and this tarnished his image as reformer. Although the Senate Ethics Committee eventually concluded that Brooke had made no more than minor infractions of the Senate professional conduct rules, for which no prosecution was warranted, this revelation came in 1979, too late to help in his failed attempt to win a 1978 reelection.

Brooke retired from politics, but he was named the chairman of the Boston Bank of Commerce in 1984.

Further Reading

Buckmaster, Henrietta. *The Fighting Congressmen: Thaddeus Stephens, Hiram Revels, James Rapier, Blanche K. Bruce*. New York: Scholastic Book Services, 1971.

Cutler, John Henry. *Ed Brooke: Biography of a Senator*. Indianapolis, Ind.: Bobbs-Merrill, 1972.

Hartshorn, Elinor C. *The Quiet Campaigner: Edward W. Brooke in Massachusetts*. Amherst: University of Massachusetts, 1974.

Swain, Carol M. *Black Faces, Black Interests: Representation of African Americans in Congress*. Cambridge, Mass.: Harvard University Press, 1995.

Bruce, Blanche Kelso
(1841–1898) *senator*

Blanche Kelso Bruce was the second African American appointed to serve in the U.S. Senate and the first to serve a full six-year term.

Bruce was born a slave on March 1, 1841, in Farmville, Virginia, but shortly thereafter moved as a slave to Missouri. His slave master's son tutored him sufficiently so that at the outbreak of the Civil War he was able to move to Ohio to attend Oberlin College for two years. After that, with Reconstruction governments in place throughout the South, Bruce was able to move to Mississippi and purchase a large plantation.

Since there were virtually no other educated and wealthy African Americans in Mississippi at the time, he filled a leadership vacuum for African Americans in the state. He worked as a teacher briefly, but he quickly moved into politics, filling several state and local government positions, such as sergeant at arms of the state senate, Bolivar County property assessor, and sheriff from 1870 to 1875.

In 1874, the Reconstruction government state legislature elected him to the U.S. Senate where he served for a full term. When the North was no longer interested in expending the political capital to maintain the Reconstruction governments, it became increasingly clear that he could not be re-elected. He nonetheless fought vigorously for African-American voting rights in the South, fair treatment for Native Americans, and improved navigation and flood control on the Mississippi.

Bruce also saw the importance of applying the Fourteenth Amendment to the case of Chinese and other Asian American immigrants who were being excluded from the United States. He further opposed granting pensions to former Confederate soldiers.

After his term ended, he was named the register of the treasury in 1881 by President JAMES ABRAM GARFIELD. He lost that position under President STEPHEN GROVER CLEVELAND, but President BENJAMIN HARRISON named him the District of Columbia's Recorder of Deeds in 1889. He continued in this position even through Grover Cleveland's second term. President WILLIAM McKINLEY

reappointed him the register of the treasury in 1897, the position in which he served until his death on March 17, 1898.

Further Reading
Buckmaster, Henrietta. *The Fighting Congressmen: Thaddeus Stephens, Hiram Revels, James Rapier, Blanche K. Bruce.* New York: Scholastic Book Services, 1971.
Swain, Carol M. *Black Faces, Black Interests: Representation of African Americans in Congress.* Cambridge, Mass.: Harvard University Press, 1995.
———. *Blanche K. Bruce: Politician.* Cambridge, Mass.: Harvard University Press, 1989.

Bryan, William Jennings
(1860–1925) *secretary of state, candidate for president, representative*

One of the great orators of his age, William Jennings Bryan was the youngest person ever nominated for president by a major party's nominating convention and the only person nominated by a major political party for three runs for the presidency. He is best remembered for the stunning effect of his famous "Cross of Gold" speech at the 1896 Democratic convention and for the remarkable campaign that followed.

Bryan was born on March 19, 1860, in Salem, Illinois. Living with family friends, he managed to finance a college education at Illinois College, from which he graduated in 1881. While studying law at the Union College of Law in Chicago, he improved his already growing debating and oratorical skills. He practiced law briefly before moving to Nebraska where he saw the opportunity to advance his career faster than he could in the already settled and established political life of Illinois.

By the age of 30, he had already been elected to the U.S. House of Representatives from Nebraska. He was reelected in 1892, but he chose to run for the U.S. Senate in 1894. During this race, the Democratic Party was so badly split that almost any Democratic candidate would have lost. The state was heavily Republican and Democratic unity and Republican disunity were required before a Democrat could win.

With his defeat, he was named the editor of the *Omaha World Herald*, a vehicle that gave him room to expand his political base. Over the next two years, he immersed himself in the question of currency reform and became convinced of the economic wisdom of the United States returning to the backing of currency with both silver and gold. In the hard economic times, Bryan's ability to explain the arcane issues involved—even more than his oratorical skills—allowed him to move to the forefront of the national debate.

The 1896 Democratic National Convention was badly divided on the issue of whether the nation should abandon the gold standard in favor of a bimetallic basis for currency. The incumbent Democratic President STEPHEN GROVER CLEVELAND was solidly committed to the gold standard, as were many Eastern democrats, but the South and West favored the inflationary stimulus of a bimetallic system. There were other advocates of the free coinage of silver, but they all were either too old (as in the case of RICHARD PARKS BLAND), had made too many enemies, or were too obscure.

Still Bryan was not the most likely nominee. On the morning of his nomination, everyone else—except Bryan—had counted him out. At breakfast that day he predicted to his small groups of friends that he would be nominated because the timing was right. Unbelievably, at just the right moment in the convention, when the initial favorites were deadlocked in a situation in which none could muster enough ballots to win the nomination, Bryan rose to give his famous "Cross of Gold" speech. The speech was not new or even particularly specific on the remedies it would provide for the nation's economic ills. It was, however, beautifully delivered and brilliantly timed. The speed at which the events were unfolding at the convention was such that if the speech had been given an hour earlier, it would have been too early; if an hour later, it would have been too late. As it was, it was impeccably timed.

Contemporary accounts suggest that, as the speech was being delivered, the entire audience knew they were attending a nominating convention at a critical moment. Observers say they felt a growing sense of the impending significance of what Bryan was doing in the closing moments of his speech. When Bryan finally completed it, everyone sat in stunned silence as they realized he had seized exactly the right moment to capture the nomination. Then the crowd broke loose with such an overwhelming demonstration of support that a man who had been counted out at breakfast time had captured a major party nomination before the end of the day. Bryan did so not by backroom maneuvering but through a public address. At 36 years of age, Bryan was the youngest major party nominee for president, a mere one year older than the minimum required age of 35 given in the U.S. Constitution.

The popular impression that Bryan focused only on the bimetallism question obscures the rest of his program, which he had carefully developed in his two years in Congress and as he presented it during the campaign. Bryan set the agenda for change in American politics for the next generation. Some of his reforms were realized during the two terms of President THOMAS WOODROW WILSON, but some were not adopted until the coming of President FRANKLIN DELANO ROOSEVELT's New Deal in the 1930s.

Bryan's progressive ideas seemed radical to the so-called Gold Democrats, such as Grover Cleveland, and were anathema to the leadership of the Republican Party. Under the direction of MARK ALONZO HANNA, the Republicans pulled out all the stops in the 1896 presidential campaign to elect their nominee, WILLIAM McKINLEY. In terms of fund-raising, the Republicans admitted spending 30 times as much as the Democrats and may have spent even more in ways they could not admit, for the secret ballot was not widely used. This made very plausible the threat of Republican business owners in the Northeast who argued that they would fire anyone discovered to have voted for Bryan. Some also threatened that, if Bryan won, their entire businesses would be closed on the following day.

Bryan did remarkably well against such long odds, but McKinley was elected by a narrow majority. As if to prove the truth of Bryan's arguments about the need for a more expansive currency, the Republicans dumped extra gold on the market before the election to ease the economic hard times. Over the next four years, the discovery of new sources of gold in Alaska gave the economy the liquidity it needed—at least temporarily.

Bryan had done so well in 1896 that the Democratic nomination was his for the asking in 1900. The expanded currency and the improvement in economic conditions made it harder for him to argue the bimetallism case four years later. Bryan did develop other important issues, but none had as strong a popular appeal among farmers and workers as the free coinage of silver issue. He lost by a wider margin to McKinley in 1900 than in 1896.

In 1904, the Democrats passed over Bryan to nominate conservative attorney Alton B. Parker in his losing effort against the progressive incumbent Republican President THEODORE ROOSEVELT. When Roosevelt chose not to run for another term in 1908, the Republicans followed Roosevelt's recommendation and selected WILLIAM HOWARD TAFT as their standard-bearer. The Democrats turned again to Bryan, but the third time was not a charm, and Bryan lost by the widest margin of any of his three tries.

With Bryan's support, the Democrats chose New Jersey Governor Woodrow Wilson to lead them in 1912. The Democrats benefited from a serious feud between former President Theodore Roosevelt and the current incumbent, President Taft. Roosevelt sought the Republican nomination, but Taft controlled the party machinery and was able to block Roosevelt's attempt to win the presidential nomination. Roosevelt then became the Progressive or Bull Moose nominee for president, allowing Wilson to win—with Roosevelt second and Taft a distant third. Bryan had worked hard for Wilson and was named secretary of state in return. Bryan's strong pacifist streak was to doom him as secretary of state, but he supported as much of Wilson's aggressive foreign policy as he could, eventually resigning when he was ordered to send a stern note to the Germans protesting the sinking of the *Lusitania* in 1915.

Although he failed to win the presidency, he represented the fondest hope of a generation of Democratic Party supporters. For those who liked him, he was always the "Great Commoner," making appeals for the improvement of the common.

He supported women's suffrage, the graduated income tax, anti-imperialism, world peace and disarmament, and prohibition (because of his genuine personal fundamentalist Christian religious beliefs).

Although he suffered from diabetes and a heart condition, he undertook a major campaign against the teaching of evolution in 1925. He undoubtedly believed his oratorical skills would carry the day when he agreed to be the special state prosecutor in the trial of John Scopes, who was accused of teaching evolution in a classroom in Dayton (Rhea County), Tennessee. Bryan's oratorical skill with a large audience was up against the polished legal skills of Clarence Darrow, whose oratorical style was better suited to the courtroom. Bryan managed to win the conviction, but Darrow maneuvered him into taking the stand himself to defend biblical fundamentalism. Once on the stand, Darrow destroyed Bryan as a serious thinker for the great mass of Americans. Worse still, Bryan's fundamentalist religious allies turned on him for not being able to defend fundamentalism adequately.

Shortly after the conclusion of the Scopes Monkey Trial, William Jennings Bryan's health problems overwhelmed him and he died in his sleep on July 26, 1925.

Further Reading

Bryan, William Jennings. *The First Battle*. Chicago: W. B. Conkey Company, 1896.

———. *The Memoirs of William Jennings Bryan*. Philadelphia: John C. Winston Company, 1989.

Ciment, James. "William Jennings Bryan" in *The Encyclopedia of Third Parties in America*, edited by Immanuel Ness and James Ciment. Armonk, N.Y.: M. E. Sharpe, Inc., 2000.

Coletta, Paolo Enrico. *William Jennings Bryan*. Lincoln: University of Nebraska Press, 1964.

Curti, Merle Eugene. *Bryan and World Peace*. New York: Garland Publishers, 1971.

Glad, Paul W. *The Trumpet Soundeth*. Lincoln: University of Nebraska Press, 1966.

Koenig, Louis William. *Bryan*. New York: Putnam, 1971.

"William Jennings Bryan" in *The Presidency A to Z: Second Edition*, edited by Michael T. Nelson. Washington, D.C.: Congressional Quarterly Press, 1998.

Brzezinski, Zbigniew Kazimierz
(1928–) *national security adviser, author*

As an international relations specialist, Zbigniew Brzezinski served as an aide to Presidents JOHN FITZGERALD KENNEDY and LYNDON BAINES JOHNSON before being named President JAMES EARL CARTER's assistant for national security affairs.

Born on March 28, 1928, in Warsaw, Poland, Zbigniew Kazimierz Brzezinski received early training in international affairs since his father was a diplomat. His father was abroad much of the time while Brzezinski was growing up, so he received a varied education while living in France and Germany. While Brzezinski was abroad, he avoided capture by the German Nazis when they overran Poland in 1939. By then, the Brzezinski family had already settled in Canada. Brzezinski received his bachelor's and master's degrees at McGill University in Montreal, Canada, but transferred to Harvard to complete his doctorate in 1953. From 1953 to 1960, he taught at Harvard. In 1960, he was named professor of public law and government at Columbia University, and a year later he was named the director of Columbia's Institute on Communist Affairs.

Brzezinski was one of President John Kennedy's preinaugural foreign policy specialists in 1960. Six years later, President Lyndon Johnson appointed him to be a member of the Policy Planning Council at the Department of State. In 1968, he was writing foreign policy papers for HUBERT HORATIO HUMPHREY. Brzezinski consistently took a hard line on communism and the Soviet Union. He supported the U.S. involvement in the Vietnam War arguing that, without American resistance, the wars in Asia would be unending.

With the election of President Jimmy Carter in 1976, Brzezinski emerged as a key adviser to the president when he was named the top assistant for national security affairs. This brought him into conflict with Carter's secretary of state CYRUS ROBERTS VANCE over a variety of issues. Generally, Brzezinski favored a harder line against the Soviet Union. On Iran, Brzezinski supported clearly informing the shah and his military advisers that the United States would not oppose the use of military force against the Muslim fundamentalists. Vance disagreed. In the end, an ambiguous message was sent, and U.S. policy failed by giving ambiguous conflicting instructions. Still later, Brzezinski favored a rescue mission to attempt to free the hostages taken by the Islamic fundamentalists in their takeover in Iran. Vance opposed it. When the mission failed, Vance resigned.

After the end of the Carter administration, Brzezinski resumed his academic career at the Johns Hopkins University's School for Advanced International Studies in Washington, D.C.

Further Reading
Brzezinski, Zbigniew K. *Between Two Ages*. New York: Penguin Books. 1976.
———. *Dilemmas of Change in Soviet Politics*. New York: Columbia University Press, 1969.
———. *The Fragile Blossom*. New York: Harper & Row, 1972.
———. *The Grand Chessboard*. New York: Basic Books, 1997.
———. *Out of Control: Global Turmoil on the Eve of the 21st Century*. New York: Scribner's, 1993.
———. *Power and Principle: Memoirs of the National Security Adviser, 1977–1981*. New York: Farrar, Straus & Giroux, 1985.

Buchanan, James
(1791–1868) *president, secretary of state, diplomat, senator, representative*

When James Buchanan became president, he had a long record of positive public accomplishments, but he has been the president most often given low marks for his failure to take steps to avoid the U.S. Civil War. Among Buchanan's positive achievements were his support of a transcontinental railroad, an increase in the navy, and a reduction in the public debt, but these are dwarfed by his massive failure to do anything to stop the Civil War.

Born on April 23, 1791, near Mercersburg, Pennsylvania, he was the son of a shopkeeper prosperous enough to support him in college. After graduating from Dickinson College in 1809, Buchanan studied law and was admitted to the bar in 1811. He began his political career as a Federalist and was elected to the Pennsylvania legislature in 1814 and reelected in 1815. He was elected to the U.S. House of Representatives in 1820, but he became a Democrat and a supporter of ANDREW JACKSON in 1824.

Buchanan left his seat in the House of Representatives in the middle of 1831 to be the U.S. ambassador to Russia, where he remained until 1833. When he returned from Russia, the Pennsylvania state legislature named him a U.S. senator from 1834 until 1845.

Buchanan was first mentioned as a candidate for president of the United States in 1844. He lost the nomination to JAMES KNOX POLK, but he worked hard for Polk's election. Polk rewarded Buchanan by naming him secretary of state, but the two did not get along well. As secretary of state, Buchanan successfully negotiated with the British to determine the boundary between Oregon and Canada.

Buchanan helped draft the peace treaty after the war with Mexico and insisted that Polk vigorously enforce the Monroe Doctrine in Central and Latin America. He had a long-term interest in seeing the United States acquire the island of Cuba, a conviction he retained throughout his life.

Although Buchanan had promised not to run for president in 1848 if he were named secretary of state, he reneged on his promise and sought the nomination. Lewis Cass, who later ran unsuccessfully against ZACHARY TAYLOR, defeated Buchanan for the Democratic presidential nomination. Out of a job in the Whig administration until 1852, Buchanan tried and failed in a presidential bid when FRANKLIN PIERCE was nominated and elected instead. Buchanan helped Pierce win and this time was rewarded by being named ambassador to Great Britain. While in Britain, Buchanan assisted in the development of the controversial Ostend Manifesto, which urged the United States to acquire Cuba, but he avoided being tarnished by the controversy over the 1854 Kansas-Nebraska Act. In 1856, Buchanan was the Democratic compromise choice for president and straddled the slavery issue well enough to be elected.

President James Buchanan is remembered for his failure to act to stop southern secession and the Civil War. *(Library of Congress)*

The major issue of the day was whether slavery would be allowed into the territories that were not already states. Buchanan thought the issue could be settled if the U.S. Supreme Court would rule on the question. The Dred Scott case seemed to provide a way to get a clear ruling. Dred Scott was a slave who sought his freedom on grounds that he had been taken into areas where slavery was banned. Buchanan lobbied hard with members of the Court on the case and got the clear ruling he sought, but the result was disastrous.

Instead of avoiding the case, as the Court could have easily done, or deciding on limited grounds that Scott was still a slave, the Court reached far beyond those issues. The Court declared that the Compromise of 1820, setting a geographical limit to the expansion of slavery, was unconstitutional. The Court further declared that slaves had virtually no rights and Congress had no right to end slavery in any U.S. territories. Instead of quieting the issue, the decision provoked uproar in the North, incited abolitionist sentiment, and brought on a series of events that rapidly moved the country toward war.

Buchanan also supported the admission of Kansas into the United States under the so-called Lecompton Constitution, fraudulently drafted by pro-slavery forces in a convention that barred antislavery delegates. The decision was so pro-slavery that even Senator STEPHEN ARNOLD DOUGLAS, a Democrat generally in favor of allowing slavery into the territories, split with Buchanan. The Buchanan-Douglas dispute split the Democratic Party and hastened the war.

Buchanan fared poorly on other issues as well. He supported the 1857 Tariff Bill, which angered his supporters in Pennsylvania and helped the development of the Republican Party. He clung to outdated Jacksonian principles on economic matters when a fresh approach was needed.

Buchanan is most criticized for his failure to take steps to reduce the danger of secession after the election of ABRAHAM LINCOLN. He also failed to reinforce Union garrisons in the South because he felt he did not have the authority to do so. Since Buchanan had announced he would serve only a single term as president, he had declining authority over time so he was unable to take steps needed to avoid war.

After he retired from the presidency, he returned to private life at his home in Pennsylvania and died on June 1, 1868.

Further Reading

"Buchanan, James," Available online. URL: http://www. whitehouse.gov/history/presidents/jb15.html. Downloaded on October 20, 2001.

Gienapp, William E. "James Buchanan" in *The American Presidents,* edited by Frank N. Magill, John L. Loos, and Tracy Irons-Georges. Pasadena, Calif.: Salem Press, 2000.

Hermon, Joseph Martin. *Profiles in Character: Hubris and Heroism in the U.S. Senate—1789–1990.* Armonk, N.Y.: M. E. Sharpe, 1997.

"James Buchanan" in *The American President,* by Philip B. Kunhardt, Jr., Philip B. Kunhardt III, and Peter W. Kunhardt. New York: Riverbend Books, 1999.

"James Buchanan" in *The Presidency A to Z: Second Edition,* edited by Michael T. Nelson. Washington, D.C.: Congressional Quarterly Press, 1998.

Moore, John Basset, ed. *The Works of James Buchanan.* Philadelphia: J. B. Lippincott Company, 1908–11.

Burger, Warren
(1907–1995) *chief justice of the United States*

Chief Justice Warren Burger followed Chief Justice EARL WARREN, who presided over one of the most expansive periods in Court history. Some conservatives hoped Burger would roll back many of the Warren Court decisions, but the Burger legacy was much more modest.

Born on September 17, 1907, in St. Paul, Minnesota, Warren Earl Burger acquired his college education by taking extension courses from the University of Minnesota from 1925 to 1927. Over the next four years, he went to night school at the Billy Mitchell School of Law (then known as the St. Paul College of Law), while making a living as an insurance salesman. Finally admitted to the Minnesota bar in 1931, he combined an active law practice with a teaching career at the Mitchell School of Law. Burger had one of the most modest sets of academic credentials of any nominee for the Supreme Court in the latter half of the 20th century.

Long active in Minnesota state Republican activities, Burger assisted in organizing the Young Republicans and supported Harold Stassen for governor in 1938 and reelection in 1940. After World War II, Burger faithfully supported Stassen for president in both 1948 and in 1952. However, when it was clear Stassen could not win the Republican nomination in 1952, Burger switched his support to DWIGHT DAVID EISENHOWER and carried the Minnesota delegation for him.

In 1953, Eisenhower rewarded Burger with the post of assistant attorney general in charge of civil litigation in the U.S. Department of Justice. In 1956, Eisenhower appointed him to the federal bench as a judge on the U.S. Circuit Court of Appeals for the District of Columbia, a court often seen as a stepping-stone to the Supreme Court.

Since he was known as a safely conservative judge whose opinions often departed from those of the more liberal Warren Court, Burger was in an excellent position to be named chief justice when Earl Warren chose to resign in 1969. Although Warren had tried to resign during the administration of LYNDON BAINES JOHNSON so that a Democrat could make the appointment of his successor,

Johnson's initial choice of Abe Fortas was so fraught with difficulties that Warren had to stay on until after President RICHARD MILHOUS NIXON was inaugurated. Burger seemed in many ways to be exactly the kind of judge Nixon said he wanted to support, and he was appointed to the Supreme Court in 1969.

On the bench, Burger was a moderate-to-conservative justice. The Burger Court upheld many Warren Court rulings in the areas of civil liberties and civil rights, and it even extended the Warren Court's desegregation rulings by approving busing to reduce de facto school segregation. The Burger Court retreated from Warren Court rulings that expanded the rights of those accused of crimes so that the powers of law enforcement were somewhat strengthened.

Burger was best known for his efforts to streamline the administration of the federal courts, but his improvements were not revolutionary. Burger retired from the Supreme Court in September 1986 and President RONALD WILSON REAGAN named the clearly more conservative associate justice WILLIAM HUBBS REHNQUIST to be chief justice.

Warren Burger died on June 25, 1995.

Further Reading

Bryson, Joseph E. *The Supreme Court and Public Funds for Religious Schools: The Burger Years.* Jefferson, N.C.: McFarland, 1990.

Burger, Warren E. *It Is So Ordered.* New York: W. Morrow & Co, 1995.

Galub, Arthur. *The Burger Court,* Millwood, N.Y.: Associated Faculty Press, 1985.

Maveety, Nancy. *Representation Rights and the Burger Years.* Ann Arbor: University of Michigan Press, 1991.

Schwartz, Bernard. *The Ascent of Pragmatism: The Burger Court in Action.* Reading, Mass.: Addison-Wesley, 1990.

Burr, Aaron

(1756–1836) *vice president, senator, Revolutionary War leader*

Aaron Burr had a distinguished political career, but his many positive contributions to the United States are overshadowed by the fact that he killed ALEXANDER HAMILTON in a duel and was the first vice president of the United States to be tried for treason.

The descendant of a prominent colonial family and a long line of religious and intellectual leaders, Burr was born on February 6, 1756, in Newark, New Jersey. His grandfather was Jonathan Edwards, the famous religious leader in New England. His father was one of the founders of Princeton University (originally called the College of New Jersey) and Princeton's second president, but he died when young Burr was only two. Raised by a stern relative and educated at home by tutors, he rebelled against their authority. Very bright, he fled the tight family control by entering Princeton at age 13. Graduating in three years, he joined the American Revolutionary Army during the siege of Boston.

At first, Burr served on the staff of General Benedict Arnold, who was subsequently found guilty of treason. Fortunately, he was able to transfer to the command of GEORGE WASHINGTON briefly and then to serve under General Israel Putnam. Burr was given command of the regiment in the summer of 1777. When he fought at the battle of Monmouth, Burr made an error that led Washington to criticize him. Burr became very angry, and, two years later, he used an illness as an excuse to quit the army. For this, Washington never forgave him.

Burr became a lawyer in New York in 1792. He had already developed hostility toward Alexander Hamilton. The two had served together briefly in the army and had had a falling out at that time. Both were intelligent and ambitious, and no doubt personal rivalry lay behind their long-standing hatred. New York State politics were divided between the factions headed by GEORGE CLINTON and Alexander Hamilton. Since working with Hamilton was out of the question, Burr naturally sided with Clinton. To make matters worse, Clinton supported Burr for attorney general and aided Burr in his successful attempt to win a U.S. Senate seat that was held by Philip Schuyler, Hamilton's father-in-law.

Burr's good fortune soon turned around when he was defeated for reelection in 1797. Fighting back, Burr helped Clinton create a powerful Democratic Republican Party political machine in New York City that gained sufficient strength to control the state legislature. This group controlled not only the naming of the U.S. senators from New York but also the presidential Electoral College votes. So THOMAS JEFFERSON, the leading candidate for president on the Democratic Republican ticket, decided he had to take Burr as his vice presidential running mate to secure the New York vote.

In 1800, the Federalist Party was split between JOHN ADAMS and CHARLES COTESWORTH PINCKNEY so it seemed that Jefferson would win easily. Under the original Electoral College, all electors voted separately for president and vice president. The individual with the highest vote became president and the one with the second-highest became the vice president. Everyone recognized that, if a president and vice president ran as a team, the winning ticket would have produced a tie. Therefore, informally it was agreed that a few electors would refrain from casting ballots for the intended vice president to avoid a tie developing. It was important that this practice was infrequent or else the presidential candidate for the other team would be elected vice president, as had happened in 1796 when Jefferson became Adams's vice president. This agreement had been made in 1800, but Burr had secretly arranged for everyone to believe that someone else was responsible for not voting for vice president and, therefore, they should all vote for him. When all the Democratic Republican electors voted for both Jefferson and Burr, the result was a tie.

The tie was referred to the House of Representatives for the members to vote for a winner among the top three candidates—Jefferson, Burr, and Adams. Since the Federalists would not abandon their own candidate, Adams, and since Burr did not drop out, the House was deadlocked. The deadlock continued through 36 ballots. Negotiations between the Federalists and Burr took place, although Burr denied starting them. When Hamilton got wind of it, he was furious. Much as he disagreed with Jefferson, he despised Burr. Hamilton finally persuaded some of the Federalists to shift from Adams to Jefferson, breaking the deadlock and blocking Burr from seizing the presidency. Jefferson was elected president and Burr, with the second-highest number of votes, became the vice president. After the controversy, Jefferson never trusted Burr.

Two years later, Burr tried to run for governor of New York, but Hamilton fought hard and brought about his defeat. After years of hostility, Burr was insulted by a derogatory remark Hamilton made in a letter that was later and perhaps accidentally made public. He challenged Hamilton to a duel, which they arranged to conduct in New Jersey where the laws against dueling were less strict. The two faced off on July 11, 1804; Hamilton was seriously wounded and died shortly thereafter.

The public outcry and the attempts to indict Burr for murder caused him to flee both New York and New Jersey to Philadelphia. When the furor subsided, Burr returned to the Senate where he presided as if there were no controversy. His break with Jefferson meant he had no political future in a Jefferson administration, and he was out of office at the end of Jefferson's first term.

Burr, apparently believing he was acting with the support of President Jefferson, then became associated with a plan to create a perfectly legal society of non-slaveholders in Louisiana. This plan fit with Burr's long opposition to slavery. While Burr thought the land had been properly purchased for that purpose, he was unaware that some legal problems existed over the deed.

Burr traveled with about a dozen lightly armed frontier settlers down the Ohio and Mississippi Rivers to this new property. There he sought to recruit various non-slaveholders to join him in developing the area. Burr did not realize the depth of the hatred the southern slaveholders had to his plan of a non-slaveholding plantation. Nor did he realize that these southerners had secretly approached their fellow southern slaveholder, President Jefferson, with a highly exaggerated tale about a plot to lead a revolt of southwestern territories to form a new country.

During his journey south, Burr discussed his plan with James Wilkinson, the governor of Louisiana territory. A thoroughly disreputable man, Wilkinson pretended to support Burr while reporting false stories about Burr's plans to the federal authorities. Burr was arrested and tried for treason in Washington in 1807. The framers of the U.S. Constitution specifically limited the definition of treason to avoid the purely political prosecutions for treason that had occurred in England. U.S. Supreme Court Justice JOHN MARSHALL, a Federalist opponent of Jefferson (but no particular friend of Burr) insisted that the definition of treason be followed strictly and Burr was not convicted. Still Burr's political reputation in the United States was ruined and he had fallen on hard times.

After the treason trial, Burr fled to Europe to escape all the people to whom he owed money—and perhaps to seek new financial supporters for his schemes. By 1812, he decided to return to New York where he spent the last quarter century of his life, living privately as a modestly successful attorney. Aaron Burr died on September 14, 1836.

Further Reading

Fleming, Thomas J. *Duel: Alexander Hamilton, Aaron Burr, and the Future of America.* New York: Basic Books, 1999.

Lomask, Milton. *Aaron Burr, The Conspiracy and Years of Exile, 1805–1836.* New York: Farrar, Straus & Giroux, 1982.

Kennedy, Roger G. *Burr, Hamilton, and Jefferson: A Study in Character.* Oxford: Oxford University Press, 2000.

Kunstler, Laurence. *The Unpredictable Mr. Aaron Burr.* New York: Vantage Press, 1974.

Rogow, Arnold A. *A Fatal Friendship: Alexander Hamilton and Aaron Burr.* New York: Hill & Wang, 1998.

Bush, George Herbert Walker

(1924–) *president, vice president, director of the Central Intelligence Agency, diplomat, representative, author*

George Herbert Walker Bush's presidency reflected both the sudden ups and downs of personal popularity in the office. Bush received the highest presidential popularity approval ratings in the polls of any president since World War II shortly after the U.S. Armed Forces won a decisive victory in a two-day war over the Iraqi army in 1991. Shortly after that, his presidential popularity ratings plummeted, paralleling the economic slowdown, and he was defeated for reelection to the presidency two years later.

Born in Milton, Massachusetts, on June 12, 1924, Bush was raised in Greenwich, Connecticut. After attending Phillips Andover Academy, he enlisted in the U.S. Naval Reserve. In 1943 he became the youngest naval pilot while serving in World War II, and he acted heroically by landing his crippled plane on the deck of an aircraft carrier. After the war, he enrolled in Yale University and graduated in only three years. Leaving New England, he decided to make his career in the Texas oil business. Bush learned of the oil business firsthand and established a number of different oil businesses before he went into politics in the early 1960s.

Following in the footsteps of his father, Senator Prescott Bush of Connecticut, Bush sought election to the U.S. Senate in 1964. He won the Republican nomination but lost the general election in a 1964 Democratic landslide. He was seeking to win a statewide race as a Republican in the same year that LYNDON BAINES JOHNSON, a Texas Democrat, was running for reelection as president of the United States.

Two years later, Bush was elected to the U.S. House of Representatives where he served for two terms. In the House Bush took a generally conservative stance on fiscal issues as a member of the House Ways and Means Committee. However, his stance on social issues, such as civil rights and granting 18-year-olds the right to vote, proved too liberal for the comfort of his conservative Texas constituents.

In 1970, he decided not to seek reelection to the House of Representatives but instead to make another run for the Senate. Conservative Democrat Lloyd Bentsen defeated him, but his strong effort earned him respect in Republican Party councils. President RICHARD MILHOUS NIXON appointed him the U.S. ambassador to the United Nations. After two years in New York, he became the chairman of the Republican National Committee. Bush defended Nixon in the Watergate scandal until the release of the presidential tapes clearly demonstrated that Nixon had been in on the cover-up of the Watergate scandal.

Nixon's successor, President GERALD RUDOLPH FORD, then named Bush to be the U.S. liaison to the People's Republic of China where he remained for two years. After that, he returned to the United States to become a director of the Central Intelligence Agency (CIA). Since the CIA had been subject to embarrassing involvement in destabilizing Third World countries, Ford thought naming someone with Bush's reputation would improve the agency's standing, though he served for only eight months.

Out of office at the end of the Ford administration, Bush sought to establish himself as a Republican presidential candidate. In 1980, he sought the Republican presidential nomination, even though he was a long shot against a well-established front-runner, future President RONALD WILSON REAGAN. Bush pulled an upset in the Iowa

George Herbert Walker Bush was the second president (after John Adams) to see his son inaugurated as president of the United States. *(Library of Congress, Official White House photo)*

caucuses and came much closer than expected to Reagan, who eventually went on to gain the Republican nomination. This success was attributed to his campaign manager, JAMES ADDISON BAKER III.

After trying unsuccessfully to persuade former president Gerald Ford to accept the vice presidential nomination, Reagan turned to his popular primary challenger, George Herbert Walker Bush, for his vice presidential running mate. They won the election (and the 1984 reelection) with Bush serving eight years as vice president. Bush loyally supported the Reagan administration to the extent of becoming involved in the Iran-Contra Scandal and spending the last two years, with mixed success, arguing that he was not involved.

Bush's term as vice president was successful enough that he became a leading contender for the Republican presidential nomination in 1988. As the best financed candidate, he outdistanced his competitors and won the nomination. His Democratic opponent was Massachusetts Governor Michael Dukakis. Although the national race was reasonably close, Bush was a comfortable victor.

The first two years of the Bush presidency were filled with amazing foreign policy developments. First, Bush concluded that the government of Panama, headed by General Manuel Noriega, had turned the country into a base for drug smuggling. When a domestic revolt failed to capture Noriega, Bush carried out a military operation in Panama that resulted in the capture of Noriega and his removal to the United States for trial and conviction.

In 1989, Chinese student demonstrations and the eventual Chinese government crackdown outraged public opinion to such a degree that other Communist regimes concluded they must meet their own demonstrators with concessions, not repression. This destabilized the already weakened Soviet Union's empire in Eastern Europe. Over the next two years, all of the Communist regimes in Eastern Europe collapsed, including the Soviet Union itself. The successes were credited to the Bush administration, although they likely would have occurred without American intervention.

One consequence of the changing European power relationships was that Soviet-influenced regimes in the Middle East saw European instability as a chance to advance their international aims. In 1990, one Middle Eastern dictator, Saddam Hussein, saw American preoccupation in Europe as an opportunity for him to settle a border dispute with a small oil-rich neighbor by taking over the entire country.

Saddam Hussein badly miscalculated the American response to a seizure of Kuwait. First, the United States engaged in an expansive creation of a coalition of Saddam Hussein's neighbors to counter his threat to another small neighbor, Saudi Arabia. Second, the United States began a prolonged buildup of military forces designed to deter Saddam Hussein from taking any other territory in the area. Ultimately, the large collection of American troops, supplemented by European allies, created a mass military force to expel Saddam Hussein's forces from Kuwait.

Although the Iraqi army was rated as the fifth largest army in the world, it was no match for the technologically advanced American troops and their allies already in place in the Middle East. The actual fighting, in an operation called Desert Storm, was over in less than two days and the Iraqi army was completely routed. Curiously, Bush then decided to order American troops to stop their advance, allowing enough of the Iraqi army to escape punishment that Saddam Hussein was able to maintain himself in power. He maintained that he had promised the Russians that he would not destroy Saddam Hussein entirely. He also anticipated that Saddam Hussein would be so weakened that he would inevitably fall.

However, Saddam Hussein was able to hang onto power, recover from the war, and restore some of his political and military strength. Bush was criticized at the time for failing to push through to complete victory, but the ability of Saddam Hussein to survive for more than a decade was not fully perceived by anyone. At the time, the success of the U.S. armed forces was so great that George Bush received the highest presidential popularity rating since such polling began.

Bush's foreign policy success may have contributed to his downfall by creating the belief that he could solve any problem—even domestic and international problems largely beyond his control. By 1991, the United States economy had enjoyed

a very long successful expansion. Following a typical business cycle, a downturn was likely by 1991 or 1992. As Bush benefited from fortuitous foreign policy events, so he was punished for an economic slowdown beyond his control.

Bush also emphatically promised in his 1988 presidential campaign that he would not raise taxes, pledging, "Read my lips: No new taxes." The economic downturn required new revenue and Bush reneged on his promise by signing a tax increase. This became the fundamental basis for the Democratic campaign attack in 1992.

Worse, Bush faced an attack from two candidates. The first was Democrat WILLIAM JEFFERSON CLINTON, who had served nearly two decades as the governor of Arkansas. Although Arkansas was a small state, Clinton had compiled a successful record. The second was HENRY ROSS PEROT, a political maverick who saw the slowdown in the economy and the failure to dislodge Saddam Hussein as an opportunity for him to jump into the presidential race as an independent. An extremely wealthy individual, Perot offered to pay for his entire presidential campaign out of his own pocket. Although Perot could not win the presidency on his own, he threatened to take so many votes away from Bush that Clinton would win. Sophisticated election analyses failed to show that Perot cost Bush the election directly, but Perot complicated the campaign for Bush. Overall, Bush's popularity fell sharply after his incredible post–Gulf War high in one of the most spectacular declines in recent history.

Bush retired from the presidency to his home state of Texas, where he acted behind the scenes as he attempted to advance the political careers of his two sons. The Bush family calculated that their younger son, Jeb, was the better candidate and pushed hard for his election as governor of Florida. They anticipated that, after winning the Florida gubernatorial race, the younger Bush would be a prominent candidate for president in 2000. Unfortunately, Jeb Bush lost his first try for governor of Florida and the focus of the Bush family efforts shifted to the older son, GEORGE WALKER BUSH, who was successful in winning the governor's office in Texas. Although Jeb won the governor's office in Florida on his next try, the political momentum was on the side of George W., who won reelection as governor in 1998 and was elected president in 2000. Former President Bush has been careful to avoid having any public statements on his sons presidency that might seem to represent undue or improper influence.

Further Reading

Bush, George. *A World Transformed.* New York: Knopf, 1998.

"Bush, George Herbert Walker," Available online. URL: http://www.whitehouse.gov/history/presidents/gb41.html. Downloaded on October 20, 2001.

Bush, George H. W. *All the Best, George Bush.* New York: A Lisa Drew Book/Scribner, 1999.

Campbell, Colin, and Bert Rockman. *The Bush Presidency.* Chatham, N.J.: Chatham House Publishers, 1991.

Goldman, Peter, Tom Matthews, and the Newsweek Special Election Team. *The Quest for the Presidency 1988.* New York: Simon & Schuster, 1989.

Graubard, Stephen R. *Mr. Bush's War.* Hill & Wang, 1992.

Greene, John Robert. *The Presidency of George Bush.* Lawrence: University Press of Kansas, 2000.

Mervin, David. *George Bush and the Guardianship Presidency.* New York: St. Martin's Press, 1996.

Parmet, Herbert S. *George Bush: The Life of a Lone Star Yankee.* New York: Scribner, 1997.

Woodward, Bob. *Shadow.* New York: Simon & Schuster, 1999.

Bush, George Walker

(1946–) *president, governor*

George W. Bush is the only man, besides JOHN QUINCY ADAMS, to be elected president after his father (GEORGE HERBERT WALKER BUSH) served as president.

Born on July 9, 1946, while his father was a student at Yale University, George Walker Bush was raised in east Texas as his father was engaged in the oil business. Following in his father's footsteps, George W. attended Yale University, graduating with a degree in history in 1968. He went on to earn a master's in business administration at Harvard University in 1975.

George W. Bush worked at a variety of different business ventures in oil and the professional sports field before being elected governor of Texas in 1994. He was reelected in 1998.

While governor, he sought to improve education performance in Texas and made his record of education reform one of the hallmarks of his presidential campaign. The institution of the Texas governor has limited authority when compared with other states, but the state is large and has many wealthy industries, such as oil. These industries can offer the opportunity of raising large campaign donations. By combining his father's fund-raising skills as president with his brother's fund-raising skills in Florida and his own considerable resources in Texas, George W. Bush amassed such a large sum of campaign finance money that he was able to avoid taking federal matching funds. This allowed him to pay for his primary campaign without many of the usual campaign finance restrictions.

Although he was the front-runner because of his tremendous campaign funds, securing the Republican nomination did not prove easy. Conservative Republican Senator JOHN MCCAIN, who had an attractive Vietnam War record, opposed him. McCain won the New Hampshire primary by a wide margin and constituted a serious challenge to Bush in several subsequent primaries, winning, for example, the Michigan Republican primary. McCain failed to win the crucial Republican primary in South Carolina and was unable to win enough other states, despite making a strong showing. In the end, Bush's tremendous campaign war chest and his father's connections and organizational skills proved decisive, and McCain was forced to withdraw from the race. The Democratic primary race was between former U.S. Senator Bill Bradley and incumbent Vice President ALBERT ARNOLD GORE JR., a contest which Gore won easily.

Neither party started out with a decisive edge in the general election. The Democrats had the advantage of White House incumbency, which normally would help their nominee in fund-raising and the ability to generate favorable news coverage. However, the advantage is often limited because the necessary decisions of governing almost always have a negative impact on some domestic groups, who develop a long-lasting hostility against the "in" party. This situation gets worse particularly after a second term (or eight years) when weariness with the "in" party may also set in. The Democrats benefited from a strong economy, but there was an underlying concern that the prosperity might be coming to an end, thereby limiting the appeal.

The Republicans had the advantage of being the "out" party, but this was also limited. Since the economy was strong, they could not simply point to the problems and make vague promises about fixing them. They needed to articulate a more sophisticated positive program. The Republicans were weakened in offering a positive approach since they had controlled both houses of Congress for the preceding six years. They were identified with using this control in the very unpopular attempt to impeach President WILLIAM JEFFERSON CLINTON for alleged perjury and obstruction of justice in connection with sex-related encounters with Monica Lewinsky. Throughout the impeachment, the polls consistently showed that a solid majority of the American people approved of the job Clinton was doing—even though they disapproved of his private life—and did not want him impeached. Nonetheless, the Republican congressional leadership persisted in impeaching and trying Clinton, failing to convict only because they could never meet the constitutional requirement of a two-thirds vote in the Senate as long as the Democrats held nearly half the seats in the body. The evidence for this conclusion lies not in ephemeral poll numbers but in the result of the 1998 congressional elections. Any party that controls the White House for two terms often loses seats in the election held in the sixth year of their tenure—and usually in very large numbers. In the 1998 elections, however, the Democrats gained seats. This happened only once before in U.S. history—in 1834, almost a century and a half earlier.

Complicating the election further was the fact that neither major party candidate seemed to be obviously superior to the other. Vice President Al Gore was an intelligent man with a 24-year record of distinguished national service in the House of Representatives, Senate, and vice presidency, and he was almost entirely untouched by the scandals that surrounded President Clinton. He was unable

to transform this reputation to the mass electorate, despite repeated attempts to learn how. Most frequently accused of making "wooden" speeches, it is more accurate to say that he could not overcome his own awareness of his intelligence and he patronized his national audience. As a result, he was respected for his intelligence but disliked.

As governor of Texas for six years, Bush had a much less extensive public record. He was likeable, but he had to overcome the impression that he was not substantial enough for the job. However intelligent he may be, he has had a tendency to mispronounce words or use the wrong words frequently on subjects both large and small, which does not generate confidence.

The public opinion polls showed a close race throughout the campaign with one candidate and then the other taking a narrow lead. This was especially true during the presidential and vice presidential debates. Bush was relatively more successful in gaining or maintaining his strength during the debate period.

Gore "won" all three of the debates according to the experts who concentrated on the debating points and according to those polled specifically on the debates. Bush gained ground in those polls that asked for whom the voters would vote. Expectations for Bush's performance in the debates were low, given his reputation for making verbal blunders, but ironically the debates helped him some since he did better than expected—even when he "lost." Gore was extremely well informed in the first debate, but he was so confident that he came across as an arrogant "know-it-all." This impression was made even worse when the vice presidential debate took place in a more relaxed format. Republican candidate Dick Cheney and Democratic nominee Joe Lieberman both conducted such a civil debate that they offered a stark contrast to the strident tone of the first presidential debate. The second presidential debate (and the third debate of the series) took place in a more relaxed format. Faced with criticism that he was too aggressive in the first debate, Gore was more subdued in the second debate, with the result that he was criticized for being too passive. He achieved the proper balance in the third debate, but the momentum had been lost.

Bush's gains appeared to have been a less important factor, however, since he continued to make mistakes. Overconfident, Bush took a day off to rest from the campaign in the last two weeks, which cost him campaign time. At one point, he made a strange blunder by saying that Social Security was not a federal program. And it was later discovered that Bush failed to disclose early in the campaign a decades-old arrest for driving under the influence of alcohol—when disclosing such a fact would have done little harm. The arrest was discovered in the last weekend before the election, when Bush had little chance to recover.

Both candidates struggled to the finish line with the momentum being in the Gore campaign. On election night, the television networks declared Gore the winner in Michigan, Pennsylvania, and Florida—the three states Gore had said would be likely to put him over the top. Indeed, had Gore carried all three states, he would have been elected president even if he had lost the popular vote. As it was, Gore's momentum caused him to receive more than 500,000 more votes than Bush nationwide. Also, more people came to the polls in Florida intending to vote for Al Gore than those who came to polls to vote for Bush. The question was whether they cast valid votes when they arrived or, through their own error, invalidated their ballots. Only a careful recount could have determined the result, and that was foreclosed by a Supreme Court decision.

After declaring that Gore carried Florida (in an announcement made before all the polls had closed in Florida), the networks came under heavy criticism from the Republicans and withdrew their declaration, moving Florida and the entire election into the "too close to call" category. Florida remained undecided until the early hours of the morning when the networks, following the lead of the Fox television network, declared for Bush. Given the remaining returns, this made it very likely that Bush had won the election.

However, almost as soon as the networks declared Florida for Bush, the Bush lead began to slip. In the interim, Gore called Bush to congratulate him and then headed to a gathering of supporters to concede. Before he got there, he got a call urging him not concede on grounds that the Florida totals were just a few hundred votes apart. Gore called Bush and told him he was not going to concede because of the close vote and did not address the crowd that gathered.

The Florida election was more than close; it was riddled with irregularities. Most Florida counties used a punch card voting system, an inexpensive system that used an older computer technology subject to a variety of errors. The first and most widely discussed of these was a ballot layout known as a "butterfly" ballot, in which arrows pointed to the holes for the appropriate candidates. Such a ballot layout was illegal under Florida law, although local officials from both parties had approved its use in advance. The ballot layout may have confused some voters and led them to vote for candidates other than those they preferred. In other cases, the Votomatics, or punching boards for the ballots, may have been clogged with the punched out pieces of paper from previous users so that the ballots could not be punched completely.

In both cases, the solution to determining whom the voters actually preferred depended on a time-consuming hand recount of the ballots. Florida law provided a precertification ballot examination procedure and a postcertification contested election recount procedure. Holding a lead of just a few hundred votes, Bush opposed any further counting of the ballots and said that his opponent should not use the courts to try to win the election and demanded that the initial tally be accepted. Gore naturally requested a recount in areas in which irregularities occurred and was granted some recounts in those areas as provided by Florida law.

Ironically, Bush sued first by trying to block further recounts. Bush lost the main suit in the Florida courts and sued in federal courts, offering a novel, untested legal theory that the recount law violated the equal protection clause of the Fourteenth Amendment because not every ballot was recounted—only ballots in areas in which irregularities occurred. When the Florida Supreme Court heard the lawsuit, the court ruled that a recount could go forward under the existing state law and extended a deadline set out in state law for such a recount to take place.

Bush then appealed to the U.S. Supreme Court, which overturned the Florida Supreme Court and ordered the recount halted, using the novel equal protection clause argument as its basis. The Supreme Court decided the question by a narrow five to four decision in which the five most conservative justices—all Republican appointees—decided the issue. The decision was remarkable from a conservative legal point of view. Instead of following the conservative philosophy of respecting federalism and granting deference to state courts to allow them to interpret their own laws, the decision overturned a state supreme court ruling on grounds of a violation of the equal protection clause—a clause usually avoided by conservatives because it leads to expansions of judicial power normally associated with liberals. That the most conservative justice would adopt such a stance led to widespread criticism that the Court was acting out of mere partisan political concerns. Even conservative legal scholars criticized the decision. It led to acrimonious debate among the justices, for the two Democratic appointees and two Republican appointees of moderate views dissented vigorously and objected publicly. The internal debate among the justices was especially bitter and apparently continued for months after the decision. Recognizing that there was not a higher court to which he could appeal, Gore made a gracious concession speech and the election was over.

Bush began his administration by carrying out a campaign promise to push through a 10-year, across-the-board tax cut of $1.3 trillion as a "refund" (as he called it)—taxes overpaid by the citizens. Although Bush had promised the tax cut would not lead to deficits or to using the Social Security trust fund, the economy had slowed down so much that it became necessary to use a portion of the Social Security trust fund to pay for government services because of the tax cut.

On September 11, 2001, four groups of hijackers—all apparently numbers of Al Qaeda, a radical Muslim group—seized four planes and used them as flying missiles aimed at important buildings in the United States. Two of the planes flew into the towers of the World Trade Center in New York City, starting a fire so intense that it caused the buildings to collapse. A third plane was crashed into the Pentagon in Washington, D.C. The last plane was crashed before hitting its intended target because the passengers apparently struggled with the hijackers, managing to cause the plane to crash in a remote area where no one on the ground was killed.

Bush responded to this tragedy by making a well-received speech to a joint session of Congress and the nation. He also initiated a widely supported war against terrorism, which initially focused on the Taliban. This was an extreme fundamentalist Muslim regime that controlled Afghanistan and harbored the Al Qaeda terrorist group. Led by wealthy former Saudi Arabian Osama bin Laden, Al Qaeda had been linked to a number of terrorist and attempted terrorist acts against the United States or its personnel in Africa, Europe, Asia, and the Middle East.

In a matter of weeks, the U.S. Air Force attacked, dominating the skies over Afghanistan and bombing suspected Taliban and Al Qaeda positions heavily. New U.S. allies—Afghan warlord ground forces who opposed the Taliban, known as the Northern Alliance—were supported in their fight against the Taliban. By the beginning of 2002, the Taliban regime had been overthrown, and many Taliban and Al Qaeda troops had been killed or captured. However, Osama bin Laden and the religious head of the Taliban had not been captured.

The apparent success of the early efforts in this war on terrorism resulted in a soaring presidential popularity rating for President Bush, which helped him overcome the cloud on his legitimacy as the result of his contested 2000 election. His military success was not matched by a corresponding success in domestic affairs.

U.S. government economic advisers officially declared the continued slowdown in the economy to be a recession in fall 2001. The recession reduced tax receipts and the war on terrorism increased government expenditures so that the budget deficit, the shortfall created by the 2001 tax cuts, was aggravated. What were supposed to be continued revenue surpluses became a significant deficit. Enron, a large energy firm, with political ties to the Bush administration and the Republican Party (with some connection to the

Democrats as well), collapsed into the biggest bankruptcy in U.S. history in January 2002.

At the end of George W. Bush's first year and a half in office, it was hard to ignore the parallels between his father's presidency and his own. Both had seen astronomical presidential popularity ratings as the result of an apparently successful war effort coupled with an uncertain domestic economic situation. The domestic economic situation had doomed his father's presidency, but it was not clear whether parallel events would doom his own first term.

From the first, Bush announced that the war on terrorism would take time. Initially, although Osama bin Laden and most of his highest level associates were not killed or captured in the first months of the war, the Bush administration could point to a partial success in the overthrow of the Taliban regime in Afghanistan. Taking out an old regime was easier than creating a stable successor. This had yet to be accomplished.

In Spring 2002, Israel launched a major military offensive into Palestinian areas in the Gaza Strip and West Bank in an effort to break up terrorist networks and confiscate bomb-making materials and other armaments. The Israeli action provoked strong criticism in the Muslim world and criticism by some in Europe and the United States. During Spring 2002, the Israeli-Palestinian conflict overshadowed the rest of the war on terrorism, and it complicated U.S. plans to deal vigorously—and perhaps forcefully—against Saddam Hussein and his Iraqi regime, which Bush had declared was a key source of terrorism. Bush sent Colin Powell to the Middle East to a negotiate, but Powell returned without solid results. Clearly, foreign policy was to be a major issue in the Bush presidency.

Further Reading

Bush, George W. *A Charge to Keep.* New York: Morrow, 1999.
"Bush, George Walker," Available online. URL: http://www.whitehouse.gov/history/presidents/gb43.html. Downloaded on October 20, 2001.
Hatfield, James. *Fortunate Son: George W. Bush and the Making of an American President.* New York: Soft Skull Press, 2000.
Ivins, Molly. *Shrub: The Short But Happy Political Life of George W. Bush.* New York: Random House, 2000.
Minutaglio, Bill. *First Son: George W. Bush and the Bush Family Dynasty.* New York: Times Books, 1999.
Mitchell, Elizabeth. *W: Revenge of the Bush Dynasty.* New York: Hyperion, 2000.

Butler, Benjamin Franklin
(1818–1893) *candidate for president, representative*

Benjamin Butler was a Democratic politician in Massachusetts state politics who sympathized with the South but was strongly opposed to secession. After the Civil War began, he switched to support the Republican administration of Abraham Lincoln. His administrative success early in the war led to his appointment as military governor of Louisiana, where his harsh treatment of white southerners earned him the nickname "Beast Butler." After the war, he officially switched to the Republican Party and served as a Radical Republican in Congress. Gradually falling out with the Republicans, he switched to the Greenback Party under whose label he won two nonconsecutive terms in Congress before switching back to the Democratic Party without winning any more elections.

Benjamin Franklin Butler was born on November 5, 1818, in Deerfield, New Hampshire. After the death of his father, Butler and his mother moved to Massachusetts where she operated a boardinghouse for women who worked in the textile mills. Butler graduated from Colby College (then known as Waterbury College) in 1838, "read in the law," and was admitted to the bar in 1840. A capable lawyer, he quickly earned a fortune from his law practice and investments.

In his 30s, Butler turned his attention to politics and was elected to the Massachusetts House of Representatives in 1853 and to the Massachusetts Senate in 1859. Butler was a Democrat who sympathized with the Southerners and backed the Southern Democratic faction in supporting JOHN CABELL BRECKENRIDGE for president in 1860. While he sympathized with the South, he strongly opposed secession. After secession, he recruited a unit of Union troops and played a critical role in preventing Maryland from seceding from the Union. As a result, President ABRAHAM LINCOLN appointed Butler a major general of a unit of volunteers. He was a failure as a field commander but was useful as a wartime administrator. Butler conceived of the idea of treating as contraband of war the slaves who fled their Southern slaveholding masters across Union lines.

Butler earned his nickname "Beast Butler" during his assignment as a military governor of New Orleans. He created an international law incident when he seized the Confederate gold supply, which had been stored in the French government's consulate. He also ordered that any New Orleans woman who did not show proper respect for the Union flag should be regarded as a prostitute plying her trade. Southerners detested Butler so much that, in addition to his uncomplimentary nickname, they spread rumors that Butler was so low that he stole silverware from the houses he was occupying while performing his duties.

After the war, Butler switched from the Democratic to the Republican Party and became a member of the Radical Republican congressional faction. Following the leadership of Representative THADDEUS STEVENS, he supported the most severe Reconstruction program. Butler was one of the managers, selected by the House of Representatives, charged to try the impeachment case against President ANDREW JOHNSON, an effort that failed by only one vote in the Senate. As Radical Republicanism went out of fashion, Butler's string of political successes was diminished. He was defeated in two runs for Massachusetts governor in 1871 and 1872. He also failed in a reelection bid to Congress in 1875.

Butler joined the Greenback Party because he believed that the U.S. economy needed to be supported by the printing of paper money without the backing of either gold or silver, as had been done during the Civil War. Under the Greenback Party label, Butler was elected to Congress in 1876. Butler again lost races for governor in 1878 and 1879, but he was elected to a one-year term in 1882. When he failed to be reelected, he decided to seek the Democratic nomination for president in 1884.

Butler was unable to defeat STEPHEN GROVER CLEVELAND for the Democratic presidential nomination, but he did receive the presidential nomination for two small political parties: the Anti-Monopoly Party and the National or Greenback Party. Although he received almost 200,000 popular votes, he garnered no Electoral College votes.

Butler retired from public life and never ran for office again. Nine years later on January 11, 1893, he died in his Washington, D.C., home.

Further Reading

Butler, Benjamin Franklin. *Butler's Book: A Review of his Legal, Political and Military Career.* Boston: Thayer, 1892.

Hearn, Chester G. *When The Devil Came Down to Dixie: Ben Butler in New Orleans.* Baton Rouge: Louisiana State University Press, 1997.

Holzman, Robert S. *Stormy Ben Butler.* New York: Collier Books, 1961.

Nolan, Dick. *Benjamin Franklin Butler: The Damnedest Yankee.* Novato, Calif.: Presidio, 1991.

Trefousse, Hans Louis. *Ben Butler: The South Called Him Beast!* New York: Octagon Books, 1974.

Werlich, Robert. *"Beast" Butler: The Incredible Career of Major General Benjamin Franklin Butler.* Washington, D.C.: Quaker Press, 1962

West, Richard Sedgwick. *Lincoln's Scapegoat General: A Life of Benjamin F. Butler, 1818–1893.* Boston: Houghton Mifflin, 1965.

Byrnes, James Francis

(1879–1972) *secretary of state, associate justice of the Supreme Court, senator, representative, governor, author*

As a U.S. representative, senator, and associate justice of the Supreme Court, James Francis Byrnes held successively important posts and was widely regarded as a prospect for the 1944 Democratic vice presidential nomination and a presidential bid after that. However, his secretiveness resulted in his being distrusted, and he was passed over for vice president in favor of HARRY S. TRUMAN in 1944. After Truman became president, he selected Byrnes to be his secretary of state. Truman also came to distrust Byrnes and fired him. Byrnes's aspirations for national office were dashed and he ended his career as governor of South Carolina.

James Francis Byrnes was born on May 2, 1879, in Charleston, South Carolina. Byrnes began working as a court reporter, and he used the opportunity to study the law and to be admitted to the South Carolina bar in 1903. On top of his legal work, Byrnes edited and published a newspaper in Aiken, South Carolina.

At age 32, Byrnes began his political career by serving in the U.S. House of Representatives from South Carolina as a Democrat. He ran for the U.S. Senate in 1924 but was defeated. Although he was no longer serving in the Congress, he continued to be active in politics and was elected to the Senate in 1930 and reelected in 1936.

Initially, Byrnes supported President FRANKLIN DELANO ROOSEVELT's New Deal programs, but after 1963 he turned conservative, worried about direct welfare payments, and opposed Roosevelt's domestic policies. He continued to support Roosevelt's foreign policy of helping the Allies without joining the war. He helped repeal the Neutrality Act of 1935 and pass the Lend-Lease Act in 1941, both of which aided Britain.

Byrnes supported Roosevelt for a third presidential term in 1940, and Roosevelt rewarded him with an appointment as an associate justice of the Supreme Court. After the United States entered World War II, Roosevelt asked Byrnes to leave the court to help Roosevelt manage the domestic economy. During the war, Byrnes proved masterful at generating tremendous quantities of war supplies while holding the line on domestic inflation. He developed strong ties to Senator Harry S. Truman, who headed a U.S. Senate committee on the conduct of the domestic economy during the war. By 1944, Byrnes was regarded as one of the most powerful men in Washington. Byrnes believed he had strong support to replace incumbent Vice President Henry A. Wallace, who was unacceptably liberal for many southern and border state Democrats. Byrnes was too conservative to receive Roosevelt's enthusiastic support and was opposed by labor and the northern liberals.

In a compromise move, Roosevelt agreed to accept Truman as his vice presidential running mate. When Roosevelt died, Truman became president and needed the help of an experienced Washington hand, such as Byrnes. Truman named Byrnes secretary of state early in his presidency and Byrnes's advice was critical in the early months.

While Roosevelt was alive, Byrnes took a conciliatory line toward the Soviet Union, even supporting Roosevelt's agreement at the Yalta Conference at the end of World War II to give Stalin a large role in the control of Eastern Europe. After Truman became president, Byrnes abruptly switched to a hard line against the Soviet Union. On learning that the United States was about to possess an atomic bomb, Byrnes urged Truman to withhold important knowledge about the atomic bomb from the Soviets. He urged Truman to drop the bomb on Japan in an attempt to threaten the Soviets into becoming more cooperative.

Scholars of the decision to drop the atomic bomb are now convinced that Japan could have been defeated quickly without any significant loss of American life. This could have been accomplished if the United States had relaxed the terms of unconditional surrender to allow the Japanese to keep their emperor as a mere national symbol and made it clear that the Soviets were prepared to enter the war against Japan in August 1945.

Nonetheless, Byrnes persistently refused to accept any advice modifying the terms of surrender and to prevent anyone from using diplomatic channels through the Swedes to inform Japan of the ultimate intentions of the United States. Byrnes's strategy of threatening the Soviets increased the chances that a cold war arms race would result. His critics often called him "conniving," and in the end, Truman agreed with that assessment. He replaced Byrnes as secretary of state after the two men had a bitter falling out.

After he was fired as secretary of state, Byrnes became one of Truman's hardest critics. Byrnes returned to South Carolina where he was elected governor in 1951. In that role and as a Southern segregationist, he fought school desegregation viciously from 1951 to 1955. Byrnes was apparently so bitter against Truman and the Democrats that he supported DWIGHT DAVID EISENHOWER for president in 1952.

At the end of his term as governor, Byrnes retired from public life, and he died on April 9, 1972.

Further Reading

Alperovitz, Gar. *The Decision to Use the Atomic Bomb.* New York: Knopf, 1995.

Byrnes, James Francis. *All in One Lifetime.* New York: Harper, 1958.

———. *Speaking Frankly.* New York: Harper, 1947.

Messer, Robert L. *The End of an Alliance.* Chapel Hill: University of North Carolina Press, 1982.

Robertson, David. *Sly and Able: A Political Biography of James F. Byrnes.* New York: Norton, 1994.

Ward, Patricia Dawson. *The Threat of Peace: James F. Byrnes and the Council of Foreign Ministers, 1945–1946.* Kent, Ohio: Kent State University Press, 1979.

Byrns, Joseph Wellington
(1869–1936) *Speaker of the House, representative*

Joseph Wellington Byrns was a successful conservative Democratic politician from Tennessee who rose to the office of Speaker of the House where he earned his greatest fame as a loyal Democrat advancing FRANKLIN DELANO ROOSEVELT's New Deal legislation.

Joseph Wellington Byrns was born near Cedar Hill, Tennessee, on July 20, 1869. Although he was raised in a farm family, he earned his law degree at Vanderbilt University in 1890. Quickly admitted to the bar, he established a law practice in Nashville in 1891. Still a young man, he began his political carrer in 1894 in the Tennessee legislature. Reelected in 1896 and in 1898, he was named Speaker in 1899. Although he was elected to the state senate in 1900, he was defeated soon after that in an attempt to be the district attorney general in Nashville, Davidson County, Tennessee.

Byrns began his national carrer in the House of Representatives by winning a surprise upset against a Republican in 1908. Byrns promised to secure federal money for building a dam and locks on the Cumberland River near Nashville. He kept his promise and the voters of Nashville reelected him 13 more times so that he served a total of 28 years.

Byrns was personally conservative and supported fiscal economy in government, but he shared the Democratic Party position in favor of lower tariffs. He was a strong supporter of President THOMAS WOODROW WILSON. By the 1930s, he had moved up to majority leader of the Democrats in the House and was instrumental in passing President Franklin Delano Roosevelt's New Deal legislation, even though it went against many of his own basic philosophical principles. Rewarded for his long-term loyalty, he was appointed Speaker of the House of Representatives in 1935, but he died suddenly on June 4, 1936.

Further Reading

Davis, Kenneth S. *FDR: Three Volumes.* New York: Random House, 1993.

McJimsey, George T. *The Presidency of Franklin Delano Roosevelt.* Lawrence: University Press of Kansas, 2000.

Morris, Jeffrey. *The FDR Way.* Minneapolis: Lerner Publications, 1996.

C

Calhoun, John Caldwell

(1782–1850) *vice president, secretary of state, secretary of war, senator, representative*

Regarded as one of the greatest U.S. senators of all time, John Caldwell Calhoun also served as a vice president under two presidents and as a powerful cabinet officer. However, his greatest fame came as the expositor of the philosophical justification for Southern resistance to Northern opposition to slavery and the author of Southern nullification and secession doctrines.

John Caldwell Calhoun was born on March 18, 1782, in a rural area in the uplands near the Savannah River in South Carolina. He graduated from Yale in 1804, was admitted to the bar in 1807, and began practicing law near his native home in Abbeville, South Carolina.

In 1808 he was elected to the South Carolina legislature as a member of the Democratic Republican Party. Two years later he was elected to the U.S. House of Representatives. Initially, he was an outspoken advocate of the expansion of the United States, hoping that the acquisition of Florida would protect South Carolina's southern flank. To achieve this, he joined with those in the Congress who hoped for a war with Great Britain to annex both Canada and Florida, although this meant that the underdeveloped military forces of the United States would be pitted against the most powerful nation on earth. These aggressive congressmen, including HENRY CLAY and DANIEL WEBSTER, were known as the "War Hawks." When the war came, the United States lost heavily and was saved from defeat mainly by British war weariness.

Calhoun supported the War of 1812 despite its many disasters. As a nationalist, Calhoun also supported Clay and his "American System," which called for spending federal money on internal improvements such as roads and canals, creating a national bank, and using tariffs to protect infant American industries from foreign competition. After Calhoun's six years in Congress, President JAMES MONROE asked him to be his secretary of war. In that post, Calhoun worked to strengthen the U.S. military forces, which needed rebuilding after the War of 1812.

In 1824, John C. Calhoun reluctantly agreed to be the vice president under President JOHN QUINCY ADAMS. Though ANDREW JACKSON had received the largest number of popular votes, the Electoral College deadlocked and Adams had won election by a vote in the House of Representatives. Calhoun decided that Jackson was the more popular political figure and distanced himself from Adams. He even condemned President John Quincy Adams in speeches to endear himself to Jackson. When Jackson was nominated for president in 1828, Calhoun agreed to serve as his vice president, hoping that the vice presidency would be a stepping-stone to the presidency for himself.

Soon conflicts with President Jackson made it increasingly impossible to remain as vice president. Calhoun's wife took a strong dislike to the wife of

Secretary of War John Eaton. Eaton and his wife had strong support from Jackson. Among the Jackson's cabinet, only MARTIN VAN BUREN was willing to treat the Eatons civilly. Jackson gradually switched his allegiance to Martin Van Buren, who later became Jackson's vice president (and successor as president).

President Jackson also discovered that Calhoun had been viciously critical of him during the Indian wars in 1818 and this infuriated Jackson. Calhoun also changed his mind about tariffs, concluding that they harmed the South. Joining with other Southerners, Calhoun began to discuss the concept of nullification. Under this doctrine, states could refuse to follow laws passed by the federal government if they thought the laws were unconstitutional.

In 1828, Calhoun published his *South Carolina Exposition* at the request of the South Carolina legislature. In this essay, Calhoun argued that because the states had once been sovereign nations, they could not be compelled to follow laws passed by the national Congress that they believed to be unconstitutional.

When Congress declared tariffs essential for American prosperity in 1832, the nullification crisis came to a head when South Carolina's legislature determined that the tariffs were not binding in their state. A strong nationalist, President Jackson informed South Carolina that nullification would not be tolerated. Calhoun could no longer follow party interests and be loyal to the South, so he resigned as vice president. He was the first vice president ever to resign and one of only two in all of U.S. history. Sensing a dangerous national constitutional crisis, both sides agreed on a compromise that lowered the tariffs. That crisis was avoided, but Calhoun was completely committed to the Southern cause from then on. Calhoun remained in the Senate except for a brief stint as the secretary of state under JOHN TYLER.

Calhoun began to express ever more forcefully that the federal system had to protect the interest of minorities better. He argued for the creation of a "concurrent majority" system to protect Southern interests and moved very close to justifying secession. He continued to support

Over his legendary Senate career, John C. Calhoun formulated the intellectual basis for the southern states' secessions that led to the Civil War. *(Library of Congress)*

the annexation of Texas, but he opposed the war with Mexico. When the Wilmot Proviso was proposed to ban slavery in the territory taken from Mexico, Calhoun began to advance the view that slaves were the constitutionally protected property of the slave owner and could be legally taken into any territory since territories were owned in common by all states, thereby repudiating the Missouri Compromise of 1820.

In 1849, Calhoun tried to arouse the Southern senators to the peril they faced from abolitionists, but they did not agree. He used up a great deal of his strength fighting to protect Southern rights in the drafting of the Compromise of 1850. Too weak to deliver the last speech he drafted, he had it published. Calhoun died on March 31, 1850.

Further Reading

Bartlett, Irving H. *John C. Calhoun: A Biography*. New York: Norton, 1993.

Coit, Margaret L. *John C. Calhoun*. Columbia: University of South Carolina Press, 1970.

Niven, John. *John C. Calhoun and the Price of Union: A Biography*. Baton Rouge: Louisiana State University Press, 1993.

Peterson, Merrill D. *The Great Triumvirate: Webster, Clay, and Calhoun*. New York: Oxford University Press, 1987.

Von Holst, Hermann. *John C. Calhoun*. New York: Chelsea House, 1980.

Cameron, Simon

(1799–1889) *secretary of war, diplomat, senator*

Simon Cameron was a leading figure in the creation of the Republican Party through the use of patronage, but his personal desire for great wealth led him into many patronage practices that encouraged corruption. In the midst of the Civil War, his mishandling of contracts for military supplies was so outrageous that the U.S. House of Representatives censured him.

Simon Cameron was born on March 18, 1799, in Lancaster County, Pennsylvania. He learned the printing business in Pennsylvania's state capitol of Harrisburg, but he left for Washington, D.C., in 1822 to work in the printing house that compiled congressional debates. In 1824, he went back to Harrisburg, purchased a newspaper, and began building a solid political following. He followed the conventional political wisdom of the business class and consistently gave strong support to protective tariffs.

Always seeking more money, Cameron quit the newspaper business and made a fortune in various other businesses, such as banking, insurance, and construction. He remained politically active and used his political position for financial gain. In 1838, while he was a government commissioner in charge of settling claims with the Winnebago Indians, he made a substantial profit by running the claims through his own bank.

In 1845, Cameron won a seat in the U.S. Senate as a Democrat, but he was defeated in two other tries in 1849 and in 1855. Cameron had switched to the Republican Party and ran successfully for the Senate in 1857. Thereafter, always a Republican, he committed himself to organizing the Pennsylvania Republicans. At the 1860 Republican convention, he delivered Pennsylvania to ABRAHAM LINCOLN in return for Lincoln's promise to name him a member of the cabinet. Lincoln honored his promise and named Cameron secretary of war, but complaints of favoritism, corruption, and mismanagement forced Lincoln to transfer Cameron to the position of U.S. ambassador to Russia in 1862. While Cameron was abroad, the House of Representatives investigated the War Department and censured Cameron for his behavior.

When Cameron returned from Russia, he was defeated when he tried to get back in the Senate, but he was later elected in 1867 and again in 1873. Cameron was powerful enough that he forced President ULYSSES S. GRANT to appoint his son secretary of war.

The corruption of the Grant administration was so bad that Grant was unable to secure the presidential nomination for a third term. The Republicans, as a part of a reform effort, nominated and elected RUTHERFORD BIRCHARD HAYES. In an attempt to clean up the administration, Hayes refused to allow Cameron's son to continue as secretary of war. Cameron retaliated by resigning his Senate seat, so that his son could be named in his place. By this time, Cameron's son had taken over the responsibilities of the Pennsylvania Republican Party, so the Camerons continued to exercise control over the Pennsylvania Republicans.

Simon Cameron retired to his farm in rural Pennsylvania in 1877 and died on June 26, 1889.

Further Reading

Bradley, Erwin Stanley. *Simon Cameron, Lincoln's Secretary of War: A Political Biography*. Philadelphia: University of Pennsylvania Press, 1966.

Crippen, Lee Forbes. *Simon Cameron: Ante-Bellum Years*. New York: Da Capo Press, 1972.

Hernon, Joseph Martin. *Profiles in Character: Hubris and Heroism in the U.S. Senate—1789–1990*. Armonk, N.Y.: M. E. Sharpe, 1997.

Page, Elwin L. *Cameron for Lincoln's Cabinet*. Boston: Boston University Press, 1954.

Campbell, Ben Nighthorse
(1933–) *senator, representative*

Ben Nighthorse Campbell is the only Native American serving in the U.S. Senate. He is the highest-ranking person of Native American background to serve in the U.S. national government with the exception of former vice president CHARLES CURTIS.

Campbell was born in Auburn, California, on April 13, 1933, into a poverty stricken family. His father was Northern Cheyenne, his mother Portuguese. Neither of his parents was employed on a regular basis, because his father abused alcohol during long absences from the family and his mother had contracted tuberculosis. As a child in California, both he and his sister, Alberta, spent time in orphanages or in sanitariums as his mother sought treatment for her disease. As a teenager, he had several clashes with the law and eventually dropped out of high school. However, after leaving high school he joined the U.S. Army where he finally found a structure to his life that his previous experiences had lacked. With a regular paycheck and a life regulated by military discipline, he developed an interest in sports, particularly in judo. He was so successful at this that he was one of the youngest U.S. citizens to acquire a fourth degree brown belt. After his stint in the army, he attended California State University at San Jose, from which he graduated in 1957. He earned a master's degree from Stanford University. He worked as an educator in the Sacramento law enforcement agency. He competed in the 1964 Olympics in judo. Campbell developed an interest in making jewelry, teaching jewelry-making as well as doing his own work.

Eventually, he moved to Colorado. In 1982, he was elected to the Colorado General Assembly where he served until 1986. He ran for the U.S. House of Representatives in 1986 and won. He was reelected in 1988 and 1990. In 1992, he ran for the U.S. Senate and was elected. In 1995, he changed his party affiliation from Democratic to Republican when the Republicans gained control of both the Senate and the House of Representatives. He was reelected to the Senate in 1998.

Throughout his legislative career, he has supported measures that have developed naturally out of his life experiences but that do not fit easily into the usual policy framework of either political party.

In line with conservative Republicanism, he is pro-business and has a strong record supporting efforts to confront crime. However, he also supports abortion rights and welfare and educational programs to help young people avoid falling into a life of crime—policies for which he would typically find more support in the Democratic Party. He has strongly supported efforts to combat the use of alcohol by pregnant women to combat fetal alcohol syndrome—a position that defies partisan labeling. He has taken stands on environmental issues that put him at odds with both political parties from time to time. Campbell continued his jewelry business and gained a reputation for his skill and design.

Further Reading
Brooke, James, "Two Political Rebels Gear Up for a G.O.P. Primary in Colorado's Senate Race." *New York Times* (24 September 1997) A14, A20.

"Colorado Primary Results: Skaggs, Campbell Look Solid," *Congressional Quarterly Weekly Report* 16, no. 33 (13 August 1988): 2268.

"Democrats Ask Bolting Senator to Repay," *New York Times* (10 March 1995): A9.

Gruenwald, Juliana, "Campbell's Party Switch Has Some Side Effects," *Congressional Quarterly Weekly Report* 53, no. 10 (11 March 1995): 764.

Henry, Christopher E. *Ben Nighthorse Campell: Cheyenne Chief and U.S. Senator.* Broomall, Pa.: Chelsea House Pub., 1994.

Hirschfelder, Arlene. "Ben Nighthorse Campbell" in *Artists and Crafts people.* New York: Facts On File: 1994.

Klein, Joe, "How the West Was Lost: Why Ben Nighthorse Campbell's Defection Signals a Democratic Disaster," *Newsweek* 125, no. 12 (20 March 1995): 31.

Moss, J. Jennings, "Defections Don't Panic the White House—Yet," *Insight on the News* 11, no. 19 (15 May 1995): 16.

"Republican Rebel Halts Showdown in Colorado," *New York Times* (21 October 1997): A12, A16.

Cannon, Joseph Gurney
(1836–1926) *Speaker of the House, representative*

Joseph Cannon served in the U.S. House of Representatives from 1903 to 1911. Although he was identified with a highly authoritarian style of managing the House, Cannon's style was the product of a 19th-century reform movement that sought to strengthen the power of the Speaker because the House of Representatives had been divided and fragmented before that.

Born on May 7, 1836, in Guilford County, North Carolina, Joseph Gurney Cannon was raised in Annapolis, Indiana. Privately educated as an attorney, he was elected attorney general for the Illinois 27th Judicial District in 1861. He was elected to the U.S. House of Representatives as a Republican in 1872 and represented Illinois in Congress almost continuously for 50 years until 1923.

During the 30 years until 1903, Cannon served on many important committees and held several leadership posts. Although he was not associated with any notable legislative accomplishments, he was well known as a dedicated conservative. He supported Speaker THOMAS BRACKETT REED in the early 1890s. He was strongly opposed to President WILLIAM HOWARD TAFT and his proposal to lower tariffs. Because Cannon controlled the rules committee absolutely, he had complete control of the passage of legislation. He also controlled who was recognized on the floor and therefore could close debate whenever he wished. President Taft disliked and wanted to curtail his powers, but Cannon's power was so great that Taft backed down.

In 1910, Representative GEORGE WILLIAM NORRIS of Nebraska led a successful coalition of Progressive Republicans and a few Progressive Democrats in approving a resolution to change the House rules governing the selection of the crucial rules committee. The passage of this resolution deprived Cannon of many of his powers.

Joseph Cannon's style of leadership was a direct result of the reforms Speaker Thomas "Czar" Reed introduced in the late 19th century to save the House from its practice of permitting dilatory minority tactics. In the 1830s JOHN QUINCY ADAMS introduced these dilatory minority tactics, again as a reform of the preexisting practices. In turn, the House reforms that took power away from Joseph Cannon led to excessive power in the hands of standing committee chairmen. In the 1990s, Speaker NEWTON LEROY GINGRICH reformed the House again in order to strengthen the Speaker against the chaotic, centrifugal forces in the House.

Once his powers as Speaker were limited, Cannon was vulnerable to defeat at home. He lost a seat in Congress in 1912 (when the race for president was divided three ways), but he managed to win reelection in 1914 and remained a member of the House for 10 more years. However, he never regained his former power in Congress and he retired in 1923. Joseph Cannon died on November 12, 1926.

Further Reading

Bolles, Blair. *Tyrant from Illinois: Uncle Joe Cannon's Experiment with Personal Power.* Westport, Conn.: Greenwood Press, 1974.

"Cannon, Joseph" in *Congress A to Z: Third Edition,* edited by David R. Tarr and Ann O'Connor. Washington, D.C.: Congressional Quarterly, 1999.

Cannon, Joseph Gurney. *Uncle Joe Cannon: The Story of a Pioneer American.* St. Clair Shores, Mich.: Scholarly Press, 1970.

Gwinn, William Rea. *Uncle Joe Cannon, Arch Foe of Insurgency: A History of the Rise and Fall of Cannonism.* New York: Bookman Associates, 1957.

Hatch, Carl. *The Big Stick and the Congressional Gavel.* New York: Pageant Press, 1967.

Cardozo, Benjamin Nathan
(1870–1938) *associate justice of the Supreme Court*

Regarded as one of the most powerful intellects of the U.S. Supreme Court, Benjamin Cardozo left his mark on American constitutional law, although he served for only six years.

Born in New York City on May 24, 1870, Benjamin Nathan Cardozo earned his B.A. degree at age of 19 in 1889 and his master's degree at the age of 20 in 1890 from Columbia University. A year later, he was admitted to the New York bar. A specialist in commercial loans and an "attorney for attorneys," he practiced primarily before the New York Court of Appeals, the highest court in that state's judicial system.

Cardozo was elected as a reform candidate to the New York Supreme Court in 1913. Four years later, he ran as a candidate of both the Democratic and Republican parties for a 14-year term on the New York Court of Appeals. His mastery of legal logic led him to a special role of adapting laws that were created in largely rural society for use in an industrial society. He became widely read and quoted by lawyers throughout the English-speaking world for this critical transformation he brought about.

In 1932, President HERBERT CLARK HOOVER appointed Cardozo to succeed Associate Justice OLIVER WENDELL HOLMES, JR., on the high Court. The 1930s were a particularly unsettled time for the U.S. Supreme Court. Although appointed by a conservative Republican president, Cardozo voted mainly with the more liberal justices, such as LOUIS DEMBITZ BRANDEIS and Harlan Stone. In this, he was following the logic of transforming the law from an agrarian society to an industrial society. Cardozo was in the minority on several critical decisions that struck down parts of President FRANKLIN DELANO ROOSEVELT's New Deal program, but his dissents laid the basis for a new majority.

Cardozo served long enough to see President Roosevelt's plan to pack the U.S. Supreme Court defeated in the Congress and long enough to see his minority view become majority positions on the Court. He died on July 9, 1938, before the full consequences of all the legal revolution of which he was a part could take place.

Further Reading

Goodhart, Arthur Lehman. *Five Jewish Lawyers of the Common Law.* Freeport, N.Y.: Books for Libraries Press, 1971.

Hellman, George Sidney. *Benjamin N. Cardozo: American Judge.* New York: Russell & Russell, 1969.

Kaufman, Andrew L. *Cardozo.* Cambridge, Mass.: Harvard University Press, 1998.

Levy, Beryl Harold. *Cardozo and the Frontiers of Legal Thinking.* New York: Oxford University Press, 1938; rev. ed. 1969.

Pollard, Joseph Percival. *Mr. Justice Cardozo: A Liberal Mind in Action.* Westport, Conn.: Greenwood Press, 1970.

Carmack, Edward Ward
(1858–1908) *senator, representative, prominent newspaper editor*

Edward Ward Carmack was a social reformer and prohibitionist in Tennessee, a state deeply divided on a variety of social issues. As a symbol of the state's division, Edward Carmack is honored with a statue at the Tennessee State Capitol immediately above a Capitol tunnel entrance named after one of the creators of Jack Daniel's whiskey. The long-standing social division in the state has led to the joke that Tennessee cannot decide whether Carmack was dominant over the whiskey interests or whether the whiskey industry supported Carmack. This obscures the story of Carmack's assassination, the reason for which the statue was erected.

Born near Castalian Springs, Tennessee, on November 5, 1858, Edward Ward Carmack was the son of a minister in the Disciples of Christ (also known as the Christian Church or the Campbellites). His father died when he was just a child, and Carmack had to work as a farmer and a laborer in a brickyard. He studied diligently in the public county schools and was helped by family friends to attend the Webb schools in Culleoka, Tennessee, as well as Jacinto Academy in Mississippi.

By reading the law at home and at a lawyer's office, Carmack learned enough to be admitted to the Tennessee bar in 1879. He practiced law only briefly and entered politics at age 26 as a Democratic state representative. In the same year, he took over the editorship of the local newspaper in Columbia, Tennessee. Four years later, he became the editor of the *Nashville American* and four years after that, *The Memphis Commercial Appeal.* He used his skills as a writer and a newspaperman to poke fun mercilessly at corrupt and inefficient politicians.

Over time he became convinced that political corruption and abuse of alcohol were connected. After the 1890s, Carmack had clearly become a prohibitionist.

Carmack was elected to the U.S. House of Representatives as a Democrat in 1897 and re-elected in 1899. While in Congress, he voted to prohibit liquor sales in Alaska, ban the sale of liquor to American Indians in newly admitted states, and prohibit the shipment of alcohol in interstate commerce to states where prohibition was the law. In 1900, Carmack was elected to the U.S. Senate where he continued his attacks on the liquor industry as well as branching out on other reforms, such as opposition to imperialism and monopolistic corporations.

He failed to be reelected in 1906 to the Senate, but he ran for governor in 1908 on a strong prohibition platform. Although he lost a primary to the incumbent governor, M. R. Patterson, Carmack finally united the reformers and prohibitionists. While Patterson won reelection narrowly, he found that his political control of the legislature had been broken.

By this time, Carmack had moved on to the editorship of the Nashville *Tennessean*. As the largest paper in the central part of the state, it was the perfect forum for him to begin fierce personal attacks on his political enemies, including Governor Patterson. One of his editorials also enraged Duncan Cooper, a former friend turned against him.

On November 9, 1908, Duncan Cooper and his son, Robin, met Carmack in a shootout on a Nashville city street. Although Carmack shot first, Robin Cooper shot straighter. Carmack was hit and died almost immediately. Carmack's assassins were convicted and sentenced to 20-year prison terms, but they never served any time because they had sufficient political support to avoid prison.

Carmack became a martyr of the temperance movement, and the legislature was intimidated into passing a prohibition law over the veto of Governor Patterson. The controversy ruined Patterson's political career, and Carmack's desire to see Tennessee as a dry state was fulfilled.

Further Reading

Majors, William R. *Editorial Wild Oats.* Macon, Ga.: Mercer University Press, 1984.
Summerville, James. *The Carmack-Cooper Shooting: Tennessee Politics Turns Violent, November 9, 1908.* Jefferson, N.C.: McFarland, 1994.

Carter, James Earl

(1924–) *president, governor*

Probably no president in American history has been as highly regarded for his humanitarian efforts as former President Jimmy Carter. He was the first president to be elected from a Deep South state since Zachary Taylor in 1848. While Carter could claim many accomplishments during his single term as president, his administration was dogged with economic and foreign policy problems that led to his defeat for reelection in 1980.

Born on October 1, 1824, in Plains, Georgia, James Earl Carter grew up on the family farm nearby. After spending a year studying at Georgia Southwestern College and the following year at Georgia Institute of Technology from 1941 to 1942, he received an appointment to the U.S. Naval Academy in Annapolis.

Upon graduation in 1946, he entered the navy. In 1948, he began his career as a submarine officer on conventional submarines. However, because of his intelligence and skill, he was selected to work as a commander in the nuclear submarine program created by Admiral Hyman Rickover. In 1953, Carter returned to run the family farm and other businesses after his father's death.

The 1960s were controversial because of the Civil Rights movement aimed at ending segregation for African Americans in the South. Carter later criticized himself for not doing more to end segregation. However, he refused to join the White Citizens Council and, along with only one other person, voted against the prohibition of blacks attending services at the local Baptist church in 1965.

Carter's political career began in a variety of local governmental posts. In 1962, he ran for the Democratic nomination for the state senate and lost a narrow race as the result of what he called ballot box stuffing by his opponent. However, he managed to persuade the Georgia Democratic Party committee to place his name on the general election ballot and he won. He served a single term and then ran for governor. Losing his first time out in 1967, he won in 1970.

Carter consolidated about 300 state agencies into 22 new departments and introduced "zero-based budgeting," which required agencies to justify their budgets by actual requirements rather than by simply carrying forward the previous year's budget. Carter sponsored anticrime, conservation, and environmental legislation. Georgia adopted "sunshine" or open meetings legislation under his direction. Perhaps most significantly, he opened his administration to African Americans and women to an unprecedented degree.

Touted as a vice presidential candidate with GEORGE STANLEY MCGOVERN in 1972, he was passed over for a role that would have surely damaged his reputation. Carter's term as governor ended in 1975, since he was barred by Georgia's convention from serving more than a single consecutive term. So as he prepared to leave the governor's mansion, Carter began running for president.

With only a single term in the state senate and a single term as governor, Carter did not seem to be a formidable candidate for president. However, Carter realized that the nation was demoralized by the failed presidencies of Presidents LYNDON BAINES JOHNSON and RICHARD MILHOUS NIXON. Both of these men had years of experience, yet they failed to deal effectively with the Vietnam War, the Civil Rights movement, or even the integrity of their own administrations. Carter also sensed that the country might be ready for an outsider. Therefore, he pitched his campaign to the grass roots. To save campaign money, he stayed in the homes of supporters. To appear more like an ordinary citizen, he emphasized that he was a farmer. He carried his own luggage on airplanes. Above all, he began with the grassroots fight to organize the Iowa precinct caucuses, which replaced the Iowa presidential preference primary. Carter scored a stunning win in the Iowa caucuses, followed it up with the New Hampshire primary victory, and went on to capture the Democratic nomination with the delegates he won in 30 state presidential primary victories.

Carter initially started off the general election campaign with a strong lead in the polls, but incumbent President GERALD RUDOLPH FORD waged a vigorous campaign and the final popular vote was close. Carter also narrowly won the Electoral College by only 297–240 votes. In that election, a shift of a few thousand votes in only two states would have given Ford a victory in the Electoral College even though he would have lost the popular vote.

At his inauguration, Carter again portrayed himself as an ordinary citizen by reaching back to the inauguration of THOMAS JEFFERSON for the

precedent of walking to the White House from the swearing-in ceremony at the national Capitol. As refreshing as this was, later events seemed to suggest that Carter was so much of an outsider that he could not get a grip on the operation of the government itself.

To be sure, Carter faced extraordinary difficulties with high unemployment, high inflation, and oil shortages. The economic situation was poor when Carter came into office and unfortunately became worse before he left, contributing to his failure to be reelected. Much of the underlying economic problem facing the Carter administration came as a result of the oil shocks produced by restraints on oil production caused by the Organization of Petroleum Exporting Countries oil cartel. All Carter could do was to recommend energy

Jimmy Carter, the first president to be elected from a Deep South state since Zachary Taylor in 1848, negotiated the Israeli-Egyptian peace treaty and has compiled a distinguished humanitarian record as a former president. (Library of Congress, Official White House photo)

conservation measures that, by their very nature, took a long time to show results and were a significant inconvenience in the short run. These oil shortages aggravated the unemployment problem and the inflationary pressure that was largely external to the U.S. economy.

Carter had considerable success in foreign affairs in the beginning. He successfully negotiated a new treaty with Panama over the Panama Canal and pushed it through the Senate, winning passage by only a single vote. Carter also negotiated a peace treaty between Egypt and Israel in the Middle East, one of the very few successful agreements negotiated in that entire region since the end of World War II.

These successes were overshadowed by the Islamic revolution in Iran, the capture of U.S. embassy personnel in Tehran, and the Soviet military activity in Afghanistan. When Islam militants threatened to overthrow the government of the Shah of Iran, Carter's advisers–National Security Advisor ZBIGNIEW KAZIMIERZ BRZEZINSKI and Secretary of State CYRUS ROBERTS VANCE—were divided on their recommendations. The United States thus gave muddled instructions to the Shah through the U.S. embassy. The Shah, already depressed by the news that he suffered from cancer, reacted to all of the news ineffectually, and the revolution took off. Finally, the Shah fled Iran to avoid capture by the revolutionaries who threatened to execute him for what they saw as his crimes against the country. Since the United States was perceived as the major prop for the Shah, the militants were outraged when the Shah escaped from the country, briefly took refuge in Central America, and was finally admitted to the United States for medical treatment. Carter saw his allowing the Shah to come to the United States as a mere humanitarian gesture. He saw no need to take extraordinary steps, such as evacuating the U.S. embassy in Iran. He seriously misjudged the Islamic militants, who took the admission of the Shah into the United States as an attack on their revolution. They took out their anger against the U.S. embassy. Despite the immunity normally granted to an embassy, they invaded the embassy grounds, captured the remaining staff, and held them hostage for 444 days.

Contemporaneously, the Soviet Union faced a threat from the Islamic militants in their client state, Afghanistan. The Soviets reacted with force. Since Afghanistan is immediately next door to Iran, Carter feared the Soviets might expand their military operations into Iran. Carter saw this as a double threat and ordered a grain embargo with the Soviet Union, which had the unfortunate impact of hurting American farmers almost as much as the Russians. He announced that the United States would not participate in the 1980 Olympic Games, causing a four-year cycle of American athletes to miss an important event in their own athletic development. As costly as these measures were on the United States and its citizens, they appeared to have absolutely no effect on the Soviet Union.

Carter's earlier accomplishments were dwarfed by these failures. Massachusetts Senator EDWARD MOORE KENNEDY immediately faced him with a primary challenge. As the younger brother of former president JOHN FITZGERALD KENNEDY and former senator ROBERT FRANCIS KENNEDY and last remaining brother to lead the famous Kennedy clan, he seemed a formidable adversary. An incumbent president almost always has complete control of his own party's machinery, however, so Carter was able to defeat Kennedy for the nomination. The Kennedy challenge nonetheless weakened Carter as he approached the general election.

In spite of these complications, Carter still seemed to be in the lead for reelection, because the Republicans chose RONALD WILSON REAGAN for their nominee. Reagan represented the most conservative element within the Republican Party and had been criticized severely by his Republican primary opponents. Further, one of Reagan's Republican primary opponents, JOHN BAYARD ANDERSON, lost a Republican presidential nomination and then announced that he would run as an independent. This appeared to open the possibility that Anderson would split votes off from Reagan and help Carter win reelection. Unfortunately, Anderson was attractive to many Democrats who were disappointed with Carter's performance in office, and Anderson appeared to pull almost as many votes from Carter as from Reagan.

Carter made a number of mistakes in the campaign, including refusing initially to debate Reagan because he would have to share a platform with Anderson. Reagan seized on this circumstance to imply during a debate with Anderson that Carter was a coward. This only increased Reagan's national recognition. Carter was finally forced to debate Reagan a few days before the election. When Carter did relatively poorer than expected in the debate, Reagan capitalized on the experience and went on to win very comfortably.

Carter retired to his farm in Plains, Georgia. He not only developed his presidential library and wrote his memoirs but also began to reinvigorate his image with a series of humanitarian efforts in the United States and around the world. At home he lent his prestige to a previously little-known charity named Habitat for Humanity that builds homes for poor families. Internationally, he served as an observer in a series of elections in countries that had previously been troubled by election irregularities and fraud. For these efforts, Carter has earned considerable popular support as a distinguished former president.

Further Reading

Bourne, Peter G. *Jimmy Carter: A Comprehensive Biography from Plains to Post-Presidency.* New York: Scribner, 1997.

Brinkley, Douglas. *The Unfinished Presidency: Jimmy Carter's Journey Beyond the White House.* New York: Penguin Books, 1999.

"Carter, James Earl," available online. URL: http://www.whitehouse.gov/history/presidents/jc39.html. Downloaded on October 20, 2001.

Carter, Jimmy. *Turning Point: A Candidate, a State, and a Nation Come of Age.* New York: Times Books, 1992.

———. *Keeping Faith.* Norwalk, Conn.: Easton Press, 1985.

Carter, Rosalyn. *First Lady from Plains.* New York: Ballantine Books, 1985.

Garrison, Jean A. *Games Advisors Play: Foreign Policy in the Nixon and Carter Administrations.* College Station: Texas A&M University Press, 1999.

Skidmore, David. *Reversing Course: Carter's Foreign Policy, Domestic Politics, and the Failure of Reform.* Nashville, Tenn.: Vanderbilt University Press, 1996.

Strong, Robert A. *Working in the World: Jimmy Carter and the Making of American Foreign Policy.* Baton Rouge: Louisiana State University Press, 2000.

Casey, William Joseph
(1913–1987) *director of the Central Intelligence Agency, undersecretary of state, Securities and Exchange commissioner*

William Joseph Casey, a prominent attorney long active in both Republican politics and espionage work for the U.S. government, achieved his greatest prominence when he successfully managed the 1980 presidential campaign of RONALD WILSON REAGAN. Rewarded with the directorship of the Central Intelligence Agency (CIA), he was involved in a scandal known as Iran-Contra, but he died before the full extent of the scandal became public.

Born on March 13, 1913, in Elmhurst, New York, William Joseph Casey attended Fordham University. After graduation, he did postgraduate work at Catholic University in Washington, D.C. Shifting to law, he graduated from St. John's University Law School in 1937 and was admitted to the New York bar in 1938.

William Casey was an intelligence officer in the Office of Strategic Services (OSS) in World War II and directed spy activities in German-occupied Europe. After the war, he became a prominent attorney with both Washington, D.C., and New York law firms. Long a Republican Party activist, he was instrumental in President RICHARD MILHOUS NIXON's 1968 presidential campaign. In 1971, Nixon named him to the Securities and Exchange Commission (SEC) and later undersecretary of state for economic affairs. Continuing in national politics under President GERALD RUDOLPH FORD, Casey was Export-Import Bank chairman in 1974–75 and Foreign Intelligence Advisory Board member in 1976.

Casey remained active in Republican politics during the administration of Democratic President JAMES EARL CARTER, and he managed Ronald Reagan's 1980 presidential campaign. In 1981, President Reagan appointed him the director of the CIA and raised the prestige of the position by making it a cabinet-level post. As the CIA director, Casey was frequently involved in undercover operations in countries hostile to the United States.

Key among these was the U.S. relationship with the Nicaraguan revolutionary government that had taken over from a brutal dictatorship run by the Somoza family and long endorsed by the United States. This Sandinista government was particularly distasteful to Reagan, and he dispatched Casey to do what he could to bring it down. Casey went so far as to mine the Nicaraguan harbors covertly to stop Soviet-bloc ships from delivering arms to the government—and incidentally endangering any neutral shipping that might wish to have ordinary commercial relations with the Nicaraguan government. He also allowed undercover American operatives to carry out acts of violence against civilian officials in the Sandinista government. Some of these were contrary to congressional policy, but none were as significant as the circumstances that developed in the Iran-Contra scandal.

In the mid-1980s, U.S. foreign relations with Iran were also poor. In an attempt to improve those relations, Casey was involved in exchanging armament with the Iranian government in return for the release of American hostages held in various countries in the Middle East. He also favored providing funding and covert military support for the anticommunist rebels in Nicaragua, better known as the Contras. Since Congress refused to provide aid for the Contras, Casey devised a scheme for selling arms to the Iranians for a higher price than they were worth, skimming the profits off the sales, and using the money to fund the Contras. Much of this was illegal under U.S. law. Nonetheless, Casey endorsed the program and worked through a White House military aide named Oliver North.

When this came to light, there was a lengthy investigation in the U.S. Congress. By the time of the investigation, Casey had fallen prey to a brain tumor and was unable to testify or even be deposed by attorneys. He died on May 6, 1987.

Further Reading

Casey, William J. *The Secret War against Hitler.* Washington, D.C.: Regnery Gateway, 1988.
Persico, Joseph E. *Casey: From the OSS to the CIA.* New York: Viking, 1990.
Woodward, Bob. *Veil: The Secret Wars of the CIA.* New York: Simon & Schuster, 1987.

Chase, Salmon Portland
(1808–1873) *chief justice of the United States, secretary of the treasury, senator*

Salmon Chase was the secretary of the treasury in President ABRAHAM LINCOLN's cabinet during the Civil War. Because of his service in creating a national banking system and assisting in the financing of the war, Lincoln nominated him for chief justice of the U.S. Supreme Court. He served on the Court for almost 10 years until May 7, 1873. He also presided ably and impartially over the impeachment trial of President ANDREW JOHNSON.

Born on January 13, 1808, in Cornish, New Hampshire, Salmon Portland Chase graduated from Dartmouth College in New Hampshire by the age of 18. He was named the head of a boy's school in Washington, D.C., shortly thereafter. By the age of 21, he had read in the law sufficiently to be admitted to the bar.

Chase moved west and settled in Cincinnati, Ohio, where he was almost immediately caught up in antislavery activities, for Cincinnati was an important stop for runaway slaves on the underground railroad. He represented so many of these fleeing slaves that he was nicknamed "attorney general" for such persons.

Chase began his political career as a Whig, but he supported JAMES GILLESPIE BIRNEY's Liberty Party in 1841. Seeking a stronger political vehicle, he organized the Free-Soil Party in 1848 and used this connection—with cooperation of some Democrats—to win a seat in the U.S. Senate in 1849. He opposed the spread of slavery to the territories so thoroughly that he spoke out against both the Compromise of 1850 and the Kansas-Nebraska Act.

When he assisted in the founding of the Republican Party in 1854, Chase carried as much of his Free Soil Party as he could along with him. He used this new organization to help him be elected governor of Ohio in 1855, and he was reelected in 1857. Chase was a candidate for the Republican presidential nomination in both 1856 and in 1860, but he could never get the unified support of the Ohio delegation.

Elected to the Senate in 1860, Chase resigned to become Abraham Lincoln's secretary of the treasury in 1861, a role in which his contribution to the war was singular. He created a national banking system and provided for an adequate currency supply. Although he favored hard money, he came to realize that only through the issuance of government currency not backed by gold or silver could the war be financed.

Chase was a thorn in Lincoln's side in the cabinet. He was self-righteous and unbending. He criticized Lincoln for being too lax in his administration and too slow in prosecuting the war. Chase would seek to win arguments by threatening to resign, but Lincoln ignored this. Carrying out his threat, Chase would resign and Lincoln would ignore that. Finally, when Chase appeared to be working behind Lincoln's back to win the Republican presidential nomination in 1864, Lincoln accepted one of his letters of resignation. Apparently hoping that he could move Chase out of the political arena, Lincoln appointed him chief justice of the United States.

Undeterred by the notion that the chief justice of the United States should avoid political activities, Chase sought the Republican nomination for president in 1868. When he failed to receive the Republican nomination, he proceeded to seek the Democratic nomination for the same office in the same year.

Chase served impartially as the presiding officer at the impeachment trial of Andrew Johnson, for which the Radical Republicans criticized him viciously. Chase also authored the important decision in *Ex parte Milligan* (1866), which concluded that Lincoln had erred in allowing civilians to be tried in military courts during the Civil War. The precise ruling was that military courts could not try civilians unless the civilian courts were completely inoperative or martial law had been declared, neither of which applied in *Milligan*.

Chase upheld the power of President Johnson and his appointees to enforce the Reconstruction Acts and thereby temporarily muted the conflict between the president and the Congress on Reconstruction. He also argued that, since secession had been invalid, there was no basis for barring Confederates from holding public office. He even concluded that the Legal Tender Act of 1862 was unconstitutional, though he had administered the act while he was secretary of the treasury.

Chase also dissented from the majority opinion in the *Slaughterhouse Cases*, finding that the majority had adopted an overly narrow interpretation of the Fourteenth Amendment, a view that is generally regarded as accurate today. In the *Slaughterhouse Cases*, the U.S. Supreme Court interpreted the newly ratified Fourteenth Amendment, which provided that the states could not "abridge the privileges and immunities of citizens of the United States; . . . [or] deprive any person of life, liberty or property without the due process of the law; nor deny any person within its jurisdiction equal protection of the law." A large group of individual New Orleans butchers filed suit to overturn a law passed by the corrupt Louisiana legislature giving a monopoly on meat processing to a single slaughterhouse, a seemingly clear violation of the language of the Fourteenth Amendment. A five to four majority on the Court gave the Fourteenth Amendment such a narrow interpretation that it rendered it virtually useless for the protection of African Americans, white minorities, or any other disadvantaged groups for the next five decades. When the *Slaughterhouse Cases'* majority had its interpretation overturned in the five decades following the 1920s, the estimation of all four dissenters rose substantially. Chase did not live to see his views vindicated, but historians have found his record at the Treasury Department and on the Court on the whole commendable.

Chase was unable to succeed in his repeated attempts to be elected president or even to be nominated by one of the two major parties. However, he had a distinguished career as the secretary of the treasury during the troubled years of the Civil War and as chief justice of the United States, the office he still held when he died on May 7, 1873.

Further Reading

Blue, Frederick J. *Salmon P. Chase: A Life in Politics.* Kent, Ohio: Kent State University Press, 1987.

Hart, Albert Bushnell. *Salmon P. Chase.* New York: Chelsea House, 1980.

Niven, John. *Salmon P. Chase: A Biography.* New York: Oxford University Press, 1995.

Schuckers, Jacob W. *The Life and Public Services of Salmon Portland Chase.* New York: Da Capo Press, 1970.

Chase, Samuel

(1741–1811) *associate justice of the Supreme Court, Revolutionary War leader*

Samuel Chase was the brightest U.S. Supreme Court justice until JOHN MARSHALL, and some of his decisions stand as valid principles today. A long-term and outspoken Federalist, Chase aroused the animosity of many members of the opposite political party, the Democratic Republicans, including President THOMAS JEFFERSON. The opposition against Chase became so great that the U.S. House of Representatives impeached him for his behavior while serving as a judge on the bench in a trial. In retrospect, the charges appear to be mainly political and Chase was not convicted in the Senate, thereby setting a precedent that impeachment should not be used as a political tool.

Born on April 17, 1741, in Somerset County, Maryland, Chase was the son of an Anglican minister. After reading in the law in Annapolis, he was admitted to the bar at the age of 21. By the time he was 23, he was deep into politics as a member of the Maryland Colonial Assembly where he served until 1785.

In 1765, he was an active opponent of the Stamp Act, along with his contemporaries in Massachusetts, such as SAMUEL ADAMS and JOHN ADAMS. As a member of the Committee of Correspondence for his state, he soon developed a reputation as an outspoken revolutionary. He successfully pushed Maryland into supporting independence and earned the wrath of the loyalists.

He was a delegate to the First Continental Congress from 1774 to 1778. In the distinguished company of Benjamin Franklin and Charles Carroll, he was sent to Canada to try unsuccessfully to persuade the Canadians to declare independence. He served a single term in the Second Continental Congress in 1784. Four years later he moved to Baltimore where he was named the chief justice of the criminal court. In 1791, he became the chief justice of the general court of Maryland and created an uproar when he declined to step down from the other judicial post, believing he could serve in both simultaneously.

Chase opposed the adoption of the U.S. Constitution because it lacked a Bill of Rights. After the Bill of Rights was adopted, he became a strong supporter of the federal union. By 1796, his devotion to the U.S. Constitution was so steadfast that President GEORGE WASHINGTON appointed him to the U.S. Supreme Court.

Chase wrote the opinions in the early, pre-Marshall Court on several important questions. He asserted the necessity of the supremacy of treaties negotiated by the United States over state laws in *Ware v. Hylton* (1796). He provided the basic definition of a direct tax in *Hylton v. United States* (1796). Finally, he defined and analyzed ex post facto laws in *Calder v. Bull* (1798).

This distinguished record of service did not help much when he ran afoul of his political opponents. Chase supported the Federalist Party in Congress in its adoption of the Alien and Sedition Acts. Taking the view of no less an authority than Blackstone that freedom of the press was protected as long as there was no prior restraint, Chase accepted the Federalist view that there was no prior restraint in the Alien and Sedition Acts since all prosecutions occurred only after publication had occurred. This view is no longer widely accepted, but it was an arguable position in the late 1700s. Chase was also accused of being overzealous from the bench in prosecuting Jeffersonians under the Alien and Sedition Acts.

In 1804, Chase was impeached for these allegedly partisan acts while serving on the bench. By a very narrow margin, he avoided impeachment in the Senate. His trial is taken as a precedent that judges should not be impeached for political reasons. Chase remained on the Supreme Court until his death on June 19, 1811.

Further Reading

Elsmere, Jane Shaffer. *Justice Samuel Chase.* Muncie, Ind.: Janevar Publishing Company, 1980.

Rehnquist, William H. *Grand Inquests: The Historic Impeachments of Justice Samuel Chase and President Andrew Johnson.* New York: Morrow, 1992.

Chisholm, Shirley Anita St. Hill

(1924–) *representative, candidate for president, author*

Shirley Chisholm was one of the first African Americans to serve in the U.S. House of Representatives after the end of the Reconstruction period. She was the first African-American woman to serve in the House of Representatives and to make a serious race for a major party nomination for president of the United States.

Born Shirley Anita St. Hill on November 30, 1924, in Brooklyn, New York, she was the daughter of Charles and Ruby Seal St. Hill. Her father, who was born in Guyana, worked as a laborer, and her mother was a maid and a seamstress. Her family was so poor that she was sent to live with her maternal grandmother in Barbados during her early childhood. She returned to New York for junior high and graduated from a New York City junior high school in 1939 and three years later with an excellent record from Girl's High School in Brooklyn. Although she received offers from both Vassar and Oberlin, her poverty led her to continue her schooling in New York City. She graduated from Brooklyn College cum laude in 1946. After receiving a master's degree in elementary education from Columbia University in 1949, she began teaching in the New York City public schools. In 1950, she married Conrad Chisholm, a private security agency detective and a New York City Department of Hospital Services investigator.

Soon Chisholm was a recognized authority on early childhood education and became a director of day-care centers. More important, she became active in local political affairs. By 1964, she had been elected to the New York Assembly (the state legislature)—the first African-American woman so elected from Brooklyn—and she remained in the assembly for four years. Throughout her service in the legislature, she was the only woman and one of only eight African Americans in the body.

After the 1960s reapportionment revolution, a 1968 reapportionment led to the creation of a new 12th congressional district in New York, an area with a 70 percent majority of African Americans and Puerto Ricans. Despite these favorable numbers, Chisholm knew she faced an uphill fight for Congress in that district since she opposed James Farmer, one of the founding members of the Congress of Racial Equality (CORE). Moreover, Farmer sought to use her gender against her by suggesting that the district needed to be repre-

sented by a strong male presence. As an indication of the future of such gender-based campaign attacks, Chisholm defeated Farmer by 34,885 votes to 13,777—a margin of better than two to one.

Her neighborhood was so poor that it was not even well represented by the Democratic Party structure in the city. As a result, she promised she would be independent and speak out for her constituents. As a freshman in Congress, she would normally have had little to say about her initial committee assignment in the House. Indeed, as a female African American from a poor urban district in a northern state, she had little leverage. She was assigned to the subcommittee on rural villages and forests of the House Agricultural Committee. Unlike others who quietly accepted their fate at the hands of the southern-dominated Democratic leadership in Congress, she protested and received national attention. The assignment was so absurd that the Democratic Party's congressional leadership took the unusual step of changing her assignment to the Veterans Committee, which was an improvement but not what she had hoped for. She was reelected in 1970.

Chisholm's bold step opened the door for future similar challenges such as that of BELLA SAVITSKY ABZUG, who successfully challenged her committee assignment two years later. Chisholm herself finally achieved membership on the Education and Labor Committee, which she most desired. She stayed in Congress until she retired in 1982.

In 1972, she became the first African-American woman to seek the presidential nomination of a major political party when she ran for the Democratic nomination. Surprisingly, she received 10 percent of the Democratic delegates after her name was placed in nomination. Because she also filed to run for reelection to Congress, she retained her seat in the House of Representatives. Before the Supreme Court's *Roe v. Wade* decision declaring laws banning abortion unconstitutional, she worked for the repeal of laws banning abortion on the national level. She also fought for increases in the minimum wage, for Social Security and Medicare increases, and for the creation of the Office of Economic Opportunity (OEO). From 1972 to 1976, Chisholm served on the Democratic National Committee.

Shirley Chisholm was the first African-American woman to serve in the U.S. Congress and to receive a substantial number of delegate votes for a major party presidential nomination. *(Library of Congress, Congressional Portrait Collection)*

She also cosponsored and secured the passage of a bill to erect a memorial in Washington, D.C., to Mary McLeod Bethune, the first woman president of the National Association for the Advancement of Colored People (NAACP). This was the first time that federal funds had been used to erect a monument to an African American.

In 1993, President WILLIAM JEFFERSON CLINTON nominated her to serve as the U.S. ambassador to Jamaica.

Further Reading

Brownmiller, Susan. *Shirley Chisholm: A Biography.* New York: Pocket Books, 1972.

Chisholm, Shirley. *The Good Fight.* New York: Harper Row, 1973.

———. *Unbought and Unbossed.* New York: Avon Books, 1972.

Drotning, Philip T., and Wesley W. South. *Up from the Ghetto.* New York: Cowles, 1970.

Rennert, Richard Scott, ed. *Female Leaders.* New York: Chelsea House, 1993.

Scheader, Catherine. *Shirley Chisholm: Teacher and Congresswoman.* Hillsdale, N.J.: Enslow, 1990.

Cisneros, Henry

(1947–) secretary of Housing and Urban Development

Henry Cisneros was the first Mexican American to serve as a member of a presidential cabinet. Although he served with distinction in this office, he was forced by scandal to resign before the end of his term.

Born on June 11, 1947, in San Antonio, Texas, Cisneros attended school in Texas and received his bachelor's degree from Texas A&M University in 1969. He continued there, receiving his master's in urban and regional planning in 1970. While he was still in school, he served as assistant to the city manager in San Antonio, Texas, in 1968 and as assistant to the city manager in Bryan, Texas, from 1969 to 1970. He also served as the assistant director in the Department of Model Cities in San Antonio from 1969 to 1970.

Cisneros was named a White House fellow to the secretary of the Department of Health, Education, and Welfare for 1971 to 1972. He then moved to the northeast to continue his education, receiving his master's degree in business administration at Harvard University in 1973. From there, he moved back to Washington, D.C., to attend George Washington University, where he received his doctorate in public administration in 1975.

His formal education complete, he returned to San Antonio where he was elected to the city council, on which he served from 1975 to 1981. He moved up to the office of mayor of San Antonio in 1981 and remained in that position until 1989.

In 1993, President Bill Clinton nominated him to serve as the secretary of Housing and Urban Development. He served in that capacity until 1997. At that time he was forced to resign because of the disclosure that he had not accurately reported to the FBI the total amount of money he had paid to a mistress with whom he was associated while he was mayor of San Antonio.

After he left public service, he was named the president of Univision Communications in Los Angeles, California, a position he has held since 1997.

Further Reading

Diehl, Kemper. *Cisneros: Portrait of a New American*. San Antonio, Tex.: Corona Publishing Company, 1985.

Henry, Christopher E. *Henry Cisneros*. New York: Chelsea House, 1994.

Martinez, Elizabeth Conrad. *Henry Cisneros: Mexican-American Leader*. Brookfield, Conn.: Millbrook Press, 1993.

Gillies, John. *Senor Alcalde: A Biography of Henry Cisneros*. Minneapolis: Dillon Press, 1988.

Clark, James Beauchamp
(Champ Clark)
(1850–1921) *Speaker of the House, candidate for president, representative*

Champ Clark was a long-term member of the U.S. House of Representatives who became Speaker of the House of Representatives and then ran for president in 1912. While he established a leading legislative role, he was unable to generate a broad national appeal.

Born on March 7, 1850, in Lawrenceburg, Kentucky, James Beauchamp Clark went to college in West Virginia and graduated from Bethany College in 1873. Settling in Bowling Green, Missouri, he was admitted to the Missouri bar in 1875. Clark ran for the Missouri state legislature as a Democrat in 1889 and served there until he was elected to the U.S. House of Representatives in 1892. He was not reelected in 1894 but came back to win in 1896. From then on, he served in the House of Representatives until his death in 1921.

Showing real talent for debating and public speaking, he was elected the Democratic minority leader in 1907. History credits him most for his role in unseating the powerful Republican House Speaker JOSEPH GURNEY CANNON. In 1910, Clark worked with Progressive Republicans, such as Nebraska's GEORGE WILLIAM NORRIS, and most of the Democrats to strip from the Speaker's office the

key power to control the House Rules Committee and the Speaker's absolute control over debate. Thus weakened, Cannon was eventually removed from his job. Clark himself ascended to the Speaker's post in 1911 and held it for eight years.

As a Progressive and as a border state Democrat, Clark was able to offer the necessary compromises between different legislative factions. This stood him in good stead in the Congress where compromise was the key attribute but was less helpful in his race for president.

In 1912, Clark went to the Democratic National Convention with the largest number of delegates committed to him. He led in the voting on the first ballot, but he was unable to stop New Jersey Governor THOMAS WOODROW WILSON, who had executive experience and could state a clear political vision. In particular, this appealed to WILLIAM JENNINGS BRYAN, who threw his support to Wilson on later ballots and put Wilson over the two-thirds rule used by the Democratic Party to name its nominees.

As a loyal Democrat, Clark supported Wilson's domestic programs avidly in Congress, but he refused to support the national draft for the armed forces even after the United States entered World War I. Since the reforms he introduced in the House of Representatives reduced the power of the Speaker, he was less powerful than some of his predecessors and was not able to prevail on many issues. But he remained a popular congressional figure throughout his career.

In 1918, the Republicans reclaimed control of the House of Representatives and Clark had to step down as Speaker. He then became the Democratic minority leader. Reelected to the House from his home district in 1920, he was not reelected the minority leader by the Democrats in 1921. He died shortly thereafter on March 2, 1921.

Further Reading

Clark, Champ. *My Quarter Century of American Politics*. New York: Harper, 1920.

"Clark, James B. 'Champ'" in *Congress A to Z: Third Edition*, edited by David R. Tarr and Ann O'Connor. Washington, D.C.: Congressional Quarterly, 1999.

Krahn, Carole Ellen. *Champ Clark: Presidential Candidate*. Carbondale: Southern Illinois University, 1965.

Clay, Henry

(1777–1852) *secretary of state, candidate for president, Speaker of the House, senator, representative*

Henry Clay wanted to be president of the United States so much he could taste it, but he never succeeded. Clay failed to see that his contributions to the Congress over a 30-year period would have made him more popular and better remembered historically than some of those who won the office he cherished most. Except for ANDREW JACKSON, Clay was the foremost spokesman for the new West. Because of this common background, the two men were competitors for the leadership of the West and often in conflict with each other. Many of their struggles in the first half of the 19th century turned on their personal competitiveness.

Henry Clay was born on April 12, 1777, in Hanover County, Virginia. Largely self-educated, he studied law and was admitted to the bar by the time he was 20. By the age of 21, he had moved to Lexington, Kentucky, and opened his own practice. He acquired a strong reputation for defending those accused of crimes because, it was said, he never had any of his clients executed.

Clay was identified with three different political parties over his career. The selection of these parties reflected the looseness of party affiliations over Clay's lifetime. He started as a follower of THOMAS JEFFERSON and his Democratic Republican Party and ran under that label for the Kentucky state legislature in 1803. Elected, he stayed there until 1807, when he was elected to fill an unexpired Senate term. He was also elected to fill an unfinished Senate term from 1810 to 1811.

Clay preferred to be closer to the people and so decided to run for the House of Representatives in 1810. Winning the seat, he moved quickly to the position of Speaker of the House where he actively promoted his aggressive foreign policy views. He was one of the so-called War Hawks of the period who favored war with Great Britain in order to annex territory in Canada and Florida. He joined JOHN CALDWELL CALHOUN and DANIEL WEBSTER in this effort.

During the War of 1812, President JAMES MADISON named Clay one of the negotiators of the peace treaty with Britain. After Clay helped the negotiators bring the war to a successful end, he returned to the House, was renamed the Speaker, and stayed until 1820. The high point of this period of Clay's service was his skillful guiding of the Compromise of 1820 through the Congress. This act provided about 30 years of relative peace over the slavery issue. It admitted Maine as a free state and Missouri as a slave state to keep the balance between North and South. It prohibited slavery in the territory of the Louisiana Purchase north of the 36-degree 30-minute line.

Clay badly wanted to be elected president so he hoped President JAMES MONROE would appoint him secretary of state since that post was regarded as a stepping-stone to the presidency. When Monroe selected JOHN QUINCY ADAMS, Clay became furious and refused to let Adams take the oath in the House chamber, as had been the customary practice.

At the end of Monroe's second term, Clay ran for president against ANDREW JACKSON, John Quincy Adams, and William Crawford. Jackson got the highest number of popular votes, but no one received a majority of either the popular or the Electoral College votes. Clay finished last. When the election was sent to the House of Representatives, Clay used his influence as Speaker of the House to throw the election to Adams as the second-highest vote getter. Adams showed his gratitude by making Clay his secretary of state.

If Clay figured he would now be in line for the presidency, he did not reckon with Andrew Jackson and his supporters. Although the Adams-Clay arrangement was legal and constitutional, Jackson and his supporters called it a "corrupt bargain." Not very personable to begin with, Adams had virtually no success in achieving any of his objectives in office. Clay conceived of an interesting international objective called the Pan-American Conference only to discover that it could not be held, because the hatred of Jackson's supporters toward Clay led them to block it in Congress. Jackson easily defeated Adams for president in 1828.

Clay was elected to the U.S. Senate in 1831 and used this as a springboard to run against Jackson as a National Republican in 1832, but Jackson beat him badly. With the National Republicans dead as a party, Clay sought the nomination for president as a Whig in 1840, 1844, and 1848. Although the Whigs nominated him in 1844, President JAMES KNOX POLK defeated him in the general election.

Clay retired in 1849, but he saw that a sectional war over slavery was brewing and tried to help the country avoid war. He returned to the U.S. Senate where he fashioned and pushed through a package of bills known collectively as the Compromise of 1850. This compromise was necessary because the Compromise of 1820—also largely fashioned by Clay—had outlived its effectiveness. The 1820 measure had solved the question of whether slavery would be permitted in the territories by creating an arbitrary line (36 degrees 30 minutes) north of which slavery would not be allowed.

The new territory taken by the Mexican War disrupted the amount of land in question, and the population of California was so large that if it were admitted as a free state, there was no comparable area that could be admitted as a corresponding slave state. Clay gained a critical concession from the southerners on the admission of California as free state by providing that Utah and New Mexico could decide whether they wished to be free or slave, based on the idea of popular sovereignty. Southern worries about fugitive slaves were partially satisfied by a tough new fugitive slave law, and the South was reassured that the District of Columbia would be permitted to retain slaves, but slave trade was stopped within its borders. This package included something for everyone, but it did not satisfy anyone completely. Although Clay's compromise staved off war for 10 years (helping the North more than the South, because the North grew much stronger during the next decade), it was not sufficient to provide a permanent peace. Clay died two years later on June 29, 1852.

While the 1850 compromise was touted as Clay's best single effort, his longer-term contribution came from his so-called American System, a set of proposals that were influential even if they were never adopted in full. He articulated a genuine national program for the United States. The American System called for the federal government to support the building of canals and roads and other transportation links between the different sections of the country. He also favored high protective tariffs in order to build up native "infant" industries. Finally, he supported a national bank to provide a system for borrowing capital to build the nation.

In retrospect, it is clear that Clay's program was sound. At the time, Clay had to struggle against the notion that the U.S. Constitution did not provide explicitly for these goals. He argued that the Constitution permitted these activities and they would be good for the nation. Clay's programs were designed to please different sections of the country; each section was expected to compromise by seeing the benefit of part of a program for them and to be willing to accept the disadvantages of other parts of the program. In a legislative setting, Clay was often successful, and the essence of his American System became the system of legislating for most of the 19th century.

Henry Clay, a legendary congressional figure, served as U.S. representative, Speaker of the House, and senator. (Library of Congress)

Further Reading

Baxter, Maurice G. *Henry Clay: The Lawyer.* Lexington: University Press of Kentucky, 2000.
————. *Henry Clay and the American System.* Lexington: University Press of Kentucky, 1995.
Remini, Robert V. *Henry Clay: Statesman for the Union.* New York: Norton, 1991.
Watson, Harry L. *Andrew Jackson vs. Henry Clay: Democracy and Development in Antebellum America.* Boston: Bedford/St. Martin's 1998.

Cleveland, Stephen Grover
(1837–1908) *president, governor, mayor*

Grover Cleveland was the only U.S. president to serve two nonconsecutive terms, having been elected in 1884 and 1892 but having lost in 1888. He won the popular vote in all three elections. Until he was elected president in 1884, no president had been able to win on the Democratic Party banner since before the Civil War. Cleveland was able to win because he used the traditional Democratic Party link between the rural southern (and later the western states) and the big cities in the Northeast.

The son of a minister, Cleveland was born on March 18, 1837, in a parsonage in Caldwell, New Jersey. In 1841, Cleveland's father moved to a new church in Fayetteville, New York, and again moved to a new church in Clinton, New York, in 1850, taking his family with him on each move. After his father died when Cleveland was 16, his mother's financial situation worsened. Cleveland went to work at the New York Institution for the Blind. With help from an uncle, he studied law so that he was admitted to the New York bar at the age of 22. By 1863, he had become the assistant district attorney for Erie Country. Since he had to care for his mother and sister, he could not fight in the Civil War and had to hire a substitute to go in his place. This would later be held against him politically.

In 1881, Cleveland became the Democratic reform mayor of the city of Buffalo. He was successful so quickly that he was elected as the Democratic reform governor of New York in 1882. Two years later, Cleveland's reputation for integrity

brought him quick success. In 1884, he was nominated as the Democratic candidate for president of the United States. Cleveland succeeded when the public perception of widespread corruption in the Republican Party led voters to reject the party that had won the Civil War.

The Republicans strengthened this perception when they nominated JAMES GILLESPIE BLAINE as their candidate. As Speaker of the House, Blaine had been implicated in a scandal concerning the receipt of railroad stock that he allegedly received in return for favors. Since such scandals had affected Republican candidates before, it was an easy charge to be believed. Blaine thought the scandal had occurred so long ago that it had ceased to be important, but the taint continued to affect his candidacy.

Blaine also thought he could counter the scandal by pointing out that Cleveland had agreed to pay child support to a woman who bore a child out of wedlock. Although Cleveland claimed he did not know if he was actually the father, he paid the support anyway, possibly to cover for the woman's other consorts —friends of Cleveland's who were married. Cleveland defused the charge not only with his record of integrity in his public life but also with his candid admission of the circumstances surrounding his agreement to pay the child support.

In the late 19th century, the electorate was so evenly divided between the Democrats and Republicans that, for several national elections, the outcome of the presidential election turned on as few as 50,000 voters out of millions cast. Cleveland won in 1884 because he was the Democrat from New York State. This position won him votes from big city Democrats as well as rural Southern voters who made up the backbone of the post–Civil War Democratic Party.

Blaine might still have won except for an unfortunate event late in the campaign. He attended a rally in New York City and sat through a speech in which one of his supporters condemned the Democrats as the party of "Rum, Romanism, and Rebellion." When Blaine did not quickly distance himself from that speaker, the remark was used against him, and he proceeded to lose the Catholic vote and New York state by about 5,000 votes.

New York cost him the Electoral College votes he needed to win.

Cleveland had a restrictive view of presidential power, so he did not attempt much in his first years in office, although he could have done little anyway since the Republicans controlled the Senate. Cleveland signed the Interstate Commerce Act. He also vetoed most of the veterans' pension bills, since they were largely raids on the treasury voted by congressmen who wished to buy the votes of veterans. Since Cleveland paid a substitute to serve for him in the Civil War, some held his vetoes against him. Following long-standing Democratic Party positions, he also pushed to reduce tariff rates since the rates were generating an unnecessary surplus. The Republicans opposed this because they wanted high tariffs to protect U.S. industry and not merely for revenue.

In 1888, the Republicans attempted to capitalize on these relatively small mistakes, but the most important decision they made was to select a candidate from the Midwest unassociated with any scandals. They found their man in the dour, if honest, BENJAMIN HARRISON from Indiana. Harrison lost the popular vote but was able to deny Cleveland a few thousand votes in enough large states to win the presidency in the Electoral College.

After 1888, it was the Republicans' turn to suffer. They raised tariff rates, and that provoked opposition from farmers who faced high tariffs from foreign countries who were retaliating against high U.S. tariffs on manufactured goods. Harrison was not very personable and was so straitlaced that he lost popularity within his own party. Cleveland had gone back to New York to practice law and bide his time. When Harrison failed to succeed popularly, Cleveland was ready to make a comeback. Nominated on the first ballot in 1892, he reclaimed that handful of votes needed to carry New York State and, with his strength in the South and West, went on to win his second presidential term.

Cleveland is the only American president to serve two nonconsecutive terms. He appealed to the Democrats as someone who could win, for the Democrats had been out of the White House for 24 years in 1884. However, he was essentially a conservative—almost Republican—candidate who was not able to inspire Democratic voters in economic hard times. In his second term, Cleveland confronted a deep depression. As a believer in sound currency, especially one backed by gold, he was philosophically unable to consider taking steps to increase the money supply, which would probably have eased the economic situation somewhat.

More than backing ineffectual policies, Cleveland seemed constitutionally and philosophically aligned with financial elites against ordinary citizens. He authorized the use of federal troops to quell a strike in Chicago, despite the opposition to their use by the Illinois governor of his own party. He also resisted the attempt to annex the Hawaiian Islands and opposed the recognition of a revolutionary government in Cuba, despite strong popular support from both parties. Cleveland became so deeply unpopular within his own party that he had no chance of winning the nomination for reelection. In fact, the 1896 Democratic National Convention was openly hostile to the Democratic incumbent president.

Cleveland was popular for a time, but he had no answer for economic hard times or the common man. Neither he nor any of his East Coast friends could overcome the populist appeal of a western Democrat like WILLIAM JENNINGS BRYAN, who swept the 1896 Democratic National Convention. Bryan lost the election to WILLIAM MCKINLEY while winning the enduring support of a generation of Democratic voters.

Cleveland retired to Princeton, New Jersey, where he wrote articles and gradually regained a measure of popular acceptance. He toyed with the idea of seeking the Democratic nomination for president in 1904 but accepted the nomination of Alton B. Parker, a conservative eastern Democrat with similar views to his own. Cleveland died on June 24, 1908.

Further Reading

"Cleveland, Stephen Grover" Available online. URL: http://www.whitehouse.gov/history/presidents/gc22.html. Downloaded on October 20, 2001.

Ford, Henry Jones. *The Cleveland Era: A Chronicle of the New Order in Politics.* New Haven: Yale University Press, 1921.

"Grover Cleveland" in *The American President,* by Philip B. Kunhardt, Jr., Philip B. Kunhardt III,

Grover Cleveland was the only U.S. president to serve two nonconsecutive terms, having been elected in 1884 and 1892, but having lost in 1888 in the Electoral College while winning a majority of the popular vote. *(Library of Congress)*

and Peter W. Kunhardt. New York: Riverhead Books, 1999.

"Grover Cleveland" in *The Presidency A to Z: Second Edition,* edited by Michael T. Nelson. Washington, D.C.: Congressional Quarterly Press, 1998.

Hernon, Joseph Martin. *Profiles in Character: Hubris and Heroism in the U.S. Senate—1789–1990.* Armonk, N.Y.: M. E. Sharpe, 1997.

Hollingsworth, J. Rogers. *The Whirligig of Politics: The Democracy of Cleveland and Bryan.* Chicago: University of Chicago Press, 1963.

Merrill, Horace Samuel. *Bourbon Leader: Grover Cleveland and the Democratic Party.* Boston: Little, Brown, 1957.

Nevins, Allan. *Grover Cleveland: A Study in Courage.* Norwalk, Conn.: Easton Press, 1989.

Roberts, Randy. "Grover Cleveland," in *The American Presidents,* edited by Frank N. Magill, John L. Loos, and Tracy Irons-Georges. Pasadena, Calif.: Salem Press, 2000.

Tugwell, Rexford G. *Grover Cleveland.* New York: Macmillan, 1968.

Welch, Richard E. *The Presidencies of Grover Cleveland.* Lawrence: University Press of Kansas, 1988.

Clifford, Clark McAdams

(1906–1998) *secretary of defense, assistant to the president*

Clark McAdams Clifford, a prominent Washington attorney, lobbyist, insider, and friend and adviser to several presidents, is most famous as secretary of defense for persuading President LYNDON BAINES JOHNSON to abandon the escalation of the Vietnam War and begin peace negotiations.

Born on Christmas Day in 1906 in Fort Scott, Kansas, Clark McAdams Clifford grew up in St. Louis, Missouri. He studied law at Washington University in St. Louis and was admitted to the Missouri bar in 1928. He quickly established a successful law practice in corporate and labor law. During World War II, he was commissioned a lieutenant in the U.S. naval reserve and served in Washington as an assistant to James K. Vardaman, who was a naval aide to President HARRY S. TRUMAN.

In January 1946, Clifford succeeded Vardaman and managed a number of special projects for the president. Included among these was the establishment of the Central Intelligence Agency (CIA), although it was initially referred to as the National Intelligence Authority.

In June 1946, when his military service came to an end, Clifford became special legal counsel to the president and soon one of Truman's most trusted advisers. He specialized in foreign affairs but had a wide-ranging responsibility. In particular, Clifford was generally regarded as the author of the memo laying out the critical strategy for Harry Truman's winning presidential campaign over Thomas Dewey. Two years after that critical campaign, Clifford left government service for a lucrative law practice. Throughout the 1950s, he was regarded as a critical lobbyist and Washington insider. In 1960, he assisted the president elect JOHN FITZGERALD KENNEDY during the transition from President DWIGHT DAVID EISENHOWER's administration.

In 1961, Kennedy named Clifford to the Foreign Intelligence Advisory Board, which oversaw the operations of the CIA. After Kennedy's assassination, Clifford was a close adviser to president Lyndon B. Johnson. As America's involvement in Vietnam increased and as secretary of defense ROBERT STRANGE MCNAMARA grew more disenchanted with the Vietnam War, President Johnson turned to Clifford to serve as his new secretary of defense.

Initially, Clifford was regarded as a hawk on the war in Vietnam, for he recommended renewed bombing of the North. He came to see that bombing would not succeed in winning the war and ultimately recommended that Johnson begin peace talks with the Vietnamese. Because of Clifford's stature in the Democratic Party establishment, Johnson listened to him and began the process of disengaging from Vietnam.

Serving as secretary of defense was the political high point of Clifford's official governmental career, but he remained highly active behind the scenes. Regrettably, he was involved in a financial scandal very late in his life that damaged his reputation considerably. He died on October 11, 1998.

Further Reading

Clifford, Clark M. *Counsel to the President: A Memoir.* New York: Random House, 1991.

Frantz, Douglas. *Friends in High Places: The Rise and Fall of Clark Clifford.* Boston: Little, Brown, 1995.

Clinton, DeWitt

(1769–1828) *candidate for president, senator, mayor*

DeWitt Clinton was largely responsible for the creation of the Erie Canal, a technological marvel in its age. Clinton should also be credited for creating the patronage model for filling government positions, later developed more fully by President ANDREW JACKSON.

Clinton was a scion of a wealthy, politically prominent family active in the Democratic Republican Party (now called the Democratic Party). He was born on March 2, 1769, in Little Britain, New York. Before he was 21 years old, he had graduated from Columbia College, had studied law, and was admitted to the bar. Since his uncle was GEORGE CLINTON, New York's former governor, he had special political support and won a seat in the state assembly in 1797 when he was only 28 years of age. A year later, he won a four-year term in the state senate. In 1801, Clinton was appointed to a position that allowed him to name people to state jobs. Clinton immediately proceeded to select as many Democratic Republican Party members as possible to fill posts previously held by Federalists. This may be said to be the founding of the patronage system, but the patronage system was actually a reform of the earlier patrician system of naming only descendants of prominent families to government positions. As the United States added new voters to the electorate, a change to the patronage system was inevitable.

The state legislature elected Clinton to the U.S. Senate in 1802, but he decided he would have greater patronage power as New York City's mayor, and he left the U.S. Senate in 1803 to seek that office. He served four annual mayoral terms until 1807 when he was out of office for one year. From 1808 until 1815, he served continuously as mayor except for one year from 1810 to 1811. While he served as mayor he also managed to be elected state senator from 1806 to 1811 and lieutenant governor from 1811 to 1813. In the politics of his day, he strongly supported education and health issues. As an indication of his later interest in the Erie Canal, he also had a special interest in the shipping industry.

In 1812, Clinton challenged the incumbent Democratic Republican President JAMES MADISON in his reelection bid, even though both were members of the same party. Clinton was urged to do so by a faction within the party that opposed Madison's war with Great Britain. He saw an opportunity to gain the support of this Democratic Party faction and the Federalist Party, which also opposed the war. However, the two groups' remaining policies were quite different, and he was able only to gather the support of both parties by separately telling each of the two parties exactly what they wished to hear.

Since this meant Clinton was making contradictory promises he could not possibly fulfill, Madison was able to charge Clinton with dishonesty and to win reelection. Madison earned 128 Electoral College votes to Clinton's 89. The Democratic Republicans were furious with Clinton for having tried to gain Federalist support for his campaign, and they refused to renominate him for lieutenant governor in 1813; he was also defeated for mayor in 1815.

While these events would have destroyed a political career of a lesser man, Clinton had extra political resources in New York State. In 1916, the state legislature adopted the plans for the Erie Canal as he had long urged. With his political career improved, he was elected governor in 1817. After serving two terms, he decided it would be politically prudent not to seek a third term, but he had the wisdom to retain the post of canal commissioner. This angered his opponents, who finally removed him from the canal post in 1824. However, Clinton was so closely identified with the Erie Canal that he was able to use his ouster as a cause for him to be reelected governor. He was, therefore, able to preside as governor over the opening of the Champlain and Erie Canals in 1825.

His long and checkered political career ended with his death on February 11, 1828.

Further Reading

Cornog, Evan. *The Birth of Empire: DeWitt Clinton and the American Experience, 1769–1828.* New York: Oxford University Press, 1998.

Fitzpatrick, Edward A. *The Educational Views and Influence of DeWitt Clinton.* New York: Arno Press, 1969.

Hanyan, Craig. *DeWitt Clinton and the Rise of the People's Men.* Montreal and Buffalo: McGill-Queen's University Press, 1996.

Renwick, James. *Life of DeWitt Clinton.* New York: Harper, 1970.

Siry, Steven E. *DeWitt Clinton and the American Political Economy: Sectionalism, Politics, and Republican Ideology.* New York: P. Lang, 1990.

Clinton, George

(1739–1812) *vice president, governor, Revolutionary War leader*

George Clinton is often referred to as the father of New York State because of his efforts early in the state's history to create a strong state government. He may also properly be referred to as one of the founders of the Democratic Republican Party, now known as the Democratic Party. Clinton's decision to join forces with THOMAS JEFFERSON and JAMES MADISON in the mid-1790s created a fundamental political alliance between the rural South and the big cities in the North, which has survived to the 21st century.

Clinton was born on July 26, 1739, in Little Britain, New York, and was self-educated in the law. He was undistinguished professionally until he was elected to the legislature for the British colonial provincial assembly for New York in 1768. In competition with Philip Schuyler, he sought to lead the pro-Revolutionary forces. He served in the Second Continental Congress and would have signed the Declaration of Independence except that he left the congress early in order to become a general in one of the revolutionary army units.

He was not a success as a military man. Still, when he returned to New York and was elected governor, he proved an effective wartime leader. Faced with a difficult financial situation, he kept the state afloat and managed to retain popular support by taking a hard-line approach toward the loyalists who remained in the state.

Clinton feared that New York might be rendered excessively weak if there was a strong national government, and he fought against the ratification of the U.S. Constitution. He wrote some anti-Federalist essays under the title of "Cato," but he was up against the arguments advanced by JOHN JAY, James Madison, and ALEXANDER HAMILTON in the *Federalist Papers*. Hamilton, in particular, was related by marriage to the Schuylers, giving a personal dimension to this political struggle.

Clinton lost the battle over ratification of the Constitution, but he remained an important political force and was inclined in the anti-Federalist dimension. This made him a natural ally for Madison and Jefferson as they came to fear the excesses of a centralized government in the hands of the Federalist Party.

In the middle of the 1790s Madison and Jefferson took a botanical expedition up the Hudson River to Albany. While they were genuinely committed to gathering new species of plants to take back to Virginia, they also had a political agenda. When they stopped in Albany, they were able to forge an alliance with George Clinton that formed the core of the Democratic Republican Party. While there have been changes in this alliance over the past two centuries, the essential outlines of this alliance are still present in American politics.

In 1800, Jefferson selected AARON BURR, a Clinton ally, as his vice presidential running mate, but Burr attempted to take the presidency away from Jefferson in the Electoral College. Burr was allowed to serve as vice president, but the Democratic Republicans never trusted him again. A new vice presidential candidate was needed when Jefferson ran for reelection in 1804. Since New York was vitally important to Jefferson's prospects for winning a second term, he selected George Clinton as a powerful New York political figure for his vice presidential running mate.

Throughout Clinton's service as vice president, he sought to build political support for his own run for president, but Jefferson was convinced that Madison should be his successor. After Clinton failed to secure sufficient support for the 1808 presidential nomination, he accepted the vice presidency under Madison. This was not a happy arrangement, and increasingly Madison felt that Clinton was disloyal. In fact, in 1811, Vice President Clinton cast a tie-breaking vote in the Senate, favoring of the rechartering of the Bank of the United States even though Madison was opposed to this proposal.

Clinton had long been ill and died on April 20, 1812, becoming the first vice president to die in office. His nephew, DeWitt Clinton, took up the challenge and unsuccessfully attempted to defeat Madison in the presidential election in 1912. His own political problems in forging a difficult alliance between the Federalists and a faction within the Democratic Republican Party meant that the Clintons were never able to win the presidency.

Further Reading

Hastings, Hugh, and J. A. Holden, eds. *Public Papers of George Clinton, First Governor of New York, 1777–1795, 1801–1804.* New York: AMS Press, 1973.

Kaminski, John P. *George Clinton: Yeoman Politician of the New Republic.* Madison, Wis.: Madison House, 1993.

Spaulding, Ernest W. *His Excellency George Clinton, Critic of the Constitution: Second Edition.* Port Washington, N.Y.: I. J. Friedman, 1964.

Clinton, Hillary Rodham
(1947–   ) *first lady, senator, author*

Hillary Rodham Clinton is the first first lady to win a political office. She won her bid to be elected the U.S. senator from New York in the campaign of 2000.

Born on October 26, 1947, in Park Ridge, Illinois, Hillary Rodham graduated from Maine Township High School South and went to Wellesley, from which she graduated in 1969. She then went to Yale Law School and graduated in 1973. She worked as legal counsel for the Children's Defense Fund and Carnegie Council on Children from 1973 to 1974. She also worked on the impeachment inquiry staff of the Judiciary Committee of the House of Representatives in 1974.

She married WILLIAM JEFFERSON CLINTON in October 1975, after his first unsuccessful race for Congress, but before his successful career took off. She taught law at the University of Arkansas Law School, both in Fayetteville and in Little Rock, until she entered the Rose law firm in 1977.

She stayed in private practice with that law firm until 1992, when she supported her husband's race for president. This was an unusually demanding role since she was required to defend her husband against various charges that he had had extramarital affairs during their marriage. She is generally credited with having aided him substantially in his defense.

Upon her husband's election as president, she took over the management of his proposed legislative program dealing with health care, a growing concern in the nation. Health-care reform included not only the comparatively simple issue of worker ability to transfer health insurance from one job to another but such intractable issues as high doctors' salaries, hospital costs, and pharmaceutical prices that led to ever increasing budgets for both Medicare (for the elderly) and Medicaid (for the poor of all ages).

Hillary Clinton led a commission that devised a complicated program that required a large federal bureaucracy plus either high taxes or high employer payments to pay for it. While the national polls showed substantial concern over improved health care, the details of such a massive undertaking soon produced a strongly adverse political reaction. As this prospect became clear, American public opinion turned against comprehensive health-care reform, and Clinton's proposals were defeated in the Congress, where they died without being brought up for a final vote. Only comparatively modest proposals were passed, allowing workers who change jobs to transfer their health insurance coverage without penalty. Hillary Clinton temporarily withdrew from having such an active political profile. During this time, she wrote a successful book, *It Takes a Village to Raise a Child,* and donated the proceeds to charity.

Taking a less public role was not easy, since the Clintons' opponents were unending in their quest for discovering something scandalous about them. Hillary Clinton was investigated almost continually for eight years at a cost of millions of dollars, but no indictment—let alone a conviction—was ever brought against her. The investigators first examined the Whitewater land deal, a failed real estate venture in which the Clintons lost money, for evidence that the Clintons improperly influenced the granting of bank loans. This was expanded into an inquiry into the firing of the White House travel office, into the handling of FBI files, and, eventually, to the personal sex life of the president. Hillary Clinton was heavily involved in her husband's financial dealings and could not be oblivious to his personal life. Although none of the investigations found any serious—let alone indictable—wrongdoing on the part of Hillary Clinton, the dynamic of needing to find something to justify the expense kept the investigation going.

Regarding the president's extramarital affairs, Hillary Clinton defended her husband. Curiously, her own popularity tended to be lower when his was higher and vice versa. Her defense of her husband throughout the investigation and the subsequent impeachment proceedings led to a significant increase in her popularity. Ironically, the scandal over the president's relationship with Monica Lewinsky may have strengthened the first lady politically and made her race for the Senate a reality. In any event, once her husband survived conviction on the impeachment charges, the first public discussion of her as a candidate for the Senate from New York began.

In 1999, New York's Democratic senator, DANIEL PATRICK MOYNIHAN, announced his decision to retire after the 2000 election and all but openly endorsed Hillary Clinton from the outset. Although she was born in Illinois and lived in Arkansas during all the years that her husband was the governor of Arkansas, she had sufficient national recognition and sufficient political funding to seek and secure the Democratic nomination for the U.S. Senate in New York. Since neither the U.S. Constitution nor state law prohibited individuals from moving into New York and running for the Senate office, Clinton's largest challenge was to convince New Yorkers that she would do more for New York than any of her opponents, even though she was not born there.

Initially, she expected to run against Rudy Giuliani, the Republican mayor of New York City, who attracted national attention by considerably reducing the level of crime in the largest city in the United States. As an opponent, Giuliani was a mixed bag. He was clearly popular within New York City, but many Republicans in upstate New York were skeptical of any Republican candidate from the city itself. Giuliani had also made enemies and even alienated important groups during his service as mayor. While Hillary Clinton had negative attributes for not being a native New Yorker, Giuliani had high negatives as a result of his controversial tenure as mayor.

In the midst of the campaign, Giuliani announced he would not run since he faced cancer surgery and had marital problems. Immediately, Republican Governor George Pataki urged that his party select Long Island Republican congressman Rick Lazio (someone Pataki had long preferred as the candidate since Pataki and Giuliani were not on good terms). Although Lazio had a late start, Hillary Clinton was so hated by Republicans across the country that he was amply funded. Since Lazio did not have the negative attributes of Giuliani, he was a real threat to Hillary Clinton.

Clinton proved that she was not merely a first lady but also a formidable political campaigner on her own. She campaigned aggressively and effectively not only in New York City with its strong Democratic majority but also in upstate New York with its strong Republican core. The outcome of the race hinged on the strong showing of Vice President ALBERT ARNOLD GORE, JR., as the Democratic presidential nominee running against Republican GEORGE WALKER BUSH. Gore ran substantially ahead of Hillary Clinton in New York and apparently had sufficiently longer "coattails" to carry Clinton into the office. This fact does not diminish Hillary Clinton's achievement: She won a major political office, something no other first lady in American history has done.

Historically, new senators have been encouraged to limit their national public utterances to avoid the appearance of upstaging other senators with greater seniority. While the current trend is for new senators to speak out nationally earlier than in the past, this longstanding norm remains in effect. Senator Clinton has appeared to follow this pattern quite closely, speaking out mainly on issues of great concern to her own state. Given her stature as a former first lady, her statements concerning the terrorist attacks of September 11, 2001, made national headlines, but this was acceptable since it directly concerned New York.

By early 2002, Senator Clinton increasingly spoke out on national issues in the process of addressing issues of concern to New Yorkers since New York is such a large state. For example, the historically significant 1996 welfare reform legislation must be reauthorized in 2002. In a major statement on welfare reform—a subject for which she was criticized for discussing as first lady—she has staked out a moderate position, but one considerably to the left of the Republican White House.

Even without making public pronouncements, Democratic senators—and some moderate Republican senators—sought her advice and support for amendments to the various proposals to reauthorize the welfare reform legislation. In addition, senatorial staff members of both parties were in contact with her staff to glean information she gained while in the White House as to the meaning and import of various provisions in the 1996 legislation. Although she did not serve on the Senate Finance Committee, which crafts any new welfare reform measures, her influence was felt through these contacts. Education, social services, and health care are other issues on which she has impact privately and should be expected to have public impact in the future.

As a candidate for the Senate in 2000, she ruled herself out of the presidential contest in 2004 and repeated that position as a newly elected senator. Still, national polls in April 2002 showed her ahead of all the announced and probable candidates for the Democratic nomination for president except Albert Gore. Gore, the Democrat's presidential nominee in 2000, continued to have the greatest Democratic support of any of the announced or probable candidates, but he also had the greatest number of respondents who thought he should not run again. Even Senator Clinton's statement that she would not be a presidential candidate in 2004 might be subject to reversal in the event of a genuine draft from among stalwarts in the Democratic Party.

Further Reading

Andersen, Christopher P. *Bill and Hillary: The Marriage.* New York: Morrow, 1999.

Cocco, Marie. "Welfare Reform Back on the Hill—With Hillary," *The Sacramento Bee.* April 15, 2002, B5.

Conason, Joe. *The Hunting of the President: The Ten-Year Campaign to Destroy Bill and Hillary Clinton.* New York: St. Martin's Press. 2000.

Hubbell, Webb. *Friends in High Places: Our Journey from Little Rock to Washington, D. C.* New York: Morrow, 1997.

Ingraham, Laura. *The Hillary Trap: Looking for Power in All the Wrong Places.* New York: Hyperion, 2000.

Milton, Joyce. *The First Partner—Hillary Rodham Clinton.* New York: Morrow, 1999.

Radcliffe, Donnie. *Hillary Rodham Clinton: The Evolution of a First Lady.* New York: Warner Books, Inc., 1999.

Sheehy, Gail. *Hillary's Choice.* New York: Random House, 1999.

Clinton, William Jefferson
(William Jefferson Blythe)
(1946–   ) *president, governor, state attorney general*

William Jefferson Clinton, better known as Bill Clinton, is only the second president to be impeached. Clinton was not convicted and had one of the most consistently high presidential popularity ratings, especially for one who was engulfed in controversy throughout his presidency. His presidential term abounded with remarkable ups and downs.

Bill Clinton was born William Jefferson Blythe on August 19, 1946, in Hope, Arkansas. He never knew his father, who died in a car accident. Clinton's mother, a nurse, moved to Hot Springs, Arkansas, where she remarried, and her children took the last name of her second husband. Clinton spent most of his youth in Hot Springs.

The frequently told story of how he, as a high school student, met President JOHN FITZGERALD KENNEDY on a school-connected trip to Washington, D.C., suggests an early inclination toward politics. This Washington trip apparently influenced his choice of colleges, for he entered Georgetown University, largely because it was located in the nation's capital. After graduating from college, Clinton was selected to be a Rhodes scholar and studied at Oxford University in Great Britain from 1968 to 1970. After completing that program, he returned to the United States to attend Yale Law School, from which he graduated in 1973.

Completing law school, he returned to Arkansas to begin his political career. He practiced law and taught at the University of Arkansas Law School at Fayetteville from 1973 to 1976. He first ran unsuccessfully for Congress as a Democrat in 1974 at the age of 28. The race gave him sufficient recognition so he was able to win the post of state attorney general two years later, a post in which he served from 1977 to 1979.

He used the exposure of his statewide race for Arkansas state attorney general to make a successful bid for governor of Arkansas in 1979. He stumbled over several issues during his first term, particularly endorsing ideas too advanced for his constituents, and failed to win reelection two years later. Reexamining that loss, he became a more determined political leader and won the governor's office back in 1982. He remained governor consistently until he was elected president in 1992.

The Clinton presidency abounded with contradictions reflecting the underlying ironies of the politics of the age. In 1992, he became the first "baby boomer"—someone born in the post-World War II birth surge—to be elected president. He defeated President GEORGE HERBERT WALKER BUSH, a man old enough to be his father and someone whose son GEORGE WALKER BUSH was older than Clinton.

Their personal histories were profoundly different. President Bush was a distinguished and heroic veteran of World War II, which ended before Clinton was born. Clinton was never in the armed services and failed to serve—some say "draft dodged"—during the Vietnam War. Still, American voters elected him the commander in chief of the U.S. armed forces in preference to Bush, who had received record high popularity two years earlier as the commander in chief during America's short and decisive military victory in the Gulf War.

Political contradictions also dogged Clinton's predecessor and confounded his opponents during the period. Immediately following the successful 48-hour-long Gulf War, President Bush achieved the highest job approval ratings in the public opinion polls of any president since World War II. But when Bush was unable to provide a dramatic recovery from the economic recession in his last two years, his popularity rating plummeted at the fastest rate of any post–World War II president.

Clinton capitalized on the relatively slow recovery during the Bush administration by promising "change" if he were elected. This vague promise allowed Clinton to intimate that his administration would be different in ways that would please a wide variety of groups. Liberals and conservatives alike could believe they would favor the "change" in the offing. Even a moderate status quo supporter could hypothesize that Clinton would follow Bush's generally moderate goals while showing greater competence than Bush in achieving them. Such a campaign promise ran the risk that many would be disappointed when their policy preferences were not achieved.

His most famous campaign admonition was: "It's the economy, stupid." While the economy was recovering from the recession during the last Bush year, the recovery was not dramatic enough to generate voter confidence, and Clinton won the election. Clinton and his Democratic allies wanted to stimulate more economic growth without generating inflation and to reduce the deficit. They offered an economic stimulus package, the restoration of relatively higher tax rates on the wealthy, and some modest middle-class tax cuts. The Republicans opposed this, but they were strong enough only to defeat the stimulus package with conservative Democratic support. The resulting compromise stimulated an already growing economy to produce long-term growth and deficit reduction.

Clinton's accomplishments in reducing the budget deficit while providing for economic recovery were overshadowed by other issues. Clinton promised comprehensive universal health care for all Americans in the 1992 campaign, but the details of his proposals—prepared by a commission headed by his wife, HILLARY RODHAM CLINTON—generated a strong reaction, and the final proposal was not even submitted for a vote. While there was support for a universal health-care program, drafting the details of such a program divided so many different groups that no such comprehensive proposal could be enacted. Other secondary issues also overshadowed Clinton's economic success, such as his pro-choice stance on abortion and his support for the right of gays to serve in the armed forces.

In the 1994 congressional elections, the Republicans, led by their minority leader NEWTON LEROY GINGRICH, campaigned on a new nation-wide program called the "Contract with America," a 14-point political and intellectual proposal for reducing the size of government and restoring "family values" in American political life. One novel part of the program was that it promised a national solution rather than the piecemeal kinds of promises typically made by both parties' congressional candidates, which are tailored to the public opinions polls for that district. The Republicans said, in effect, that a vote for their candidates in any district would result in a specific result through this "contract." This campaign strategy appeared to work because the Republicans made startling gains in both the House of Representatives and the Senate, and they reclaimed both houses of Congress for the first time in 42 years.

The election returns made it appear that there had been a seismic shift in the country toward the

Bill Clinton was only the second president (after Andrew Johnson) to be impeached, and, like Johnson, he was not convicted. *(Library of Congress, Official White House photo)*

conservative direction, although the underlying policy preferences reflected in other public opinion polls did not indicate this. In fact, no fundamental shift had occurred. Instead, the Republicans benefited from other factors. From the mid-1960s until the reapportionment after the 1990 census, the Democrats had been able to achieve a majority of seats in the House of Representatives by constructing congressional district boundaries so that they held a sufficient number of safe seats to gain a majority. A certain portion of these seats had solid Democratic majorities because there were so many white Democratic Party identifiers and African-American party identifiers that the Republicans could not win.

African Americans began to demand that the post-1990 congressional districts be drawn so that they acquired a large number of "safe seats" for African Americans. To be sure, these would be overwhelmingly Democratic, but they would not be seats taken away from Republicans; they would be seats taken away from other Democrats. In the end, so many of these were constructed that the total number of Democratic "safe" seats fell below the number needed to hold a majority in the House. In 1994, the Republicans also benefited by turning out a higher percentage of their voters than the Democrats did, as often happens in congressional elections.

The Republican congressional leadership did not see this but behaved as though there had been a revolutionary conservative shift. The House passed virtually all of the "Contract with America." The Republican Senate passed some of it but modified parts of it. Much of the "contract" was sent to Clinton, who signed some but vetoed more of it. Some of the "contract" became law only to be declared unconstitutional by the Supreme Court. Some of the Republicans' "contract" survived— but not as much as would have if a genuine revolution has occurred.

The second two years of Clinton's first term were characterized by Republican initiatives led principally by Newt Gingrich, the former minority leader who had become the new Speaker of the House. Meanwhile, Clinton bided his time. He correctly perceived that the Republican congressional leadership had misread national public opinion and that their political agenda would be rather quickly perceived to be too radical. He also seemed to sense that they were about to overreach. They did this when the Republican Congress failed to pass a compromise budget acceptable to Clinton. The Republicans then sought to show that Gingrich was the most powerful man in America by shutting down the government. They succeeded in shutting down the government, but that only meant that they got the lion's share of the blame for a situation that dragged on for several weeks at the end of 1995 and early in 1996.

Clinton then deftly countered their initiatives with a mainstream program of his own in the context of peace abroad and economic recovery at home. The political advantage then shifted to Clinton, who attacked Republican extremism. When the Republicans nominated Senate majority leader ROBERT JOSEPH DOLE as their Republican presidential nominee, Clinton was able to portray Dole as a member of the radical Republican congressional leadership.

Despite having no major opportunity to demonstrate his ability in foreign or military affairs, Clinton defeated Bob Dole, a distinguished World War II veteran, in the 1996 presidential campaign. He thereby became the first Democratic presidential candidate to win reelection since FRANKLIN DELANO ROOSEVELT 60 years earlier and the first Democratic president to be reelected without winning at least one house of Congress in the 80 years since THOMAS WOODROW WILSON.

Clinton successfully won reelection for himself but was unable to carry either house of Congress, so his second term was structurally a repeat of the last two years of his first term. The president was forced to compromise with Republican majorities, but this situation was still useful to him because it allowed him to rein in the extremists in his own party. Divided government, sometimes called gridlock, was as typical of most of the Clinton years as it was during the Reagan-Bush years. In a longer historical perspective, Americans have apparently accepted this kind of division with one party controlling the White House while the other party controlled the Congress.

Within weeks of his first inauguration, conservative Republicans began an attack on Clinton. Bumper stickers calling for his impeachment first circulated in 1993, sometimes cleverly attacking both Clinton and his wife, saying "Impeach Clinton and her husband, too." Once the Republicans took control of both houses of Congress in 1995, the investigations began in earnest and continued throughout his presidency. The first investigation focused on financial dealings regarding a real estate venture known as Whitewater in which Bill and Hillary Clinton had been involved while he was governor. The investigations raised some questions about the Clintons' involvement but never provided any proof to refute their claim that they lost money on the venture and that Whitewater was simply a failed real estate deal typical of the 1980s.

As for the character issue, the first-term controversy over Clinton's involvement in Whitewater was complicated in the second term by concerns over excessive campaign contributions. Although campaign finance reform had been promised by both political parties for years, and violations of the campaign laws could be found in the records of both political parties, the main focus was on the Clinton White House. Still, the attack on the Clintons was balanced by Speaker Newt Gingrich's improper use of funds from a tax-exempt foundation to finance an "educational" course appearing to have unacceptable partisan overtones at a college in Gingrich's home district.

The long investigation of Clinton resulted from a federal law, enacted in the wake of the Watergate scandal, that created the office of special prosecutor. This special prosecutor was called into play when circumstances arose in which the attorney general of the United States could not prosecute an executive branch official because of a potential conflict of interest. The most obvious conflict of interest was when charges of wrongdoing were leveled against a president of the United States, the very person who named the attorney general in the first place. In the case of the Whitewater scandal, a special prosecutor had been named and began the investigation. However, he withdrew and another special prosecutor was named.

The special prosecutor statute called for that individual to be named by a panel of three federal judges, who would presumably be impartial in the matter. Unfortunately, a controversy arose because the three judges on this panel contained a clear majority of members with strong personal animus toward President Clinton. Further, these judges apparently had a series of meetings with the president's political enemies before they decided whom to select. It was not surprising that they selected a conservative Republican as a special prosecutor, but the particular choice was of concern. The selection of Kenneth Starr was notable because of his connection to a network of far right-wing attorneys, some of whom had received special funding from a foundation funded by an extremely wealthy individual who hated Clinton. None of this suggested that an impartial judicial proceeding was taking place.

The circumstances set a strong partisan tone to the Whitewater investigation. Years went by and millions of dollars were spent on what appeared to be an inconclusive investigation. At best, the investigation had resulted in the indictment and conviction of a few low-level individuals involved in the Whitewater land deal, none of whom provided any real evidence that directly connected President Clinton or his wife to specific wrongdoing.

Partisan political charges against Starr included the accusation that he deliberately imprisoned Susan McDougal for refusing to fabricate stories against the Clintons. As the partisan charges bounced back and forth between the special prosecutor's office and the White House, the special prosecutor's office apparently sought to move the investigation into a different direction, trying to find something to justify the time and money invested in the case.

Rumors had long circulated that Clinton had been romantically involved with women other than his wife. In particular, Paula Jones had charged that Clinton, while he was the Arkansas governor and she was a low-level Arkansas state employee, had made a sexual advance toward her when she went to his hotel room. She was not fired, so she could not sue on that basis, but she felt she was entitled to pursue a harassment claim. Whether her sexual harassment claim was strong or not, her lawsuit had to be dealt with.

Clinton sought to delay the legal proceeding, asserting that his official duties precluded a person from suing him for incidents outside his official duties. Although heard in lower court, the case was of such a nature that it would inevitably be appealed to the U.S. Supreme Court, which unanimously ruled that Clinton's special status did not preclude the Jones litigation from being heard while he was in office. Clinton had delayed the legal proceedings beyond his first term and reelection campaign, but he had to face the issue in his second term.

As the litigation progressed, Clinton faced a deposition, or questioning under oath. This meant that if Clinton made deliberately untrue statements material to the case in the deposition, it might be grounds for a felony conviction for perjury. The Jones lawyers had heard that Clinton had recently had a sexual relationship with Monica Lewinsky, a 24-year-old intern at the White House. Lewinsky discussed her sexual relationship with Linda Tripp, a female coworker at the Pentagon. Tripp had secretly tape-recorded conversations with Lewinsky, providing at least circumstantial evidence that the president had sexual relations with someone other than his wife. This might not, strictly speaking, be relevant to a sexual harassment case, but such charges, if true, might tend to confirm the charges of someone alleging sexual harassment. In addition to attorneys for both sides being present, the federal judge hearing the case was listening by telephone to rule on the propriety of the questions. In the course of the deposition, the Jones attorneys asked the president if he had had sexual relations, defined in a very special and convoluted definition, with a person other than his wife. Because of the precise wording of the definition, the president believed he could give a negative answer without committing perjury, even though a negative answer would mislead the lawyers and the federal judge listening on the phone.

The Jones lawyers directly or indirectly leaked the circumstances to the press. Clinton felt obliged to go on national television to deny that he had had sexual relations with Lewinsky, an answer that was truthful only if one accepted Clinton's definition of sexual relations as being sexual intercourse—an activity that apparently did not take place.

Special prosecutor Starr then argued that Clinton committed perjury and obstructed justice by persuading Lewinsky to file a false affidavit in the Jones litigation, stating she had not had sexual relations with Clinton. Since this affidavit contradicted her comments over the telephone as secretly tape recorded by Tripp, Lewinsky faced perjury charges. Starr hoped that, facing a perjury conviction and a possible prison sentence, Lewinsky would turn on Clinton and expose him to a perjury conviction. Lewinsky then retained various attorneys who sought to obtain her immunity from prosecution before she would talk to the special prosecutor. Although the negotiations were lengthy, she finally agreed to testify before a federal grand jury. Under the circumstances, she had no choice but to describe in detail the sexual activity she had with Clinton.

When her grand jury testimony was compared with Clinton's answers in the Jones deposition, Starr argued that Clinton had committed perjury and subpoenaed him to appear before a special grand jury. Because of the special status of the president, he was allowed to answer in a videotaped proceeding.

Before beginning his grand jury testimony, Clinton read a statement acknowledging that his initial testimony was misleading and that his relationship with Lewinsky had been wrong. However, Clinton maintained he did not commit perjury, arguing that he simply declined to volunteer information in the deposition as he had a right to do. Starr was not satisfied by this answer, but Clinton stuck to this defense throughout the months to come. Starr felt that he had grounds to report to the House of Representatives that Clinton had perjured himself and engaged in obstruction of justice. After lengthy hearings, the House of Representatives voted in committee and in the full body along strict party lines to impeach Clinton for perjury and obstruction of justice.

Impeachment, similar to the word *indictment*, means a formal questioning or charging an individual with a crime, but it does not mean the individual has been convicted. Under the U.S. Constitution, the House of Representatives may vote impeachment by a simple majority vote. Given that the Republicans had a majority in the House, they easily impeached Clinton, but they faced the difficulty of convicting him in the Senate where a two-thirds vote was required to convict since they had only a bare majority. After voluminous testimony and much acrimonious debate, the Senate voted essentially along party lines to acquit Clinton.

Public opinion polls showed that most Americans did not want Clinton impeached even though they disapproved of his actions, but the Republicans proceeded with the impeachment and trial nonetheless, perhaps hoping it would help them in the 1998 congressional elections. Any party that controls the White House for two term usually loses seats in the election held in the sixth year of their tenure—and often in very large numbers. One would have expected the Clinton scandal to make the situation even worse for the Democrats. However, the Democrats gained seats in the 1998 elections, something that happened only once before in U.S. history—in 1834, a century and a half earlier.

This stunning reversal of expectations can be attributed only to the reaction against the Republicans for the impeachment effort. While the public opinion polls showed Clinton had high negative ratings for his personal life, the same polls showed that the voters approved of Clinton's job performance. The polls also showed that the American people were strongly opposed to the impeachment effort. This reversal of the normal voting pattern suggests that the voters took their opposition to impeachment out on the Republican candidates for the House and Senate.

Clinton's last two years in the presidency were comparatively peaceful. However, in the closing days of his administration, Clinton granted pardons and commuted sentences for a large number of people who had been convicted of crimes. Some of these were perhaps understandable if questionable. Clinton pardoned his half-brother, Roger, of a drug conviction after Roger Clinton had served his sentence. Clinton also pardoned Susan McDougal, who had gone to jail rather than give negative—and, she said, fabricated—testimony against Clinton under pressure from Special Prosecutor Ken Starr. However, some of the pardons and commutations appear to have been given in return for large legal fees paid to Clinton's brother-in-law for intervention on behalf of the pardoned individuals. Clinton also pardoned Marc Rich, a fugitive from justice, who was convicted of fraudulent stock transactions and tax evasion. There was only a very weak legal justification for this. Clinton was further criticized since he had received large campaign contributions and donations to his presidential library from Marc Rich's former wife, who continued to have some kind of continuing financial relationship to Rich himself. These events on Clinton's last day in office finally led to a serious decline in his presidential approval ratings, which had remained high throughout all the other controversies of his administration.

Clinton and his wife moved to New York State, which his wife represented in the U.S. Senate, and he retired to write his autobiography, for which he was said to be paid $10 million, the highest sum ever paid for presidential memoirs.

Further Reading

Birnbaum, Jeffrey. *The Madhouse.* New York: Times Books, 1996.

Campbell, Colin, and Bert Rockman. *The Clinton Presidency: First Appraisals.* Chatham, N.J.: Chatham House, 1996.

Campbell, James E. *Cheap Seats: The Democratic Party's Advantage in U.S. House Elections.* Columbus: Ohio State University Press, 1996.

Ceaser, James W., and Andrew E. Busch. *Losing to Win: The 1996 Elections and American Politics.* Lanham, Md.: Rowman & Littlefield, 1997.

"Clinton, William Jefferson." Available online. URL: http://www.whitehouse.gov/history/presidents/bc42.html. Downloaded on October 20, 2001.

Dionne, E. J., Jr., and William Kristol, eds. *Bush V. Gore: The Court Cases and the Commentary.* Washington, D. C.: Brookings, 2001.

Drew, Elizabeth. *On the Edge: The Clinton Presidency.* New York: Simon & Schuster, 1994.

———. *Showdown: The Struggle between the Gingrich Congress and the Clinton While House.* New York: Simon & Schuster, 1996.

Maraniss, David. *First in His Class.* New York: Simon & Schuster, 1994.

Morris, Dick. *Behind the Oval Office.* New York: Random House, 1997.

Stephanopoulos, George. *All Too Human: A Political Education.* Boston: Little, Brown, 1999.

Weaver, R. Kent. *Ending Welfare as We Know It.* Washington, D. C.: Brookings, 2000.

Woodward, Bob. *The Agenda: Inside the Clinton White House.* New York: Simon & Schuster, 1994.

Colfax, Schuyler

(1823–1885) *vice president, Speaker of the House, representative*

Schuyler Colfax was the Speaker of the House of Representatives and the vice president under President ULYSSES S. GRANT. His career was ruined by the Crédit Mobilier scandal in the 1870s.

Colfax was born on March 23, 1823, in New York City and moved to Indiana in 1836. He was a newspaper writer who began his political career in a variety of local appointed offices, such as auditor and clerk. At the age of 22, he bought a part interest in a South Bend, Indiana, newspaper and became an editor. He gradually transformed that paper into a leading Whig newspaper in the northern section of the state.

A year before he bought the newspaper, he made campaign speeches for HENRY CLAY, the leading Whig candidate of the day. Colfax did not seek elected office in his own name until 1851, when he ran and lost a race for the U.S. House of Representatives as a Whig. Since the Whig party was already showing the strains over slavery that would destroy it in just a few years, Colfax became a Republican. Starting in 1855, he won seven straight terms in the U.S. House of Representatives as a Republican.

While the friends of Colfax urged President ABRAHAM LINCOLN to name him postmaster general, Lincoln decided that he ought to remain in the House of Representatives since he was a young man with a promising career there.

By 1863, Colfax was elected Speaker of the House, in which office he was a strong supporter of the political rights of African Americans. President Ulysses S. Grant selected him to be his vice presidential running mate in 1868, and Colfax served as Grant's vice president during his first term. While Speaker of the House, Colfax was involved in the Crédit Mobilier scandal, which became public only after he was vice president. The Crédit Mobilier construction company received huge federally subsidized contracts to help build the Union Pacific Railroad. However, the arrangement fraudulently allowed a few stockholders to pocket the money without the company doing any work. In a failed attempt to head off a congressional investigation, the company had officials pay off key politicians, including Colfax, with blocks of stock in the company. Colfax was allowed to finish his term on grounds that the scandal occurred before he became vice president, but he was so tarnished by it that he never held public office again. He withdrew from public life and died on January 13, 1885.

Further Reading

Hollister, Ovando James. *Life of Schuyler Colfax.* New York: Funk & Wagnalls, 1886.

"Schuyler Colfax" in *The Presidency A to Z: Second Edition,* edited by Michael T. Nelson. Washington, D. C.: Congressional Quarterly Press, 1998.

Smith, Willard H. *Schuyler Colfax: The Changing Fortunes of a Political Idol.* Indianapolis: Indiana Historical Bureau, 1952.

Conkling, Roscoe

(1829–1888) *senator, representative*

Roscoe Conkling was well known for developing the patronage policies of the Republican Party after the Civil War. As the head of the so-called Stalwart faction, his career was marred by allegations of corruption in patronage matters.

Conkling was born on October 30, 1829, in Albany, New York. He went to school briefly at Mount Washington Collegiate Institute in New

York City, but after studying law, he was admitted to the New York bar in 1850.

At the age of 21, he was appointed district attorney for Albany and became the mayor of Utica in 1858. He was elected to Congress in 1859, served until 1863, was out of Congress from 1863 to 1865, and then returned for two years from 1865 to 1867.

Conkling supported the Radical Republicans on plans for a harsh Reconstruction program for the South after the Civil War. When President AN-DREW JOHNSON resisted those plans, Conkling supported Johnson's impeachment. He took control of the New York Republican Party in 1867, was elected to the U.S. Senate in that year, and was reelected twice in 1873 and 1879.

Conkling believed that patronage was the key to maintaining the Republican Party, since it was still new in national politics. He tightly controlled New York's Republican Party federal patronage during the administration of President ULYSSES S. GRANT. This patronage became so tainted with corruption that reformers, such as Maine's Republican Senator JAMES GILLESPIE BLAINE, sought to purge corrupt patronage officeholders from the party. Conkling became the leader of the faction known as the Stalwarts; Blaine became the leader of the Half-Breeds.

Since Grant ended his second term with his administration under the cloud of corruption, he did not seek a third term in 1876. RUTHERFORD BIRCHARD HAYES was nominated and won. Although Hayes came into the presidency as the result of a controversial election, he was a man of great personal integrity and was determined to root out corruption. Conkling tried to convince Hayes to allow him to continue to control federal patronage in New York, but Hayes had little in common with Conkling. Hayes further incensed him by supporting civil service reform and initiating an investigation of the New York City customs house headed by Conkling crony, future President CHESTER ALAN ARTHUR. When Arthur refused to cooperate with Hayes's investigation, Hayes fired him. With that, the struggles between the Stalwarts and the Half-Breeds verged on open warfare. Hayes kept his promise to serve only one term, leading to an open race in 1880.

Conkling and the Stalwarts supported the nomination of former President Grant for an unprecedented third term, but Grant was passed over and JAMES ABRAM GARFIELD won instead. The badly disappointed Stalwarts were forced to settle for Chester Arthur as vice president. Conkling disliked Garfield but thought he could intimidate him. Early in the Garfield administration, Conkling insisted that if the Half-Breed Blaine was going to be secretary of state, then the secretary of the treasury should be a Stalwart. Garfield could not accept Conkling's candidate for treasury but offered Conkling some other appointments, which Conkling stubbornly refused. Conkling then persuaded his supporters to boycott the administration.

At this point, Blaine persuaded Garfield to nominate William H. Robertson to be the customs collector of the Port of New York, the post that controlled 90 percent of the customs receipts for the United States and the post that Chester Arthur had been forced out of during the Hayes administration. Since Robertson was a Conkling foe, the battle was now joined. Conkling furiously protested Garfield's decision and demanded that the Senate uphold him on grounds of personal privilege belonging to senators, known as senatorial courtesy. Conkling was sure he would win since senatorial courtesy had been absolute before that time, but Garfield stubbornly insisted that an office collecting 90 percent of the nation's customs revenue ought to be under the control of a president's administration rather than be the personal fiefdom of one senator. The other senators were generally in favor of senatorial courtesy but were concerned that only one of them, Conkling, was controlling too much of the money. They came to see that they might do better to back Garfield, so Conkling lost. Conkling then resigned from the U.S. Senate in 1881, foolishly believing that the New York State legislature would simply reappoint him. However, national events turned against Conkling. On July 2, 1881, a disappointed office seeker assassinated Garfield, and patronage was in disrepute. Chester Arthur succeeded to the presidency, but he did an about-face and endorsed civil service reform. Civil service reform was an idea whose time had come, and Conkling's reputation for patronage at its worst led the New York legislature to appoint someone else. His political career was over, and he lived in quiet retirement until his death on April 18, 1888.

Further Reading

"Conkling, Roscoe" in *Congress A to Z: Third Edition,* edited by David R. Tarr and Ann O'Connor. Washington, D.C.: Congressional Quarterly, 1999.

Brigham, Johnson. *Blaine, Conkling and Garfield: Reminiscence and a Character Study.* New York: G. E. Stechert, 1970.

Chidsey, Donald Barr. *The Gentleman from New York: A Life of Roscoe Conkling.* New Haven, Conn.: Yale University Press, 1935.

Hernon, Joseph Martin. *Profiles in Character: Hubris and Heroism in the U.S. Senate—1789–1990.* Armonk, N.Y.: M. E. Sharpe, 1997.

Jordan, David M. *Roscoe Conkling of New York: Voice in the Senate.* Ithaca, N.Y.: Cornell University Press, 1971.

Coolidge, Calvin
(1872–1933) *president, vice president, governor*

Looking back at two generations of activist presidents, it is hard to appreciate that Calvin Coolidge best represented the idea that the president should be the passive head of a very limited government. Coming to power after the death of President WARREN GAMALIEL HARDING, Coolidge was granted a long honeymoon in office by the public. Coolidge was popular because he gave the impression of integrity just as the corruption of the Harding administration came to light after Harding's death. However, gaining the confidence of the congressional leaders took some time.

Calvin Coolidge was born on July 4, 1872, in Plymouth Notch, Vermont. He grew up there and attended a private school in nearby Ludlow, Vermont. He then attended Amherst College in Massachusetts, graduating in 1895. By 1905 he had moved to Massachusetts where he passed the bar and began raising his family.

Although he claimed to wish to do nothing more than be a shop owner like his father, Coolidge seemed to be drawn into politics. In 1898, he served as an unpaid city councilman. In 1905, he suffered his only electoral defeat when he lost a race for school committeeman. By 1906, he had been elected to the Massachusetts House of Representatives. After serving two terms as mayor of North Hampton, Massachusetts, he won a seat in the state senate and quickly moved up to the office of president of the senate in 1913. Coolidge more fully moved into the public spotlight when he ran for lieutenant governor in 1915. His statewide exposure and his image as an honest, frugal conservative Republican captured the popular imagination in Massachusetts. He was easily reelected in 1917 and moved up to the governor's office in 1918.

During his term as governor, the Boston police officers went out on strike. Under state law, public employees, such as police officers, lost their jobs by striking. The police officers were convinced that Coolidge would reinstate them in order to maintain domestic harmony, but they did not realize that Coolidge would stick to his conservative philosophy. Coolidge refused to rehire the officers, saying that he believed that there was no right to strike against public safety. His statement, "There is no right to strike against the public safety by anybody, anywhere, any time" delivered in a telegram to the president of the American Federation of Labor made him instantly famous.

Although Coolidge was afraid his strong stand against the police would ruin him, that stand catapulted him into national fame. He was easily reelected in 1918 and then promoted as a presidential candidate in 1920. He did not succeed in winning the presidential nomination, but he was the perfect choice for vice president to balance the ticket with Warren Harding. He was spontaneously nominated over Wisconsin senator Irvine Lenroat on the first ballot.

After the Harding-Coolidge ticket won the election, Coolidge served quietly in what started out as a successful administration—at least until scandals began to emerge shortly before Harding's death in 1923. When Harding died, no Hollywood screenwriter would have dared to write a script as quaint as the actual circumstances surrounding Coolidge's taking of the oath of office as president. Coolidge was fishing with his father at a cabin in a remote corner of Vermont when a telegraph messenger rode a bicycle to the cabin to give him the news that President Harding had died and that Coolidge was now the president. Coolidge was sworn in as president by his father, who held no higher office than that of a notary public in Vermont. The swearing in was conducted by the light of an oil lamp after midnight on August 2, 1923.

The simplicity of his swearing in seemed a fitting symbol for his presidency, which was characterized by honesty, integrity, frugality, and passivity. In the wake of the Harding scandals, these were seen as very positive attributes. He dismissed those cabinet members involved in the scandals as the scandals came to light, and he defended the Republican Party against charges of its complicity. He was able to regain the public's confidence in the Republican administration. He also succeeded in dominating the Republican Party machinery sufficiently to be nominated for a full term in June 1924.

In July, Coolidge suffered a personal tragedy when his younger son, Calvin, Jr., died of blood poisoning as the result of an injury received while playing on the lawn of the White House. In spite of the tragedy, Coolidge soldiered on defeating the Democratic presidential nominee, John W. Davis, and the Progressive Party nominee, ROBERT MARION LA FOLLETTE, in the general election. His opponents exhausted themselves decrying the scandals and the other failings of the administration, but Coolidge's equanimity and the evident prosperity in the country led to an easy victory.

During his second term, Coolidge achieved his major legislative goals—limited as they were for such a passive president. Coolidge had retained the best of Harding's cabinet members, and his administration was untouched by scandal. Secretary of the Treasury Andrew Mellon and Secretary of Commerce HERBERT CLARK HOOVER were especially helpful in pushing Coolidge's domestic program through Congress.

Becoming president after the death of President Warren Harding, Calvin Coolidge gave the impression of integrity just as the corruption of the Harding administration became public. *(Library of Congress)*

Coolidge reduced the national debt and lowered income tax rates. The combined impact of these measures was to increase the amount of money available for consumer spending, and this contributed to the prosperity of the mid-1920s.

The agricultural sector was unfortunately left behind in this general economic upsurge. Coolidge did support some limited cooperative proposals to attempt to solve farm problems and supported the expansion of services available from the Department of Agriculture, but he successfully blocked enactment of the McNary-Naugen legislation that would have allowed the sale of discounted farm surpluses in overseas markets to raise domestic prices. Coolidge opposed its cost as well as its price fixing characteristics. The failure of American farms to share in the general prosperity meant that the farm crisis would be far more severe during the next decline in the business cycle—the Great Depression.

Boosting consumer spending without limiting business excesses also contributed to the Great Depression. This failure limited the success of Coolidge's otherwise sound domestic policies. His administration supported the orderly development of aviation, the regulation of the broadcast industry, the augmentation of waterways, increased flood control, and the expansion of Commerce Department services, positive steps—but clearly insufficient—to meet the growing problem of corporate irregularities during the excessive boom that led to the depression.

Coolidge's foreign policy seemed on the whole successful while he was in office, but it, too, contained the seeds of problems that would only be seen much later. Coolidge restored diplomatic relations with Mexico that had been terminated during the THOMAS WOODROW WILSON administration and eased around a difficult situation that developed over the recognition of the new government of Nicaragua and restrictions on oil rights and the Catholic Church in Mexico. In some respects, Coolidge anticipated the Good Neighbor policy of FRANKLIN DELANO ROOSEVELT. This modest success was not duplicated in the larger world scene. He failed to obtain Senate permission for the United States to join the World Court and Anglo-British cooperation for another round of disarmament. His administration's highly touted success—the Kellogg-Briand Pact of 1928 renouncing war as an instrument of national policy—was to become a symbol of American simpleminded foolishness when the international crises of the 1930's developed.

Coolidge moderated the immediate problem of German reparations with the Dawes Plan to attempt to make German payments manageable, and he negotiated a reduction in the interest payments owed to the United States by the victors in World War I. However, again, these steps were mere palliatives that did nothing to relieve the underlying problems that would explode in the Great Depression. He tidied up another issue left over from the First World War when he released the remaining political prisoners convicted under the Wilson administration's Sedition Act.

The nation did not initially appreciate how devastated Coolidge had been by the death of his younger son in 1924 and they were shocked when he announced he did not wish to run for reelection in 1928. The people came to understand that his rather simple man was grieving greatly at the death of his son and so they accepted his wish to retire from politics.

Coolidge retired to his modest home in Northampton, Massachusetts, and died of a heart attack on January 5, 1933.

Further Reading

"Coolidge, Calvin." Available on line. URL: http://www.whitehouse.gov/history/presidents/cc30.html. Downloaded on October 20, 2001.

Coolidge, Calvin. *The Autobiography of Calvin Coolidge.* New York: Cosmopolitan, 1929.

Ferrell, Robert H. *The Presidency of Calvin Coolidge.* Lawrence: University Press of Kansas, 1998.

Fuess, Claude Moore. *Calvin Coolidge, The Man from Vermont.* Westport, Conn.: Greenwood Press, 1976.

McCoy, Donald R. *Calvin Coolidge: The Quiet President.* Lawrence: University Press of Kansas. 1988.

Murray, Robert K. *The Politics of Normalcy: Governmental Theory and Practice in the Harding-Coolidge Era.* New York: Norton, 1973.

White, William Allen. *A Puritan in Babylon: The Story of Calvin Coolidge.* Norwalk, Conn.: Easton Press, 1986.

Cox, James Middleton
(1870–1957) *candidate for president, representative, governor*

James Cox capped his long political career by running as a Democrat for president in 1920. He ran a very energetic campaign but was defeated at a time when almost no Democrat could have won.

Born on March 31, 1870, in Jacksonburg, Ohio, James Middleton Cox came from a family so poor that he was unable to afford to go to college. Nonetheless, he educated himself well enough on his own to become a schoolteacher. This education also served him nicely when he chose to be a newspaper reporter. He made a name for himself by discovering a host of things that he found "astounding." With this optimistic point of view, he was nicknamed "Astounding Cox." While some critics ridiculed him for this, Cox's optimism was popular, for he became editor and then publisher of several Ohio papers estimated to be worth several million dollars.

By the time he was 38 years old in 1908, he had made so much money that he could afford to run for Congress, and he was elected to the first of two terms as a Democrat in the U.S. House of Representatives. In 1912, he successfully ran in the Ohio gubernatorial race. As Ohio's governor he became a champion for the rights of labor and other reforms. Although the conservatives defeated him in 1914, he bounced back with strong victories in 1916 and 1918.

"Astounding Cox" then proceeded to astound everyone by winning the 1920 Democratic presidential nomination on the 44th ballot after days of deadlock. The optimist Cox chose as his running mate was future President FRANKLIN DELANO ROOSEVELT, whose highest political office at that point was only as an assistant secretary of the navy.

These two optimists set off on a campaign remarkable for more than just its optimism in the face of certain defeat. Cox and Roosevelt not only defended domestic progressivism but supported internationalism. They urged the United States to join the League of Nations in the face of a public mood that wished to abandon international responsibilities and simply enjoy a return to peace after World War I.

President WARREN GAMALIEL HARDING captured the national mood much better in his campaign to return to what he called "normalcy." Startled—one might even say astounded—by his overwhelming defeat in both the popular and Electoral College counts, Cox returned home and never reentered politics.

After Franklin Roosevelt was elected president, he honored Cox by naming him to serve as a U.S. delegate to the World Monetary and Economic Conference in 1933, his only public service after the 1920 campaign. He had a long retirement before his death on July 15, 1957.

Further Reading

Babson, Roger Ward. *Cox: The Man.* New York: Brentano's, 1920.

Cebula, James E. *James M. Cox: Journalist and Politician.* New York: Garland, 1985.

Cox, James M. *Journey through My Years.* New York: Simon & Schuster, 1946.

Hernon, Joseph Martin. *Profiles in Character: Hubris and Heroism in the U.S. Senate—1789–1990.* Armonk, N.Y.: M. E. Sharpe, 1997.

Curtis, Charles
(1860–1936) *vice president, senator, representative*

Charles Curtis is the highest-ranking person of Native American descent in American history. Not only did he have a distinguished political career of more than 35 years in the U.S. Congress, but he also served a four-year term as vice president under President HERBERT CLARK HOOVER from 1929 to 1933.

Born on January 25, 1860, in North Topeka, Kansas, Curtis was part Kaw Indian on his mother's side. Curtis attended Indian reservation mission schools as well as public schools. He was admitted to the Kansas bar after having studied law. By the time he was 24 he was serving as the Shani County (Kansas) attorney, a position he held for four years.

In 1892, Clark was elected to the U.S. House of Representatives as a Republican and remained there until he was elected to the Senate in 1907. He failed to be reelected in 1912, but he succeeded in wresting a Republican nomination away from the incumbent Kansas Senator Joseph Bristow in 1914. Curtis easily won the general election later that year.

For 15 years, from 1914 until 1929, Curtis served in the Senate. While some of his critics considered him mediocre, he had a reputation as a conciliator among his colleagues in the Senate. He was named Republican Senate majority leader in 1924.

Curtis tried to win a Republican nomination for president in his own right in 1928. When that failed, he accepted the vice presidential nomination offered to him by Hoover. Curtis was 73 years old when he finished his vice presidential term in 1933. He retired from politics and died on February 8, 1936.

Further Reading

"Charles Curtis" in *The Presidency A to Z: Second Edition,* edited by Michael T. Nelson. Washington, D.C.: Congressional Quarterly Press, 1998.

Ewy, Marvin. *Charles Curtis of Kansas, Vice President of the United States.* Emporia: Kansas State Teachers College, 1961.

Seitz, Don Carlos. *From Kaw Teepee to Capitol: The Life Story of Charles Curtis, Indian.* New York: Frederick A. Stokes Company, 1928.

Unrau, William E. *Mixed-Bloods and Tribal Dissolution: Charles Curtis and the Quest for Indian Identity.* Lawrence: University Press of Kansas, 1989.

D

Daschle, Thomas
(1947–) *Senate minority leader, senator*

Tom Daschle became the Senate Democratic majority leader in 2001 as the result of a Republican senator leaving the party to become an independent. Daschle served as majority leader with one of the slimmest majorities in the history of the Senate.

Born in Aberdeen, South Dakota, on December 9, 1947, Thomas Daschle attended college at South Dakota State University where he received his bachelor's degree in 1969. Four years later, he began working as a field coordinator for South Dakota's Senator James Abourzek. He later moved up to become the chief legislative aide.

In 1976, Daschle was elected to the U.S. House of Representatives from the first congressional district of South Dakota. He was reelected in 1978 and in 1980. When South Dakota lost one of its congressional seats as a result of the 1980 U.S. census, he ran for and won the remaining at-large congressional seat in 1982. He was reelected in 1984. This district required Daschle to campaign throughout the state and gave him an advantage in any future race for a statewide office, such as governor or U.S. senator.

In 1986, Daschle ran for the U.S. Senate and was elected to a six-year term. He was reelected in 1992 and in 1998. Because of his extraordinary skills as a conciliator, he was selected to be the Democratic minority leader in 1995.

In the 2000 election year, the presidential election was so close that neither party had an advantage in the congressional elections, which ended in a virtual draw. In the Senate, the result produced an exact 50–50 split. Since the Republicans won the presidency, the Republican vice president Dick Cheney cast the tie-breaking vote to allow the Republicans to organize the Senate, thereby giving them control of the majority leader's office and majority control on each of the committees. However, the conservative Republicans assumed that they did not need to compromise with more moderate members of the Senate from their party, and some of these moderates felt alienated. One of them, Senator James Jeffords of Vermont, left the Republican Party in spring 2001 and became an independent. This gave the Democrats a 50–49 vote majority (with Jeffords as the lone independent) and made Daschle the new majority leader of the Senate.

In the aftermath of the terrorist attack on September 11, 2001, Daschle's office and the office of Senator Patrick Leahy of Vermont were the object of a different kind of terrorist attack when letters laced with deadly anthrax powder were mailed to them. At the same time, similar letters were mailed to various national news media offices. While the infected members of the congressional staffs were cured, several of those infected by the letters sent to the news media died, including postal workers—as well as two women with no media connection. Despite an exhaustive investigation by the Federal Bureau of Investigation (FBI) and the Central Intelligence Agency (CIA), the perpetrators had not been apprehended by the middle of 2002. However, the investigation had apparently determined that the source of the anthrax was domestic rather than foreign.

Daschle was so successful as the new majority leader in working with such a slender majority that many prominent Democrats began to discuss him as a potential Democratic presidential nominee in 2004. As the highest-ranking Democratic office-holder in the United States, Daschle was called on to be the major spokesperson for the party, but such a role has always had the potential of conflicting with the legislative demeanor that favors avoiding strong public pronouncements. When Daschle criticized the seemingly open ended nature of the war on terrorism, Republican congressional leaders attacked his patriotism. Daschle did not make further statements of that kind, and his moderate stance seemed to preserve his stature as a national leader. Daschle's success may be measured by the outpouring of attacks on him from the far right, but this did not affect his standing in mainstream politics.

Further Reading

Crowley, Michael. "Tom Daschle's Struggle to Save the Dems," *The New Republic* (March 26, 2001).

Kaiser, Robert G. "The Smiling Majority: Tom Daschle Is at the Top of the Political Game," *The Washington Post* (June 6, 2001): C1.

Mencimer, Stephanie. "Tom Daschle's Hilary Problem," *Washington Monthly*, January/February 2002. Available online. URL: www.washingtonmonthly. comfeatures/2001/02. Downloaded June 17, 2002.

Daugherty, Harry Micajah
(1860–1941) *attorney general, author*

Harry Daugherty was most notorious for the charges of abuse leveled against him in the Teapot Dome scandal and the other irregularities of the administration of President WARREN GAMALIEL HARDING. However, he is given credit for being almost prophetic in seeing how Harding would emerge as the Republican presidential nominee in 1920. It was Daugherty who accurately predicted that Harding would win the nomination of a dead-locked national convention after a decision was made in a smoke-filled room.

Born in Washington Courthouse, Ohio, on January 26, 1860, Harry Micajah Daugherty practiced law in his hometown after earning his law degree from the University of Michigan in 1881. Active in Republican Party politics from the start, he was elected to two terms in the Ohio state legislature in 1890 and 1892. He never won any additional state or federal offices, but he was active in the Ohio Republican Party when Ohio was regarded as a critical state in the election of presidents. Daugherty's influence outstripped his official public posts, for he served as the Ohio campaign chairman for WILLIAM HOWARD TAFT in both 1908 and 1912. He had previously served as an important campaign worker for WILLIAM McKINLEY in 1896.

Daugherty was an early and devoted supporter of Harding, and he was rewarded with an appointment as attorney general. A strong pro-business and antilabor conservative, he issued a broad injunction against a strike brought by railroad workers in 1922. Having alienated labor support, he became a high-profile target when the first rumors of the Teapot Dome scandal emerged. The scandal involved giving private oil companies highly beneficial leases to oil reserves on land that was supposed to be protected as a reserve for the U.S. Navy.

Daugherty used his power over the Federal Bureau of Investigation to harass the senator who had publicly denounced him over Teapot Dome. He was further accused of taking money from people who had violated the prohibition laws and improperly supervising the disposal of confiscated property from World War I.

President CALVIN COOLIDGE demanded his resignation in 1924 as these charges emerged. Three years later, Daugherty was tried on a variety of charges but was not convicted because successive juries failed to produce unanimous verdicts.

Although his political reputation was irreparably destroyed, he spent the rest of his life writing a book and attempting to prove his innocence. He died on October 12, 1941.

Further Reading

Daugherty, Harry M. *The Inside Story of the Harding Tragedy.* Freeport, N.Y.: Books for Libraries Press, repr. 1971.

Giglio, James N. *H. M. Daugherty and the Politics of Expediency.* Kent, Ohio: Kent State University Press, 1978.

Hernon, Joseph Martin. *Profiles in Character: Hubris and Heroism in the U.S. Senate—1789–1990.* Armonk, N.Y.: M. E. Sharpe, 1997.

Davis, Jefferson

(1808–1889) *secretary of war, senator, representative, president of the Confederate States of America*

Jefferson Davis is remembered for his valiant attempt to lead the Confederacy during the Civil War. Even without his service as president of the Confederacy, his career as secretary of war, U.S. senator, and member of the House of Representatives as well as his distinguished U.S. military career make him an important American political leader. Davis's long, distinguished record of public service before the Civil War far exceeds that of President ABRAHAM LINCOLN, who served only a single term in the U.S. House of Representatives before reaching the presidency.

Born on June 3, 1808, near Fairview, Kentucky, Jefferson Davis was raised in Wilkinson, Mississippi. A brilliant student, Davis attended private schools before winning an appointment to West Point at the age of 16 in 1824. Emotionally high-strung and extremely disciplined, Davis thrived in the military. When he graduated at the age of 20, he was sent to the northwestern front where he served in the Black Hawk War. He was close to his commander, General ZACHARY TAYLOR, and married Taylor's daughter. After his marriage in 1835, he left the military and went back to Briarfield, a 1,000-acre plantation he owned in Mississippi. His wife lived only three months after their return to Mississippi. Davis remarried in 1845.

Davis was strongly convinced that blacks were biologically inferior to whites and that the Bible sanctioned slavery. He also believed that slavery was mutually beneficial, with slaves benefiting greatly from the system. His slaves themselves acknowledged that he treated them very well.

In 1845, he won a seat in the U.S. House of Representatives as a Democrat, but he resigned soon after that to fight in the Mexican War where he was a hero at the Battle of Buena Vista. By 1847, the Mississippi state legislature elected him to the U.S. Senate. He supported President JAMES KNOX POLK in his expansionist policies, except that he opposed admitting California to the Union as a free state. He also opposed the Wilmot Proviso, which sought to ban slavery in any of the territories won in the Mexican War.

Along with his former father-in-law, President Zachary Taylor, Davis was skeptical of the Compromise of 1850, a package of bills including a tough fugitive slave law (favored by the South) as well as the admission of California as a free state, which he saw as a fatal blow to the South since it gave the free states two more senators than the slave states had. Davis resigned his Senate seat to try to become Mississippi's governor, but he lost. In 1852, Davis supported the successful election of Democratic presidential candidate FRANKLIN PIERCE and was named secretary of war in return.

Davis served exceptionally well as secretary of war. He improved the salaries, rules, and equipment of the military. He even tried unsuccessfully to eliminate seniority as the basis for promotion and to substitute a merit system. He also strongly supported the development of a transcontinental railway. Since he hoped the railroad would take a southern route, he worked hard to achieve the Gadsden Purchase. Whether it was a northern, central, or southern route, such a railway was possible only because Davis authorized exploration parties that surveyed the various possible routes. In line with southern interests, he supported the acquisition of Nicaragua and Cuba.

At the end of Pierce's term, Mississippi sent Davis back to the U.S. Senate where he became the leading spokesman for the South. Davis strongly supported the spread of slavery to the territories. Indeed, he thought that slave owners had a constitutional right to take their slaves anywhere in the United States—a position that meant there could be no free states. By the late 1850s, Davis had become the South's leading spokesman, but he departed from the earlier views of South Carolina's former Senator JOHN CALDWELL CALHOUN. Davis did not believe in nullification. Rather, he was convinced the United States was a compact of sovereign states. While no single state could nullify the terms of the compact, any state could secede.

Davis opposed STEPHEN ARNOLD DOUGLAS, a fellow Democrat, for president in 1860, and he supported JOHN CABELL BRECKINRIDGE for president after the Democrats split. When ABRAHAM LINCOLN won, Davis knew that secession—now favored by most southerners—would likely mean war, so he struggled hard, but fruitlessly, to find a compromise. When Mississippi voted to secede in 1861, he dutifully resigned from the U.S. Senate and joined the Confederacy.

David hoped to be named the commander in chief of the Confederate armies, but the convention elected him president because they were unable to settle on an alternative. Davis persisted in trying to run the army and frequently clashed with his generals. Based on his experience as Pierce's secretary of war, he knew how strong the North was and how necessary it was for the South to be united under a strong government.

Jefferson Davis held several high offices in the U.S. government before becoming the only president of the Confederacy. *(Library of Congress)*

However, the nature of the Confederacy rested on its strong view of states' rights and its fear of a strong central government. Davis was in a constant struggle with other southerners who saw him as too authoritarian.

Davis was also stubborn. When southerners pressed Davis to fire his secretary of war, JUDAH PHILIP BENJAMIN, Davis complied and then appointed Benjamin to be his secretary of state, thereby further alienating some of his support in the Confederacy.

Always prone to bold, uncompromising positions, Davis would only negotiate for peace on the basis of the South continuing as a separate nation, which left no room for compromise with President Lincoln. As the confederate capital at Richmond fell, Davis tried to flee to the southern coast so he could escape to Cuba and thereby somehow stave off final defeat. However, he was arrested by federal troops as he neared the coast. He spent two harsh years in northern custody before being released. Northern authorities twice threatened him with a trial for treason—a capital offense. He was eventually released, but he was never granted a pardon, which he refused to ask for.

Davis was often berated for his conduct in the war and blamed for the defeat—often by those who did not heed his warnings about the dangers of the South's failure to unite. Eventually, the opposition softened as they observed how strongly he supported the South and how badly northerners treated him. He survived principally through the sale of *The Rise and Fall of the Confederacy*, his account of the war that was published in 1881. He lived to be 81 years old and died in 1889.

Further Reading

Allen, Felicity. *Jefferson Davis: Unconquerable Heart.* Columbia: University of Missouri Press, 1999.

Chadwick, Bruce. *The Two American Presidents: A Dual Biography of Abraham Lincoln and Jefferson Davis.* Secaucus, N.J.: Carol Publishing Group, 1999.

Davis, Jefferson. *Jefferson Davis: Constitutionalist: His Letters, Papers, and Speeches.* New York: AMS Press, 1973.

———. *The Rise and Fall of the Confederacy.* New York: D. Appleton and Company 1881. Reprint, Richmond, Va.: Garrett & Massie, 1938.

Harsh, Joseph L. *Confederate Tide Rising: Robert E. Lee and the Making of Southern Strategy.* Kent, Ohio: Kent State University Press, 1998.

Kennedy, James R. *Was Jefferson Davis Right?* Gretna, La.: Pelican Publishing Company, 1998.

Denby, Edwin
(1870–1929) *secretary of the navy, representative*

Edwin Denby is remembered as one of those accused of wrongdoing in the Teapot Dome scandal in the 1920s, but questions about his guilt and the level of his involvement still exist. It seems likely that he may have been the unfortunate victim of the scandalous acts of others.

Born in Evansville, Indiana, on February 18, 1870, Denby graduated from high school and then went to China where his father was the U.S. ambassador. He worked for 10 years in the Chinese customs service. After he returned to the United States, he earned his law degree from the University of Michigan in 1896. Denby began to practice law in Detroit in 1898, after spending two years in the U.S. Navy.

In 1903, Denby was elected as a Republican to the Michigan legislature. In 1905, he won the first of three consecutive terms in the U.S. House of Representatives. A long-term Republican, President WARREN GAMALIEL HARDING appointed him secretary of the navy in 1921. Because of Denby's rather weak credentials for the position, many people were surprised by the appointment.

As secretary of the navy, Denby had very little influence on the navy and would not be remembered at all except for his indirect involvement in the Teapot Dome scandal. This scandal involved oil company executives who sought to acquire oil belonging to the government at below market value by avoiding public bidding. The main culprits were Edward L. Doheny and Secretary of the Interior ALBERT BACON FALL, who conspired to have the navy's emergency reserve oil lands declared surplus and turned over to the Department of the Interior, which granted oil leases to favored oil companies without competitive bidding.

In order to hide their intention to sell oil leases at low prices to important oil executives, the conspirators decided that Denby should sign off on the leases as well. That appears to be the extent of his involvement. His good judgment might be questioned, but, absent other information, his participation in the fraud was far from proved.

When the scandal broke in 1924, the Senate investigators were unable to get their hands on former Secretary of the Interior Fall, who had retired from the government. Needing someone to blame, they seized on Denby and demanded that President CALVIN COOLIDGE fire him from the cabinet, but Coolidge refused. Denby protested his innocence and challenged the House of Representatives to impeach him if they had any evidence of his wrongdoing. The House did not do so, but the pressure was so great on Denby that he ultimately resigned his office in March 1924 in order to avoid embarrassing President Coolidge. Coolidge had refused to fire Denby but accepted his resignation.

Denby returned to Michigan and retired from public life. He died on February 8, 1929.

Further Reading

Davis, Margaret L. *Dark Side of Fortune: Triumph and Scandal in the Life of Oil Tycoon Edward L. Doheny.* Berkeley: University of California Press, 1998.

Stratton, David H. *Tempest over Teapot Dome: The Story of Albert B. Fall.* Norman: University of Oklahoma Press, 1998.

Noggle, Burl. *Teapot Dome: Oil and Politics in the 1920's.* Westport, Conn.: Greenwood Press, 1980.

De Priest, Oscar Stanton
(1871–1951) *representative, city council member*

Oscar De Priest, a Republican, was the first African American ever to be elected from the northern states to serve in the House of Representatives.

Born in Florence, Alabama, on March 9, 1871, Oscar Stanton De Priest moved to Kansas with his parents, who were former slaves. De Priest graduated from Salina Normal School in 1888. He then moved to Chicago where he made a fortune managing real estate. Since the Republicans under ABRAHAM LINCOLN's leadership had freed the slaves, De

Priest followed the long-standing practice of African Americans of his generation and became a Republican. However, Chicago's Southside had become a Democratic stronghold and even the African Americans became Democrats there.

Nonetheless, De Priest managed a large number of city offices because of his ability to organize and deliver the votes of other African Americans. He also showed considerable skill in playing Democratic and Republican Party factions off against one another.

De Priest became the first African American elected to the Chicago City Council in 1915. Six years later, he was appointed assistant Illinois Commerce Commissioner, a post that controlled many patronage appointments, in return for his support of a successful Republican candidate for governor.

In 1928 De Priest supported a white Republican candidate for Congress over a black Republican candidate in a primary. The white candidate died after winning the nomination, and the appropriate Republican Party committee appointed De Priest in his place. De Priest went on to win the general election for a seat in the House of Representatives.

In Congress, De Priest sponsored a number of pieces of legislation to benefit African Americans. He also traveled extensively in the South to urge African Americans to organize. Even though he was not well received in the southern states, he refused to back down or be frightened off.

Reelected to Congress in 1930, De Priest even managed to win in the face of the landslide victory of President FRANKLIN DELANO ROOSEVELT in 1932. Despite his tremendous popularity, De Priest ultimately lost in his attempt to win a fourth term in Congress to a black Democratic leader in 1934. Nonetheless, De Priest stayed active in local politics and was elected alderman for the four years from 1943 to 1947.

He retired from public life after 1947 and died on May 12, 1951.

Further Reading
Buckmaster, Henrietta. *The Fighting Congressmen: Thaddeus Stephens, Hiram Revels, James Rapier, and Blanche K. Bruce.* New York: Scholastic Book Services, 1971.
Gosnell, Harold Foote. *Negro Politicians: The Rise of Negro Politics in Chicago.* Chicago: University of Chicago Press, 1967.
Swain, Carol M. *Black Faces, Black Interests: Representation of African Americans in Congress.* Cambridge, Mass.: Harvard University Press, 1995.

Dewey, Thomas Edmund
(1902–1971) *candidate for president, governor, district attorney general, author*

As one of the few Americans ever to be nominated more than once for the presidency by a major party, Thomas Dewey is best remembered as the man who lost the upset election to President HARRY S. TRUMAN in 1948.

Thomas Edmund Dewey was born in Owosso, Michigan, on March 24, 1902. At the age of 21, he graduated from the University of Michigan and then moved to New York, where he studied at Columbia University law school, graduating in 1925. Hard working and precocious, Dewey was appointed the chief assistant U.S. attorney for the southern district of New York when he was only 28 years of age.

When Dewey was 33, the Democratic New York governor Herbert H. Lehman appointed him a special prosecutor for the elimination of organized crime. Dewey was so successful that only two years later he was elected district attorney for New York County.

He received national recognition for his prosecution of underworld figures, particularly the infamous organization Murder, Inc. In 1938, Dewey sought to parlay his fame into election as governor of New York. He failed by a narrow margin but clearly signaled that he was a force to be reckoned with in New York Republican politics.

Successfully elected governor in 1942, Dewey set his sights on being elected president of the United States. Throughout his years as governor, his main focus was on winning the presidency. In 1944, he captured the Republican nomination for president, but he faced the most formidable vote getter in American history, President FRANKLIN DELANO ROOSEVELT. Dewey lost, but he seemed like an odds-on favorite to win the election for president four years later.

When President Roosevelt died in office in 1945, Vice President Harry S. Truman assumed the office. Truman initially seemed unable to master the job, and Dewey thought he should be able to win the presidency easily in 1948. The Republican Party was anxious to win the presidency since they had been out of national executive leadership since 1932. Dewey was clearly the front-runner, but he faced primary challenges from Minnesota's governor Harold Stassen, who challenged Dewey in a number of primary fights.

After Dewey won the Republican nomination, he felt secure. His security was buoyed by national public opinion polls, which showed him with a long lead over Truman. However, this security turned to overconfidence, and the Dewey campaign sought the safest possible course throughout the campaign. Dewey declined to take stands on controversial issues and delivered bland speeches and press releases.

On the other hand, President Truman knew he was in a fight for his life. The Democratic Party was split, with the liberals supporting former Vice President Henry A. Wallace, who left the Democratic Party and accepted the presidential nomination of the Progressive Party, which by this time had fallen into the hands of left-wing groups apparently including Communist Party operatives.

Southern Democrats also were uncertain about Truman, who had a long record of opposing the Ku Klux Klan and supporting the civil rights of African Americans. The issue came to a head when the young mayor of Minneapolis, Minnesota, HUBERT HORATIO HUMPHREY, offered the first ever civil rights plank at a Democratic National Convention. This caused southern conservative Democrat JOHN STROM THURMOND to lead other southern Democratic delegates out of the convention to form a new political party, called the Dixiecrats.

All this disorder in the Democratic Party seemed ready-made for a Dewey victory. At the same time, Dewey did not perceive his own weakness, for many Republicans were not enthusiastic in supporting him. The polls showed a long lead for Dewey until the first of October, when most pollsters decided to avoid the expense of additional polling since they concluded Dewey had already won the election. A few pollsters who continued to poll did notice that the race was tightening but assumed that the race would never tighten enough for Truman to win. Only a single pollster who polled until Election Day concluded that the election was too close to call. On election night a number of newspapers and commentators declared Dewey was the winner. The following morning they faced the embarrassment that Harry Truman had done very well on the West Coast and had won reelection.

Although he was not elected president, Dewey was reelected governor in 1950. He compiled an excellent record in New York, for his administration was always first rate. He endorsed a large highway construction plan and pursued all government activities with efficiency. He was a strong supporter of racial and religious freedom and promoted passage of antidiscrimination legislation. He also favored the creation of a labor mediation board and called for improved unemployment and disability benefits.

He retired from the governor's office and public life in 1954. He died on March 16, 1971.

Further Reading

Beyer, Barry K. *Thomas E. Dewey: A Study in Political Leadership.* New York: Garland Publishing Company, 1979.

Dewey, Thomas E. *The Case against the New Deal.* New York: Harper, 1940.

Donaldson, Gary. *Truman Defeats Dewey.* Lexington: University Press of Kentucky, 1999.

Karabell, Zachary. *The Last Campaign: How Harry Truman Won the 1948 Election.* New York: Knopf, 2000.

Smith, Richard N. *Thomas E. Dewey and His Times.* New York: Simon & Schuster, 1982.

Stolberg, Mary M. *Fighting Organized Crime: Politics, Justice, and the Legacy of Thomas E. Dewey.* Boston: Northeastern University Press, 1995.

Dickinson, John

(1732–1808) *Revolutionary War leader, governor, colonial officeholder*

John Dickinson was an important American political leader who held high political offices both before and after the American Revolution, but he is best remembered for his writing on political matters. This earned him the reputation of "Penman of the Revolution."

Dickinson was born on November 8, 1732, in Talbot County, Maryland, but his family moved to Delaware in 1746. He studied law in Philadelphia and traveled to London to study at Middle Temple, one of the most famous British legal institutions of the day.

With this background, it was easy for him to establish a successful law practice in Philadelphia, beginning in 1757. In 1760, he was elected to the Delaware assembly (Delaware was a subunit of Pennsylvania at that time). Two years later, he was elected to the Pennsylvania legislature, where he served until 1765 and again from 1770 to 1776. His historical reputation, however, rests on his writings, which include his most famous *Letters from a Farmer in Pennsylvania to the Inhabitants of the British Colonies*, written in 1767, which turned public opinion in Britain and America against the Townshend Acts, which imposed taxes on the colonies to pay the salaries of royal officials. His *Essay on the Constitutional Power of Great Britain over the American Colonies*, written in 1774, set out the legal basis for resistance to British policy.

Dickinson served in the Continental Congress from 1774 to 1776. However, he did not sign the Declaration of Independence. Not only was Dickinson a strong conservative but also he thought it was rash for the colonies to declare independence from Great Britain without having a foreign ally to back them up. His patriotism is clearly shown in his *Address to the Inhabitants of Quebec*, its *Petitions to the King*, and, most importantly, his *Declaration . . . Setting Forth the Causes and Necessity of Their Taking up Arms*. Moreover, he hoped it would be possible to find some compromise with Great Britain. He was a patriot nonetheless, for he did fight as a brigadier general with the Delaware militia during the Revolution. While in the Continental Congress, he helped draft the Articles of Confederation. He likewise aided in drafting the U.S. Constitution during the Constitutional Convention in 1787. Although he retired from active politics in 1787, he supported the ratification of the U.S. Constitution writing a series of essays signed *Fabius*. Before that he served as president of Delaware from 1781 to 1782 and as a governor of Pennsylvania from 1782 to 1785.

Since the American Revolution was successful, it is easy to focus on those early revolutionaries who fought the Revolutionary War to its conclusion. Dickinson is particularly important since he symbolizes that large minority of Americans who were both conservatives and reluctant revolutionaries.

He died on February 14, 1808. In his home state of Pennsylvania, Dickinson College in Carlisle was chartered in 1783 and named in his honor.

Further Reading

Ahern, Gregory S. "The Spirit of American Constitutionalism: Johns Dickinson's *Fabius Letters*" in *Humanitas*, Volume XI, number 2. Washington, D.C.: National Humanities Institute, 1998.

Dickinson, John. *Letters from a Farmer in Pennsylvania to the Inhabitants of the British Colonies*. New York: Kraus, 1970.

Flower, Milton E. *John Dickinson: Conservative Revolutionary*. Charlottesville: University Press of Virginia, 1983.

Jacobson, David L. *John Dickinson and the Revolution in Pennsylvania*. Berkeley: University of California Press, 1965.

Ryn, Claes G. *Democracy and the Ethical Life*. Washington, D.C.: Catholic University of America Press, 1998.

Stille, Charles J. *The Life and Times of John Dickinson, 1732–1808*. New York: B. Franklin, 1969.

Dirksen, Everett McKinley
(1896–1969) *senator, representative*

As Senate minority leader during the Democratic administrations of the mid-1960s, Everett McKinley Dirksen was the principal spokesman for the Republican Party. He had a distinctive speaking voice, and his language style made him immediately recognizable on both radio and television, but he was most famous for switching sides on the issue of civil rights and helping pass the Civil Rights Act of 1964.

Dirksen was born on January 4, 1896, in Pekin, Illinois. Before he enlisted in the U.S. Army during World War I, he attended the University of Minnesota for three years but did not graduate.

Returning from the war, he ran successfully for local office in 1926 but was defeated when he tried to win a seat in Congress four years later. In 1932, he was elected to the U.S. House of Representatives and won reelection every two years thereafter until 1948 when he decided to retire because he thought he was losing his eyesight.

Ten months later after medical treatment improved his vision, he decided to run for the U.S. Senate. In what was a remarkable political comeback, he defeated the Democratic incumbent and took his seat in the Senate in 1951. Later that year, his daughter Joy married HOWARD HENRY BAKER, JR., the son of a congressional friend.

Although he was philosophically conservative, he had a pragmatic streak. Since this fit particularly well with the philosophy of President DWIGHT DAVID EISENHOWER, the Republicans selected Dirksen to be their minority leader and chief congressional spokesperson before the 1952 election.

After 1960 with the election of President JOHN FITZGERALD KENNEDY, Dirksen was the highest-ranking Republican official in the nation. He was so conservative that he strongly resisted the 1960s Supreme Court decisions on reapportionment and unsuccessfully sought passage of a new constitutional amendment to overturn those decisions.

He was on good terms with many southern Democratic senators who favored segregation and had himself never shown any particular interest in civil rights questions. After the Kennedy assassination and the elevation of his old friend (but political opponent) LYNDON BAINES JOHNSON to the presidency, Dirksen changed his mind. The 1964 Civil Rights Act had majority support in both houses of Congress but faced a determined filibuster by Southern segregationist senators, who might have won were it not for Dirksen. Pressured by President Johnson and by his own conviction that the civil rights revolution was an idea whose time had come, he changed sides. He carried a handful of Republican votes with him to break the filibuster, and this led to eventual passage of the 1964 Civil Rights Act.

Dirksen thereby became something of a hero to the liberals briefly, but his conservative principles meant that he opposed most welfare proposals of the Democrats, so the liberals were quickly disillusioned. During the Vietnam War he was a strong supporter of the policies of President Johnson until Johnson decided to enter into peace negotiations with the North Vietnamese. He then turned against him. Everett Dirksen died on September 7, 1969, while still serving in the Senate.

Further Reading

Dirksen, Everett McKinley. *The Education of a Senator.* Urbana: University of Illinois Press, 1998.

Dirksen, Louella. *The Honorable Mr. Marigold: My Life with Everett Dirksen.* Garden City, N.Y.: Doubleday, 1972.

MacNeil, Neil. *Dirksen: Portrait of a Public Man.* New York: World Publishing Company, 1970.

Schapsmeier, Edward L. *Dirksen of Illinois.* Urbana: University of Illinois Press, 1985.

Dole, Elizabeth Hanford

(1936–) *candidate for president, secretary of labor, secretary of transportation, author*

Elizabeth Dole was the first woman to mount a serious campaign for a major political party's presidential nomination. While she was unsuccessful in 2000, she decided to run for the U.S. Senate from North Carolina in 2002 and could be a presidential contender in the future. She served in every presidential administration from LYNDON BAINES JOHNSON through GEORGE HERBERT WALKER BUSH and has been identified as a Democrat, an independent, and a Republican throughout the years.

Elizabeth Hanford was born on July 29, 1936, in Salisbury, North Carolina. After graduating from Duke University in 1958, she spent the summer of 1959 at Oxford University. She returned to the United States where she received her master's degree in education at Harvard University in 1960 and her law degree in 1965.

By the age of 30 in 1966, she began as a staff assistant to the assistant secretary of education in the Department of Health, Education and Welfare. In 1968, she joined President Johnson's Committee on Consumer Interests as an associate director for legislative affairs.

In 1971, Hanford became a Republican so she could serve as deputy director of RICHARD MIL-

HOUS NIXON's Office of Consumer Affairs. While she held this position, she became acquainted with Senator ROBERT JOSEPH DOLE, and they were married in 1975. In 1973, Nixon appointed her to a seven-year term on the Federal Trade Commission (FTC), on which she served until 1976 when she took a leave to support her husband's campaign for vice president. After the election, Dole returned to the FTC where she served under President JAMES EARL CARTER. She resigned from the FTC in 1980 so she could campaign for her husband when he ran for president.

Dole served as the assistant for public liaison to President RONALD WILSON REAGAN from 1981 to 1983. Reagan appointed her to be the secretary of transportation in 1983. In 1987 she resigned her cabinet post to help her husband campaign for the 1988 Republican presidential nomination. Although President Bush won the Republican presidential nomination and the election in 1988, Bush appointed her secretary of labor. In 1990 Elizabeth Dole resigned from Bush's cabinet to head the American Red Cross, a position she held until she ran for president of the United States in 2000.

In September 2001, Elizabeth Dole announced that she would seek the Republican nomination for the U.S. Senate from her home state of North Carolina since long-term incumbent Jesse Helms made it known that he would not seek reelection in 2002.

Although she was a nationally known figure with clear front-runner status in the senate race, she faced opposition from seven other Republicans. One wealthy conservative Republican primary opponent, Jim Snyder, characterized Dole as the equivalent of Senator HILLARY RODHAM CLINTON for being a "carpetbagger" and having views too liberal for North Carolina. Snyder's attacks signaled that Dole would not receive a free ride to the nomination and that the more moderate views on gun control and abortion she expressed in her presidential campaign might come back to haunt her.

Dole was different from Clinton in that she was born and raised in North Carolina while Clinton had been born and raised in Illinois (not New York). Nonetheless, Dole had lived in Washington, D.C., for 30 years prior to entering the North Carolina race, and she took great pains to emphasize

all of her North Carolina roots whenever she could. She also did not emphasize her views on abortion and gun control, which differed substantially from Republican Senator Jesse Helms's, whose place she proposed to take.

Other parallels to Clinton were inescapable and for more than being one of the best-known women in America. Despite having held two cabinet posts, Dole was still best known as the spouse of her more famous husband, just as Hillary Clinton had been. She also chose to run for a senate seat previously held by a very prominent member of their respective parties in an election in which their party's hopes to maintain control of the senate were on the line in the race. National attention, not always welcome in a state contest, was inevitable.

Significantly, the national scandal over the collapse and eventual bankruptcy of Enron—previously the seventh-largest corporation in America—had already intruded into the campaign when it was revealed that Dole had had Enron's controversial former chairman, Kenneth Lay, host a fund raiser for her in Texas just a week after the terrorist attack on September 11, 2001, and just a short time before Enron collapsed. While Dole claimed to be ignorant of Enron's imminent collapse, it was a negative issue to arise so early in the campaign.

As an indication of the importance of the race, President George W. Bush had already announced that he would actively campaign for Dole in the primary and general election despite the presence of others in the Republican primary. The White House endorsement of Dole stood in sharp contrast to Bush's position in other states that he would not play favorites in a Republican primary.

Just as Senator Clinton declined to have her more famous husband campaign extensively for her—probably fearing a backlash from voters—so too Dole avoided having her husband enter the public arena in the campaign. She did not shy away from using her other national connections to advance her contention that she could do more for North Carolina than any of her opponents. She frequently pointed to her service as the head of the Red Cross and her two stints as a member of a presidential cabinet. She emphasized that she had served in a previous cabinet with Vice President

Dick Cheney and worked closely with Secretary of Defense Donald Rumsfeld. She also frequently commented that Secretary of Labor Elaine Chao had previously worked for her.

Not only did Dole have opposition in the Republican primary, but she was guaranteed opposition from the Democrats in the general election. Indeed, one of her prominent potential Democratic opponents was North Carolinian Erskine Bowles, the former chief of staff for President WILLIAM JEFFERSON CLINTON. While early polls showed her in a long lead over her seven Republican primary opponents and modestly ahead of any of the potential Democratic candidates, the race was still early and likely to tighten up as the national press and both parties made it a key race for control of the Senate in 2002.

Further Reading

Berke, Richard L. "Echoes Aside, Dole Insists She Is No Clinton." *New York Times,* April 8, 2002, A20(L), col 1.

Bumiller, Elisabeth, "Two Political Rebels Gear Up for a G.O.P. Primary in Colorado's Senate Race." *New York Times,* February 10, 2002, A24, col 4.

Dole, Robert J., and Elizabeth Dole. *Unlimited Partners: Our American Story.* New York: Simon & Schuster, 1996.

Kozar, Richard F. *Elizabeth Dole.* Philadelphia: Chelsea House, 1999.

Lucas, Eileen. *Elizabeth Dole.* Brookfield, Conn.: Millbrook Press, 1998.

Mitchell, Allison, "Enron's Many Strands: The Politics; In Commercial Elizabeth Dole is Chastised For Enron Ties." *New York Times,* February 1, 2002, C5, col. 6.

Mulford, Carolyn. *Elizabeth Dole: Public Servant.* Hillside, N. J.: Enslow, 1992.

Sanger, David E. "Bush Campaigns for Mrs. Dole in North Carolina Race." *New York Times,* February 28, 2002, A18, col. 3.

Dole, Robert Joseph

(1923–) *candidate for president and vice president, senator, representative, author*

For a quarter of a century, Robert Dole was a leading figure in the Republican Party. From 1985 until 1996, he led the Senate Republicans as either the majority or minority leader.

Robert Joseph Dole was born on July 22, 1923, in Russell, Kansas, where he went to public schools. After two years at the University of Kansas, he entered the armed forces in World War II. He was so seriously wounded in Italy that he has never regained the use of his right arm. Undeterred by this handicap, Dole completed his undergraduate degree at the University of Arizona. He returned to Kansas to earn his law degree from Washburn University in Topeka, Kansas, in 1952.

Before he graduated from law school, Dole had already been elected as a Republican to the Kansas state legislature, where he served from 1951 to 1952. He was Russell County attorney from 1953 to 1961. In 1960, he was elected to the U.S. House of Representatives from Kansas and reelected to four more terms until 1969 when he moved up to the U.S. Senate where he remained until he resigned in 1996. He held a succession of important Senate and party posts before becoming the majority leader of the Senate Republicans in 1985.

Dole was conventionally conservative, although he did endorse civil rights legislation and a few federal programs that benefited agricultural interests. This record was sufficient to make him conservative enough to win conservative votes for a national party nomination and moderate enough to run for national office. In 1976, incumbent President GERALD RUDOLPH FORD selected Dole as his vice presidential running mate. In that race, Dole helped improve the poll standings of the Ford-Dole ticket, although that improvement was insufficient to carry the ticket to victory.

In 1980 and again in 1988, Dole sought a Republican nomination for president but was unsuccessful in both tries. He served as the Senate Republican majority leader until 1996, when he finally succeeded in gaining the Republican nomination for president. That year he decided he should retire from the Senate to campaign more effectively against incumbent Democratic President WILLIAM JEFFERSON CLINTON. He was defeated anyway.

After the 1996 presidential campaign, Dole retired from politics. He continued to be a member of a prominent law firm in Washington, D.C., and became a paid spokesman and made television commercials for several businesses. While avoiding a prominent public role, he assisted in the unsuccessful presidential candidacy of his wife, ELIZABETH HANFORD DOLE and was expected to play a similar role in her race for the Senate from North Carolina. In the wake of the terrorist attack on September 11, 2001, Dole joined his earlier political opponent, former President Clinton, in a fundraising effort for the victims of the tragedy.

Further Reading

Cramer, Richard Ben. *Bob Dole*. New York: Vintage Books, 1995

Dole, Robert J., and Elizabeth Dole. *Unlimited Partners: Our American Story*. New York: Simon & Schuster, 1996.

Hilton, Stanley G. *Senator for Sale: An Unauthorized Biography of Senator Bob Dole*. New York: St. Martin's Press, 1995.

Shogan, Robert. *The Fate of the Union: America's Rocky Road to Political Stalemate*. Boulder, Colo.: Westview Press, 1998.

Thompson, Jake H. *Bob Dole: The Republicans' Man for All Seasons*. New York: Primus, 1996.

Woodward, Bob. *The Choice: How Clinton Won*. New York: Simon & Schuster, 1997.

Stephen Arnold Douglas is most famous as Abraham Lincoln's opponent in the Lincoln-Douglas debates. *(Library of Congress)*

Douglas, Stephen Arnold

(1813–1861) *candidate for president, senator, representative, state supreme court judge*

Stephen Douglas is most famous as the opponent of ABRAHAM LINCOLN in the Lincoln-Douglas debates. More than any other political figure in the 19th century, Douglas symbolized the tragedy of the national political split that led to the American Civil War. He was a compromiser and thus achieved many legislative goals. However, the divisions over slavery were so great that his attempts at compromise only made him hated by both the slave owners and the abolitionists and ultimately destroyed his career.

Born on April 23, 1813, in Brandon, Vermont, Stephen Arnold Douglas was raised in New England. He received very little formal education and studied law on his own. In 1834, he moved to Illinois and was admitted to the Illinois bar. While he

established a law practice there, he loved politics more than anything else. By 1835, he had been elected state's attorney in the first judicial district.

A Democrat, Douglas served briefly in the state legislature in 1836 and then ran for the U.S. House of Representatives in 1838. He lost, but it was a close race and the loss actually advanced his career. By 1840, he was in charge of the Democratic Party's statewide campaigns and served as Illinois secretary of state.

In 1841, he was elected to the Illinois Supreme Court, and it was this service that earned him the title "judge," a nickname he carried for the rest of his life. In 1842, he ran unsuccessfully for the U.S. Senate without resigning his seat on the Illinois Supreme Court. The following year he was elected to the U.S. House of Representatives from a newly drawn congressional district and he won reelection in 1845. In 1847, the Illinois legislature elected him to the U.S. Senate (since U.S. senators were not directly elected until 1913).

At the start of the 1850s, Douglas reached the peak of his national popularity. Always an able conciliator, he had his first success in guiding the Compromise of 1850 through the Congress. The Compromise of 1850, a package of bills that admitted California as a free state and included a tough fugitive slave law among other elements, diffused a crisis that threatened to bring on disunion in 1850. Douglas achieved widespread acclaim for his efforts in this difficult task, and he almost won the 1852 Democratic presidential nomination. After 1852, the margin for compromise in American politics had diminished. Douglas at first attempted a compromise by supporting the 1854 Kansas-Nebraska Act. To aid its passage, he espoused what he called his doctrine of popular sovereignty. Under this view, territorial settlers were to be granted their own right to determine whether they wished to live in slave or free states.

Popular sovereignty as a compromise doctrine might have worked in normal circumstances as a legitimate moderate position, but the division had grown to the point that any compromise was seen as fence straddling. Southerners supported the 1854 Kansas-Nebraska Act, because it repealed the antislavery provisions of the Compromise of 1820, but it angered northerners for the same reason. Douglas sought to win back support in the North with his opposition to the Lecompton Constitution, but he only succeeded in making southerners very angry. The Lecompton Constitution was largely fraudulent because it had been written at a convention in which antislavery people were excluded.

In 1858, Abraham Lincoln challenged Douglas to a series of seven debates in Illinois as a part of Lincoln's campaign to unseat him as the U.S. senator from Illinois. The debates made both men nationally famous because they clearly set out the arguments about slavery. Unfortunately, Douglas's compromise position became so convoluted that it was not acceptable to either the North or South. Particularly confusing was his attempt at Freeport, Illinois, to offer a doctrine that explained why the U.S. Supreme Court's Dred Scott decision did not mean that slavery could be spread to all the territories of the United States. The Freeport Doctrine,

as it became known, led to his ridicule in the North and his condemnation in the South.

The Democrats won the Illinois legislature in 1858, and they reelected Douglas to the Senate seat. However, Douglas was weakened as the battle lines were drawn for the 1860 presidential contest. Lincoln won the Republican presidential nomination and Douglas won the Democratic nomination. However, the southern Democrats broke from the northern Democrats and nominated their own candidate, JOHN CABELL BRECKINRIDGE. At the same time, a new fourth party nominated JOHN BELL of Kentucky. With the pro-slavery forces split in varying ways among the three other candidates, Lincoln—with the united antislavery forces—won the presidency.

Lincoln's election created so much fear in the South that disunion and the Civil War followed. Although Douglas had been Lincoln's opponent, he supported the Union and spoke against secession in speeches all across the country until his death on June 3, 1861.

Further Reading

Jaffa, Harry V. *Crisis of the House Divided: An Interpretation of the Issues in the Lincoln-Douglas Debates.* Chicago: University of Chicago Press, 1982.

Johannsen, Robert W. *The Frontier, the Union, and Stephen A. Douglas.* Urbana: University of Illinois Press, 1989.

———. *Stephen A. Douglas.* Urbana: University of Illinois Press, 1997.

Lincoln, Abraham. *The Complete Lincoln-Douglas Debates of 1858.* Chicago: University of Chicago Press, 1991.

Sigelschiffer, Saul. *The American Conscience: The Drama of the Lincoln-Douglas Debates.* New York: Horizon Press, 1973.

Wells, Damon. *Stephen Douglas: The Last Years, 1857–1861.* Austin: University of Texas Press, 1971.

Douglas, William Orville
(1898–1980) *associate justice of the Supreme Court, Securities and Exchange Commission chairman, author*

William O. Douglas served more years on the U.S. Supreme Court than any other individual in

American history. During his tenure he was widely perceived as the Court's most liberal member. In the late 1940s and 1950s Douglas was in the minority and often wrote stinging dissents, but he lived long enough to see most of his ideas adopted as majority positions.

The son of a poor Christian minister, William Orville Douglas was born on October 16, 1898, in Maine, Minnesota. He moved with his family to California and then Yakima, Washington. At the age of seven he was stricken with polio but recovered. He became an outdoor sports enthusiast, a hiker, and a mountain climber to rebuild his strength.

Douglas attended Whitman College and graduated in 1920. Traveling to the East, he studied law at Columbia University Law School from which he received his degree in 1925. He practiced corporate law on Wall Street for a time, but he preferred being a professor so he returned to Columbia. Douglas was soon recruited for a new program at Yale, where he took part in innovative teaching, particularly in the area of financial law.

With the coming of the Great Depression and the administration of President FRANKLIN DELANO ROOSEVELT, Douglas's advice on financial legal matters made him invaluable as a national resource. In 1936 Roosevelt appointed him to the Securities and Exchange Commission, and nine months later Douglas became its chairman.

In 1939, at 41 years of age, Douglas was appointed to the U.S. Supreme Court where he served for 36 years—longer than anyone else in U.S. history. During the early years, Douglas was often in the majority with other Roosevelt appointees on the Court. After a series of deaths and retirements in the late 1940s, President HARRY S. TRUMAN appointed members to the Court who were decidedly more conservative than the Roosevelt appointees had been. At that point, Douglas found himself frequently in the minority and began writing strong dissenting opinions. Particularly on questions of freedom of expression, Douglas often found himself allied only with Justice HUGO LAFAYETTE BLACK.

Undeterred, Black and Douglas united in the string of dissents that still stand as a monument to the defense of free speech, and their logic supports the current constitutional law on freedom of expression. After the newly elected President DWIGHT DAVID EISENHOWER appointed EARL WARREN as chief justice, the political character of the Court began to shift in the direction of Black and Douglas. While Black and Douglas were still often in the minority during the 1950s, they picked up another new ally when President Eisenhower appointed WILLIAM JOSEPH BRENNAN, JR., an associate justice. These four justices still found themselves in the minority, but their dissents took on an increasingly confident point of view. Occasionally they acquired supporters from the other more moderate members on the Court, and they were able to restrain and then gradually overturn the decisions of the Court during the era of JOSEPH RAYMOND MCCARTHY.

Douglas was a strong defender of the idea that the first 10 amendments to the United States Constitution, collectively known as the Bill of Rights, should be applied to the states as well as to the federal government even though they were originally applied only on the federal level. Douglas believed that the language of the Fourteenth Amendment meant that the Bill of Rights was incorporated and should be applied to the states so that neither the state governments nor the federal government could infringe on the rights stated in these 10 amendments. Douglas did not go as far as his colleague Hugo Black, who believed in the total incorporation of the Bill of Rights, but he certainly took an expansive view of it.

Douglas also extended freedom of expression as an absolute in dealing with pornography. Although he personally opposed pornography, he maintained there was an absolute right of free expression that limited the government's ability to control pornography. For many years, some Supreme Court justices felt it necessary to view pornographic films to decide whether they were protected free speech or unprotected obscene productions. Douglas refused to watch movies, saying that he was sure they were terrible but that it would not affect his decision not to censor them.

Douglas was also a strong defender of the rights of those accused of crime, since their rights were similarly protected by the Bill of Rights. While some justices were willing to endorse a balancing of those rights against the government's need to control, Douglas felt that the rights stood on their own and should be granted to everyone.

Douglas broke new ground with his majority opinion in the case of *Griswold v. Connecticut,* where he found that the Ninth Amendment and its unenumerated rights could be combined with rights found in the First, Fourth, and Eighth Amendments so that there was a right of privacy in the Constitution. Although the *Griswold* decision was limited to a doctor's right to provide information about contraceptives to patients, Justice HARRY ANDREW BLACKMUN used the logic of the decision in his landmark *Roe v. Wade* decision that overturned the state laws banning abortions.

Douglas strongly supported all the cases that provided civil rights for African Americans and other minorities. He also defended the rights of all citizens to be equally represented in elections for the House of Representatives and the state legislatures. On *Baker v. Carr* and the other cases of the Reapportionment Revolution, Douglas was solidly behind the principle of one person, one vote.

In poor health for his last few years, Douglas eventually retired from the Court in 1975 and died on January 19, 1980.

Further Reading

Ball, Howard. *Of Power and Right: Hugo Black, William O. Douglas, and America's Constitutional Revolution.* New York: Oxford University Press, 1992.

Douglas, William O. *An Almanac of Liberty.* Westport, Conn.: Greenwood Press, 1973.

———. *America Challenged.* Princeton: Princeton University Press, 1960.

———. *Being an American.* Freeport, N.Y.: Books for Libraries Press, 1971.

———. *The Court Years, 1939–1975: The Autobiography of William O. Douglas.* New York: Random House, 1980.

———. *Justice Douglas and Freedom of Speech.* Metuchen, N.J.: Scarecrow Press, 1980.

Duram, James C. *Justice William O. Douglas.* Boston: Twayne Publishers, 1981.

Hoyt, Edwin Palmer. *William O. Douglas: A Biography.* Middlebury, Vt.: P. S. Eriksson, 1979.

Simon, James F. *Independent Journey: The Life of William O. Douglas.* New York: Harper & Row, 1980.

Wasby, Stephen L. *"He Shall Not Pass This Way Again": The Legacy of Justice William O. Douglas.* Pittsburgh, Pa.: University of Pittsburgh Press, 1990.

Dulles, Allen Welsh
(1893–1969) *director of the Central Intelligence Agency, diplomat, author*

No person supervised American espionage activities longer than Allen Dulles, who directed, or was associated with directing, spy activities during World War I, World War II, and the cold war. Successful for most of these years, his luck ran out in the late 1950s and early 1960s when he was involved in two unsuccessful intelligence operations that ended his career.

Born on April 7, 1893, in Watertown, New York, Allen Welsh Dulles was educated at Princeton University, receiving his bachelor's degree in 1914 and his master's degree in 1916. Before World War I, he entered the U.S. Foreign Service and was assigned to Switzerland. Operating out of Bern, Switzerland, he was involved in espionage activities and controlled agents in Austria-Hungary, the Balkans, and elsewhere in Eastern Europe. At the end of the war, he was a member of the American Commission to Negotiate the Peace and helped draw the boundaries for many Eastern European countries.

After the negotiations were complete, Dulles attended George Washington University Law School and graduated in 1926, while still working at the State Department. After obtaining his law degree, he left the State Department and began his legal career with a prominent law firm. He was active in politics as an internationalist and repeatedly warned about the threat from Adolf Hitler.

With his extensive espionage experience, he was recalled to service in World War II in the new Office of Strategic Services (OSS) headed by William Donovan. Initially, he headed the New York OSS office, but he was soon sent to Bern, Switzerland, where he ran the intelligence-gathering activities behind enemy lines in Germany. His greatest apparent success was in obtaining the surrender of the Italians in World War II without prior consultation with the Soviet Union, an ally of the United States at the time. This simplified the surrender negotiations for the United States and Great Britain initially but led to hard feelings on the part of the Russians who felt their interests were betrayed.

After World War II, President HARRY S. TRU-MAN disbanded the OSS, and Dulles returned to his New York law practice. By 1947, the cold war between the United States and the Soviet Union had developed, and Truman decided there was a renewed need for spy activities. He called on Dulles to assist in drafting the legislation creating the Central Intelligence Agency (CIA). After Dulles worked part-time for three years on the project, in 1950, Truman asked him to develop the agency under the legislation he had drafted. From 1950 to 1953, Dulles was the deputy director while the agency was under direct military control.

In 1953, President DWIGHT DAVID EISEN-HOWER named Dulles the first civilian director of the CIA. Since Eisenhower also named Allen's older brother, JOHN FOSTER DULLES, secretary of state, U.S. foreign policy appeared to be a closely held, almost family, affair. The Dulles brothers had a string of early successes in matching the Soviet Union's tactics in fighting the cold war. Dulles was active in overthrowing a legitimate government in Iran in 1953 because it was pursuing a domestic and foreign policy different from that in the United States. He also had a hand in overthrowing the elected but nonaligned Guatemalan govern-ment in 1954. By 1958, Dulles's tactics were no longer as effective, and he failed to control the government in Indonesia then under the power of an independent nationalist named Sukarno.

Dulles was also heavily involved in the deci-sions to send U-2 flights over the Soviet Union. Before the development of unmanned spy satel-lites, the United States relied on aerial reconnais-sance provided by manned aircraft. In the 1950s, the most advanced of these was the U-2, a very high-altitude plane capable of flying above the range of the Soviet Union's antiaircraft batteries and missiles for many years. As the 1950s pro-gressed, the Soviet Union developed a new sur-face-to-air missile (SAM), and the U-2 became increasingly vulnerable. However, apparently be-cause the intelligence was so valuable, the risk was discounted and the flights continued until 1960.

As the time approached for a long-planned Paris Peace Conference in 1960, a U-2 flight was sent out despite the risk of its being shot down. The Soviets shot the plane down, made no public

announcement, and waited for the United States to release its routine cover story that a plane (often said to be studying the weather) was missing and presumed crashed.

When Eisenhower arrived in Paris, he issued the standard denial that the United States was spying on the Soviet Union. Eisenhower, and the world, were stunned when the Soviet Union an-nounced that the plane did not crash because of a malfunction but that Soviet forces had shot it down. They produced photographic evidence of the crashed plane, its reconnaissance equipment, and the pilot who had bailed out and failed to take the poison pill he was supposed to take if he was captured. Soviet leader Nikita Khrushchev then denounced the United States, walked out of the Paris Peace Conference, and proceeded to put the pilot, Francis Gary Powers, on trial in the Soviet Union. Convicted of spying, Powers was only re-leased when exchanged for an American-held Rus-sian spy. The entire incident was one of the most embarrassing losses for the United States in the cold war.

Dulles escaped blame for this incident, but an-other incident in 1961 ended his career. After the success of Fidel Castro in taking over the govern-ment of Cuba, Dulles participated in the develop-ment of plans—at the end of the Eisenhower administration—to overthrow Castro's govern-ment. The plan involved landing about 1,500 CIA-trained right-wing Cuban refugees on a beach in Cuba in the belief that this small group would instigate a successful uprising of the Cuban people to overthrow Castro. The plan overestimated the Cuban people's dissatisfaction with Castro and un-derestimated the power of Castro's 250,000-man army to cope with the 1,500 invaders. Dulles ap-parently knew the initial force was likely to fail, but he thought the new president, JOHN FITZGER-ALD KENNEDY, would use the failed landing as a pretext for sending in regular U.S. armed forces to overthrow Castro in a massive invasion. When the landing failed, Kennedy refused to involve the United States in a wider war, and about 1,200 of the original landing force were killed or captured. Eventually, the United States paid for the release of the captured Cuban refugees with a sizable transfer of heavy equipment to Cuba. Publicly,

Kennedy took the responsibility for the failure, but privately he let it be known that he blamed Dulles and determined that he had to go.

Under pressure, Dulles retired from public life in 1961 and died on January 30, 1969.

Further Reading

Dulles, Allen Welsh. *From Hitler's Doorstep: The Wartime Intelligence Reports of Allen Dulles, 1942–1945.* University Park: Pennsylvania State University Press, 1996.

Grose, Pete. *Gentleman Spy: The Life of Allen Dulles.* Boston: Houghton Mifflin, 1994.

Mosley, Leonard. *Dulles: A Biography of Eleanor, Allen and John Foster Dulles and their Family Network.* New York: Dial Press, 1978.

Srodes, James. *Allen Dulles: Master of Spies.* Washington, D.C.: Regnery, 1999.

Dulles, John Foster
(1888–1959) *secretary of state, U.S. ambassador, diplomat, senator, author*

John Foster Dulles had a U.S. diplomatic career of more than 50 years, but he was best known for his more than six years as President DWIGHT DAVID EISENHOWER's secretary of state during the 1950s. Dulles was a fervent anti-Communist and developed the doctrine of massive retaliation and the policy of brinksmanship in attempting to cope with the Soviet Union during the cold war.

Dulles was born on February 25, 1888, in Washington, D.C., into a family of prominent religious leaders. While he initially intended to follow in the family tradition and become a clergyman, his early experiences led him into a life devoted to diplomatic affairs. Some observers, however, see continuity between his early religious proclivities and the fervor with which he attacked Communism.

In 1907, Dulles's grandfather took him to the Hague Peace Conference, where the young man became the secretary to the Chinese delegation. These events introduced him to international affairs. After graduating from Princeton in 1908, he studied at the Sorbonne in Paris and returned to Washington, D.C., to earn a law degree from George Washington University in 1911. He began

practicing law in New York City but soon became the legal counsel to the War Trade Board in World War I. Based on his international experience, he was selected to be one of the members of the delegation headed by President THOMAS WOODROW WILSON that went to the Versailles Peace Conference at the end of World War I. After the conference, Dulles returned to New York City and became a prominent international lawyer.

In 1946, President HARRY S. TRUMAN chose Dulles as one of the bipartisan delegates to the conference that drafted the United Nations Charter, and he served there until 1948. He also served as a special adviser to the U.S. secretary of state at a series of foreign ministerial conferences from 1945 to 1947. In July 1949, New York Governor THOMAS EDMUND DEWEY appointed him to finish out a Senate term made vacant by the death of an incumbent, but he served only a few months because he was unable to win a special election held late in that year. Truman reappointed him to the U.S. delegation to the United Nations in 1950. In 1951, Truman granted him the rank of U.S. ambassador to the meetings that negotiated with the Japanese the treaty that formally ended World War II.

In 1953, Eisenhower named Dulles the secretary of state and appointed his younger brother, ALLEN WELSH DULLES, to be the first civilian director of the Central Intelligence Agency. Since these two posts are the most important in the determination of U.S. foreign policy, the Dulles brothers appeared to dominate the field throughout most of the Eisenhower administration.

Dulles was convinced that Communism, backed by the armed forces and aggressive activities of the Soviet Union, was the greatest threat to the United States. This threat was complicated by what was believed to be the massive number of men the Soviets had under arms, and it was made worse by the millions of Chinese added to the Communist empire after the fall of Chiang Kai-shek's pro-Western Nationalist government in 1949. The Korean War from 1950 to 1953 served to confirm that the Communists had both the capability and will to engage in aggression around the world.

Dulles sought to find a policy to balance the large army the Communists were believed to have and to avoid the heavy American casualties that would result from a conventional war. Further, since the Communists seemed able to seize control of governments through subversion without the direct, overt action on the part of the Russians, the United States was not equipped to fight everywhere at the same time. Dulles devised what he called a doctrine of massive retaliation, which held that the United States would regard aggression against its allies—whether external with conventional weapons or internal as the result Soviet-inspired subversion—as originating with the Soviet Union and respond with "massive retaliation," using any weapons possible, including nuclear ones.

To more carefully identify the U.S. allies, Dulles sought and negotiated a series of regional military alliances around the world that almost completely encircled the Soviet Union. Some of the alliances were the Australia, New Zealand, and United States pact (ANZUS), the Baghdad Pact or Central Treaty Organization (CENTO), and the South East Asia Treaty Organization (SEATO). Along with other smaller treaties, these pacts were modeled after the NATO alliance, which had been created during the Truman administration as a part of its "containment policy" toward the Soviet Union.

Dulles was not interested in a merely defensive posture in which the United States simply halted further aggression on the part of the Communists, and he refused to be bound by the static, defensive sounding "containment" policy. Instead, he wanted an active foreign policy that would liberate areas that had already fallen to the Communists. Hence, Dulles added to the "massive retaliation" policy the notion of liberation, or of a "rollback," of Communist possessions.

To those critics who argued that this set of policies could lead to war, Dulles made it plain that he did not intend to fight a war—at least not a major or world war. Instead, he believed that much of the Communist success had rested on a policy of intimidation or "bluff," so if the United States stood firm and showed a willingness to go to war, the Russians would back down. This required that the United States take some risks by going to the "brink of war," but Dulles though that "brinksmanship" would pay off in the long run.

Given that a part of the threat was also brought about by Communist-inspired and -supported internal subversion, Dulles, with the help of his brother Allen, proposed to counter that as well, Dulles supported his brother Allen in destabilizing a legitimate Iranian government in 1953. That government was socialistic and nationalistic (but not necessarily communist), but Dulles considered it a risk and it was overthrown. By implication, Dulles suggested this rollback had worked because a socialist government had been "rolled back" and a capitalist government reinstalled. In another rollback, Dulles also acted to overthrow a legitimate nonaligned Guatemalan government in 1954, because it was communist-influenced in his view. By 1958, these tactics were no longer as effective, and Dulles failed to control the Indonesian government then headed by an independent nationalist named Sukarno.

As for his brinksmanship tactic, it seemed successful in the truce (not a peace treaty because that has never been signed) agreed to by the North Koreans and their allies in 1953. Privately, through unofficial channels, Eisenhower and Dulles let the Communists know that the United States was prepared to use nuclear weapons if necessary to break the stalemate that had stalled the peace talks in Korea. While there may have been other reasons for the Communists to soften their stance and begin to negotiate, Dulles took this event as a validation of his policy. Eisenhower clearly used the implicit threat of nuclear weapons to break the two-year deadlock over Korea, gaining the truce agreement that the Truman administration had failed to obtain. However, when Dulles and others tried to persuade Eisenhower to use the threat of nuclear war to relieve the French garrison under siege at Dien Bien Phu in North Vietnam, Eisenhower declined to do so.

This massive retaliation policy looked better when it was enunciated in 1953 than it did later in the decade. The United States was the only country that had built an atomic bomb until 1949 when the Russians detonated one. The United States developed the hydrogen or thermonuclear bomb shortly after building the atomic bomb and maintained its monopoly until 1953 when the Soviets detonated their first thermonuclear device. For some years after that, the United States had a larger stockpile and a better delivery system, so the United States would presumably win a nuclear war, although Europe would be destroyed. As the Russian stockpile increased and their delivery systems improved, the United States became vulnerable to Russian retaliation against American cities. While the United States might still win a nuclear war, the costs would be staggering. For the United States to threaten to begin a nuclear war in response to a purely conventional attack ceased to be believable. Dulles, however, continued to make this threat implicit in his diplomacy.

The events of 1956 cast considerable doubt on the effectiveness of Dulles's policies. As a part of rolling back Communism, the United States engaged in a wide range of activities designed to encourage people in Eastern Europe to rebel against the Russians. For example, from aircraft flying over Hungary, the United States dropped medallions promoting freedom and used Radio Free Europe to encourage rebellion. In 1956, the Hungarians revolted against the native Hungarian communist rulers and selected a reform-minded moderate Communist named Frederick Nagy as their new leader. Nagy demanded that the Russians withdraw the troops they had stationed in Hungary, and the Hungarians appeared to have won their independence, if not from Communism, then at least from direct Soviet domination. After a few days, the Russians reentered Hungary with fresh troops to reconquer Hungary. The Hungarians fought back fiercely and waited anxiously for the United States to intervene, but no intervention—and no threats of nuclear attack—occurred. Whether Dulles wished to intervene or not, Eisenhower would have none of it. The risk of nuclear war was simply too great when compared with the value of Hungarian freedom.

In 1956, the nonaligned government of Egypt nationalized the Suez Canal, removing it from British and French control. Egypt promised to keep the canal open to international sea traffic, but the British and French wanted an excuse to retake the canal. They urged the Israelis to find a pretext to fight Egypt, attack across the Sinai Desert, and threaten the canal. The British and French would then invade the canal area in Egypt, presumably to protect the canal and keep it open to international shipping. The Israeli attack was so successful (and the Anglo-French forces were so slow) that the Israelis reached the canal before the Anglo-French forces did. Worse, the Egyptian resistance to the Anglo-French force was more effective than against the Israelis. The whole British-French strategy depended on speed. When their forces became bogged down, international pressure—including thinly veiled nuclear threats from the Soviet Union—grew for them to withdraw.

The British and French thought they had cleared the matter with Dulles and that they could count on the United States coming to their rescue. Dulles may have hoped that, since Eisenhower was ill, he would allow Dulles to make the decision and the United States would then help out their NATO allies. Eisenhower refused to support the Anglo-French invasion of Egypt and even threatened to use U.S. economic power to ruin the British pound if they would not withdraw. Since Britain and France were NATO allies and since the Russians had threatened them with nuclear weapons, this was a strong stand to take. However, Eisenhower perceived—apparently better than Dulles—that massive retaliation and brinksmanship had very real limits at a time when both the Soviet Union and the United States had nuclear weapons.

Eisenhower was clearly the decisive voice against the U.S. involvement in the Suez crisis. While it is true that Eisenhower was ill with a heart attack in 1956, no one suggests that he would have favored risking a major war if he were in better health. Rather, the supposition is that he would have put his foot down earlier and clearly warned the Anglo-French governments of his opposition before they became so deeply involved. Had he been in better health, he might have muted some of the more extreme statements that emanated from others in his administration during the crisis and the Hungarian revolt. After 1956, Dulles's policies of massive retaliation and brinksmanship appeared increasingly empty.

In 1959, Dulles was diagnosed with cancer and he was forced to resign for health reasons in April. He died about a month later on May 24, 1959.

Further Reading
Dulles, John Foster. *War or Peace.* New York: Macmillan, 1950.

Guhin, Michael A. *John Foster Dulles: A Statesman and His Times.* New York: Columbia University Press, 1972.

Hoopes, Townsend. *The Devil and John Foster Dulles.* Boston: Little, Brown, 1973.

Immerman, Richard H. *John Foster Dulles: Piety, Pragmatism, and Power in U.S. Foreign Policy.* Wilmington, Del.: Scholarly Resources, 1999.

———, ed. *John Foster Dulles and the Diplomacy of the Cold War.* Princeton: Princeton University Press, 1990.

Kahin, Audrey. *Subversion as Foreign Policy: The Secret Eisenhower and Dulles Debacle in Indonesia.* New York: Norton, 1995.

Marks, Frederick W. *Power and Peace: The Diplomacy of John Foster Dulles.* Westport, Conn.: Praeger, 1993.

Mosley, Leonard. *Dulles: A Biography of Eleanor, Allen and John Foster Dulles and Their Family Network.* New York: Dial Press, 1978.

Pruessen, Ronald W. *John Foster Dulles: The Road to Power.* New York: Free Press, 1982.

Ehrlichman, John
(1925–1999) *White House staff adviser*

John Ehrlichman reached the peak of his political career as the domestic affairs adviser to President RICHARD MILHOUS NIXON from 1969 to 1973. With his friend HARRY ROBBINS HALDEMAN, the White House chief of staff, he was regarded as one of the two most powerful men in Washington besides the president. At the apex of his power, he became involved in the Watergate scandal. As events unfolded, he was forced to resign, was convicted of felonies, and spent time in prison.

Born on March 20, 1925, in Tacoma, Washington, he served as a navigator on bombers in Europe in World War II. After the war, he attended the University of California at Los Angeles and graduated with a bachelor's degree in 1948. He went on to law school at Stanford University and obtained his law degree in 1951.

Moving to the state of Washington, he established his law practice in Seattle. In 1967, he became a law instructor at the University of Washington. His old friend Haldeman persuaded him to become an adviser to Richard Nixon during the 1968 presidential contest. Rising quickly in the Nixon campaign, Ehrlichman was named the domestic affairs adviser after Nixon became president. With Harry Robbins Haldeman, Nixon's chief of staff, Ehrlichman's critical job was to protect the reclusive Nixon from unwelcome visitors. Together Haldeman and Ehrlichman were often called the Berlin Wall. They also were heavily involved in highly sensitive political matters, such as the Watergate breakin, campaign dirty tricks, and the coverup.

In 1973, two members of the White House staff implicated Ehrlichman in the Watergate scandal, and he was forced to resign. In January 1975, he was convicted of conspiracy, obstruction of justice, and two counts of perjury. Ehrlichman served 18 months in a federal penitentiary in Safford, Arizona. After leaving prison, he was a writer and did volunteer legal counseling for local Indian and Hispanic groups. Ehrlichman was also a radio commentator. He died in a nursing home on February 14, 1999, of complications from diabetes.

Further Reading
Ehrlichman, John. *Witness to Power: The Nixon Years.* New York: Simon & Schuster, 1982.

Genovese, Michael A. *The Nixon Presidency.* New York: Greenwood, 1990.

Safire, William. *Before the Fall.* Garden City, N.Y.: Doubleday, 1975.

Sussman, Barry. *The Great Cover-up: Nixon and the Scandal of Watergate,* Arlington, Va.: Seven Locks Press, 1992.

Eisenhower, Dwight David
(1890–1969) *president, author*

Dwight David Eisenhower was one of the most successful military men ever elected president of the United States. He was the supreme commander of allied forces during World War II, was responsible for the massive June 6, 1944, D-Day invasion of Europe, and successfully led those troops to victory over the Axis powers—Nazi Germany and Fascist Italy. After the war, he was elected president by a comfortable margin in 1952 and reelected by landslide in 1956. He was highly popular during both terms.

Born on October 14, 1890, in Denison, Texas, Eisenhower was raised in Abilene, Kansas. After high school, he was admitted to the U.S. Military Academy at West Point from which he graduated in 1915. He remained in the United States during World War I and managed an armored vehicle training school in Pennsylvania.

His administrative skills were identified early, and he served as an assistant to General Douglas MacArthur in 1920s. Although unknown at the time, Eisenhower was sharply critical of General MacArthur for his use of excessive force in handling a demonstration of former servicemen—

Dwight David Eisenhower was the supreme commander of allied forces during World War II before he became president in 1952. *(Library of Congress)*

called Bonus Marchers—who applied for extra pensions after the start of the Great Depression. After this incident, General MacArthur was dispatched to the Philippines in the 1930s to build up Philippine military forces. Lieutenant Colonel Eisenhower accompanied him and served as his chief aide. Before World War II began, Eisenhower was recalled to the United States where he had a number of opportunities to demonstrate his administrative skills separate from those of MacArthur.

Eisenhower first gained prominence as a result of conducting very successful coordinated tank, infantry, and air support maneuvers in Louisiana in the early 1940s. Shortly thereafter promoted to brigadier general, he was brought to Washington after Pearl Harbor to serve as General George C. Marshall's assistant chief of staff. In that role, Eisenhower laid out detailed plans for the conduct of U.S. military strategy in the European theater during World War II, including an extremely complicated and detailed plan for an amphibious Allied invasion of France across the English Channel. Because of his demonstrated administrative skills, Eisenhower was selected by General Marshall to serve as the supreme commander of the Allied Expeditionary Forces in Europe during World War II. Eisenhower then directed the Allied invasions of North Africa, Italy, France, and finally Germany.

Early in his career as supreme allied commander, he took the courageous step of negotiating the surrender of the Vichy French naval forces under the command of Admiral Darlan. Because the Vichy French government was a puppet government controlled by the Germans, British and American elected political leaders would have been criticized for negotiating with Darlan. Eisenhower, by seeming to defy orders (but actually doing what the political leaders really wanted him to do), finally established his credentials as a subtle master diplomat as well as a military leader.

After World War II, Eisenhower oversaw reduction in American forces in Europe and held military posts with important foreign and diplomatic duties until he left the army in 1948 to become the president of Columbia University. Two years later, President HARRY S. TRUMAN persuaded him to become the supreme commander of the North Atlantic Treaty Organization (NATO). He resigned that post to become the Republican candidate for president in 1952.

Until 1952, Eisenhower refused to declare a political party preference and avoided taking any political stands outside of military questions. In the late 1940s, President Truman even tried to persuade him to become the Democratic nominee for president, but he declined to become involved in politics. Eisenhower probably would have stayed out of politics altogether, but several Republican Party leaders convinced him that unless he ran for the Republican presidential nomination in 1952, Republicans would select Ohio Senator Robert Taft. Since Taft was a well-known isolationist, who had opposed U.S. preparedness before World War II and continued to oppose U.S. involvement in world affairs, his views were dramatically different from Eisenhower's. Further, Taft seemed likely to win the general election since Truman had become very unpopular because of the Korean War. Eisenhower agreed to campaign for the Republican presidential nomination.

Eisenhower won a number of primary election contests, but primaries were not yet decisive for winning presidential nominations. He needed to prevail in the 1952 Republican National Convention, which was still dominated by state delegations under the control of various party leaders. He successfully maneuvered among competing candidates and emerged the winner on an early ballot. This convention turned out to be the last presidential nominating convention in the 20th century to take more than one ballot to select a nominee.

Eisenhower ran an excellent campaign, topping it with the promise that he, as a former successful military man, would go to Korea in order to bring that war to an end. He easily defeated Illinois governor ADLAI EWING STEVENSON, the Democratic presidential nominee, in the general election campaign. He received 6 million more popular votes than Stevenson and overwhelmed him 442–89 in the Electoral College.

In domestic politics, Eisenhower appeared to adopt the general Republican Party policy preference for a restrained role of the federal government in domestic affairs. He was not identified with any major legislative proposal other than the develop-

ment of the interstate highway system, which was presented as a defense proposal under the name of the "Interstate Defense Highway System." Although expensive, this program resembled public works projects long supported by both parties and did not resemble the welfare programs supported by the previous Democratic administrations. Still, Eisenhower did not roll back or discontinue the previously adopted Democratic programs, as many Republicans wanted, because he recognized their popularity. He appeared to continue the welfare state with marginal improvements but with no dramatic new initiatives. Subsequent investigation has shown that Eisenhower was a much more activist president than was recognized at the time, but he avoided taking stands on controversial domestic issues, seeking always to preserve his popularity so that he might act decisively if the need arose.

For example, Eisenhower was widely believed to oppose the U.S. Supreme Court's efforts to desegregate the public schools, but later evidence has shown that he had a proposal for integrating the public schools, which in certain respects was more activist than that adopted by the Court. His activism was hidden from public view until 1957, when Arkansas governor Orville Faubus sought to block integration of the Little Rock, Arkansas, high school. Eisenhower federalized the Arkansas National Guard and sent U.S. army paratroopers into Little Rock to prevent violence and integrate the schools.

In foreign affairs, the Eisenhower administration was generally successful. President Truman's policy of containment of the Soviet Union was continued during the Eisenhower administration, with the United States maintaining a clear military superiority over the Soviet Union and its allies. While the Soviet Union had a few spectacular space achievements in the late 1950s, these were essentially public relations stunts, and the solid military strength of the United States was never at issue.

In diplomatic policy, the Eisenhower administration seemed to be dominated by the leadership of the U.S. Secretary of State JOHN FOSTER DULLES and his brother, Central Intelligence Agency Director ALLEN WELSH DULLES. John Foster Dulles was a fervent anti-Communist who believed that the advances the Soviet Union had made in Eastern Europe and Asia should be "rolled back." Since the Russians and Chinese had large conventional armies, a conventional war to roll back Communist advances would be bloody. As an alternative, Dulles proposed to threaten the Russians with nuclear destruction. Since the United States had more nuclear weapons than the Russians, the United States would presumably win such a war. By 1953, the Russians had developed both atomic and hydrogen bombs, so even if the Russians were ultimately destroyed, they would still do a great deal of damage destroying Europe and perhaps a few cities in the United States. Since the United States was not prepared to accept such damage, Dulles intended merely to threaten war by taking confrontations to the "brink of war." Dulles soon became associated with the phrases *massive retaliation* and *brinksmanship,* policies increasingly seen as merely a bluff.

Although the policies enunciated by Dulles were administration policies, it is not clear to what extent Eisenhower personally believed in them. The record seems to indicate some skepticism on Eisenhower's part. He clearly used the implicit threat of nuclear weapons to break the two-year deadlock over Korea, gaining the truce agreement that the Truman administration had failed to obtain. However, a short time later, some of his advisers tried to persuade him to threaten to use nuclear weapons to relieve the French garrison under siege at Dien Bien Phu in North Vietnam. Eisenhower refused, saying that the United States could not conceivably use "those awful weapons" on Asians twice within a 10-year period.

Eisenhower remained leery of involvement in Southeast Asia throughout his administration, allowing no more than a handful of U.S. military advisers to be sent to Vietnam, despite pressure for greater involvement. He opposed the U.S. involvement in both the Suez and Hungarian crises in 1956. While Eisenhower was in fact suffering from a heart condition in 1956, it is doubtful that he would have favored risking a major war if he were in better health. Had his health not been an issue, he probably would have made his strong opposition more clearly known to the

Anglo-French governments before they became so deeply involved. Were it not for his illness, he might have muted some of the more extreme statements made by others in his administration during the Hungarian crisis.

Eisenhower's greatest single foreign policy setback occurred with the shooting down of the U-2 spy plane and the cancellation of the Paris Conference in 1960. Clearly, Eisenhower hoped that he might succeed with a breakthrough on arms control at the Paris Conference once he convinced Russian Premier Nikita Khrushchev that one should be held. All hopes for a breakthrough and the conference itself were destroyed by the U-2 incident.

Before the development of spy satellites in the 1960s, aerial reconnaissance required using airplanes that violated the airspace of the target countries. Antiaircraft guns, fighter planes, or missiles could shoot down airplanes that flew too low. The United States developed an extremely high altitude aircraft, the U-2, which could fly very long distances over the Soviet Union out of range of their guns, missiles, or interceptor aircraft. These U-2 planes provided valuable intelligence from reconnaissance flights over the Soviet Union and Eastern Europe throughout the 1950s. As the 1950s progressed, U-2 planes faced a growing risk that the Russians would be able to hit them with their newly developed surface-to-air missiles (SAMs).

Because the intelligence was so valuable, Eisenhower discounted the risk that the plane would be shot down and allowed one last U-2 flight in 1960. By 1960, the Russians had perfected their SAMs, shot down the plane, and waited for the standard American cover story about a weather plane being lost. As soon as Eisenhower denied that the United States was spying on the Russians, the Russians not only produced photos of the downed aircraft and displays of its photographic equipment, but also the pilot, Francis Gary Powers, who bailed out of the plane, failed to take his suicide capsule, and had been captured by the Soviets.

With the Russians prepared to put Powers on trial, President Eisenhower was ultimately forced to admit that the United States had engaged in aerial spying for years. Russian leader Khrushchev used the incident to break up the long-planned Paris Peace Conference in 1960, one of most embarrassing incidents for the United States in the cold war.

This incident not only diminished Eisenhower's legacy as president but also influenced the 1960 presidential campaign. Democratic nominee JOHN FITZGERALD KENNEDY campaigned on the theme that he would get this country going again, implying that the Eisenhower administration was at a standstill. The failed Paris Peace Conference contributed to the notion that the Eisenhower administration was falling behind. However, Kennedy also asserted that the Russians had gained a numerical advantage over the United States in the total number of intercontinental ballistic missiles (ICBMs) it possessed. While Kennedy may actually have believed that this was true, the United States had hundreds of ICBMs while the Russians had only about a dozen. This latter charge provoked one of Eisenhower's very few angry public statements when he flatly denied that he had failed to provide for the military defense of the United States.

Eisenhower suffered several illnesses while in office, including heart attacks, strokes, and an ileitis operation. He retired from the White House to a farm in Gettysburg, Pennsylvania, where he wrote his memoirs, played golf, and took up painting. He suffered another massive heart attack in 1965 but lived four more years. He died on March 28, 1969.

Further Reading

Arnold, James R. The First Domino: Eisenhower, the Military, and America's Intervention in Vietnam. New York: William Morrow, 1991.

Bowie, Robert R. Waging Peace: How Eisenhower Shaped an Enduring Cold War Strategy. New York: Oxford University Press, 1998.

Broadwater, Jeff. Eisenhower and the Anti-Communist Crusade. Chapel Hill: University of North Carolina Press, 1992.

Clarfield, Gerard H. Security with Solvency: Dwight D. Eisenhower and the Shaping of the American Military Establishment. Westport, Conn.: Praeger, 1999.

Craig, Campbell. Destroying the Village: Eisenhower and Thermonuclear War. New York: Columbia University Press, 1998.

"Eisenhower, Dwight David." Available on line. URL: http://www.whitehouse.gov/history/presidents/de34.html. Downloaded on October 20, 2001.

Greenstein, Fred I. The Hidden-Hand Presidency: Eisenhower as Leader. Baltimore, Md.: Johns Hopkins University Press, 1994.

Murray, G. E. Patrick. Eisenhower Versus Montgomery: The Continuing Debate. Westport, Conn.: Praeger, 1996.

Parmet, Herbert S. Eisenhower and the American Crusades. New Brunswick, N.J.: Transaction Publishers, 1999.

Perret, Geoffrey. Eisenhower. New York: Random House, 1999.

Pickett, William B. Dwight David Eisenhower and American Power. Wheeling, Ill.: Harlan Davidson, Inc., 1995.

Snead, David L. The Gaither Committee, Eisenhower, and the Cold War. Columbus: Ohio State University Press, 1999.

Ellsworth, Oliver
(1745–1807) *chief justice of the United States, senator, diplomat*

Oliver Ellsworth was the fourth chief justice of the United States. But he is more famous for his service in the 1787 U.S. Constitutional Convention, where he assisted in promoting the famous Connecticut Plan or Great Compromise by breaking a key deadlock. He is also known for drafting the Judiciary Act of 1789, which established the Supreme Court, the federal circuit and district courts, and the attorney general of the United States.

Ellsworth was born on April 29, 1745, in Windsor, Connecticut, into a prominent New England family. He began his advanced education at Yale, but he graduated from Princeton (then called the College of New Jersey) in 1766. He originally intended to become a clergyman but shifted over to law, studied largely on his own, and was accepted to the bar in 1771. He was very successful and soon became wealthy by his own efforts. He strongly supported the independence of the colonies from England, and he entered politics, serving in a variety of local offices and in the

Second Continental Congress from 1776 to 1783. During this time, he also became a member of the Connecticut governor's council.

Because of his excellent legal background, he served on the Second Continental Congress's court of appeals. He had a major role in overturning a Pennsylvania decision concerning the British ship *Active*. This complex case was eventually resolved by the U.S. Supreme Court as the *United States v. Peters* in 1809. After leaving the Second Continental Congress, he entered the Connecticut Supreme Court.

A determined Federalist, he supported a strong central government. He was a delegate from Connecticut to the 1787 Constitutional Convention, where he assisted Roger Sherman in devising and pushing through the Connecticut Plan or Great Compromise, which broke the deadlock that threatened to destroy the convention.

The convention was stalemated over whether the legislature should represent states as states, with each state having the same number of representatives or the same vote (popular with the small states) or having the states represented in proportion to their population (popular with the large states). The Great Compromise created a bicameral (or two-house legislature) with the Senate represented by two senators from each state and the House apportioned on the basis of population. The compromise saved the Convention and may well have been Ellsworth's greatest contribution to U.S. history.

Ellsworth contributed in other ways as well. The Connecticut legislature elected him to the Senate, and he served in the first Congress where he was the principal draftsman of the Judiciary Act of 1789. The U.S. Supreme Court was authorized in the body of the original Constitution, but it was not fully developed. The Constitution further specified that Congress would create additional courts. This seminal Judiciary Act of 1789 created 13 district courts, three circuit courts, and a six-member U.S. Supreme Court, and it laid out the detailed rules necessary to make the federal courts operational.

Ellsworth's contribution to the first Senate varied across the host of legislative matters that confronted a new nation. He drafted the Senate rules of procedure, wrote the legislation that first established the consular service, created the U.S. attorney general's office, and initiated the bill to admit North Carolina as a state. Significantly, he also served on, and made the presentation from, the joint House-Senate conference committee that drafted the final language for the first 10 amendments to the Constitution, known popularly as the Bill of Rights.

In 1796, GEORGE WASHINGTON appointed him the chief justice of the United States, and he served until ill health forced his resignation in 1800. On the Court, he tried to persuade his fellow justices that the Court would be vastly more effective if it issued *per curiam* (or single) opinions rather than the *seriatim* (or series of individual opinions) that prevailed to that point. He was not successful in this effort, but he set the stage for the compromise position effectively introduced by his successor, JOHN MARSHALL. Without Ellsworth's efforts, it would have been more difficult for Marshall to have prevailed.

Ellsworth's impact on the Court was limited not only because he was ill but also because President JOHN ADAMS prevailed on him to assist in the negotiations with the French over the undeclared naval war of 1799. He performed this duty without resigning from the Court, but this responsibility limited his service on the Court. The result of these negotiations, the Treaty of 1800, was not particularly favorable for the United States, but it did stave off a war the country was ill prepared to fight. While abroad he became very ill, resigned as chief justice, and withdrew from public service entirely upon his return to the United States.

He died on November 26, 1807.

Further Reading

Brown, William G. *The Life of Oliver Ellsworth*. New York: Da Capo Press, 1970.

Casto, William R. *The Supreme Court in the Early Republic: The Chief Justiceships of John Jay and Oliver Ellsworth*. Columbia: University of South Carolina Press, 1995.

Flanders, Henry. *The Lives And Times of the Chief Justices of the Supreme Court of the United States*. Philadelphia: Lippincott, 1855–58.

Ervin, Samuel James, Jr.
(1896–1985) *senator, representative, author*

Sam Ervin's career in politics was capped by his service as the chairman of the U.S. Senate committee investigating the Watergate scandal, but that brief experience—significant as it was—understates his long-term service to the United States as a conservative senator from North Carolina.

Samuel James Ervin, Jr., was born on September 27, 1896, in Morganton, North Carolina. He attended the University of North Carolina and then served in France in World War I. After the war, he went to Harvard Law School. He was elected to the North Carolina state legislature in 1923 and served a total of three terms over the next decade.

In 1935, Ervin became a county judge, moving up to Superior Court judge in 1937. He was elected to the U.S. House of Representatives in 1946 before being named to the North Carolina Supreme Court in 1948. In 1954, Ervin was appointed to fill a Senate vacancy in North Carolina. He proved so popular that he was reelected consistently thereafter until he decided to retire in 1974.

Sam Ervin was a strong conservative segregationist from the southern state. He consistently opposed civil rights legislation, Medicare, Model Cities, Head Start, and other social welfare legislation. However, he was regarded as a great constitutional legal scholar. He supported the 1964 Criminal Justice Act, which provided free legal counsel for poor defendants in federal criminal suits. Ervin also took a strong stand on the separation of church and state, and he opposed the 1965 constitutional amendment that attempted to restore prayer in the public schools.

As a conservative southern Democrat with years of experience on the Senate Judiciary Committee, Ervin was a logical choice to head the Senate committee investigating Watergate in 1973. He was suitably conservative so that any findings against the Nixon administration could not be attributed to ideological opposition to conservative administration. At the time, Ervin became something of a hero to liberals, but they were disillusioned when they discovered the totality of his conservative positions on a wide range of subjects.

Ervin chose not to run for reelection in 1974. He wrote books in retirement and died on April 23, 1985.

Further Reading

Clancy, Paul R. *Just a Country Lawyer: A Biography of Senator Sam Ervin.* Bloomington: Indiana University Press, 1974.

Dabney, Dick. *A Good Man: The Life of Sam J. Ervin.* Boston: Houghton Mifflin, 1976.

"Ervin, Sam. J." in *Congress A to Z: Third Edition*, edited by David R. Tarr and Ann O'Connor. Washington, D.C.: Congressional Quarterly, 1999.

Ervin, Sam J. *Preserving the Constitution: The Autobiography of Senator Sam J. Ervin, Jr.* Charlottesville, Va.: Michie, 1984.

———. *The Whole Truth: Watergate.* New York: Random House, 1980.

Stem, Thad, Jr. *Senator Sam Ervin's Best Stories.* Durham, N.C.: Moore Publishing Company, 1973.

F

Fall, Albert Bacon
(1861–1944) *secretary of the interior, senator*

Albert Fall was the first U.S. presidential cabinet officer ever to be convicted and imprisoned for a felony committed while in office. He was convicted of taking a bribe as a part of his involvement in the Teapot Dome scandal in the administration of President WARREN GAMALIEL HARDING.

Born on November 26, 1861, in Frankfurt, Kentucky, Albert Bacon Fall moved to Clarksville, Texas, 20 years later. Six years after that, Fall visited the area around La Cruces, New Mexico, on a mining expedition. He liked the area and purchased a ranch. Self-educated in the law, he built a corporate law practice for industries dealing with land development, mining, and timber.

Fall began his career as a Democrat, serving from 1892 to 1897 and from 1902 to 1904 in the New Mexico territorial legislature. He also served as a justice on the supreme court for the territory of New Mexico and served two terms as the territorial attorney general.

In 1908, Fall switched parties and became a Republican. After 1912, when New Mexico was admitted to the Union, Fall became one of its first two U.S. senators. He remained in the Senate until President Warren Harding appointed him secretary of the interior.

Early in the administration, Fall persuaded President Harding and Secretary of the Navy EDWIN DENBY to transfer to the Department of the Interior all of the oil lands held in reserve for the U.S. Navy. Fall accepted a bribe of $400,000 from Harry Sinclair and other oil executives in return for giving them drilling rights to the Teapot Dome Naval Oil Reserve lands in Wyoming.

In early 1923, conservationists forced Fall out of office because of his proposal to transfer the forestry division from the Department of Agriculture to the Department of the Interior, where he would control the U.S. timberlands. Although his activity on the oil leases was not known at the time, it became apparent after a lengthy congressional investigation in October 1923.

Under oath, Fall said that he did not receive a bribe, but eventually everyone who gave Fall the bribe confessed to the crime. In 1931, at the age of 69, he was convicted and sentenced to a year in prison. After being released from prison, he returned to private life and died on November 30, 1944.

Further Reading
Daugherty, Harry M. *The Inside Story of the Harding Tragedy.* Freeport, N.Y.: Books for Libraries Press, 1971.

Giglio, James N. *H. M. Daugherty and the Politics of Expediency.* Kent, Ohio: Kent State University Press, 1978.

Noggle, Burl. *Teaport Dome: Oil and Politics in the 1920's.* Westport, Conn.: Greenwood Press, 1980.

Stratton, David H. *Tempest over Teapot Dome: The Story of Albert B. Fall.* Norman: University of Oklahoma Press, 1998.

Farley, James Aloysius

(1888–1976) *postmaster general, national party chairman*

With a reputation for an almost perfect memory of faces and names, James Aloysius Farley excelled at personal campaigning. As such, he was the successful campaign manager for President FRANKLIN DELANO ROOSEVELT's first two gubernatorial and first two presidential campaigns in 1932 and 1936. In 1940, Farley broke with Roosevelt and ran for the presidency himself in 1940. Failing badly, he retired from politics.

James Aloysius Farley was born on May 30, 1888, in Grassy Point, New York. He grew up there and moved to New York City in 1905 to train as a bookkeeper. While there, he worked for the Universal Gypsum Company. Within seven years, he moved back to his home area and served as the township clerk for three terms from 1912–1919.

Farley's phenomenal gift for remembering names and faces and buoyant good humor carried him far in politics. By 1918, he helped ALFRED EMANUEL SMITH become governor and was named the warden for the port of New York in return for his assistance. The office of warden was discontinued in 1919, but Farley continued to work for Universal Gypsum. His political prospects were limited since Smith was not reelected governor in 1920. This was a bad year for Democrats everywhere since they were forced to run against the national trend of the landslide for Republican presidential candidate, WARREN GAMALIAL HARDING, in 1920.

Within the party, Farley moved up to the post of chairman of the Rockland County Democratic Committee. He masterminded Smith's reelection as governor and won a seat for himself in the legislature in 1922. He served only a single term before being appointed to the state athletic commission in return for his services to the Smith gubernatorial campaign. His political and business career had been sufficiently successful for Farley to leave Universal Gypsum and set up a company of his own. He subsequently made a fortune in business.

His political career was about to reach a new level when Farley was appointed the secretary of the New York State Democratic Committee. In this capacity, he became involved in the political career of Franklin Roosevelt early in 1928. Farley engineered Roosevelt's election to the office of governor of New York in 1928 and 1930. In 1930, he became chairman of the New York State Democratic Committee.

At this point, he set out on a nationwide political tour touting the benefits of Roosevelt for president. Such an effort was used since Roosevelt was unable to walk as the result of his legs having been paralyzed by polio. In this way, Roosevelt got the benefit of greater exposure.

By the time of the 1932 Democratic convention, Roosevelt was the frontrunner for the nomination. However, the Democrats were still operating under the requirement that they could only nominate a presidential candidate with a two-thirds vote. With many southerners firmly committed to Texas representative and U.S. House Speaker JOHN NANCE GARNER, Roosevelt risked being locked out of the nomination by a new dark horse who might emerge. At this point, Farley arranged a deal through Texas representative (and future House Speaker) SAMUEL TALIAFERRO RAYBURN whereby Garner would withdraw urging his supporters in Texas and California to switch to Roosevelt in return for the vice presidential nomination of Garner. While Garner ultimately regretted this deal that made him vice president, it was a brilliant move by Farley and Roosevelt, guaranteeing southern support for the Democratic presidential contest.

After securing the presidential nomination for Roosevelt in 1932, he was named Democratic National Party chairman, from which position he managed both of Roosevelt's 1932 and 1936 campaigns. In recognition of these accomplishments, President Roosevelt made Farley the U.S. postmaster general in 1933. This gave Farley a critical force in the control of patronage. He did his job well but inevitably made some enemies as there were always more applicants than jobs. Still, Farley's optimistic good humor allowed him to remain a popular figure.

Although he was a valuable source of political skill for Roosevelt, the two were never close friends. As a businessman, Farley was skeptical of many of Roosevelt's New Deal programs. Farley disliked a number of the members of President Roosevelt's "brain trust" because he doubted that they were good Democrats. Still, Farley stuck with Roosevelt hoping to receive his blessing for his own run for president in 1940, when Roosevelt would have served two full terms.

When Farley finally learned of Roosevelt's decision to seek a third term as president in 1940, ending the tradition that went back to George Washington, he broke with Roosevelt, believing he was entitled to run for president after Roosevelt had served two full terms. Farley resigned from the post of postmaster general in the cabinet.

Farley overrated his own political skills and did not appreciate that more than glad-handing was required to be elected president, especially in an age in which Roosevelt had mastered the critical new campaigning power of radio. Farley failed badly in the attempt to get the 1940 Democratic nomination. He continued as the New York State Democratic Committee Chairman from which position he also opposed Roosevelt's subsequent fourth term bid in 1944.

Failing in this effort to block Roosevelt in 1944, Farley had by now alienated too many New York Democrats to remain a successful chairman. Farley dropped out of politics and accepted a post as an executive with Coca-Cola Company. He thereafter was active only in business until he retired in 1973. He died on June 9, 1976.

Further Reading

Casey, John T., and James Bowles. *Farley and Tomorrow.* Chicago: Reilly & Lee, 1937.

Davis, Kenneth S. *FDR: Three Volumes.* New York: Random House, 1993.

Farley, James A. *Behind the Ballots: The Personal History of a Politician.* New York: Harcourt Brace, 1938.

———. *Governor Al Smith.* New York: Vision Books, Farrar, Straus & Cudahy, 1959.

———. *Jim Farley's Story: The Roosevelt Years.* New York: Whittlesey House, 1948.

McJimsey, George T. *The Presidency of Franklin Delano Roosevelt.* Lawrence: University Press of Kansas, 2000.

Morris, Jeffrey. *The FDR Way.* Minneapolis: Lerner Publications, 1996.

Newquist, Gloria W. *James A. Farley and the Politics of Victory, 1928–1936.* Los Angeles: University of Southern California, 1966.

Ferraro, Geraldine Anne

(1935–) *candidate for vice president, representative, author*

Geraldine Ferraro was the first woman to be nominated for vice president by a major political party. Less frequently recognized is that she was also the first Italian American similarly nominated. Although the Mondale-Ferraro Democratic ticket did not win, she no doubt improved the prospects for women in public service by her performance in a demanding campaign.

The daughter of Italian immigrant parents, Geraldine Anne Ferraro was born in Newburgh, New York, on August 26, 1935. She was only eight years old when her father died, a circumstance that imposed real hardships on her early years. She attended Marymount Manhattan College on scholarship and taught school after graduation in 1956. While teaching she attended Fordham University's law school at night, graduated in 1960, and was admitted to the New York bar in 1961. When she married John Zaccaro in 1960, she retained her maiden name in honor of her mother.

Initially, she practiced law part-time for 10 years while she raised her children. When her youngest child started school in 1974, she became an assistant attorney general in Queens. In 1978, she was elected to the House of Representatives and was reelected for two consecutive additional terms.

In 1984, Walter Mondale, the Democratic presidential nominee, selected her as his vice presidential running mate. As a Catholic and feminist, she worked out a compromise position on abortion generally acceptable to her constituents and appealing to a national audience. She offered moderately liberal views compatible with Mondale's campaign.

The intertwining of her campaign finances with her husband's business interests complicated her financial status. He had been involved in two questionable real estate deals, and she was forced to spend valuable campaign time defending herself in the press.

She largely retired from public office after her failed vice presidential bid, but she ran an unsuccessful campaign for the Senate in 1992. She also wrote a book on her experiences and has been a commentator on national television shows.

On June 19, 2001, Ferraro announced that she had been diagnosed with a rare form of cancer of the blood two years before, but that the disease had been in remission for several months (with her blood count normal) as the result of taking an experimental drug regime using the drug thalidomide. She came forward with this information in part to help publicize the positives of thalidomide, which had caused a string of serious birth defects in Europe in the 1950s, at which time it was given for morning sickness. While no longer approved for use by pregnant women, it was tentatively determined to be effective against some forms of cancer.

Further Reading

Breslin, Rosemary. *Gerry!: A Woman Making History.* New York: Pinnacle, 1984.

Drew, Elizabeth. *Campaign Journal.* New York: Macmillan, 1985.

Ferraro, Geraldine. *Ferraro, My Story.* New York: Bantam Books, 1985.

————. *Framing a Life: A Family Memoir.* New York: Scribner, 1998.

Katz, Lee M. *My Name Is Geraldine Ferraro: An Unauthorized Biography.* New York: New American Library, 1984.

Witt, Linda, Karen M. Paget, and Glenna Matthews. *Running as a Woman: Gender and Power in American Politics.* New York: Free Press, 1993.

Fillmore, Millard
(1800–1874) *president, vice president, representative*

Millard Fillmore made his greatest contribution to U.S. history when he threw the weight of his administration behind the Compromise of 1850, ensuring its passage and forestalling the Civil War for a decade. His opportunity to make this contribution came when he was elevated to the presidency upon the death of President ZACHARY TAYLOR. His career was marred by other compromises he made

Millard Fillmore is best known for supporting the Compromise of 1850, which staved off the U.S. Civil War for a decade. *(Library of Congress)*

at a time when politics was increasingly polarized over the issue of slavery.

Fillmore was born on January 7, 1800, in Summerhill (then called Locke), New York. Although his family was very poor, a local judge, who saw his extraordinary intelligence, ambition, and talent, aided him. With the judge's help, he studied the law and was admitted to the New York bar in 1823. He was elected to the New York legislature in 1828.

Two years later he moved to Buffalo, New York, to open a more promising practice. Joining the Whig Party, he served three more terms in the state legislature where he compiled a progressive record supporting the development of the public school system. Elected to the U.S. House of Representatives in 1832, he served there from 1833 to 1835 and again from 1837 to 1843. In 1844, he was considered as a vice presidential candidate but was not nominated. He ran for New York governor later that year but was defeated. His star began to rise again when he was elected state comptroller in 1847. In 1848, he was selected to balance the ticket with the Whig Party's presidential nominee Zachary Taylor, and the Taylor-Fillmore ticket went on to win.

Fillmore strongly believed in compromise in solving political problems, but he found that slavery was an issue about which the American people increasingly could take only uncompromising positions. With the politicians of his day, he was unable to find a long-term compromise on the question, but in 1850 Fillmore played a special role in finding a compromise that postponed the war between North and South for a decade—long enough for the North to build up its industrial strength so it could win the coming conflict.

By 1850, the lines between North and South were sharply drawn. The South wanted to preserve slavery at all costs. Southern extremists, such as JEFFERSON DAVIS, believed slavery was good for the slaves and slave owning was a constitutionally protected property right. By extension, they felt that slave owners should be able to take their slaves with them when they moved into any state or territory in the United States, and they opposed the existence of free states. The abolitionists believed slavery was bad for slaves and wrong according to moral laws higher than the U.S. Constitution. Many politicians tried to find a middle ground, but the various compromise positions became as strongly held as the extreme positions. Lines had hardened by 1850 to the degree that secession and war seemed likely.

Directly at issue was the fate of California, which had experienced such a surge of immigrants as the result of the 1849 Gold Rush that it was large enough to be a state in its own right. California was strongly inclined to be a free state and the North favored its admission as a free state. The South opposed California's admission because that meant the South would also be outvoted in the Senate (where an exact balance existed). This was important since the South had a smaller population and was already outvoted in the House of Representatives.

Northern extremists favored the Wilmot Proviso that banned slavery in any of the territories gained by the United States in the Mexican War, while the South favored unrestricted movement of slavery into the territories. Northerners favored ending slavery in the nation's capitol, Washington, D.C., and the South opposed this. The southerners wanted passage of a strong fugitive slave law, and the northerners opposed having to return escaped slaves to the South when they could be beaten or killed.

Given these divisions, any compromise would be difficult and would have to be as comprehensive as possible. The Compromise of 1850 sought to meet all these needs in one effort. California was admitted as a free state. A tough new fugitive slave law would be passed and imposed on the North. Slave trade, but not slavery itself, would be banned in the District of Columbia. The Arizona and New Mexico territories would be allowed to choose whether they would be free or slave.

There was something for everyone in the proposal, but the package satisfied no one very much. One problem was that President Taylor did not accept it and threatened to veto it. Everyone recognized that the votes were only barely there for passage and that no possibility of overriding a presidential veto existed.

A stalemate existed until Taylor died. Fillmore succeeded to the presidency, and he strongly supported the compromise. He quickly removed the members of Taylor's cabinet and named more moderate Whigs in their place. He then used all the resources of his administration to push for passage. The stalemate was broken, the Compromise of 1850 was passed and signed, and the Union was saved.

Fillmore's problems were not over, however. The tough fugitive slave law was difficult to implement. Many states passed state laws working against its effective enforcement. The South was angry with Fillmore for not enforcing the fugitive slave law more vigorously, and the North was angry with him for enforcing it as rigorously as he did. The issue clearly damaged his political reputation.

Fillmore sought the Whig Party presidential nomination in 1852, but HENRY CLAY opposed him. Since both Fillmore and Clay represented the moderate wing of the Whig Party prepared to compromise with the South, they split the moderate faction. This enabled the more radical, antislavery faction to nominate their candidate, General WIN-FIELD SCOTT. Scott went on to lose the general election to FRANKLIN PIERCE, the Democratic Party nominee.

In 1856, with the Whig Party essentially destroyed, Fillmore became a member of the Know-Nothing Party and accepted their presidential nomination. The Know-Nothing Party was distinguished by the secrecy surrounding its activities and its members' practice of answering questions about the party by saying, "I know nothing." Central to the party's existence was an antiforeigner bias, which was directed mainly at foreign-born Catholic immigrants to the United States and which garnered its main support in the northern section of the country. The Know-Nothing Party was a possible successor to the now disintegrated Whig Party, but it had to contend with the rise of another third party, the Republican Party, which had replaced the Free Soil Party and was also attractive to many former Whigs. The Republicans nominated General JOHN CHARLES FREMONT and made a very strong showing, but the Democrats won the election with Franklin Pierce. Fillmore came in a distant third, carrying only one state, and his political career was over.

Fillmore largely retired from public service and became the first chancellor of the new University of Buffalo. Although he entertained president-elect ABRAHAM LINCOLN on his journey to the White House, Fillmore opposed Lincoln's handling of the secession crisis and supported the Democratic Party nominee, General GEORGE BRINTON MCCLELLAN in 1864. He supported President ANDREW JOHNSON, however, and his moderate reconstruction policies after Lincoln's death.

Fillmore died on March 8, 1874.

Further Reading

Austerman, Wayne R. "Millard Fillmore" in *The American Presidents*, edited by Frank N. Magill, John L. Loos, and Tracy Irons-Georges. Pasadena, Calif: Salem Press, 2000.

Barre, W. L. *The Life and Public Services of Millard Fillmore.* New York: B. Franklin, 1971.

"Fillmore, Millard." Available on line. URL: http://.whitehouse.gov/history/presidents/mf13.html. Downloaded on October 20, 2001.

"Millard Fillmore" in *The American President,* by Philip B. Kunhardt, Jr., Philip B. Kunhardt III, and Peter W. Kunhardt. New York: Riverhead Books, 1999.

Grayson, Benson L. *The Unknown President: The Administration of President Millard Fillmore.* Washington, D.C.: University Press of America, 1981.

Griffis, William E. *Millard Fillmore: Constructive Statesman, Defender of the Constitution, President of the United States.* Ithaca, N.Y.: Andrus & Church, 1915.

"Millard Fillmore" in *The Presidency A to Z: Second Edition,* edited by Michael T. Nelson. Washington, D.C.: Congressional Quarterly Press, 1988.

Rayback, Robert J. *Millard Fillmore: Biography of a President.* Norwalk, Conn.: Easton Press, 1989.

Severance, Frank H. *Millard Fillmore Papers.* New York: Kraus, 1970.

Smith, Elbert B. *The Presidencies of Zachary Taylor and Millard Fillmore.* Lawrence: University Press of Kansas, 1988.

Snyder, Charles M. *The Lady and the President: The Letters of Dorothea Dix and Millard Fillmore.* Lexington: University Press of Kentucky, 1975.

Ford, Gerald Rudolph
(Leslie King, Jr.)
(1913–) *president, vice president, representative*

Gerald Ford is the only person to have served as both vice president and president without having been elected to either office. In addition, he is the only president to issue a pardon for another president. He is most often credited with helping heal the nation's wounds after the Watergate scandal, but he had few other memorable achievements.

Ford was born on July 14, 1913, in Omaha, Nebraska, and named Leslie King, Jr. Less than two years later, his mother divorced his father and moved to Grand Rapids, Michigan. After his mother remarried, Leslie was adopted by his stepfather and renamed Gerald Rudolph Ford. He was an excellent football player while at the University of Michigan, and he graduated in 1935. He was the collegiate boxing coach and assistant football coach while attending Yale University where he graduated in 1941.

Ford passed the Michigan bar exam later that year but did not get to practice law very long because World War II began. He joined the navy and was both an assistant navigator and a gunnery officer on the USS *Monterey,* an aircraft carrier that saw service in almost every major battle in the South Pacific. Ford earned 10 battle stars for his service in World War II, a remarkably high number and one that outstripped the military records of other presidents who have been regarded as military heroes.

After he left the navy in 1946, Ford joined a major law firm in Grand Rapids. In 1948, he ran for the U.S. House of Representatives as a Republican against an incumbent Republican congressman, Bartel C. Jonkman, who had a reputation as a reactionary conservative and an isolationist on international questions. Ford defeated him in the Republican primary and went on to win the general election in what was regarded as a safe Republican district. On entering the House of Representatives, he recalled that his first acquaintance was RICHARD MILHOUS NIXON with whom he formed a long-lasting political association.

As an internationalist, he supported generally the foreign policy of Democratic President HARRY S. TRUMAN, including the Marshall Plan, the Four Point Program, and increases in defense spending. As a Republican, he opposed most of Truman's domestic programs, particularly the pro-labor bills, such as minimum wage hikes and the repeal of the Taft-Hartley Act. He also supported the veto override of the McCarran-Walter Act, which contained a number of anti-Communist provisions about which Ford later became skeptical. Ford said later that he was disappointed that he did not speak out against the excesses of Senator JOSEPH RAYMOND MCCARTHY.

In 1952, Ford supported DWIGHT DAVID EISENHOWER over his rivals for the Republican presidential nomination. Following his friendship with Richard Nixon, Ford used his influence to try to keep Nixon on the ticket in 1956 and backed him for the Republican presidential nomination in 1960. His career steadily advanced in the House of Representatives, and he was named the chairman of the Republican Conference in the House in 1963. President LYNDON BAINES JOHNSON named

him, as one of only two Republicans, to the Warren Commission after the assassination of President JOHN FITZGERALD KENNEDY.

In the House, Ford compiled a conservative voting record, opposing Medicare and most of Johnson's Great Society and War on Poverty programs. He generally supported civil rights legislation for African Americans, although some civil rights leaders believe he tried to weaken some bills by amendment. His generally mainstream conservative Republican voting record stood him in good stead with his colleagues, and he was named the Republican minority leader in 1965.

Ford backed Nixon for president in 1968 and supported his administration in both foreign and domestic policy. He favored cutting back on social welfare programs and reluctantly agreed that wage and price controls were necessary after the oil-producing nations raised oil prices in the early 1970s. In foreign policy, he supported Nixon's Vietnamization program, his development of détente with the Soviet Union, and the opening of relations with the People's Republic of China.

As a part of his strong support for, and at the behest of, the Nixon administration, he attempted to impeach WILLIAM ORVILLE DOUGLAS, a liberal member of the Supreme Court. Douglas was suspected of irregularities in receiving financial support from a charity known as the Parvin Foundation, an organization said to receive some of its money from organized crime. This effort was apparently undertaken in response to the failure of the U.S. Senate to approve two of President Nixon's appointments to the Supreme Court. The rather apparent political motivation of the Douglas impeachment effort doomed its success from the outset, and Ford later said that he was sorry that he had taken part in it.

When Vice President SPIRO THEODORE AGNEW was forced to resign and pled no contest to charges of bribe taking and corruption, Nixon needed to name a new vice president under the terms of the Twenty-fifth Amendment to the U.S. Constitution. Nixon's first choice was former Texas governor John Connelly, a Democrat turned Republican, but Nixon recognized that there was insufficient support of Connelly in the Congress. The terms of the Twenty-fifth Amendment put so much power in the hands of the House of Representatives that a choice from the Congress was highly advisable. Ford became the most obvious candidate who could muster a majority vote, since both the House of Representatives and the Senate had Democratic majorities, partly because he did not seem to be a potential candidate for the presidency. Indeed, Ford promised Nixon that he would not run for president in 1976 if he were picked as vice president and served out his vice presidential term. Nixon picked Ford, and his confirmation was forthcoming in a reasonably short period of time.

Ford steadfastly defended Nixon throughout the Watergate scandal, both as a member of Congress and as vice president, but it became increasingly clear that Nixon's prospects for continued tenure were increasingly dim. A few days before Nixon resigned, ALEXANDER MEIGS HAIG, the White House chief of staff, called Ford and told him new evidence linking Nixon to the Watergate scandal was about to be released. Haig said it was so damaging that he expected Nixon would either resign or be impeached. Haig advised Ford to be ready. Nixon resigned in August 1974, and Ford assumed the presidency—the first vice president elevated to the presidency who had not been elected in the first place.

Ford was then required to select a new vice president, and he chose New York's long-term Republican governor, NELSON ALDRICH ROCKEFELLER. The period from late 1974 to January 1977 was the only time in U.S. history when both the president and vice president were unelected to their respective offices. The choice of Rockefeller, a well-known figure from the most liberal wing of the Republican Party, was problematic for Ford and may have been the result of harmful machinations carried out by former Nixon associates whom Ford retained during his presidency. Many believe Ford would have been wiser to select his own staff rather than keep the old Nixon people because it made his presidency look too much like a continuation of the Nixon years. As such, it damaged Ford's efforts to heal the nation's wounds after Watergate and Nixon's resignation.

In office, Ford set as his first objective the restoration of confidence in government. The first month was a large success with accolades from all sides and high presidential approval ratings in the polls. Had Ford selected more mainstream Republican, such as GEORGE HERBERT WALKER BUSH, as vice president and perhaps named Rockefeller a new secretary of state while naming more conservative Republican as secretary of defense, he would have fared better, especially in view of his granting a pardon to Nixon.

Part of Ford's conception of restoring confidence was the final resolution of all the issues surrounding Watergate. One remaining item of concern was the prosecution of Nixon for his role in Watergate. Since a large number of his associates had pled guilty or been convicted of felonies, the prospect that Nixon would be indicted and tried was high. Ford apparently viewed the prospect of having his staff of Republican holdovers preoccupied with gathering evidence either for or against Nixon (or both) as being too disruptive. Ford also seemed genuinely concerned for Nixon's physical and mental health, fearing a nervous breakdown or suicide as possibilities. Finally, Ford concluded that Nixon had suffered enough and granted Nixon a "full, free, and absolute pardon" for any and all of his activities while he was president, including any that might not yet have come to light. Since this pardon was granted without even a confession of guilt or admission of wrongdoing on Nixon's part and since Nixon had not actually been tried, this pardon was open to a great deal of criticism from many legal and political points of view.

Ford badly underestimated the terrible political result of this pardon. His critics immediately asserted that the pardon was part of a bargain in which Ford got to be president in return for a pardon. Some believed that the arrangement was made between Nixon and Ford directly, while others speculated that the terms may have been worked out through the White House chief of staff, Alexander Haig. Nixon, Ford, and Haig all denied that a deal was struck, but skeptics pointed out that they naturally would deny any such an arrangement. Others naturally thought it unlikely that a deal was necessary since Nixon and Ford must have known by late July that Nixon would be leaving either through resignation or impeachment, and Ford would have no reason to make a deal.

Still, the damage was done to Ford in all but his closest circle of advisers. Even Jerald terHorst, his newly named press secretary, resigned in protest. Coupled with the large number of Nixon appointees Ford retained, the albatross of Nixon and his White House was hung on Ford. In retrospect, even Ford acknowledged that his failure to win the 1976 election was the result of the pardon.

Ford inherited more than the Watergate scandal from Nixon. The economy was still reeling from the impact of the sudden rise in oil prices brought on by the renewed strength and determination of the Oil Producers and Exporters Cartel (OPEC), and both unemployment and inflation were on the rise.

To deal with inflation, Ford rejected wage and price controls like those tried in the Nixon years.

Gerald Ford was the first person appointed vice president under the Twenty-fifth Amendment and the only vice president to succeed a president who resigned the office. (Library of Congress, Official White House photo)

Instead, he used a national television address to attempt a large public relations campaign, encouraging voluntary compliance with a national goal of retarding inflation. Under the slogan, "Whip Inflation Now," this campaign was even complete with its own set of campaign buttons with the slogan shortened to the acronym, "WIN." The WIN button campaign did not whip inflation and it did not win Ford any popular support. It quickly became the butt of jokes, showing that such public relations campaigns have little impact on underlying economic realities.

Ford sought merely to ease and not to solve the unemployment problem by extending the existing unemployment benefits to 65 weeks. This assisted the unemployed but did not win him much support since the basic unemployment rate continued to stand at 9.2%. Given his conservative orientation, it was probably unrealistic to expect Ford to offer the kinds of relief that Democrats favored.

Ford did support some progressive legislation, such as $4.8 billion for mass transit to ease the U.S. dependence on foreign oil and $25 billion in federal aid to education.

Ford also supported the 1974 Federal Campaign Reform Act, which provided for public funding of presidential campaigns. This legislation was motivated by the realization that RICHARD MILHOUS NIXON had his campaign treasurer collect very large amounts of money—some of it illegal. His campaign used some of this money to pay the burglars who broke into the Democratic National Committee headquarters in what became known as the Watergate scandal.

As a conservative midwestern congressman, Ford had spent his entire public life trying to cut government spending, not only by Democratic presidents but often by Republicans as well. It would have been too much to expect that he would change upon entering the White House—the place with the power to cut spending through impoundments and the veto. The national economic recession was all the more reason for a conservative Republican to cut spending. Ford cast 48 regular vetoes in his little more than two years in the White House—a modern record for so short a time. The Democrats managed the necessary two-thirds vote to override in both houses only 12 times in those same two years. The 36 vetoes sustained cut $9.2 billion dollars and cut the rate of growth of federal spending in half. Included in those were bills that effectively killed by sustained vetoes were two social services appropriations, a jobs bill, and $7.9 billion in additional federal aid to education.

Ford planned to do more cutting in the 1976 budget. Cutting federal spending was aimed at cutting taxes, which presumably would have stimulated the economy as long as the cuts were in the hands of those wealthy enough to invest the money. Ford sponsored $28 billion in tax cuts for individuals and corporations and paid for them with $28 billion cut from existing programs. Conservative Republicans were thrilled, but this record did not have much to offer the electorate at large in a recession. Since this budget was planned for the 1976 election year, Ford found the Democratic Congress less enthusiastic than he was, and the proposal was not adopted.

Ford had even less going for him in international affairs. Nixon's Vietnamization program came down to a proposal to withdraw all U.S. troops and let the South Vietnamese go it alone. Since they had trouble going it alone before the United States committed ground troops, the prognosis was not good. In fact, one of Nixon's successors—sooner or later—was going to confront North Vietnam in control of the South. Ford was the unfortunate successor who presided over the evacuation of Saigon (the capitol of South Vietnam), removing as many Americans and U.S. South Vietnamese supporters as possible. This was not a large number. Left behind were millions of South Vietnamese and thousands of American servicemen still missing and unaccounted for.

In the wake of the fall of Saigon, another incident occurred that did Ford little good. The *Mayaguez*, a ship flying the American flag but actually foreign owned with foreign crew, was captured by Communist rebels from Vietnam's neighbor, Cambodia. Not wanting to be blamed for the loss of this ship so soon after the fall of South Vietnam, Ford gave the Cambodians a very short time in which to release the ship and crew before the United States took military action. When the Cambodians did not appear to respond affirma-

tively, Ford sent in the U.S. Marines. Unfortunately, the Marines were misinformed about the location of the *Mayaguez* and landed on the wrong island. The island was heavily defended and the Marine casualties virtually exceeded the number of crew members on the *Mayaguez*. Worse, a delay in communications meant that the Cambodian decision to return the *Mayaguez,* which had been made before the Marines landed, did not reach the White House in time to call off the attack.

In the 1976 election campaign, Ford could offer little in either foreign or domestic policy. The polls showed him vulnerable and a large number of Democrats were set to challenge him, but Ford first faced a major challenge from within his own party. Conservative California governor RONALD WILSON REAGAN mounted a serious challenge that was successful in several primary states and left Reagan only a little more than 100 votes from commanding a majority in the Republican National Convention, the closest convention fight in the last half of the 20th century and one of the closest in American history. Historically, incumbent presidents are in control of the convention. In the end, Ford had enough strength to defeat Reagan narrowly, but it was not a good omen for the general election.

The Democratic field was crowded, but the more prominent primary candidates all fell before JAMES EARL CARTER, a comparatively unknown candidate who had served only a single term as Georgia's governor. Carter actually used his lack of Washington experience as an asset, arguing that he was not a part of the national political scene that had become too corrupt. A deeply religious Southern Baptist and a farmer, Carter managed to defeat all of his better known Democratic rivals and win the Democratic presidential nomination by a wide margin. Early in the campaign, Carter also had a strong lead over Ford in the public opinion polls.

Ford had selected another moderate-to-conservative midwesterner, Kansas's senator ROBERT JOSEPH DOLE, as his vice presidential running mate, satisfying his conservative Republican base without unduly aggravating the moderates he needed to win a general election campaign. The poll margin between Ford and Carter narrowed, at least until an unfortunate event occurred in the second presidential debate held that year. In the debate, Ford responded to a question about Poland in which he asserted that Poland, a country clearly still under the domination of the Soviet Union, was not dominated by them. This improbable statement was virtually indefensible, but Ford stubbornly attempted to defend it for several days after the debate.

This contributed to the image of Ford as a bumbler. In 1975, Ford had made international news by slipping on a wet stairway while exiting Air Force One on a trip to Austria and almost falling at the feet of the Austrian chancellor. He had also once bumped his head while exiting a helicopter. Although Ford was a well-known athlete and as well or better coordinated than most men his age, the image of him as a bumbler was established in the popular mind, so his error was not simply dismissed. Rather, it served to underscore an unfavorable image that had emerged.

Ford, however, had enlisted the support of JAMES ADDISON BAKER III, someone with a strong record as a campaign manager. In the end, Ford mounted a come-from-behind campaign that almost succeeded. Ford lost the popular vote 40.3 million—38.5 million and the Electoral College by 297–240. A shift of a few thousand votes in two states would have given Ford the White House in the Electoral College even thought he would have had fewer popular votes than Carter.

Ford retired to southern California and has remained active in a variety of business and public service activities.

Further Reading

Cannon, James M. *Time and Chance: Gerald Ford's Appointment with History.* New York: HarperCollins, 1994.

"Ford, Gerald." Available on line. URL: http://www.whitehouse.gov/history/presidents/gf38.html. Downloaded on October 20, 2001.

Ford, Gerald R. *A Time to Heal: The Autobiography of Gerald R. Ford.* Norwalk, Conn.: Easton Press. 1987.

Greene, John R. *The Limits of Power: The Nixon and Ford Administrations.* Bloomington: Indiana University Press, 1992.

———. *The Presidency of Gerald R. Ford.* Lawrence: University Press of Kansas, 1995.

Hartmann, Robert T. *Palace Politics: An Insider's Account of the Ford Years.* New York: McGraw-Hill, 1980.

Hersey, John. *Aspects of the Presidency.* New Haven: Ticknor & Fields, 1980.

Howell, David. *Gentlemanly Attitudes: Jerry Ford and the Campaign of '76.* Washington, D.C.: HKJV Publications, 1980.

Randolph, Sallie G. *Gerald R. Ford, President.* New York: Walker, 1987.

Reichley, James. *Conservatives in an Age of Change: The Nixon and Ford Administrations.* Washington, D.C.: Brookings Institution, 1981.

Reeves, Richard. *A Ford, Not a Lincoln.* New York: Harcourt Brace Jovanovich, 1975.

Rozell, Mark J. *The Press and the Ford Presidency.* Ann Arbor: University of Michigan Press, 1992.

Schapsmeier, Edward L. *Gerald R. Ford's Date with Destiny: A Political Biography.* New York: P. Lang, 1989.

Frankfurter, Felix
(1882–1965) *associate justice of the Supreme Court*

Felix Frankfurter was the justice most identified with the doctrine of judicial self-restraint. His commitment to this position made him one of the most controversial justices on the Supreme Court. A well-known liberal legal activist for decades before he was named to the Court, his name struck fear in the hearts of many businessmen and conservatives. By the time he was named to the Court, the legal temperament of the times had changed. Increasingly, Frankfurter found that many liberals saw him as an obstacle to change, particularly in the areas of civil rights and civil liberties. In reality, Frankfurter's fundamental belief that the Supreme Court should exercise judicial restraint was the consistent hallmark of his legal career.

Frankfurter was born on November 15, 1882, in Vienna, Austria. He immigrated to the United States with his parents when he was 12 years old in 1894. He was an excellent student and learned English quickly. In 1902, he graduated third in his class at City College of New York; he then went to Harvard Law School where he graduated in 1906 at the very top of his class.

Frankfurter began his legal career in the U.S. Attorney's Office in New York, serving as an assistant U.S. attorney from 1906 to 1910. He also served as the legal officer in the Bureau of Insular Affairs from 1911 to 1914. When he left there, he joined the faculty of the Harvard Law School and retained that position until 1939. However, Harvard allowed him the flexibility to hold a wide variety of public posts on a part-time basis throughout those years.

During World War I, Frankfurter was legal counsel for industrial issues for the secretary of war, NEWTON DIEHL BAKER. He was also named the secretary, and later counsel, for the War Mediation Commission. By 1918, he was the chairman of the War Labor Policies Board. In these jobs, he was involved in a number of controversial strikes, often taking the side of the workers to such a degree that he incurred the wrath of conservative industrialist. But these activities did not harm his career, and people kept appointing him to ever more important positions. By 1919, he had become President THOMAS WOODROW WILSON's legal adviser at the Versailles Peace Conference in France. After the conference, he returned to Harvard. The succession of Republican administrations in the 1920s did not call on his services, but he taught a generation of students—many of whom filled high positions in the administration of President FRANKLIN DELANO ROOSEVELT.

During the 1920s, Frankfurter helped created the American Civil Liberties Union, although later his decisions often differed from what became the standard position of this organization on many issues. He helped found the liberal magazine *The New Republic* and frequently took up liberal causes. His support of Sacco and Vanzetti, who were anarchists convicted of murder during a robbery, led to his acquiring a national reputation as a strong liberal spokesman, which again angered many conservatives.

He supported President Franklin Roosevelt and his New Deal programs and was a frequent adviser to the president and others in the administration. It was hardly surprising when Roosevelt appointed him to the Supreme Court in 1939. The widespread assumption was that he would continue to advance the liberal legal agenda on the Court.

In this regard, many misunderstood Frankfurter. From the start of the 20th century until the mid-1930s, the predominant liberal legal agenda was frustrated by an activist Supreme Court majority that struck down what would be called liberal or progressive legislation passed by Congress and signed by the president. This was especially true during the Great Depression and the early Roosevelt years. This judicial activism by conservative judges frustrated popular will and led to ringing dissents by Justices OLIVER WENDELL HOLMES, JR., and LOUIS DEMBITZ BRANDEIS who called for judicial restraint. Frankfurter wholeheartedly agreed with those positions. He clearly followed the judicial restraint doctrine of Holmes, and he was an especially close friend with Brandeis.

After the mid 1930s, however, Roosevelt had appointed enough justices so that, coupled with some liberal holdovers, his positions were generally defended by a majority on the Court. This new majority now wished to be as activist as their predecessors—but in a liberal direction. Frankfurter, however, continued to see real dangers in the Court exceeding its authority and damaging the system of separation of powers set out in the U.S. constitution. This gave the appearance that Frankfurter had changed his mind and become a leader of the conservatives. In reality, Frankfurter was consistent; it was the others who changed.

Frankfurter was always a teacher, and he saw the role of the Supreme Court as that of a teacher for the lower federal courts, the state courts, and the various elected officials. Sometimes his teaching led him to give long dissertations on the law to his colleagues on the Court, none of whom would tolerate being lectured to as if they were schoolchildren. Frankfurter particularly irked Justice WILLIAM ORVILLE DOUGLAS, who often made fun of Frankfurter. Frankfurter, for his part, accused Douglas of being intellectually lazy.

Frankfurter's controversies with Justice HUGO LAFAYETTE BLACK—a frequent supporter of Douglas's positions—were still more hostile and constituted one of the most long-standing personal antagonisms on the Court. Both were appointees of Roosevelt, both opposed the extreme reactionaries who preceded them, both were liberal on the basic policy questions, but each represented a very different judicial philosophy, which was especially evident in their treatment of the Bill of Rights and the Fourteenth Amendment. Frankfurter always balanced competing rights and competing sources of law; Black took the formalist or textualist position that the text should be the essential guide whenever possible.

On the First Amendment, Frankfurter maintained the right of free speech had to be balanced against society's interest, which naturally included the value of the free exchange of ideas but did not raise individualism to an absolute value. Black, on the other hand, looked at the language of the text and concluded that, when the framers said, "Congress shall make no law . . . abridging freedom of speech" that that is exactly what they meant. As for balancing, Black asserted that the Constitutional framers had done all the balancing that needed to be done when they set the balance entirely to the side of free and unfettered speech.

Frankfurter carefully endorsed the idea that some of the values in the Bill of Rights were incorporated by the Fourteenth Amendment and applied to the states, a view that was called "selective incorporation"; Black was convinced that the Fourteenth Amendment incorporated the Bill of Rights as a whole, or total incorporation.

The men also differed on federalism, with Frankfurter deferring to the elected representatives of the states in line with his deference to coordinate branches on the national level. Black would defer to the states on some issues but not on the key issues of civil liberties, where he was convinced that the language of the Fourteenth Amendment settled issues regarding the nationalization of the Bill of Rights. This difference showed clearly in the last major issue to divide them: the reapportionment revolution. For Black, the failure of the state legislatures to reapportion clearly violated the Fourteenth Amendment. For Frankfurter, the court's venturing into the redrawing of legislative district lines was a failure to give proper deference to elected officials, the height of judicial arrogance, overweening judicial activism, and a journey into a "political thicket" that would ultimately damage the Court. Clearly their disputes were philosophical at their core and not easy to re-

solve. However, to the credit of both men, they became reconciled to one another toward the end of their lives.

In one regard, Frankfurter failed to be completely consistent on the issue of judicial restraint. He was not restrained about giving political advice to presidents. He was a trusted adviser of Roosevelt and continued to advise him long after he joined the Court. Such behavior always runs the risk of biasing judicial judgment, and many scholars frown on Frankfurter's lack of judicial restraint in his freedom in giving political and policy advice. However, this may have been consistent with the value he placed on studying the law and teaching it to others.

Although not conventionally religious as an adult, he requested that a Jewish prayer be recited at the time of his death. Frankfurter said that he was born a Jew and wished to die as one. He supported secular Jewish causes throughout his life. As was his mentor, Justice Brandeis, he was a Zionist.

Felix Frankfurter died on February 22, 1965.

Further Reading

Baker, Leonard. *Brandeis and Frankfurter: A Dual Biography.* New York: New York University Press, 1986.

Burt, Robert. *Two Jewish Justices: Outcasts in the Promised Land.* Berkeley: University of California Press, 1988.

Dawson, Nelson L. *Louis D. Brandeis, Felix Frankfurter, and the New Deal.* Hamden, Conn.: Archon Books, 1980.

Goldstein, Leslie F. *In Defense of the Text: Democracy and Constitutional Theory.* Lanham, Md.: Rowman & Littlefield, 1991.

Hockett, Jeffrey D. *New Deal Justice: The Constitutional Jurisprudence of Hugo L. Black, Felix Frankfurter, and Robert H. Jackson.* Lanham, Md.: Rowman & Littlefield, 1996.

Lash, Joseph P. *From the Diaries of Felix Frankfurter.* New York: Norton, 1975.

Mendelson, Wallace. *Justices Black and Frankfurter: Conflict in the Court.* Chicago: University of Chicago Press, 1966.

Murphy, Bruce Allen. *The Brandeis/Frankfurter Connection: The Secret Political Activities of Two Supreme Court Justices.* New York: Oxford University Press, 1982.

Silverstein, Mark. *Constitutional Faiths: Felix Frankfurter, Hugo Black, and the Process of Judicial Decision-Making.* Ithaca, N.Y.: Cornell University Press, 1984.

Simon, James F. *The Antagonists: Hugo Black, Felix Frankfurter and Civil Liberties in Modern America.* New York: Simon & Schuster, 1989.

Urofsky, Melvin I. *Felix Frankfurter: Judicial Restraint and Individual Liberties.* Boston: Twayne, 1991.

Frémont, John Charles

(1813–1890) *candidate for president, senator, explorer*

Often called "Pathfinder of the West" for his exploits as a military explorer in the Far West, Frémont can also be considered a "Pathfinder" as the first presidential candidate of the new Republican Party in 1856.

John Charles Frémont was born on January 21, 1813, in Savannah, Georgia, and grew up in Charleston, South Carolina. After his father died in 1818, an attorney supported him with his education. Frémont entered Charleston College at age 16 and graduated two years later. In 1831, he joined the U.S. Navy.

His career took off in 1835 when he left the navy in order to become a surveyor. He earned the rank of second lieutenant in the United States Topographical Corps in 1838. In 1842, he became famous for writing a memoir of the trip he made with Kit Carson, the famous scout, as they sought to find the best way to reach Oregon.

In 1841 he married Jesse Benton, the daughter of U.S. Senator THOMAS HART BENTON, who aided his career still more. Jesse Benton also assisted by helping Frémont write his articles and memoirs. In 1843, Frémont was granted the important job of surveying the Oregon Territory, which was much larger than the current state of Oregon and comprised much of what is today the northwestern United States. After a year in the wilderness, he showed up in St. Louis in August 1844 to deliver an exciting account of his adventure. His account included scientific measurements and detailed maps.

In 1845, while Frémont was on assignment to explore Northern California, President JAMES KNOX POLK sent word that war with Mexico was about to begin. On June 14, 1846, Frémont responded by traveling to Sonoma, California, and encouraging the local American settlers there to revolt against Mexico. He then took command of what he called the Bear Flag Republic, which carried a new state flag with a picture of a grizzly bear in the center. In July 1846, Navy Commodore Robert S. Stockton sailed to California and proclaimed himself governor of what he said was a new U.S. territory called California.

At this point, there was a serious breakdown in communication within this new government. Commodore Stockton appointed Frémont the territorial governor of California, but General Stephen W. Kearney arrived, claiming dominance based on order from Washington. When Frémont refused to take orders from Kearney, he was arrested and court-martialed. His trial for disobedience and mutiny was held in Washington amid widespread publicity. Ultimately, Frémont was sentenced to dismissal from the army. President Polk later overrode the judgment against Frémont, but Frémont angrily resigned from the army anyway.

After Frémont left the army, he raised money from private donors and set out on an expedition to prove that the Sangre de Cristo and San Juan Mountains in California could be made usable for railroad traffic in the winter, but he failed to find such a route. However, while he was on the exploration, gold was discovered in July on land Frémont had purchased as a result of gifts made to him by various friends. Suddenly he was a very wealthy man. He made extensive investments in San Francisco and bought a large ranch in Mariposa County.

In December 1850, the California legislature named Frémont one of its first two U.S. senators. However, serving in the Senate was too constraining for Frémont, and he resigned after only a few months. He traveled to Europe, where he stayed two years. Returning to the United States, he made another winter expedition to attempt to find a railroad route to the Pacific, this time farther south in California.

Frémont's greatest political success came in 1856 when he was nominated as the first presidential candidate of the new antislavery Republican

Party. The party officials hoped that Frémont's national reputation would overcome their general disorganization. Campaigning on the slogan called "Free soil, free speech, and Frémont," they tried to make the party into a national political force. Although joined by distinguished intellectuals such as Ralph Waldo Emerson, William Cullen Bryant, and Henry Wadsworth Longfellow, they were not able to overcome fears that the South would secede if Frémont were elected president. JAMES BUCHANAN, the Democratic nominee, defeated Frémont 174 electoral votes to 114. Frémont returned to California but proceeded to lose his fortune there when his gold mine petered out. What little remained after the mine closed he spent trying to find a new source of gold.

When the Civil War began, Frémont rejoined the army and was named the head of the Department of the West. He exceeded his instructions by freeing the slaves of the Confederates in his district without first seeking approval from President ABRAHAM LINCOLN. Fearing that Frémont's precipitous action might provoke the secession of slaveholding border states that had not yet left the Union, Lincoln had no choice but to remove Frémont. At the same time, Frémont was a poor administrator and questions arose over corrupt army contracts that had been issued in his department.

Frémont was transferred to western Virginia. He soon resigned again from the army. A group of Radical Republicans tried to get him to run for president in 1864, but he dropped out of the race after only four months. Frémont served as governor of the Arizona territory from 1878 to 1883. He spent most of the rest of his life in private business. Frémont invested heavily in railroads and lost all this money in speculative ventures. Congress finally voted him a pension in 1890 shortly before he died on July 13 of that year.

Further Reading

Bartlett, Ruhl Jacob. *John C. Frémont and the Republican Party*. Columbus: Ohio State University, 1974.

Brandon, William. *The Men and the Mountain: Frémont's Fourth Expedition*. New York: Morrow, 1955.

Egan, Ferol. *Frémont: Explorer for a Restless Nation*. Reno: University of Nevada Press, 1985.

Hawthorne, Hildegarde. *Born to Adventure: The Story of John Charles Frémont*. New York: D. Appleton-Century Co., 1947.

Johnson, Kenneth M. *The Frémont Court Martial*. Los Angeles: Dawson's Book Shop, 1968.

Nevins, Allan. *Frémont: Pathmaker of the West*. Lincoln: University of Nebraska Press, 1992.

Rolle, Andrew F. *John Charles Frémont: Character as Destiny*. Norman: University of Oklahoma, 1991.

Fulbright, James William
(1905–1995) *senator, representative, author*

James William Fulbright served for 30 years in the U.S. Senate and had a distinguished career that made him a leading expert on foreign relations. He was eventually named the chairman of the prestigious Senate Foreign Relations Committee where he became a leading opponent of continuing U.S. involvement in the Vietnam War. He also was responsible for creating a student and faculty foreign exchange program that still carries his name.

Fulbright was born in Sumner, Missouri, on April 9, 1905, but moved with his parents to Fayetteville, Arkansas, in 1906. He attended public schools up through graduation at the University of Arkansas in 1925 at the age of 20, and then he was accepted as a Rhodes scholar at Oxford that same year. After returning to the United States, he attended the George Washington University Law School, graduated in 1934, and was admitted to the bar. He worked in the U.S. Department of Justice antitrust division for a year before returning to the George Washington University Law School to teach.

Fulbright returned to Arkansas where his career began a dramatic rise. He was active in farming, lumbering, banking, and newspaper work, but his principal occupation was teaching law for four years at the University of Arkansas. Almost immediately successful in an academic setting, he was named the president of the university in 1939. He resigned three years later because he was elected to the U.S. House of Representatives as a Democrat. After one term in the House, he won election to the Senate in 1944 and remained there for six terms, spanning 30 years.

As an indication of his later interest in international relations, he sponsored legislation creating an international exchange program for students—a program named for him. Expanded with various amendments in the 1950s and 1960s, the Fulbright program, which now provides for faculty and other professional exchanges, remains the premier government-sponsored and -funded exchange program. That he succeeded in obtaining its passage as a freshman senator is a tribute to his legislative skills.

As a southern senator he was conservative on domestic issues and opposed civil rights legislation throughout the 1950s and 1960s, calling for a very gradual pace of reforms. To have done otherwise would have meant his political demise. His stands on international issues cast doubt as to whether these conservative domestic stands were truly his own. In fact, by being conventionally conservative on domestic issues, particularly the rights of African Americans, he was freed to take far more liberal stands on other issues. For example, he was an early critic of Republican Senator JOSEPH RAYMOND McCARTHY and his tactics in investigating reputed Communist influence in the federal government. Senators in other parts of the country did not have that flexibility, and Fulbright was able to aid in bringing about McCarthy's downfall.

As a conventional conservative domestically, Fulbright advanced in the southern-dominated Democratic hierarchy in the Senate. By 1955, he had been named as the chairman of the Senate Banking and Currency Committee and served in that role from 1955 to 1959. His prime interest was in international relations, and he seized an opportunity to move over to become the chairman of the Senate Foreign Relations Committee in 1959. He remained on that committee until he retired in 1974.

During his long tenure as Foreign Relations Committee chairman, he grew increasingly skeptical of U.S. foreign and military policy, particularly of the U.S. proclivity to try to solve complex international issues with military force. He sought to end the blind deference that the Senate had long given to presidents over the use of force abroad, and he tried to reassert the Senate's influence in international affairs. To educate the public, he held frequent open hearings, which received widespread coverage in the press. He also wrote six books on foreign policy and international affairs.

Fulbright opposed the Bay of Pigs invasion (1961) and U.S. intervention in the Dominican Republic (1965). He voted for the 1964 Tonkin Bay Resolution, authorizing the president to use force in Southeast Asia, but later regretted having done so and claiming he was misled by President LYNDON BAINES JOHNSON. From then on, he opposed the escalation of the war in Vietnam.

His liberal stands became increasingly controversial in Arkansas by the early 1970s, and he ultimately paid the price for being so far ahead of his constituents. In the 1974 Democratic primary in Arkansas, he was defeated for the senatorial nomination by Dale Bumpers. He resigned the Senate on December 31, 1974, to enable his successor to take his oath of office early and improve his seniority rank. After this retirement, he remained in Washington and continued writing and lecturing.

In the late 1960s and early 1970s, he hired a young man from Arkansas, who had attended Georgetown University and been a Rhodes scholar at Oxford as he had. He subsequently helped him in some ways to avoid military service. That young man, WILLIAM JEFFERSON CLINTON, later elected governor of Arkansas and president of the United States, awarded Fulbright the Presidential Medal of Freedom in 1993.

He died of a stroke in Washington, D.C., on February 9, 1995.

Further Reading

Brown, Eugene. *William Fulbright: Advice and Dissent.* Iowa City: University of Iowa Press, 1985.

Fulbright, J. William. *The Arrogance of Power.* New York: Random House, 1967.

———. *The Crippled Giant.* New York: Random House, 1972.

———. *Old Myths and New Realities.* New York: Random House, 1964.

———. *The Pentagon Propaganda Machine.* New York: Vintage Books, 1971.

———. *The Price of Empire.* New York: Pantheon Books, 1989.

———. *Prospects for the West.* Cambridge, Mass.: Harvard University Press, 1963.

Powell, Lee Riley. *J. William Fulbright and His Time: A Political Biography.* Memphis, Tenn.: Guild Bindery Press, 1996.
Woods, Randall B. *Fulbright: A Biography.* New York: Cambridge University Press, 1995.

Fuller, Melville Weston

(1833–1910) *chief justice of the United States*

Melville Fuller served 22 years as chief justice of the United States and succeeded in improving the administration of the Court during his tenure. He was one of the most obscure men to be appointed to the Court, but he was also one of the first to have any significant academic training in the law. He reflected the conservative legal views of the day and was generally very popular.

Born on February 11, 1833, in Augusta, Maine, Melville Weston Fuller was part of a family with a long history in the legal profession. His father and both his grandfathers were attorneys, and his maternal grandfather was the chief justice on the Maine Supreme Court. His parents divorced when he was only two months old, and his mother took him to live with her father. While she later remarried, Fuller stayed with his grandfather, who aided his education.

After attending Bowdoin College, where he graduated Phi Beta Kappa in 1853, he attended Harvard University's legal program. Although his stay was brief, he studied law on his own and at the law office of one of his uncles. He was admitted to the bar in 1855, and he began to practice law. Since his law practice was not very busy, he also wrote for a local newspaper owned by his uncle. That paper had a Democratic slant, and he and his family were active in Democratic politics throughout then lives. Fuller ran for and was elected the president of the Common Council of Augusta in 1856 and seemed to have a promising career in Maine politics.

Either as the result of a failed romance or because of the attractiveness of the business opportunities in the West, he moved to Chicago late in 1856 and began a real estate and commercial law practice there. He became involved almost immediately in Illinois politics and actively supported

STEPHEN ARNOLD DOUGLAS, both for the Senate against ABRAHAM LINCOLN in 1858 and for president against Lincoln in 1860. In the early 1860s, he served on an Illinois constitutional convention and later in the Illinois state legislature from 1863 to 1864. He was a delegate to the Democratic National Convention in 1864, 1872, 1876, 1880, and 1884.

During the Civil War, Fuller supported the Union, but his politics had never been antislavery, and he was certainly no Republican. He backed General GEORGE BRINTON MCCLELLAN in 1864. Some Republicans accused him of being a disloyal "copperhead," but no evidence of disloyalty was ever found. Rumors of this nature continued for years and complicated his confirmation to the Supreme Court.

He actively supported STEPHEN GROVER CLEVELAND against JAMES GILLESPIE BLAINE in 1884, and Cleveland appreciated his efforts. Cleveland met Fuller during the campaign and was impressed that Fuller's views on hard currency and low tariffs complemented his own. Cleveland offered him a position either on the civil service commission or as solicitor general, but Fuller declined. In 1888, Chief Justice Morrison R. Waite died. Cleveland determined that he wanted to appoint an Illinois attorney to the Court since Illinois and the other states in the circuit had not been represented for several years and Illinois was likely to be crucial in the upcoming presidential campaign. Cleveland initially offered the post to another Illinoisan who declined to serve, and then he turned to Fuller.

Fuller's political record complicated his confirmation. He was not particularly well known outside Illinois, and some critics said he was too obscure for the post. Some Democrats and populists were concerned that Fuller had strong ties to corporate interests, but they were in a poor position to buck their own party's president. The Republicans were concerned about rumors of his disloyalty to the Union during the Civil War, but these rumors were quieted when former president Abraham Lincoln's son, Robert Todd Lincoln, testified to his loyalty. After two and a half months, the Senate confirmed by a comfortable, but not overwhelming, vote of 41–20.

Fuller worked hard on the Court and wrote an appropriate, but not the highest, number of opinions. Few are highly regarded today and virtually none remain valid precedents in current law. Fuller, popular on the Court, was a good administrator and drew high praise from other justices, most notably OLIVER WENDELL HOLMES. He served 22 years and established cordial relations with most justices, so he was able to reduce tensions on controversial questions.

Fuller followed the conservative legal philosophy of his age. He wrote the opinion ruling that an income tax violated the Constitution's prohibition of direct taxes unless they were in proportion to population—a view that appears questionable today. He also wrote the opinion in the case that construed the Sherman Antitrust Law so narrowly that it could not even break up the notorious sugar trust. He reached this conclusion by deciding that manufacturing a product for sale was not commerce, a conclusion that was so dubious that it was steadily eroded over the years. For the benefit of employers, Fuller endorsed the views that limited their liability for injuries to their workers on the job. He also found that the antitrust laws could not regulate the giant trusts, but they were strong enough to break up labor unions.

Fuller was convinced that the Fourteenth Amendment actually worked no fundamental change in the Constitution at all, and therefore he was untroubled by the many violations of the rights of African Americans that occurred in the South during his tenure. He was in the majority in the notorious *Plessy v. Ferguson* (1896) decision, which validated segregation in the South for nearly six decades. He held the view that children born in the United States to Chinese couples were not citizens of the United States.

On commercial questions, he persuaded the Court to accept his view that states could not regulate products that were shipped across state lines in their original package, another distinction that has not stood the test of time. As popular as Fuller was in his own age, few if any of his legal views survive today.

Cleveland lost the 1888 presidential campaign but was reelected in 1892. At the start of his second term, he offered the post of secretary of state to Fuller. Fuller apparently considered the position seriously but declined because he thought it would lower the Court's prestige for someone to resign as chief justice to take a temporary political post.

Fuller had an interest in international affairs, and he agreed to serve on the Venezuela–British Guiana Border Commission in 1899. He also served on the Permanent Court of Arbitration in The Hague from 1900 to 1910.

He died of a heart attack while vacationing in Maine on July 4, 1910.

Further Reading

King, Willard L. *Melville Weston Fuller: Chief Justice of the United States, 1888–1910*. New York: Macmillan, 1950.

Kosma, Montgomery N., and Ross E. Davies. *Fuller and Washington at Centuries' End*. Washington, D.C.: Green Bag Press, 1999.

G

Gadsden, James
(1788–1858) *diplomat*

James Gadsden is best known for negotiating the Gadsden Purchase, the purchase of a strip land in the southwestern United States on which a railroad could be built, linking California to the rest of the nation.

Born on May 15, 1788, into a prominent family in Charleston, South Carolina, Gadsden graduated from Yale University when he was only 18 years old. His early career was in the military where he served in the War of 1812 and again in the war against the Seminole Indians in Florida.

President JAMES MONROE appointed Gadsden to be the commissioner in charge of moving all the Seminole Indians onto a special Indian Reservation in Florida in 1823. Despite his success in clearing Florida for white settlement, Gadsden lost several races for the U.S. House of Representatives from Florida. Finally, in 1839, Gadsden moved back to Charleston, South Carolina, and began his career as a railroad executive.

As president of the South Carolina Railroad Company, Gadsden envisioned a great railroad network created across the South that would make the region a commercial success on a scale similar to that of the North, but he was never able to persuade enough southerners of this idea. He was ultimately removed from his post when he became too preoccupied with this attempt.

Undeterred by this setback, Gadsden continued to push for his idea of a railroad stretching from the Atlantic to the Pacific along the southern part of the United States. In 1853, President FRANKLIN PIERCE appointed him to be U.S. ambassador to Mexico and empowered him to negotiate the purchase of a large tract of land in north Mexico for up to $50 million.

At first Gadsden was sure that the Mexican leader Santa Anna was so desperate for money that he would sell him all the land he wanted. However, he misjudged the issue and was able to secure only a small strip of land along the southern edge of what is now Arizona and New Mexico for the price of $10 million. This land was sufficient to build a railroad, and Gadsden achieved at least part of his dream.

Gadsden died on December 26, 1858.

Further Reading
Gara, Larry. *The Presidency of Franklin Pierce*. Lawrence: University Press of Kansas, 1991.

Garber, Paul Neff. *The Gadsden Treaty*. Gloucester, Mass.: P. Smith, 1959.

Nichols, Roy F. *Franklin Pierce: Young Hickory of the Granite Hills*. Newtown, Conn.: American Political Biography Press, 1993.

Garfield, James Abram
(1831–1881) *president, representative*

Preacher, lawyer, professor of ancient languages, college president, military hero, Civil War general, eight-term congressman, and national party conciliator, James Garfield probably entered the presidency better prepared for the job than any president since JOHN QUINCY ADAMS. Even without his election to the presidency, he had accomplished more in his short 50 years of life than many of his predecessors in this nation's highest office. Horatio Alger, the writer of many "rags to riches" inspirational tales in the late 19th century, wrote one of his campaign biographies. Garfield's career was so dramatic that his life might have been taken from one of Alger's novels.

James Abram Garfield was born in Orange, Ohio (near Cleveland), on November 19, 1831, into a poor pioneer family. Unlike other presidential aspirants who inaccurately claimed to have been born in a log cabin, Garfield actually was born in such humble surroundings and was the last president so born. His father died before he was two years old and his mother struggled to maintain a small farm and raise Garfield and three older siblings.

As a youth he worked at a variety of odd jobs, including farmer and carpenter. He attempted unsuccessfully to become a Great Lakes sailor, but he did eventually work as a canal boy driving a horse-drawn barge along the Ohio canal. Garfield humorously described that six-week adventure as falling, "into the canal just fourteen times and had fourteen almost miraculous escapes from drowning." He did not drown, but he did contract malaria. At this time (about age 19), he had a profound religious conversion and became a convert to—and later evangelist for—the Disciples of Christ.

When he recovered from malaria, Garfield entered Geauga Seminary in a nearby town. Following his first term, he supported himself by teaching in the district school. At 20 years of age, he enrolled in Hiram College (then called Western Reserve Eclectic Institute) near Cleveland. He studied and taught some classes there for three years, until he saved enough money to transfer to Williams College in Massachusetts.

For the next two years, Garfield described himself as having been personally tutored by the Williams College president, Mark Hopkins, until he broadened his interests substantially and more fully matured. In 1856, after graduation from Williams, Garfield returned to Hiram College as a

James Abram Garfield, perhaps one of the most capable men ever elected president, was assassinated by a disappointed office seeker before he could demonstrate his skill in office. *(Library of Congress)*

professor of ancient languages and literature. He was so good at classical languages that he could actually stand at the blackboard and simultaneously write the same material in Greek with one hand and in Latin with the other. In that same year, Garfield made his first foray into politics by supporting the antislavery candidate JOHN CHARLES FRÉMONT for president on the newly founded Republican Party ticket.

The following year, Garfield was chosen president of Hiram College when he was only 26 years of age. While president, Garfield studied law and became a part-time evangelist for the Disciples of Christ. During the next four years, he also was romantically linked to two women but eventually settled on one of his students, Lucretia Rudolph (whom he called "Crete"), and they were married in 1858. In 1859, he was elected to the Ohio state senate.

When the Civil War began, the Ohio governor named Garfield a lieutenant colonel in command of a group of state volunteers. Garfield won a battle in Middle Creek, Kentucky, in January 1862 and was elevated to the rank of brigadier general, the youngest in the Union Army. On April 7, 1862, he took part in the Battle of Shiloh and in the skirmishes near Corinth in Tennessee. He fell ill in the summer of 1862 and returned to Ohio. While recuperating, he was nominated and elected to the U.S. House of Representatives, even though he made it clear that he would not resign from the army nor serve in Congress while he was needed in the war.

In early 1863, he returned to active service as chief of staff under General William S. Rosecrans. In that capacity, and over objections of other officers, he recommended that Rosecrans attack Confederate General Braxton Bragg's forces at Chickamauga, Georgia. Rosecrans followed his advice, but the attack was a disaster. Rosecrans was discredited, but Garfield became a hero by riding under heavy fire to deliver an important message to U.S. General George H. Thomas. He was promoted to major general after the battle. After his promotion in December 1863, he resigned his commission in the army and took his seat in the U.S. House of Representatives.

Garfield was elected to the House eight times and never lost an election. He served as chairman of the appropriations committee and as a member of the committees on military affairs, ways and means, and banking and currency. He supported harsh Reconstruction plans and was disappointed by ABRAHAM LINCOLN's moderate reconstruction, but he supported the president's reelection in 1864. He joined the Radical Republicans on their military reconstruction of the South, was horrified by the more moderate plans of President ANDREW JOHNSON, and voted for his impeachment.

When THADDEUS STEVENS, the House Republican floor leader, retired in 1868, two men with very different personalities, JAMES GILLESPIE BLAINE and James A. Garfield, jointly replaced him. Despite their differences, they were very effective in that role.

In 1872, Garfield was among those congressmen (including Blaine) accused of accepting gifts of stock from the Crédit Mobilier, a corporation that had received government-subsidized contracts to build a transcontinental railroad, allowing the company to receive huge amounts of money while doing little or no work. Garfield's involvement—which was never really proven—extended to receiving a check for $329. He had never purchased any stock in the company, but this $329 was a dividend check. Garfield defended himself by claiming he thought it was a campaign contribution. Garfield was also criticized for accepting a $5,000 fee from a paving company for contract work in the city of Washington, D.C. Admitting he received the fee, he contended that his services were proper.

In 1876, Blaine was elected to the Senate. Garfield probably could also have been elected to the Senate that year, but RUTHERFORD BIRCHARD HAYES asked him to stay in the House where he could serve in a badly needed leadership role. Garfield also served on the commission that settled the disputed Hayes-Tilden election of 1876, thereby participating in the questionable arrangements that took the presidency from SAMUEL JONES TILDEN and gave it to Hayes. During the Hayes administration, the Democrats controlled the House, so Garfield was the minority floor leader.

The Hayes administration coincided with a deep division in the Republican Party, most frequently linked to the two main Senate protagonists: ROSCOE CONKLING and Blaine. Conkling believed that patronage was the key to maintaining the Republican Party, since it was still new in national politics. He tightly controlled New York's Republican Party federal patronage during the administration of President ULYSSES S. GRANT. This patronage became so tainted with corruption that reformers, such as Maine's Republican Senator Blaine, sought to purge corrupt patronage officeholders from the party. Conkling became the leader of the faction known as the Stalwarts; Blaine became the leader of the Half-Breeds. Since Grant ended his second term with his administration under the cloud of corruption, he did not seek a third term in 1876.

Hayes was nominated and won the controversial 1876 election. Although Hayes came into the presidency as the result of controversy, he was a man of great personal integrity and was determined to root out corruption. Conkling tried to convince Hayes to allow him to continue to control federal patronage in New York, but Hayes had little in common with Conkling. Hayes further incensed him by supporting civil service reform and initiating an investigation of the New York City customs house headed by Conkling crony future President CHESTER ALAN ARTHUR. When Arthur refused to cooperate with Hayes's investigation, Hayes fired him. With that, the struggles between the Stalwarts and the Half-Breeds verged on open warfare. Though closer to the Half-Breeds, Garfield stood between the two factions and remained on speaking terms with both groups. Hayes kept his promise to serve only one term, leading to an open race in 1880.

The Ohio legislature elected Garfield to the U.S. Senate in 1880. Before he could take his Senate seat, he led his state's delegation to the Republican National Convention to support the "favorite son" candidacy of John Sherman. By 1880, Hayes had aggravated critical party constituencies to such a degree that he could not be renominated, even if he had not promised to run for only a single term. Conkling's Stalwart faction (of which Arthur was a member) tried to renominate Grant for a third term, but the Grant administration's reputation for corruption led the anti-Grant forces to push for their leader, Blaine. The Stalwarts and the Half-Breeds deadlocked, which might have set the stage for Sherman (the apparent compromise dark horse), except that Conkling could not tolerate Sherman since he had supported Hayes over the firing of Arthur.

Garfield faithfully nominated Sherman at the convention with a rousing speech. As a lay minister, he put his evangelistic best into nominating Sherman. Garfield's speech may have been one of the most effective until the famous "Cross of Gold" speech of WILLIAM JENNINGS BRYAN in 1896. The net result was that Garfield captured the attention of the convention, and several observers told him that they wished he were the favorite son candidate instead of Sherman.

The convention remained deadlocked. On the 34th ballot, suddenly the Wisconsin delegation shifted 16 delegate votes to Garfield. The convention sat in stunned silence and then broke into cheers. On the 35th ballot, dozens more moved to Garfield until, on the 36th ballot, the nomination was Garfield's—to the cheering voices of the thousands present. Garfield was not firmly attached to either faction, but he seemed closer to the Half-Breeds. As a concession to the Stalwarts, Chester Arthur, Conkling's lieutenant in the New York Republican machine, was nominated for vice president.

This was very helpful to Garfield and the Republicans because Arthur was regarded as the cleverest political operative in the country. During the campaign, he organized the publicity, raised the cash, and managed the campaign orators. Garfield defeated his Democratic Party opponent, Winfield Scott Hancock, by just a few thousand votes nationwide. Garfield, with his past support for a harsh Reconstruction, was hated in the South and received not a single Electoral College vote there, but he was so strong in the North that he defeated Hancock 214–155 in the Electoral College. Since the national election was so close, it is likely that any other Republican would have lost and underscored the importance of party unity for them. Garfield realized this but did not foresee how vicious the fighting would be in the opening days of his administration.

After the election, party quarrels flared again. Garfield supported an investigation by Postmaster General Thomas L. James, who found fraud in the awarding of contracts to transport the mail (the so-called Star Routes matter), even though it implicated some prominent Republicans. This made Conkling uncomfortable. Conkling did not really like Garfield but thought he could intimidate him. Early in the Garfield administration, Conkling insisted that if the Half-Breed Blaine was going to be secretary of state, then the secretary of the treasury should be a Stalwart. Garfield could not accept Conkling's candidate for treasury, but he offered Conkling some other appointments, which Conkling stubbornly refused. Conkling then persuaded his supporters to boycott the administration.

Conkling and the Stalwarts had been passed over for several important appointments and would normally have received some now except that Conklins persisted stubbornly in fighting Garfield. Frustrated with Conkling and the Stalwarts, Garfield now accepted the Half-Breed Blaine's recommendation of William H. Robertson to become the Port of New York's customs collector. Not only did this post control 90 percent of the customs revenue for the United States, but also this was the very post from which the Stalwart Chester Arthur had been fired during the Hayes administration. Conkling hated Robertson and furiously protested Garfield's decision. He demanded that the Senate uphold him on grounds of a personal privilege (known as senatorial courtesy)—a privilege previously guarded jealously by all senators. Since senatorial courtesy had been absolute before that time, Conkling was sure he would win.

However, Garfield would not give up. He argued that an office collecting 90 percent of the nation's revenue ought to be under the control of a president's administration rather than be the personal fiefdom of one senator. The other senators were generally in favor of senatorial courtesy but were concerned that only one of them, Conkling, would control too much of the government's money if he won on this issue. A majority came to see that they might do better backing Garfield, and Conkling lost. Outraged, Conkling then resigned from the U.S. Senate in 1881, foolishly believing that the New York state legislature would simply reappoint him. However, after Garfield was assassinated, national events turned against Conkling, and the New York legislature simply nominated someone else.

On July 2, 1881, as Garfield was about to leave the Capitol for a long-awaited 25th reunion of his class at Williams College, he walked through a reception room in the railroad station when Charles J. Guiteau fired two pistol shots at him. Garfield fell, and Guiteau cried: "I am a Stalwart and Arthur is President now!" Guiteau was arrested immediately. He held a grudge because Garfield had refused to appoint him U.S. consul in Paris. There was no evidence that he was truly an agent of the Stalwarts, but the national mood swung in the direction of deciding that, if the patronage system could generate so much hostility that a deranged person could seize on a failed appointment as grounds for an assassination, then the system must need reforming. At his trial Guiteau acted like a madman. His attorney argued

that he was innocent by reason of insanity, but a jury convicted him. He was hanged in 1882.

Garfield was gravely ill for 80 days. While one of the bullets merely scratched his arm, the other had lodged near his spine. When surgeons could not find it, Alexander Graham Bell was called in and tried unsuccessfully to locate the bullet with a new electrical device he had just invented. Surgeons would have done better to leave the wound alone, for it was developing a protective cyst around the bullet. Garfield might have lived with the bullet in his body for several years, as President ANDREW JACKSON had done. However, the doctors proceeded to probe for the bullet, and their efforts led to an infection that killed Garfield.

Garfield remained in Washington throughout the hot summer. A primitive air-conditioning system—using 100 pounds of ice an hour—was devised to cool the White House during that time. He did almost no official business, but the Constitution did not provide any effective way to deal with presidential disability until the Twenty-fifth Amendment was approved in the middle of the 20th century, so there was no way for Vice President Arthur to step in. Since Arthur was a Stalwart and there was so much hostility between the factions, he would have had great political difficulties doing so in any case.

Eventually, the doctors concluded that even with the primitive air conditioning, Garfield was suffering too much in Washington. Arrangements were made for him to be taken to a seaside cottage in Elberon, New Jersey. As an indication of the government's concern for Garfield, they arranged for a special railroad line to be constructed by 300 men at night, so that Garfield could be delivered right to the door of the cottage. For a short while, Garfield was allowed to enjoy the sea air in the company of his wife. The infection did not stop, however, and he died on September 19, 1881.

Chester Arthur was now president, but his reputation as a crafty manager became a serious liability when Garfield died. Since the assassin had openly proclaimed that he shot Garfield in order to make Arthur the president, Arthur faced a difficult situation. With his reputation as a Stalwart conniver, the assassin's shout created the sort of rumor that risked destroying Arthur. There was no evidence that Arthur had anything to do with the assassination plot. In fact, he reputedly prayed for Garfield's recovery and was devastated by Garfield's death.

Further Reading

Alger, Horatio. *From Canal Boy to President: The Boyhood and Manhood of James A. Garfield.* New York: Street & Smith, 1901.

Bates, Richard O. *The Gentleman from Ohio: An Introduction to Garfield.* Durham, N.C.: Moore Publishing Company, 1973.

Caldwell, Robert G. *James A. Garfield.* New York: Dodd, Mead & Company, 1931.

Doenecke, Justus D. *The Presidencies of James A. Garfield and Chester A. Arthur.* Lawrence: Regents Press of Kansas, 1981.

"Garfield, James Abram." Available on line. URL: http://www.whitehouse.gov/history/presidents/jg20.html. Downloaded on October 20, 2001.

"James A. Garfield." *American Heritage* 15, no. 5 (August 1964).

Leech, Margaret. *The Garfield Orbit.* New York: Harper & Row, 1978.

Peskin, Allan. *Garfield: A Biography.* Norwalk, Conn.: Easton Press, 1987.

Simpson, Brooks D. *The Reconstruction Presidents.* Lawrence: University Press of Kansas, 1998.

Smith, Theodore C. *The Life and Letters of James Abram Garfield.* New Haven, Conn.: Yale University Press, 1925. Reprint, Hamden, Conn.: Archon Books, 1968.

Taylor, John M. *Garfield of Ohio: The Available Man.* New York: Norton, 1970.

Garner, John Nance
(1868–1967) *vice president, Speaker of the House, representative*

John Nance Garner lived longer than any other president or vice president of the United States. As a 30-year veteran of the U.S. House of Representatives, as a former House Speaker, and as vice president, he was most responsible for pushing President FRANKLIN DELANO ROOSEVELT's legislative program through the Congress during the famous First One Hundred Days of the Roosevelt

administration. Had his advice been followed, Roosevelt might have avoided the serious mistakes of his second term. Had Roosevelt not run for a third term, Garner would have been the leading candidate to succeed him. Even without service as a president, Garner made an important contribution to U.S. history and particularly to the development of the modern vice presidency.

Garner was born the son of a former Confederate soldier near Detroit, Texas, on November 22, 1868. Although some public relations people tried to make much of the claim that he was born in a log cabin, he came from a fairly well-to-do family since his mother was the daughter of the town banker. At age 18, young Garner set off to enroll at Vanderbilt University in Nashville, Tennessee, but he suffered from respiratory problems (which were aggravated in Tennessee), and he found he was not well prepared for a liberal arts education. Garner decided to return to Texas and began studying the law on his own in a Clarksville, Texas, law office. Through his own efforts, he learned enough to be admitted to the bar in 1890. At age 21, he ran for city attorney in Clarksville, but he lost.

Still troubled with his respiratory condition, he moved to Uvalde, Texas, where the climate was drier. He bought a local newspaper and soon had established a political base in the area. A shrewd businessman, he ultimately bought thousands of acres of land, three banks, and numerous other businesses, which made him a millionaire while still quite a young man.

In 1893, he ran for and won a race for judge of Uvalde County, and he served as county judge from 1893 to 1896. He then had a stint in the Texas state legislature from 1898 to 1902. Texas gained an additional congressional seat after the 1900 census, and that meant a new district had to be drawn. Since Garner was chairman of the committee drawing the new lines, he was able to fashion a congressional district from which he could win easily. He was elected to the U.S. House of Representatives in 1902, and he was successfully reelected continuously up to and including 1932 when he won reelection to the House the same day he was elected vice president.

Garner followed the traditional route of rising southern members of Congress by avoiding the limelight and carefully displaying party loyalty during the early years. He was eventually rewarded with committee appointments, such as Ways and Means, on which he became the highest-ranking Democrat by the mid-1920s. Even more powerful was his position as chairman of the House Democratic Committee on Committees, which chose that party's members for all House committees.

The 1928 presidential campaign between Democrat ALFRED EMANUEL SMITH and Republican HERBERT CLARK HOOVER resulted in a Republican landslide that reduced the Democratic membership in the House to new lows. It elevated Garner, however, who became the floor leader of the House Democratic Party in 1929. Garner's strategy as floor leader was to give his colleagues credit wherever possible. He was so successful at this that he sponsored only four major bills to Congress under his own name during his entire three decades in the House.

Throughout the one-year period from the 1930 midterm elections and the start of the following Congress in December 1931, an unusually large number of congresspersons (14) died. Since the Great Depression made Republicans very unpopular, the Democrats won a large enough number of the special elections to give the Democrats a 219–214 majority and to elevate Garner to the Speaker's office. The emergency of the Great Depression sharpened differences between the two parties and made Democratic cohesion more important. Since the Democrats had grown sloppy on party discipline when they were a minority, Garner found it necessary to become a ruthless leader, and he rose to the occasion.

The Great Depression caused Garner to soften his conservative opposition to federal intervention. Initially he tried to forge a bipartisan program with Hoover, supporting business proposals he had never before considered. As Hoover grew increasingly rigid—and increasingly unpopular—Garner broke out on his own and pushed through the Congress a huge public works program. Hoover vetoed it with a particularly harsh veto message, and Garner was never on good terms with Hoover again.

Garner was now the titular head of his party as its highest national officeholder. Given that

Hoover was increasingly unpopular, it is not surprising that a "Garner for President" movement began in January 1932. While Garner did not push it, neither did he ask his supporters to stop. Key among his backers was the prominent newspaper publisher William Randolph Hearst, who saw Garner as the least objectionable of the prospective Democrats.

Garner was closer to Hearst's conservative economic views and his isolationism than the others. Many conservative southern and western politicians were personally more comfortable with Garner than an easterner such as Roosevelt or Smith. Some backed him only as a way to try to stop the growing Roosevelt bandwagon. Garner was personally most concerned with finding a Democrat who could win so handily as to carry a number of Democrats in the Congress to strengthen the narrow majority necessary to keep him as Speaker.

Privately, Garner decided that Roosevelt's candidacy offered the best chance for the party, but he did not disavow his supporters and was still an unannounced candidate when the 1932 Democratic National Party Convention opened. On the first ballot. Garner ran third behind Roosevelt and Smith. After two more ballots saw only a small increase in Garner's support and a continuing deadlock between Roosevelt and Smith, it was time for a deal. Although Roosevelt had a majority of the delegates, he could not get the two-thirds necessary under the Democratic Party rules unless Garner withdrew. Although both Roosevelt and Garner denied any deal, it is a virtual certainty that Garner agreed to withdraw in return for being nominated vice president.

Garner played only a limited role in the 1932 campaign (since he almost always shunned the spotlight), but Roosevelt consulted him frequently between the election and inauguration day on matters of both strategy and substance. Curiously, Garner espoused one of the more liberal proposals—government-guaranteed bank deposits—and Roosevelt resisted until he learned how popular the idea was. This early support for the Federal Deposit Insurance Corporation indicates that Garner was hardly the reactionary he was often portrayed as being.

While becoming vice president was a step down from the powerful office of Speaker, Garner soldiered on for Roosevelt. Garner had as many as 20 friends in the Senate whom he had met during his House days and who had moved over to the Senate. He called in old favors and, more important, was a master in the mechanics and traditions of the Congress.

Garner did not always agree with Roosevelt's policies, but he encouraged his friends to support the president out of patriotism during this crisis. While he was a master of legislative process, he declined to take a public role in speaking out on administration policy. This was not disloyalty but a practical recognition that the press would try to find differences between Roosevelt and Garner— to the disadvantage of the administration. Garner did not agree with all of the New Deal even in the first term, for he doubted the wisdom of the National Recovery Act, the recognition of Russia, and parts of the Neutrality Act. In the first 100 days, he swallowed his differences and brought many skeptical southern conservatives into line behind Roosevelt's program. In 1936, Garner was helpful to Roosevelt in his attempt to repeal the two-thirds rule required by the Democrats to nominate a president and vice president. Garner was such a safe choice that delegates who otherwise would have balked at the repeal of the two-thirds provision went along with it. The Roosevelt-Garner ticket easily defeated the Republican nominee ALFRED MOSSMAN LANDON in the general election.

During Roosevelt's second term, he increasingly ignored Garner's sound advice, to Roosevelt's detriment, and Garner fell out with Roosevelt over the issues. It was inevitable that a conservative, such as Garner, would oppose the large increase in the role of the federal government in providing ever larger amounts of federal welfare aid. Garner naturally opposed much of the pro-labor legislation Roosevelt felt he had to support for the benefit of the northern liberal, pro-labor wing of the party.

All previous disputes paled in comparison to the rift caused by Roosevelt's 1937 Court-packing proposal, a plan that was Roosevelt's greatest domestic defeat. Roosevelt's first term New Deal pro-

gram suffered a series of Supreme Court decisions that overturned its provisions. At that time, the Court was dominated by justices appointed mainly by Roosevelt's conservative Republican predecessors, and Roosevelt went through his entire first term being unable to make any appointments to the Court. Emboldened by his landslide victory in 1936, Roosevelt seized on an idea that had been floated some months previously that the size of the U.S. Supreme Court should be increased. Since the Constitution does not specify the size of the Court, Congress must determine its size. In the past, political decisions had often determined the congressional enactments, so Roosevelt apparently thought his proposal would not arouse such deep hostility. The proposal called for one new justice to be appointed for every current justice over 70 years of age who was on the Supreme Court and refused to resign. Although constitutional, it smacked of an attempt to control the Court.

Garner was not opposed to the plan because he thought it would succeed in controlling the Court, for he was convinced no president could control the Court. Rather, he objected that Roosevelt introduced it without proper consultation. When the bill was introduced in the Senate, Garner stood in the Speaker's dais, held his nose, and gave a thumbs-down sign, dramatically signaling his disapproval. He then went to Texas for an extended vacation, the first he had taken while Congress was in session. He returned to Washington later, since Senate Democratic Majority Leader Joseph Robinson died and someone had to take over the Court-packing legislation. Garner was assigned the task of pushing the bill through. He clearly did not like the bill, but it is doubtful he could have aided its passage even if he had favored it. His apparent dislike for the bill led to his being blamed for its defeat, thereby worsening his relations with Roosevelt.

Since Garner's friends in the House and Senate regularly praised him, he had good press. Roosevelt seemed jealous of this. He believed that if he could replace the conservative southern and western Democratic senators and representatives with loyal New Dealers, his legislative proposals would sail through the Congress. In 1938, he set out to purge the Democratic Party, despite Garner's clear warning that he could never unseat the southern conservative members of Congress who had safe seats and could only help Republicans replace Democrats in the North.

Roosevelt ignored the Garner's advice, and Garner's prediction came true. Roosevelt defeated precisely one of his targets, Representative John J. O'Connor, and that was probably because O'Connor was from New York where Roosevelt had a local or "hometown" advantage. Roosevelt did manage to defeat 81 Democrats in the House and eight Democrats in the Senate. He then blundered by appointing the losers to prominent posts in his administration, thereby rubbing salt in the wounds of the Democrats and Republicans who had recently been elected. The upshot was that Roosevelt had fewer Democrats to call on, and those that remained deeply distrusted him. Garner estimated that there were at least 20 Democrats in the Senate who would vote against Roosevelt on almost any issue. After the 1938 elections, Roosevelt could not get any new reform legislation passed, and the economic system had taken a downward turn into recession. In 1939, Congress denied virtually everything Roosevelt requested. Roosevelt blamed Garner for his own failings and set his supporters to work on Garner's reputation. Garner's salty language and country background made it comparatively easy to attack him in urban areas, although it was less successful in rural areas. Overall, Garner continued to lead in the public opinion polls among the possible alternatives to Roosevelt if he did not run.

Increasingly, it seemed likely that Roosevelt would run. The outbreak of war in Europe and the ongoing war in China were the pretext Roosevelt used to assert how indispensable he was and to justify breaking the two-term custom. Garner decided that he should announce that he would not actively seek the 1940 Democratic presidential nomination but would not turn it down, whether or not Roosevelt chose to run. This challenge to the president was the only time in the 20th century that a vice president directly opposed the sitting president of his own party for the nomination. Garner recognized that he could not be nominated by campaigning so passively, but he thought he was the only one who could gather enough strength to persuade Roosevelt not to run again.

He may have been the only one who had a chance to block Roosevelt, but his efforts were not enough. In early 1940, the Germans captured Denmark and Norway. Then they attacked France through Belgium and Holland. In six short weeks, the British evacuated from the Continent, France fell, and the British endured the bombardment from the air known as the Battle of Britain. These dramatic events caused such an outpouring of patriotic concern that no one could stop Roosevelt. Not needing to garner two-thirds of the delegates also made it easier for him and harder for anyone else to start. Roosevelt won the nomination on the first ballot at the Democratic National Convention by a vote of 946 for him, 72 for JAMES ALOYSIUS FARLEY, and only 61 for Garner. Garner refused to campaign for Roosevelt and did not even vote in the election.

With his strong background in the Congress, Garner was a true asset to the president in the first term. As such, he represented one of the strongest vice presidents up to that time in terms of legislative craftsmanship. That same skill appeared to be an obstacle for Roosevelt in his second term when the personal and policy disputes became so great and Garner's skill—rightly or wrongly—appeared to be pitted against the president. No subsequent president has allowed his vice president to have that much leeway in the legislative process. Instead, the vice presidency evolved in a way quite different from what Garner was capable of doing. Garner shunned the spotlight and the modern vice president has often been pushed to play that role, although almost always on a short leash to be sure that administration policy is not derailed.

Garner retired to Texas where had a long retirement before his death on November 7, 1967. He died just two weeks before his 99th birthday.

Further Reading

Davis, Kenneth S. *FDR: Three Volumes.* New York: Random House, 1993.

"Garner, John Nance" in *The Presidency A to Z: Second Edition,* edited by Michael T. Nelson. Washington, D.C.: Congressional Quarterly Press, 1998.

McJimsey, George T. *The Presidency of Franklin Delano Roosevelt.* Lawrence: University Press of Kansas, 2000.

Morris, Jeffrey. *The FDR Way.* Minneapolis: Lerner Publications, 1996.

Timmons, Bascom N. *Garner of Texas: A Personal History.* New York: Harper, 1948.

Gephardt, Richard Andrew
(1941–   ) *House minority leader, House majority leader, representative, author*

Richard Gephardt was the second highest-ranking Democrat in the U.S. House of Representatives (following then Speaker Thomas Foley) from 1989 until 1994. He would normally have become Speaker of the House after Foley was defeated in his 1994 reelection bid from Washington State. However, the Democrats lost their majority to the Republicans in that election, so Gephardt has been the House Minority leader, even though he was the highest-ranking Democrat in the chamber.

Richard Andrew Gephardt was born in St. Louis, St. Louis County, Missouri, on January 31, 1941. He represented in Congress the same neighborhood in which he was raised. He graduated from South West High School—the local high school—in 1958, and he did his undergraduate work at Northwestern University in Evanston, Illinois, where he graduated in 1962. He then moved to Michigan where he attended the University of Michigan Law School. He graduated from law school in 1965 and was admitted to the Missouri bar in 1965.

Gephardt was in the Missouri Air National Guard from 1965 to 1971, part of the time serving in the reserves. He began his political career as a precinct captain and moved up to Democratic Party committeeman for St. Louis from 1968 to 1971. He was one of a group of young reformers who ran for the St. Louis City Board of Aldermen in 1971, where he supported a wide range of reforms.

Upon being elected to the Congress, he became an understudy to Representative Richard Bolling, also of Missouri, who helped him receive the prime committee assignment on the House Ways and Means Committee. Simultaneously, he served on the House Budget Committee, which was an unusually good vantage point from which

to gain expertise in a wide range of tax and budget issues, including the financing of health care. In 1984, he was named the chairman of the House Democratic Caucus, the fourth-ranking Democratic Party position in the House.

Gephardt ran for the Democratic presidential nomination in 1988 and helped to set the political agenda for the national debate on economic questions, which were dominant that year. He did not win, but he gained a much wider recognition. As a border state Democrat, he has not been found on the extreme left of party issues. Coming from a state with a fairly strong labor union constituency, he has been a favorite of the labor movement in recent years.

In 1989, he became the Democratic majority leader, the second highest position in the House. When the Republicans gained a majority of the seats in the House in 1994, he became the House minority leader, a position he has continued to hold since then.

Further Reading
Crowley, Michael. "Tom Daschle's Struggle to Save the Dems," *The New Republic* (March 26, 2001).

"Gephardt, Richard A." In *Congress A to Z: Third Edition,* edited by David R. Tarr and Ann O'Connor. Washington, D.C.: Congressional Quarterly, 1999.

Kaiser, Robert G. "The Smiling Majority: Tom Daschle Is at the Top of the Political Game," *The Washington Post* June 6, 2001: Co1.

Loomis, Burdett A. *Esteemed Colleagues: Civility and Deliberation in the U.S. Senate.* Washington, D.C.: Brookings Institution, 2000.

Gerry, Elbridge
(1744–1814) *vice president, governor, diplomat, representative, Revolutionary War leader*

Elbridge Gerry is best known for contributing his last name to the word *gerrymander,* a practice of drawing legislative district lines in such a way as to improve the chance of one party to secure more than its fair share of the legislative seats based on the votes in an election. While the extent to which Gerry was personally involved in drawing the lines for the 1812 Massachusetts legislature is unclear, as the Massachusetts governor at the time, his name was linked to the plan and the word has now been added to the English language. This single incident should not obscure the more than 50 years of public service Gerry gave to the colonies in the Revolutionary War and in the founding of the United States.

Gerry was born on July 17, 1744, at Marblehead, Massachusetts, into a wealthy merchant and shipping family. He attended Harvard and graduated in 1762. Gerry then joined the family shipping business, which participated in trade between the West Indies and Europe. Because this business had frequent conflicts with the British on the high seas, it was not surprising that he developed strongly anti-British views. These put him in good stead with the electorate that sent him to the colonial legislature in 1772 where he served for two years.

While in the Massachusetts colonial legislature, he befriended SAMUEL ADAMS and supported his call for the development of committees of correspondence to spread the word about British abuses. Gerry worked for both the Massachusetts and Marblehead committees of correspondence. When the British Parliament passed the Coercive Acts, which closed the Boston harbor in June 1774 (in reaction to the Boston Tea Party), Marblehead became one of the alternative ports used to unload materials donated by revolutionary supporters elsewhere in the colonies to aid Boston. Gerry used ships from the family business to pick up and deliver the supplies.

In 1774, he served on the First Provincial Congress, a forerunner to the Continental Congress, and followed this up by joining the Second Provincial Congress in 1776. He was indefatigable in revolutionary causes and served with Samuel Adams and JOHN HANCOCK on the Council of Safety. In that role he used his background in shipping to supply the troops with supplies. On April 18, 1775, he was almost captured by the British while attending a Council of Safety meeting at a tavern on the road between Lexington and Concord, while the British troops were marching toward their famous battle at that location.

In 1776, Gerry was elected to the Second Continental Congress and signed the Declaration of Independence. He also served on the critically important treasury board, where he earned the moniker the Soldier's Friend because of his support for higher pay and better equipment for the troops. He was not a blind advocate for them, however, as he did not support military pensions. While he urged that the Congress adopt longer term enlistments, he did not support the concept of a standing army—a fact that may explain his reluctance to endorse military pensions.

Gerry always strongly supported the rights of the states and objected to what he called the Second Continental Congress's infringement on states' rights. He withdrew from active participation for the next three years. His controversy with the Congress may also have been motivated by the fact that he was a supplier of materials for the army and felt the Congress was not paying a fair price for them. He did not drop out of politics or the war, for he continued to serve in the revolutionary Massachusetts legislature. He also used his family shipping business to engage in privateering as well as trade. Eventually, he also returned to the Second Continental Congress for the period from 1783 to 1785.

He left politics for a year and returned to the family business full-time. By 1786 he decided to retire from an active business career and was elected to the Massachusetts legislature. From there he was sent as a delegate to the Constitutional Convention of 1787, where he was one of the most outspoken delegates. He chaired the committee that produced the Connecticut Plan, which became the basis for the Great Compromise, but he was not a supporter of the compromise himself. He antagonized many because he seemed to be inconsistent and to object to anything he did not suggest.

Gerry had earlier walked out of the Second Continental Congress when he felt it infringed on states' rights, but he started out in the Constitutional Convention supporting a strong central government. Yet he ultimately rejected the U.S. Constitution and refused to sign it. His most consistent objection was that the document lacked a bill of rights, which he characteristically said meant it was a threat to republicanism. He opposed ratification of the Constitution in Massachusetts, objecting to its vagueness, ambiguous legislative powers, insufficient separation between the executive and the legislative, overly strong judicial branch, and inadequate provision for democratic election of all representatives. To his credit, Gerry did see some good in the Constitution and thought it could be amended to repair its problems.

After ratification, Gerry came around to see the usefulness of the Constitution, promised to support it, and was elected to the First Congress in 1789. Having opposed the ratification of the Constitution, he surprised many by supporting the financial policies of ALEXANDER HAMILTON, the arch Federalist, against some of his old anti-Federalist friends. Still, as a merchant from Massachusetts and someone who long fought for sound government finance, his support of Hamilton's program was not beyond reason.

Gerry retired from the U.S. House of Representatives in 1793 and largely withdrew from politics for four years. During this time, he became enamored of the French Revolution. Since he correctly perceived that many Federalists wanted to ally with Britain against France, he became distrustful of his sometime Federalist friends. President GEORGE WASHINGTON was convinced that the United States was too small and weak to become embroiled in the conflict between Britain and France and wisely adopted a neutrality policy. President JOHN ADAMS attempted to follow this neutrality policy, but events made this very difficult. France, regarding the United States as ungrateful for not coming to their aid against Britain, began attacking U.S. shipping in the late 1790s. Adams selected three emissaries to go to France to try to resolve the conflict. He selected JOHN MARSHALL and CHARLES COTESWORTH PINCKNEY (both strong Federalists) but felt he needed to balance the group with someone not so clearly identified with the Federalists. Since Gerry was not as rabid as other Democratic Republicans, Adams selected him as the third member.

In Paris, the French refused to meet the group unless the United States loaned France $10 million and paid a $250,000 bribe. Adams stated that the United States had been insulted. In order to prove the incident had occurred, Adams supplied documents on which the names of the French agents had been blacked out and replaced with the letters "XYZ"—thereby creating the name by which the affair was called. Adams's popularity soared as the result of the XYZ affair and his prompt efforts to strengthen national defense.

Unfortunately, Gerry decided to follow the advice of the French Foreign Minister Talleyrand, who convinced him that if he stayed in France, he would prevent war. When Marshall and Pinckney left in anger, Gerry stayed behind long after their departure. Eventually, Adams became so embarrassed by Gerry that he recalled him. Gerry met severe censure from the Federalists upon his return, and he was forced into the firm embrace of the Democratic Republicans.

The Massachusetts constitution provided for annual terms for governor, and Gerry ran as a Democratic Republican four times for the office between 1800 and 1803, failing in each attempt. By 1810, his political fortunes had changed and he won two consecutive terms. Toward the end of his second term, he supported a bill to redistrict the state senate. The plan called for all the Federalist areas to be lumped together in the smallest number of districts. The Federalists would, of course, win all of those seats, but their remaining votes would be spread thinly in the other districts, enabling a larger than proportionate share of Democratic Republicans to win. The resulting districts had a peculiar shape, and one of them looked like a salamander. The Federalist newspapers drew a cartoon, which took the shape of one district, added a head and some wings, and called the concoction a "Gerry Mander." Eventually, the phrase evolved into the word *gerrymander*, which is used today to describe any purportedly unfair districting plan.

Although he was only in his 60s when he was nominated for vice president with JAMES MADISON in 1812, Gerry was in poor health and had financial problems because of his many years of neglecting the family business. Still, Madison needed him, and Gerry agreed to run. Since he was a Democratic Republican from Massachusetts—still a Federalist bastion—he was a real asset to the ticket because Madison had fallen out with GEORGE and DEWITT CLINTON of New York. Madison did not want to come up short in New England if he could help it. Gerry served as vice president in 1813 and 1814, but he collapsed and died on his way to the Senate chamber on November 23, 1814. His widow, who lived until 1849, was the last surviving spouse of a signer of the Declaration of Independence.

Gerry was like several of the Revolutionary War leaders who had difficulty with the critical job of governing after they won the Revolution. He was intelligent, experienced, and worked very hard, but he made more enemies than necessary by being humorless, suspicious of others' motives, and overly fearful of political and military tyranny.

Further Reading

Austin, James T. *The Life of Elbridge Gerry.* Boston: Wells & Lilly, 1828.

Billias, George A. *Elbridge Gerry: Founding Father and Republican Statesman.* New York: McGraw-Hill, 1976.

"Gerry, Elbridge." in *The Presidency A to Z: Second Edition,* edited by Michael T. Nelson. Washington, D.C.: Congressional Quarterly Press, 1998.

"Gerrymandering" in *Congress A to Z: Third Edition,* edited by David R. Tarr and Ann O'Connor. Washington, D.C.: Congressional Quarterly, 1999.

Morison, Samuel Eliot. "Elbridge Gerry, Gentleman-Democrat," in *By Land and by Sea.* New York: Knopf, 1953.

Gingrich, Newton Leroy

(1942–   ) *Speaker of the House, representative*

In 1995, Newt Gingrich was the most powerful Speaker of the U.S. House of Representatives that the United States had seen since the earliest days of the 20th century. He misjudged the nature of his power and was forced to resign both the Speaker's office and his seat in the House as the result of one of the worst losses sustained by his party in the 1998 midterm congressional elections. Initially famous for forcing the resignation of former Democratic Speaker James Wright over a few thousand dollars in ethically suspect financial transactions, Gingrich was forced to pay a $300,000 fine for his own financial irregularities, including a $4.5 million book deal and the misuse

of large sums of tax-exempt money for political purposes. As Speaker, he presided over the impeachment of President WILLIAM JEFFERSON CLINTON for having not been forthcoming about an extramarital affair at the same time that he was conducting an extramarital affair of his own. His hypocrisy, as much as his lack of skill, was responsible for his political demise.

Newton Leroy Gingrich was born in Harrisburg, Pennsylvania, on June 17, 1943. He attended school at various military installations, because his father was a career military officer. He ended up graduating from Baker High School in Columbus, Georgia, in 1961, because his father was posted nearby at the time.

After receiving his B.A. degree from Emory University in 1965, Gingrich studied modern European history at Tulane, receiving his M.A. in 1968 and his Ph.D. in 1971. He moved back to Georgia where he began teaching history and environmental studies at West Georgia College in Carrollton, Georgia.

Gingrich was first elected to the U.S. House of Representatives in 1978 and, almost from the start, began to advocate a policy of confrontation rather than cooperation with the Democrats as a method of political success. His strategy seemed popular at the time, and he was elected as the Republican minority whip in 1989. Almost immediately he began a tenacious pursuit of Democratic Speaker Jim Wright. Gingrich believed that if an investigation were unrelenting enough, some kind of irregularities could be found that would bring Speaker Wright down.

Gingrich was correct. Wright had written a book under a contract that had allowed him to receive a few thousand dollars in income, thereby circumventing House rules that limited the amount of outside income someone could receive. The House Ethics Committee agreed to have an outside attorney investigate Wright's financial affairs and, in April 1989, the committee determined that they wished to hold hearings on 69 instances in which Wright might have violated House rules. Rather than face long, dragged out public hearings over these matters, Wright resigned as Speaker in the middle of his term—the first time this happened in U.S. history.

Gingrich's strategy paid off, and his star was on the rise. In 1994, Gingrich was the prime mover behind a national Republican campaign strategy known as the "Contract with America," a political and intellectual proposal for moving the United States in a conservative direction by reforming the legislative procedures in the House as well as making policy changes, such as lowering taxes while reducing domestic spending and yet increasing defense expenditures. Its novelty rested on its promise of a comprehensive national approach rather than the piecemeal proposals tailored to the public opinion polls for individual districts so typical of past campaigns. Using his strategy, Republicans made such large gains in both the House of Representatives and the Senate that they won control of both houses of Congress for the first time in 42 years.

While the election returns made it appear that the U.S. citizenry had suddenly become overwhelmingly conservative, no fundamental shift in national ideology had really taken place. Instead, the Republicans benefited from a series of decisions to allow African Americans to draw more "safe seats" from which African Americans could be elected. While these new districts would likely be safe for Democrats, they could only be constructed by weakening other districts from which Democrats had previously been elected. These new seats would not be taken away from Republicans; they would be taken away from other Democrats. As the result, the total number of Democratic "safe seats" fell below the number needed to hold a majority in the House, and the Republicans captured the House. The Republicans also benefited from the typically higher Republican turnout in congressional elections.

Gingrich and the Republican congressional leadership ignored this prosaic, if accurate, explanation and acted as if there had been a revolutionary shift in U.S. public opinion in a conservative direction. As the newly elected Speaker, Gingrich fulfilled his promise by forcing the new Republican majority to pass almost the entire "Contract with America." The less tightly controlled Republican Senate paid lip service to the contract but modified many parts of it. Despite these changes, Gingrich declared he had kept his promise, and the

new legislation was sent to President Clinton, who signed some of it but vetoed the rest. Later, the Supreme Court declared still more parts of the contract unconstitutional. Some of the contract survived but not as much as if a genuine revolution had occurred.

In 1995, Gingrich not only controlled action on the House floor but also controlled the Republican Conference so he could name the committee chairpersons and assign the new members to their committees. In short, the Republicans dismantled the seniority system for their members. Congresspersons now discovered they had to vote as Gingrich's lieutenants instructed or risk removal from either the chairperson's job or the committee. It was this power that enabled Gingrich to forced the "Contract with America" through the House on an expedited schedule.

However, Gingrich overplayed his hand, and his power dissipated greatly during the next two years. He blundered initially by accepting a $4.5 million advance payment on a book. This contract, though apparently legal, made Gingrich look bad since he had previously hounded former Speaker Jim Wright out of office for taking a few thousand dollars for a book contract. Facing a storm of criticism, Gingrich relented and accepted only a one-dollar advance against royalties to settle the matter.

Gingrich then faced charges from the House Ethics Committee—the same committee that Gingrich had used to bring charges against Speaker Wright—that Gingrich had used tax-exempt money for political purposes. In responding to inquiries from members of the committee, Gingrich gave them information, which the committee later determined to be "inaccurate, incomplete, and unreliable." Gingrich then admitted he gave the committee false information but said he did not intend to do so.

Gingrich's success in leading the Republicans to control of the House for the first time in more than 40 years caused him to make political misjudgments as well. Gingrich seemed very proud of the press reports that implied he was now the most powerful man in the United States and the fact that *Time* magazine named him the 1995 Man of the Year. He reacted by ruling with an iron hand, but this worked only briefly and ultimately led to resentment. Further, while Gingrich's press coverage might eclipse the president's coverage briefly, the Speaker of the U.S. House of Representatives is simply not more powerful than the president.

During all this, Clinton kept a low profile, correctly perceiving that the mainstream of the U.S. electorate would eventually find the Republican political agenda too radical. He also seemed to sense that the Republicans were about to overreach. This they did when they sought to show that Gingrich was the most powerful man in America by shutting down the government when Clinton refused to sign the budget that the Republicans forced through the Congress. They succeeded in shutting down the government, but that only meant that they got the lion's share of the blame for a situation that dragged on for several weeks at the end of 1995 and early 1996.

The political advantage then shifted to Clinton, who attacked Republican extremism while presenting a somewhat more mainstream program, which he said would bring peace abroad and economic recovery at home. When the Republicans nominated Senate majority leader ROBERT JOSEPH DOLE as their 1996 presidential nominee, Clinton was able to portray Dole as a member of the radical Republican congressional leadership, even though he was a senator and Gingrich was Speaker of the House.

Ironically, Clinton defeated Dole, a distinguished World War II veteran, in the 1996 presidential campaign even though he had still not had a major opportunity to demonstrate his ability in foreign or military affairs. Clinton successfully won reelection for himself, but he was unable to carry either house of Congress, so that he faced the same political disadvantage during his second term that he had during the last two years of his first term. Clinton was forced to compromise with Republican majorities, but this situation was still useful to him because it allowed him to rein in the extremists in his own party.

In early 1997, Gingrich felt compelled to make a much more humble address when he resumed his duties as Speaker at the start of a new session of Congress. Gingrich essentially maintained that he had learned his lesson and that he was going to abandon his past confrontational tactics. There were no rousing cheers for the speech, and nine Republicans had decided not to vote for Gingrich's reelection. Within a month, the entire House voted to impose a $300,000 fine on Gingrich for his ethics violations—the first time this kind of a penalty had been imposed on a sitting Speaker. Still, the Republican congressional leadership continued their confrontations with the White House.

Conservative Republicans had attacked Clinton almost from the moment of his election. By 1993, bumper stickers circulated calling for Clinton's impeachment, sometimes attacking both Clinton and his wife, saying "Impeach Clinton and her husband, too." When the Republicans captured control of both houses of Congress in 1995, they began to investigate both Clintons over the so-called Whitewater real estate venture, in which Bill Clinton and his wife, HILLARY RODHAM CLINTON, had been involved while he was Arkansas governor. While the investigators raised some questions about the Clintons' involvement, they were never able to provide any proof to refute the Clintons' claim that they lost money on the venture and that Whitewater was simply a failed real estate deal typical of the 1980s.

A special prosecutor named Kenneth Starr had been appointed to investigate charges made against the president and his cabinet officials, pursuant to a statute passed years earlier after the Watergate scandal. Unfortunately for the perceived fairness of the investigation, partisan charges that Starr's appointment had been political dogged the investigation from the first. As the partisan charges bounced back and forth between the special prosecutor's office and the White House, the special prosecutor's office apparently sought to move the investigation into a different direction, trying to find something to justify the time and money invested in the case. Eventually the investigation turned to an examination of Clinton's extramarital sex life. None of these investigations were a problem for Gingrich until Special Prosecutor Starr concluded that grounds existed to impeach Clinton for lying under oath about a romantic involvement with a 24-year-old woman named Monica Lewinsky.

At that point, the law required Starr to report his findings to Congress. The more radical Republicans demanded that Speaker Gingrich support their efforts to impeach Clinton. Gingrich likely had mixed feelings about this, rightly fearing that the end result might be the discovery of his own extramarital affair with a member of his congressional staff. By 1997, Gingrich's political strength had dissipated to the point that he could not block the impeachment effort even if he had wanted to do so.

To impeach a president requires that the House of Representatives vote to do so by a simple majority of those present and voting. Since the Republicans controlled a majority of seats in the House, they were able to impeach Clinton on almost a perfectly straight party line vote. However, conviction requires that the Senate hold a trial and vote to convict by a two-thirds vote. The Republicans had a majority in the Senate but did not control two-thirds of the seats so that Clinton would escape conviction as long as no significant number of the Democrats deserted him. After voluminous testimony and much acrimonious debate, the Senate voted essentially along party lines to acquit Clinton.

Throughout the entire impeachment process, most Americans indicated in public opinion polls that, even though that they disapproved of his actions, they wanted Clinton neither impeached nor convicted. The Republicans proceeded with the impeachment trial nonetheless, believing that it was the right thing to do and perhaps hoping it would help them in the 1998 congressional elections. However, the impeachment effort hurt the Republicans badly. Normally, the Democrats would have lost seats in the 1998 congressional elections. Historically, the party that controls the White House for two terms has lost seats in the midterm elections in the sixth year of their White House tenure, usually in very large numbers. It is generally believed that the electorate simply tires of the control of one party in the White House and that the electorate then vents its discontent on the representatives of that party in Congress. This phenomenon makes the 1998 congressional election outcome startling since the Democrats gained seats. This had happened only once before in U.S. history. In 1834, the Whig Party—precursors of the Republican Party—attacked Andrew Jackson so viciously that their campaign backfired and allowed the Democrats to gain seats when they normally would have lost them.

This stunning reversal of expectations can most likely be attributed to the popular reaction against the Republicans for the impeachment effort. While the public opinion polls showed Clinton had high negative ratings for his personal life, the same polls showed that the voters approved of his job performance and strongly opposed the impeachment effort.

Clinton survived impeachment, but Gingrich did not. In the summer of 1997, Gingrich had beaten back a challenge to his leadership by conservative Republican House members who were disappointed by his failure to defeat Clinton in the budget battles. Three days after the 1998 election, when it became clear that the Republican majority had been reduced to only a few votes, Republican House Appropriations Chairman Robert L. Livingston issued a statement that he would challenge Gingrich for the post of Speaker. Press reports about Gingrich's extramarital affairs were already circulating, so Gingrich, apparently to avoid intense scrutiny over the issue, resigned both as Speaker and as a member of the House (even though he had just won reelection to his House seat by a wide margin). The bottom line for Gingrich must have been the knowledge that since the Republicans had only a five-seat majority at that point, any five Republicans could defeat Gingrich by simply not voting when the vote for Speaker came up in the next Congress.

The same slender margin also affected Gingrich's putative successor. Only a few days later, Robert Livingston rose in the House chamber to announce that he would not seek to become the Speaker and that he, too, was resigning. Attempting to avoid the destructive power of the press, he now admitted that he had had extramarital affairs and confessed that that was why he was resigning. Sometime later, the Republicans selected DENNIS HASTERT as their new leader, and he became the Speaker of the House at the start of the next Congress.

After his retirement, Gingrich went into private business as a management consultant. He became a senior fellow at the American Enterprise Institute and a visiting fellow at the Hoover Institution at Stanford University. He has appeared on television as a political analyst and has written a number of books.

Further Reading

Drew, Elizabeth. *Showdown: The Struggle between the Gingrich Congress and the Clinton White House.* New York: Simon & Schuster, 1996.

Gingrich, Newt, et al. *Contract with America.* New York: Times Books, 1994.

———. *Lessons Learned the Hard Way: A Personal Report.* New York: HarperCollins, 1998.

———. *1945.* Riverdale, N.Y.: Baen Publishing Enterprises, 1995. A novel.

———. *To Renew America.* New York: HarperCollins, 1995.

Jones, Charles O. *Clinton and Congress, 1993–1996: Risk, Restoration, and Reelection.* Norman: University of Oklahoma, 1999.

Maraniss, David. *"Tell Newt to Shut Up!"* New York: Simon & Schuster, 1996.

Steely, Mel. *The Gentleman from Georgia: The Biography of Newt Gingrich.* Macon, Ga.: Mercer University Press, 2000.

Williams, Dick. *Newt! Leader of the Second American Revolution.* Marietta, Ga.: Longstreet Press, 1995.

Wilson, John K. *Newt Gingrich: Capitol Crimes and Misdemeanors.* Monroe, Maine: Common Courage, 1996.

Goldberg, Arthur Joseph

(1908–1990) *associate justice of the Supreme Court, secretary of labor, diplomat*

Arthur Joseph Goldberg had a varied career as a labor lawyer, secretary of labor, associate justice of the U.S. Supreme Court, and ambassador to the United Nations. He is one of the very few justices of the Supreme Court ever to resign a lifetime term on that exalted bench for a limited term political post.

Goldberg was born on August 8, 1908, in Chicago, Illinois. He attended Northwestern University School of Law where he received his LL.B. in 1928 and his J.D. in 1929. Admitted to the bar in 1929, he began a long period of private practice that lasted until he became the U.S. secretary of labor in the administration of President JOHN FITZGERALD KENNEDY in 1961. Initially his law practice was in Chicago until 1952, although he did serve as the special assistant in the Office of Strategic Services in 1942 and 1943.

His legal practice was as a labor lawyer, and he attained a succession of increasingly important positions. He served as the general counsel to the United Steelworkers and the Congress of Industrial Organizations after 1948. In the mid 1950s, he had a major role in the merger of the American Federation of Labor (AFL) with its former archrival, the Congress of Industrial Organizations (CIO). Goldberg was rewarded for his efforts by being named the general counsel to the new American Federation of Labor-Congress of Industrial Organizations (AFL-CIO) after the two major labor groups merged in 1955. By 1952, Goldberg had moved his law practice to Washington, D.C., where he could be in better communication with the national headquarters of his most important clients.

When Kennedy was elected president in 1960, he repaid a large debt to organized labor by appointing Goldberg his secretary of labor. He served in that capacity until Kennedy nominated him to be an associate justice of the U.S. Supreme Court on August 31, 1962. FELIX FRANKFURTER, a member of the Jewish faith, had held this seat until he resigned in ill health. Since he had replaced the first Jewish justice on the Court, LOUIS DEMBITZ BRANDEIS, this seat had come to be considered a "Jewish" seat and Goldberg, also Jewish, was a logical candidate for the post. The Senate confirmed Goldberg easily on September 25, 1962, and he joined the Court just three days later on September 28, 1962.

On the court, he was considered a regular member of its liberal wing. The change from Frankfurter to Goldberg was considerable and gave the liberal wing a dependable five-vote majority. Frankfurter espoused the judicial restraint philosophy that limited the degree of change that the Court was entitled to make. Goldberg took the more activist view that the Court had a responsibility to protect any permanent minority that might not be able to use the political process to redress its grievances. Goldberg's most important long-lasting contribution may well have been his concurrence in the case of *Griswold v. Connecticut* (1965), which overturned a state law prohibiting doctors from providing birth control information to married couples. The implications extended far beyond the issue of the case, for *Griswold* provided the basis for the Court's landmark abortion decision in *Roe v. Wade*. Goldberg's concurrence set some of the issues in sharper relief than did the majority opinion in *Griswold*.

Goldberg wrote the majority opinion in *Escobedo v. Illinois* (1964), which laid the basis for the Court's later decision in *Miranda v. Arizona* (1966), mandating that those who are accused of a crime have a right to remain silent unless they have their attorney present. While both *Miranda* and *Escobedo* have been either overturned or eroded, certain significance still remains attached to them.

In *Gibson v. Florida Legislative Investigation Commission* (1963), Goldberg found that the right of the state to limit the right of association required that the state show a compelling state interest before doing so. In *Aptheker v. Secretary of State*, Goldberg found that laws revoking passports had to be strictly drafted, thereby freeing the Communist Party member whose passport had been revoked because of his association with the Communist Party.

These rulings take on special significance given Goldberg's short tenure on the Court. President LYNDON BAINES JOHNSON was determined to name his old friend, Abe Fortas, to the Court. Since Fortas was also Jewish, the best way to do this was to persuade Goldberg to resign. Johnson convinced Goldberg that he could have a lasting impact on resolving the war in Vietnam if he would resign from the Court to become the U.S. ambassador to the United Nations. Under intense pressure from Johnson, Goldberg reluctantly agreed to do so in 1965 and regretted the decision ever after. As it turned out, Goldberg's influence on the Johnson administration's Vietnam policy was so limited that he felt compelled to resign as UN ambassador in 1968.

After resigning as ambassador, Goldberg returned to private practice in New York. He ran for governor of New York in 1970 but lost, and that

defeat effectively ended his political career. A year later he moved his law practice back to Washington, D.C. His only other political appointment came when President JAMES EARL CARTER appointed him U.S. ambassador-at-large, and he served in a variety of troubleshooting roles from 1977 to 1978. He continued in the private practice of law in Washington, D.C., until his death on January 19, 1990.

Further Reading

Goldberg, Arthur J. *The Defenses of Freedom: The Public Papers of Arthur J. Goldberg.* New York: Harper & Row, 1966.

Goldberg, Dorothy K. *A Private View of a Public Life.* New York: Charterhouse, 1975.

Lasky, Victor. *Arthur J. Goldberg, The Old and the New.* New Rochelle, N.Y.: Arlington House, 1970.

Stebenne, David. *Arthur J. Goldberg: New Deal Liberal.* New York: Oxford University Press, 1996.

Goldwater, Barry Morris
(1909–1998) *candidate for president, senator, author*

More than a senator and an unsuccessful candidate for president, Barry Goldwater became a cultural icon for many conservatives and has been credited with paving the way for the eventual conservative revolution led by President RONALD WILSON REAGAN in the 1980s.

Barry Morris Goldwater was born on January 1, 1909, in Phoenix, Arizona, at a time when Arizona was still a territory. His grandfather had come there as an immigrant peddler to sell goods to miners during the gold rush. His parents built that business into a thriving department store operation in Phoenix. In 1928, Goldwater graduated from Staunton Military Academy in Phoenix. He attended the University of Arizona in Tucson but dropped out to work in the family business. He became president of Goldwater's Department Store in 1937. He was named chairman of the board in 1953 and remained in that position until the stores were sold.

During World War II, he was the commander of the Ninetieth Air Base Squadron and, later, chief of staff of the Fourth Air Force. He flew in the first flight of P-47s from the United States to Europe. He also served as the chief pilot in the Air Transport Command in North Africa and India. Goldwater continued to serve in the Air Force Reserve after the war and rose to the rank of major general by the time he retired in 1967. Goldwater was a skillful pilot and persuaded the air force to allow him to fly several of its newest airplanes as they were being developed. He was the first person who was not officially a test pilot to fly the U-2, SR-71, and B-1 planes.

After the war, he started out in politics as a founder of the Charter Government party formed by Phoenix business leaders to eliminate corruption in the city. In the 1949 municipal election, he won a seat on the city council with more votes than any of the other candidates. His service resulted in his being named the first Phoenix Man of the Year. He was again the top vote getter when he ran for reelection in 1951 as a Charter Government candidate.

Within a year, the Republicans were pushing Goldwater to run against Ernest W. McFarland, the Democratic Senate majority leader whose term was up in 1952. In September 1952, Goldwater ran as a Republican Senate candidate and defeated McFarland by a vote of 132,063–125,338.

In the Senate, Goldwater served on the Armed Services Committee, the Commerce, Science and Transportation Committee (then known as the Aeronautical and Space Science Committee), and the Intelligence Committee. However, he was not well known for his legislative achievements, but rather he used the Senate as a platform for his attempts to reinvigorate the conservative cause. He made it clear that he felt the United States had lapsed into a dangerous accommodation with liberalism during the administration of President DWIGHT DAVID EISENHOWER. In 1960, he wrote and published his well-known book, *The Conscience of a Conservative,* long a standard statement of conservative principles.

In 1964, Goldwater pursued the Republican nomination for president. His candidacy badly divided the moderates in the party who were forced to choose among the conservative Goldwater, the liberal New York Governor NELSON ALDRICH ROCKEFELLER, and the moderate Pennsylvania governor William Scranton. During the ill-fated 1964 campaign, when moderate and conservative Republicans were tearing the party apart, Goldwater uttered his most famous line: "Extremism in the defense of liberty is no vice. Moderation in the pursuit of justice is no virtue." This was meant as a defense of his efforts to revitalize conservatism.

While the statement was true enough, his opponents seized on this remark as a defense of extremism, indicating that Goldwater would persist in making statements urging the use of nuclear weapons in war and obstructing the achievement of civil rights for African Americans. These positions solidified his credentials for his followers on the far right but alienated voters in the middle of the spectrum. Goldwater lost the popular vote for president to LYNDON BAINES JOHNSON by 16 million votes. In percentage terms, he lost by the largest percentage of the two-party vote in the 20th century. He also lost the Electoral College vote by 52–486 for Johnson, one of the largest Electoral College losses in the 20th century.

His 52 Electoral College votes came from several southern states and his home state of Arizona. The election results represented a critical shift in which previously solid Democratic states in the South voted Republican for the first time. It was Goldwater's vote against the 1964 Civil Rights Act that allowed him to carry the South and advanced the realignment of America's two political parties.

Despite the defeat, many observers have suggested that Goldwater's loss set the stage for the conservative revolution that accompanied the election of President Reagan in 1980. Goldwater was out of office after his presidential defeat, but he won election to the U.S. Senate again in 1968. He thus served throughout the Nixon presidency—but without acquiring any friendship with Nixon, whom he once said was the "most dishonest individual I ever met in my life."

Goldwater was one of the Republican leaders who went in a group to the White House to tell Nixon that he had to resign or he would be impeached. Despite Watergate, Goldwater was reelected in 1974 and 1980, but his 1980 reelection was so close that it may have led to his decision to retire at the end of that term in 1986.

It was in Goldwater's last term that he achieved what he regarded as his greatest legislative accomplishment: passage of a military reorganization bill he pushed through the Senate in May 1986. Also in May 1986, President Reagan awarded Goldwater the Presidential Medal of Freedom, the nation's highest civilian award.

After retiring from a 30-year Senate career in 1986, Goldwater lectured at Arizona State University and supported local Republican candidates, but his political activities continued to be controversial. In October 1987, he called on Arizona's governor, Evan Mecham, a Republican, to resign for his corrupt activities, and this provoked outrage among Republicans.

Goldwater's bluntness often made many Republicans very angry. He took a dim view of the religious right and publicly castigated the Reverend Jerry Falwell. He endorsed a woman's right to have an abortion and the right of gays to serve in the military. He endorsed Democrat Karan English for Congress over her Republican opponent in 1992. He also urged Republicans to lay off WILLIAM JEFFERSON CLINTON over the Whitewater scandal.

In August 1996, Goldwater horrified Republicans by suggesting he would choose Clinton over Republican ROBERT JOSEPH DOLE, but he later said he was joking. In September 1996, he was hospitalized for two weeks after suffering a minor stroke. Even in the hospital he got national headlines, with visits by Clinton, GOP presidential challenger Dole, and Colin Powell, former head of the Joint Chiefs of Staff. During his retirement he survived 15 major surgeries but died on May 29, 1998.

Further Reading

Edwards, Lee. *Goldwater: The Man Who Made a Revolution.* Washington, D.C.: Regnery, 1995.

Goldberg, Robert A. *Barry Goldwater.* New Haven, Conn.: Yale University Press, 1995.

Goldwater, Barry Morris. *The Conscience of a Conservative.* New York: Hillman, 1960.

———. *Goldwater.* New York: Doubleday, 1988.

———. *People and Places.* New York: Random House, 1967.

———. *Where I Stand.* New York: McGraw-Hill, 1964.

———. *Why Not Victory? A Fresh Look at American Foreign Policy.* New York: McGraw-Hill, 1962.

———. *With No Apologies.* New York: Morrow, 1979.

Iverson, Peter. *Barry Goldwater: Native Arizonan.* Norman: University of Oklahoma Press, 1997.

Novak, Robert D. *The Agony of the G.O.P. 1964.* New York: Macmillan, 1965.

Rovere, Richard. *The Goldwater Caper.* New York: Harcourt, Brace & World, 1965.

White, Theodore H. *The Making of the President, 1964.* New York: New American Library, 1965.

Gore, Albert Arnold, Jr.

(1948–) *candidate for president, vice president, senator, representative, author*

Albert Arnold Gore, Jr., had a distinguished career as an eight-year veteran of the House of Representatives and as an eight-year veteran of the Senate before being elected vice president in 1992. After eight years as vice president, he was the Democratic nominee for president in 2000. Gore won the popular vote for president in 2000 by more than a half million votes, a reasonably close margin but by no means the closest popular vote margin in U.S. history. He also would have received a majority of the Electoral College votes if Florida's Electoral College votes had been discarded as irredeemably tainted. He would also have received Florida's Electoral College votes (and therefore been elected president) if the votes of all those who turned out to vote for him in Florida had been counted. However, many of his supporters failed to cast unambiguous ballots for him, and Florida officials in a variety of ways eliminated the ballots of enough people that the election in Florida—and therefore the nation—was given to President GEORGE WALKER BUSH. Gore then joined Democrats ANDREW JACKSON, SAMUEL JONES TILDEN, and STEPHEN GROVER CLEVELAND as the only Americans who received a majority of the popular votes but not the majority of the Electoral College votes needed to be elected president.

Gore was born in Washington, D. C., on March 31, 1948. His father, a moderate to liberal Democrat, represented Tennessee in the U.S. House and Senate for more than 30 years. Educated in private schools in Washington while his father served in Congress, Gore received a bachelor of arts degree in government from Harvard in 1969. Facing the draft, he volunteered for the army and served as an army reporter in Vietnam. He was one of the few sons of Congress members to serve in Vietnam rather than evade military service. He then studied religion and law at Vanderbilt University, but he was not satisfied with either career. He began working as a reporter for the Nashville *Tennessean* and wrote a number of important journalistic pieces before entering politics in 1976.

Gore was elected to the U.S. House of Representatives as a Democrat from Tennessee's Fourth Congressional District in 1976, a district that his father once represented. After serving four terms, Gore was elected to the U.S. Senate in 1984 (but not to the seat his father once held). In the Congress, Gore focused his attention on arms control, the development of technology, facilitating the use of the Internet, and the protection of the environment. In 1992, he wrote *Earth in the Balance: Ecology and the Human Spirit,* which went on to become a best-seller. In it, he set out the need to protect the earth's ozone layer, to clean up toxic waste, and to take specific steps to meet that goal.

Gore first ran for the Democratic presidential nomination in early 1988 when he was 39 years old. In his congressional career, he positioned himself as a moderate on most of the important issues to voters in the South. At the same time, he staked out a more progressive posture on the environment, arms control, and technology where progressive ideas would attract southern and border state support while not offending most southern voters. The strategy worked well in the South, where he won seven Democratic primaries and caucuses. He even received the backing of some leading Democratic moderates and, in advance of the New York primary, from then New York City mayor Edward Koch. However, in a crowded field, he could not stretch his regional support into a genuine national base, and he eventually dropped out of the race.

Two years later, he ran for reelection to the Senate and won by such a landslide that he carried every county in the state—a feat unparalleled in a two-party race in recent Tennessee history. Gore debated about entering the presidential race in 1992 but decided against it, citing family reasons.

But the apparent recent success of President GEORGE HERBERT WALKER BUSH in handling the Gulf War may well have played a role in his deciding not to run.

Gore reemerged as a national candidate when the Democratic presidential nominee, WILLIAM JEFFERSON CLINTON, selected him as his vice presidential running mate. Defying the usual convention of selecting a running mate from a different geographic location or ideological background, Clinton chose Gore, a senator from Tennessee, a state adjacent to his own home state of Arkansas, and a moderate from the same faction in the Democratic Party. Key among the considerations must have been the fact that Gore actually served in the armed forces in Vietnam when Clinton did not serve in the armed forces at all (and was accused by some of draft dodging).

The Clinton-Gore ticket won the election by a comfortable margin. Gore then began one of the most successful vice presidencies in recent history by becoming a trusted adviser to Clinton. He was given a significant role in reforming the federal government by reducing its size and increasing its efficiency under the banner of "Reinventing Government." He also continued to lead on environmental issues, the expanded use of technology, and education.

After winning reelection, the Clinton-Gore team encountered new difficulties that ultimately strained their relationship. One of Gore's campaign responsibilities had been to focus on fundraising, some of which appeared to skirt the law in the eyes of his opponents. Gore made fund-raising telephone calls from government buildings in violation of an obscure 19th-century law of uncertain application to current practices and attended some questionable political fund-raising events. Critics demanded that the U.S. attorney general, Janet Reno, appoint a special prosecutor to investigate these matters, but Reno decided that there was insufficient evidence to do so. Gore claimed to have been cleared, although his critics continued to question these events and implied that the nonprosecution was a cover-up.

The difficulties over Gore's campaign activities were seen against the background of the extensive investigations of President Clinton and his wife,

HILLARY RODHAM CLINTON, that had dragged on inconclusively throughout the first term. In 1998, these investigations took a dramatic new turn when President Clinton was accused of having an affair with 24-year-old woman who worked in the White House and then lying and obstructing justice to cover up these activities. Gore had no role in these events, but it was an obviously awkward time for him. The allegations were initially unproven. After the affair was acknowledged, doubt persisted as to whether the president's actions to cover up the affair constituted criminal wrongdoing. Gore would have had difficulty attacking the president while the charges were in doubt without appearing disloyal, but he could not remain absolutely silent without appearing to have any independent judgment at all. Gore's attempt to salve the situation by expressing disapproval of Clinton's behavior did not satisfy his critics.

Clinton survived the impeachment scandal, and Gore, despite the past difficulties, ran for the 2000 Democratic presidential nomination. Former Senator Bill Bradley opposed him for the nomination, managed to make some inroads with the liberal wing of the Democratic Party, and raised a considerable campaign fund. But Bradley was unable to win any primaries, and Gore eventually coasted to the nomination at the Democratic National Convention. Making a well-received nomination speech, Gore got a boost in the polls. The Republicans nominated George W. Bush, son of former President George Herbert Walker Bush.

The 2000 presidential campaign became the most controversial in U.S. history, but it gave no indication of the controversy ahead when it started. While both candidates had some strong features in their backgrounds, neither seemed so strong as to obviously overwhelm the other. Gore was regarded as an intelligent man with a 24-year record of distinguished national service and was almost entirely untouched by the scandals that surrounded Clinton. However, he seemed to have difficulty relating to the mass electorate despite repeated attempts to change his approach. Most frequently accused of making wooden speeches, it might be more accurate to say that he could not overcome his own awareness of his intelligence and ended up appearing to patronize his audience.

As a result, he was respected for his intelligence but disliked. Bush, who had been elected to two terms as governor of Texas, was regarded as likeable but had compiled a record of misstatements that raised some questions about his intelligence. The closeness of the election was reflected in public opinion polls, which showed the lead shifting back and forth between the candidates, a situation that continued even during the presidential and vice presidential debates.

Gore won all three of the debates according to the experts who concentrated on the debating points as well as those polled specifically on the debates, but Bush gained ground slightly in the polls that asked for whom the voter intended to vote. Expectations for Bush's performance were low given his reputation for making verbal blunders, but ironically this helped him during the debate period because he did better than expected. Gore was so well informed in the first debate that he came across as a strident, arrogant know-it-all. Gore's stridency seemed even worse after the vice presidential debate because both Republican Dick Cheney and Democrat Joe Lieberman conducted such a civil debate (in a more relaxed format) that they offered a stark contrast to the harsh tone of the first presidential debate. Faced with criticism that he was too aggressive in the first debate, Gore was more subdued in the next presidential debate (which took place in a more relaxed format) with the result that he was criticized for being too passive. He achieved the proper balance in the third debate, but Bush seemed to have gained critical momentum.

Bush's short-term strength became less important because he continued to make mistakes. Overconfident, Bush took a day off to rest in the last two weeks and then made a strange statement that Social Security was not a federal program. Bush had also failed to disclose a decades-old drunk-driving arrest early in the campaign (when disclosure would have done little harm) only to be placed on the defensive when the arrest suddenly came to light four days before the election.

Gore reached Election Day with slight momentum in his favor in a very tight campaign. Early on election night, all major television networks declared Gore the winner in Michigan,

Pennsylvania, and Florida—three states thought to provide him with the margin of victory. Indeed, had Gore carried all three states he would have been elected president even if he had lost the popular vote. As it was, Gore received 500,000 more votes than Bush nationwide, but he was not awarded a win in Florida, costing him the majority in the Electoral College.

In retrospect, it appears that more people went to the polls in Florida intending to vote for Gore than for Bush, but a sufficient number of these voters apparently invalidated their ballots, perhaps as the result of machine failure or confusing ballot layout. Only a careful official recount could have determined the result for certain, and that was preempted by a U.S. Supreme Court decision that gave the election to Bush.

The confusion began on election night when the television networks first declared Florida had voted for Gore after most polls had closed but before a handful of northwest Florida counties had finished voting. Vehemently criticized by Republicans, the networks then switched Florida—and the entire national election—into the "too close to call" category. Florida remained undecided until the early hours of the morning when the networks, following the lead of the Fox television network, declared for Bush. Given the returns from the other states, this made it very likely that Bush had won the election. Gore then telephoned Bush to congratulate him on his victory, but almost as soon as he did, Bush's lead began to slip. While Gore was heading to a gathering of supporters to concede, he received a phone call urging him not to concede since the Florida total was just a few hundred votes apart. Gore then telephoned Bush again to tell him the concession speech was on hold given the closeness of the vote.

The Florida election was also riddled with irregularities. Most Florida counties used a punch card voting system, an inexpensive system that used an older computer technology subject to a variety of errors. Punch card ballot layout is complicated, and one ballot layout variant, known as "butterfly" ballot, was misleading because it had arrows pointing to holes for the wrong candidates. Although such a ballot layout was illegal, both parties' local officials had foolishly approved its use in advance, leading some voters to vote for candidates other than those they wanted to vote for. In other cases, the punching boards for the ballots may have been clogged with small bits of paper from previous users so that the voter could not punch the ballot properly. Elsewhere, Republicans were given a special privilege not given to Democrats that helped them gain more absentee ballot applications and therefore more votes than the Democrats.

In ideal circumstances, the proper solution for determining the actual voter preference would have required a hand recount of the ballots. Florida law provided a pre-certification ballot examination procedure and a post-certification contested election recount procedure. Holding a lead of just a few hundred votes, Bush opposed any further counting of the ballots, said that his opponent should not use the courts to try to win the election, and demanded that the initial tally favoring his election be accepted. Gore naturally requested a recount in areas in which irregularities occurred and was granted some recounts in those areas as provided by Florida law.

Having initially said that the courts should not be used to determine the outcome, Bush was the first to file suit, trying to block further pre-certification ballot examination. Bush lost the suit related to the ballot counting process in the Florida courts and then sued in federal courts, offering a novel, untested legal theory that the recount law violated the equal protection clause of the Fourteenth Amendment because not every ballot was recounted—only ballots in areas in which irregularities occurred. The federal courts initially demurred. When the Florida Supreme Court decided the matter, they ruled that a recount could go forward under the existing state law and extended a deadline set out in state law for such a recount to take place.

Bush then appealed the lower federal court demurral to the U.S. Supreme Court, which overturned the Florida Supreme Court and ordered the recount halted using the equal protection clause argument as its basis. The Supreme Court decided the question by a narrow five-to-four decision in which the five most conservative justices—all Republican appointees—decided the issue. Instead of following the more conservative philosophy of respecting federalism and granting deference to state courts to allow them to interpret their own state constitution and laws, the five conservatives overturned a state supreme court ruling on grounds of a violation of the equal protection clause—a clause usually avoided by conservatives because it leads to expansions of judicial power normally associated with liberals.

That the most conservative justices would adopt such a stance led to widespread criticism that the Court was acting not out of a respect for the Constitution but out of mere partisan political concerns. Many conservative legal scholars criticized the five conservatives. The two Democratic appointees and two Republican appointees of moderate views dissented vigorously and objected publicly, apparently causing hard feelings that lasted for months. Recognizing that there was no higher court to which he could appeal, Gore made a gracious concession speech and the election was over.

Gore had achieved much with his candidacy. Some observers had thought he would lose the presidential race by a wide margin early in 2000. Gore surprised many with his strong campaign finish, which found him winning 50.2% of the vote and a raw popular vote margin of victory of more than a half million votes. Had Florida's Electoral College vote not been counted, as it could have been under some interpretations of the rules, Gore would have had a majority of the Electoral College vote and been elected president.

Gore did not retire from public life although he grew a beard and receded from public view for a while. He continued to make a few political appearances while accepting a teaching position at Columbia University in New York City and Vanderbilt University in Nashville. By 2002, media accounts reported that Gore was planning to run for president again in the 2004 presidential election. In April 2002, Gore shaved off his beard and made a rousing speech to a Democratic gathering in Florida—in what many observers said clearly signaled Gore's intention to enter the 2004 presidential contest, although there had been no official announcement.

Further Reading

Alston, Chuck, and Will Marshall. *Building the Bridge: Ten Big Ideas to Transform America.* Lanham, Md.: Rowman & Littlefield, 1997.

Baden, John A. *Environmental Gore: A Constructive Response to Earth in the Balance.* San Francisco: Pacific Research Institute for Public Policy, 1994.

Gore, Albert. *Common Sense Government: Works Better and Costs Less.* New York: Random House, 1995.

———. *Earth in the Balance: Ecology and the Human Spirit.* New York: Plume, 1993.

Grant, Ulysses S.
(Hiram Ulysses Grant)
(1822–1885) *president*

The greatest U.S. general in the Civil War and one of the greatest U.S. generals of all time, Ulysses S. Grant was a controversial and, at best, mediocre president.

Grant was born on April 27, 1822, in Pleasant Point, Ohio. His mother initially named him Hiram Ulysses Grant. Although some biographers have asserted that the S. stands for "Simpson," Grant insisted that he had no middle name beyond the letter "S." His father was in the leather tanning business, but young Grant disliked the trade. He did like to travel and often replaced his father on business trips so he could travel as widely as possible. Traveling widely became a dominant personal characteristic of Grant throughout his life. He attended public schools, but he did not do well until his father arranged for him to attend West Point. Young Grant was convinced he was not a good student, so he feared he would not even pass the entrance exams for the military academy. To his surprise, he passed easily, managed the military curriculum well, and graduated in the upper quarter of his class.

For two years after West Point, he pursued his duties in the infantry in Missouri, where he met and became engaged to his future wife, Julia Dent, the sister of one of his West Point classmates. After two years in peacetime service in Missouri and Louisiana, Grant joined the army under the command of General ZACHARY TAYLOR to fight in the Mexican War. The military life agreed with Grant, and he stayed in the army after the war was over, even though most of his West Point classmates returned to civilian life. He held the rank of captain, a high position in a peacetime army, but could not support his family. He eventually returned to civilian life, working at first for his father-in-law and then on his own. He was not successful in any of these business ventures. He was working with his brothers in their father's tanning and leather goods business when the Civil War broke out.

The Illinois governor, Richard Yates, appointed Grant to lead a ragtag volunteer unit, and he quickly turned it into a disciplined fighting force. In September 1861, Grant was elevated to the rank of brigadier general. After Grant's success in taking the Confederate strongholds at Fort Henry and Fort Donelson in February 1862, President ABRAHAM LINCOLN named him to the rank of major general.

Ulysses S. Grant, considered by many the greatest general of the Civil War, although personally honest, presided over a scandal-ridden administration. *(Library of Congress)*

Grant's success was the result of his conclusion that the existing theories of combat in his day were incomplete. The previous European model spent excessive attention on clockwork drill, polished dress, and maneuver. Grant simplified this to a strategy of seeking the best ground, massing his forces, and then fighting until the opposing army broke. His strong point in this strategy was his excellent administrative skill. At the same time, the strategy was expensive in terms of casualties, but it worked. Grant did not always win easy battles. The battle at Shiloh was one of the bloodiest of the Civil War, and some of Grant's critics wanted Lincoln to remove him. Lincoln turned aside that demand by asserting that Grant was one of the few northern generals who actually fought battles.

Grant continued to pursue his strategy of seeking to control the Mississippi, and he cut the Confederacy in two by capturing Vicksburg, the key city on the river. He next focused on the key rail center of Chattanooga, where the Union army was under siege. Grant's strategy there, as elsewhere, was to mass his troops and fight his way out. After he had broken out at Chattanooga, the entire state of Georgia laid almost completely undefended before Union troops. Grant assigned General William T. Sherman to drive through Georgia, cutting the Confederacy into two more parts. Grant then used the Army of the Potomac to isolate General Robert E. Lee's Army of Northern Virginia. Lincoln appointed Grant general-in-chief in March 1864. By April 9, 1865, Lee surrendered at Appomattox. Grant, for his part, wrote out generous terms of surrender that forestalled treason trials against his opponents.

After the assassination of President Lincoln, Grant was the most popular man in the northern United States following the Civil War, and he was courted by all political groups. His own inclination was to avoid political stands based on abstract ideas and to make his decisions on concrete facts. Thus, he was not interested in the states' rights position of politicians such as President ANDREW JOHNSON, because that would lead to the hard fact that the leaders of the Confederacy would be restored to power in the southern states. Nor was Grant interested in an abstract principle, such as the racial justice ideal pursued by the Radical Republicans, because that created a number of impractical demands on government. Grant was closest to the practical approach of the moderate Republicans (sometimes referred to as the conservatives) who were prepared to insist that the South grant suffrage (or voting rights) to African Americans but would not push racial justice beyond that.

While Grant avoided political discussions and left himself open to all groups, he was the conservative Republicans' logical candidate for president in 1868. Because he had taken so few stands, many others concluded that he agreed with them whether he did or not. Intellectuals and reformers were particularly likely to assume that he shared their view that what the country needed was stable, well-administered government. Since wartime organization and administration were Grant's strengths, he was able to attract their support as well. The Radical Republicans were suspicious of him, but the effort to impeach President Johnson and the contentious struggle with the South reduced their popularity to the point where they had to support Grant or lose the election and have even less influence.

The Democratic Party nominated New York Governor Horatio Seymour as their presidential nominee. Even with Grant as their presidential nominee and their record of successfully prosecuting the war, the Republicans were only able to win by about 300,000 votes out of 5.7 million votes cast (53% of the popular vote). Grant began his administration with a reservoir of goodwill, given the popular sentiment for an end to the war and wartime controversies, but it dissipated as he attempted to grapple with the problems of Reconstruction and the economic problems the nation faced by the necessity of paying wartime debts.

Grant's strong suit would seem to have been administration, but administration would not answer the real political problems at stake. Reconstruction was not yet complete. Virginia, Mississippi, and Texas had not yet complied with the readmission requirement that they ratify the Fourteenth Amendment and write a state constitution providing for racial civil and political equality. The Radical Republicans continued to add stiffer conditions in these states, but the conserva-

tive Republicans and the Conservatives (meaning former Democratic and Whig opponents of the Radical Republicans) resisted them. In addition, the white Georgia legislators had expelled the African-American members from the legislature, which cast serious doubt on the degree to which political equality existed there.

In the international sphere, there was the important issue of settling claims with the British for their sometime unofficial support of the Confederacy. The British had built ships for the Confederacy and allowed Confederate raiders to use their harbors. Their ships had damaged U.S. shipping, so the United States sought reparations. Initially, CHARLES FRANCIS ADAMS, U.S. ambassador to Great Britain, had negotiated a settlement during the administration of President Johnson, but the Radical Republicans thought the result was too conciliatory, and the proposed treaty was rejected. Some Radical Republicans wanted war with Great Britain; others thought that the United States ought to receive the entire province of Canada as compensation. Fortunately, an international arbitration court in Geneva, Switzerland, finally resolved the issue peacefully in 1871.

The successful prosecution of the Civil War led to an exuberant desire for foreign adventure. The Spanish colony of Cuba was the scene of nearly continuous unrest from slave revolts. Having ended slavery in the United States, some reformers thought they should end it elsewhere in the hemisphere. Opinion was divided, so moderates were able to derail the Cuba initiative. There was less division initially over the annexation of Santo Domingo (now called the Dominican Republic), but eventually divisions arose and this initiative also became sidetracked.

Regarding the U.S. economy, a number of interrelated issues called for resolution, but the Grant administration did not make much progress on them. The Civil War was financed largely through issuing bonds and printing paper currency unbacked by precious metals. To make the bonds attractive investments, they carried a high rate of interest and were made free from either federal or state taxation. The paper currency or "greenbacks" were declared to be legal tender for all debts. These policies together led to inflation throughout the war years. After the war, bondholders, backed by the intellectual economic opinion of the day, demanded a return to the use of specie (coins made of precious metals, such as gold or silver) or to currency backed by precious metals.

During the war, most of the wealth was in the northeastern part of the United States, so most of the bonds were sold there. These bondholders naturally wanted their bonds paid off in the hardest currency available, so they demanded a return to a currency backed by gold or silver. However, to repay the bonds meant taxes had to be raised. This tax increase applied to direct as well as indirect taxes, such as the tariff. The United States traditionally depended on tariffs for revenue, and the northeastern manufacturing interests were delighted to have high tariffs because it protected their markets within the country. The northeastern areas also favored the tightest banking system, a federal system in which federally chartered banks could buy bonds and issue bank notes on them. Again, such a system favored the northeast because that is where most of the banks were located.

In areas in the South and west of Ohio, all of these policies were devastating to business and farm interests alike. The lack of local banks in the South and West reduced the money supply. Shifting from greenbacks to hard currency also contracted the money supply. The tariff, on the other hand, raised prices that were harder to pay because of the contracted money supply.

Into this sectional controversy, Grant blundered badly. Grant was by all evidence personally honest, but prior to becoming president he had accepted some very large gifts from wealthy businessmen in the Northeast. In Philadelphia he was given a beautiful, fully furnished house, while New York businessmen came up with $100,000 in cash (a magnificent sum in those days). Not wishing to fall behind, businessmen in Washington, D.C., gave Grant a house and $75,000 in cash. When Grant followed the policies recommended by financial interests in the northeastern states, the knowledge that he had accepted these gifts created doubts about his impartiality.

The most egregious incident involved the financial speculators Jay Gould and Jim Fisk. These men formed a partnership with Grant's brother-in-

law and a treasury official to take advantage of a treasury policy to corner the market on gold. The speculators thought they had Grant's concurrence, but he was, in fact, ignorant of their intentions. When it became clear that the speculators were about to corner the gold market, Grant suddenly ordered his treasury secretary to sell gold, flooding the market and destroying the scheme. Considerable economic damages still occurred. Worse for Grant was the fact that he had been seen with the speculators shortly before the scheme came to light, and this made it appear that he responded correctly only because he was caught.

None of these issues required Grant's administration skills. Instead, they required political skill to resolve. Though Grant was not strong in politics, he had appointed a cabinet filled with able personalities, except for his first secretary of the navy (who was quickly replaced). In spite of their capabilities, however, Grant did not give them clear direction on the issue of patronage and civil service reform. Some cabinet officers attempted civil service reform, but others found it easier to yield their patronage issues to the Congress.

Indeed, the Congress had written the laws to strengthen the cabinet's power. The Tenure of Office Act, which had been passed to control President Andrew Johnson, was still on the books, and Congress refused to repeal it. The practical result was that Grant could not permanently remove any cabinet officer without congressional approval. If he did so, the Congress could refuse to confirm his new appointment and the old appointee would remain in place. Grant could be faulted for not using his prestige to have this law repealed, but he did not do so. With the law on the books, Congress was free to abuse the patronage power and they did—often with Grant taking the blame.

Still, the problems of the first Grant administration paled before the disaster of the second administration. Grant easily won the 1872 election against Democrat HORACE GREELEY, but in his second term, the economy collapsed, a situation caused in part by the currency contraction policies of his first term. On top of poor economic times, Americans were treated to the spectacle of repeated, serious corruption scandals within the Grant administration. That Grant did not personally benefit from them did not excuse him from the responsibility he had for the administration in which they occurred. To be sure, Congress's patronage policies were often the biggest culprit, but Grant never used his power and influence to restrain the Congress. As a result, there was little enthusiasm for giving Grant a third term in 1876.

After leaving the White House in 1877, Grant—an inveterate traveler—visited Europe and received a warm welcome wherever he went. Buoyed by this, he decided to extend the trip around the world over the next two years. This tour—the first of its kind by a U.S. president—also created goodwill for the United States. Upon returning to America, Grant again considered politics. The reform efforts of his successor, President RUTHERFORD BIRCHARD HAYES, were courageous but so angered the old guard Republicans that they begged and badgered Grant to attempt a run for a third term as president in 1880. Regardless of this enthusiasm, the Republicans were ultimately divided between Grant (backed by a faction known as the Stalwarts) and JAMES GILLESPIE BLAINE (backed by another faction known as the Half-Breeds) and the nomination and the election went to JAMES ABRAM GARFIELD.

After the 1880 election, Grant became a partner in a Wall Street investment firm with his son and his son's friend, Fred Ward. Ward was a charlatan and simply absconded with Grant's money. Grant was bankrupt and was forced to sell many of his Civil War mementoes to raise money. When that was not enough, he undertook to write his memoirs. These memoirs concentrated on his military exploits and avoided his presidential years. They were published by Mark Twain, became a best-seller, and are still regarded as a model for memoirs of this type. Unfortunately, shortly after beginning the memoirs, Grant learned that he had throat cancer. Still, he continued to write despite the pain and finished the manuscript less than a month before he died on July 23, 1885.

Further Reading

Anderson, Nancy S. *The Generals—Ulysses S. Grant and Robert E. Lee.* New York: Knopf, 1988.

Arnold, James R. *Grant Wins the War: Decision at Vicksburg.* New York: John Wiley, 1997.

Arnold, Matthew. *General Grant.* Kent, Ohio: Kent State University Press, 1995.

Boothe, F. Norton. *Ulysses S. Grant.* New York: Gallery Books, 1990.

Catton, Bruce. *Grant Moves South.* Boston: Little, Brown, 1988.

———. *Grant Takes Command.* New York: Book-of-the-Month Club, 1994.

Conger, A. L. *The Rise of U. S. Grant.* New York: Da Capo Press, 1996.

"Grant, Ulysses S." Available online. URL: http://www.whitehouse.gov/history/presidents/ug17.html. Downloaded on October 20, 2001.

Grant, Ulysses S. *Personal Memoirs of U. S. Grant.* New York: Penguin Books, 1999 (reprint).

Hankinson, Alan. *Vicksburg 1863: Grant Clears the Mississippi.* London: Osprey, 1993.

Kaltman, Al. *Cigars, Whiskey, and Winning: Leadership Lessons from General Ulysses S. Grant.* Paramus, N.J.: Prentice Hall Press, 1998.

Lowry, Don. *Fate of the Country: The Civil War from June to September 1864.* New York: Hippocrene Books, 1992.

———. *No Turning Back: The Beginning of the End of the Civil War: March–June 1864.* New York: Hippocrene Books, 1992.

———. *Towards an Indefinite Shore: The Final Months of the Civil War, December 1864–May 1865.* New York: Hippocrene Books, 1995.

Mauck, Jeffrey G. *The Education of a Soldier: U. S. Grant in the War with Mexico.* Carbondale, Ill.: American Kestrel Books, 1996.

Perret, Geoffrey. *Ulysses S. Grant: Soldier and President.* New York: Random, 1997.

Scaturro, Frank J. *President Grant Reconsidered.* Lanham, Md.: University Press of America, 1998.

Simpson, Brooks D. *The Reconstruction Presidents.* Lawrence: University Press of Kansas, 1998.

———. *Ulysses S. Grant: Triumph over Adversity.* Boston: Houghton Mifflin, 2000.

Greeley, Horace
(1811–1872) *candidate for president, representative, author*

Horace Greeley was the most prominent journalist in the mid-1800s and set the agenda for many of the reform efforts of the day. He was more of a social reformer than a politician throughout his life, particularly when he ran for president in 1872.

Greeley was born on February 3, 1811, in Amherst, New Hampshire. His family was very poor, and his father earned what little he could farming and working as a day laborer. While Horace was still an infant, his father fled with his family to Westhaven, Vermont, to avoid imprisonment for debt. Greeley's mother was literate and encouraged her precocious son, who by the age of five had read the entire Holy Bible. He attended school only irregularly until he was 14 when he entered a four-year apprenticeship with Amos Bliss of the *Northern Spectator* in East Poultney, Vermont. When this newspaper failed, young Greeley moved with his family to Erie County, Pennsylvania, for about a year where he again worked as a printer.

By August 1831, Greeley had managed to save $25, so he moved from Pennsylvania to New York City where he worked as a newspaper typesetter and printer. In January 1833, he started the New York *Morning Post* with another printer, and he operated a job printing office on the side. After the first paper failed and his partner died in a tragic accident, Greeley and a new partner founded the *New Yorker*, a weekly journal covering literature, arts, and sciences. While he made no money, he did build a circulation among a literary elite and earned a positive literary reputation over the next seven years. He essentially survived by writing regularly for the *Daily Whig* and by editing Whig campaign broadsides.

By 1838, Greeley had established himself well enough in Whig circles to become the editor of the Whig campaign weekly called *The Jeffersonian*. He used this paper to help elect WILLIAM HENRY SEWARD governor of New York. In alliance with Seward and Thurlow Weed, Greeley then started another Whig paper, which had a large circulation of more than 85,000 copies and went a long way toward helping elect President WILLIAM HENRY HARRISON in 1840.

By the age of 30, Greeley was so well established that he founded the *New York Tribune* as a "penny paper" on April 10, 1841. He edited this paper for the next 30 years, turning it into the greatest single newspaper in the country. His purpose was to provide a paper for working people that was as cheap as those of his rivals but less sensational than the other penny papers of the day. In 1846, Charles A. Dana joined the paper and remained as his chief editorial assistant for 15 years. In 1849, George Ripley started a new section in the *Tribune*, the first regular literary and book review department in a U.S. newspaper, and he continued it for 30 years. Carl Schurz, Whitlaw Reid, Henry James, William Dean Howells, Margaret Fuller, and even Karl Marx were contributors to the paper, and Greeley was the first journalist to allow writers to use their own bylines. Greeley's own concise, current, and vigorous editorials were the hallmark of the *Tribune* and provided it with its national reputation.

Greeley used his newspaper as a voice for a wide variety of reforms. The abolition of slavery, improvement in the status of women (but not women's voting rights), a variant of socialism known as Fourierism, prohibition, tariffs for revenue only, and ending capital punishment all were featured topics of reform over the years. Greeley advocated such an advanced agenda that he could hardly hope to be much of an electoral success. In 1848, Greeley held his only public office when he was appointed to fill a vacancy in the House of Representatives from December 1848 to March 1849, but he was unable to win election on his own, although he tried repeatedly.

Horace Greeley was politically active in other ways. For many years, he was a Whig, but he switched to the Free Soil Party because of its clearer stand against slavery. Finally, as a delegate to the national organizing convention in February 1856, Greeley was one of the first members of the new Republican Party. Because he was warring with the New York state leaders, including Seward, he had to attend the 1860 Republican convention as a representative of Oregon. He managed to block his enemy Seward from the presidential nomination and eventually threw his support to ABRAHAM LINCOLN. (Seward later returned Greeley's kindness by blocking Greeley's attempt to be elected to the U.S. Senate.)

Greeley pursued an erratic course in the Civil War. At first, his antiwar humanitarianism led him to suggest that the Confederate states should be allowed to secede rather than risk war. Later, this view gave way to a demand for vigorous prosecution of the war. One constant in this period was Greeley's criticism of Lincoln for not freeing the slaves in the border states—a move Lincoln would not consider since it would have risked forcing still more states to secede. Greeley wrote a public letter to Lincoln that probably did Lincoln a favor by bringing the issue into the open. Lincoln then answered the charge in his famous August 25, 1862, reply, which stated that his war objective was to save the Union and not to abolish slavery directly. Greeley then was overjoyed when Lincoln signed the Emancipation Proclamation. Greeley pushed for peace negotiations with Confederate leaders, but the Confederate President JEFFERSON DAVIS and his unalterable demand that there could only be two separate nations doomed the effort from the start. Finally, only with reluctance and very late in the 1864 campaign, Greeley endorsed Lincoln's reelection.

Greeley's postwar policies were even more erratic. He supported not only black suffrage but also full black equality. He backed the Thirteenth, Fourteenth, and Fifteenth Amendments to the Constitution. Not surprisingly, he pushed for the impeachment of ANDREW JOHNSON. Those who followed him in all these efforts were then asked to "understand" his humanitarian gesture in signing the bond to release Jefferson Davis from prison. About half of the paying readership of his *Weekly Tribune* did not understand, and they canceled their subscriptions.

Greeley supported ULYSSES S. GRANT early on but changed his mind as soon as he perceived that Grant was allowing Senator ROSCOE CONKLING to control patronage in New York. Falling out with Grant, Greeley encouraged the formation of a new political movement known as the Liberal Republican Party and actively pursued the new party's nomination for president. Since the Democrats saw no hope for any nominee of their own, they endorsed Greeley as well. However, it was hard for many Democrats to support someone who had opposed most of their principles for so many years.

During the campaign, all Greeley's shortcomings were caricatured, and he was denounced as a traitor and a crank. Despite Greeley's vigorous

campaigning, Grant won by 3.6 million votes to Greeley's 2.8 million votes. Greeley carried only six southern and border states, and the Electoral College landslide for Grant was overwhelming.

Greeley's wife was ill toward the end of the campaign, and he returned home to care for her. She died a few days before the election. Whether from grief, because of his massive electoral defeat, or due to his loss of control to Whitlaw Reid at the New York *Tribune* during his campaign absence—or a combination of all three—Greeley went completely insane and died less than a month later on November 29, 1872.

Further Reading

Chamberlin, Everett. *The Struggle of '72: The Issues and Candidates of the Present Political Campaign.* Chicago: Union Publishing, 1976.
Greeley, Horace. *The Autobiography of Horace Greeley.* New York: Treat, 1977.
Horner, Harlan H. *Lincoln and Greeley.* Westport, Conn.: Greenwood Press, 1971.
Ingersoll, Lurton Dunham. *The Life of Horace Greeley.* New York: Beekman Publishers, 1974.
Maihafer, Harry J. *The General and the Journalists: Ulysses S. Grant, Horace Greeley, and Charles Dana.* Washington, D.C.: Brassey's, 1998.
Sotheran, Charles. *Horace Greeley and Other Pioneers of American Socialism.* New York: Haskell House Publishers, 1971.
Welch, F. G. *That Convention: Or, Five Days a Politician.* Chicago: F. G. Welch, 1974.

Greenspan, Alan

(1926–   ) *chairman of the Federal Reserve Board, chairman of the Council of Economic Advisers, economist*

Alan Greenspan became the best-known chairman of the U.S. Federal Reserve Bank in U.S. history since he was credited with following policies that resulted in the longest economic boom in U.S. economic history until in ended in a recession beginning in March 2001.

Alan Greenspan was born in New York City on March 6, 1926. He graduated summa cum laude with a bachelor of science degree in economics from

New York University in 1948 and continued there, receiving a master's degree in economics in 1950. Greenspan also did advanced graduate study in economics at Columbia University. Influenced by the philosophy of Ayn Rand, Greenspan has been a strong supporter of the free market and an opponent of government intervention in the economy.

In 1954, Greenspan opened a private economic consulting firm known as Townsend-Greenspan and Company in New York City. He served as its chairman and president from 1954 to 1974 and again from 1977 to 1987. From 1974 to 1977, he served as chairman of the President's Council of Economic Advisers under Presidents RICHARD MILHOUS NIXON and GERALD RUDOLPH FORD. Greenspan received a Ph.D. in economics in 1977 as he was completing his tour of duty on the Council of Economic Advisers.

In 1981, President RONALD WILSON REAGAN appointed Greenspan the chairman of the National Commission on Social Security Reform, which improved the financing of the U.S. Social Security system to assure its solvency.

In 1987, President Reagan appointed him chairman of the Federal Reserve System, replacing Paul Volker and filling his unexpired term. Dr. Greenspan was reappointed to the board for a full 14-year term, which began February 1, 1992. He was designated chairman by Presidents Reagan, George H. W. Bush, and Clinton.

Dr. Greenspan also served as chairman of the Federal Open Market Committee, the system's principal monetary policymaking body. As Federal Reserve chairman, he emphasized controlling inflation over promoting economic growth and has won widespread praise for his deft manipulation of interest rates. He faced criticism in the last years of both the Bush and Clinton presidencies for failing to ease credit enough to forestall an economic downturn.

His previous presidential appointments have also included participation in the president's Foreign Intelligence Advisory Board, the Commission on Financial Structure and Regulation, the Commission on an All-Volunteer Armed Force, and the Task Force on Economic Growth.

Further Reading

Beckner, Steven K. *Back from the Brink: The Greenspan Years.* New York: Wiley, 1996.

Lindsey, Lawrence. *Economic Puppetmasters: Lessons from the Halls of Power.* Washington, D.C.: AEI Press, 1999.

Sicilia, David B. *The Greenspan Effect: Words that Move the World's Markets.* New York: McGraw-Hill. 2000.

H

Haig, Alexander Meigs
(1924–   ) *secretary of state, White House staff adviser*

Alexander Haig came close to serving as the unofficial president of the United States during the closing days of the administration of RICHARD MILHOUS NIXON. Haig's career also included serving as Nixon's White House chief of staff and as secretary of state under President RONALD WILSON REAGAN.

Born on December 2, 1924, in Philadelphia, Pennsylvania, Alexander Meigs Haig entered the U.S. military academy at West Point after high school and graduated as an army officer in 1947. He served briefly as an assistant to General Douglas MacArthur in Japan before returning to the United States and earning a master's degree from Georgetown University in 1961.

After two years as a Pentagon staff officer, Haig became a special assistant to Secretary of Defense ROBERT STRANGE MCNAMARA in 1964. In 1966 and at his own request, Haig served a year in South Vietnam as an infantry battlefield commander. Haig was named deputy commandant at West Point when he returned to the United States in 1967. In 1969, after the start of the Nixon administration, Haig returned to Washington as a staff aide at the White House. Advancing quickly, he became a military assistant to National Security Affairs Assistant HENRY ALFRED KISSINGER. By 1971, Haig advanced to become the deputy assistant to the president for national security affairs.

Nixon selected Haig to serve as the chief negotiator at the Vietnam peace talks in Paris and promoted him to major general. Haig was appointed a four-star general when he moved up to being vice chief of staff at the Pentagon. Shortly thereafter, Haig was called back to the White House to serve as chief of staff after the resignation of HARRY ROBBINS HALDEMAN. It was during the rest of 1973 and the first half of 1974 that Haig acted as an unofficial president of the United States because of the inability of Richard Nixon to focus on the duties at hand. Nixon could only concentrate on defending himself against the charges raised by the Watergate investigation, and he failed even at that as he was forced to resign in August 1974.

After President GERALD RUDOLPH FORD took over the presidency in August 1974, Haig was transferred to Europe as the supreme allied commander of the North Atlantic Treaty Organization (NATO). After five years, Haig resigned as NATO commander and from the army, choosing to work as a business executive.

Haig's principal interest was in government service, and he accepted the appointment to secretary of state under President Ronald Reagan in 1980. At the time of the assassination attempt on President Reagan, Vice President GEORGE HERBERT WALKER BUSH was away from Washington, and secretary of state Haig thought he could reassure the nation by going to the White House situation room and announcing that he was in charge. Since Haig, as secretary of state, was not next in the line of succession to become president in the event that Reagan died, this was taken as a presumption on his part. Shortly thereafter, perhaps because he could not affect foreign policy in the way he wished, but probably as a result of his presumption, Haig resigned.

Haig returned to private business but made an attempt to be elected president of the United States in 1988, an effort at which he failed badly.

Further Reading

Haig, Alexander M. *Caveat: Realism, Reagan, and Foreign Policy*. New York: Macmillan, 1984.
———. *The Future of Deterrence*. Washington, D.C.: Heritage Foundation, 1987.
———. *Inner Circles: How America Changed the World: A Memoir*. New York: Warner Books, 1992.
Streissguth, Thomas. *Soviet Leaders from Lenin to Gorbachev*. Minneapolis, Minn.: Oliver Press, 1992.

Haldeman, Harry Robbins

(1926–1993) *White House chief of staff*

Harry Robbins Haldeman has the distinction of having served in the most scandal-ridden White House of any president in the 20th century.

Born on October 27, 1926, into a prominent, conservative family in Los Angeles, California, Haldeman grew up there and graduated from the University of California at Los Angeles in 1948. Initially he served as an advertising executive for the J. Walter Thompson Agency. In 1956, he did volunteer work for RICHARD MILHOUS NIXON during his vice presidential reelection bid. Two years later, he worked for the Republican congressional campaigns and won sufficient notice of his efficiency to be selected as the chief advance man for Richard Nixon's presidential campaign in 1960.

After Nixon lost the presidency, Haldeman returned with Nixon to California. Nixon made a bid for a comeback by running for governor of California in 1962. Although Haldeman had tried to discourage him from the effort, he bravely served as Nixon's campaign manager in that losing effort.

Although it must have seemed to both of them as if Nixon's career in politics were over, Haldeman stuck with Nixon. When Nixon ran for

president in 1968, Haldeman was the campaign manager who created the strategy of putting forth the "new" Nixon. This strategy called for managing Nixon's public appearances very carefully so that Nixon would not become too exhausted and make "off the cuff" sarcastic or brusque remarks. Haldeman showed real creativity in learning how to use the power of television to maximum effect. The same techniques were used in Nixon's winning 1972 reelection campaign.

Because of his devotion to Nixon, Haldeman was an obvious choice as chief of staff in 1969. Following the strategy of the campaign, Haldeman carefully managed Nixon's time and was a ruthless gatekeeper. In the last half of the 20th century, no other chief of staff has had as much control over access to a president as H. R. Haldeman had.

Haldeman's downfall began with a bungled burglary on June 17, 1972, at the Democratic National Committee's headquarters in the Watergate complex. In the investigation that followed, Haldeman played a key role in covering up the scandal until after Nixon's reelection in November 1972.

In 1973, the cover-up came apart as first the burglars and then other members of the White House staff began to reveal how the Nixon administration had worked. In April 1973, Haldeman and JOHN EHRLICHMAN, a close friend who served as Nixon's domestic affairs adviser, were forced to resign in a futile attempt to save President Nixon. They sought to take complete responsibility for the scandal, but tape recordings were later discovered—made by Nixon himself for personal use—which clearly implicated Nixon in a cover-up. Nixon attempted to keep these tape recordings from reaching the courts or being made public, but the U.S. Supreme Court ultimately ruled that they were evidence that could be considered by a criminal court. Upon their full disclosure, Nixon was forced to resign in August 1974 or face impeachment, conviction, and removal from office.

Ultimately, Haldeman was convicted of obstruction of justice, conspiracy, and perjury. He was sentenced to 18 months in a federal penitentiary. He served his time at Lompoc, California, in a minimum-security facility from June 1977 until December 1978. After his release from prison, he returned to private life. He died of cancer at his home in Santa Barbara, California, on November 12, 1993.

Further Reading

Ehrlichman, John. *Witness to Power: The Nixon Years.* New York: Simon & Schuster, 1982.

Genovese, Michael A. *The Nixon Presidency.* New York: Greenwood, 1990.

Safire, William. *Before the Fall: An Inside View of the Pre-Watergate White House.* Garden City, N.Y.: Doubleday, 1975.

Smith, J. Y. "H. R. Haldeman Dies," *The Washington Post* (November 13, 1993): A12.

Sussman, Barry. *The Great Cover-up: Nixon and the Scandal of Watergate,* Arlington, Va.: Seven Locks Press, 1992.

White, Theodore H. *Breach of Faith: The Fall of Richard Nixon.* New York: Athenaeum, 1975.

Wicker, Tom. *One of Us: Richard Nixon and the American Dream.* New York: Random House, 1991.

Hamilton, Alexander

(ca. 1755–1804) *secretary of the treasury, Revolutionary War leader, author*

Alexander Hamilton has the rare honor of having his likeness imprinted on U.S. currency (the ten-dollar bill), although the highest rank he held was as a member of a presidential cabinet. The honor was accorded to him because of his outstanding service as the first secretary of the treasury. His historical reputation also rests on his service in the Revolutionary War Army, his participation in the creation of the U.S. Constitution, and his role in its ratification.

Hamilton was born the illegitimate son of a financially impoverished British aristocrat and his common-law wife on the West Indies island of Nevis. The most commonly accepted date for his birth is January 11, 1755 (given in some sources as 1757), but absolute certainty is impossible under the circumstances. His mother moved him to the nearby island of St. Croix, where he grew up. After his mother died when he was young, he was abandoned by his father but taken in by various influential people on the island. He worked for a

Alexander Hamilton provided such an outstanding service as the first secretary of the treasury that his likeness is imprinted on the U.S. $10 bill. *(Library of Congress)*

trading company in Christiansted, St. Croix, and proved so adept at the work that powerful island leaders decided he should be sent to New York for a formal education.

In 1772 Hamilton traveled to New York for his formal education, beginning with elementary school, but in just a few years had moved through the curriculum so that he was able to attend Columbia University (then called King's College). While a teenager at King's College, he was caught up in the revolutionary fervor and opposed the British policies in the North American colonies.

Going beyond merely advocating independence, he joined the Revolutionary Army. Assuming his birth date is correct, Hamilton would have been a soldier commanding artillery troops in the important Revolutionary battles fought at White

Plains, New York City, and Princeton—all before he turned 20. After Hamilton displayed his brilliance, General GEORGE WASHINGTON took him in as his aide-de-camp, a role he served from 1777 to 1781.

Despite his high honor, Hamilton chaffed at having merely a staff position and begged Washington to give him a field command. Hamilton had become Washington's most trusted aide and Washington needed him so badly that he refused to let him go into the field until the war's end. Washington finally allowed him to take command of a regiment that took part in the siege of Yorktown. In the final assault on Yorktown, Hamilton personally led his troops in the fighting over the ramparts and into the fort.

By his mid-twenties, he was selected for the Continental Congress, in which he served from 1782 to 1783. He left the Congress to begin his own law practice in New York City in 1783. As the weakness of the Articles of Confederation—the first U.S. constitution—became clear, Hamilton strongly urged significant strengthening of the central government. He attended the Annapolis Convention as a delegate in 1786, at which time a call for a constitutional convention was issued. Hamilton also served in the New York State legislature in 1786 and, a year later, attended the Constitutional Convention in Philadelphia as a delegate from New York.

At the convention, Hamilton clearly stood for a very strong national government and advocated a strong executive, such as a monarch. His views were not well received in the convention, and there is little indication that he was responsible for much of the language in the document. Still, Hamilton's arguing for an even stronger executive or a stronger national government may have influenced the proceedings, resulting in the final product being more in the direction he desired than if he had not been present at all. Some delegates who found their views passed over by the convention abandoned the effort, but Hamilton stayed to the end, supported the final product, and worked diligently for its ratification.

With JAMES MADISON and JOHN JAY, Hamilton wrote a series of essays published in the New York newspapers—collectively known as the *Federalist Papers*—to justify ratification. They are now

regarded as one of the most significant contributions to American political philosophy. Hamilton was such an ardent advocate and such a prolific writer that he wrote almost two-thirds of the papers. In 1788, Hamilton also served another term in the Congress of the Confederation (still popularly known as the Continental Congress) in what turned out to be the last session under the old Articles of Confederation.

After the first Congress created the Department of the Treasury, Washington appointed Hamilton, who served from September 11, 1789, until January 31, 1795. Still in his early 30s, Hamilton quickly grasped the essentials of national finance that would have eluded other national figures much his senior.

His fundamental political objective was the creation of a strong central government, which required the payment of taxes to the national government. In office for barely a month, he proposed establishment of a seagoing arm of the military to secure the revenue from imported goods. By the summer of 1790, the Congress authorized 10 ships to be revenue cutters in a maritime force that ultimately became the U.S. Coast Guard. He also strongly supported the Naval Act of 1794 that created the navy. Hamilton even advocated the creation of a naval academy, although this was an idea ahead of its time.

A strong national government, in Hamilton's view, required that the wealthy creditor, commercial, and manufacturing classes firmly support the new government and that the United States be respected among the nations of the world. This required that the United States pay its war debts in full. Hamilton made his case on this issue and many others in his famous "Report on the Public Credit" published in January 1790—only four months after taking over the Treasury. This report, although less well known than the *Federalist Papers*, may have been even more important for the future of the nation.

Hamilton's plan, while fiscally sound, had a political downside. Much of the debt was owed to former soldiers who were so desperate for cash that they had sold their promissory notes to speculators for mere pennies on the dollar. Hamilton's plan would enrich the speculators yet would provide little for those who had risked their lives in the war. Nonetheless, Hamilton saw the need for national credit-worthiness as critical for the nation's future. THOMAS JEFFERSON and James Madison opposed Hamilton's plan and aligned themselves with the poor soldiers who had sold off their promissory notes, but Hamilton's plan passed overwhelmingly.

Hamilton's plan also provided for assumption not only of the domestic and the foreign debts from the war but of the state debts as well. This issue set loose sectional discord because some states, such as Massachusetts, had huge debts since they were the scenes of most of the fighting. Other states, as in the South, saw little warfare and had only small debts, some of which had been paid in full. For Hamilton, the Revolutionary War had been a national effort no matter where it was fought, and debts from that war needed to be paid by everyone—particularly if the United States was going to be one nation.

Both Madison and Jefferson again strongly opposed Hamilton's plan (largely on sectional grounds), but they settled the issue in a private meeting on July 21, 1790. During this meeting, Hamilton agreed to the future location of the nation's capital on the Potomac River (the current location of Washington, D.C.), in return for their support of the assumption of state debts. This compromise clearly showed Hamilton's capacity to reach beyond the financial issues to the highest concerns of state policy.

That Hamilton was right about this issue is shown by one of history's great ironies. Only a dozen years later, when Jefferson had an opportunity to buy the Louisiana Purchase from the French, he was able to do so only because the credit of the United States—thanks to Hamilton—had risen from the bottom to the top of the European money markets.

Hamilton's proposals also called for import duties and excise taxes for raising revenue, for the congressional creation of the first Bank of the United States, and for placing the revenues and expenditures on firm ground. His financial program gave the infant nation good credit, a sound currency, and mature financial machinery.

Still, Hamilton faced political opposition. In 1794, the "Whiskey Rebellion" broke out in western Pennsylvania and Virginia. This protest was led to oppose the collection efforts of excise taxes on spirits since this type of tax was a direct tax (as opposed to an indirect tax such as a tariff). From Hamilton's point of view, compliance with the enforcement of a direct federal tax was critical. Not only did Hamilton prevail on Washington to use force to quash the rebellion, but he also persuaded Washington to let him accompany the troops in an advisory capacity to put down the insurrection.

In retrospect, Hamilton's decisions were fundamentally sound, but they were not popular. By 1795, he had fought so many battles and made so many enemies that he concluded he would serve President Washington better by resigning from Treasury but continuing as an unofficial adviser. While he resumed his private law practice, he retained the inside track with the remaining members of Washington's cabinet and, of course, with Washington himself.

Hamilton was a rival of his fellow Federalist, Vice President JOHN ADAMS, and he privately opposed Adams for president in 1796. When he realized he could not succeed in blocking Adams, he settled for controlling Adams's cabinet. Hamilton had been so astute in his private advisory capacity that Adams, as Washington's successor, was unaware of the extent of Hamilton's control. When Adams retained Oliver Wolcott, TIMOTHY PICKERING, James McHenry, and Charles Lee from Washington's cabinet, he did not realize that, for most of his presidency, a majority of these men were strongly influenced by Hamilton. Only late in his presidency did Adams discover the truth, fire many of Hamilton's associates, and take command of his own cabinet.

Having been exposed as a behind-the-scenes manipulator of Adams's cabinet, Hamilton felt he had little to lose by supporting CHARLES COTESWORTH PINCKNEY against Adams in the election of 1800. The Federalists had much to lose, and they indeed lost the presidency to the Democratic Republicans. At first it was not clear which Democratic Republican had been elected since Thomas Jefferson and his vice presidential running mate, AARON BURR, tied in the Electoral College. At that point, Burr declined to step aside, and some Federalists sought to cut a deal to make Burr president because they hated Jefferson so much. Hamilton would not support that since his hatred of Burr was greater than his hatred of Jefferson, and Hamilton finally swung enough votes to Jefferson for his victory.

Hamilton then aggravated the situation with Burr by opposing him for governor of New York in 1804. In a private letter that somehow became public, Hamilton made very unflattering statements about Burr. Burr challenged Hamilton to a duel. Hamilton, although publicly on record as opposed to dueling, apparently felt obliged to accept.

Hamilton and Burr had a personal rivalry probably born during the Revolutionary War itself. In one sense, the two men were complete opposites. Burr came from an extremely high-ranking colonial family including famous clerics, such as Jonathan Edwards, and famous scholars, such as his father and grandfather who founded or headed Princeton University (then called the College of New Jersey). By the circumstances of his birth, Hamilton lacked all that Burr had. Despite the differences, both men had great intelligence, a willingness to compromise for political objectives, and extreme ambition. The two men served nearby in the war and held comparable rank. Yet while Hamilton rose higher and higher in Washington's estimation, Burr clashed badly with the general and ultimately left the army.

Their rivalry carried over into local politics in New York. Hamilton married into the Schuyler family, which had a long-standing struggle for dominance with the GEORGE CLINTON clan. Burr naturally gravitated to the Clintons. The Schuyler-Hamilton alliance was a key factor in the Federalist Party. The Clinton-Burr axis became the bedrock of the Democratic Republican Party in New York.

Still, the duel might have been avoided through the actions of talented intermediaries. Those who did try unfortunately did not succeed. Some scholars have even speculated that Hamilton's political career was in such a shambles that he might have seen the duel as a way to die with "honor" rather than commit suicide or fade from active political life. Whatever the truth, Hamilton wasted his first shot; Burr did not. Hamilton was fatally wounded and died in New York City on July 12, 1804.

Further Reading

Brookhiser, Richard. *Alexander Hamilton, American.* New York: Free Press, 1999.

Fleming, Thomas J. *Duel: Alexander Hamilton, Aaron Burr, and the Future of America.* New York: Basic Books, 1999.

Flexner, James T. *The Young Hamilton: A Biography.* New York: Fordham University Press, 1997.

Gordon, John Steele. *Hamilton's Blessing: The Extraordinary Life and Times of our National Debt.* New York: Penguin Books, 1998.

Kennedy, Roger G. *Burr, Hamilton, and Jefferson: A Study in Character.* New York: Oxford University Press, 2000.

Lodge, Henry Cabot. *Alexander Hamilton.* Broomall, Pa.: Chelsea House, 1997.

McDonald, Forrest. *Alexander Hamilton.* New York: Norton, 1982.

McNamara, Peter. *Political Economy and Statesmanship: Smith, Hamilton, and the Foundation of the Commercial Republic.* DeKalb: Northern Illinois University Press, 1998.

Miller, John C. *Alexander Hamilton and the Growth of the New Nation.* New York: Harper & Row, 1964.

Morris, Richard B. *Witnesses at the Creation: Hamilton, Madison, Jay, and the Constitution.* New York: New American Library, 1989.

Rogow, Arnold A. *A Fatal Friendship: Alexander Hamilton and Aaron Burr.* New York: Hill & Wang, 1998.

Hancock, John
(1737–1793) *Revolutionary War leader, governor*

John Hancock was the president of the Second Continental Congress and the first to sign the Declaration of Independence. When he did so, he announced that he would sign it so large that the King of England could read it without his eyeglasses. That act has led to his name becoming an unofficial synonym for one's "signature." To affix your "John Hancock" to a document means to sign your name.

Hancock was born on January 23, 1737, in Braintree (now Quincy), Massachusetts. His father was a clergyman but died when John was very young. Hancock was raised by a wealthy uncle who arranged for his education at Harvard, where he graduated in 1754, and also for some brief business training in London. He joined his uncle's firm, Thomas Hancock and Company, upon his return to the United States. When his uncle died in 1764, he inherited the company and became the wealthiest merchant in New England. As a merchant he was naturally opposed to the Stamp Act, the Sugar Act, and other British taxation and retaliatory measures.

Hancock initially became well known in Massachusetts in 1768 because the British sought to make an example of him. He owned a ship named the *Liberty*, which had wine as a part of its cargo. Without Hancock's knowledge, some merchants brought the wine ashore in a violation of the Sugar Act, which assessed a tax on products made with sugar. While Hancock had not engaged in the smuggling, he was technically liable for its cargo. British customs agents seized the *Liberty* and towed it out to a British warship for impoundment. To Bostonians, this appeared to be a deliberate vendetta of the British against Hancock because he had spoken out against their policies. Boston came alive with public demonstrations on his behalf. Hancock refused to give in and hired JOHN ADAMS to defend him. Hancock was anxious to face down the charges, but the British thought the spectacle of a trial would be dangerous and dropped the prosecution. At about the same time, a mob drove the British tax commissioners out of the city temporarily. This action led the British to station troops in Boston, which precipitated the Boston Massacre in 1770.

SAMUEL ADAMS saw the importance of persuading a prominent merchant to join in the independence movement, and he apparently had a great deal of influence on Hancock. With Adams in the background, Hancock was put forward as a leading figure in the revolutionary movement. In 1774, Hancock was chosen president of the Massachusetts Provincial Congress, and the following year he became the leader of the Boston patriot committee.

By now, Hancock and Adams had become such prominent protesters against the British that their arrest was ordered. When their arrest was imminent, Paul Revere warned them and they escaped from Lexington just as the battles of Lexington and Concord occurred, setting off the Revolutionary War.

Hancock joined the Second Continental Congress and was elected its president. In that capacity, he was the first to sign the Declaration of Independence with the flourish for which he is most famous. Later, he hoped to be named the commander in chief of the Continental Army, but the Congress—at the urging of John Adams—turned to GEORGE WASHINGTON instead. Hancock was bitterly disappointed and resigned as president, but he remained in Congress for three years after relinquishing the presidency in 1777. As it turned out, Adams was right in urging the selection of Washington. Not only was it important that a Virginian, such as Washington, should lead the army to bind southern colonies to the war, but also Hancock did not prove to be a good military man. In 1778, Hancock was put in charge of about 5,000 Massachusetts troops who were to attack the British in Rhode Island. The attack was mismanaged, and the Massachusetts losses were heavy.

Nonetheless, Hancock was an active figure in Massachusetts's politics, and he was elected governor for nine annual terms between 1780 and 1793. He dropped out of the governor's office in 1785, allegedly because he suffered from an attack of gout. However, it is possible that the economic depression in those years and Shays's Rebellion in western Massachusetts were events he was reluctant to face. He remained popular and returned to the governor's office when these difficulties had been overcome.

Shays's Rebellion and the economic hard times were both proximate causes of the Constitutional Convention held in 1787 to create a stronger central government. While Hancock might have been thought to favor such a development, he was initially critical of the proposed Constitution. Apparently Hancock was persuaded to support ratification by the promise that he would be nominated for the first presidency if George Washington decided not to serve. He presided over the Massachusetts constitutional ratification convention in 1788, and it is generally believed that his support for ratification was crucial to the favorable outcome in Massachusetts.

Most scholars have held that Hancock was a vain, flamboyant man, unduly influenced by

Samuel Adams, but there is no denying that he risked his fortune and his life for the American Revolution. Hancock devoted himself to Massachusetts, and his great popularity there led him to hold on to the governor's office for most of the period from 1780 until his death in Quincy, Massachusetts, on October 8, 1793.

Further Reading

Baxter, William T. *The House of Hancock: Business in Boston, 1724–1775*. New York: Russell & Russell, 1965.

Brandes, Paul D. *John Hancock's Life and Speeches: A Personalized Vision of the American Revolution*. Lanham, Md.: Scarecrow Press, 1996.

Fowler, William M. *The Baron of Beacon Hill: A Biography of John Hancock*. Boston: Houghton Mifflin, 1980.

Nolan, Jeannette C. *John Hancock: Friend of Freedom*. Boston: Houghton Mifflin, 1966.

Sears, Lorenzo. *John Hancock: The Picturesque Patriot*. Boston: Gregg Press, 1972.

Umbreit, Kenneth Bernard. *Founding Fathers: Men Who Shaped our Tradition*. Port Washington, N.Y.: Kennikat Press, 1969.

Hanna, Mark Alonzo

(1837–1904) *senator*

A wealthy entrepreneur and political operative, Mark Hanna was responsible for the eight-year campaign to make WILLIAM MCKINLEY president of the United States and for introducing into U.S. politics the practice of gathering delegates well in advance of presidential nominating conventions.

Mark Alonzo Hanna was born in New Lisbon, Ohio, on September 24, 1837, and moved with his family to Cleveland when he was 15. Although he went to college briefly, he was self-taught in business and soon amassed a large fortune in coal, iron, and shipbuilding. Moving beyond that into the public arena, he acquired the Cleveland Opera House, the Cleveland streetcar system, and the *Cleveland Herald* newspaper.

Impressed with the interconnections between business and politics, he was a conservative supporter of the gold standard (or hard currency) and the high tariff. He departed from the conservative catechism only in that he thought it legitimate for workers to unionize. His first foray into national politics was backing fellow Ohioan John T. Sherman for the Republican presidential nomination in 1888. Sherman lost to BENJAMIN HARRISON, but Hanna had the good fortune to meet Ohio congressman William McKinley, in whom Hanna saw great potential. Hanna set out on a successful eight-year campaign to make McKinley president.

With Hanna's organizational genius and money, McKinley was elected Ohio's governor in 1891 and 1893. Hanna then began lining up potential delegates to the 1896 Republican National Convention. He was so successful that McKinley swept to the nomination on the first ballot. Hanna then became the Republican national chairman and organized the massive fund-raising effort and the vicious political campaign used to defeat the charismatic Democratic nominee, WILLIAM JENNINGS BRYAN, who was painted as an anathema to business, labor, and urban interests in the United States. Upon McKinley's election, Hanna became his most trusted adviser. Hanna easily persuaded the Ohio legislature to elect him to the U.S. Senate in 1897 and reelect him in 1903.

After McKinley's assassination, Hanna continued to advise the new president, THEODORE ROOSEVELT, but had a falling out with him, referring to him privately as "that damned cowboy." Hanna probably would have run for president against Roosevelt in 1904 if he had not died suddenly on February 15 of that year.

Further Reading

Beer, Thomas. *Hanna, Crane and the Mauve Decade*. New York: Knopf, 1941.

Croly, Herbert D. *Marcus Alonzo Hanna: His Life and Work*. Hamden, Conn.: Archon Books, 1965.

Hernon, Joseph Martin. *Profiles in Character: Hubris and Heroism in the U.S. Senate—1789–1990*. Armonk, N.Y.: M. E. Sharpe, 1997.

Stern, Clarence A. *Resurgent Republicanism: The Handiwork of Hanna*. Ann Arbor, Mich.: Edwards Brothers, 1968.

Thompson, Charles W. *Presidents I've Known and Two Near Presidents (Mark Hanna)*. 1956. Reprint, Freeport, N.Y.: Books for Libraries Press, 1970.

Harding, Warren Gamaliel
(1865–1923) *president, senator*

In 1920, Warren Gamaliel Harding was elected president by one of the highest percentages of the two-party popular vote in the 20th century. After the strenuous years of the THOMAS WOODROW WILSON presidency, the country hoped for a more relaxed time. Harding wished to give it to them and make his presidency one of the most popular in history. Although personally honest, he was a poor judge of his friends and appointees. His administration was so beset with scandal that it is often regarded as one of the worst presidencies of all time.

Harding was born on November 2, 1865, in Blooming Grove, Ohio. His father was a Civil War veteran who tried his hand at being a farmer, a horse trader, and a rural doctor. He was never very successful in any of these efforts, even though his wife assisted his medical practice by acting as a midwife. As a student, Harding showed some talent for music and an even greater talent for public speaking. When Harding was 10 years old, his family moved the town of Caledonia, where he learned to play a musical instrument and worked part-time for a small local newspaper his father acquired as the result of a trade. In 1879, he moved to Iberia, Ohio, and entered Ohio Central College—a small, undistinguished institution with fewer than a hundred students and only three teachers. He managed the school paper there and graduated two years later.

At one point, Harding's father moved to Marion, hoping to establish a new medical practice, but he failed. After graduating from college in 1882, young Harding came to live in Marion—the place he called home for the rest of his life. Harding was active in civic affairs and helped organize the Marion People's Band, in which he played a number of instruments and which won the top prize in a state tournament. He tried teaching school briefly but decided against making a career of it. He also attempted to become a lawyer, but he found that reading the legal texts was beyond his capability. He failed at being an insurance salesman because he was unable to calculate the rates correctly.

He even tried railroad work, but he eventually turned to the youthful hobby that became his life's career: newspaper work. He was a part-time reporter for a local Democratic political newspaper, but he decided he favored the election of a Republican, JAMES GILLESPIE BLAINE, and that put him at odds with the management. After the election of 1884, Harding finally hit on a winning proposition. With two friends, he raised enough cash to buy out the *Marion Star,* a small local paper that had fallen on hard times. Subsequently, he bought out his friends and gradually, over a five-year period, turned it into the most successful paper in the county and one of the most successful small town papers in the state. By the time Harding served in the Senate, his newspaper holdings were providing him with a comfortable supplemental income of $20,000 a year.

Appearances to the contrary, Harding seems always to have had a troubled personal life. He suffered a number of nervous breakdowns as a young man, both before and after he married. His early employment career suggests a lack of discipline. Perhaps realizing that, when he was 25 years old he entered into a strong marriage with a domineering woman five years older than himself. Florence Kling DeWolfe was divorced and had a son, but she was the daughter of the leading banker in town and a shrewd businesswoman. She helped run his business and managed a large part of his political career.

Despite her reputation for being domineering, she was unable to prevent Harding from having a number of affairs, including one 15-year liaison with Carrie Phillips, the wife of a Marion businessman. Among many others, Harding had an affair with Nan Britton, a headstrong young woman, 31 years younger than he, who visited him in Washington when he was a senator. They had a daughter, Elizabeth Ann, who was born in 1919.

Harding's strongest political skill was in public speaking. He did not say much of substance, but he said it very well. He lost his first race for county auditor, but he was elected to the state senate as a Republican in 1899. Never a legislative draftsman, he was successful by being friendly and cooperative. He worked agreeably with both of the major factions in the state Republican Party and eventually was mentored by HARRY MICAJAH DAUGHERTY, an Ohio lobbyist and political operator. In 1901, he was chosen as the Republican Party's floor leader. In the following year he was elected lieutenant governor.

In 1910, the Republicans split into two factions: The conservatives were followers of incumbent president WILLIAM HOWARD TAFT, and the progressives were followers of former president THEODORE ROOSEVELT. The conservatives nominated Harding for governor, but he sustained such a massive defeat that it could have ended his career except that he was asked to nominate Taft for reelection at the 1912 Republican National Convention. This strengthened his ties with Taft, but Harding never ceased to be friendly with Roosevelt. During World War I, for example, Harding sponsored an amendment that would have allowed Theodore Roosevelt to raise a private military force, as he had in the Spanish-American War, to fight in Europe. President Wilson defeated the plan, but Roosevelt was so grateful that, had Roo-

Warren G. Harding, elected president by a wide margin, was unable to control his corrupt friends in office. (*Library of Congress*)

sevelt been able to run for president in 1920, he was expected to have chosen Harding as his running mate. Despite the lack of legislation that carries Harding's name, his careful amiability was an important political skill.

This friendliness paid off in 1914 when the two Republican factions tried to patch things up and needed a unity candidate to run for the U.S. Senate. Harding fit the bill. Harding was even pleasant to his Irish Catholic opponent, Timothy S. Hogan, then Ohio's Democratic state attorney general, and never attacked Hogan for his Catholic religion. (Harding's supporters were not so kind and played the religious issue so skillfully in rural areas that Harding won handily.)

Harding continued his winning ways during his six years in the Senate. He was much in demand as a speaker at Chautauqua educational institutes and he was able to bridge the gap between conservatives and progressives during the split. He was loyal to his party, but he was open and friendly with the schismatics. By 1916, he was one of the few men agreeable to all sides, and he became chairman of the Republican National Convention after CHARLES EVANS HUGHES was nominated for president. Since Hughes was defeated, Harding's stature as party boss was even higher. Initially it was expected that Theodore Roosevelt would once again try for a third term as a Republican in 1920, but his sudden death in January 1919 threw the nomination into the open.

In 1920, the two leading Republican candidates appeared to be General Leonard Wood and Illinois's reform governor Frank Lowden. Wood had a slender lead, but Daugherty saw the probability of a deadlocked convention and the possibility that Harding could be nominated. Daugherty, with difficulty, persuaded Harding to announce his candidacy and to name him the campaign manager. Daugherty then toured the country, securing second- and third-choice delegate votes for Harding. When the deadlock occurred, as Daugherty anticipated, a majority of delegates were already in place to nominate Harding. The myth of Harding's selection in a "smoke-filled room" in Chicago was just that: a myth. Daugherty already had the votes and the famous meeting that took place in the Blackstone Hotel merely ratified Harding as the nominee. Harding was nominated on the 10th ballot, and CALVIN COOLIDGE, a puritanical governor from New England, was chosen to balance the ticket.

Harding conducted a so-called front porch campaign, avoiding clear stands on controversial issues and making rhetorically grand speeches. The opposing Democratic ticket of JAMES MIDDLETON COX and FRANKLIN DELANO ROOSEVELT toured the country vigorously but only garnered 9,147,353 popular votes to Harding's 16,153,785. In the Electoral College, Harding swamped his opponents by 404 votes to 127.

Harding was the first president to be born after the Civil War, and he was the first American president to take office after World War I. Woodrow Wilson's first term had been filled with energetic domestic reforms, and his second term was dominated by World War I and plans for an organization to guarantee world peace. After such a supercharged agenda for such a long time, the country was ready for a slower political pace. There was probably more than a little truth in Harding's statement that what the country needed was a return to "normalcy," even if Harding had to create an entirely new word to express the idea.

Harding's administration started off in a most promising direction. He called for a special session of Congress shortly after his inauguration and set a remarkable agenda for Congress to consider. Harding wanted to move the country away from a wartime stance by reducing the size of government in many, but not all, ways. He called for the repeal of the wartime excess profits tax and the lowering of taxes generally. He did not want all the tax revenues refunded because he wanted to build an enlarged merchant marine and create a department of public welfare. This would stimulate peacetime economic growth and, to move ahead even faster, he proposed a reduction of railroad rates and the promotion of agricultural interests.

Setting the agenda was not enough, and Harding would have had to lobby hard to achieve all of his goals. As a conservative Republican, he was hampered by his limited conception for what a president was entitled to do. He did not push very hard, and Congress did not do very much. His proposal for a national budget system, institutionalized through the Bureau of the Budget, was passed.

Harding initiated this office properly by making one of his best appointments. As its director, he named Charles G. Dawes, the former comptroller of the currency under WILLIAM MCKINLEY.

Harding himself took great pride in his international achievements, typified by the treaties negotiated following the Washington Conference on disarmament in 1921. While Secretary of State Charles Evans Hughes must be given the credit for hammering out the many details, it is to Harding's credit that he appointed Hughes in the first place and listened to him in the second. At this conference, the United States, Britain, France, Italy, and Japan had agreed to limit all further naval construction for 10 years and to scrap many of their existing warships. This was a useful agreement. That it failed to stop World War II a decade and a half later is simply a testimony to how difficult it was to deal with dictators, such as Hitler, Mussolini, Stalin, and the Japanese militarists. The success of these dictators should not take away from the achievement in international arms limitation that the Washington Conference represented.

Harding also took some strong stands on important issues. He vetoed an American Legion–sponsored soldiers' bonus bill, a notorious raid on the treasury that most politicians lacked the courage to oppose. Since Harding had been accused throughout his political career of having African-American ancestry, he showed exceptional courage in traveling into the South and calling for improved civil rights for African Americans. His speech in Birmingham, Alabama, which called for political, economic, and educational equality for the races, was one of his best in terms of its boldness. He was roundly cursed in the South for delivering it. By executive order, he reversed President Wilson's racist practice of excluding African Americans from federal appointments.

In addition to Budget Director Charles G. Dawes and Secretary of States Charles Evans Hughes, Harding made other distinguished cabinet appointees at Treasury (Andrew Mellon), at Commerce (HERBERT CLARK HOOVER), and at Agriculture (Henry C. Wallace). He also made an outstanding appointment when he named former president William Howard Taft chief justice of the United States.

In spite of these key cabinet appointments, he failed dramatically in other executive positions. It is perhaps understandable (but still unfortunate) that he followed an all-too-common practice of appointing a close associate as his attorney general. Harry Daugherty had never held a public office before, and his legal credentials hardly qualified him to be the attorney general of the United States. Worse still, he was corrupt and only escaped conviction for his wrongdoing because of the failure of juries to reach a unanimous verdict against him. With Daugherty as attorney general, there was little, if any, executive authority to reign in corruption. Far less understandable was Harding's appointment of Charles R. Forbes as director of the newly created Veterans' Bureau. And the worst appointment turned out to be Senator AL-BERT BACON FALL of New Mexico as secretary of the interior. Despite a strong record against conservation, Fall generated almost no great dissent at the time of his appointment.

That Harding made such poor appointments was made worse by his inability to control his subordinates—no doubt a part of his general desire to be loved and his reluctance to say no. Corruption ran rampant, and some of it was so blatant that it gradually became public. While the full extent was not known until after Harding's death, there was so much wrongdoing in Daugherty's Department of Justice and particularly within the Justice Department's Bureau of Investigation (later reorganized as the Federal Bureau of Investigation, or FBI), in the Treasury Department's Prohibition Bureau, in Forbes's Veterans' Bureau, and in Fall's Interior Department that there was a definite sense of sleaziness about the administration. At the same time, the government retrenchment and monetary deflation led to collapse of the war boom, wage cuts, unemployment, agricultural price drops, and other farming area distress. With Prohibition, voters could not even drown their sorrows legally. However, they could still vote. In the 1922 congressional midterm elections, Harding found his popularity sharply diminished, and his Republican legislative colleagues faced a strong rebuke.

Surprisingly, Harding tried to bounce back and showed real leadership on some issues. He had earlier taken ambiguous stands on the League of Nations, allowing haters of Wilson's league to assume he was with them. Apparently, he was never as isolationist as many thought, for he suddenly proposed that the United States should join the league's World Court. When Congress resisted, he decided to take his case to the voters. Perhaps he even imagined that changing the public discourse to international affairs could shift the focus away from his domestic failings. In any case, he embarked on a cross-country tour that took him to the West Coast and then on up to Alaska in June 1923. He was actually on his way back across the country when his heart condition, no doubt aggravated by the stress of the trip, turned into a fatal thrombosis in a San Francisco hotel on August 2, 1923.

By all accounts, Harding's funeral procession was accompanied by an outpouring of grief that rivaled that of ABRAHAM LINCOLN, JAMES ABRAM GARFIELD, and William McKinley, all presidents who did not simply die in office but were assassinated.

Harding's hope to be remembered as the "best-loved" U.S. president did not long survive his funeral. With Harding gone, the scandals surfaced, one after another. Secretary of the Interior Fall had received $400,000 from oilmen Harry Sinclair and Edward Doheny in return for giving them leases—without competitive bids—on the naval oil reserves in California and at Teapot Dome, Wyoming. The very name Teapot Dome became synonymous with corruption.

Fall denied that he ever took a bribe. However, when all those involved testified that they gave him one, the jury sent him to jail, a first for a presidential cabinet officer. Forbes and others followed him. Daugherty, finally fired by Coolidge, survived on the strength of hung juries. Others, perhaps innocent participants, such as Secretary of the Navy EDWIN DENBY, had their reputations permanently ruined.

As the years went by, more and more stories surfaced. Harding's name was further blackened when Nan Britton wrote an expose of their affair, presumably to raise money for her daughter. The discovery that Harding's widow had burned his correspondence and had refused to allow an autopsy of his body led to rumors that he had committed suicide or been murdered. Harding's failings were certainly many, but focusing solely on them has caused his accomplishments to be overlooked. No evidence of his personal corruption has surfaced, but evidence that he was thrust into a job beyond his capacities has been abundant.

Further Reading

Anthony, Carl S. *Florence Harding: The First Lady, the Jazz Age, and the Death of America's Most Scandalous President.* New York: William Morrow, 1998.

BaKhufu, Auset. *The Six Black Presidents: Black Blood, White Masks, USA.* Washington, D.C.: PIK2 Publications, 1993.

Britton, Nan. *Honesty or Politics.* New York: Elizabeth Ann Guild, 1932.

Daugherty, Harry M. *The Inside Story of the Harding Tragedy.* Freeport, N.Y.: Books for Libraries Press, 1971.

Downes, Randolph C. *The Rise of Warren Gamaliel Harding, 1865–1920.* Columbus: Ohio State University Press, 1970.

Giglio, James N. *H. M. Daugherty and the Politics of Expediency.* Kent, Ohio: Kent State University Press, 1978.

"Harding, Warren." Available online. URL: http://www.whitehouse.gov/history/presidents/wh29.html. Downloaded on October 20, 2001.

Kurland, Gerald. *Warren Harding: A President Betrayed by Friends.* Charlotteville, N.Y.: SamHar Press, 1971.

Mee, Charles L. *The Ohio Gang: The World of Warren G. Harding.* New York: M. Evans, 1981.

Murray, Robert K. *The Politics of Normalcy: Governmental Theory and Practice in the Harding-Coolidge Era.* New York: Norton, 1973.

Russell, Francis. *The Shadow of Blooming Grove: Warren G. Harding in His Time.* Norwalk, Conn.: Easton Press, 1988.

Trani, Eugene P. *The Presidency of Warren G. Harding.* Lawrence: Regents Press of Kansas, 1977.

Harlan, John Marshall

(1833–1911) *associate justice of the Supreme Court*

Often ranked in the top 10 of all U.S. Supreme Court justices throughout history, John Marshall Harlan is the only justice to have had a close relative—his grandson and namesake, John Marshall Harlan II—serve on the Court as well. Harlan was a remarkable political leader on several other grounds as well. He was a slave owner as a young man, a proslavery Union supporter during the Civil War, and a conservative Republican opponent of the Radical Republican Reconstruction of the South, but on the Court, he became an outstanding supporter of civil rights of African Americans. Often standing entirely alone, he was such a strong voice for civil rights that he has been called one of the great dissenters of all time.

Harlan was born into a well-to-do, slave-owning family in Boyle County, Kentucky, on June 1, 1833. His father was a prominent lawyer and successful Whig politician who was not only a friend of HENRY CLAY but also a U.S. congressman and holder of such Kentucky state offices as secretary of state, attorney general, and state legislator. Young Harlan attended Centre College in Danville, Kentucky, and graduated in 1850. After studying law at Transylvania University and having a period of self-study in his father's law office, he was admitted to the bar in 1853 and began practicing law.

With the deaths of Henry Clay and DANIEL WEBSTER, the Whig Party fell on hard times, and young Harlan followed his father into the Know-Nothing Party. This resulted in his winning his first elective office as a county judge in 1858. Harlan was later deeply embarrassed by some of the nativist and racist statements he made during this period.

At the start of the Civil War, he clearly sided with the North and served as a colonel in the Union army until 1863, when he returned home to settle the affairs of his recently deceased father. Finishing those matters, he was elected attorney general of Kentucky on the Constitutionalist Union Party ticket (the successor of the Whigs in Kentucky). As the Unionist Party declined, he joined the Republicans and became a leader of the conservative Republicans (which faction opposed the Radical Republican plan for Reconstruction in the South). He was defeated for the governorship as a conservative Republican in 1872 and again in 1875. As head of the Kentucky delegation to the Republican National Convention in 1876, he played a leading role in the nomination of RUTHERFORD BIRCHARD HAYES by leading the delegation to switch to Hayes at just the right moment.

After Hayes was elected president as the result of the contested election of 1876, he appointed Harlan to serve on a new five-member commission in 1877 to determine which of two rival Louisiana governments was the legitimate one. This post came with an unmistakable political requirement that Harlan agree with Hayes's post-inaugural policy that gave control of Louisiana to the Democrats as a part of the deal that made him president. This commission was to decide that the Louisiana counting board, which declared the electors that made Hayes president, was right in electing the Republican Hayes but wrong in declaring the Republicans elected in the state government. Harlan did as he was instructed. In return, Hayes appointed him an associate justice on the U.S. Supreme Court in October of that year.

If Hayes thought that appointing Harlan to the Supreme Court would give him a vote he could control, he was mistaken. Harlan's vote on the Louisiana commission is apparently the last time he ever voted as instructed. On the Court, Harlan became a judge of strong and independent convictions. Harlan, like his namesake JOHN MARSHALL, was a textualist and a strict constructionist. Perhaps, above all, he became known as a judge not afraid to dissent—alone if necessary. In fact, it was frequently necessary for him to vote alone, and he did so courageously.

Perhaps because he was forced to vote to abandon the newly freed slaves to their fate at the hands of white southern Democrats in Louisiana, Harlan made a dramatic switch to defending African Americans in a string of stinging dissents. The first of these dissents was in the 1883 civil rights cases. When the majority struck down the key provisions of this case, holding that Congress did not have the right to forbid segregation in public accommodations, Harlan, as a former slave owner, ironically declared that Congress had precisely that power. The ironies did not end there; Harlan wrote his dissent with the same pen and inkwell that Chief Justice ROGER BROOKE TANEY used to write the infamous pro-slavery Dred Scott decision.

This dissent was a forerunner for his most famous dissent in *Plessy v. Ferguson* (1896), in which the Supreme Court majority enunciated the "separate but equal" doctrine justifying segregation. Harlan's most famous line, "Our Constitution is color blind and neither knows nor tolerates classes among citizens," came from that eloquent dissent.

Modern legal thinkers also recognize his progressive legal thinking in his dissent in *Pollack v. Farmer's Loan and Trust Co.* (1895). In this case, the majority found that income tax unconstitutionally violated the Constitution's prohibition of direct taxes not apportioned to a state's population. While the Sixteenth Amendment overturned this decision in 1913, it is very difficult now to follow the Court majority's logic in striking down the income tax law. Harlan's dissent, however, has a very modern ring to it. So, too, was his dissent in the "Insular Cases" (1901), when he protested against the majority's decision that did not give the residents of the new U.S. possessions the national benefits of the Constitution.

Harlan also argued that the Court had no right to read the word *unreasonable* into the Sherman Act in the decisions against the Standard Oil and American Tobacco trusts. In these dissents, he was popular with antitrust reformers of his day, although he was never as consistent on property rights as he was on civil rights, and his opinions in other property rights cases made him seen contradictory.

Harlan also participated in international law tribunals. In 1893, President BENJAMIN HARRISON appointed him to the Bering Sea Arbitration Tribunal that met in Paris.

He was not always consistent, and OLIVER WENDELL HOLMES, JR., the great jurist who joined him in some later dissents, often pointed to his weaknesses, among them being that he was "the last of tobacco chompers." Harlan not only chewed tobacco, but he also drank bourbon, loved baseball, played golf, and wore outlandishly colorful outfits not typical of Supreme Court justices. Harlan alone among the justices of his era was comfortable socializing with African Americans and Asians, another unique characteristic that made him a significant U.S. political leader.

Harlan died on October 14, 1911.

Further Reading

Beth, Loren P. *John Marshall Harlan: The Last Whig Justice.* Lexington: University Press of Kentucky, 1992.

Clark, Floyd Barzilia. *The Constitutional Doctrines of Justice Harlan.* Baltimore: Johns Hopkins Press, 1989.

Latham, Frank Brown. *The Great Dissenter: John Marshall Harlan, 1833–1911.* New York: Cowles Book Co., 1970.

Przybyszewski, Linda. *The Republic According to John Marshall Harlan.* Chapel Hill: University of North Carolina Press, 1999.

Yarbrough, Tinsley E. *Judicial Enigma: The First Justice Harlan.* New York: Oxford University Press, 1995.

Harrison, Benjamin
(1833–1901) *president, senator*

During his single term as president, Benjamin Harrison gave the people of the United States honest, progressive government that achieved much in both the international and domestic spheres. Since he began his term exactly 100 years after GEORGE WASHINGTON, he became known as the "Centennial President." He is the only president whose grandfather also served as president. His great grandfather, also Benjamin Harrison, signed the Declaration of Independence.

Benjamin Harrison's grandfather was President WILLIAM HENRY HARRISON, and the Harrison family had given a century and a half of distinguished service to the United States before Harrison was elected. Five successive generations of Harrisons, with the first name of Benjamin, amassed distinguished careers as attorneys, military officers, educated gentlemen, and public officials between 1632 and 1791. If one adds his grandfather's long career and his father's service in the U.S. Congress, the record for the Harrison family—through Benjamin Harrison's presidency—is continuous for 150 years. Typically, the rankings of historians rate Harrison as merely average, but the times simply did not demand more from him. On a personal level, his independence, intelligence, and sense of justice made him a president of great character.

Harrison was the son of John Scott Harrison, the only man to be the son of one president and the father of another. Benjamin Harrison was born at North Bend, Ohio—a two 2,000-acre rural estate—on August 20, 1833. When he was 14 years of age, Benjamin Harrison was sent to Farmers'

Benjamin Harrison, grandson of William Henry Harrison, was elected president with fewer popular votes than his opponent, as the result of an anomaly of the Electoral College. *(Library of Congress)*

College (then known as Cary's Academy) in Cincinnati, Ohio. After two years there, he transferred as a junior to Miami University— one of the leading colleges in the West during its day—in Oxford, Ohio, where he was active in the forensic society and the Presbyterian Church, as well as excelling in his studies. Upon his graduation in June 1852, Harrison was awarded the top honors. While he considered the ministry, he ended up studying law with one of the leading law firms in Cincinnati. When Benjamin married in the fall of 1853, his father, who had just been elected to the House of Representatives as a Whig, allowed him to live at the North Bend estate when he left for Washington, D.C.

When Harrison was admitted to the bar in 1854, he moved to Indianapolis where, within a year, he joined a law partnership with the son of a former Indiana governor and the brother of Lew

Wallace, who later became a famous author. Harrison had moderate success as an attorney and still more success in politics. Although his father warned him against politics and specifically against the Republican Party, Benjamin Harrison campaigned for JOHN CHARLES FRÉMONT, the 1856 Republican presidential candidate. He was also elected the city attorney of Indianapolis as a Republican in 1857. Serving as secretary of the Republican Party's state central committee in 1858, he gained critical exposure and was elected the state supreme court reporter in 1860 and reelected two more times to this profitable post.

In the summer of 1862, Indiana's governor asked Harrison to establish and train an Indiana regiment and become its colonel. Trained with Harrison's strict discipline, this unit fought successfully in the Georgia campaign during the Civil War. Because of his personal heroism in one battle, General Joseph Hooker recommended, and President ABRAHAM LINCOLN granted, Harrison a promotion to brigadier general. Harrison then led his troops in action in Tennessee, the Carolinas, and Virginia. While his grandfather had a reputation as a fighter of American Indians Benjamin Harrison has a vastly more extensive military record.

A genuine war hero, Harrison returned to his successful law practice in Indianapolis. He was active in politics but did not seek a major office until he ran unsuccessfully for the governor of Indiana in 1876. While he did not win, he was credited with helping elect President RUTHERFORD BIRCHARD HAYES. Hayes then appointed him to a two-year term on the Mississippi River Commission. Harrison became the Republican leader in Indiana in 1877 and successfully backed JAMES ABRAM GARFIELD for the Republican presidential nomination in 1880. Having been elected to the U.S. Senate in 1880, Harrison declined a post Garfield offered him in his cabinet.

In the U.S. Senate, Harrison compiled an outstanding record for a one-term senator. Not only was he a distinguished speaker, but he was also a craftsman of progressive legislation that was aimed at regulating the railroads and trusts, as well as providing for African-American civil rights, civil service reform, and fair treatment for Asian immigrants. In line with the dominant position of his party, he favored high tariffs for industrial growth. As one would expect of a Civil War general, he strongly criticized Democratic President STEPHEN GROVER CLEVELAND for vetoing the dozens of veterans' pension bills that were perennial raids on the treasury. At the time, that made him the "soldiers' friend," and he gained the staunch support of the Grand Army of the Republic (GAR).

Nonetheless, the Democrats won control of the Indiana state legislature, and Harrison was denied reelection to the Senate by a single vote. Having lost a close contest to Cleveland in 1884, JAMES GILLESPIE BLAINE wisely decided against another presidential bid, creating an open campaign for the Republican nomination. Harrison was generally acceptable to all factions, and he was nominated along with Levi P. Morton for vice president. The Democrats nominated Cleveland for a second term.

The politics of the late 1800s found both parties almost equally divided in national politics, so that the shift of a fairly small number of votes in key states could tip the balance one way or the other in the presidential contest. The Democrats had wide margins of victory in southern and western states, which meant they often were at a disadvantage in the Electoral College. Both Harrison and Cleveland were honest, intelligent, conservative gentlemen, so there were not many issues that separated them, other than the tariff and veterans' pensions. Harrison and the Republicans were for high tariffs and more pensions; Cleveland and the Democrats were for low tariffs and less pensions. The campaign turned on who could get the vote out in the key northern industrial states. The Republican Party bosses were hungry after being without presidential patronage for four years and thought they could control Harrison. They worked hard and carried Indiana, New York, and all of the necessary doubtful states by slim margins. In the end, Harrison won the Electoral College vote by 233–168, even though Cleveland garnered 90,000 more popular votes in the nation as a whole.

The Republicans captured both houses of Congress in the election, so Harrison was able to push through four significant pieces of legislation in his first two years. In line with Republican promises, Harrison raised the tariffs and provided for more pensions. These may have been somewhat counterproductive for his economic goals, but they were expected of a Republican. Harrison even deviated from a single-minded high tariff stance by supporting negotiated reciprocal trade agreements.

In progressive domestic legislation, Harrison supported the Sherman Antitrust Act, which took limited steps to outlaw trusts and monopolies and tried to meet the demands of small businessmen and farmers for protection from some predatory corporate practices. Harrison also supported the Sherman Silver Purchase Act, which increased the amount of silver that could be coined and was modestly inflationary, thereby reassuring farmers who feared failing farm prices would lead to foreclosures and bankruptcy.

In the international sphere, he favored an improved merchant marine and the building of a two-ocean navy. In 1889, he sponsored the first Pan-American Conference in Washington to build good relations between the United States and Latin America. Harrison reached an agreement with Britain in the Bering Sea fur seal controversy. He negotiated a peaceful settlement of the Samoan island controversy between Britain and Germany. Smaller diplomatic crises with Italy over the lynching of three Italians in New Orleans and with Chile over the killing of two U.S. sailors were also resolved peacefully. Only Harrison's desire to annex Hawaii was thwarted.

In 1892, Harrison was nominated again. Whitelaw Reid, U.S. ambassador to France and editor of the New York *Tribune,* replaced Vice President Levi Morton as his running mate. The Democrats once again nominated Cleveland. Harrison had a strong record on which to run. The economy was reasonably good, although farmers were perennially discontented. However, Harrison was scrupulously honest and did not get along well with the corrupt congressional leadership of his party in that period. Harrison limited congressional control of patronage to the extent he was able. In consequence, many Republican Party bosses, who worked hard for him in 1888, sat on their hands during the 1892 election.

A significant number of farmers voted for the Populists as a protest against falling prices, and James B. Weaver, the Populist candidate, received more than a million votes. Some workers were disgruntled over the Harrison administration's support of business during the Homestead steel strike at Homestead, Pennsylvania, and elsewhere. Opposition to the rates under the McKinley Tariff also was a drag on his popularity. Prior to the election, neither major candidate took to the stump. Harrison avoided campaign speaking because his wife was ill (she died shortly before the election), and Cleveland declined to campaign in deference to Harrison's grief. Harrison, who trailed Cleveland by 90,000 popular votes in 1888, now trailed him by more than 350,000 votes. Worse, he lost votes in the doubtful states he could not afford to lose. This time the Electoral College result matched the popular result, with Cleveland winning 277, Harrison 145, and Weaver 22 votes.

In retirement, Harrison continued to write, lecture, and practice law. He even argued before the Supreme Court. Asked to participate in the international legal dispute over the boundary between Venezuela and British Guiana, he successfully defended Venezuela against the British. He died on March 13, 1901.

Further Reading

"Benjamin Harrison" in *The American President,* by Philip B. Kunhardt, Jr., Philip B. Kunhardt III, and Peter W. Kunhardt. New York: Riverhead Books, 1999.

Fickle, James E. "Benjamin Harrison" in *The American Presidents,* edited by Frank N. Magill, John L. Loos, and Tracy Irons-Georges. Pasadena, Calif.: Salem Press, 2000.

"Harrison, Benjamin." Available online. URL: http://www.whitehouse.gov/history/presidents/bh23.html. Downloaded on October 20, 2001.

Harrison, Benjamin. *Public Papers and Addresses of Benjamin Harrison.* Washington, D.C.: Government. Printing Office, 1893.

"Harrison, Benjamin" in *The Presidency A to Z: Second Edition,* edited by Michael T. Nelson. Washington, D.C.: Congressional Quarterly Press, 1998.

Sievers, Harry J. *Benjamin Harrison.* Norwalk, Conn.: Easton Press, 1989.

Socolofsky, Homer E. *The Presidency of Benjamin Harrison.* Lawrence.: University Press of Kansas, 1987.

Wallace, Lew. *Life of General Ben Harrison.* Philadelphia: Hubbard Brothers, 1888.

Harrison, William Henry
(1773–1841) *president, senator, representative*

William Henry Harrison was the oldest person elected president at that time in history, and he was the first to die in office. Living only 30 and one-half days after his inauguration, he served a shorter period of time than any other president. He was the father of John Scott Harrison, who served in the House of Representatives, and the grandfather of president BENJAMIN HARRISON.

Harrison was born in the family home at Berkeley Plantation in Charles City County, Virginia, on February 9, 1773. His father, the fifth in a line of Benjamin Harrisons whose collective distinguished service stretched back to 1632, signed the Declaration of Independence. William Henry Harrison was tutored at home and was bright enough to pass the entrance exams at Hampden-Sydney College in the late 1780s, but he quit college before completing the program to study medicine in Richmond in 1790 and Philadelphia in 1791.

On August 16, 1791, he abandoned all these educational efforts and joined the army as a junior officer. Although he was only 18 years of age, he recruited a company of somewhat less than 100 men, who were willing to risk their lives fighting American Indians for glory and a $2-a-day salary. He marched his troops from Philadelphia to Pittsburgh, where they boarded boats that carried them down the Ohio River to Fort Washington at what is now Cincinnati, Ohio.

For the next quarter century, Harrison was an American Indian fighter and negotiator of Indian treaties, who, as much as any single individual, opened the Northwest Territory for settlement. In 1794, General Anthony ("Mad Anthony") Wayne cited Harrison for courage during the Battle of Fallen Timbers. In 1795, he was briefly the commandant to Fort Washington. Having risen to the rank of captain, Harrison resigned the army in 1798 and moved his family a few miles down the Ohio River from Fort Washington to a place called North Bend, where he bought a modest farm that he developed into a large estate over time.

When Harrison was out of military service for only about a month, President JOHN ADAMS appointed him secretary of the Northwest Territory. In 1796, the territorial legislature elected him as their delegate to Congress, where he vigorously supported their interests in opening land on generous terms. In 1800, President Adams appointed him the territorial governor of the Indiana portion that had been subdivided from the Northwest Territory. This required his moving to the territorial capital in Vincennes, where he built a mansion reminiscent of his family home in Virginia. As a Virginian, he had ties to newly elected President THOMAS JEFFERSON, though they belonged to different parties, so Jefferson reappointed him territorial governor. Jefferson's interest in Harrison stemmed from the fact that Harrison hoped to introduce slaveholding into the Northwest Territory, even though that would have meant repealing the antislavery provisions that had been inserted in 1787.

Harrison did not succeed in allowing slavery into the Northwest Territory, but he did succeed in opening it for white settlement by negotiating a series of Indian treaties over the next eight years. Collectively, the Delaware, Miami, Potawatomi, and Eel Indians sold about 3 million acres for annual payments of $200 to $500 for each tribe. This was solemnized in the Treaty of Fort Wayne in 1809. The treaties did not solve the Indian problem, however, for white settlement aroused Indian enmity. The British, who still harbored hopes of reclaiming the land they lost in the Revolutionary War, incited the area tribes to join with the Shawnee warriors Tecumseh and his brother, the Prophet, to protect Indian hunting grounds. Harrison conducted negotiations with the Shawnee brothers, including a dramatic meeting at his own home, but he failed to settle the question.

Sometime later, Harrison decided a show of force was necessary and led about 800 troops toward the Shawnee settlement. Stopping overnight on November 6, 1811, at Tippecanoe Creek, Harrison did not calculate his campsite well. At dawn on the following day, the Shawnee attacked. Although Harrison beat them back, he suffered 61 dead and 127 wounded. In retaliation, Harrison went to the nearby village and razed it, although it was empty when he got there. The Shawnee and their allies were now firmly on the side of the British and fought with them in the War of 1812.

Objectively, Harrison's "success" at Tippecanoe was ambiguous, but he continued to use it for political advantage for years to come.

If Tippecanoe was ambiguous, Harrison's success in the War of 1812 was not. After the British captured Detroit, President JAMES MADISON appointed Harrison a brigadier general and placed him in charge of the Northwestern Army. Appointed a major general the following spring, he fortified Fort Meigs near Detroit and withstood two sieges by the British and the American Indians. After Captain Oliver Perry defeated the British on Lake Erie and took control of the Great Lakes, Harrison was able to take Detroit from the British and chase them into Canada. On October 5, 1813, Harrison's army convincingly defeated British and American Indian forces on the Thames River. Tecumseh was killed, the British fled, and the northwestern border was effectively secured.

Retiring again from the army, Harrison parlayed his military success into a seat in the U.S. House of Representatives where he served from 1816 to 1821, representing the Ohio district in which his estate was located. Over the next four years, he tried without success to be elected governor, U.S. congressman, and U.S. senator before finally succeeding in election to the U.S. Senate in 1825. In the Senate, he served three years and was chairman of the committee on military affairs. In 1828, as a supporter of the Adams administration, Harrison was rewarded with an appointment as minister to Colombia, but he served only one month before he was recalled by Adams's successor, ANDREW JACKSON.

Harrison suffered political and personal reverses throughout the years of Jackson's administration. After 1834, he served as a clerk of the court of common pleas in Hamilton County, Ohio, while he struggled with financial troubles. Having decided to run for president, he went on speaking tours throughout Indiana and Illinois in 1835, and he later garnered support from Whig conventions in Pennsylvania, Maryland, Kentucky, and Indiana. When Jackson chose not to run after two terms, the open election invited a large number of candidates to challenge Jackson's hand-picked successor, MARTIN VAN BUREN. DANIEL WEBSTER's friends tried to talk Harrison into running as Whig vice presidential running mate, but Harrison refused and ran for president himself. During the summer of 1836, he broke with tradition and openly campaigned at rallies throughout the country. The Whigs failed to agree on a single candidate and split their vote among Harrison, Webster, and Hugh L. White. The Democrat Van Buren won handily in the Electoral College with 170 votes over 73 for Harrison. Still, Harrison carried seven states and received almost as many popular votes in the North as Van Buren, making him a leading candidate for 1840.

Since Harrison did well in the 1836 losing effort, he continued to campaign for the next four years by visiting veterans, Whig, and anti-Masonic groups. He was so effective that at their convention the Whigs turned on their long-term leaders, Daniel Webster and HENRY CLAY, and nominated Harrison. To avoid controversy the Whigs did not produce a platform, and they insisted Harrison not

William Henry Harrison, renowned as an Indian fighter, served the shortest term of any president, dying only one month after taking his oath of office. *(Library of Congress)*

repeat his controversial views on slavery, tariffs, and the national bank. To broaden party appeal they selected JOHN TYLER, a former Democratic senator from Virginia, as Harrison's vice presidential running mate, thereby rounding out the slogan "Tippecanoe and Tyler, Too." Apparently, little thought was given to the possibility that Tyler might become president and might retain his Democratic views in the White House.

The Democrats nominated their incumbent president, Martin Van Buren, despite the fact that he was increasingly blamed for the economic downturn that followed the Panic of 1837. Complicating the campaign, an openly antislavery Liberty Party made its appearance with their nominee, JAMES GILLESPIE BIRNEY. Democrats tried to exploit the fact that the Whigs had passed over their recognized leaders, Clay and Webster, but the Whigs had been out of power so long that they stuck together. Democrats also tried to ridicule Harrison's war record and exploit his age, but one of their attempts to suggest that Harrison lived in a log cabin and drank hard cider backfired. Instead of negative characteristics, Whigs realized that these charges would serve to give a common touch to their candidate—who was actually a Virginia blueblood whose "log cabin" had entirely been made over into a mansion.

Slogans and slander were everywhere. While Democrats mistakenly picked on Harrison over hard cider, the Whigs unfairly portrayed Van Buren as a dandy who preened himself in front of silver mirrors. Slander was not new, but it was intensified in this campaign. Several new features of political campaigning were added in 1840. In Cleveland, some Whigs fashioned a large tin ball and rolled it relay fashion down to the state capitol in Columbus waving a banner extolling, "Keep the Ball Rolling." The campaign also added rallies with barbeque, coonskin hats, hard cider, and so on. Apparently, everyone had a good time, and the turnout was a record 83% of the voters, or a total of 2,400,000. This was a 50% increase over that of 1836 and a record high to that time, but the election was close. Harrison defeated Van Buren with a popular vote margin of only about 150,000 votes.

The Electoral College vote was a landslide for Harrison, however, who won 19 of the 26 states, for an electoral vote total of 234 to Van Buren's 60. To counter the charge that he was too old, Harrison traveled widely and campaigned vigorously. Newspapers were filled with stories of how vigorous he seemed for such an old man. Some of this was unfortunately deceptive, for Harrison was exhausted when he reached Washington for his inaugural. On March 4, 1841, giving one of the longest inaugural addresses on record, Harrison caught cold. He aggravated this by beginning a round of meetings with demanding office seekers, while still trying to manage everything in the government, including procurement for the White House kitchen. One rainy day later in the month, he went out to buy vegetables for the kitchen, was chilled, and developed pneumonia. About a week later, on April 4, 1841, he died in Washington, D.C.

Further Reading

"Harrison, William Henry." Available online. URL: http://www.whitehouse.gov/history/presidents/wh9.html. Downloaded on October 20, 2001.

"Harrison, William Henry," *American Heritage* 15, no. 5 (August 1964).

Cleaves, Freeman. *Old Tippecanoe: William Henry Harrison and His Time.* Norwalk, Conn.: Easton Press, 1986.

Fickle, James E. "William Henry Harrison" in *The American Presidents,* edited by Frank N. Magill, John L. Loos, and Tracy Irons-Georges. Pasadena, Calif.: Salem Press, 2000.

Goebel, Dorothy B. *William Henry Harrison: A Political Biography.* Indianapolis: Historical Bureau of the Indiana Library and Historical Department, 1926.

"Harrison, William Henry" in *The Presidency A to Z: Second Edition,* edited by Michael T. Nelson. Washington, D.C.: Congressional Quarterly Press, 1998.

Hudson, Randall O. *American Diplomacy in Action: William Henry Harrison in Colombia.* Wichita, Kans.: Wichita State University, 1973.

Peterson, Norma Lois. *The Presidencies of William Henry Harrison & John Tyler.* Lawrence.: University Press of Kansas, 1989.

"William Henry Harrison" in *The American President,* by Philip B. Kunhardt, Jr., Philip B. Kunhardt III, and Peter W. Kunhardt. New York: Riverhead Books, 1999.

Young, Stanley. *Tippecanoe and Tyler, Too!* New York: Random House, 1957.

Hastert, Dennis
(1942–) *Speaker of the House, representative*

A modest Midwesterner of moderate views, Dennis Hastert was suddenly named the Republican Party's designee for Speaker of the U.S. House of Representatives after back-to-back resignations by Speaker NEWTON LEROY GINGRICH and his newly designated replacement, Congressman Robert Livingston, in the wake of the disastrous Republican electoral debacle in the fall of 1998.

Hastert was born on January 2, 1942, in Aurora, Illinois, and he grew up not far away in Oswego, Illinois. He went to college in the suburbs of Chicago, graduating in 1964 from Wheaton College where he earned a bachelor's degree in economics. He also attended graduate school at Northern Illinois University in DeKalb, Illinois, where he earned a master's degree in the philosophy of education in 1967.

For the first 16 years of his career, he was a government and history teacher at Yorkville High School. He also coached football and wrestling and led the school team to a victory in the 1976 Illinois State Wrestling Championship. A former high school and college wrestler himself, Hastert was named Illinois Coach of the Year and inducted as an Outstanding American into the National Wrestling Hall of Fame in Stillwater, Oklahoma. In 2001 the United States Olympic Committee named him honorary vice president of the American Olympic movement.

In 1980, Hastert was elected to the Illinois House of Representatives and served six years in the Illinois General Assembly, where he sponsored child abuse prevention and educational reform legislation. He also worked for property tax reform, economic development, and a new public utilities act.

Hastert was elected to the U.S. House of Representatives in 1986. He served as chairman of the House Government Reform and Oversight Subcommittee on National Security, International Affairs, and Criminal Justice. In this capacity, he had broad oversight for the State, Defense, and Justice Departments, as well as the drug war and the 2000 census. On the House Commerce Committee,

Hastert had jurisdiction over a broad range of interstate and foreign commerce issues.

During his years in Congress, Hastert compiled a moderate to conservative record in line with the general predisposition of his constituents. In 2000, they reelected him with 74% of the overall vote. His legislative record includes working to balance the budget, cut taxes, streamline government, and preserve the environment.

Hastert joined U.S. Senator JOHN MCCAIN to repeal the previous Social Security earnings limit that prevented senior citizens from working, a long-term project only completed after he became Speaker. Hastert was entrusted by the House Republicans to be a leader in their position on health care reform. This effort required a bipartisan approach, which resulted in legislation passed by the Congress and signed by President WILLIAM JEFFERSON CLINTON in 1996. Hastert chaired the committee that produced the 1998 Patient Protection Act, expanding medical choices for citizens.

In 1994, Hastert served as chief deputy majority whip, a leadership position that he held until elevated to Speaker. While this is an important party post and is in line for promotion when a vacancy occurs higher up in the hierarchy, it is unlikely that anyone anticipated that Hastert would emerge as the new Speaker in the fall of 1998. In that campaign, the historical record would lead to the expectation that the Republicans would make large gains in Congress since the opposition Democrats had held the White House for the previous six years. Since 1834, every party that has held the White House for two terms has lost seats in such an election. Worse for the Democrats would seem to be the negative publicity from the incumbent Democratic president having had an extramarital affair and his having just survived a lengthy impeachment effort.

Contrary to expectations, the Democrats did not lose seats but gained them and almost took control of the House of Representatives from the Republicans. With the Republican majority down to single digits, a decision by a handful of Republicans to switch sides or sit out the vote for Speaker would have endangered the election of a Republican to the post. The incumbent Speaker Newt Gingrich had been challenged previously and was clearly vulnerable. As soon as Congressman Robert Livingston announced that he would challenge Gingrich for Speaker, Gingrich resigned not only as Speaker but from his House seat as well.

The key factor in Gingrich's sudden withdrawal was apparently the growing knowledge that he had been having an extramarital affair at the same time he was presiding as Speaker over the impeachment of President Clinton. With Gingrich's resignation, the Republicans chose Livingston as the new Speaker-designate. Shortly thereafter, Livingston rose in the House chamber to announce that he would not be accepting the Speakership and that he too was resigning because the press was about to disclose that he had been having an extramarital affair as well. In this context, Hastert, who faced no such scandal and ranked high in the party hierarchy, became the Republicans' choice for Speaker.

Upon becoming Speaker, Hastert behaved very differently from his predecessor, Gingrich. Following the traditional behavior pattern of Speakers of both parties, Hastert worked behind the scenes to produce majority support for his position rather than attracting attention to himself with attention-grabbing public pronouncements.

Hastert had a moderate to conservative voting record that fit with his moderate to conservative district. Both factors gave him the flexibility to compromise in order to manage his party's slim, single-digit hold on control of the House.

Unlike his predecessor, Gingrich, or even his Senate counterpart, Senator TRENT LOTT, he sought to moderate positions to maintain power. Clearly threatened by the loss of control in the extremely close 2000 election, Hastert helped his party hang on to a slim majority while the Republican leadership in the Senate led their party from a small majority to a tie. (Lott's leadership provoked Senator James Jeffords of Vermont to leave the Republican Party causing Republicans to lose control to the Democrats.) Hastert led the House in support of most of President GEORGE WALKER BUSH's 2000 legislative proposals.

Hastert had his failures, however. The Republican House majority was opposed to the Shays-Meehan campaign finance reform bill (a close copy of the Senate's McCain-Feingold proposal).

Hastert led the Republican attempt to stop this proposal from being enacted by the simple expedient of preventing the proposal from reaching the floor. Despite strenuous efforts, a sufficient number of Republicans joined a majority of Democrats to force the proposal out of committee and onto the floor, where it passed narrowly.

The Republicans who bolted from the Hastert-led opposition recognized that the bankruptcy of the ENRON corporation had altered the political landscape so that failure to enact campaign finance reform threatened the Republicans in the November 2002 election.

Hastert apparently responded to this setback by moderating the House Republican position on welfare reform. Instead of adopting the very conservative Bush administration position, Hastert positioned the House Republicans in between the White House and the more liberal Democratic Party position.

Hastert has shown considerable success by returning to the more traditional form of the Speaker's office than that used by the predecessor, Gingrich.

Further Reading

"Hastert, Dennis" in *Congress A to Z: Third Edition,* edited by David R. Tarr and Ann O'Connor. Washington, D.C.: Congressional Quarterly, 1999.

Hastert, Dennis. "Welfare Reform, New and Improved." *New York Times,* April 11, 2002, A33, col. 1.

Mitchell, Alison. "House Vote is Set on Campaign Bill," *New York Times,* January 25, 2002, A1, col. 3

———. "While Hastert Turns to Bush, Backers of Campaign Overhaul Mull Delay of Its Effect," *New York Times,* February 8, 2002, A19, col.1

Loomis, Burdett A. *Esteemed Colleagues: Civility and Deliberation in the U.S. Senate.* Washington, D.C.: Brookings Institution, 2000.

Hayes, Rutherford Birchard
(1822–1893) *president, representative, governor*

Rutherford Birchard Hayes became president as a result of one of the most disputed elections in U.S. history, since he received fewer popular votes for president and fewer uncontested Electoral College votes than his opponent. As the result of a controversial Congressional commission, he was awarded all contested Electoral College votes and thereby the presidency. Inspite of the circumstances by which he was elected, Hayes was a man of great personal integrity and compiled an excellent record of public service both in and out of the presidency.

Hayes was born on October 4, 1822, in Delaware, Ohio, about 10 weeks after the death of his father. Hayes had distinguished lineage traceable back to the *Mayflower*, and all four of his great-grandfathers fought in the Revolutionary War. His older brother died when he was only two, so Hayes's mother and older sister doted on him as the only male in the family. His sister apparently had a very strong affection for him and drove him to excel. Unfortunately, her ambition and constant attention made him a very nervous young man, but, as the result of the stable influence of a maternal uncle, he survived this situation and matured well.

His family provided him with a remarkably good education for those living in early 19th-century Ohio. After attending a Methodist seminary in Norwalk, Ohio, he was sent to Middletown, Connecticut, where he entered a private school that was later absorbed into Wesleyan University. He returned to Ohio to attend Kenyon College. After graduation, apparently at the urging of his sister, he went back to New England to study law at Harvard Law School, which he finished in 1845. Initially Hayes appears neither to have liked being a lawyer nor to have prospered as one. In 1849, he broke from his family's influence and moved to Cincinnati. Three years later, he married Lucy Ware Webb and started a family.

A Whig by temperament and background, Hayes was not heavily involved in politics and, at first, avoided taking strong stands on slavery. He focused on his legal career and was particularly successful in a number of criminal cases. He began volunteering his services to the Underground Railroad, helping fugitive slaves win their freedom. Perhaps the plight of the runaway slaves began to affect him, because by 1856, he was openly opposed to slavery and helped found the Ohio Republican Party. Since founding such a third-party effort was risky, he seems not to have entered politics for ambition, power, or money. He was, however, successful in winning the office of Cincinnati city solicitor in 1858.

When the Civil War broke out, Hayes was 38 years old, the father of three sons, and certainly had enough money to employ a substitute. He could easily have avoided military service, but he volunteered and served four years, most of it with the Twenty-third Ohio Volunteers, a unit in which WILLIAM MCKINLEY also served. During the war, Hayes was wounded five times, cited for bravery, and promoted to the rank of major general.

While still in service, he was nominated for the U.S. House of Representatives in 1864 and elected without his needing to campaign. In the House, he was mainly aligned with the Radical Republicans and accepted the ultra-Radical THADDEUS STEVENS as leader. But he showed independence by sponsoring an unsuccessful attempt to amend the draft of the Fourteenth Amendment to include a literacy test for both whites and blacks as a condition for voting. Although just a freshman, he succeeded in passing legislation to develop the Library of Congress.

He was reelected in 1866 but resigned very early in his term, because he had been nominated for governor of Ohio. In 1867, he won easily because he was believed to be a staunch follower of Radical Republicanism and supported ratification of the Thirteenth, Fourteenth, and Fifteenth Amendments. Reelected to two more two-year terms, he was a strongly reformist governor who worked to establish mental hospitals, modern prisons, a welfare bureau, and the state education system. He was particularly active in creating the land-grant agricultural school that later became Ohio State University.

By 1873, Hayes had inherited his uncle's estate at Fremont, Ohio, and he decided to retire from politics. His retirement was brief, because the Ohio Democrats had staged a comeback, relying on discontent over the Republicans' deflationary policies and agitating over some of the Reconstruction issues as well. William Allen, a popular greenback advocate and a Democrat, had taken the governor's office and looked like a sure bet for reelection. Desperate, the Republicans urged Hayes to come out of retirement and make an-

Rutherford B. Hayes, elected president in the most controversial election until the 2000 election, received fewer votes than his opponent. *(Library of Congress)*

other bid for governor. It was expected to be a difficult race, but Hayes won and thereby became a national figure and a potential presidential candidate for 1876.

While often thought of as a "dark horse" candidate in 1876, Hayes was a serious contender. To be sure, others, such as JAMES GILLESPIE BLAINE, ROSCOE CONKLING, Benjamin H. Bristow, and Oliver P. Morton, were better known, but they were also scarred by previous battles. Blaine and Conkling were particularly bitter enemies as the leaders of the Half-Breeds and the Stalwarts, respectively. Benjamin Bristow was anathema to party regulars since he had led many Republicans into the Liberal Republican Party that had backed HORACE GREELEY against ULYSSES S. GRANT in the previous election. Morton was considered a moderate Stalwart who was principally attractive to the southern Republicans because of his continued

support of Radical Reconstruction. Each had a dedicated base of support, but none could pick up votes from any of the others.

Hayes was well known to the delegates and had the ability to pick up second-choice votes from many of them. On the first ballot, Hayes came in fifth. By the seventh ballot, when Morton, Bristow, and Conkling dropped out, Hayes was the beneficiary and went on to defeat Blaine. The Republicans chose Representative William A. Wheeler of New York as Hayes's vice presidential running mate. The Democrats chose SAMUEL JONES TILDEN of New York and balanced their ticket by picking Thomas A. Hendricks of Indiana as their vice presidential nominee.

Hayes ran a rather passive campaign, allowing political operatives to do the electioneering for him. When the results came in, his Democratic opponent led him in the popular vote by 4,284,000–4,036,000. Counting the Electoral College votes for all those states that were uncontested, Tilden led Hayes 184–165. In short, if the contested states had had their votes thrown out, Tilden would have won the presidency in both the popular and Electoral College votes. But, if the contested states were not thrown out, the minimum number of Electoral College votes for the majority needed to win would be 185. If Tilden were to pick up even one of the four contested states (Oregon, Louisiana, South Carolina, and Florida), he would win the presidency. Hayes could only win in the unlikely event that all of the contested states were given to him.

This last scenario was a remarkable undertaking, but it is exactly what the Republican political operatives set out to do. On election night, Hayes thought he had lost. The three major states—Louisiana, Florida, and South Carolina—were sure to vote Democratic if the white voters, who were in the majority, had their way. However, the existing counting or "returns" boards had Republican majorities that were a holdover from the previous Reconstruction regimes. Acting on his faith that the Republican counting boards would know what to do, Republican Party Chairman Zack Chandler made his bold pronouncement that Hayes had 185 Electoral College votes and was elected. Chandler then set out to make his statement come true.

The raw votes indeed appeared to be for Tilden, but Republicans sought out affidavits accusing Democrats of fraud in several counties in those states (or parishes in Louisiana), and the Republican-controlled counting boards threw out enough votes in those Democratic counties that Hayes was the winner. Screaming fraud, the minority Democrats on the counting boards sent in returns showing that Tilden was the winner.

Congress then was forced to decide which set of returns should be honored but had few precedents to follow. The Democrats controlled the House while the Republicans controlled the Senate, and they deadlocked on which set of returns should be accepted. After much debate, a compromise was thrashed out. An electoral commission would be created to conduct an "impartial" investigation. Five members were chosen from each house and five more from the Supreme Court. The Republican Senate picked three Republicans and two Democrats; the Democratic House picked three Democrats and two Republicans. The Supreme Court picked two Democrats and two Republicans and a final crucial member, David Davis, the only member of the Supreme Court thought to be an independent.

This commission might have produced an impartial result, except that the Illinois legislature elected Davis to the U.S. Senate, so he resigned from the Court and withdrew from the commission. Seeking a replacement, the Supreme Court picked Joseph P. Bradley, a Republican but the member thought to be the most fair-minded. Bradley may indeed have been the most impartial Republican that could be found, but he was still a Republican, and he ended up voting a straight party line. All contested cases, no matter what the diverse facts may have been, were decided in favor of Hayes.

The matter still required the confirmation of Congress, and the Democrats controlled the House and could use the filibuster in the Senate. The Democrats delayed for a long time, but eventually the pressure was on them to accept the commission's findings because they had voted for the commission in the beginning. Sensing that they would lose if the issue dragged out past the scheduled inauguration, they finally cut a deal. They would drop their objections to the commission's findings for Hayes if Hayes would agree to end Reconstruction in the South, appoint a Democrat to his cabinet, and support subsidies for a southern transcontinental railway. Operatives for Hayes agreed to these terms as long as the southerners promised not to punish the southern Republicans and to treat African Americans fairly. Perhaps this was the best compromise that could be fashioned, but several parts of it were clearly not enforceable.

It was ironic that Hayes, who had a well-earned reputation for honesty, should have come into office under such a cloud. The doubtful title clearly limited his political resources, but he soldiered on as independently as he could. He had personally avoided involvement in the decisions, but parts of the compromise would have been acceptable to him in any case. Hayes, and the northerners generally, were ready for an end to Reconstruction. And Hayes, recognizing the need to build bipartisan alliances, was open to having a Democrat in his cabinet.

Hayes chose David Key, a Democrat and former Confederate colonel, as postmaster general, a post that clearly allowed Democrats and even former Confederates to receive federal jobs. This distressed Republican Party regulars, but they probably concluded that that was the price of having a Republican in the White House. The rest of Hayes's choices were distinguished but set the stage for a major struggle with Roscoe Conkling and the Stalwart faction of the Republican Party.

Hayes chose William Evarts to be his secretary of state. Evarts was a distinguished New York lawyer who had previously served as attorney general in a Republican administration. However, that Republican administration was ANDREW JOHNSON's, and Evarts had led the defense of Johnson in his Senate impeachment trial, a fact that did not endear him to the Radical Republicans. He had long opposed Conkling over patronage matters. Hayes then chose CARL SCHURZ, a distinguished reformer, for secretary of the interior. Schurz's reform credentials were also impeccable, for he had been one of the reform Republicans who left the party and opposed the reelection of President Grant in 1872, again a fact that did not endear him to many party regulars. Hayes understandably chose John Sherman, his very old friend and an acknowledged fiscal expert, for secretary of the treasury, but he, too, had clashed with Conkling. Conkling and the Stalwarts were furious and set out to block the entire cabinet, but Hayes managed to prevail over the Stalwarts with the help of Senate independents and reformers.

The battle over cabinet choices was only the first Hayes battle against Conkling. In 1877, Hayes promised civil service reform, and after his inauguration he issued an executive order forbidding active political participation by federal civil servants. Alonzo B. Cornell, a Conkling crony, defied Hayes's order and Hayes fired him. Hayes then began an investigation of corruption in the New York customhouse. The port collector, CHESTER ALAN ARTHUR, another Conkling crony and future president, resisted and Hayes fired him. Hayes pleased reformers, but he had started a war with Conkling that lasted for two years before Hayes won. Hayes was not particularly astute in this political struggle, and he used up a great deal of goodwill. However, he prevailed and set the stage for further advances in civil service reform by Arthur, as well as JAMES ABRAM GARFIELD, STEPHEN GROVER CLEVELAND, and BENJAMIN HARRISON.

In domestic affairs, aside from his attempt at reconciliation with the South and the start of civil service reform, his administration was noteworthy for his resumption of the use of precious metals to back up the paper currency and bonds that financed the Civil War. Secretary Sherman received much of the credit for the return to sound currency, but he could hardly have succeeded without Hayes's support. Hayes was clearly disappointed that his attempts to reconcile with the South while protecting African Americans often led to sacrificing African Americans. While Hayes thought that the southerners had agreed to vote with Republicans to install Garfield as Speaker, the southerners were successful in increasing their strength in the midterm elections and declined to do so. Hayes then refused to support subsidies for the southern transcontinental railroad. Much of the compromise that brought Hayes into office was now in shambles.

Hayes was modestly successful in international affairs, which did not command his attention the way that domestic struggles did. He established the broad outlines of a policy for creating a U.S.-controlled canal across Panama, although the building of the canal was still decades away. Chinese immigration into California became a divisive issue, and Hayes took a compromise position. His fairness was influential in settling the problem amicably. He vetoed a Chinese exclusion bill enacted by Congress because, in his view, it violated the terms of the Burlingame Treaty. He then sent a commission to China to negotiate a new agreement with the Chinese government, which permitted the United States to regulate immigration of Chinese laborers.

Hayes had pledged to serve only one term, but it is doubtful, given his struggles with the members of his own party, that he could have been renominated. Hayes was gratified that Garfield was elected, although Hayes did not aid in the campaign much, perhaps fearing he would be a drag on Garfield's chances. After leaving the White House in 1881, he avoided further public participation in electoral politics. For the last 12 years of his life, he promoted such causes as mental hospitals, prison reform, aid to African Americans (particularly in southern schools), and public education, especially the building of various universities, such as Ohio State.

Beyond this, he was influenced by Mark Twain, William Dean Howells, and Henry George, and he voiced his concerns about the rise of monopolies, the decline of fair market competition, the dismal conditions of laborers, and the corruption brought about by accumulations of enormous wealth. All of these positions made him one of the most advanced liberal reformers of his age—and the most advanced of any president until the onset of the Progressive movement a decade after his death. Hayes died of a heart attack on January 17, 1893, at his estate, Spiegel Grove, in Fremont, Ohio.

Further Reading

Davison, Kenneth E. *The Presidency of Rutherford B. Hayes*. Westport, Conn.: Greenwood Press, 1972.

Eckenrode, H. J. *Rutherford B. Hayes: Statesman of Reunion*. Norwalk, Conn.: Easton Press, 1988.

"Hayes, Rutherford B." Available online. URL: http://www.whitehouse.gov/history/presidents/rh19.html. Downloaded on October 20, 2001.

Hoogenboom, Ari A. *Rutherford B. Hayes: Warrior and President*. Lawrence: University Press of Kansas, 1995.

Simpson, Brooks D. *The Reconstruction Presidents.* Lawrence: University Press of Kansas, 1998.

Williams, Charles R. *The Life of Rutherford Birchard Hayes: Nineteenth President of the United States.* New York: Da Capo Press, 1971.

Henry, Patrick
(1736–1799) *Revolutionary War leader, governor*

Long recognized as one of the greatest orators in U.S. history, Patrick Henry's famous lines—"If this be treason, make the most of it" and "Give me liberty or give me death"—have been widely recognized by all Americans. Henry was one of the earliest advocates of American independence, governor of Virginia during the Revolutionary War, and a determined supporter of the addition of the Bill of Rights to the U.S. Constitution.

Patrick Henry was born on May 29, 1736, at Studley, a small village in Hanover County, Virginia. His father was John Henry, a Scotsman who was educated at Aberdeen University and immigrated to Virginia where he was a judge, surveyor, and army officer. Young Henry was largely educated by his father and studied on his own before becoming a lawyer.

His first revolutionary clash with the British came when he was a colonel in the Virginia militia. The British-appointed colonial governor seized a large quantity of gunpowder that the colonial legislature had set aside for the Virginia militia and stored it aboard his ship anchored in a Virginia harbor. Henry, with a regiment of Virginia colonial militia, then marched on the Virginia capitol, forcing the governor to return the gunpowder to the militia's control. This event came to be known as the famous "Gunpowder Affair."

Henry was elected as a delegate to the Virginia House of Burgesses, where he served from 1765 to 1774. He became a radical and one of the first to speak out against England in that country's attempt to impose taxation without representation. In 1765, during a heated debate in the House of Burgesses on the Stamp Act, he said, "If this be treason, make the most of it," while the other delegates shuddered.

Ten years later in 1775, his most famous speech occurred at St. John's Church in Richmond when he said, "Is life so dear or peace so sweet as to be purchased at the price of chains and slavery? Forbid it Almighty God! I know not what course others may take, but as for me, give me liberty or give me death." He had already been elected to the Second Continental Congress in 1774 at that time and continued there until 1776. He also had overlapping service in the Virginia provincial (constitutional) convention in 1775. While there, he personally drafted the religious freedom section of the state constitution at the time of Virginia's independence.

Henry was elected governor of Virginia in 1776 and stayed in that position until 1779. As governor, he was not able to lead troops in the field, but he supplied men from Virginia for GEORGE WASHINGTON's army as well as for his state's militia forces. Henry aided Daniel Boone and his westerners in Kentucky (then a part of Virginia) in holding the territory for the Revolution against British and Indian attacks. He also supported Colonel George Rogers Clark in the winning of the Northwest Territory. Clark's victories in Ohio, Indiana, and Illinois clinched that territory for America during the negotiations that ended the war with England.

After the Revolutionary War was over, Henry continued working for individual freedom. He was elected Virginia's governor again in 1784 and led the fight for the Virginia Religious Freedom Act of 1785. Initially he opposed ratification of the U.S. Constitution, principally because it did not contain a Bill of Rights. After successfully working for the adoption of the Bill of Rights, he became a Federalist. In 1794, he retired and resumed private legal practice. He was offered several important posts, such as chief justice of the U. S. Supreme Court, secretary of state, and U.S. minister to Spain and to France, but he declined them because of failing health. He even turned down a sixth term as governor. Despite Patrick Henry's illness, George Washington persuaded him to become a candidate for the state legislature in 1799, but he died on June 6 of that year.

Further Reading
"Henry, Patrick." Available online. URL: http://libertyonline.hypermall.com/henry-liberty.html. Downloaded October 20, 2001.

"Henry, Patrick." Available online. URL: http://
webpages.homestead.com/revwar/files/HENRY.
HTM. Downloaded October 20, 2001.

Mayer, Henry. *A Son of Thunder: Patrick Henry and the
American Republic.* Charlottesville: University Press
of Virginia, 1991.

Tyler, Moses C. *Patrick Henry.* New York: Chelsea House,
1980.

Vaughan, David J. *Give Me Liberty: The Uncompromising
Statesmanship of Patrick Henry.* Nashville, Tenn.:
Cumberland House Publishers, 1997.

Holmes, Oliver Wendell, Jr.

(1841–1935) *associate justice of the Supreme
Court, chief justice of the Massachusetts
Supreme Judicial Court, author*

Oliver Wendell Holmes, Jr., is the best-known associate justice to serve on the U.S. Supreme Court and the best-known member of any kind on the Court with the exception of Chief Justice JOHN MARSHALL. Holmes led the legal profession in the new direction of legal realism. As a leader, he often stood alone in opposition to his colleagues, and he is known as "The Great Dissenter" for the extraordinary quality and quantity of his dissents.

Holmes was born on March 8, 1841, in Boston, Massachusetts, into a prosperous, intellectual family. His father, Oliver Wendell Holmes, Sr., was a famous 19th-century poet and author as well as being a Harvard professor of medicine and a physician. Young Holmes attended private schools in Boston and went to college at Harvard. Accused by faculty members of being disrespectful, Holmes deserted Harvard for a Civil War training camp. Since his unit was not called up for immediate combat, Holmes finally returned to Harvard and received his degree in 1861 before returning to his unit.

Holmes had a distinguished war record, joining the fighting in Bali's Bluff, Antietam, and Fredericksburg. He was wounded three times and rose to the rank of captain by the time he left the army in 1864 to return to Harvard to study law. Graduating in 1866, he was admitted to the bar in 1867. While he was in private practice for more than 15 years, he seemed almost always more interested in legal scholarship than in the routine practice of law. He spent four grueling years editing the *Kent's Commentaries: Twelfth Edition*, which he published in 1873. During these years, he edited the *American Law Review* and lectured occasionally at Harvard. He worked for several years in trying to find a rational, systematic conceptualization of the law.

After several years of research, he gave a series of 12 lectures that were published in 1881 as *The Common Law*. This became his most famous work, challenging the historical underpinnings of much of Anglo-American jurisprudence by arguing that legal theories must yield before changing economic, social, and political realities. In this book, Holmes wrote one of his most famous quotations, "The life of the law has not been logic; it has been experience." This statement might be taken as a very general summary of the work itself.

The lectures and the publication of this work led to Holmes being invited to take an endowed chair at Harvard, which he accepted, in early 1882. However, before the year was out, he was appointed to the Supreme Judicial Court of Massachusetts, the state's highest court, and he accepted this post—much to the displeasure of Harvard, which had gone to some lengths to provide him with the endowment for his teaching post. However, he was rushed into this choice since the vacancy on the court developed as a Republican governor was about to be replaced by a Democrat. Holmes served on the Massachusetts high court for 20 years, wrote more than 1,300 opinions, and rose to the position of chief justice in 1899.

His opportunity for even greater accomplishment came in 1902, when Holmes received the ultimate legal appointment: nomination to the U.S. Supreme Court. As with his appointment to the top Massachusetts court, accident played a large role. A vacancy on the Court developed in the so-called "New England seat" (Supreme Court justices originally rode geographically defined circuits, hearing individual appeals from federal district courts, and became identified with different regions of the country) during a Republican presidential administration. As it happened, Massachusetts Senator Henry Cabot Lodge was a friend both with Holmes and President THEODORE ROOSEVELT. Lodge assured Roosevelt that Holmes would be compatible with Roosevelt's progressive policies and the deal was done. "Compatible with" did not mean "subservient to," so Roosevelt was disappointed that some of his efforts met with Holmes's dissents when cases reached the Court.

Holmes served on the Supreme Court for 30 years, longer than almost any other justice, but it is the quality and not just the quantity that made him renowned. For more than a decade, until LOUIS DEMBITZ BRANDEIS joined him on the Court, Holmes was often in dissent and often alone. While Brandeis joined him in many later dissents, it was Holmes's vision of the law expressed in those opposing views that made him "The Great Dissenter."

Holmes resigned due to ill health in 1932, at age 90. He was the oldest man ever to serve on the U.S. Supreme Court. He died on March 6, 1935, just two days shy of his 94th birthday.

Further Reading

Aichele, Gary J. *Oliver Wendell Holmes, Jr.—Soldier, Scholar, Judge.* Boston: Twayne Publishers, 1989.

Baker, Liva. *The Justice from Beacon Hill: The Life and Times of Oliver Wendell Holmes.* New York: Harper-Collins, 1991.

Burton, David H. *Taft, Holmes, and the 1920s Court: An Appraisal.* Madison, N.J.: Fairleigh Dickinson University Press, 1998.

Cohen, Jeremy. *Congress Shall Make No Law: Oliver Wendell Holmes, The First Amendment, and Judicial Decision-Making.* Ames: Iowa State University Press, 1989.

Dane, Bob. "The Man Who Was Touched With Fire." Available online. URL: http://www.historynet.com/AmericasCivilWar/articles/2001/0301_cover.html. Downloaded October 20, 2001.

Gordon, Robert W. *The Legacy of Oliver Wendell Holmes, Jr.* Stanford, Calif.: Stanford University Press, 1992.

Holmes, Oliver Wendell, Jr. *The Essential Holmes.* Chicago: University of Chicago Press, 1996.

"Holmes, Oliver Wendell, Jr." Available online. URL: http://www.arlingtoncemetery.org/historical_information/oliver_wendell_holmes.htm. Downloaded October 20, 2001.

"Holmes, Oliver Wendell, Jr." Available online. URL: http://www.harvardregiment.org/holmes.html. Downloaded October 20, 2001.

Novick, Sheldon M. *Honorable Justice: The Life of Oliver Wendell Holmes.* New York: Dell Publishing, 1990.

Pohlman, H. L. *Justice Oliver Wendell Holmes: Free Speech and the Living Constitution.* New York: New York University Press, 1991.

White, G. Edward. *Justice Oliver Wendell Holmes: Law and the Inner Self.* New York: Oxford University Press, 1995.

Hoover, Herbert Clark

(1874–1964) *president, secretary of commerce, diplomat, author*

A mining engineer millionaire by age 40, Herbert Clark Hoover shifted his focus to international relief work, bureaucracy reform, economic development, and politics. His genius and his luck ran out when he, as president and at the apex of his public career, encountered the Great Depression.

Hoover was born on August 10, 1874, in West Branch, Iowa, into a Quaker family. His father died when he was six years old and his mother be-

Herbert Hoover is principally remembered as the president who was in office at the start of the Great Depression. *(Library of Congress)*

fore he was 10. In 1884, he was sent to live with Quaker relatives in Newberg, Oregon, where he attended a Quaker school affiliated with his relatives. In 1888, when he was 14, his relatives moved to Salem, Oregon, where young Hoover began attending night school while working as an office boy. At age 17, Hoover started Stanford University where he displayed skill in mathematics and geology. He graduated with a degree in engineering in May 1895 and began working in the California gold mines, later as a mining engineer in Colorado, and then as a staff member to a San Francisco mining engineer.

Starting in 1897, at age 23 and for the next 17 years, Hoover traveled around the world five times, ascending the professional and corporate ladder until he was an internationally known expert in the mining field. During those 17 years, he compiled an extraordinary record. He explored Western Australia as chief of gold-mining operations for the British mining firm of Bewick, Moreing and Company.

As chief engineer of the Chinese Engineering and Mining Company in 1899 and 1900, Hoover took his new wife to China where, after a year and a half, they found themselves in the middle of a two-month-long siege in Tianjin, China, surrounded by antiforeign Chinese during the Boxer Rebellion. Characteristically, Hoover organized the resistance and rationed the supplies with such efficiency that he was named the general manager of the reorganized mining company after the rebellion was over. From 1901 to 1908, Hoover was a junior partner with Bewick, Moreing and Company, and he worked on their operations mostly in the field and thus traveled extensively.

In 1908, at the age of 34, Hoover was wealthy and had a worldwide reputation in his profession, so he struck out on his own with chairmanships in a number of mining companies. The following year, he also lectured at both Columbia and Stanford Universities and then published his lectures as a book, *Principles of Mining.*

By chance, Hoover was in London when World War I began. Since about 120,000 Americans were stranded in Europe, Walter Hines Page, the U.S. ambassador to Great Britain, asked Hoover to organize and run a relief effort for them.

After Hoover succeeded at that, the international recognition of his efforts led European leaders to appoint him the head of the Commission for Relief in Belgium, which operated in German-occupied Belgium and northern France to feed the residents who were starving there. Over the next four years, Hoover's commission spent nearly $1.5 billion caring for some 10 million civilians.

In the middle of this effort, the United States joined the war, and President THOMAS WOODROW WILSON asked Hoover to return to the United States to become the U.S. food administrator. Hoover was then in charge of increasing food production, improving distribution, eliminating waste, and stabilizing prices in the U.S. food supply. After the war ended in 1918, the French, British, Italian, and American leaders asked him to direct relief and rehabilitation efforts during Europe's postwar famine. Altogether, the programs Hoover managed fed and clothed more than 200 million people by 1920. Especially for the millions of children left underfed and diseased by the war, Hoover established the American Relief Administration, which used a congressional appropriation of $100 million to feed children. From 1921 to 1923, there was a famine in parts of Russia, and the American Relief Administration also fed millions of adults as well as children there.

Since he had been abroad for so many years, Hoover's party affiliation was unknown. Still, his efforts to feed hungry people were so much more popular than the activities of most politicians that it is not surprising that many people wanted him to become involved in politics. Returning to the United States in September 1919, Hoover discovered that some supporters had mounted an unofficial campaign to have him named either the Republican or Democratic Party nominee for president in 1920.

Pressed to declare a party affiliation, Hoover finally stated that he always though of himself as a Republican, but this announcement came shortly before the national nominating conventions were held. HARRY MICAJAH DAUGHERTY had already arranged for WARREN GAMALIEL HARDING to receive the Republican presidential nomination (although this was not publicly known until much later), so Hoover did not get either party's nomination.

After he was elected, Harding was pleased to appoint Hoover the secretary of commerce. Over the next seven years and under both Warren Harding and CALVIN COOLIDGE, Hoover used the commerce post to extend his influence far beyond the traditional limits of that position. Many considered that he was the most important member of the cabinet throughout those years. He also had time in 1922 to write *American Individualism,* a book in which he set forth his personal and political philosophy.

Once President Coolidge announced he would not seek reelection in the summer of 1927, Hoover became the front-runner for the Republican presidential nomination, which he received easily on the first ballot at the 1928 Republican National Convention. The Democrats nominated New York governor ALFRED EMANUEL SMITH, the first Roman Catholic nominated by a major party. Since Smith spoke with a strong New York accent and favored the end of Prohibition, he was far from an ideal candidate to run in the South, the strongest Democratic area in the nation. Hoover was personally opposed to attacks on Smith's religion, but it hardly mattered, for many others made those attacks anyway. Hoover barely campaigned at all and made very few speeches, but he won by a popular vote of 21,430,743–15,016,443—a margin larger than any previous president had received. Hoover carried all but eight states and won the Electoral College vote by a landslide vote of 444–87.

In March 1929, Hoover began his term under the most favorable circumstances. The Republicans had won both houses of Congress by large majorities. He called a special session of Congress to pass legislation to help the farmers and to make small changes in the tariff. Congress passed the farm bill Hoover wanted. However, the industries that could benefit by higher tariffs to protect their manufactures saw a chance to increase their protection (and therefore their prices), and they pushed through the Hawley-Smoot Tariff, the highest peacetime tariff rates in history. Hoover said he opposed the high rates but signed the bill anyway, because it gave him the leeway to reduce rates by up to 50 percent if a tariff commission so recommended. This tariff restricted international trade and arguably contributed to the severity of the Great Depression, which began on October 29, 1929, when the stock market crashed.

From October 1929 on, nothing positive that Hoover did on other fronts mattered very much. This economic catastrophe left upwards of 14 million U.S. citizens unemployed by the end of his administration. In the 1930 congressional elections, Democrats seized control of the House of Representatives and came within one vote of taking over the Senate.

Hoover had succeeded throughout his life by believing in the power of voluntary contributions (or private charity) to relieve the problems of people being hungry. It had, after all, worked for him in the period from 1914 to 1920. It would not work this time—at least not quickly enough—and Hoover did not have the flexibility to change. He also believed in federalism, so he looked to state and local governments, not the federal government, to help the "deserving poor." Hoover was willing to help businesses recover in the hope that they would then hire workers and relieve unemployment. The theory was that if money were put into the economic system at the top, it would trickle down to those at the bottom. Following this philosophy, in January 1932 Hoover recommended and Congress created the Reconstruction Finance Corporation to give half a billion dollars in aid to major businesses to stimulate economic growth. Not only was this aid very late, but also Hoover continued to oppose any direct federal welfare payments to the great mass of the unemployed.

In foreign policy, Hoover claimed progress toward world peace with a minor, and ultimately ineffectual, international treaty that limited small navy ships, and he also made marginal improvements in U.S. relations with Latin America. The biggest foreign policy crisis occurred when Japan invaded the section of China known as Manchuria. Had Hoover taken a strong, consistent stand against Japanese aggression at that point, Japan might have been prevented from the much larger aggression it committed later. Hoover instead took the totally ineffective step of simply expressing disapproval of the takeover by refusing to recognize the territorial conquest under the "Stimson Doctrine," which carried the name of his secretary of state, HENRY LEWIS STIMSON.

Hoover received his party's renomination easily, but the general election pitted him against the popular Democratic nominee, New York Governor FRANKLIN DELANO ROOSEVELT. With the Great Depression so severe, there was little question of the outcome. Hoover went from winning all but eight states in 1928 to losing all but six states in 1932. The popular vote went to Roosevelt by a total 22,821,857–15,761,841. The landslide vote in the Electoral College was 472–59.

Out of office, Hoover severely criticized Roosevelt's domestic New Deal program as excessive federal government intervention in the states and in the private sector. Hoover recommended a noninterventionist foreign policy course. Neither view gained Hoover much popularity, and Roosevelt was able to ignore him.

After Roosevelt's death, President HARRY S. TRUMAN called on Hoover to take various trips around the world to recommend ways to avoid food shortages after the war. In 1947, Truman named Hoover chairman of the Commission on Organization of the Executive Branch of Government to make use of Hoover's administrative skills. President DWIGHT DAVID EISENHOWER also asked Hoover to head up a similar commission in 1955. Even when Hoover was quite elderly, he kept up a formidable writing schedule. In 1958 and at age 83, Hoover published *The Ordeal of Woodrow Wilson*, what many have considered his best book and the first book written by one president about another, especially important since Hoover had served under Wilson during World War I.

Hoover died in New York City on October 20, 1964. Living past his 90th birthday, Hoover lived longer after his term of office than President JOHN ADAMS. In total number of years, he lived longer than any other president except John Adams and RONALD WILSON REAGAN.

Further Reading

Clements, Kendrick. *Hoover, Conservation, and Consumerism: Engineering the Good Life*. Lawrence: University Press of Kansas, 2000.

Hoff-Wilson, Joan. *Herbert Hoover: Forgotten Progressive*. Prospect Heights, Ill.: Waveland Press, 1992.

"Hoover, Herbert." Available online. URL: http://hoover. nara.gov/. Last updated December 13, 2001.

"Hoover, Herbert." Available online. URL: http://www. whitehouse.gov/history/presidents/hh31.html. Downloaded January 18, 2002.

Hoover, Herbert. *The Ordeal of Woodrow Wilson*. New York: McGraw-Hill, 1958; Baltimore: Johns Hopkins University Press, reprint 1992.

———. *Memoirs: Three Volumes*. New York: Macmillan, 1951.

Nash, George H. *The Life of Herbert Hoover: Master of Emergencies*. New York: W.W. Norton, 1996.

Liebovich, Louis. *Bylines in Despair: Herbert Hoover, the Great Depression, and the U.S. News Media*. Westport, Conn.: Praeger, 1994.

Lisio, Donald J. *The President and Protest: Hoover, Macarthur, and the Bonus Riot*. New York: Fordham University Press, 1994.

Wueschner, Silvano A. *Charting Twentieth-Century Monetary Policy: Herbert Hoover and Benjamin Strong*. Westport, Conn.: Greenwood Press, 1999.

Hoover, John Edgar
(J. Edgar Hoover)
(1895–1972) *director of the Federal Bureau of Investigation, author*

A consummate bureaucratic politician, J. Edgar Hoover created the modern Federal Bureau of Investigation (FBI) and built it into a national crime-fighting organization. He also used the power of his secret investigative files to maintain control over the agency until his death. A master at public relations, he managed to keep his personal lifestyle out of the press while using the press to destroy many citizens' careers and threatening to destroy many others. Only after his death did the full extent of his activities become known.

John Edgar Hoover was born in Washington, D.C., on January 1, 1895. When his father suffered a nervous breakdown and was sent to a mental institution, young Hoover was forced to leave school and start working. While he worked days as a messenger for the Library of Congress, he went to night school and earned a law degree at George Washington University.

After Hoover received his law degree in 1917, his uncle arranged for him to work in the U.S. Department of Justice where he skillfully moved up to become special assistant to U.S. Attorney General Alexander Mitchell Palmer in two years. Hoover was in charge of investigating members of revolutionary groups, particularly left-wing groups such as communists, and arranging for their deportation whenever possible. This was the start of his lifelong obsession with punishing those with left-wing views.

Perhaps using his experience from working at the Library of Congress, Hoover created a massive card indexing system of 450,000 names of people with presumed left-wing political views and detailed biographies of some 60,000 that Hoover considered the most dangerous. Hoover then advised Palmer to have these people rounded up and deported.

On November 7, 1919, the second anniversary of the Russian Revolution, more than 10,000 suspected left-wingers were rounded up in 23 different cities. Since the overwhelming majority were American citizens, they were eventually released, but Hoover now had the names of hundreds of lawyers who were willing to represent left-wingers, and he inserted those names into his files. Hoover succeeded in winning a high-profile case against Emma Goldman on dubious grounds and used his victory to deport her and more than 200 other people to Russia.

In 1921, Hoover was rewarded by being promoted to the post of assistant director of the Bureau of Investigation. The original Bureau of Investigation was created under the Justice Department in 1908 and was given the very limited function of investigating violations of federal law and assisting other law enforcement agencies. Law enforcement in the United States was essentially a state activity, not a federal one, and the bureau agents were not allowed to carry guns or to make arrests.

Because of the corruption in the administration of President WARREN GAMALIEL HARDING, his successor, CALVIN COOLIDGE, was determined to run a clean administration. His new attorney general (and future Supreme Court justice) Harlan Fiske Stone appointed Hoover to be director of the Bureau of Investigation in 1924. Hoover decided the organization needed to improve the quality of its staff. He fired those who were in the agency as the result of political appointments, and he began hiring agents on merit, especially seeking out those

with degrees in accounting and law. In 1926, Hoover established a fingerprint file that eventually became the largest in the world.

By 1935, Hoover was able to persuade Congress to establish the Federal Bureau of Investigation and allow its agents to carry firearms and make arrests. Hoover then set about establishing a first-class crime-fighting organization. He clearly succeeded in significant innovations, such as the formation of a scientific crime-detection laboratory and the highly regarded FBI National Academy.

In a significant development for the rest of Hoover's career, he persuaded FRANKLIN DELANO ROOSEVELT to give the FBI the task of investigating both foreign and domestic espionage in the United States. Hoover now had the authority to collect information on those with radical political beliefs. With the help of a few defectors from left-wing groups, Hoover began to assemble more files. He was particularly concerned with the political influence that motion pictures were having on society. By working closely with the members of Congress who shared his views, he was able to use the House Un-American Activities Committee (HUAC) to investigate the entertainment industry. Using names supplied by Hoover, the committee held hearings in which those subpoenaed either gave the committee more names or were found in contempt of Congress. On top of this, the committee and the FBI pressured the major entertainment industries to blacklist artists who were known to hold left-wing political views.

In 1950, some former FBI agents used FBI files to publish a small book that contained the names of more than 100 writers, performers, and directors—all of whom were purported members of subversive groups who had so far not been blacklisted. The book was sent to entertainment industry employers who were urged to blacklist those named unless they came before HUAC and convinced the committee they were no longer left-wingers. By the late 1950s, it was estimated that hundreds of artists had been blacklisted and were unable to find work in television and the cinema.

In the 1960s and 1970s, Hoover and the FBI carried out detailed investigations into any prominent person whom he thought held dangerous political views. Included were leaders of the civil rights movement and those opposed to the Vietnam War. Hoover also conducted investigations into political corruption, but he produced few indictments or convictions because he was mainly interested in using the information as a way to gain control over powerful politicians. Beyond criminal activities, however, Hoover also collected merely embarrassing information—often of a sexual nature—on as many leading politicians as possible. It has long been asserted that Hoover used such damaging information so none of the eight presidents under whom he served would remove him as the head of the FBI.

At the same time, Hoover virtually ignored organized crime, devoting only scant resources to the Mafia while using massive resources against left-wing groups. After his death and as more information has become available, the answer appears to be that certain members of the Mafia—Meyer Lansky is most frequently mentioned—had gathered photographs that proved Hoover's homosexual relationship with his assistant director Clyde Tolson, and Hoover was fearful of being exposed. Curiously, early in Hoover's career, one journalist had hinted at the possibility, and Hoover had investigated him, released damaging information about him, and frightened other journalists from pursuing the story. Hoover managed to keep this story from widespread publication although many political insiders apparently were aware of the situation and allowed it to continue.

Hoover was still in office as the FBI director when he died in his Washington, D.C., home on May 2, 1972. He was 77 years old.

Further Reading

Bardsley, Marilyn. "J. Edgar Hoover." Available online. URL: http://www.crimelibrary.com/hoover/hoovermain.html. Downloaded October 20, 2001.

DeLoach, Cartha. *Hoover's FBI: The Inside Story by Hoover's Trusted Lieutenant.* Washington, D.C.: Regnery, 1995.

Garrow, David J. *The FBI and Martin Luther King, Jr.* New York: Penguin Books, 1983.

Gentry, Curt. *J. Edgar Hoover: The Man and the Secrets.* New York: Norton, 1991.

"Hoover, J. Edgar." Available online. URL: http://foia.fbi.gov/hoover.htm. Downloaded October 20, 2001.

"Hoover, J. Edgar." Available online. URL: http://www.zpub.com/notes/znote-jeh.html. Downloaded October 20, 2001.

"Hoover, J. Edgar." Available online. URL: http://www.geocities.com/WestHollywood/Heights/8255/hoover.html. Downloaded October 20, 2001.

North, Mark. *Act of Treason: The Role of J. Edgar Hoover in the Assassination of President Kennedy.* New York: Carroll & Graf, 1991.

McKnight, Gerald. *The Last Crusade: Martin Luther King, Jr., the FBI, and the Poor People's Campaign.* Boulder, Colo.: Westview Press, 1998.

Potter, Claire Bond. *War on Crime: Bandits, G-Men, and the Politics of Mass Culture.* New Brunswick, N. J.: Rutgers University Press, 1998.

Powers Richard G. *Secrecy and Power: The Life of J. Edgar Hoover.* New York: Free Press, 1987.

Summers, Anthony. *Official and Confidential: The Secret Life of J. Edgar Hoover.* New York: G. P. Putnam's Sons, 1993.

Theoharis, Athan G. *J. Edgar Hoover, Sex, and Crime: An Historical Antidote.* Chicago: Ivan R. Dee, 1995.

Unger, Robert. *The Union Station Massacre: The Original Sin of J. Edgar Hoover's FBI.* Kansas City: Andrews McMeel Publishing, 1997.

Hopkins, Harry Lloyd
(1890–1946) *secretary of commerce, White House staff adviser, diplomat*

Harry Lloyd Hopkins was the key figure in FRANKLIN DELANO ROOSEVELT's depression relief efforts, first in New York State while Roosevelt was governor and then in the nation when he was president. As World War II began in Europe, Hopkins—although ill with cancer—moved into the White House where he was Roosevelt's closest adviser during the remainder of his administration.

Harry Lloyd Hopkins was born in Sioux City, Iowa, on August 17,1890, and his family then moved to Grinnell, Iowa, where he grew up. After graduating from Grinnell College in 1912, he moved to New York City and became a social worker. After the Great Depression began in 1929, Hopkins came to the attention of Roosevelt, who, as governor of New York, needed someone with skill in managing economic relief efforts. In 1931,

Roosevelt named him to head the New York State Temporary Emergency Relief Administration.

When Roosevelt became president in 1933, he again called on Hopkins to work for him—this time as head of the Federal Emergency Relief Administration (FERA). Hopkins continued to stay on after FERA was renamed the Works Progress Administration (WPA) in 1935. In 1938, Hopkins moved up to a cabinet-level position as the secretary of the Department of Commerce, where he stayed until 1940 when he became seriously ill with the cancer that killed him six years later.

Despite his illness, Roosevelt needed Hopkins so badly that he urged him to come back into White House service. Roosevelt had Hopkins move into the White House where he could have the best medical attention and did not have to commute to work or worry about any living arrangements that would detract from the work at hand. Hopkins worked on the lend-lease program, which was established in 1941 to aid Britain and later Russia, countries already at war with Germany and Italy.

After the Pearl Harbor attack on December 7, 1941, Hopkins became Roosevelt's top adviser and assistant throughout the war. Hopkins understood so well that Roosevelt trusted him to react to new events as he would. Since Roosevelt was confined to a wheelchair as the result of his affliction with polio, having someone like Hopkins to act in his behalf was of incredible importance to Roosevelt and the government.

During the war, Hopkins traveled abroad and represented Roosevelt in a number of top-secret meetings with the British Prime Minister Winston Churchill and Russian dictator Joseph Stalin. Since Hopkins carried no official title and was free from having any bureaucratic responsibilities (as he would have had as a cabinet officer), he was free to travel with the minimum of attention paid to him and with maximum effectiveness.

After Roosevelt's death, President HARRY S. TRUMAN designated Hopkins to be his representative to Moscow in settling problems that had arisen over Poland and the organization of the United Nations. However, Hopkins was never as close to Truman as he had been to Roosevelt. When one considers that Hopkins was terminally ill and in great pain nearly every day throughout the wartime years, his devoted service to Roosevelt and the United States was especially heroic. Eventually, the illness took its toll, and he was forced to retire from public life in July 1945.

Officially, he took a private industry position as the chairman of the Woman's Cloak and Suit Industry, but he was too ill to work very hard. Hopkins died of cancer on January 29, 1946.

Further Reading

Adams, Henry H. *Harry Hopkins: A Biography.* New York: Putnam, 1977.

Charles, Searle F. *Minister of Relief: Harry Hopkins and the Depression.* Syracuse, N. Y.: Syracuse University Press, 1963.

Hopkins, June. *Harry Hopkins: Sudden Hero, Brash Reformer.* New York: St. Martin's, 1999.

Kurzman, Paul A. *Harry Hopkins and the New Deal.* Fair Lawn, N. J.: R. E. Burdick, 1974.

McJimsey, George T. *Harry Hopkins: Ally of the Poor and Defender of Democracy.* Cambridge, Mass.: Harvard University Press, 1987.

Olson, James S. "Hopkins, Harry Lloyd." Available online. Discovery Channel School; original content provided by World Book Online. URL: http://www.discovery school.com/homeworkhelp/worldbook/atozhistory/ h/262310.html. Downloaded October 20, 2001.

Sherwood, Robert E. *Roosevelt and Hopkins.* New York: Harper, 1950.

Tuttle, Dwight William. *Harry L. Hopkins and Anglo-American-Soviet Relations, 1941–1945.* New York: Garland Publishing, 1983.

Wills, Matthew B. *Wartime Missions of Harry L. Hopkins.* Raleigh, N. C.: Pentland Press, 1996.

House, Edward Mandell
(1858–1938) *White House staff adviser, diplomat, author*

Edward Mandell House was an unofficial campaign manager and adviser to President THOMAS WOODROW WILSON for almost his entire presidency. House had a mandate to deal with a wide range of domestic and international matters, but Wilson and House had a falling out at the end of Wilson's presidency that may have worked to Wilson's serious disadvantage in his last months in office.

House was born into a wealthy family in Houston, Texas, on July 26, 1858. Raised in Texas, he attended Cornell University and later returned to Texas to manage his father's business affairs after his father's death. By 1890, House had made so much money that he was able to sell the family cotton plantations and live off his investments for the rest of his life. Now independently wealthy, he could pursue his love of politics freely. In 1892, he managed the reelection campaign of Texas governor James S. Hogg. The governor took him on as a special adviser and gratefully named him a "colonel" in the Texas military—a title that stuck with him throughout his life.

After the Democrats won a congressional victory in 1910, House moved into national politics. He met Wilson in 1911 and helped him win the support of the Texas delegation in the 1912 Democratic National Convention. Even more important, House persuaded WILLIAM JENNINGS BRYAN to urge his supporters to join him in endorsing Wilson for president at the convention. After winning the three-way race for president (against WILLIAM HOWARD TAFT and THEODORE ROOSEVELT), Wilson turned to House to become a member of his cabinet. House declined and opted instead to become Wilson's unofficial and confidential adviser. He quickly became known as Wilson's silent partner in negotiating with congressional leaders and with the various pressure groups in national politics.

Of particular value was his relationship with secretary of State William Jennings Bryan. Despite Bryan's support for Wilson's nomination, Bryan and Wilson were not close. House was able to smooth out the working relationship, but increasingly House began to handle international relations himself. House was a much stronger supporter of Great Britain than Wilson, but House worked within the confines of Wilson's preferences. Wilson sent House to Europe in 1914 in an unsuccessful attempt to stave off war. In 1915, Wilson sent House to the various war participants to propose a peace conference, again unsuccessfully.

After the U.S. entry into World War I, House was Wilson's most trusted representative at the conferences coordinating Allied activities. House even helped author Wilson's famous war aims, known as the Fourteen Points. As the war came to an end, House garnered information for the peace conference, was Wilson's delegate to negotiate the armistice, and served the U.S. peace commission.

However, House began to sense that Wilson had become somewhat more distant after his marriage to Edith Galt Wilson (the first Mrs. Wilson died early in Wilson's first term), and this increased distance eventually took its toll during the peace negotiations. Also, House did such a good job that he seemed in some ways to upstage the president himself—a dangerous situation for a trusted presidential adviser. House took a more realistic view of what the Versailles Peace Conference could accomplish, and this seemed to place House on the side of the British and French during the negotiations. Finally, after the Versailles Treaty was drafted and submitted to the U.S. Senate, the treaty ran into stiff opposition from some senators. House recommended some minor concessions, but Wilson became angry and simply stopped talking to House.

Wilson needed House more than he realized at that point. With the treaty in serious trouble in the Senate, Wilson set out on a cross-country speaking tour. While on the trip, Wilson suffered a stroke but refused to recognize his disability. Hanging on to the presidency, Wilson's stubbornness unnecessarily alienated many of his own supporters and assisted his enemies mightily. Wilson's treaty was defeated in the Senate, and his presidency ended on a much-weakened basis. House might well have helped Wilson if Wilson had not turned him aside.

House remained active in political and intellectual circles throughout the 12 years of Republican dominance in the 1920s. In 1932, he supported FRANKLIN DELANO ROOSEVELT for president. While he met with Roosevelt, he never became a trusted member of Roosevelt's inner circle. In a way, it was HARRY LLOYD HOPKINS who performed the role with Roosevelt that House had played with Wilson.

House died just a few months short of his 80th birthday on March 28, 1938.

Further Reading

Ambrosius, Lloyd E. *Wilsonian Statecraft: Theory and Practice of Liberal Internationalism During World War I.* Wilmington, Del.: SR Books, 1991.

Auchincloss, Louis. *Woodrow Wilson: A Penguin Life.* New York: Viking Penguin, 2000.

Blum, John Morton. *Woodrow Wilson and the Politics of Morality.* New York: HarperCollins, 1990.

Clements, Kendrick A. *Woodrow Wilson: World Statesman.* Chicago: I. R. Dee, 1999.

Floto, Inga. *Colonel House In Paris: A Study of American Policy at the Paris Peace Conference 1919.* Princeton, N. J.: Princeton University Press, 1980.

George, Alexander L. *Woodrow Wilson and Colonel House: A Personality Study.* New York: Dover Publications, 1964.

House, Edward M. *Philip Dru: Administrator.* Upper Saddle River, N. J.: Literature House, 1969.

Neu, Charles E. "House, Edward Mandell." Available online at the Handbook of Texas Online: http://www.tsha.utexas.edu/handbook/online/articles/view/HH/fho66.html. Downloaded October 20, 2001.

Noogle, Burt. "Woodrow Wilson," in *The American Presidents,* edited by Frank N. Mangill, John L. Loos, and Tracy Irons-Georges. Pasadena, Calif.: Salem Press, 2000.

Seymour, Charles, ed. *The Intimate Papers of Colonel House.* Boston: Houghton Mifflin, 1926–28.

Smith, Arthur Douglas H. *Mr. House of Texas.* New York: Funk & Wagnalls, 1940.

Viereck, George. *The Strangest Friendship in History: Woodrow Wilson and Colonel House.* Copyrighted 1932, reprinted Westport, Conn: Greenwood Press, 1976.

Williams, Joyce G. *Colonel House and Sir Edward Grey: A Study in Anglo-American Diplomacy.* Lanham, Md.: University Press of America, 1984.

Hughes, Charles Evans

(1862–1948) *chief justice of the United States, associate justice of the Supreme Court, candidate for president, secretary of state, governor*

Charles Evans Hughes was the only member of the Supreme Court to serve two separate terms on the Court—one as an associate justice and the other as the chief justice. In the interim, he was an unsuccessful presidential candidate, a secretary of state, and an attorney in private practice. His stint on the Supreme Court as chief justice is generally thought to have been his period of greatest service to the nation, since he attempted to bridge the gap between liberals and conservatives during this turbulent time.

Hughes was born in Glens Falls, New York, on April 11, 1862. He attended Colgate University (then known as Madison College) briefly but transferred to Brown University where he graduated in 1881. After teaching for a time in a small town in New York, he entered Columbia Law School where he graduated in 1884. Admitted to the bar in the same year, he began practicing law in New York City and became quite successful.

In 1905, Hughes served as the prosecuting counsel for the Stevens Gas Commission, a committee of the New York state legislature that investigated the electric light and gas utilities in New York City. His success was so great that he was selected later that year as counsel for the Armstrong Commission, another New York State investigating committee, which looked at corruption in New York State insurance companies. Not only did he achieve national prominence through these efforts, but also the Republican Party nominated him for governor of New York in 1906 and he won that election.

As a reform governor, he frequently clashed with leaders in his own party, but he was reelected in 1908. Over his nearly four years of service from 1907 to 1910, Hughes's record of reform was remarkable. Not only did he institute administrative reforms and enforce the New York State constitution's ban on race track gambling, but he also pushed through legislation to create the Public Service Commission, to provide new welfare legislation, to give workers the protection of much more progressive labor laws, and to protect consumers from various corrupt practices in the insurance industry. He also took steps to institute the direct primary.

With Hughes's record of success, President WILLIAM HOWARD TAFT appointed him associate justice of the U.S. Supreme Court, and he resigned the governorship in 1910 to take the post. Since he was on the Court, he was insulated from the bitter fight between the regular Republican Party and those who followed former President THEODORE ROOSEVELT into the Progressive (or Bull Moose) Party. This split the Republican vote and helped elect President THOMAS WOODROW WILSON in 1912.

By 1916, the Republicans realized how costly their 1912 fight had been. They had reunited for the most part, but they needed a candidate who could bridge the gap between the factions. Having avoided the fight while on the Court, Hughes was the perfect candidate, but he did not want to run. He refused to be a candidate, but his supporters pushed ahead anyway, securing the Republican nomination and then the Progressive nomination (Theodore Roosevelt declined to run again and reluctantly endorsed Hughes). At this point, Hughes decided no man could decline such a high honor. He resigned from the Court and ran for president in a hard-fought campaign.

Wilson defeated Hughes by a fairly large popular vote of 9,129,606–8,538,221, but it was one of the closest presidential contests in American history in terms of the Electoral College vote of 277–254. California's Electoral College vote decided the election, and it went for Wilson by less than 4,000 votes. The election was not decided for several days because the ballots from a small county in the Sierra Nevada Mountains could not be delivered to the central counting facility due to a sudden snowstorm. After the event, the town renamed itself Wilsonia. Sadly for Hughes, the Progressives led by HIRAM WARREN JOHNSON and regular Republicans were still at war with one another in California, and their split gave the state to Wilson.

Defeated for president and off the Court, Hughes again devoted himself to his law practice. He also served as chairman of the New York Draft Appeals Board. In the Wilson administration, he was even given the opportunity to investigate the aircraft industry as a special investigator for the U.S. attorney general. As an example of his commitment to civil liberties, he courageously defended the socialists who were excluded from their duly elected seats in the New York legislature because of their beliefs during the infamous "Red Scare" in 1919 and 1920.

In 1921, President WARREN GAMALIEL HARDING selected him to be secretary of state, and CALVIN COOLIDGE retained him when he assumed office upon Harding's death. Hughes urged that the United States sign the Versailles Treaty and enter the League of Nations or at least join the World Court, but he failed on both issues. He then negotiated a separate peace treaty with Germany, and he was responsible for the Washington Conference and its naval arms limitation agreement. In this treaty, the major powers, for the first time ever, agreed to limits on existing capital (or major) warships according to a set ratio. Further, they agreed to scrap or dismantle any exiting ships that exceeded the ratio. This agreement failed in the end, but it was useful for a few years. When France occupied the German Ruhr Valley because Germany could not pay its reparations, Hughes created the Dawes plan to use private banking funds to restructure German debt and diffuse the crisis. These steps vastly increased his prestige and that of the U.S. State Department. He also worked to improve U.S. relations with Latin America. He resigned in 1925 to return to private practice, but he continued to be active in international affairs. He served on the Permanent Court of Arbitration from 1926 to 1930 and was appointed a judge of the Permanent Court of International Justice from 1928 to 1930.

In 1930, President HERBERT CLARK HOOVER nominated Hughes to be chief justice of the United States. Since he had served with distinction before on the Court, his confirmation ought to have been routine. However, the Democrats had been energized by the prospects of electoral success since the Great Depression had started during a Republican administration. Many Democrats balked at what they perceived as Hughes's conservative support for corporate interests, apparently forgetting his early career in investigating corporate abuses. The Senate vote on his confirmation was closer than expected but still a comfortable 52–26.

As chief justice Hughes was moderately conservative, and often he was the decisive vote on those economic decisions that split between the four conservative and four liberal judges. On civil liberties, Hughes was a strong defender of the free press. He wrote the very important majority opinion *Near v. Minnesota* (1931), in which the Court asserted the critical principle of no prior restraint by the government in advance of press publication. This decision also incorporated the freedom of the press into due process and applied it to the states as well as the federal government. In this way, *Near v. Minnesota* helped develop the modern notion of free press and free speech.

Although Roosevelt attacked Hughes as one of the conservative obstacles to his New Deal programs, Hughes voted more often with Roosevelt than against him. However, he wrote the majority opinion in *Schechter Poultry Corp. v. United States* (1935), which declared the National Industrial Recovery Act (NIRA) unconstitutional as an excessive delegation of power to the executive branch by the Congress. He also voted with the conservatives in the *Panama Refining* and *Carter Coal Company* cases, stating that the National Recovery Administration (NRA) was unconstitutional on similar grounds.

These decisions apparently angered Roosevelt greatly, and he devised his infamous 1937 Court-packing plan in which he proposed to add one new justice (up to six for a total of 15 on the Court) for every justice over 70 years of age who did not retire. Hughes was the most eloquent and effective opponent of Roosevelt on this issue, and he was also a positive force in realigning the Court in a more moderate direction after the Court-packing scheme was defeated. Hughes voted to sustain a number of liberal labor laws in Roosevelt's legislative proposal, and it would be wrong to see him as a die-hard reactionary.

Hughes retired from the Court in 1941, and he died on August 27, 1948.

Further Reading

Auchincloss, Louis. *Woodrow Wilson: A Penguin Life.* New York: Viking Penguin, 2000.

Glad, Betty. *Charles Evans Hughes and the Illusions of Innocence: A Study in American Diplomacy.* Urbana: University of Illinois Press, 1966.

Hendel, Samuel. *Charles Evans Hughes and the Supreme Court.* New York: Russell & Russell, 1968.

Hughes, Charles Evans. *The Autobiographical Notes of Charles Evans Hughes.* Cambridge, Mass.: Harvard University Press, 1973.

Lovell, S. D. *The Presidential Election of 1916.* Carbondale: Southern Illinois University Press, 1980.

Matsude, Mari J. "Charles Evans Hughes" in *The Oxford Companion to the Supreme Court,* edited by Kermit J. Hall. New York: Oxford University Press, 1992.

Perkins, Dexter. *Charles Evans Hughes and American Democratic Statesmanship.* Boston: Little, Brown, 1956.

Pusey, Merlo J. *Charles Evans Hughes.* New York: Columbia University Press, 1963.

Ransom, William L. *Charles E. Hughes: The Statesman.* New York: E. P. Dutton, 1980.

Smith, Daniel M. "Hughes, Charles Evans." Available online. URL: http://lawbooksusa.com/supremecourt/hughes.htm. Downloaded October 20, 2001.

Wesser, Robert F. *Charles Evans Hughes: Politics and Reform in New York, 1905–1910.* Ithaca, N.Y.: Cornell University Press, 1967.

Hull, Cordell

(1871–1955) *secretary of state, senator, representative*

Cordell Hull served as secretary of state for nearly 12 years, which is longer than any other person has held the position. Although he had not seemed to have strong credentials in international affairs while he was a U.S. senator from Tennessee, he was from a southern state, and FRANKLIN DELANO ROOSEVELT needed a southerner to balance the overwhelmingly northern liberal cast to his cabinet. Since Roosevelt relished being his own secretary of state, he and Hull were not close. Hull often found himself excluded from Roosevelt's highest policy advisers both before and during World War II, and he was shunted aside into drafting documents for the proposed postwar international organization. This work, however, resulted in Hull's being referred to as the "Father of the United Nations" and his receiving the Nobel Peace Prize in 1945.

Hull was born on October 2, 1871, near Byrdstown, Tennessee, in a section of the state so remote that today it is still uncertain in which county Hull was actually born. He came from a family of farmers, lumbermen, and moonshiners. He studied in a series of private academies before attending the National Normal University in Lebanon, Ohio, from 1888 to 1889. He returned home and enrolled at Cumberland Law School in Lebanon, Tennessee. In less than half a year of study, he received his law degree in 1891.

Before practicing law, he had already been elected in the Clay County Courthouse as the Democratic Party Chairman. He won a seat in the Tennessee House of Representatives in a special election held in 1892 when he was only 20—before he was constitutionally allowed to hold the office. In January 1893, he was sworn in, just three months after his 21st birthday, making him the youngest person ever to take a seat in the Tennessee legislature to that point.

He remained in the legislature until 1897 when he resigned to become a captain in the Tennessee volunteers who served in the Spanish American War. After the war, he returned to Tennessee to practice law. In 1903, he was appointed a state circuit court judge, and for the rest of his life often referred to as "judge." He resigned the judgeship when he was elected to the U.S. House of Representatives in 1907, where he remained until he was defeated for reelection in 1920, a victim of the landslide election of President WARREN GAMALIEL HARDING.

As compensation for his loss, he was named the Democratic National Chairman in 1921, and he served for four years. Two years later, he won back his seat in the House and stayed there until elected to the U.S. Senate in 1930 in the reaction against the administration of President HERBERT CLARK HOOVER and the coming of the Great Depression. He supported Roosevelt in the 1932 Democratic National Convention, undercutting the strength of former New York governor ALFRED EMANUEL SMITH and going against the most prominent southern candidate, JOHN NANCE GARNER.

After Roosevelt won the election, he named Hull his secretary of state. Hull was probably selected because Roosevelt needed a southern moderate to balance the large number of northern liberals in his cabinet. Having served only two years in the Senate, Hull was not a Senate insider, and thus Roosevelt knew he could not do much damage by undercutting his legislative program the way a true conservative southern Senate insider could have.

Almost from the start, Roosevelt made it clear that he wished to be his own secretary of state. Hull was pushed aside into Latin American relations, where he did some good in advancing the so-called Good Neighbor Policy.

As the tensions leading to World War II in Europe increasingly preoccupied Roosevelt, Hull was allowed a somewhat greater role in the Pacific. Some recent scholarship appears to show that Hull may have been given too much authority and may have been too inflexible with the Japanese, thereby bringing about the onset of war in the Pacific earlier than a more capable diplomat might have. Roosevelt excluded Hull from most of the important international conferences and allowed him to draft the early proposals for the anticipated postwar international organization, but this was not a high priority while the war was still in doubt. This allowed Hull to take some credit for the creation of the United Nations and earned him the Nobel Peace Prize, but it was not a sign of his influence in the Roosevelt administration.

Before and during the war, Roosevelt depended on Undersecretary of State Sumner Welles, rather than Hull, to conduct all the important affairs at the State Department. Later in the war Hull apparently saw an opportunity for revenge and threatened to expose Welles as a homosexual. Welles resigned from the State Department, but then Roosevelt had the last word. While Hull was 74 and was no doubt ill from time to time, his announced illness was probably not the real reason he resigned in November 1944 (he was certainly not fatally ill since he lived almost 11 years longer). Roosevelt was happy to call Hull the "Father of the United Nations" and happier still that he no longer had to call him secretary of state. Roosevelt carefully chose the obscure Edward Stettinius as Hull's replacement so that he would no longer have a secretary of state with any political following whatsoever.

Hull died in Bethesda, Maryland, on July 23, 1955.

Further Reading

Butler, Michael A. *Cautious Visionary: Cordell Hull and Trade Reform, 1933–1937.* Kent, Ohio: Kent State University Press, 1998.

Gellman, Irwin F. *Secret Affairs: Franklin Roosevelt, Cordell Hull, and Sumner Welles.* Baltimore: Johns Hopkins University Press, 1995.

Hinton, Harold B. *Cordell Hull.* Garden City, N. Y.: Doubleday, Doran, 1991.

Hull, Cordell. *The Memoirs of Cordell Hull.* New York: Macmillan, 1948.

"Hull, Cordell." Available online. URL: http://worldatwar. net/biography/h/hull/. Downloaded October 18, 2001.

"Hull, Cordell." Available online. URL: http://www.nobel.se/peace/laureates/1945/hull-bio.html/. Updated April 17, 2001.

Utley, Jonathan G. *Going to War with Japan, 1937–1941.* Knoxville: University of Tennessee Press, 1985.

Wright, Carl. "Cordell Hull." Available online. URL: http://www.payson.tulane.edu/cordellhull/prod04.htm. Updated February 2, 2001.

Humphrey, Hubert Horatio

(1911–1978) *candidate for president, vice president, senator*

Hubert Horatio Humphrey was a key leader in the liberal wing of the Democratic Party in the U.S. Senate in the 1950s and 1960s until his election as vice president in 1964. As the Democratic nominee for president in 1968, he campaigned so vigorously that he went from being an obvious loser to being within a hair's breadth of winning one of the closest elections in U.S. history.

Humphrey was born in Wallace, South Dakota, on May 27, 1911. His family moved a short time later to Doland, South Dakota, where he attended public school and participated as a star debater in the National Forensic Society. After graduation in the late 1920s, he went to St. Paul, Minnesota, to attend the University of Minnesota but was forced to drop out because of the Great Depression.

He returned to Doland to help his father manage the family drugstore, but he was able to take enough time off to attend and graduate from the Capitol College of Pharmacy in Denver, Colorado. From 1933 to 1937, he worked as a pharmacist at his father's store, which was then located in Huron, South Dakota.

Eventually he saved enough money to return to the University of Minnesota, where he earned a B.A. degree in 1939. He then studied political science at Louisiana State University, where he earned an M.A. in 1940. That year, he returned to Minneapolis to teach as an assistant instructor of political science at the University of Minnesota and pursue further graduate study. In 1941, he began working for the Works Progress Administration. After Pearl Harbor and the U.S. entrance into World War II, he became the Minnesota state director of war production training and reemployment as well as the Minnesota state chief of the war service program.

In 1943, he ran for mayor of Minneapolis but lost. He then returned to teaching as a visiting professor of political science at Macalester College in St. Paul, Minnesota, for the 1943–1944 academic year. Humphrey continued to teach at Macalester but also worked as a news commentator for radio station WTCN and managed an apartment building. In 1945, he again ran for mayor of Minneapolis and was elected; he served a four-year term until 1948.

In 1948, at the Democratic National Convention, he gained national recognition when he delivered a ringing speech in favor of a strong civil rights plank in the Democratic Party's national platform. In November of 1948, voters in Minnesota elected Humphrey to the U.S. Senate. While in the Senate, he was known as a liberal, working on the issues of civil rights, social welfare, and fair employment. However, he developed a close friendship with Senator LYNDON BAINES JOHNSON, who entered the Senate the same year that Humphrey did. It was Johnson who explained that, unlike other Senate liberals, Humphrey had a pragmatic nature and actively tried to pass legislation instead of simply making speeches.

As a recognized leader of the Senate's liberal wing, Humphrey ran for president in the Democratic primaries in 1960. Initially he was thought to have a lead over Senator JOHN FITZGERALD KENNEDY since he had served in the Senate longer and had compiled a better legislative record. However, he was underfinanced and up against the considerable resources of the Kennedy family. Kennedy pulled out a narrow victory in Wisconsin, the neighboring state to Humphrey's home state of Minnesota, in part due to the substantial Catholic vote in the eastern part of the state near Milwaukee. This damaged Humphrey, but he hoped to recover with a victory in West Virginia, which had no substantial Catholic population. When Kennedy also won West Virginia, Humphrey was forced to abandon his campaign.

Kennedy won the Democratic presidential nomination and selected Lyndon Johnson as his vice presidential running mate. Senator MICHAEL

JOSEPH MANSFIELD then became the Democratic Senate majority leader, which allowed Humphrey to move up the Senate hierarchy and become the Senate Democratic whip from 1961 to 1964. He served as the chairman of the Select Committee on Disarmament, where he helped to secure the ratification of the 1963 Nuclear Test-Ban Treaty, a significant accomplishment because it required a two-thirds vote, and there was substantial opposition from conservative Republicans and southern Democrats.

In 1964, at the Democratic National Convention, Johnson selected Humphrey as his vice presidential running mate. The ticket was elected that November in a Democratic landslide. In 1968, Humphrey was the Democratic Party's candidate for president, but he was narrowly defeated by RICHARD MILHOUS NIXON in a race in which former Democrat GEORGE CORLEY WALLACE ran as an American Independent Party candidate and siphoned off Democratic votes in southern states. After the defeat, Humphrey returned to Minnesota to teach at the University of Minnesota and Macalester College.

He was elected in 1970 to the U.S. Senate and won reelection in 1976. He was a member of the prestigious Senate Foreign Relations Committee and the chairman of the Joint Economic Committee. After he was diagnosed with cancer, a mark of the respect of his peers came when they created the post of deputy president pro tempore of the Senate for him. He held that post from January 5, 1977, until his death in Waverly, Minnesota, on January 13, 1978. In another honor granted by the government, he lay in state in the Rotunda of the Capitol in Washington, D.C.

Further Reading

Berman, Edgar. *Hubert: The Triumph and Tragedy of the Humphrey I Knew.* New York: Putnam, 1979.

Cohen, Dan. *Undefeated: The Life of Hubert H. Humphrey.* Minneapolis, Minn.: Lerner Publications, 1978.

Fleming, Daniel B. *Kennedy vs. Humphrey, West Virginia, 1960: The Pivotal Battle for the Democratic Presidential Nomination.* Jefferson, N.C.: McFarland, 1992.

Garrettson, Charles Lloyd III. *Hubert H. Humphrey: The Politics of Joy.* New Brunswick, N.J. Transaction Publishers, 1993.

"Humphrey, Hubert H." Available online. URL: http://www.lbjlib.utexas.edu/johnson/archives.hom/FAQs/Humphrey/HHH_home.asp. Downloaded October 18, 2001.

"Humphrey, Hubert H." Available online. URL: http://bioguide.congress.gov/scripts/biodisplay.pl?index=h000953. Downloaded October 18, 2001.

Humphrey, Hubert H. *The Education of a Public Man: My Life and Politics.* Minneapolis University of Minnesota Press, 1992.

———. *Hubert Humphrey: The Man and His Dream.* New York: Methuen, 1978.

Lichtenstein, Nelson, ed. *Political Profiles: The Johnson Years.* New York: Facts On File, Inc., 1976.

Manfred, Frederick F. *Prime Fathers.* Salt Lake City, Utah: Howe Brothers, 1988.

Polsby, Nelson W. *The Citizen's Choice: Humphrey or Nixon.* Washington, D.C.: Public Affairs Press, 1968.

Sherrill, Robert. *The Drugstore Liberal.* New York: Grossman Publishers, 1968.

Solberg, Carl. *Hubert Humphrey.* New York: Norton, 1984.

Thurber, Timothy N. *The Politics of Equality: Hubert H. Humphrey and the African American Freedom Struggle.* New York: Columbia University Press, 1999.

Waldrup, Carole Chandler. *The Vice Presidents: Biographies of the 45 Men Who Have Held the Second Highest Office in the United States.* Jefferson, N.C.: McFarland, 1996.

I

Inouye, Daniel Ken
(1924–) *senator, representative*

When Hawaii entered the Union in 1959, Daniel Ken Inouye was the first elected member from that state to the U.S. House of Representatives. Upon his election to the U.S. Senate in 1964, he also became the first Asian American to serve in both houses of the U.S. Congress.

Inouye was born in Honolulu, Hawaii, on September 7, 1924. In 1943, during World War II, he enlisted as a private in the U.S. Army. He served in France and Italy until April 21, 1945. On that day, he was leading his platoon against an entrenched enemy position in the mountains. With his unit caught in the cross fire from three machine-gun nests, he crawled within a few yards of one of the guns, threw hand grenades to eliminate it, and fired his gun to eliminate the second. Although wounded by a sniper bullet, he was still firing on the third when a hand grenade destroyed his right arm. He refused to be evacuated until the third gun emplacement was eliminated and his men were safe again. For this and other heroic acts, he received the Distinguished Service Cross, the Bronze Star, and the Purple Heart. After a very long delay, the army finally recognized his heroism in Italy and awarded him the Congressional Medal of Honor.

Inouye stayed in the army until 1947 when he left the service with the rank of captain. He attended the University of Hawaii and graduated with a bachelor's degree in government and economics in 1950. After receiving a law degree from George Washington University in 1952, he started his law practice in Hawaii in 1953.

In 1953, Inouye began his public service as an assistant in the prosecutor's office in Honolulu. By 1954, he had been elected to Hawaii's territorial House of Representatives, where he served until 1958 when he became a member of the territorial Senate. When Hawaii became a state in 1959, Inouye was elected as their first representative to the U.S. House of Representatives and reelected in 1960. In 1962, he won election to the U.S. Senate and has been consistently reelected to the Senate six times since then.

His Senate service includes membership on the committees on Appropriations; Commerce, Science, and Transportation; Rules and Administration; and the Joint Committee on Printing. He has also chaired the Committee on Indian Affairs and the Select Committee on Intelligence. In 1973, Inouye served on the select committee investigating the Watergate scandal. In 1987, he was the chairman of the select committee investigating the Iran-contra affair. In 1988, Inouye supported legislation to allow casino gambling on Indian reservations and has also pushed for legislation to regulate it more carefully.

Inouye played an important role in 1993 as the state of Hawaii regained control over the island Kahoolawe, which had been used as a target practice site by the U.S. military. Despite some criticism that Inouye compromised too much on issues surrounding the environmental clean-up of the island, the example of Kahoolawe was brought up repeatedly in circles debating the Vieques Island bombing site in Puerto Rico and may have influenced President George W. Bush's decision in June 2001 to discontinue naval bombing exercises on the island by May 2003.

In 2002, Inouye was serving his seventh consecutive term in the Senate.

Further Reading

Goodsell, Jane. *Daniel Inouye.* New York: Crowell, 1977.

Inouye, Daniel K. *Journey to Washington.* Englewood Cliffs, N.J.: Prentice-Hall. 1967.

"Inouye, Daniel K." Available online. URL: http://www.homeofheroes.com/moh/citations_1942_nisei/inouye.html. Downloaded January 18, 2002.

"Inouye, Daniel K." Available online. URL: http://www.senate.gov/~inouye.html. Downloaded January 18, 2002.

J

Jackson, Andrew
("Old Hickory")
(1767–1845) *president, senator, representative, Revolutionary War leader*

Andrew Jackson was the first president who was not a member of the colonial aristocracy, and he transformed the very conception of the U.S. presidency during his two terms. Jackson's support for measures to increase the number of people eligible to vote, break the power of the congressional "King Caucus" to control nomination of candidates, and promote many democratic reforms led his administration to be called the era of "Jacksonian Democracy."

Jackson was born on March 15, 1767, in a remote area near the border between North and South Carolina. The area is so remote that the exact site has never been located, and a popular custom has arisen as an unofficial solution. The appropriate counties in North and South Carolina have high schools whose football teams play an annual game with the county and state of the winning team claiming Jackson's birthplace as their own for the year.

A few weeks before Jackson was born, his father died, so his strong mother raised Jackson with almost no formal schooling. Jackson's mother moved from the family log cabin in North Carolina to the South Carolina home of her sister to raise young Andrew and his two older brothers. Young Jackson and his two brothers served in the Continental army in the Revolutionary War, and their mother served by nursing American prisoners of war. All except Andrew died—either from wounds or war-induced illness—in the service of their country during the Revolutionary War.

By age 14, Jackson was an orphan without any living members of his immediate family. Jackson was 12 when his oldest brother died after the Battle of Stono Ferry, South Carolina, in 1779, and he was only 13 years old when he joined the Continental army as a messenger. In 1781, Andrew and his other brother, Robert, were captured by the British and held as prisoners for most of the month of April 1781. Once, while they were prisoners, a British officer ordered the Jackson boys to clean his boots and they refused. When the officer raised his sword against them, young Andrew tired to defend his brother and himself, and the officer's sword cut Jackson's hand to the bone. He carried the scars from that encounter throughout his life.

Given this record of mistreatment, Jackson had an abiding hatred of the British. It is this hatred that explains the curious paradox of Jackson's personal respect for the Native Americans—he adopted and raised an Indian child as his own—and his pursuit of policies inimical to the welfare of many Native American tribes. Many American Indian tribes sided with the British during both the Revolutionary War and the War of 1812. Jackson treated those tribes as enemies of the United States. He was disappointed in his personal hope that the Native Americans would abandon their tribal ways and become assimilated into the rest of American society.

Andrew Jackson transformed the U.S. presidency with an expansion of the electorate that has been called "Jacksonian Democracy." *(Library of Congress)*

As an orphan, Jackson was raised by relatives for about year and a half and apprenticed to a saddle maker for about six months. Jackson briefly used his limited formal education to teach school, but at age 17 he decided to study law instead. In September 1787, he was admitted to the North Carolina bar, and soon after he moved to Nashville (in what is now Tennessee but then was still in the western section of North Carolina) to become the prosecuting officer for a local superior court.

During this period, Jackson supported the local groups who favored the western section of North Carolina splitting off into a new state. In 1796, when Tennessee became the 16th state of the Union, Jackson was elected Tennessee's first member of the House of Representatives. In 1797, the Tennessee legislature selected him for the U.S. Senate, but he had faced some financial reverses and felt he could not afford to serve in the Senate,

so he resigned after only one session. When Jackson came home, he served as a justice on the Tennessee Supreme Court for the next six years until he restored his finances.

In 1802, and overlapping with his judicial service, Jackson was elected major general of the Tennessee state militia. When the War of 1812 broke out, Jackson led the militia on two expeditions to suppress the Creek Indian uprising in Mississippi. When he finally defeated the Creek at the Battle of Horseshoe Bend in 1814, he earned the nickname "Old Hickory" as well as a promotion to major general of the regular U.S. Army. He forced the Creek to sign a treaty in which they ceded more than 20 million acres of land to the United States.

These Indian wars made Jackson a secondary national hero, but his victory at New Orleans against seasoned British regulars made him into a national icon. This reputation was perfectly understandable due to Jackson's independence, courage, and sheer willpower in this campaign. Everyone anticipated that the British—battle-hardened in the long wars with France—would use their superior sea power to land troops at New Orleans, the critical gateway to the interior of the United States. Jackson, in charge of the southern frontier, first fought the British in a skirmish at Mobile Bay, then marched eastward to destroy the British base at Pensacola, and finally rushed back westward past Mobile to take up a position south of New Orleans on both sides of the Mississippi.

When the British arrived and disembarked, they spent two weeks trying to find a weakness in Jackson's line. Feeling overconfident against Jackson's ragtag band, the British commander ordered a frontal assault, which left the British with 2,000 casualties while Jackson suffered about a dozen dead and a few dozen wounded. Across the Atlantic Ocean, U.S. negotiators had already concluded the Treaty of Ghent (ending the war), but that did not diminish the nationalistic pride at learning that the U.S. Army had finally defeated the battle-tested British regulars in face-to-face combat. Earlier U.S. victories in both the American Revolution and the War of 1812 had been either guerrilla attacks or assisted by European forces. At New Orleans, Jackson helped earn the United States a new respect from the Europeans.

New Orleans was the last battle that Europeans fought against Americans on U.S. soil.

Jackson was soon to add to his fame with another military victory. He stayed in the army after the War of 1812 and continued to protect the white southerners from the Indians. In December 1817, President JAMES MONROE sent Jackson to crush the remaining Creek and Seminole Indians who were preying on the settlers along the Georgia border. Going beyond merely stopping the raids, Jackson chased the Indians to their villages in Florida, continued on to capture Pensacola, removed the Spanish colonial governor, and executed two British citizens he blamed for stirring up the Indians. Britain was furious, and Monroe and his secretary of war, JOHN CALDWELL CALHOUN, fearfully denied authorizing Jackson's actions and considered reprimanding him.

Secretary of State JOHN QUINCY ADAMS had a better idea. Since Jackson was in effective control of Florida, Adams thought this would be a good time to suggest to Spain that, instead of fruitlessly trying to control such a distant parcel as Florida, they should sell it to the United States. Spain agreed in the following year, and Jackson's reputation for boldness got another boost. Monroe then named Jackson governor of the Florida territory, but Jackson disliked living so far from Tennessee and resigned to accept the Tennessee legislature's selection as U.S. senator in 1822. Jackson was then positioned to run for president in 1824.

In 1824, the last of the Revolutionary War military leaders and heroes had left the political arena, for none of the plausible candidates had been adult participants during the war. This meant there was no inevitable front-runner as there had been in most of the previous presidential contests. Three "establishment" figures sought to be elected. Two had served in the cabinet of the incumbent, President James Monroe: John Quincy Adams of Massachusetts, who had served as Monroe's secretary of state, and William H. Crawford of Georgia, who was Monroe's secretary of the treasury. The third, HENRY CLAY of Kentucky, was the Speaker of the U.S. House of Representatives.

Since the "eastern establishment" had always won the presidency, these three candidates were considered the prime competitors, and they overlooked the person regarded as something of a country bumpkin. Since Andrew Jackson had fought in the Revolutionary War as a teenager and followed it up with spectacular military successes, they apparently missed the threat he represented. While they were splitting the establishment vote among them, Jackson was claiming the great mass of U.S. voters who did not perceive themselves as the eastern elite. Jackson won the highest number of popular votes and the highest number of Electoral College votes, but he did not win the majority (or 50 percent plus one of the total votes cast) of the Electoral College votes needed to win the presidency. As required by the U.S. Constitution, the election was thrown into the House of Representatives where the eastern establishment was in control.

Since Crawford had suffered a stroke, his candidacy did not seem plausible, so the question of which establishment candidate would win turned on Adams and Clay. Since Adams had outpolled Clay, Clay threw his support to Adams, and Adams was declared the president in legal conformity with the Constitution. General Jackson took his loss graciously—until he learned Adams named Clay as his secretary of state. Since THOMAS JEFFERSON, JAMES MADISON, Monroe, and John Quincy Adams had served as secretary of state before becoming president, this role was thought to be the obvious stepping-stone to the presidency. To Jackson and his supporters, it now seemed obvious not only that Clay was named secretary of state as a payoff to Clay for his support of Adams as president, but also that Adams would back Clay for president when he left office.

While it might have seemed reasonable to members of the political elite that such "arrangements" would be proper if made within the elite, it looked to many Americans in the lower classes and the West like a "corrupt bargain," which is what they chose to call it. In retrospect, it is clear that Adams's hopes for election to a second term were gone before he even started his first term due to the Clay selection.

Jackson began a four-year campaign for election to the presidency in 1828. It was clear wherever he went in the West and South that he was the front-runner. It was obvious that Jackson had the initiative, and various elite members thought their future would be damaged if they were associated with Adams and his proposals.

One of the most obvious defectors from the Adams camp was Vice President John C. Calhoun. He had agreed to serve with Adams, but now he decided not only to vote against Adams whenever he had the chance as vice president to break a tie in the Senate but also to speak out publicly against President Adams. Calhoun was rewarded for his conversion to Jackson's side by being given the opportunity to run for vice president again as Andrew Jackson's running mate. Jackson won in a landslide, carrying all of the western and southern states along with Pennsylvania and New York.

The campaign was as dirty as the result was one-sided. In an attempt to counter the power of the Jackson campaign's "corrupt bargain" charge, Adams's supporters revealed the circumstances of Jackson's marriage. Jackson's wife, Rachel, had been married before—briefly and unhappily to Lewis Robards. After she returned to live with her parents, Robards applied to the Kentucky legislature for permission to divorce. His request was granted in 1790. Hearing that, Jackson and Rachel assumed that Robards had completed the divorce, and they got married.

In 1794, they discovered that Robards had waited until 1793 to sue for divorce and then did so on grounds of Rachel's adultery with Jackson. The Jacksons remarried, but the unpleasant gossip continued for years. In the hands of Adams's supporters, Jackson was an adulterer and Rachel was a bigamist. When Rachel died suddenly after the election but before Jackson's inaugural, Jackson was grief-stricken and angry at the thought that the stress of the campaign had brought about her death. These emotions may have colored several issues in his presidency.

If the elite missed the fact that change was coming, Jackson's inaugural should have removed any doubts. Jackson had an inaugural party that included throwing open the doors to the White House to a disorderly crowd of supporters who ran through the president's house with muddy boots, stood on the furniture, and were otherwise unruly.

Change came on several levels and over several issues. Some seemingly minor issues took on significance that colored other policies. Washing-

ton society under the eastern elite had already acquired a definite character, despite the newness of the nation, and this was made evident in the case of John and Peggy Eaton. Secretary of War John Eaton was Andrew Jackson's closest friend in his cabinet, and he had married his wife shortly after her first husband committed suicide. To the gossips in Washington, this was taken as evidence of her promiscuity. Since the charge was leveled against the wife of a close friend and resembled the charge against his own deceased wife, Jackson took up Peggy Eaton's social cause and pressed the members of his cabinet to force their wives to be sociable to her. They refused, and so did the wife of Vice President Calhoun. Only Jackson's secretary of state, MARTIN VAN BUREN, a widower, was able to support the Eatons without provoking domestic strife. Van Buren thereby ingratiated himself with Jackson, while Calhoun was placed at a disadvantage. Since Calhoun and Van Buren both were presidential hopefuls for the post-Jackson period, this rift was bound to have political consequences.

Calhoun was soon disadvantaged on a second issue. Calhoun had publicly supported Jackson regarding his seizing of Florida in the Seminole War, but privately he had recommended that Jackson be reprimanded. When Jackson discovered private correspondence to this effect in the government files, he believed Calhoun was guilty of treachery, and their personal relations were never close again.

These two seemingly personal issues became entwined with major policy issues. Calhoun adopted the standard southern position that tariffs should be for revenue only and not for the protection of infant industries (which raised the costs to southern planters and led to foreign retaliation against their produce). Van Buren favored moderate tariffs, but these tariffs were still higher than those preferred in the South. In the midst of the other more personal issues, the tariff came to the fore. The South had been opposed to high tariffs almost since the inception of the Union and, feeling ignored for most of the previous four decades, now became desperate. As their champion, Calhoun authored a doctrine that allowed individual states to nullify congressional enactment within their state boundaries. Calhoun liked to say that his policy would save the Union from inevitable secession. To Jackson, nullification was the close equivalent of secession.

Calhoun hid his authorship of the nullification doctrine as long as possible, but eventually he owned up to it. At a banquet to celebrate Thomas Jefferson's birthday, several toasts were given, including one by Jackson who looked straight at Calhoun and said, "Our Federal Union, it must be preserved." In response, Calhoun toasted, "The Union: Next to our liberty most dear; may we all remember that it can only be preserved by respecting the right of the states and distributing equally the benefit and burden of the union." The rift between Jackson and Calhoun was almost complete by this point.

The Congress pushed through even higher tariffs in 1832, and South Carolina passed nullification ordinances. Jackson issued a proclamation threatening force against South Carolina, but he also compromised by pushing lower tariffs through the Congress. The immediate crisis was diffused, but Calhoun was then suspicious that the South had lost critical parity with the North, and he resigned as vice-president in 1832. Jackson replaced Calhoun with Van Buren as his vice presidential running mate during the 1832 presidential campaign.

Another issue in which the personal and policy questions became entwined concerned the Second Bank of the United States. Jackson favored the original view of Jefferson and Madison that creating a national bank exceeded the authority of the Congress under the Constitution. While Madison and Jefferson later abandoned that rigid view, Jackson continued to hold the view, despite considerable evidence that the bank was helpful to the government. Jackson's vehemence about the bank issue is hard to understand unless one includes his well-known antipathy to the bankers as a class and their political allies Henry Clay and DANIEL WEBSTER. They foolishly persuaded NICHOLAS BIDDLE, the National Bank president, to challenge Jackson on the bank issue before the 1832 presidential campaign. The bank became the major campaign issue, but Jackson won the election. Jackson managed then over the course of his second term to eliminate the national bank without offering an effective alternative to it. After Jackson left office in 1837,

an economic depression developed that his successor, President Martin Van Buren, had to manage.

Jackson remained active in politics in his retirement. In 1840, despite ill health, he actively worked for Van Buren's unsuccessful reelection. Four years later, when Van Buren opposed the admission of Texas into the Union, Jackson turned against him and his renomination. Instead, Jackson pushed for the election of his younger Tennessee protégé, JAMES KNOX POLK, when he supported the annexation of Texas that Jackson desired. After Polk's successful election, Jackson's health suffered badly, and he died at the Hermitage near Nashville, Tennessee, on June 8, 1845.

Jackson transformed the very conception of the U.S. presidency itself by asserting an increasingly powerful mandate. Instead of using the official department heads in the cabinet as key advisers, he chose his own advisers who became known as his "Kitchen Cabinet." The earlier presidents believed that they could only veto legislation passed by Congress if it were clearly unconstitutional, but Jackson vetoed bills on his own discretion, a conception that has survived to the present. He also instituted the "pocket veto" by refusing to sign some legislation passed by Congress if Congress adjourned before the time limit for signing bills.

Andrew Jackson was also the first president to serve in the military at age 13, to be a prisoner of war, to marry a woman who had been divorced, to have a vice president (John C. Calhoun) resign (in 1832), and to use a national convention (in 1832) as a vehicle for the nomination of himself and his choice for vice president.

Further Reading

Belohlavek, John M. *Let The Eagle Soar! The Foreign Policy of Andrew Jackson.* Lincoln: University of Nebraska Press, 1985.

Cole, Donald B. *The Presidency of Andrew Jackson.* Lawrence: University Press of Kansas, 1993.

Heidler, David S. *Old Hickory's War: Andrew Jackson and the Quest for Empire.* Mechanicsburg, Pa.: Stackpole Books, 1996.

"Jackson, Andrew." Available online. URL: http://www. whitehouse.gov/history/presidents/aj7.html. Downloaded October 20, 2001.

"Jackson, Andrew." First Inaugural Address. Available online. URL: http://www.bartleby.com/124/pres23.html. Downloaded January 18, 2002.

"Jackson, Andrew." Second Inaugural Address. Available online. URL: http://www.bartleby.com/124/pres24.html. Downloaded January 18, 2002.

Ratner, Lorman. *Andrew Jackson and His Tennessee Lieutenants: A Study in Political Culture.* Westport, Conn.: Greenwood Press, 1997.

Remini, Robert V. *Andrew Jackson.* New York: Harper, 1999.

Schlesinger, Arthur M. *The Age of Jackson.* Boston: Little, Brown, 1945.

Tregle, Joseph G. *Louisiana in the Age of Jackson: A Clash of Cultures and Personalities.* Baton Rouge: Louisiana State University Press, 1999.

Watson, Harry L. *Andrew Jackson vs. Henry Clay: Democracy and Development in Antebellum America.* Boston: St. Martin's, 1998.

Liberty and Power: The Politics of Jacksonian America. New York: Hill & Wang, 1990.

Jay, John

(1745–1829) *chief justice of the United States, governor, diplomat, Revolutionary War leader, author*

John Jay was the one of the diplomats who negotiated the 1783 treaty that ended the Revolutionary War, authored some of the *Federalist Papers,* and served as the first chief justice of the United States.

Jay come from a distinguished New York family and was born on December 12, 1745, in New York City. He was educated at Columbia University (then known as King's College) from which he graduated in 1764. In 1768, he was admitted to the bar, married the daughter of William Livingston, a member of a prominent New York family, and briefly joined other family members in the practice of law, thereby advancing his career and giving him wealth and social position.

In 1774, Jay was elected to the First Continental Congress and in 1775 to the Second Continental Congress, where he represented the views of the conservative colonial merchant class. He urged moderation and wrote a famous address to

the people of Great Britain. Before the Revolution, he did not favor independence and did not sign the Declaration of Independence. Once the Declaration of Independence was signed, however, he strongly supported the cause of the new nation.

Returning to the provincial congress of New York, he drafted the first constitution of New York State and was appointed chief justice of the state in 1777. In the following year, he was again elected to the Continental Congress and was chosen its president in 1778. This forced him to resign from the New York high court. In 1779, he went as minister plenipotentiary to Spain, where he secured some financial aid but failed to win recognition for the colonial cause.

In 1782, Benjamin Franklin, JOHN ADAMS, and Jay were sent to Paris to negotiate the Treaty of Paris with Great Britain to end the American Revolution. While the three commissioners were told only to insist on independence of the 13 colonies and to follow the lead of France on all other matters, France was so busy with other issues that the group went ahead on its own. By their own efforts, Jay, Franklin, and Adams bargained for a much better treaty than the military progress of their army entitled them to obtain. They managed to secure U.S. independence, the entire territory east of the Mississippi River, and North Atlantic fishing rights.

In 1784, the Second Continental Congress (sometimes called the Congress of the Confederation after 1783) had appointed Jay as secretary of foreign affairs. He served in that post until the Articles of Confederation ended. He negotiated some minor treaties, but he could not settle any major issues with Britain and Spain, because the Articles of Confederation were so weak. He wrote five papers on foreign affairs in *The Federalist,* as testimony to the disunity of the 13 original states and the weakness that produced in foreign affairs.

After the Constitution was ratified, GEORGE WASHINGTON nominated Jay the chief justice in September 1789, and he was promptly confirmed. Washington chose Jay because he had always been widely respected as a just and reasonable man. Jay did a great deal to establish the Supreme Court, but he was away much of the time. He did, however, concur in Justice James Wilson's opinion in

Chisholm v. Georgia, which led to the passing of the Eleventh Amendment. He also took out time from his duties to run unsuccessfully against GEORGE CLINTON for governor of New York in 1792.

In 1794, Washington sent Jay (even while serving on the Court) to Britain to settle some of the issues left over from the Treaty of Paris, because Britain was threatening war. Jay was not successful in getting good terms, and the result, called Jay's Treaty, was not well received, although it kept the United States out of a war it could not win.

On returning from England, Jay was surprised to learn that he had been elected New York's governor in 1795, since he never agreed to serve. Jay was forced to retire from the Supreme Court, though he would not have chosen to do so, because he felt he could not let his friends in New York down. He served ably and was reelected governor. At the end of his second term, he retired from public life.

Jay was in poor health for the last years of his life, and he died on May 17, 1829.

Further Reading

Casto, William R. *The Supreme Court in the Early Republic: The Chief Justiceships of John Jay and Oliver Ellsworth.* Columbia: University of South Carolina Press, 1995.

"Jay, John." Available online. URL: http://www.encyclopedia.com/article/06598.html. Downloaded January 18, 2002.

"Jay, John." Available online. URL: http://www.gradesaver.com/classicnotes/author/about_john_jay.html. Downloaded January 18, 2002.

Johnson, Herbert A. *John Jay: Colonial Lawyer.* New York: Garland, 1989.

Monaghan, Frank, *John Jay: Defender of Liberty against Kings and Peoples, Author of the Constitution and Governor of New York.* New York: AMS Press, 1972.

Morris, Richard B. *John Jay, The Making of a Revolutionary.* New York: Harper & Row, 1975.

———. *Witnesses at the Creation: Hamilton, Madison, Jay, and the Constitution.* New York: New American Library, 1989.

Pellew, George. *John Jay.* New York: Chelsea House, 1980.

Smith, Donald Lewis. *John Jay: Founder of a State and Nation.* New York: Teachers College Press, Columbia University, 1968.

Jefferson, Thomas

(1743–1826) *president, vice president, secretary of state, governor, diplomat, Revolutionary War leader, author, scientist, architect, philosopher*

Thomas Jefferson specified that his tombstone should state three of his accomplishments: his authorship of the Declaration of Independence, his authorship of the Virginia statute for religious freedom, and his founding of the University of Virginia. These would be singular successes for any man, but they seem almost absurdly modest for a man who was also an important diplomat for the United States at a critical period, the founder of the longer lasting of the nation's two major political parties, the first secretary of state, the second vice president, the third president, a state governor, and a key participant in four different legislatures. This

Thomas Jefferson, the third president, founder of one of the nation's two major political parties, was the first secretary of state, the second vice president, a state governor, and a member in four legislative bodies. *(Library of Congress)*

listing of political accomplishments omits his varied achievements as a linguist, farmer, inventor, paleontologist, botanist, chemist, architect, writer, philosopher, and supporter of the advancement of arts and sciences. With the possible exception of Benjamin Franklin, he was the closest person to the most universal man in American history.

On April 13, 1743, Thomas Jefferson was born at Shadwell, the Jefferson family estate in Albemarle County (then called Goochland County), Virginia. His mother, Jane Randolph Jefferson, came from one of the most distinguished families in Virginia, and his father was a landowner-surveyor and had served in several local colonial government offices. When Jefferson was 14 years old, his father died, and as the oldest son, he inherited an estate of a few thousand acres of land and some slaves, which was managed for him until he came of age.

After studying at home with a tutor, Jefferson went to live in various private boarding arrangements or schools until he was 16 and able to go to college. In 1760, he went to Williamsburg to attend the College of William and Mary. There he met William Small, who taught him mathematics and gave him a view of the sciences. Small introduced him to Judge George Wythe, who was considered the most knowledgeable legal authority in the colony. Small and Wythe, in turn, introduced Jefferson to Governor Francis Fauquier. These gentlemen apparently taught Jefferson a great deal on an informal basis. As an indication of the ferment of the times, he was present when PATRICK HENRY gave his famous speech against the Stamp Act containing the line, "If this be treason, make the most of it." Without graduating from William and Mary, Jefferson left college in 1762 and studied law with George Wythe. He was admitted to the bar in 1767 and was a successful attorney, at least until politics began to take up all his time.

In 1772, Jefferson married Martha Wayles Skelton, a young widow who was the daughter of John Wayles, a prominent Williamsburg lawyer. When Wayles died, Jefferson inherited his estate and slaves, although the estate was heavily mortgaged. Among the slaves were the Hemings children, slaves who were born of Wayles's relationship with their mother, one of his house slaves. These

slaves were light skinned, possibly having less than one-quarter African ancestry. Martha was less troubled by her father's relationship with his slave than with his second wife, because she was on poor terms with her stepmother. Although the main house was not yet finished, Jefferson brought his wife and her retinue of slaves to live at Monticello. They lived happily for 10 years and had six children, but only two of them (Martha born in 1772 and Mary born in 1778) lived to adulthood.

In 1782, Martha Jefferson became seriously ill. Before she died, she extracted a promise from Jefferson—which he kept—that he would not remarry, because she did not want her daughters to suffer as she had suffered from her father's second marriage. This deathbed promise has taken on new importance now that the Thomas Jefferson Memorial Foundation has reported—after a lengthy study of all relevant evidence, including DNA results, plantation records, and contemporary accounts—that Jefferson and Sally Hemings very likely had a long-term relationship and that he was the father of one, if not all, of her children. Since DNA is not conclusive, the foundation appears to have been persuaded by the other facts, including that Hemmings conceived her children only while Jefferson was in residence at Monticello. The foundation also noted that Hemings and her children were the only slaves Jefferson emancipated upon his death.

Since there has never been a question that John Wayles was the father of both Martha Wayles Skelton Jefferson and Sally Hemings, Sally, who was seven-eighths white and the half-sister of Martha, may well have resembled Martha quite closely. Sally Hemings was undoubtedly a trusted member of the Jefferson household. When Jefferson went to Paris as the U.S. minister to France, he took his older daughter, Martha, with him, but six-year-old Mary was left behind with relatives. Two years later, when Jefferson asked to have Mary sent over, it was the teenaged Sally Hemings who was entrusted to be Mary's sole guardian on the sea trip to France. It should be noted that the relationship was on some level consensual, because France did not permit slavery, and thus Sally was free to leave Jefferson at any point while they lived in Paris.

In 1769, Jefferson began his political career when he was elected to the House of Burgesses in colonial Virginia. Influenced by the climate of Williamsburg, particularly by the fiery Patrick Henry, he became a leader of the patriot faction. He remained in the Virginia House of Burgesses until 1774, helped found the Virginia Committee of Correspondence, and wrote for that group. In 1774, he also drafted *A Summary View of the Rights of British America*, a pamphlet that set forth the theory of Parliament having no authority over the colonies and the colonies being tied to Britain only by voluntary allegiance to the king. Jefferson gained great respect for the resolutions and documents he drafted, but he never became an effective orator.

Based on his efforts in Virginia, he was elected to the Continental Congresses in 1775 and 1776. A recognized master of prose, he was appointed to a committee to draft the Declaration of Independence. The others on the committee, such as JOHN ADAMS and Benjamin Franklin, and the Congress as a whole made only a few changes in Jefferson's draft before it was adopted.

In 1777, Jefferson returned to the Virginia legislature to help establish a new state government. He succeeded in abolishing the practices of entail (inheritance to direct descendants) and primogeniture (inheritance to eldest sons) to prevent the exclusively continuance of an aristocracy, although primogeniture lasted until 1785. By ending entail and primogeniture, great colonial estates could be broken up, which meant that more people could own property. The more people who owned property, the more people who could vote (since only people who owned property could vote at this time). Jefferson pushed an expansion of the electorate through another bill, which provided that immigrants who lived in Virginia for two years could become naturalized. He also proposed ending the established Anglican Church as the preferred Virginia church and establishing religious freedom, but this was not successful until 1786, when Patrick Henry and JAMES MADISON were able to push these ideas through to completion.

In 1779 and 1780, Jefferson was elected to two one-year terms as governor of Virginia. It was his misfortune to become Virginia's governor immediately following the dynamic and successful Patrick Henry, with whom he was unfavorably compared. The Virginia governor, following the colonial fear of executive power, had little authority or money. This worked well enough as long as there were no threats to public safety with which to contend, but it was inconvenient when the Virginia citizenry expected the governor to defend the newly created state from the British, who had shifted their attacks from the northern states to Virginia during this period. Virginia had generously given the few resources it had to GEORGE WASHINGTON, who was defending the North. During this time, Jefferson was severely criticized for failing to stop the British attacks. An official inquiry was even impaneled after he left office to investigate his lack of success, but he was completely vindicated in the end.

Between the end of his term as governor and his return to public life at the Continental Congress (or the Congress of the Confederation as it was also called), Jefferson wrote his only book, *Notes on the State of Virginia*. Writing it in French, one of his purposes was to provide it as a source for some officials in the French government. It was during this period that Jefferson's wife died. Apparently, he returned to public life and a heavy work regimen as a way to relieve his grief.

In 1783 and 1784, Jefferson was again elected to the Continental Congress, where he drew up the plan for the decimal system of money still in use in the United States today. He also drafted a proposed ordinance for governing the Northwest Territory, which was not adopted then but was the core of the 1787 Northwest Ordinance.

In 1785, the government under the Articles of Confederation sent him as the ambassador to France where he succeeded Benjamin Franklin. He ingratiated himself to the consecutive governments there since he spoke fluent French. He negotiated some important commercial treaties of benefit to the U.S. government, and he expanded his own understanding of Europe and its affairs.

Jefferson sympathetically watched the outbreak of the French Revolution. He tried and failed to negotiate a trade treaty with England with John Adams, his colleague in London, and he became especially embittered with the British. Since he was in France while the new U.S. Constitution was drafted and adopted, he had no role in its creation. He initially had reservations, particularly because of the lack of a Bill of Rights, but strongly supported the document with the promise of an addition of a Bill of Rights after the government was established.

When Jefferson returned to the United States from France in November 1789, he received a letter from President Washington, urging him to become the first U.S. secretary of state. Jefferson regretted receiving this invitation, but he finally accepted it. Having been abroad for a few years, initially Jefferson did not realize that Hamilton had become much more influential and now, in the service of northern financial elites, had plans that threatened the agrarian interests most important to Virginia and the rest of the South. Following Washington's lead, Jefferson declined to label himself either a Federalist or an anti-Federalist but was anxious to unify the new government and ensure its success.

Hamilton devised a plan for funding all the war debts of the previous national governments, including those debts that had been sold by desperate Revolutionary War veterans to currency speculators. While many anti-Federalists opposed this, Jefferson went along. When Hamilton argued that the new government should also accept responsibility for the war debts of the states, he ran into a hornet's nest of outrage from southern states such as Virginia, that had paid off much of its debt and did not want to pay the debts of other states. Jefferson initially opposed Hamilton on this issue, but finally he compromised by agreeing to the federal assumption of state debt in return for having the national capital located in the South—in fact, at its current location as the District of Columbia. Jefferson, along with James Madison, persuaded other southerners to go along.

Jefferson, however, differed with Hamilton over the best way to persuade England to turn over the British forts in what would become the Northwest Territory, as the government had promised to do in the 1783 Treaty of Paris. Jefferson wanted to block British imports as a way to put economic pressure on England, but Hamilton opposed this since the loss of tariff revenue would threaten his

plans to rebuild the nation's financial strength. Jefferson then opposed Hamilton's plans to create the first Bank of the United States, because the Constitution did not specifically authorize it in Article One, section eight, where the powers of the federal government were set forth. In this way, Jefferson rejected Hamilton's theory of implied powers. To Jefferson's surprise and disappointment, Hamilton persuaded Washington and a majority of the members of both houses of Congress to adopt his point of view.

Jefferson and Hamilton moved from being mutually mistrustful of each other to becoming openly hostile. Even President Washington, who had patched up many of their differences before, was unable to bridge the gap now. In 1793, Jefferson resigned from the cabinet. Later he bitterly criticized the treaty with England negotiated by JOHN JAY (known as Jay's Treaty), which compromised the outstanding foreign policy issues with Great Britain in ways essentially devised by Hamilton, although no one could have done much better than Jay under the circumstances.

Fearing the nearly monarchial plans of Hamilton, or at least an overly powerful national government in the hands of the northern financial interests, Jefferson became the informal leader of the forces opposing Hamilton and his Federalist supporters. He drew to himself a group of those who shared his ideas, and they began to call themselves Democratic Republicans (or often just Republicans). This group evolved into the present Democratic Party. In 1791, this organization began by starting a newspaper to set out its views. Edited by Philip Freneau, it was called the *National Gazette*.

Jefferson only reluctantly allowed this new informal party to put forward his name for president in 1796 against John Adams. Despite his reluctance, Jefferson came within three votes of defeating Adams, and this was sufficient—under the Electoral College rules then in place—to elect him vice president (since that office was still filled by the person who ran second in the presidential race). He took little part in the Adams administration but presided over the Senate as required by the U.S. Constitution and found time to write *A Manual of Parliamentary Practice*. Published in 1801, this manual is a set of rules that are the basis for the current U.S. Senate rules and that have been copied in other legislative bodies around the globe.

Jefferson and his followers kept improving their popularity and eventually even formed an alliance with New York Governor GEORGE CLINTON and others. The Federalists were increasingly divided and, fearing they might lose, passed the Alien and Sedition Acts to stifle criticism of the Adams administration and the Federalist majority in Congress. The Alien and Sedition Acts placed restrictions on new immigrants to the United States and made critics of the president, cabinet officers, and members of Congress subject to criminal liability for their statements. Curiously, the law permitted criticism of the vice president—at that time Thomas Jefferson. These laws seemed to be such a threat to the Democratic Republicans that Jefferson drafted the Kentucky Resolutions. The resolutions protested the Alien and Sedition Acts and laid out the first interpretation of states' rights in the Constitution as well as the concept of nullification. James Madison contemporaneously wrote the Virginia resolutions. Neither Jefferson nor Madison publicly admitted authorship of the documents at the time. The Alien and Sedition Acts proved to be very unpopular with the population at large and influenced the outcome of the next election and the eventual demise of the Federalist Party.

In 1800, the Democratic Republicans nominated Jefferson for president and AARON BURR for vice president. This team easily won enough states to earn a majority of Electoral College votes over Adams, but some electors were supposed to leave Burr's name off their ballot so there would not be a tie for president. For reasons that are still controversial, every Democratic Republican elector voted for both Jefferson and Burr, producing a tie. This meant the final selection was automatically made in the House of Representatives among the three top vote-getters (including Adams). Burr did not remove his name, and some Federalists preferred Burr to Jefferson, so the issue was not decided for 36 ballots. Jefferson was elected after a long deadlock, but only because Hamilton hated Burr worse than he did Jefferson and managed to switch some Federalist votes off Burr and to Jeffer-

son. Burr's apparent lack of cooperation led to a split between Burr and Jefferson that continued throughout the next four years and beyond. The Twelfth Amendment was subsequently added to the U.S. Constitution, changing the rules so a tie for president and vice president of the same party could not happen again.

Jefferson was the first president inaugurated in Washington, D.C. His election was called the "Revolution of 1800" with some justification. In line with his general philosophy, he instituted a number of practices that he felt represented Republican simplicity. He cut expenditures in all branches of government, and he succeeded in cutting the federal debt by one-third, even though he also pushed through the repeal of Hamilton's hated excise tax on whiskey. He replaced some Federalist appointees with Democratic Republicans, but he did nothing on the scale of the patronage turnovers that characterized the administrations of ANDREW JACKSON and ABRAHAM LINCOLN. He also attempted to limit the power of the judiciary, because he felt that the Federalists were attempting to entrench their philosophy by judicial fiat. He believed that the federal government should be concerned mostly with international affairs. In line with this, he sent a naval squadron to fight the Barbary pirates, who were harassing American commerce in the Mediterranean, and he at least partially reduced the threat. He believed that a strictly construed U.S. Constitution, allowing the states to administer domestic affairs, properly limited the federal government's powers.

This philosophy was not, and perhaps could not be, followed without exception. The greatest positive achievement of his administration, the Louisiana Purchase, in fact contradicted this expression of his philosophy. U.S. representatives abroad, particularly JAMES MONROE, had the foresight to act quickly when they were given the unexpected opportunity to purchase the entire tract when they had originally set out to buy only the mouth of the Mississippi River. Monroe saw the benefit quite clearly and pushed Jefferson to overcome his initial reservations, which were based on the fact that the purchase of new land was nowhere expressly authorized in the U.S. Constitution.

Jefferson wanted to acquire the land, but he at first thought that a constitutional amendment would be necessary—an act that might have delayed the purchase so long that the opportunity would be lost. In the end, the practical realities overrode his reservations and the purchase was made. Once it was completed, Jefferson's instinctive curiosity led him to push for the exploration of the West —an idea that had already caused him to plan for the Lewis and Clark expedition.

In 1804, Jefferson easily defeated CHARLES COTESWORTH PINCKNEY in the race for president by carrying every state but two. During his second administration, however, his good fortune evaporated. In foreign affairs, the main trouble resulted from the war between Britain and Napoleonic France and the attacks both countries made on neutral American shipping. Jefferson believed he could force the two warring nations to respect U.S. neutrality if the United States refused to trade with either country, and he pushed through the Nonimportation Act of 1806 and the Embargo Act of 1807.

To enforce these acts, Jefferson had to authorize the use of his limited fleet to patrol the coast to stop smuggling, thereby infringing on the individual liberty of the citizens. In economic terms, it was a disaster and produced such dislocations that the acts ended up impoverishing the lower income people who had supported his election. Shortly before the end of his term, he was forced by near rebellion to give up on his plan, although Jefferson believed in his own mind that the embargo had not been used long enough to achieve its goals.

After he retired from the presidency, Jefferson continued to advise his presidential successors, James Madison and James Monroe, from his mountaintop estate of Monticello. He achieved one of his great goals when he was able to push successfully for the founding of the University of Virginia and the design of the principal buildings on the early campus. As the president of the American Philosophical Society for 18 years from 1797 to 1815, Jefferson fostered many of the advances that were a part of his enormously varied skills as a scientist, an architect, a writer, a visionary, and a philosopher. He inherited great wealth, but he spent money freely on his varied endeavors, many of which were not financial successes. Jefferson had been often troubled by indebtedness, and after endorsing a note for a friend who failed financially, he was virtually bankrupt at the end of his life. In one of the more interesting ironies of American history, he died at Monticello on July 4, 1826, just a few hours before his friend, John Adams (from whom he was once estranged but later reconciled). Both died on the 50th anniversary of the signing of the Declaration of Independence.

Further Reading

Boorstin, Daniel J. *The Lost World of Thomas Jefferson.* New York: Holt, 1948.

Brodie, Fawn M. *Thomas Jefferson: An Intimate History.* New York: Norton, 1998.

Chase-Riboud, Barbara. *Sally Hemmings.* New York: Avon, 1980.

Commager, Henry Steele. *Jefferson, Nationalism, and the Enlightenment.* New York: G. Braziller, 1986.

Ellis, Joseph J. *American Sphinx: The Character of Thomas Jefferson.* New York: Knopf, 1998.

Gordon-Reed, Annette. *Thomas Jefferson and Sally Hemmings: An American Controversy.* Charlottesville: University Press of Virginia, 1997.

"Jefferson, Thomas." Available on line. URL: http://www.whitehouse.gov/history/presidents/tj3.html. Downloaded January 18, 2002.

"Jefferson, Thomas." Available online. URL: http://geocities.com/athens/forum/1683/ljindex.html. Downloaded January 18, 2002.

Kennedy, Roger G. *Burr, Hamilton, and Jefferson: A Study in Character.* Oxford and New York: Oxford University Press, 2000.

Koch, Adrienne. *Jefferson and Madison: The Great Collaboration.* New York: Oxford University Press, 1970.

Lewis, Jan E. *Sally Hemmings and Thomas Jefferson: History, Memory, and Civic Culture.* Charlottesville: University Press of Virginia, 1999.

Malone, Dumas. *Jefferson and His Time: Six Volumes.* Boston: Little, Brown, 1948–81.

Miller, Douglas T. *Thomas Jefferson and the Creation of America.* New York: Facts On File, 1997.

Morse, John T. *Thomas Jefferson.* Broomall, Pa.: Chelsea House, 1997.

Onuf, Peter S. *Jeffersonian Legacies.* Charlottesville: University Press of Virginia, 1993.

Owsley, Frank L. *Filibusters and Expansionists: Jeffersonian Manifest Destiny, 1800–1821*. Tuscaloosa: University of Alabama Press, 1997.

Peterson, Merrill D., ed. *The Portable Thomas Jefferson*. New York: Viking Press, 1975.

———. *Thomas Jefferson*. New York: Scribner, 1986.

Johnson, Andrew
(1808–1875) *president, vice president, senator, representative, governor*

Andrew Johnson was the first vice president to ascend to the presidency on the assassination of a president, having taken over upon the death of ABRAHAM LINCOLN. He was the only U.S. senator from a seceding southern state who stayed with the Union, and he was the first president to be impeached, although he was not convicted and served out the remainder of his term.

Johnson was born in Raleigh, North Carolina, on December 29, 1808. Johnson was only eight when his father died, and his mother then supported the family by sewing. Johnson was apprenticed to a tailor when he was 14 years of age. In 1827, he moved to Greeneville, Tennessee, hill country, where he opened a tailor shop and married Eliza McCardle, a local girl who helped him learn to read and write. By 1829, he was elected to the Greeneville town council and was elected mayor in 1831. As a follower of ANDREW JACKSON, he was elected to the state legislature in 1835, 1839, and 1841, and to the U.S. House of Representatives in 1843. Gerrymandered out of his House seat in 1852 by the Whig legislature, Johnson fought back and won the Tennessee governor's office in 1853. He served two gubernatorial terms from 1853 to 1857, when the legislature elected him to the U.S. Senate.

While Johnson owned a few slaves, he represented the non-slaveholding interests of his section of the state. His most important Senate accomplishment was the Homestead Act, which called for a 160-acre grant of western land to anyone who would live on and cultivate it for five years. Other southern congressmen opposed it because they favored only large plantations associated with slavery. In 1860, Johnson initially

Andrew Johnson was the first president to be impeached, although he was not convicted and served out the remainder of his term. *(Library of Congress)*

favored STEPHEN ARNOLD DOUGLAS, but after the southerners left the Democratic Party, Johnson supported JOHN CABELL BRECKENRIDGE, who was favored in the South.

Johnson opposed secession after Lincoln's election and fought alongside other east Tennessee unionists to stay in the Union. While eastern Tennessee voted against secession, western and central Tennessee voted to secede. Johnson followed the sentiment of eastern Tennessee and was the only senator from a seceding southern state to stay in the Union. When Union forces gained control of central Tennessee in 1862, Lincoln appointed Johnson Tennessee's military governor.

As governor, Johnson restored civil government. After Confederate troops left the state in December 1864, Johnson led Tennesseans to frame a new state constitution and elect federal and state officeholders, all within three months. In 1864,

Lincoln ran for reelection and won on the Union ticket, using Johnson as his vice presidential running mate to underscore the breadth of his appeal. At the time of his vice presidential inauguration, Johnson was ill and drank some whiskey as medicine. This made him seem rambling and incoherent during his inaugural address and led to the inaccurate charge that he was an alcoholic.

After Lincoln was assassinated and Johnson became president, he faced restoring the Union. Difficult for the northerner Lincoln, this task was even harder for the southerner Johnson. Determined to reestablish southern state governments quickly, he used a program that Lincoln had developed during the war and that provided for the speedy drafting of new state constitutions to abolish slavery and facilitate the election of new state officers. Johnson made his Reconstruction plan even harder on the South by insisting the new southern states ratify the Thirteenth Amendment, repudiate Confederate debts, and nullify secession ordinances. Acting under the temporary wartime presidential authority, Johnson offered to restore the states to the Union when they met his conditions. Southerners met his conditions quickly.

This was not enough for the Radical Republicans, since Johnson's program left the fate of African Americans completely in the hands of white Southerners. The Republican majorities in Congress refused to accept the southern states in the Union and did not seat the newly elected southern congressional representatives. Arguing that Congress was wrong in voting while the southern congressmen were excluded, Johnson vetoed the bills Congress passed to protect the rights of the former slaves in 1866. He refused to endorse the Fourteenth Amendment to the Constitution, which granted African Americans the rights of citizenship. In 1867, Congress set aside the southern governments Johnson had created and put southerners under military rule until new governments guaranteeing equal civil and political rights were established.

Johnson resisted, using his power as commander in chief to hinder the army's enforcement of the laws in the South. When Johnson tried to gain more complete control of the army in February 1868, by removing the secretary of war in an apparent violation of a recently passed tenure of office law (ultimately declared unconstitutional), he was impeached by the House of Representatives and tried before the Senate. The quality of Johnson's legal team, the tenure of office law's ambiguity, the admission of some newly elected southern congressional representatives, and Republican splintering all led to a verdict of "not guilty," but only by a single vote. Johnson served out the remainder of his term quietly and ineffectively.

On a more positive note, Johnson's foreign policy was a success largely because WILLIAM HENRY SEWARD, Lincoln's secretary of state, continued under Johnson. Seward purchased Alaska from Russia in 1867, and he pressured the French to withdraw their attempt to take over Mexico, an act begun while the United States was preoccupied by the Civil War.

Returning to Tennessee after his term was up, Johnson tried unsuccessfully to win public office and rebuild his political career. He was finally elected to the U.S. Senate in 1874, but he died on July 31, 1875, only a few months after he reentered the Senate.

Further Reading

Benedict, Michael L. *The Impeachment and Trial of Andrew Johnson.* New York: Norton, 1973.

Castel, Albert E. *The Presidency of Andrew Johnson.* Lawrence: Regents Press of Kansas, 1979.

"Johnson, Andrew." Available online. URL: http://www.whitehouse.gov/history/presidents/aj17.html. Downloaded January 18, 2002.

"Johnson, Andrew." Available online. URL: http://www.impeach_andrewjohnson.com. Downloaded January 18, 2002.

Lomask, Milton. *Andrew Johnson: President on Trial.* New York: Octagon Books, 1973.

Mantell, Martin E. *Johnson, Grant, and the Politics of Reconstruction.* New York: Columbia University Press, 1973.

Rehnquist, William H. *Grand Inquests: The Historic Impeachments of Justice Samuel Chase and President Andrew Johnson.* New York: Morrow, 1992.

Riddleberger, Patrick W. *1866, The Critical Year Revisited.* Lanham, Md.: University Press of America, 1984.

Sefton, James E. *Andrew Johnson and the Uses of Constitutional Power.* Boston: Little, Brown, 1980.

Simpson, Brooks D. *The Reconstruction Presidents.* Lawrence: University Press of Kansas, 1998.

Trefousse, Hans L. *Andrew Johnson.* New York: Norton, 1989.

Winston, Robert W. *Andrew Johnson: Plebeian and Patriot.* Norwalk, Conn.: Easton Press, 1987.

Johnson, Hiram Warren
(1866–1945) *senator, governor*

As a reform governor of California, Hiram Warren Johnson possessed a progressivism that led him to leave the Republican Party repeatedly and aid the Democrats, but his isolationism also led him into repeated conflicts with the Democrats to such a degree that he defied party labels.

Born on September 2, 1866, in Sacramento, California, Johnson went to the University of California at Berkeley for two years and then studied in his father's law office until he passed the bar in 1888. In 1902, he and his brother started their own firm in San Francisco. In 1908, Abe Ruef, San Francisco's corrupt political boss, was on trial when the prosecutor was shot. As the assistant prosecutor, Johnson took over and won the case, which involved utility corporations bribing public officials. This catapulted him into the public consciousness to such a degree that he won the Republican nomination for governor in 1910.

In one of the most remarkable campaigns in California history—or anywhere in the United States—Johnson, backed by a group of reformers in the Republican Party called the "progressives," conducted a unique campaign. Believing that the railroads, which Johnson and his supporters dubbed the "octopus," were the greatest source of corruption, he attacked them at every opportunity. He pledged to run the Southern Pacific Railroad out of politics. He charged that the railroads raised their shipping rates so they could recover the money they had to pay out in bribes. The railroads, he said, "get us every way and we foot the bill—we pick our own pockets to bribe ourselves with our own money."

Johnson not only won the gubernatorial election, but he also carried majorities of progressive reformers with him into office in both houses of the legislature. In 1911, they wasted no time instituting a broad range of reforms. For the railroads, a commission was created with complete power to set shipping rates. Parallel legislation gave this commission the authority to set the rates charged by other utilities. For the benefit of the employees, the legislation passed creating workmen's compensation and forcing the employers to take responsibility for industrial accidents. Women benefited from the establishment of an eight-hour day. Two years later, legislation was enacted to establish a minimum wage for children and women.

Of greater importance for the long term were a series of reform proposals to more fully promote the majoritarian "will of the people." These reforms included the initiative, referendum, and recall provisions that spread to many other western and midwestern states in the next decade. The initiative provided that the voters could bypass the legislature entirely to propose new laws or constitutional amendments. The referendum permitted voters to veto an act of the legislature that the people did not like. The recall allowed voters to remove an elected official from office before the end of his or her regular term. Women were given the right to vote, making California the sixth state in the United States to grant women the franchise. This decision doubled the size of the California electorate. Since California was such a large state, this meant several more congresspersons became committed proponents of amending the U.S. Constitution to allow women to vote. The California decision was a key impetus toward the adoption of the Nineteenth Amendment in 1920, giving women the vote.

Observing the California reforms from afar, former Republican President Theodore Roosevelt called them "the greatest advance ever made by a state for the benefit of its people." He further predicted that they would usher in "the beginning of a new era of popular government." Having been governor for only two years, Johnson now found himself accepted as the vice presidential running mate of Roosevelt on the Progressive (or "Bull Moose") Party label in 1912. Although defeated, Roosevelt and Johnson had the effect of splitting the vote so that incumbent President WILLIAM HOWARD TAFT—the most conservative candidate in the race—lost to another progressive, President THOMAS WOODROW WILSON in that year's general election.

In 1914, Johnson was reelected governor, and halfway through that term Johnson was elected to the U.S. Senate in 1916. Johnson was, in effect, a major factor in deciding that presidential contest as well since Johnson refused to support the Republican presidential nominee, CHARLES EVANS HUGHES. Since the 1916 contest was decided by a mere handful of votes in California, Johnson's support for Wilson became critical for the national election.

These progressive reforms rested on a great deal of populist fervor. In line with the populism found in the southern part of the United States, this populism had a dark side: racism. In appealing to the working people for support, these reformers found that workers often wanted racist laws protecting them from immigrants. While African Americans were not numerous in California's population, Asians (both Chinese and Japanese) and Asian Americans were. The progressives' opposition to large corporations fit with this, since the workers believed—with some justification—that the corporations favored the influx of immigrants to provide them with a pool of low wage workers. In 1913, the California state legislature enacted legislation banning aliens ineligible for American citizenship from purchasing land in the state. Since federal law prohibited aliens from naturalization, Asians were now eliminated as property owners. Successful Japanese farmers could now only become wage earners.

Johnson clearly was a part of this effort. As a U.S. senator after 1916, he spearheaded many of the anti-immigration efforts, including the 1924 National Origins Quota Act that stopped all subsequent Japanese immigration. This anti-immigrant view also fit with Johnson's emerging isolationist worldview of international relations.

Johnson generally supported Woodrow Wilson's domestic policies, but he only reluctantly supported him on entering World War I. Feeling misled into supporting the war, Johnson became a vehement isolationist and opposed Wilson's League of Nations and the Versailles Peace Treaty. In 1920, he was a strong candidate for the Republican presidential nomination. WARREN GAMALIEL HARDING

was nominated and offered Johnson the vice presidential nomination, but he declined. Although he at first supported the CALVIN COOLIDGE and HERBERT CLARK HOOVER administrations on foreign policy, he disagreed on domestic matters. After the Great Depression started, Johnson became Hoover's bitter opponent. He supported FRANKLIN DELANO ROOSEVELT's domestic policy but fought him bitterly over his support of aid to Britain as World War II began. Johnson was one of the most consistent and adamant of the isolationists in Congress. After Pearl Harbor, he supported the United States in World War II, but he hated foreign entanglements and voted against the United Nations in one of the last votes he cast before his death in Bethesda, Maryland, on August 6, 1945.

Further Reading

Batman, Richard D. *The Road to the Presidency, Hoover, Johnson, and the California Republican Party, 1920–1924.* Ann Arbor, Mich.: University Microfilms International, 1971.

Hernon, Joseph Martin. *Profiles in Character: Hubris and Heroism in the U.S. Senate—1789–1990.* Armonk, N.Y.: M. E. Sharpe, 1997.

"Hiram Johnson" in *Congress A to Z: Third Edition*, edited by David R. Tarr and Ann O'Connor. Washington, D.C.: Congressional Quarterly, 1999.

"Johnson, Hiram." Available on line. URL: http://www.californiahistory.net/8_pages/reform_governor.htm. Downloaded January 18, 2002.

Olin, Spencer C. *California's Prodigal Sons: Hiram Johnson and the Progressives, 1911–1917.* Berkeley: University of California Press, 1968.

Johnson, Lyndon Baines
(1908–1973) *president, vice president, senator, representative*

Lyndon Baines Johnson was the youngest U.S. senator to become Senate majority leader and one of the most effective persons to hold that post. After he became president, he used his legislative skill to pass more significant new legislation during his famous first 100 days in office than any other president except for FRANKLIN DELANO ROOSEVELT. The Vietnam War and the struggle for civil rights for African Americans created such domestic turmoil that he chose not to run for a second term in 1968

Lyndon Baines Johnson was born near Stonewall, Texas, on August 27, 1908, into a politically active family. His father and grandfather had served in the Texas legislature. In 1913, the Johnsons moved to nearby Johnson City where young Johnson attended public school, graduating from high school in 1924. In 1927, he entered Southwest Texas State Teachers College in San Marcos, where he majored in history and social science. He earned his elementary teacher's certificate in 1928 and taught Hispanic students for one year in Cotulla, Texas, before returning to college to earn his B.A. degree in 1930.

Late in 1931, he became the secretary to Texas Congressman Richard Kleberg, a position he held for four years until he became the director of the National Youth Administration in Texas in 1935. When the local incumbent congressman died in 1937, Johnson ran for and won a seat in the U.S. House of Representatives as a devoted supporter of Franklin D. Roosevelt's New Deal. He became a close ally of House majority leader (later Speaker) SAMUEL TALIAFERRO RAYBURN. In 1941, he ran for the Senate from Texas but was narrowly defeated in a special election.

When the United States entered World War II in December 1941, Johnson enlisted in the navy and toured briefly in the South Pacific. Johnson left the navy and returned to Congress when Roosevelt announced that congressmen should remain in Washington.

In 1948, Johnson ran for the Democratic nomination to the U.S. Senate against popular former governor Coke Stevenson and won a spot with Stevenson in a runoff primary. The August 1948 runoff was very close, and Johnson was declared the Democratic nominee only after extended legal battles over charges of ballot box stuffing and other irregularities. He easily won the general election against his Republican opponent. In the Senate, he ingratiated himself with powerful southern senators, including Richard Russell of Georgia, mastered the Senate rules, and became majority whip in 1951. In 1953, he was elected the youngest Democratic minority leader in Senate history.

In 1954, Johnson won reelection, and the Democrats captured the Senate, so he became the majority leader in January 1955. In the summer of 1955, he suffered a severe heart attack, but he recovered and returned to his Senate duties later that year. He followed a strategy of cooperation with Republican President DWIGHT DAVID EISENHOWER's administration.

Already planning to run for president in 1960, Johnson persuaded the Texas legislature to pass a law allowing him to run simultaneously for Senate reelection and a national office, such as president or vice president. To bolster his image as a moderate to liberal leader for a national campaign in the North, in 1957, he pushed through the first civil-rights act in more than 80 years.

Despite these machinations, he failed to win the 1960 Democratic presidential nomination, but he accepted JOHN FITZGERALD KENNEDY's offer to become his vice presidential running mate. Johnson campaigned hard in the southern and border states, helping Kennedy win Texas to clinch a narrow Electoral College victory. Many political observers credit Johnson with helping Kennedy carry as many as five southern and border states including Texas. When Johnson was elevated to the presidency after the Kennedy assassination, he used the emotional response to the assassination—and his own legislative skills—to push through the 1964 Civil Rights Act, the tax cut, and some other stalled-out Kennedy legislative programs in Congress. These succeeded and the tax cut stimulated a great deal of consumer spending to stimulate prosperity.

In the 1964 election, Johnson faced no opposition within the Democratic Party. After a contested primary between New York Governor Nelson Rockefeller and Barry Goldwater, the Republicans nominated Barry Goldwater, who had been cultivating a new formulation of conservative ideology during his 12 years as a U.S. senator from Arizona.

As a part of this new formulation, Goldwater objected to the Kennedy-Johnson administration's seeming disavowal of the first use of nuclear weapons. He implied that nuclear weapons might be used not only for deterrence against attack but also in conventional war battlefield situations. This was

Lyndon Baines Johnson, elevated to the presidency upon President Kennedy's assassination, pushed through one of the most expansive legislative programs in history but was not able to find a successful outcome to the Vietnam War. *(Library of Congress, Official White House photo)*

the basis for suggesting that he was "trigger happy" with nuclear weapons.

Goldwater also objected to the 1964 Civil Rights bill on what he regarded as principled opposition toward some of its technical provisions. To many political observers, it appeared to be a ploy to gain the votes of southerners who had traditionally voted for Democrats but who were alienated by the Democratic administration's pushing this legislation through Congress. Goldwater was one of the few nonsouthern senators who voted against the 1964 Civil Rights legislation. Over the years, he had spoken out against the supposed "socialistic" characteristics of the Tennessee Valley Authority and various other well-established social

welfare programs. Taken altogether, these positions placed him quite far to the right of the mainstream of the U.S. political spectrum.

In his acceptance speech at the Republican National Convention, Goldwater attempted to respond to these criticisms with the line "Extremism in the defense of liberty is no vice; moderation in the pursuit of justice is no virtue." However true this might be in philosophical terms, it cemented the impression that Goldwater was a dangerous extremist—an impression that the Democrats did much to reinforce. Johnson won the election with the largest popular vote margin of victory in percentage terms of any president in the 20th century.

The Democratic Party also won control of both houses of Congress by almost a two-thirds margin. On the domestic front, Johnson used the momentum from his landslide victory and his party's overwhelming control of both houses to push through the 1965 Voting Rights Act and his Great Society welfare programs, the most ambitious legislative program in the 20th century except for Roosevelt's legislation during the Great Depression.

This ambitious legislative agenda included the new Civil Rights Act of 1965 that attempted to overcome several devices white southerners had used for decades to prevent African Americans from voting. This act suspended literacy tests for voting. It also provided that federal registrars could be sent into six southern states and part of a seventh where literacy tests were accompanied by low voter registration rates. States or counties affected by the law were thereafter required to obtain approval from the U.S. Department of Justice before changing their voter registration laws or voting procedures.

Beyond the civil rights issues, Johnson developed an extensive program aimed at ending poverty, lack of education, illness, and other socioeconomic problems. Johnson labeled this collection of programs the War on Poverty. This cluster of policies included Medicare, which provided medical care for the elderly—the first major addition to the Social Security program since the Great Depression. Administered through the Social Security program, this also created a program of subsidized medical care for indigent individuals called

Medicaid. The Office of Economic Opportunity sought to increase the amount of federal aid available for all low-income individuals to find jobs, adding benefits for low-income whites as the Equal Employment Opportunity Commission aided African Americans. Recognizing that a great deal of poverty existed in the cities creating an "urban blight" that was holding back the development of cities, the Johnson administration also pushed through the Model Cities program.

This ambitious program was passed in great part because Johnson now headed an administration with nearly two-thirds control of both houses of Congress. Johnson seemed to harken back to his earliest adulthood experiences as a teacher of low-income Hispanic American students in Cotulla, Texas. In reality, Johnson's programs fit with the basic ideas he acquired during the heyday of Franklin Roosevelt's New Deal.

These programs cost a great deal of money. Federal revenues had increased somewhat as the result of the economic stimulus created by the 1964 tax cut. The money to pay for all these new programs might have been available had not the international relations situation created a war, which also made heavy demands on the federal treasury. The war in Vietnam not only made its own heavy demands on the nation's financial resources, but it created a political climate that seriously damaged Johnson's popularity.

In foreign policy, Johnson inherited the Kennedy commitment of giving military aid to South Vietnam to fight communism. In 1965, he thought increasing the use of American troops in Vietnam would bring victory, but his escalation of the Vietnam War brought about severe criticism from both left and right. The Democratic left thought the conflict was immoral, and the Republican right blamed Johnson for not unleashing the military to do its job without political interference. Domestically, the left argued that the Great Society did not go far enough, and riots and racial tension in African-American communities followed. The Republicans blamed the Great Society programs for going too far in "appeasing" radical left-wing groups.

The war in Vietnam stalemated in 1967, and the Tet offensive, which began on January 30,

1968, was a defeat for North Vietnam militarily but a blow to Johnson's weakened political standing at home. Faced with political challenges from EUGENE JOSEPH McCARTHY and ROBERT FRANCIS KENNEDY in his own party, Johnson announced on March 31, 1968, that he would not be a candidate for reelection. Instead, he devoted himself to trying without success to negotiate an end to the Vietnam War without complete capitulation.

After leaving the White House, Johnson wrote his memoirs, and he died on January 22, 1973.

Further Reading

Andrew, John A. *Lyndon Johnson and the Great Society.* Chicago: I. R. Dec, 1998.

Bernstein, Irving. *Guns or Butter: The Presidency of Lyndon Johnson.* New York: Oxford University Press, 1996.

———. *Promises Kept: John F. Kennedy's New Frontier.* New York: Oxford University Press, 1990.

Brands, H. W. *The Foreign Policies of Lyndon Johnson: Beyond Vietnam.* College Station: Texas A&M University Press, 1999.

Califano, Joseph A. *The Triumph and Tragedy of Lyndon Johnson: The White House Years.* New York: Simon & Schuster, 1991.

Caro, Robert A. *The Years of Lyndon Johnson: Means of Ascent.* New York: Knopf, 1990.

———. *The Years of Lyndon Johnson: The Path to Power.* New York: Knopf, 1990.

Dallek, Robert. *Flawed Giant: Lyndon Johnson and His Times 1961–1973.* New York: Oxford University Press, 1998.

Gardner, Lloyd C. *Pay Any Price: Lyndon Johnson and the Wars for Vietnam.* Chicago: Elephant Paperbacks, 1997.

Goldsmith, John A. *Colleagues: Richard B. Russell and his Apprentice, Lyndon B. Johnson.* Macon, Ga.: Mercer University Press, 1998.

Goodwin, Doris Kearns. *Lyndon Johnson and the American Dream.* New York: St. Martin's Press, 1991.

Gould, Lewis L. "Johnson, Lyndon." Available online. URL: http://www.tsha.utexas/handbook/Online/articles/JJ/fjo19.html. Downloaded October 20, 2001.

Hunt, Michael H. *Lyndon Johnson's War: America's Cold War Crusade in Vietnam, 1945–1968.* New York: Hill & Wang, 1997.

"Johnson, Lyndon." Available on line. URL: http://www.whitehouse.gov/history/presidents/lj36.html. Downloaded October 20, 2001.

Johnson, Lyndon B. *The Vantage Point: Perspectives of the Presidency, 1963–1969*. New York: Holt, Rinehart & Winston, 1971.

Kaiser, David E. *American Tragedy: Kennedy, Johnson, and the Origins of the Vietnam War*. Cambridge, Mass.: Belknap Press of Harvard University Press, 2000.

Mann, Robert. *The Walls of Jericho: Lyndon Johnson, Hubert Humphrey, Richard Russell, and the Struggle For Civil Rights*. New York: Harcourt Brace, 1996.

Schwab, Orrin. *Defending The Free World. John F. Kennedy, Lyndon Johnson, and the Vietnam War, 1961–1965*. Westport, Conn.: Praeger, 1998.

Shesol, Jeff. *Mutual Contempt: Lyndon Johnson, Robert Kennedy, and the Feud That Defined a Decade*. New York: Norton, 1997.

Stern, Mark. *Calculating Visions: Kennedy, Johnson, and Civil Rights*. New Brunswick, N.J.: Rutgers University Press, 1992.

Unger, Irwin. *LBJ: A Life*. New York: John Wiley, 1999.

Vandiver, Frank E. *Shadows of Vietnam: Lyndon Johnson's Wars*. College Station: Texas A&M University Press, 1997.

Jordan, Barbara Charline
(1936–1996) *representative*

Barbara Jordan was the first African-American woman elected to the U.S. House of Representatives from the Deep South. She was also the first African American elected to the Texas state senate since 1883 and one of the first two African Americans to be elected the U.S. House of Representatives since the Reconstruction Era in the late 19th century. When she spoke to the Democratic National Convention in 1976, she became the first woman to deliver a keynote address to a major political party convention.

Born on February 21, 1936, in Houston, Texas, Barbara Charline Jordan attended public schools and Texas Southern University, where she graduated magna cum laude in 1956. She earned a law degree from Boston University and was admitted to the bar in 1959. She taught at Tuskegee Institute for a year and then opened a private law practice from her home in Houston in 1960. She lost two early runs for the Texas senate in the early 1960s. After the reapportionment revolution and redistricting, she won election to the Texas senate in 1966. In 1972, Jordan ran for the U.S. House of Representatives in a four-way race with three male opponents and still won 80 percent of the total vote. She was a member of the House Judiciary Committee and earned national prominence for her eloquence in the 1974 impeachment hearings of President RICHARD MILHOUS NIXON.

The Democratic Party selected her to be the first woman to give a keynote speech at the 1976 Democratic National Convention. After three terms, Jordan retired from Congress to teach at the University of Texas at Austin, and she published her autobiography in 1979. In 1992, the Democrats once again asked her to deliver the keynote address at the Democratic National Convention. She was inducted into the National Women's Hall of Fame in 1990, and President WILLIAM JEFFERSON CLINTON awarded her the Presidential Medal of Freedom in 1994.

Jordan eventually was confined to a wheelchair because of multiple sclerosis. She also suffered from leukemia but finally succumbed to pneumonia on January 17, 1996.

Further Reading
Barnes, Lorene T. *A Comparison/Contrast of Two Black Women in Politics: Shirley Chisholm and Barbara Jordan*. Chicago, Ill.: Governors State University, 1979.

Browne, Ray B. *Contemporary Heroes and Heroines*. Detroit: Gale Research, 1990.

Blue, Rose, and Corinne Naden. *Barbara Jordan: Politician*. New York: Chelsea House, 1992.

Bryant, Ira B. *Barbara Charline Jordan: From the Ghetto to the Capitol*. Houston: D. Armstrong, 1977.

"Jordan, Barbara." Available online. URL: http://www.tsha.utexas/handbook/online/articles/JJ/fjos.html. Downloaded October 20, 2001.

"Jordan, Barbara." Available online. URL: http://www.elf.net/bjordan/. Downloaded 20, 2001.

Jordan, Barbara. *Barbara Jordan: A Self-Portrait*. Garden City, N.Y.: Doubleday, 1979.

Rogers, Mary Beth. *Barbara Jordan: American Hero*. New York: Bantam Books, 1998.

K

Kassebaum, Nancy Landon
(Nancy Kassebaum Baker)
(1932–) senator

Nancy Landon Kassebaum was the first woman who was elected to a full term in the Senate but did not succeed her husband in either the Senate or the House of Representatives. She was the only Republican woman who served in the U.S. Senate during her first term.

Born Nancy Landon on July 29, 1932, in Topeka, Kansas, she is a daughter of ALFRED MOSSMAN LANDON, a former Kansas governor and Republican presidential candidate, who lost to FRANKLIN DELANO ROOSEVELT in the 1936 landslide. In 1954, she graduated from the University of Kansas and received a master's degree from the University of Michigan in 1956. In that same year, she married John Philip Kassebaum, an attorney and businessman (she divorced him in 1979).

In 1975 and 1976, she was an aide for Kansas Republican senator James B. Pearson in his Washington office. When she learned that Pearson did not intend to seek reelection, she left his office to campaign for his newly opened seat. Because she was the daughter of Alfred M. Landon, former Kansas governor and former 1936 Republican presidential nominee, she was a leading candidate. She won both the 1978 Republican primary and the general election under the banner of "A Fresh Face, A Trusted Kansas Name." She was reelected in 1984 and 1990.

As a Republican senator from Kansas, it was almost inevitable that Kassebaum would hew to a conservative Republican voting record. She opposed raising taxes and favored cutting domestic spending while maintaining or increasing defense spending. She entered the Senate too late to vote for the original proposal of the Equal Rights Amendment, but she announced her support for it. However, she took the stance that the original seven-year deadline for ratification be adhered to, and she did not vote for the extension of the deadline for ratification when this matter came up in 1979. In this, she was not only principled in her opposition to this dubious extension but a realist in that the additional three and one-half years did not help the proposed amendment.

Notwithstanding this vote, Kassebaum was more moderate on social issues and generally supported measures to improve the status of women. She differed from the mainstream Republican stance on abortion by supporting limited federal funding for abortion. She also cosponsored, with Senator EDWARD MOORE KENNEDY, the Kennedy-Kassebaum bill, which provided that workers keep their medical insurance coverage even if they change jobs.

Kassebaum was named to the prestigious Senate Foreign Relations Committee in 1980 and used this forum to push for reductions in strategic armaments, again a stance generally outside mainstream conservative Republican positions.

In 1996, she married the former U.S. senator, Howard H. Baker, Jr., and did not run for reelection. She received appointments by both President WILLIAM JEFFERSON CLINTON and President

GEORGE WALKER BUSH. Under the Clinton administration she led a public education project on campaign reform, and in 2001 she was appointed chair of the Presidential Appointee Initiative advisory board, which recommended ways to streamline the recruitment and nomination process for appointees to the Bush government.

Further Reading

Loomis, Burdett A. *Esteemed Colleagues: Civility and Deliberation in the U.S. Senate.* Washington, D.C.: Brookings Institution, 2000.

Thornton, Lee. "Kassebaum, Nancy Landon." Available online. Discovery Channel School, original content provided by World Book Online, http://www.discoveryschool.com/homeworkhelp/worldbook/atozhistory/k/295710.html. Downloaded October 22, 2001.

Kefauver, Estes Corey
(1903–1963) *candidate for vice president, senator, representative, author*

Estes Kefauver was a rare southern political leader who is identified with the fight for civil rights, civil liberties, antitrust enforcement, and consumer protection.

Born in Madisonville, Tennessee, on July 26, 1903, Estes Corey Kefauver graduated from the University of Tennessee in 1924 and from Yale Law School in 1927. After law school, Kefauver returned to Chattanooga, Tennessee. In 1939, he served briefly as Tennessee's commissioner of the Department of Finance and Taxation before winning a congressional seat left vacant by the death of the incumbent. As a congressman, he supported New Deal programs, especially the Tennessee Valley Authority.

Kefauver successfully challenged the conservative political machine led by former Memphis mayor Ed Crump and won election to his first term in the U.S. Senate in 1948. During this Democratic primary campaign, Crump attempted to smear Kefauver, saying he was a "Communist fellow-traveler," who assisted communists like a sneaky raccoon. Wearing a coonskin cap to iden-

tify himself with the famous Tennessean Davy Crockett, Kefauver replied, "I may be a pet coon, but I'm not Boss Crump's pet coon." The coonskin cap then became his instantly recognized campaign symbol.

Appointed chairman of the Senate crime investigating committee in 1950 and 1951, Kefauver acquired nationwide attention and wrote his own account of the results of the hearing in a book entitled *Crime in America.* He was reelected to the Senate in 1954. Two years later he was the Democratic Party vice presidential nominee with presidential candidate ADLAI EWING STEVENSON. But Republican DWIGHT DAVID EISENHOWER won that race. Kefauver was one of only two southern senators (the other was his Tennessee Senate colleague, Albert Gore, Sr., father of former Vice President ALBERT ARNOLD GORE, JR.) to refuse to sign the so-called Southern Manifesto, which opposed civil rights for African Americans. His staunch support of civil-rights legislation led to a vicious Democratic campaign against Kefauver's 1960 reelection, but he won by 65 percent of the vote anyway. An early, active supporter of consumer protection, he was a principal sponsor of a 1962 law enacted to protect the consumer from dangerous or ineffective pharmaceuticals.

In 1963, Kefauver suffered a heart attack on the Senate floor, while arguing for an amendment to require a private, profit-making communications satellite corporation to reimburse NASA for the cost of research and development from which that company benefited. He died as a result of that attack on August 10 at the age of 60.

Further Reading

Brown, Theodore, Jr., and Robert B. Allen. "Remembering Estes Kefauver." Available online. URL: http://www.populist.com/96.10.kefauver.html. Downloaded January 23, 2002.

Fontenay, Charles L. *Estes Kefauver: A Biography.* Knoxville: University of Tennessee Press, 1980.

Gorman, Joseph B. *Kefauver: A Political Biography.* New York: Oxford University Press, 1971.

———. *In A Few Hands: Monopoly Power in America.* New York: Pantheon Books, 1966.

Kefauver, Estes. *Crime in America.* New York: Greenwood Press, 1969.

———. *A Twentieth-Century Congress.* New York: Essential Books, Duell, Sloan & Pearce, 1947.

"Kefauver, Estes" in *Congress A to Z: Third Edition,* edited by David R. Tarr and Ann O'Connor. Washington, D.C.: Congressional Quarterly, 1999.

"Kefauver, Estes" in *The Presidency A to Z: Second Edition,* edited by Michael T. Nelson. Washington, D.C.: Congressional Quarterly Press, 1998.

Kellogg, Frank Billings
(1856–1937) *secretary of state, diplomat, senator*

Frank Kellogg is best known in American history as one of the authors and promoters of the Kellogg-Briand Pact, which was signed in Paris in 1928 and outlawed war as an instrument of national policy. Kellogg served as U.S. ambassador to Great Britain, secretary of state, and judge on the Permanent Court of International Justice.

Born on December 22, 1856, in Potsdam, New York, Frank Billings Kellogg moved to Olmstead County, Minnesota, when he was nine years old. He worked on his father's farm and studied law until he was admitted to the Minnesota bar in 1877. In 1878, he was elected Rochester city attorney, and in 1881, he became state attorney general.

In 1887, Kellogg joined a prominent St. Paul corporate law firm and began his career representing railroads and mines. This practice made him wealthy, and soon he became a leading figure within the Republican Party. In 1904, President THEODORE ROOSEVELT appointed Kellogg a special counsel to the U.S. attorney general, and he played a major role in legal action against Standard Oil and General Paper for antitrust violations.

Kellogg was elected to the U.S. Senate in 1916 but lost his reelection bid in 1922. President WARREN GAMALIEL HARDING then appointed him the U.S. ambassador to Great Britain, a position he held from 1923 to 1925. Because Kellogg had these international affairs credentials, President CALVIN COOLIDGE appointed him secretary of state in 1925. In this position, he negotiated the end of the Tacna-Arica dispute between Chile and Peru, and he improved relations with Mexico, which

were damaged by the revolution and subsequent U.S. intervention a decade earlier.

In 1929, Kellogg was awarded the Nobel Peace Prize for his work as the author and chief promoter of the Kellogg-Briand Pact. Britain and France had asked the United States to enter into a treaty to restrain the growth of Germany, whose increased power the nations greatly feared. Well aware of how strong isolationist sentiment was in the United States, Kellogg recognized it would be difficult for the United States to enter into a typical alliance against Germany.

As an alternative, he proposed that all nations in the world sign a treaty agreeing to renounce the use of war as an instrument of national policy. The Kellogg-Briand Pact had a fatal weakness because the only way to enforce agreement was to start a war, which naturally would defeat the whole purpose of the act. Britain, France, Germany, and the other signatories recognized its weakness, but they signed it principally to appear cooperative with Kellogg and the United States. The Kellogg-Briand Pact did not stop the onset of World War II and may have aggravated the situation by holding out false hopes.

After serving a five-year term as a judge on the Permanent Court of International Justice, Kellogg retired from public life. He died on December 21, 1937, one day short of his 81st birthday.

Further Reading
Ellis, Lewis E. *Frank B. Kellogg and American Foreign Relations, 1925–1929.* Westport, Conn.: Greenwood Press, 1974.

Ferrell, Robert H. *The American Secretaries of State and their Diplomacy, Volume II: Frank B. Kellogg, Henry L. Stimson.* New York: Cooper Square, 1963.

Hernon, Joseph Martin. *Profiles in Character: Hubris and Heroism in the U.S. Senate—1789–1990.* Armonk, N.Y.: M. E. Sharpe, 1997.

Kennedy, Edward Moore
(1932–) *candidate for president, senator*

Edward Moore Kennedy, a Democratic U.S. senator from Massachusetts, is the youngest child and the only surviving son of JOSEPH PATRICK KENNEDY, SR.

His oldest brother, Joseph P. Kennedy, Jr., was killed in World War II; and his other brothers, President JOHN FITZGERALD KENNEDY and Senator ROBERT FRANCIS KENNEDY, were both assassinated in the mid-1960s. Since he has served in the Senate since 1962, he is the second-longest-serving and probably the best-known Democrat in the body, epitomizing the traditional liberalism of the Democratic Party since the New Deal.

Kennedy was born in Boston, Massachusetts, on February 22, 1932, and often goes by the nickname Ted. As the youngest son of Joseph P. Kennedy, Sr., he had a privileged upbringing. He attended private schools and then Harvard University, from which he graduated in 1956. He graduated from the University of Virginia Law School in 1959, but he entered politics so soon after graduating that he has never practiced law. In 1962, many people were surprised when he ran for and won the seat his brother John F. Kennedy vacated when he became president, since he was only 30 years old, the minimum age for a senator. John, Robert, and Edward Kennedy all served in the U.S. Senate, but only Edward Kennedy truly seemed to have the personal characteristics for a successful career in the that body. He worked hard, accommodated other senators, and gradually moved up in the party hierarchy.

From 1969 to 1971, Ted Kennedy was Democratic majority party whip in the Senate. The decade of the 1960s was particularly hard for Ted Kennedy personally. Both of his brothers were assassinated. He suffered a serious back injury—and nearly died—in a small plane crash. The tragedy at the end of the decade was the worst for him overall. In the summer of 1969, he drove his car off a narrow, unlighted bridge late at night. Kennedy was slightly injured, but Mary Jo Kopechne, the young woman traveling with him in the car, drowned despite his alleged efforts to rescue her. The incident raised many questions, but Kennedy provided almost no answers to them. This incident did a great deal of damage to his reputation, and he lost his position as Democratic majority whip to Robert C. Byrd of West Virginia in 1971.

Despite this setback, Kennedy continued to sponsor major legislation and to speak out on the issues central to the cause of the liberal wing of the Democratic Party. From 1979 to 1981, he served as chairman of the Senate's Judiciary Committee. He was chairman of the Labor and Human Resources Committee from 1987 to 1995. Kennedy has been known as a national spokesperson for liberal causes and has supported greater government spending on welfare programs for the poor, minorities, and other disadvantaged groups as well as a program of national health insurance.

A legend of the Kennedy brothers was that if one of them faltered in the effort to be president, the remaining brothers would take up the challenge in order of seniority. Despite the difficulty of defeating an incumbent president of one's own party at a time of national foreign policy crisis (after the U.S. embassy in Teheran was stormed and hostages were taken in Iran), it was not entirely unexpected when Ted Kennedy challenged President JAMES EARL CARTER in the 1980 Democratic presidential primaries. As if the circumstances of the race were not difficult enough, nearly all of the old questions about the car accident at Chappaquiddick were raised once again. The Kennedys had rarely lost election campaigns before, but Ted Kennedy consistently lost to Carter in 1980 primaries, further weakening his national stature. He lost his committee chairmanship when the Republicans took control of a majority of the seats in the Senate in 1981.

The mystique of the Kennedy family has continued to surround him and made his pronouncements something of rallying point for traditionally liberal Democrats. For the conservative wing, his stands have become targets for their opposition. He had some successes notable for the difficult circumstances in which they were achieved. In the 1995–97 term of the Congress, Kennedy pushed through a minimum wage increase despite the popular expectation that any hope of success was doomed. He also formed an alliance with the conservative Republican senator from Kansas, NANCY LANDON KASSEBAUM, to pass legislation to require portability of medical insurance for workers as they left one job and before they acquired another one. This latter act underscores what has been true of Kennedy and most genuine legislative leaders in the Senate: the willingness to form connections on specific issues of common interest across party lines. The Kennedy-Kassebaum legislation—although frequently touted as a major piece of bipartisanship—is a very limited bill that guarantees a worker medical insurance coverage if a worker loses his/her job, but the actual coverage may be less and the premium to be paid may be much higher than the coverage the worker had previously.

Kennedy's record as a successful senator is limited. After more than 40 years in the Senate, he has compiled no great record of legislative achievement. One might expect someone who began a Senate career at age 30 with all the advantages of wealth and the national recognition that came from the activities and tragedies of his brothers to have been able to do more than simply become the best known spokesperson for largely unsuccessful liberal causes in the Senate. But the continued linking of his name with national scandals has damaged his overall effectiveness. In addition to the Chappaquiddick incident, he had a messy divorce and remarriage. In 1991, he took his son and nephew William Kennedy Smith on a late night outing that resulted in his nephew being indicted for rape of a young woman. While William Kennedy Smith was acquitted, the entire incident did not make Senator Kennedy appear to be a good example for his children and other relatives. Although he was cleared of charges of harassment and drug use in a 1994 Senate Ethics Committee report, each new allegation and scandal has left its mark.

Further Reading

Burner, David. *The Torch Is Passed: The Kennedy Brothers and American Liberalism.* New York: Athenaeum, 1984.

Burns, James MacGregor. *Edward Kennedy and the Camelot Legacy.* New York: Norton, 1976.

Collier, Peter. *The Kennedys: An American Drama.* New York: Summit Books, 1984.

Clymer, Adam. *Edward M. Kennedy.* New York: Morrow, 1999.

David, Lester. *Good Ted, Bad Ted: The Two Faces of Edward M. Kennedy.* Secaucus, N.J.: Carol Publishing Group, 1993.

Goodwin, Doris Kearns. *The Fitzgeralds and the Kennedys.* New York: St. Martin's Press, 1991.

Hersh, Burton. *The Shadow President: Ted Kennedy in Opposition.* South Royalton, Vt.: Steerforth Press, 1997.

Hersh, Seymour M. *The Dark Side of Camelot.* Boston: Little, Brown, 1997.

Kappel, Kenneth R. *Chappaquiddick Revealed.* New York: St. Martin's, 1991.

Lange, James. *Chappaquiddick: The Real Story.* New York: St. Martin's Press, 1993.

Lerner, Max. *Ted and the Kennedy Legend.* New York: St. Martin's Press, 1980.

McGinniss, Joe. *The Last Brother.* New York: Pocket Star Books, 1994.

Wofford, Harris. *Of Kennedys and Kings: Making Sense of the Sixties.* Pittsburgh: University of Pittsburgh Press, 1992.

Kennedy, John Fitzgerald
(1917–1963) *president, senator, representative, author*

At the age of 43, John Fitzgerald Kennedy was the youngest man and the first Roman Catholic ever elected to the presidency. While his assassination meant that he served too short a period of time to make conclusive judgments on the overall success of his presidency in history, he became a cultural icon for two generations of Americans.

Born on May 29, 1917, in Brookline, Massachusetts, Kennedy descended from Irish Catholic immigrants. His father, JOSEPH PATRICK KENNEDY, SR., was a very aggressive businessman who became a multimillionaire as a young man. Entering politics, he supported President FRANKLIN DELANO ROOSEVELT, who in turn appointed him the head of the Securities and Exchange Commission and later the U.S. ambassador to Great Britain. When Roosevelt blocked the elder Kennedy's plan to become president, he shifted his efforts to helping one of his children attain high office. Initially, he focused on his oldest son, Joseph, until his death in World War II, after which he shifted to his second son, John.

Kennedy attended Choate, an elite private school, before graduating and moving on to Princeton University. He transferred to Harvard University where he graduated with honors in 1940. His Harvard honors thesis on the failed British foreign policies of the 1930s was published as *Why England Slept* in 1940. In 1941, shortly before the United States entered World War II,

Kennedy joined the U.S. Navy as a PT boat commander. While Kennedy was in combat in 1943, the Japanese sunk his ship, and he courageously saved his crew. He injured his back and contracted malaria, leading to his discharge in early 1945. In 1946, Kennedy was elected from Massachusetts to a seat in the U.S. House of Representatives and reelected in 1948 and 1950. As a Democrat, he backed President HARRY S. TRUMAN's domestic policies but sometimes differed with Truman on foreign policy, specifically by urging a stronger anti-Communist stand particularly in Asia. In 1952, Kennedy ran for the U.S. Senate against the Republican incumbent senator, HENRY CABOT LODGE, JR. Kennedy defeated Lodge despite the fact that the Republican presidential candidate, DWIGHT DAVID EISENHOWER, won Massachusetts in a landslide.

Kennedy was not interested in minutia and compiled no record of legislative achievement. He

John Fitzgerald Kennedy, the youngest man (aged 43) and the first Roman Catholic ever elected president, was the fourth president to be assassinated. *(Library of Congress)*

attributed this partly to illness. During 1954 and 1955, he was hospitalized with what he claimed was an old back injury, but it was actually a bout with Addison's disease. Since there was no known cure at the time, his condition had to be kept secret or it would have ended his career. The doctors found at least a temporary treatment with cortisone, but its success was not at all assured in the early 1950s. Kennedy's voting record was that of a moderate to cautiously liberal northern senator. He voiced concern for a hard line against the Communists, but he followed conventional liberal domestic policies, especially for organized labor. He supported a modest 1957 Civil Rights Act but did not oppose the anticommunist excesses of Wisconsin's Republican senator, JOSEPH RAYMOND Mc-CARTHY, on whose committee's staff his younger brother, ROBERT FRANCIS KENNEDY, served.

During his illness, Kennedy was credited with having written *Profiles in Courage*, a book of biographical profiles of U.S. politicians who behaved courageously on various political issues. Subsequent historical research has indicated that this was largely ghostwritten by others, but it won a Pulitzer Prize for biography in 1957, largely through the efforts of the famous *New York Times* correspondent Arthur Krock.

Subsequently, Kennedy began his campaign for the presidency, most notably after his landslide reelection to the Senate in 1958. Since Eisenhower was constitutionally barred from seeking a third term, the Democratic presidential field was crowded in 1960 with several well-known candidates. Kennedy realized he had no hope of winning the nomination unless he proved that a Catholic could win in the primaries. He vigorously contested the available primaries and scored several significant victories. He defeated the incumbent Senator WAYNE LYMAN MORSE in Morse's home state of Oregon. More important, he defeated Minnesota Senator HUBERT HORATIO HUMPHREY in Humphrey's neighboring state of Wisconsin. To overcome the impression that he won Wisconsin only because he was a Catholic in a Catholic state, he then challenged Humphrey in the overwhelmingly Protestant state of West Virginia and won there. This victory propelled him into a first-ballot win at the Democratic National Convention.

Recognizing that he would need political help in the southern and border states, he chose Senator LYNDON BAINES JOHNSON of Texas as his vice presidential running mate. The most notable feature of the 1960 campaign was the scheduling of four nationally televised debates. Modeled on the famous Lincoln-Douglas debates from the 1858 senatorial contest between ABRAHAM LINCOLN and STEPHEN ARNOLD DOUGLAS, they were a first for any presidential campaign. The Republicans had nominated Vice President RICHARD MILHOUS NIXON for president, and he was thought to have the advantage because of his prior debating experience. Unfortunately for Nixon, this created unrealistic expectations that he would do better than Kennedy, so even when he matched Kennedy in debating skills, he seemed less successful. Also, unprepared for the visual impact of the debate, he shunned the standard makeup and thus looked unshaven and dull compared to the more vigorous appearance of Kennedy. Since Kennedy's campaign theme was to "get the country moving again," his debate performances seemed to match the theme.

Kennedy won the election by a popular vote margin of less than 120,000 votes and an Electoral College vote of 303–219 (15 votes were cast for Senator Harry F. Byrd of Virginia). This was one of the closest presidential elections in history. At his inauguration, Kennedy gave what has come to be regarded as one of the greatest inaugural addresses ever given, sounding a cold war theme and challenging: "Ask not what your country can do for you—ask what you can do for your country." Since many southern congressional Democrats did not support his New Frontier program, the Democratic majority was too small to move many of his ideas through the Congress. In the end, much of his program passed only after he was assassinated and Lyndon Johnson became president.

Kennedy's administration and the ideals expressed in his inaugural were challenged almost immediately in the international arena. The presence of Cuba, a Communist nation just 90 miles south of the United States, had been a source of concern to the Eisenhower administration, and the Central Intelligence Agency (CIA), headed by ALLEN WELSH DULLES, had planned an amphibious

assault by right-wing Cuban refugees trained by the CIA. Dulles recognized that the plan was risky but felt that Kennedy would call for a full-scale U.S. invasion if the refugee assault did not go well, since Kennedy would not want to be responsible for a failure. Kennedy decided to let the assault go forward, based on Dulles's assurance that it would succeed, and he refused to be rushed into a full-scale war. As it turned out, the refugees were trapped on the beach, killed, or captured, and the United States had to raise money from private donors to buy the freedom of the prisoners of war. Kennedy took responsibility for the Bay of Pigs failure, and Dulles resigned. Later in his administration, Kennedy tried to diminish anti-U.S. feeling in Latin America by backing development projects under the Alliance for Progress. The Peace Corps program was developed with similar goals in mind and represented a long-lasting positive—if limited—achievement of his administration.

In June 1961, Kennedy met with Soviet leader Nikita Khrushchev in Vienna, but the Bay of Pigs fiasco made Khrushchev feel he had the upper hand. He used his momentum to try to stir up the conflict over West Berlin. He threatened to sign a separate peace treaty with communist East Germany that would have given the East Germans control over western access routes to Berlin—an action that would have threatened U.S. commitments to West Berlin and West Germany. Kennedy held firm, and Khrushchev backed down on the treaty. But a wall was erected between East and West Berlin to keep highly trained Germans from fleeing to the West.

By far the tensest overseas confrontation of the Kennedy years occurred with the Cuban Missile Crisis. In October 1962, U.S. aerial intelligence flights uncovered the fact that the Soviets were constructing offensive missile sites in Cuba. Kennedy recognized that the United States still had an advantage in missiles over the Soviets, but since the missiles could reach the United States so quickly, he had to react to such a deliberate provocation. Faced at first with two extreme options of either a full-scale invasion of Cuba or simply protesting—neither of which were acceptable—Kennedy showed real creativity. He decided that a naval and air quarantine on shipments of further missiles and other supplies to Cuba would force the confrontation at sea where the United States had a clear superiority. After making threatening noises, the Soviets relented, agreed to dismantle the missiles they had installed, and promised not to put any more there if the United States promised not to attack Cuba.

Both sides recognized the danger of nuclear war and backed off. Apparently sobered by the close call with nuclear war, both sides negotiated agreements to install a "hot line" or telegraph system for immediate communications between the countries and a treaty barring atmospheric testing of nuclear weapons. Elsewhere, the United States and Soviet Union continued to wage the cold war through other governments who acted as stand-ins for the two superpowers. In Southeast Asia, where Communist revolutionary forces were active, Kennedy gradually allowed the military to deploy 16,000 military "advisers" to Vietnam. Because the United States found its ally, the head of the government of South Vietnam, to be difficult, Kennedy authorized officials in Vietnam to cooperate with the 1963 overthrow of Ngo Dinh Diem, the South Vietnamese president, but this action only weakened the U.S. situation later.

Looking ahead to his 1964 presidential reelection campaign, Kennedy agreed to make a political trip to Texas in late November 1963. While traveling in a motorcade through Dallas, Texas, on November 22, he was shot in the head by an assassin and pronounced dead less than an hour later. When the newly sworn in President Johnson took office, he appointed a commission, headed by Chief Justice of the United States EARL WARREN, to investigate the assassination. While the commission decided that Kennedy had been assassinated by a single gunman, 24-year-old Lee Harvey Oswald, conspiracy theories have abounded over the years, especially since Oswald was himself killed by an unsavory character named Jack Ruby just a couple of days later.

Further Reading

Bernstein, Irving. *Promises Kept: John F. Kennedy's New Frontier.* New York: Oxford University Press, 1990.

Brogan, Hugh. *Kennedy.* London and New York: Longman, 1996.

Collier, Peter. *The Kennedys: An American Drama.* New York: Summit Books, 1984.

Gadney, Reg. *Kennedy.* New York: Holt, Rinehart & Winston, 1983.

Galloway, John. *The Kennedys and Vietnam.* New York: Facts On File, 1971.

Goodwin, Doris Kearns. *The Fitzgeralds and the Kennedys.* New York: St. Martin's Press, 1991.

Hersh, Seymour M. *The Dark Side of Camelot.* Boston: Little, Brown, 1997.

Kaiser, David E. *American Tragedy: Kennedy, Johnson, and the Origins of the Vietnam War.* Cambridge, Mass.: Belknap Press of Harvard University Press, 2000.

"Kennedy, John F." Available online. URL: http://www.whitehouse.gov/history/presidents/jk35.html. Downloaded on May 3, 2002.

Kennedy, John F. *Profiles in Courage.* New York: Harper, 1956.

Reeves, Richard. *President Kennedy: Profile of Power.* New York: Simon & Schuster, 1993.

Schlesinger, Arthur M. *A Thousand Days: John F. Kennedy in the White House.* Boston: Houghton Mifflin, 1965.

Schwab, Orrin. *Defending the Free World: John F. Kennedy, Lyndon Johnson, and the Vietnam War, 1961–1965.* Westport, Conn.: Praeger, 1998.

Sorensen, Theodore C. *Kennedy.* New York: Harper & Row, 1965.

Stern, Mark. *Calculating Visions: Kennedy, Johnson, and Civil Rights.* New Brunswick, N.J.: Rutgers University Press, 1992.

Wills, Garry. *The Kennedy Imprisonment: A Meditation on Power.* Boston: Back Bay Books/Little, Brown, 1994.

Wofford, Harris. *Of Kennedys and Kings: Making Sense of the Sixties.* Pittsburgh: University of Pittsburgh Press, 1992.

Kennedy, Joseph Patrick, Sr.

(1888–1969) *securities and exchange commissioner, diplomat*

Joseph Patrick Kennedy, Sr., rose from poverty to become one of the wealthiest U.S. citizens by the time he was 30. He used his wealth to advance his political career and that of his sons, one of whom, JOHN FITZGERALD KENNEDY, became the first Roman Catholic elected president of the United

States. Two other sons became U.S. senators. When he died, however, he knew that his efforts had led to tragic consequences for several members of his family.

Kennedy was born in Boston, Massachusetts, on September 6, 1888. The son of an Irish immigrant tavern owner, he learned to work hard by delivering newspapers, doing odd jobs for neighbors, and helping his family. He also did well enough in parochial school to be accepted at Harvard, where he was an academic success, but he was discriminated against socially because he was an Irish Catholic. He determined to become a millionaire by the time he was 30 and to show up the Boston "Blue Blood" Protestants who had scorned him.

In 1915, Kennedy married the daughter of the mayor of Boston and made the important connection between money and power by succeeding in both business and politics. He made a fortune in banking, shipbuilding, real estate, and by his entrepreneurship in the entirely new and untested field of motion-picture distribution. Beyond these legitimate businesses, it has been often alleged that Kennedy was involved in illegal liquor smuggling during Prohibition.

Kennedy supported ALFRED EMANUEL SMITH, an antiprohibition Catholic, for the Democratic presidential nomination in 1928 and shifted his allegiance to FRANKLIN DELANO ROOSEVELT in 1932, aiding both with significant campaign contributions. After Roosevelt was elected in 1932, he appointed Kennedy the first chairman of the Securities and Exchange Commission in 1934, where he did an excellent job in policing the securities industry. He followed that by doing a creditable job as the Roosevelt appointee as the chairman of the Federal Maritime Commission.

In 1938, Roosevelt granted him his highest honor to that time as the first Irish Catholic to serve as the U.S. ambassador to Great Britain. Given the long-standing animosity between the English and the Irish, this was an especially significant step for Roosevelt. Kennedy perceived this appointment as giving him international credentials that would assist him in his quest for the White House in 1940 when—he expected—Roosevelt would not run for a third term. In retrospect, it appears that Roosevelt intended to send

Kennedy to London so he would be out of the way during the 1940 presidential campaign because Roosevelt had already decided that he was going to seek an unprecedented third term as president.

As an Irish Catholic, Kennedy had no love for the British. Thus, his being an isolationist and calling for concessions to German leader Adolf Hitler (now seen as appeasement) was in character. His isolationism was also defended stateside as simply being a way to keep the United States out of any conflict that might develop between Britain and Germany. This position had some defenders in England itself, but the future wartime leaders, such as Churchill, were appalled. After war broke out between Germany and Britain in 1939, it was only a matter of time until Roosevelt would be forced to recall Kennedy, and he did so in 1940. Kennedy privately threatened to return from London and oppose Roosevelt for a third term. Roosevelt allegedly sent emissaries who pointed out that neither he nor any of his children would have much of a political future if Kennedy opposed a Rooseveltian third term. Kennedy then returned from London, went to the White House, and emerged to endorse Roosevelt's third-term bid.

Given his record of opposing steps to prepare for World War II because of his belief in a nonintervention policy, Kennedy's own hopes of becoming president ended when the Japanese bombed Pearl Harbor in December 1941. From that time forward, he focused on advancing the political success of his sons to the greatest degree, including making at least one of his sons president some day. Initially he centered his hopes on his eldest son and namesake, Joseph P. Kennedy, Jr., but young Joe died during a risky bombing raid on Europe in World War II.

Joseph Kennedy then shifted his attention to his second son, John F. Kennedy. He succeeded brilliantly in helping him become a member of the U.S. House of Representatives in 1946 and the U.S. Senate in 1952. The presidency was harder, of course. The younger Kennedy lost a shot at becoming vice president in 1956. However, the elder Kennedy decided that was a blessing in disguise because no Democrat was likely to win against incumbent President DWIGHT DAVID EISENHOWER in 1956, and John would only have been blamed for the defeat since he was a Catholic. Kennedy opened his coffers to guarantee John's nomination as the Democratic candidate for president in 1960. The general election was a still tougher matter, but in the end, the race was so close that Kennedy's financial aid probably was decisive for John F. Kennedy's narrow win.

Joe Kennedy succeeded in his goal of making his son president, but the road was strewn with tragedy. In addition to Joe, Jr., being killed in World War II, one of Kennedy's daughters went with the family to London, fell in love, married a British Protestant, was ostracized by her father, and then died tragically in an airplane crash in 1948. Another daughter, rightly or wrongly diagnosed as retarded, was subjected to a frontal lobotomy operation, which left her in far worse condition than before and confined her to a convent in Wisconsin for decades. These tragedies before his success in getting his son to the White House were far outstripped by the tragedies that followed.

Shortly after the Kennedy inaugural, Joseph Kennedy suffered a series of debilitating strokes that left him paralyzed, bedridden, and speechless. He nonetheless was told of the assassination of President John Kennedy. He could presumably console himself with the knowledge that the next oldest son, ROBERT FRANCIS KENNEDY, would be able to run for president someday, but those hopes ended when Robert was assassinated in 1968 while running for president. He could still wish that his youngest son, EDWARD MOORE KENNEDY, could pick up the torch and try for the ultimate political prize. But in July 1969 Edward was involved in and fled from the scene of a one-car accident on Chappaquidick Island, Massachusetts, in which a young woman was killed, thereby effectively ruining his chance to become president.

Joseph Kennedy died on November 18, 1969.

Further Reading

Beschloss, Michael R. *Kennedy and Roosevelt: The Uneasy Alliance.* New York: Perennial Library, 1987.

Bjerk, Roger Carl William. *Kennedy at the Court of St. James: The Diplomatic Career of Joseph P. Kennedy, 1938–1940.* Ann Arbor, Mich.: University Microfilms, 1974.

Collier, Peter. *The Kennedys: An American Drama.* New York: Summit Books, 1984.

De Bedts, Ralph F. *Ambassador Joseph Kennedy 1938–1940: An Anatomy of Appeasement.* New York: P. Lang, 1985.

Goodwin, Doris Kearns. *The Fitzgeralds and the Kennedys.* New York: St. Martin's Press, 1991.

Hersh, Seymour M. *The Dark Side of Camelot.* Boston: Little, Brown, 1997.

Kessler, Ronald. *The Sins of the Father: Joseph P. Kennedy and the Dynasty He Founded.* New York: Warner Books, 1996.

Koskoff, David E. *Joseph P. Kennedy: A Life and Times.* Englewood Cliffs, N.J.: Prentice-Hall, 1974.

Whalen, Richard J. *The Founding Father: The Story of Joseph P. Kennedy.* Washington, D.C.: Regnery Gateway, 1993.

Wofford, Harris. *Of Kennedys and Kings: Making Sense of the Sixties.* Pittsburgh: University of Pittsburgh Press, 1992.

Kennedy, Robert Francis
(1925–1968) *candidate for president, senator, attorney general, author*

Robert Francis Kennedy was born on November 20, 1925, in Brookline, Massachusetts. Raised in wealthy surroundings as the third son of JOSEPH PATRICK KENNEDY, SR., he attended Milton Academy and Harvard College, from which he graduated in 1948. After graduating from the University of Virginia Law School in 1951, he began his legal career in the Department of Justice's Brooklyn office.

After only brief service, he left to manage the campaign for his brother JOHN FITZGERALD KENNEDY in his successful 1952 race for the Senate. In 1953, Republican Senator JOSEPH RAYMOND MCCARTHY, a friend of Joseph P. Kennedy and chairman of the Senate Permanent Investigations Subcommittee, offered Robert Kennedy a position as council for the committee. His brother John advised Robert not to work for McCarthy, thinking that the association would damage Robert's reputation. Robert accepted the post, nonetheless, but resigned after several months because of McCarthy's ruthless tactics against suspected communists. He returned to the subcommittee later in 1954 as counsel to the Democratic minority and wrote the minority report condemning McCarthy's investigation of the army.

When the 1954 congressional elections gave the Democrats a majority in the Senate, Kennedy became the chief counsel, and the committee began to focus on white-collar crime in the federal government. Kennedy developed a reputation as a diligent hard-nosed prosecutor, especially after he became the lead counsel for the Senate Select Committee on Improper Activities in the Labor or Management Field in 1957 and began to focus on labor union racketeering. His pursuit of the Teamsters lead to convictions of two Teamster presidents in a row: Dave Beck and Jimmy Hoffa. The Labor Reform Act of 1959 also resulted from the Kennedy investigations.

Robert Kennedy managed John Kennedy's 1960 campaign for the presidency, and after the election his brother offered him the post of attorney general. While even he worried about charges that he was too young or too inexperienced, he accepted and was a good attorney general. He built an excellent staff, pushed for civil rights, and targeted organized crime and political corruption. During the 1962 Cuban Missile Crisis, Kennedy effectively argued against the premature use of excessive force and was a constructive voice in finding the ultimate compromise solution of a naval quarantine and direct negotiations that produced the peaceful resolution of the crisis. *Thirteen Days*, his personal memoir about the crisis, is still a classic of its kind.

After President Kennedy was assassinated in 1963, Kennedy stayed on as attorney general under the new President LYNDON BAINES JOHNSON. Robert Kennedy and Johnson were very different personalities and had serious disagreements on policy. Still, Kennedy hoped to be named Johnson's vice-presidential running mate in 1964, but Johnson disagreed with that idea. Kennedy then resigned, became a resident in New York, and ran for the U.S. Senate against the Republican incumbent senator, Kenneth Keating.

While Senator Kennedy had supported his brother's presidential authorization of American aid to the South Vietnamese government, he was

very concerned about Johnson's escalation of the Vietnam War. By 1968, Kennedy was advocating that a peaceful compromise with North Vietnam be found.

Kennedy wanted to run for president against Johnson, but he was afraid the incumbent Johnson was too strong until Senator EUGENE JOSEPH MCCARTHY challenged Johnson in the New Hampshire Democratic primary and almost won. On March 16, 1968, Kennedy announced he would be a candidate for president, and Johnson withdrew from the race on March 31. Johnson backed his vice president, HUBERT HORATIO HUMPHREY, who chose not to run in the primaries but to win on the basic support of Democratic Party regulars. Senator McCarthy kept many of his supporters, who opposed the Vietnam War and accused Kennedy of opportunism.

Kennedy won over McCarthy in the Indiana and Nebraska primaries, but he then lost to McCarthy in Oregon. That meant winning the June California primary was critical for both of them. Kennedy won California and then seemed able to win the Democratic Party nomination. After his California victory speech in a Los Angeles hotel, as he tried to leave the hotel by way of the kitchen, he was shot by Sirhan Sirhan, a Jordanian Arab who was angry about Kennedy's pro-Israeli views. Robert Kennedy died the next day, June 6, 1968.

Further Reading

Beran, Michael Knox. *The Last Patrician: Bobby Kennedy and the End of American Aristocracy.* New York: St. Martin's Press, 1998.

Dooley, Brian. *Robert Kennedy: The Final Years.* New York: St. Martin's Press, 1996.

Goldfarb, Ronald L. *Perfect Villains, Imperfect Heroes: Robert F. Kennedy's War against Organized Crime.* New York: Random, 1995.

Gorey, Hays. *Robert Kennedy: The Last Campaign.* New York: Harcourt Brace, 1993.

Hersh, Seymour M. *The Dark Side of Camelot.* Boston: Little, Brown, 1997.

Heymann, C. David. *RFK: A Candid Biography of Robert F. Kennedy.* New York: Dutton, 1998.

Hilty, James W. *Robert Kennedy: Brother Protector.* Philadelphia: Temple University Press, 1997.

Kennedy, Robert F. *The Pursuit of Justice*. New York: Harper & Row, 1964.

———. *Thirteen Days: A Memoir of the Cuban Missile Crisis*. New York: Norton, 1971.

———. *To Seek a Newer World*. Garden City, N.Y.: Doubleday, 1967.

Mahoney, Richard D. *Sons and Brothers: The Days of Jack and Bobby Kennedy*. New York: Arcade Publishers, 1999.

Mills, Judie. *Robert Kennedy*. Brookfield, Conn.: Millbrook Press, 1998.

Schlesinger, Arthur M. *Robert Kennedy and His Times*. Boston: Houghton Mifflin, 1978.

Schulman, Arlene. *Robert F. Kennedy: Promise for the Future*. New York: Facts On File, 1998.

Shesol, Jeff. *Mutual Contempt: Lyndon Johnson, Robert Kennedy, and the Feud that Defined a Decade*. New York: W. W. Norton, 1997.

Steel, Ronald. *In Love with Night: The American Romance with Robert Kennedy*. New York: Simon & Schuster, 2000.

Witcover, Jules. *85 Days: The Last Campaign of Robert Kennedy*. New York: Quill, 1988.

Wofford, Harris. *Of Kennedys and Kings: Making Sense of the Sixties*. Pittsburgh, Penn.: University of Pittsburgh Press, 1992.

Kirkpatrick, Jeane Duane Jordan
(1926–   ) *diplomat, author*

Jeane Duane Jordan Kirkpatrick was the first woman appointed as the U.S. ambassador to the United Nations.

Jeane Jordan was born on November 10, 1926, in Duncan, Oklahoma. She attended Barnard College and graduated in 1948 before moving on to Columbia University, from which she received her master's degree in political science in 1950. In 1955, she married Evron Kirkpatrick, a fellow political scientist who was destined to become the longtime executive director of the American Political Science Association. From 1955 to 1972, Kirkpatrick worked for various periods of time as a consultant and analyst at the U.S. Department of Defense. She joined the faculty of Georgetown University in 1967, and she completed her doctorate in political science from Columbia in 1968.

Throughout the 1970s, Kirkpatrick was active in Democratic politics working for former vice president and later Senator HUBERT HORATIO HUMPHREY during his unsuccessful race for the 1972 presidential nomination. In Humphrey's case, there was no doubt that while he was a liberal on many domestic policy matters, he was a fervent anticommunist on international affairs and foreign policy. Humphrey's and Kirkpatrick's foreign policy views were generally compatible. As late as the mid-1970s, she remained a Democrat and served on the 1976 Democratic National Convention Credentials Committee. However, her writing increasingly reflected her disillusionment with the Democratic Party in general and Democratic President JAMES EARL CARTER's foreign policy in particular.

Subscribing to the beliefs of a growing number of one-time liberals—now self-described "neoconservatives"—who felt liberalism had gone astray, Kirkpatrick was particularly critical of President Carter's decision to emphasize the human rights record in reorienting U.S. policy against the interests of various countries that had previously been regarded as U.S. allies. Kirkpatrick felt that pursuing the national interest of the United States was bound to conflict with the human rights records of various countries whose friendship was vitally important to real U.S. interests.

Kirkpatrick further criticized Carter's foreign policy, alleging that he attacked right-wing dictatorships allied to the United States while overlooking even worse abuses by Communist nations who engaged in far worse abuses while actively opposing U.S. national interests. Kirkpatrick often pushed the idea that authoritarian noncommunist regimes could be reformed but totalitarian communist regimes could not. RONALD WILSON REAGAN found this idea very attractive as a justification for the policy that he intended to follow of aiding noncommunist nations whose human rights policies might be open to criticism.

As a neoconservative, she joined the campaign of the Republican presidential candidate, Ronald Reagan, and became his 1980 foreign policy campaign adviser. After Reagan entered the White House, he named Kirkpatrick U.S. ambassador to the United Nations, where she staunchly defended Reagan's foreign policy. She served at the United Nations from early in 1981 until April 1, 1985.

In 1985, Kirkpatrick joined the Republican Party and resumed teaching at Georgetown. She continued to be an active commentator and participant in politics.

Further Reading

Gerson, Allan. *The Kirkpatrick Mission: Diplomacy Without Apology: America at the United Nations, 1981–1985.* New York: Free Press, 1991.

Harrison, Pat. *Jeane Kirkpatrick, Diplomat.* New York: Chelsea House, 1991.

Kirkpatrick, Jeane J. *Political Woman.* New York: Basic Books, 1974.

Kissinger, Henry Alfred

(1923–) *secretary of state, national security adviser, author*

Henry Alfred Kissinger was the central figure in determining foreign policy during the administrations of RICHARD MILHOUS NIXON and GERALD RUDOLPH FORD. He was awarded the 1973 Nobel Peace Prize for his efforts to negotiate an end to the Vietnam War.

Kissinger was born on May 27, 1923, in Fuerth, Germany. He immigrated with his family to the United States in 1938 and became a naturalized U.S. citizen in 1943. During World War II, Kissinger served in the U.S. Army Counter-Intelligence Corps. From 1946 to 1949, he was a captain in the Military Intelligence Reserve. After his active military service ended, he attended Harvard College, where he received his B.A. degree summa cum laude in 1950. He continued his graduate work at Harvard University, where he received his M.A. degree in 1952 and his Ph.D. in 1954.

In 1954, Kissinger joined the faculty of Harvard University both in political science and at the Center for International Affairs. At Harvard, he held a series of increasingly important academic positions from 1954 until 1969 when he entered full-time government service and took a leave of absence from Harvard. He was awarded the Woodrow Wilson Prize for the best book in the fields of government, politics, and international affairs in 1958. Kissinger has written several books and received a Guggenheim Fellowship from 1965 to 1966.

Although of conservative political views, he served as foreign policy adviser to liberal Republican NELSON ALDRICH ROCKEFELLER, the governor of New York. During the closing years of the administration of President DWIGHT DAVID EISENHOWER, Kissinger became increasingly critical of the foreign policy of the U.S. secretary of state, JOHN FOSTER DULLES, particularly his doctrine of "massive retaliation." In Kissinger's view, "massive retaliation" was not credible since the Soviet Union could always challenge the United States with conventional weapons at a level that was high enough to be dangerous but low enough not to justify the use of nuclear weapons. Kissinger called for the United States to increase its conventional war capabilities—a doctrine that became known as "flexible response."

During the administration of President JOHN FITZGERALD KENNEDY, Kissinger served as a consultant to the National Security Council from 1961 to 1962 when his view of the need for "flexible response" was increasingly adopted. After the assassination of President Kennedy, he served as a consultant to the Department of State from 1965 to 1968 during the administration of President LYNDON BAINES JOHNSON. Throughout the Kennedy and Johnson administrations, he served as a consultant to the U.S. Arms Control and Disarmament Agency.

As President Richard Nixon's assistant for national security affairs from 1969 to 1973, Kissinger became the dominant figure in the formulation of foreign policy. The position of assistant for national security affairs had become increasingly important during the Kennedy and Johnson administrations, but Kissinger carried it to new heights of prestige, as he became the principal spokesman for Nixon administration foreign policy. Nixon distrusted the career diplomats in the State Department and wanted foreign policy controlled from the White House. Kissinger was delighted to oblige. As the news media became aware of his importance, Kissinger actually became something of a media star, upstaging Secretary of State WILLIAM PIERCE ROGERS. By the start of Nixon's second term in 1973, Rogers resigned and Kissinger became secretary of state without relinquishing his position as assistant for national security affairs. Kissinger is the only person to have held both positions simultaneously.

Kissinger helped initiate the Strategic Arms Limitation Talks (SALT) with the Soviet Union in 1969 and arranged President Nixon's 1972 visit to the People's Republic of China. In 1973, he received the Nobel Peace Prize jointly with the North Vietnamese foreign minister for negotiating the cease-fire with North Vietnam. He also negotiated a cease-fire between Israel and Egypt and the disengagement of their troops after the 1973 Arab-Israeli War. Kissinger continued as secretary of state under Gerald Ford, who became president after Nixon's resignation in 1974.

Since 1977, Kissinger has lectured, served as a consultant on international affairs, and continued to write and publish books on foreign policy and international relations. He continued to be sought after as a commentator on international events for national television programs.

Further Reading

Bundy, William P. A Tangled Web: The Making of Foreign Policy in the Nixon Presidency. New York: Hill & Wang, 1998.

Cleva, Gregory D. Henry Kissinger and the American Approach to Foreign Policy. Cranbury, N.J.: Associated University Presses, 1989.

Ghanayem, Ishaq I. The Kissinger Legacy: American-Middle East Policy. New York: Praeger, 1984.

Isaacson, Walter. Kissinger. New York: Simon & Schuster, 1992.

Kimball, Jeffrey P. Nixon's Vietnam War. Lawrence: University Press of Kansas, 1998.

Kissinger, Henry. White House Years. Boston: Little, Brown, 1979.

———. A World Restored: Metternich, Castlereagh, and the Problems Of Peace, 1812–22. London: Weidenfeld & Nicolson, 1957.

———. Years of Renewal. New York: Simon & Schuster, 1999.

Schulzinger, Robert D. Henry Kissinger: Doctor of Diplomacy. New York: Columbia University Press, 1989.

Shawcross, William. Sideshow: Kissinger, Nixon, and the Destruction of Cambodia. New York: Simon & Schuster, 1987.

Strong, Robert A. Bureaucracy and Statesmanship: Henry Kissinger and the Making of American Foreign Policy. Lanham, Md.: University Press of America, 1986.

Thornton, Richard C. The Nixon-Kissinger Years: Reshaping America's Foreign Policy. New York: Paragon House, 1989.

Knox, Henry
(1750–1806) *secretary of war, Revolutionary War leader*

Henry Knox was only 26 years old when he became one of General GEORGE WASHINGTON's most trusted advisers during the Revolutionary War. Fighting at Washington's side throughout the war, he became the first secretary of war for the United States.

Knox was born in Boston, Massachusetts, on July 25, 1750, the son of Irish immigrants. Since his father died when he was young, Knox was forced to quit school to help his mother raise the family. He worked in, and later bought, a bookstore where he used his stock of books to read about military history, particularly in the management of artillery.

An early supporter of the Revolution, he became a member of the Boston Grenadier Corps in 1772 and fought at the Battle of Bunker Hill. He served under General Ward, who was in charge of the colonials around Boston. In 1775, when Washington arrived in Boston, he met Knox and realized Knox had a badly needed expertise in artillery. Knox suggested that Washington use the cannon from the recently captured Fort Ticonderoga. Washington gave Knox the rank of colonel and sent him to bring the 50 cannon from Ticonderoga to Boston, which Knox did using ox sleds over the mountains and through the forests in the winter. Knox's clever placement of these cannon allowed Washington to seize Dorchester Heights, which overlooked Boston, and force the British to flee from Boston to Canada on March 17, 1776.

After Washington captured Boston, Knox went to Connecticut and Rhode Island to organize their defense, while Washington marched his forces to defend New York where Knox joined him later. The American forces were so badly outnumbered that they were forced to retreat repeatedly until they crossed the Delaware River at Trenton, New Jersey, on December 8, 1776. Since the Americans had seized all the boats along the river, the British could not follow. Despite badly reduced numbers of poorly clad and armed troops, Washington and Knox came up with the risky, but ultimately brilliant, Christmas Eve crossing of the Delaware River followed by the early Christmas morning surprise attack on the Hessian troops at Trenton. Washington then promoted Knox to brigadier general.

Knox was involved in fighting at the battles of both Brandywine and Germantown. At Valley Forge, Knox was in charge of erecting the forts to guard Washington's winter camp from British attack. Knox assisted the German military figure Baron von Steuben in his drilling of the troops, particularly the artillery. Knox also fought at the Battle of Monmouth, New Jersey, and placed the artillery in the strategic positions the Americans used in their siege of the British at Yorktown. Knox was promoted to major general after the surrender of Cornwallis on October 19, 1781. In 1782, Knox was stationed at West Point and remained there until the British left New York. In 1783, he and other officers founded the Society of the Cincinnati, an organization made up of American officers who had fought during the Revolutionary War.

The Congress of the Articles of Confederation elected Knox secretary of war in 1785. After the adoption of the U.S. Constitution and the establishment of the new government in 1789, he was appointed secretary of war in President Washington's new cabinet. Knox found most of his service as secretary of war was devoted to dealing with growing unrest in the Indian Territory on the western frontier of the United States. In 1790, Knox proposed that a national militia (or something similar to the National Guard) be organized, but Congress rejected the plan. Knox became increasingly dissatisfied by the inattention of the Congress to military preparedness, and he resigned in 1794. TIMOTHY PICKERING, who had served as Washington's postmaster general, took his place.

In 1796, Washington wanted to appoint Knox the U.S. ambassador to St. Croix, but Knox refused. Knox retired to Thomaston, Maine, in 1796, to an area that he called "Montpelier." He was engaged in various types of businesses such as brick making, cattle raising, and shipbuilding when he died unexpectedly on October 25, 1806.

Further Reading

Brooks, Noah. *Henry Knox: A Soldier of the Revolution.* New York: Da Capo, 1974.

Callahan, North. *Henry Knox: General Washington's General.* New York: Rinehart, 1958.

Drake, Francis S. *Life and Correspondence of Henry Knox: Major General in the American Revolutionary Army.* Boston: S. G. Drake, 1873.

Nelson, Paul David. "Knox, Henry." Available on-line. Discovery Channel School, original content provided by World Book Online. URL: http://www.discoveryschool.com/homeworkhelp/worldbook/atozhistory/k/303240.html. Updated November 3, 2001.

Peck, Robert Newton. *The King's Iron.* Boston: Little, Brown, 1977.

L

La Follette, Robert Marion
(1855–1925) *candidate for president, senator, representative, governor*

Robert Marion La Follette was a prominent Wisconsin governor and U.S. senator representing the progressive wing of the Republican Party until he became convinced that the Republican Party was a hopeless vehicle for positive change and helped found the Progressive Party. He was the Progressive Party candidate for president in 1924, and he was identified with the progressive set of programs known as the "Wisconsin Idea."

La Follette was born on June 14, 1855, in Primrose, Wisconsin. He graduated from the University of Wisconsin in 1879 and was admitted to the Wisconsin bar in 1880. He began his law practice in Madison, Wisconsin, by being elected the Dane County district attorney in 1880 and being reelected in 1882. In 1884, he was elected to the U.S. House of Representatives and served three terms as a traditionally conservative Republican.

In 1890, he was defeated for reelection and began a vicious feud with Philetus Sawyer, a conservative Republican state leader and U.S. senator. Breaking with party regulars, La Follette formulated the "Wisconsin Idea," a reform package calling for a direct primary law, tax reform legislation, railroad rate regulations, and other measures. Because he appealed directly to the people and not the party leaders, he lost races for the Republican gubernatorial nomination in both 1896 and 1898. When he finally won the race for governor of Wis-

consin in 1900, he pushed through a large number of these reforms. In 1906, La Follette won a seat in the U.S. Senate, which he held until his death.

Since his reform program was clearly contrary to the conservative program of President WILLIAM HOWARD TAFT, La Follette founded the National Progressive Republican League in 1911 with the objective of winning the 1912 Republican presidential nomination. Since this required taking a virtually sure renomination away from Taft in 1912, a more powerful figure was required for success. When THEODORE ROOSEVELT announced he would run for the Republican presidential nomination, most of La Follette's supporters switched to Roosevelt.

Taft won the Republican nomination, but Roosevelt ran on the Progressive Party ticket (or Bull Moose Party as Roosevelt called it) and split the vote. The result was THOMAS WOODROW WILSON being elected president. In the U.S. Senate, La Follette usually supported President Wilson's domestic reform measures, advocating passage of the Seventeenth Amendment to the U.S. Constitution in 1913, sponsoring the act that elevated and regulated maritime employment conditions in 1915, and supporting federal railroad rate regulation.

La Follette strongly opposed the Wilson administration's foreign policy, which he increasingly saw as supporting Britain and leading the United States into an unnecessary European war. La Follette led the battle against the arming of merchant ships and voted against the U.S. declaration of war against Germany. These votes did not hurt him in Wiscon-

Robert La Follette, a progressive reformer as Wisconsin's governor and senator, helped found the Progressive Party and ran for president in 1924. *(Library of Congress)*

From 1919 to 1925, he was a force to be reckoned with in the Senate. As an isolationist, he effectively opposed the League of Nations and the World Court and fought against the U.S. postwar deflation policy. In 1924, he ran for president as the Progressive Party nominee and won more than 5 million votes but carried only his home state of Wisconsin. The strain of the campaign sapped La Follette's strength, and he died the following summer on June 18, 1925.

Further Reading

Doan, Edward N. *The La Follettes and the Wisconsin Idea.* New York: Rinehart, 1969.

Greenbaum, Fred. *Robert Marion La Follette.* Boston: Twayne, 1975.

La Follette, Robert M. *La Follette's Autobiography: A Personal Narrative of Political Experiences.* Madison: University of Wisconsin Press, 1960.

Maxwell, Robert S. *La Follette and the Rise of the Progressives in Wisconsin.* New York: Russell & Russell, 1973.

Thelen, David P. *Robert M. La Follette and the Insurgent Spirit.* Boston: Little, Brown, 1976.

Weisberger, Bernard A. *The La Follettes of Wisconsin: Love and Politics in Progressive America.* Madison: University of Wisconsin Press, 1994.

La Guardia, Fiorello Henry

(1882–1947) *representative, mayor*

Fiorello Henry La Guardia played a unique position in American politics as a New York congressman and later mayor of New York City. Always a maverick, La Guardia—whose first name Fiorello, means "Little Flower" in Italian—was a progressive politician who ran as a Republican in local politics to avoid the corruption of the Democratic Party's Tammany Hall. But he supported the Democratic presidential campaigns of FRANKLIN DELANO ROOSEVELT to combat what he perceived to be the insensitivity of the national Republican Party to the common man.

La Guardia was born in New York City on December 11, 1882, into an immigrant family with a varied background. His Roman Catholic father had immigrated to the United States from Italy; his

sin where his large number of German-descended constituents did not show much enthusiasm for fighting Germany. However, La Follette's opposition rested on his fear that the banks and munitions manufacturers were leading the country into war on the side of the British and French in order to protect the money they lent those countries to buy armaments. After war was declared, La Follette supported wartime legislation but always strove to make sure the financial burden fell on the rich.

Jewish mother had come from Trieste (then part of Austria). (Later in his life Fiorello La Guardia became a practicing Episcopalian.) The family traveled around various army outposts in the Arizona territory where his father was employed as a bandmaster. After his father died, La Guardia moved with his mother to Hungary in 1898. He was employed by the American consular service in Budapest, Trieste, and Fiume from age 19 to 23, before returning to the United States in 1906.

La Guardia worked as an interpreter on Ellis Island for the U.S. Immigration Service while studying law at night at New York University. Admitted to the New York bar in 1910, he quickly moved into politics. He was defeated in a race for the U.S. House of Representatives in 1914, but he was elected to Congress as a progressive Republican in 1916, making him the only Republican elected on the Lower East Side of Manhattan. During his first term in Congress, he joined in the successful fight for the liberalization of the House rules. Before the end of his first term, the United States entered World War I and La Guardia joined the U.S. Army's Air Corps, where his language skills quickly gave him a commanding position on the Italian-Austrian front.

After the war, La Guardia was president of the New York City board of aldermen in 1920 and 1921. In 1922, La Guardia was again elected to Congress, where he opposed Prohibition and supported women's right to vote, limits on child labor, and a variety of progressive domestic reforms. During the Republican domination of the 1920s political scene, La Guardia was a lonely voice crying in the wilderness. After the onset of the Great Depression, he was more successful. In 1932, he cosponsored with GEORGE WILLIAM NORRIS the Norris-LaGuardia Act, which restricted the courts' power to ban strikes.

With the backing of Samuel Seabury, the American jurist who headed investigations into New York politics during 1930 to 1931 that resulted in Mayor James Walker's resignation in 1932, LaGuardia successfully ran for mayor of New York City on the Fusion ticket in 1933. He was reelected New York's mayor for three consecutive terms. Over the next 12 years, he developed a reputation as an honest, progressive, and efficient ad-

ministrator. A strong supporter of Franklin Roosevelt's New Deal, La Guardia expanded the city's social-welfare services and reduced political corruption. He advanced a vast program of reform that modernized city government, beautified New York City, adopted the new 1938 city charter, introduced slum clearance projects, provided low-cost housing, and improved health and sanitary conditions.

In 1945, La Guardia decided against seeking reelection. The following year he became director general of the UN Relief and Rehabilitation Administration.

La Guardia died on September 20, 1947. His autobiography was published posthumously in 1948.

Further Reading

Bayor, Ronald H. *Fiorello La Guardia: Ethnicity and Reform*. Arlington Heights, Ill.: Harlan Davidson, 1993.

Elliott, Lawrence. *Little Flower: The Life and Times of Fiorello La Guardia*. New York: Morrow, 1983.

Heckscher, August. *When La Guardia Was Mayor: New York's Legendary Years*. New York: Norton, 1978.

Kamen, Gloria. *Fiorello: His Honor, The Little Flower*. New York: Athenaeum, 1981.

Kessner, Thomas. *Fiorello H. La Guardia and the Making of Modern New York*. New York: McGraw-Hill, 1989.

La Guardia, Fiorello H. *The Making of an Insurgent: An Autobiography, 1882–1919*. 1948; reprint, Westport, Conn.: Greenwood Press, 1985.

Manners, William. *Patience and Fortitude: Fiorello La Guardia*. New York: Harcourt Brace Jovanovich, 1976.

Moses, Robert. *La Guardia*. New York: Simon & Schuster, 1957.

Zinn, Howard. *La Guardia in Congress*. Westport, Conn.: Greenwood Press, 1972.

Landon, Alfred Mossman
(1887–1987) *candidate for president, governor*

Living to be more than 100 years of age, Alfred Mossman Landon not only served as Kansas governor and ran for president of the United States, but he also lived long enough to see his daughter, NANCY LANDON KASSEBAUM, elected to the U.S. Senate in 1979. A century of observation of American politics made him a colorful and humorous commentator on national affairs.

Born in West Middlesex, Pennsylvania, on September 9, 1887, but reared in rural Kansas, Landon received a law degree from the University of Kansas in 1908. Never practicing law, he worked in banking for about four years and established his own oil exploration and production company. When the United States entered World War I, Landon joined the army and worked in a chemical warfare division.

Although a Republican, Landon was a progressive, so he supported former President THEODORE ROOSEVELT in 1912 as the Progressive Party presidential candidate. A decade later, he became the private secretary for the Kansas governor. Six years later in 1928, he became the Kansas Republican Party central committee chairman. He was elected governor of Kansas in 1932 and was reelected in 1934. Because he cut government spending and reduced taxes, he was often referred to as the "Kansas Coolidge."

In 1934, Landon was the only Republican governor who managed to win reelection when the Democratic Party won its famous nationwide landslide in Congress. Thus, the Republicans decided he was their only hope when they faced President FRANKLIN DELANO ROOSEVELT in his reelection bid in 1936. Everyone, including Landon, knew it was hopeless. Landon managed to carry only Maine and Vermont, and he failed to win even his own home state of Kansas.

Landon remained an active Republican and operated his oil company and three radio stations in Kansas after his retirement from politics. One of his most well-known remarks was made to a reporter: "I'm an oilman who never made his million, a lawyer who never had a case, and politician who only carried Maine and Vermont." He died on October 12, 1987.

Further Reading

"Alfred M. Landon" in *The Presidency A to Z: Second Edition,* edited by Michael T. Nelson. Washington, D.C.: Congressional Quarterly Press, 1998.

Fowler, Richard B. *Alfred M. Landon: Of Deeds Not Deficits.* Boston: L. C. Page & Company, 1936.

McCoy, Donald R. *Landon of Kansas.* Lincoln: University of Nebraska Press, 1979.

Thornton, Willis. *The Life of Alfred M. Landon.* New York: Grosset & Dunlap, 1936.

White, William Allen. *What It's All About: Being a Reporter's Story of the Early Campaign of 1936.* New York: Macmillan, 1936.

Lansing, Robert

(1864–1928) *secretary of state, diplomat*

Robert Lansing served as the U.S. secretary of state before, during, and after World War I and tried with limited success to moderate the international idealism of President THOMAS WOODROW WILSON with pragmatic considerations.

Lansing was born on October 17, 1864, in Watertown, New York. He attended Amherst College, graduated in 1886, and was admitted to the New York bar in 1889. He married Eleanor Foster, the daughter of John W. Foster, the former secretary of state under President Benjamin Harrison and thereby gained access to important diplomatic circles, which advanced his career as an international lawyer. After 1892, he frequently represented the United States in international legal tribunals, including the settlement of the Alaska Boundary in the Bering Sea. Wilson named him State Department counselor in 1914. Although WILLIAM JENNINGS BRYAN was secretary of state then, Lansing wrote nearly all the state papers issued in Bryan's name. Bryan then resigned in protest when he perceived Wilson's drift toward entry into World War I.

After Bryan's resignation in 1915, Wilson appointed Lansing secretary of state. Although Wilson was less idealistic than Bryan, he was more idealistic than the disciplined pragmatist Lansing. Lansing's overriding goal was the protection of the national interest of the United States. In the context of World War I, it was clear that Lansing did not believe U.S. interests would be served by a German victory that would give Germany and Austria-Hungary domination of the European continent. Still, he did not want U.S. entry on the side of the Anglo-French alliance until U.S. domestic opinion was sufficiently aroused against the Germans to guarantee that the U.S. citizenry would support the war to its successful conclusion. Lansing felt it was imperative that Wilson be reelected in 1916. Although he lent his support to Wilson's initiative to achieve "peace without victory" through a negotiated settlement, he did not hold out much hope for its success, but saw it as a ploy to buy time to achieve his essential objectives. He also successfully urged the United States to hinder German influence in Latin America. He persuaded Wilson to recognize the Carranza government in Mexico despite its lack of democratic inclinations. He supported the U.S. military occupation of Haiti and the U.S. purchase of the Danish West Indies (the Virgin Islands) from Denmark.

To these ends, Lansing sensed that Germany's unrestricted submarine warfare would ultimately provide the reason for the United States to enter the war on the side of the Allies. When a German submarine sunk an unarmed French steamboat, Lansing obtained German assurances that they would not attack unarmed merchant ships without warning. Since the Germans badly needed the unrestricted submarine warfare to break the British blockade on their ports, Lansing was confident that this German pledge would ultimately be broken providing a reason to sever diplomatic relations, which is exactly what happened. Wilson then tried to obtain congressional approval to arm U.S. merchantmen, but the legislation ran into a Senate filibuster. Lansing sidestepped that situation by finding legal authority for the arming of the ships already in existence. When the Germans sunk three U.S. ships in March 1917, Lansing gave the final push for Wilson to declare war. During the war, Lansing remained an active diplomat negotiating an agreement recognizing Japan's interests in China and establishing a nonrecognition policy against the new Bolshevik (or Communist) government in Russia late in the war.

Unfortunately, Lansing was relatively less effective during the war. It is not uncommon for secretaries of state to become less important than military leaders once war breaks out. In this case, President Wilson expanded his own practice of making foreign policy in secret with his trusted friend, EDWARD MANDELL HOUSE. Nonetheless, Lansing served faithfully before, during, and after the war despite his reservations about Wilson's so-called idealism in international relations. Lansing attended the Versailles Peace Conference as a delegate. Concerned about the rise of communism in Russia, he urged conciliation with Germany and opposed the unreasonably high reparations ultimately imposed. He feared the League of Nations would take on the unacceptable characteristics of a new world government, but he continued to support the league and the treaty. When the league portion of the treaty ran into trouble, Lansing urged compromise on Wilson, but to no avail.

After Wilson suffered his stroke and became incapacitated, Wilson grew far more dependent on his wife, EDITH GALT WILSON. She controlled access to Wilson on grounds of protecting his health and attempted to run the government without any interference. Because of the drift in government policy, Lansing felt it was imperative to hold cabinet meetings even if Wilson did not call them. Acting on his own authority, he called the cabinet into session. Edith Wilson then—presumably acting on her husband's instruction, but possibly on her own—informed Lansing that he was fired in February 1920. The real cause may have been that Lansing finally expressed his personal skepticism over the role Wilson had devised for the United States in the proposed League of Nations in a way that became public. This would have been sufficient in itself to provoke Wilson to terminate him.

Lansing resumed his distinguished international legal career and wrote extensively until his death on October 30, 1928.

Further Reading

Beers, Burton Floyd. *Vain Endeavor: Robert Lansing's Attempts to End the American-Japanese Rivalry.* Durham, N.C.: Duke University Press, 1962.

Knock, Thomas J. *To End All Wars: Woodrow Wilson and the Quest for a New World Order.* Princeton, N.J.: Princeton University Press, 1995.

Link, Arthur Stanley. *The Diplomacy of World Power: The United States; 1889–1920.* London: Edward Arnold, 1970.

———. *The Higher Realism of Woodrow Wilson.* Nashville, Tenn.: Vanderbilt University Press, 1971.

———*The Impact of World War I.* New York: Harper, 1969.

———. *The Papers of Woodrow Wilson.* Princeton, N.J.: Princeton University Press, 1966.

———. *Wilson: The Diplomatist.* Chicago: Quadrangle Books, 1965.

———. *Woodrow Wilson: Revolution, War, and Peace.* Arlington Heights, Ill.: AHM Publishing Corporation, 1979.

Ninkovich, Frank A. *The Wilsonian Century: U.S. Foreign Policy Since 1900.* Chicago: University of Chicago Press, 1999.

Schild, Georg. *Between Ideology and Realpolitik: Woodrow Wilson and the Russian Revolution, 1917–1921.* Westport, Conn.: Greenwood Press, 1995.

Schulte Nordholt, J. W. *Woodrow Wilson: A Life for World Peace.* Berkeley: University of California Press, 1991.

Smith, Daniel M. *Robert Lansing and American Neutrality, 1914–1917.* Berkeley: University of California Press, 1958.

Lee, Richard Henry
(1732–1794) *senator, Revolutionary War leader, author*

With PATRICK HENRY and SAMUEL ADAMS, Richard Henry Lee was one of the early generation of agitators for the independence of the American colonies from Great Britain. He is most famous for his speech on June 7, 1776, in which he introduced a motion that the colonies become independent. This measure began the process that resulted in the Declaration of Independence.

Lee was born on January 31, 1732, in Westmoreland County, Virginia, into one of the most prominent Virginia families. In 1758, shortly after his election to the Virginia House of Burgesses, he spoke out against the slave trade. At this time, he clearly joined Patrick Henry and Samuel Adams in outspoken opposition to the 1765 Stamp Act. Equally outraged by the British-imposed Townshend Acts (which replaced the Stamp Act), Lee then started the neocolonial committees of correspondence in 1773.

He served in the Continental Congresses until ill health forced his resignation in 1779. He returned to the Congress of the Confederation under the Articles of Confederation where he served as president in 1783–84. He joined Patrick Henry in opposing the ratification of the U.S. Constitution in Virginia, principally because of the lack of a Bill of Rights. After the U.S. Constitution was ratified, he supported it and even served in the first U.S. Senate where he worked diligently for the passage of the Bill of Rights. Illness forced him to resign in 1794, and he died later that year on June 19.

Further Reading
Chitwood, Oliver P. *Richard Henry Lee: Statesman of the Revolution.* Morgantown: West Virginia University Library, 1967.

Hendrick, B. J. *The Lees of Virginia: A Biography of a Family,* Boston: Little Brown, 1935.

Lee, Richard Henry. *Memoir of the Life of Richard Henry Lee.* Philadelphia: H. C. Carey and I. Lea, 1825.

Mayer, Henry. *A Son of Thunder: Patrick Henry and the American Republic.* Charlottesville: University Press of Virginia, 1991.

Nagel, Paul C. *The Lees of Virginia: Seven Generations in an American Family.* New York: Oxford University Press, 1990.

Vaughan, David J. *Give Me Liberty: The Uncompromising Statesmanship of Patrick Henry.* Nashville, Tenn: Cumberland House Publishers, 1997.

Lincoln, Abraham
(1809–1865) *president, representative*

Abraham Lincoln was the 16th president of the United States in numerical order of service, but he is consistently ranked at the top of every list of great presidents, sharing the honor only with GEORGE WASHINGTON. Lincoln became president at a critical moment when the Union was in greatest danger of division from the Civil War. He prosecuted the war and was assassinated by a gunshot just days after the main Confederate Army surrendered. The longer-term implications of the war had yet to be resolved, but he must be credited with beginning the process of the emancipation of the slaves. That he did not accomplish more is the result of the shortness of his tenure rather than any personal reservations about the evil of slavery and its necessary end.

Abraham Lincoln was born in the most modest of circumstances on Sunday, February 12, 1809, in a log cabin near Hodgenville, Kentucky. His entire childhood was spent on the very edge of poverty as his family made repeated fresh starts on the western frontier. Abraham was the son of Thomas Lincoln, a carpenter and farmer, who was not a shiftless loafer as sometimes portrayed, but rather an honest, conscientious man who was trusted by his neighbors.

Thomas Lincoln had practically no education and could barely write his name. His first wife, Nancy Hanks Lincoln, who may have been of illegitimate birth, was from a still more modest background and could not write her name at all. Both of Lincoln's parents belonged to a Baptist congregation, which had broken off from another church because the Lincoln group refused to condone slavery. The family moved to Indiana in 1816, and two years later Nancy Hanks Lincoln died from a disease contracted by drinking the milk of a cow that had eaten a poisonous plant.

Abraham Lincoln, consistently ranked as one of the greatest presidents, led the nation during the Civil War. *(Library of Congress)*

Thomas Lincoln remarried in 1819, and Abraham adored his new stepmother, Sarah, who brought three children of her own and a respect for learning into the household. It was Sarah who saw to it that Abraham got enough schooling to read, write, and do simple math. Opportunities for education or cultural enrichment were meager, but Abraham made the most of them by frequently borrowing books from neighbors. Among the books Lincoln acknowledged he read during this period were *Robinson Crusoe, Pilgrim's Progress,* Aesop's *Fables,* William Grimshaw's *History of the United States,* and Mason Weems's *Life of Washington.* His family probably owned a Bible but nothing more. Lincoln's frequent use of scriptural quotations in his speeches and writings indicates he must have studied the Bible thoroughly.

In 1828, Abraham Lincoln made a flatboat trip to New Orleans. Two years later, the Lincoln family moved west to Illinois where they attempted to live in a couple of locations before settling in New Salem, Illinois, where Lincoln lived until 1837. While in New Salem, he worked at several jobs including operating a store, surveying, and serving as postmaster. He impressed the residents with his character and earned the nickname "Honest Abe" because he repaid the debts from a failed business, although it took him several years. When an Indian uprising, known as the Black Hawk War, broke out in April 1832, Lincoln volunteered and was elected captain of his volunteer company and reenlisted when his brief service was over.

Lincoln made an unsuccessful run for the Illinois legislature as an anti-Jackson Whig in 1832, the year in which ANDREW JACKSON won reelection to the presidency by a landslide. Lincoln then ran and won a seat in the state legislature four times in a row in 1834, 1836, 1838, and 1840. While in the legislature, he studied law on the side and became a lawyer in 1836. Lincoln was twice nominated as his party's candidate for House Speaker. When defeated by the perennial Democratic majority, he served as the Whig Party floor leader. His greatest achievement in the Illinois legislature, where he was a supporter of conservative business and corporate interests, was to bring about the transfer of the state capital from Vandalia to Springfield.

In 1846, Lincoln, under a trading or sharing relationship with two other Whigs, received the Whig nomination for a predominately Whig district in the U.S. House of Representatives and won the election. While in Congress, he opposed the spread of slavery and the Mexican War since any territory gained seemed likely to be opened to slavery, but he supported wartime expenditures. The war was popular in his district, and, instead of running for reelection, he chose to campaign heavily throughout New England for the Whig presidential nominee, ZACHARY TAYLOR, hoping for a significant patronage appointment if Taylor was elected. Taylor won, but the desired appointment was not forthcoming. Lincoln returned home disillusioned and resumed his law practice with vigor.

Lincoln was reactivated in politics by the passage of the 1854 Kansas-Nebraska Act. This act repealed a crucial section of the 1820 Missouri Compromise that had prohibited slavery in the land gained by the Louisiana Purchase that was north of the line of 36 degrees 30 minutes. The act substituted a provision that the people in the territories of Kansas and Nebraska could admit or exclude slavery as they chose under a concept of "popular sovereignty," which was advanced by the Illinois Democratic senator STEPHEN ARNOLD DOUGLAS. Lincoln took to the stump in the antislavery cause and challenged James Shields, who was the second Illinois Democratic senator and a Douglas follower. While Lincoln was more popular with the people of Illinois, the election was not decided by the people but by the Illinois legislature, since state legislatures named all U.S. senators prior to 1913. At this time, the Illinois legislature was dominated by Democrats.

So many Democrats were incensed at the Kansas-Nebraska Act that the antislavery Democrats could combine with the antislavery Whigs to defeat Shields. The Whigs backed Lincoln, but the antislavery (anti-Shields) Democrats supported Lyman Trumbull. Lincoln commanded more legislative votes than Trumbull, but Trumbull's supporters had pledged to never vote for a Whig. Since following this pledge would lead to Shields winning, Lincoln told his own supporters to vote for Trumbull and gave him the seat. Lincoln's grace and courage became well known. Two years later, the Whig party

split into pro-slavery and antislavery sections, and Lincoln joined the Republican Party, where he received some consideration as a vice presidential nominee to run with the Republican presidential nominee, JOHN CHARLES FRÉMONT.

After the 1856 campaign, President JAMES BUCHANAN privately pressed the U.S. Supreme Court to settle the slavery question once and for all by a favorable pro-slavery ruling in the Dred Scott decision. The Court obliged with a pro-slavery decision so strong that, instead of quieting the issue, it aroused it to a fever pitch. On June 16, 1858, Lincoln opposed the decision with his famous declaration: "'A house divided against itself cannot stand.' I believe this government cannot endure permanently *half slave* and *half free.*"

Illinois's Senator Douglas was running for reelection in 1858, and the antislavery forces recognized Lincoln was the strongest man to oppose him. Lincoln challenged Douglas to the series of seven now-famous joint debates. Douglas refused to take a position on the morality of slavery and offered his "popular sovereignty" doctrine as the solution to the problem. Lincoln condemned slavery as immoral and urged a return to the principles of the Founding Fathers, which tolerated slavery where it existed but looked to its ultimate extinction by preventing its spread. The Republicans won 4,000 more votes collectively in the election than the Democrats, but an outdated districting arrangement of the legislature permitted Douglas to win reelection to the Senate.

The debate generated national attention, and Lincoln was increasingly urged to run for president in 1860. Lincoln demurred but began speaking outside Illinois. At Cooper Union in New York City, he delivered his famous speech against the spread of slavery, evoking such enthusiasm that he finally agreed to run for president. He then won the Illinois Republican convention's decision to vote as a unit for him at the Republican National Convention.

Although the acknowledged Republican frontrunner, WILLIAM HENRY SEWARD, appeared to be ahead, Seward and other candidates all had various liabilities of some sort, and Lincoln's managers maneuvered to make him the second choice when others faltered. Seward led on the first ballot, but Lincoln got the required majority on the third ballot.

In 1860, the Democratic Party split, nominating Douglas in the North and JOHN CABELL BRECKINRIDGE in the South. A fourth candidate, JOHN BELL, candidate of the Constitutional Union Party, further split the vote, which made Lincoln an easy winner. Lincoln outpolled Douglas in the popular vote by almost 500,000 votes and the others trailed badly. In the Electoral College, Lincoln won 180 electors, Breckinridge won 72 electors, Bell won 39 electors, and Douglas won only 12 because of the way the popular vote divided among the states.

When Lincoln was elected, many southern states feared Lincoln would end slavery—despite his protestations to the contrary—and seven of them seceded from the Union. Lincoln faced great cross pressures from his supporters (some of whom were total abolitionists) as well as from the seven seceding states, four other southern states that threatened to secede, and another four pro-Union slave states that bordered the North and might secede if Lincoln made a wrong move.

Most federal forts in the South had fallen into southern hands as the result of President Buchanan's inept response to secession, but Fort Sumter still had a Union garrison. Lincoln was determined to uphold the Union by not yielding the fort, but he was equally determined not to fire the first shot of the threatened hostilities. Sumter was running out of food, and Lincoln sent an unarmed supply ship to outfit them again. Had Lincoln established the principle of supplying the Union forts without a fight, at least a faint hope would have remained that negotiations might succeed without war. The Confederates, favoring war over negotiations, opened fire. Sumter fell but Lincoln managed to hold onto the support of the four northern-most slave states as well as half of the state of Virginia (which became the new state of West Virginia).

Both sides thought they would win the war easily, but the war became the bloodiest in U.S. history, when both battle deaths and deaths from battle-related illnesses are combined. Throughout the war, Lincoln faced a hostile Congress, so he made as many decisions as possible under his assertion of his Constitutional power as commander in chief. Lincoln was not the greatest administrator at the start, but after he replaced the corrupt secretary of war SIMON CAMERON with EDWIN MCMASTERS STANTON, sufficient efficiency was achieved.

Lincoln suffered from a surplus of politically connected but inept or timid generals, and the war dragged on until he finally found General ULYSSES S. GRANT in late 1863. Lincoln was forced repeatedly to defend his policy of not abolishing slavery on the grounds that he needed to hang on to border state support. Finally, after a narrow victory at Antietam, he promulgated the preliminary Emancipation Proclamation, with the definitive Emancipation Proclamation taking effect four months later on January 1, 1863. Even this was limited to freeing slaves only in the areas of the Confederacy not under Union control.

While the war was paramount, Lincoln supported other domestic legislation, including a higher tariff, the first transcontinental railroad, the Homestead Act that allowed people in the East to obtain western land, and the National Banking Act that established a national currency and banking network. Lincoln's international policy was aimed at preventing foreign intervention in the Civil War, and it succeeded through the efforts of Secretary of State William Seward and, most especially, those of the U.S. ambassador to Great Britain, CHARLES FRANCIS ADAMS.

After Grant defeated the Confederates at Vicksburg and Chattanooga, it was becoming clear that the South would be slowly ground down. Still, Lincoln had to fear defeat at the hands of the Democrats who had regained control of Congress in 1862 and were now promoting former General GEORGE BRINTON MCCLELLAN for president. Lincoln was so concerned about the Democratic threat that he made changes in his cabinet and replaced his vice presidential running mate with ANDREW JOHNSON, a southerner and the only senator from a seceding state who did not abandon the Union. Only because Grant was able to deliver still more victories in the fall of 1864 was Lincoln reelected.

Lincoln carried every state except Kentucky, Delaware, and New Jersey. He polled more than 2.2 million popular votes to McClellan's 1.8 million and won an electoral vote victory of 212–21; however, the voters in the seceded states, the bastion of the Democratic Party, did not vote in the election. On April 9, 1865, Confederate General Robert E. Lee surrendered to Grant at Appomattox and the war was essentially over. On April 14, 1865, the Lincolns attended a play at Ford's Theater in Washington, D.C. During the play, an actor and Confederate sympathizer named John Wilkes Booth went to the president's box at the theater and shot Lincoln in the back of his head. Lincoln died the following morning and was the first president to be assassinated.

Further Reading

Basler, Roy P., ed. *The Collected Works of Abraham Lincoln, 9 Volumes.* New Brunswick, N.J.: Rutgers University Press, 1953–1955.

Catton, Bruce. *The American Heritage New History of the Civil War.* New York: Viking, 1996.

Donald, David H. *Liberty and Union.* Lexington, Mass.: Heath, 1978.

———. *Lincoln.* New York: Simon & Schuster, 1995.

"Lincoln, Abraham." Available online. URL: http://www.whitehouse.gov/history/presidents/al16.html. Downloaded October 20, 2001.

Luthin, Reinhard H. *The Real Abraham Lincoln: A Complete One Volume History of His Life and Times.* Englewood Cliffs, N.J.: Prentice-Hall, 1960.

Oates, Stephen B. *Abraham Lincoln: The Man behind the Myths.* New York: Harper & Row, 1984.

Quarles, Benjamin. *Lincoln and the Negro.* New York: Oxford University Press, 1962.

Randall, James Garfield. *Lincoln the President.* New York: Da Capo Press, 1997.

Sandburg, Carl. *Abraham Lincoln: The Prairie Years and the War Years: One Volume Edition.* New York: Harcourt Brace Jovanovich, 1974; also in 6 volumes, New York: Harcourt Brace, 1925–1939.

Thomas, Benjamin Platt. *Abraham Lincoln.* New York: Knopf, 1952.

Lodge, Henry Cabot, Jr.
(1902–1985) *candidate for vice president, diplomat, senator, author*

Henry Cabot Lodge, Jr., grandson and namesake of former U.S. Senator Henry Lodge and descendant of a famous Massachusetts family, was a U.S. senator in his own right, was the U.S. ambassador to the United Nations, and was a candidate for vice president, running with Republican presidential nominee RICHARD MILHOUS NIXON in their narrow 1960 loss.

Lodge was born on July 5, 1902, in Nahant, Massachusetts, and was educated in elite private schools. He graduated from Harvard College in 1924. For seven years, he was a reporter for the *Boston Evening Herald* and the *New York Herald Tribune.* In 1932, he was elected to the lower house of the Massachusetts legislature where he served until his election to the U.S. Senate in 1936. He was reelected in 1942 but left the Senate to serve in the U.S. Army during World War II. Reelected to the Senate in 1946, he was defeated by JOHN FITZGERALD KENNEDY in 1952.

President DWIGHT DAVID EISENHOWER appointed Lodge the U.S. ambassador to the United Nations in 1953, and he served until 1960, gaining national exposure because of his repeated television presentations in that position. Nixon selected him to be his 1960 vice presidential running mate, but the Nixon-Lodge ticket lost to that of Kennedy and LYNDON BAINES JOHNSON. President Kennedy selected Lodge to be the U.S. ambassador to South Vietnam. After Kennedy's assassination, Lodge continued in that post under President Johnson until he was appointed the U.S. ambassador to West Germany at the end of the Johnson administration. President Nixon then named Lodge to head the American delegation to negotiate the end of the Vietnam War, but he left those stalemated talks in 1970 to become the U.S. special envoy to the Vatican, where he worked intermittently until 1977. He died on February 27, 1985.

Further Reading

Blair, Anne E. *Lodge in Vietnam: A Patriot Abroad.* New Haven, Conn.: Yale University Press, 1995.

Lodge, Henry Cabot. *As It Was: An Inside View of Politics and Power in the '50s and '60s.* New York: Norton, 1976.

———. *The Storm Has Many Eyes.* New York: Norton, 1973.

Miller, William J. *Henry Cabot Lodge.* New York: Heineman, 1967.

Zeiger, Henry A. *The Remarkable Henry Cabot Lodge.* New York: Popular Library, 1964.

London, Meyer
(1871–1926) *representative*

Meyer London was one of the few members of the Socialist Labor Party ever elected to Congress. He addressed the interests of his working-class constituents and helped pave the way for the progressive enactments of the New Deal.

Born in the Russian-Polish province of Suwalki on December 29, 1871, London immigrated to the United States in 1891, settled in New York City, studied law, and was admitted to the New York bar in 1898. He became a lawyer for the garment unions in New York City and was one of their principal spokespersons. In 1910, he supported the major garment workers union's strike. Two years later, he aided the 12-week-long fur workers union strike.

The New York Socialist Party nominated London for Congress in 1910 and 1912. Although he was unsuccessful in both races, he polled better than 30 percent of the vote. Finally, uniting all the garment workers behind his campaign, he was able to win in 1914 and was reelected in 1916. In Congress, he was a loyal member of the Socialist Party, supported further unrestricted immigration, and advanced the cause of unions. He also sponsored legislation prohibiting child labor, establishing a minimum wage, and creating unemployment and old age insurance.

Along with other Socialists, London was opposed to the U.S. entry into World War I. He consistently worked against the wartime draft as well as espionage and sedition laws. Although not a strict pacifist, he believed the United States should serve only as a mediator between the warring parties in Europe. Because of his moderation on the war question, both his supporters and opponents criticized him for failing to take stronger stands on one side or the other of the issue. He failed to be reelected in 1918 but returned to the House of Representatives in 1920.

After the 1920 U.S. Census, the two major parties saw an opportunity to redraw the district lines so London could not win. Having conspired on the new district lines, they also joined together to support a rival candidate, and London was defeated in 1922. After that, he retired from public life and concentrated on his career in law. He was fatally injured in an automobile accident and died on June 26, 1926.

Further Reading
Aronowitz, Stanley. "Eugene Victor Debs" in *The Encyclopedia of Third Parties in America,* edited by Immanuel Ness and James Ciment. Armonk, N.Y.: M. E. Sharpe, Inc., 2000.

Ciment, James. "Norman Thomas" in *The Encyclopedia of Third Parties in America,* edited by Immanuel Ness and James Ciment. Armonk, N.Y.: M. E. Sharpe, Inc., 2000.

Howe, Irving. *World of Our Fathers: The Immigrant Jews of New York, 1881 to the Present.* London: Routledge & Kegan Paul, 1976.

Meyer, Gerald. "Vito Marcantonio" in *The Encyclopedia of Third Parties in America,* edited by Immanuel Ness and James Ciment. Armonk, N.Y.: M. E. Sharpe, Inc., 2000.

Miller, Penny M. "Victor Leopold Berger" in *The Encyclopedia of Third Parties in America,* edited by Immanuel Ness and James Ciment. Armonk, N.Y.: M. E. Sharpe, Inc., 2000.

Rogoff, Hillel. *An East Side Epic: The Life and Work of Meyer London.* New York: Vanguard Press, 1930.

Long, Huey Pierce
("The Kingfish")
(1893–1935) *senator, governor*

Huey Pierce Long was a flamboyant, populistic leader who built a formidable political organization in Louisiana, was elected to the U.S. Senate, and announced he was running for president. During the economic hard times of the Great Depression, "The Kingfish," as he was called, built one of the most impressive national populistic movements. Called the "Share-the-Wealth" program, it threatened the reelection of FRANKLIN DELANO ROOSEVELT until Long was assassinated by a relative of a political opponent.

Long was born on August 30, 1893, on a farm near Winnfield, Louisiana. He dropped out of high school in his senior year after a fight with the principal and became a very prosperous traveling salesman for four years. He studied law at Tulane University for only one year and was admitted to the bar in 1915.

He started practicing law in Winnfield and Shreveport, but he quickly went into politics by winning a seat on the State Railroad Commission in 1918. When it was reconfigured as the Public Service Commission, he was elected to it in 1921 and reelected in 1924. He served as its chairman as well as the attorney for Louisiana in public utility litigation.

Long lost a race for governor narrowly in 1924, but he won in 1928 while promising better roads and free school textbooks. When the state legislature blocked his economic and social reform program, he used patronage and bribery to control it. Long was responsible for the building of roads and bridges, expanding state-owned hospitals, extending schools into remote rural areas, and heavily taxing large businesses, particularly the oil companies, to pay for these projects.

In 1929, Long was impeached by a conservative dominated House on charges of bribery and gross misconduct, but he was not convicted because he persuaded 15 senators, enough to acquit, to sign a round-robin letter that they would not vote to convict. Long was so angered by the fight that he decided he had to build an impregnable machine to defeat his enemies.

In 1930, Long was in the middle of his four-year term as governor when he won a race for the U.S. Senate. His plans to move to Washington were stymied when he began feuding with Lieutenant Governor Paul Cyr and feared letting him take over as governor. Cyr then tried to force Long out as governor by declaring that Long stopped being governor as soon as he was elected to the U.S. Senate. Cyr even went to a justice of the peace to take the oath as governor. Long responded that Cyr was trying to pull off a coup d'état, and called out the National Guard, the state police, and the highway patrol to encircle the governor's mansion and office to prevent the takeover.

Then Long hit on a brilliant stroke: He insisted he was still governor since he had not taken an oath as U.S. senator, but Cyr had ceased to be lieutenant governor when he took the oath as governor. Then Alvin O. King, a Long supporter and the president of the Louisiana Senate, took over as the lieutenant governor under the state's succes-

Huey Long, legendary populist Senator from Louisiana, was assassinated just as he started his presidential campaign. *(Library of Congress)*

sion law. In a special election, King was safely elected governor and followed Long's directives on running the state. Then Long took his seat in the Senate in January 1932. In 1934, Long ordered King to begin reorganizing the state, a process that virtually abolished local government and gave Long, through Governor King, the power to appoint all state and local employees.

As senator, Long at first supported Roosevelt's New Deal, but he soon became one of Roosevelt's sharpest critics, believing that the New Deal was not attacking the fundamental need for the redistribution of wealth. As a populist leader and presidential aspirant, Long steadily gained a national following with his national economic "Share-the-Wealth" reform program, which proposed a guaranteed family annual income of $2,000 to $3,000 and a $5,000 homestead allowance for every family. These incomes would be paid for by heavy estate and income taxes that would prevent any family from owning a fortune of more than $5 million or enjoying an annual income of more than $1 million. In 1934, he proclaimed that this program would make "Every Man a King." Conservative critics called him a fascist, and this charge has been frequently leveled at him ever since, but it is more accurate to see Long as a populist descendant of General James B. Weaver, a former Civil War general turned political maverick who led a third party called the Populists in the late 1800s, with some 20th-century socialist programs added in the mix. In August 1935, Long announced he would run for president, but he was assassinated less than a month later on Sunday, September 8, 1935.

The assassination has always aroused more than the usual conspiracy theories. Long was visiting the capitol in Baton Rouge, Louisiana, to attend a special session of the state legislature, which was going to redistrict one of Long's opponents out of his legislative seat. That opponent's son-in-law, Dr. Carl Weiss, a medical doctor in Baton Rouge, greeted Long in a hallway and shot him once in the abdomen with a .22-caliber pistol. Long's bodyguards immediately killed Weiss, riddling his body with approximately 30 bullets. Long was taken to a nearby hospital, and two of the finest surgeons from New Orleans were called to operate. They were delayed by traffic, so a local doctor performed the surgery and made a very elementary mistake that eventually caused Long's death from a very small-caliber bullet wound. These irregularities have always raised the specter that others besides Weiss were really responsible.

Long's political organization continued for decades after his death. His wife served out his senatorial term, while his brother, Earl, served three terms as governor, and his son, Russell, was a member of the U.S. Senate from 1948 until his retirement in 1986.

Further Reading

Boulard, Garry. *Huey Long Invades New Orleans: The Siege of a City, 1934–36.* Gretna, La.: Pelican, 1998.

Brinkley, Alan. *Voices of Protest: Huey Long, Father Coughlin, and the Great Depression.* New York: Knopf, 1982.

Cortner, Richard C. *The Kingfish and the Constitution: Huey Long, The First Amendment, and the Emergence of Modern Press Freedom in America.* Westport, Conn.: Greenwood Press, 1996.

Dethloff, Henry C. *Huey P. Long: Southern Demagogue or American Democrat?* Lafayette: University of Southwestern Louisiana, 1976.

Graham, Hugh Davis. *Huey Long.* Englewood Cliffs, N.J.: Prentice-Hall, 1970.

Hair, William Ivy. *The Kingfish and His Realm: The Life and Times of Huey P. Long.* Baton Rouge: Louisiana State University Press, 1996.

Jeansonne, Glen. *Messiah of the Masses: Huey P. Long and the Great Depression.* New York: HarperCollins, 1993.

LeVert, Suzanne. *Huey Long: The Kingfish of Louisiana.* New York: Facts On File, 1995.

Long, Huey Pierce. *Every Man a King: The Autobiography of Huey P. Long.* New York: Da Capo Press (reprint), 1996.

Sindler, Allan P. *Huey Long's Louisiana: State Politics, 1920–1952.* Baltimore, Md.: Johns Hopkins Press, 1956.

Swing, Raymond. *Forerunners of American Fascism.* Freeport, N.Y.: Books for Libraries Press, 1969.

Williams, T. Harry. *Huey Long.* New York: Knopf, 1969.

Longworth, Nicholas
(1869–1931) *Speaker of the House, representative*

Nicholas Longworth was a long-term Republican congressman who served six years as Speaker of the U.S. House of Representatives and was widely recognized as a master of congressional rules. One of the U.S. House of Representatives office buildings was named after him.

Longworth was born on November 5, 1869, in Cincinnati, Ohio, into a prominent, wealthy family. He attended Harvard College and graduated in 1891. He returned to Cincinnati where he graduated from the University of Cincinnati Law School (then called the Law School of Cincinnati College) and joined the Ohio bar in 1894. Practicing in Cincinnati, he soon entered politics, winning a seat on the Cincinnati Board of Education and the Ohio House of Representatives, both in 1898. With the support of George B. Cox, the local Republican Party leader, Longworth was elected to the Ohio senate in 1900 and to the U.S. House of Representatives in 1902.

In 1906, he married Alice Lee Roosevelt, President THEODORE ROOSEVELT's daughter, in a White House wedding. He was reelected to Congress consistently until 1912. In that year, Longworth, a generally conservative Republican, committed himself to supporting President WILLIAM HOWARD TAFT for reelection before he knew that his father-in-law, Theodore Roosevelt, would be running for president again. Fulfilling his pledge to Taft, he still remained on good terms with Roosevelt, although the split in the Republican Party meant that he was personally defeated for reelection to the House in the general election. Out of office for two years, he was easily elected to his old seat in 1915 and continuously reelected until his death.

In 1923, Longworth became the Republican majority floor leader and was elevated to Speaker of the House in 1925. As Speaker, he restored to the office some of the power lost when Republican mavericks had stripped much of the power from former Speaker JOSEPH G. CANNON. As a conservative, he demoted 13 progressive Republicans who had bolted the Republican Party in the election. While Longworth (an old associate of Cannon) followed Cannon's pattern in depending on a handful of trusted lieutenants to run the House, he was not arbitrary in his rulings as the more dictatorial Cannon had been. He served as Speaker until his death on April 9, 1931.

Further Reading

Chambrun, Clara Longworth. *The Making of Nicholas Longworth: Annals of an American Family.* Freeport, N.Y.: Books for Libraries Press, 1971.

Longworth, Alice Roosevelt. *Crowded Hours.* New York: Arno Press, 1980.

"Longworth, Nicholas" in *Congress A to Z: Third Edition,* edited by David R. Tarr and Ann O'Connor. Washington, D.C.: Congressional Quarterly, 1999.

Lott, Chester Trent

(1941–) *senator, representative*

Chester Trent Lott, a U.S. senator from Mississippi, became the Republican Senate majority leader in June 1996 when the senators of his party chose him to be their leader after ROBERT JOSEPH DOLE resigned the Senate to run for president. Lott has been Republican Senate whip (or assistant leader) since January 1995. In 1981, Lott became the first Deep South Republican to serve as a whip in the House of Representative under Republican Minority Leader Bob Michels.

Lott, who uses his middle name Trent almost exclusively, was born on October 9, 1941, in Grenada, Mississippi. He graduated from the University of Mississippi with a bachelor's degree in 1963 and continued on in the University of Mississippi Law School, where he received his law degree in 1967. Never really practicing law, he worked as an assistant to William M. Colmer, a Democratic member of the U.S. House of Representatives, from 1968 to 1972. Lott switched from the Democratic Party to the Republican Party in 1972 and ran for Congress, being elected in the year President RICHARD MILHOUS NIXON swept the South in his landslide reelection bid.

Named to the House Judiciary Committee, Lott did not find sufficient evidence of wrongdoing on the part of Nixon to justify his impeachment in 1973 and he voted against impeaching him. (He did, however, vote for the impeachment of WILLIAM JEFFERSON CLINTON in 1999.) Lott was elected the Republican House whip in 1981.

Lott was first elected to the U.S. Senate in 1988, was elected Republican Party whip in 1995, and was elevated to Republican Senate majority leader in 1996. He lost the position as majority leader and became minority leader in 2001 when the Democrats obtained a one-vote majority. This change occurred when a moderate Republican senator decided to become an independent in protest of the heavy-handed treatment of Republican moderates by Lott and other Republican conservatives. So extreme is Lott's conservatism and so aggressive is his leadership style that some have blamed him for alienating moderate Republicans and ultimately losing the Republican majority in the U.S. Senate. Having lost the senate majority leader position to the Democrat's THOMAS DASCHLE, Lott has been less public but continues to argue a strongly conservative position. Despite his clearly conservative position, Lott has shown some willingness to compromise with

Democrats to pass legislation reforming welfare, improving water quality, and allowing workers to transfer health insurance when unemployed or changing jobs. Lott lost a major battle when he failed to secure passage of a proposed constitutional amendment that would have required the federal government to pass a balanced federal budget.

His occasional moderation aside, Lott has been the most conservative Senate Majority Leader since the 1920s.

Further Reading

Crowley, Michael. "Tom Daschle's Struggle to Save the Dems," *The New Republic* (March 26, 2001).

Kaiser, Robert G. "The Smiling Majority: Tom Daschle Is at the Top of the Political Game," *The Washington Post* (June 6, 2001): C1.

Kinsley, Michael. "Trent Lott's Stages of Grief." Tuesday, June 5, 2001. Available on-line. URL: http://www.slate.msn.com/default.aspx?id=109382. Downloaded January 23, 2002.

Loomis, Burdett A. *Esteemed Colleagues: Civility and Deliberation in the U.S. Senate*. Washington, D.C.: Brookings Institution, 2000.

"Lott, Trent" in *Congress A to Z: Third Edition*, edited by David R. Tarr and Ann O'Connor. Washington, D.C.: Congressional Quarterly, 1999.

"Trent Lott." Available on-line. URL: http://www.slate.msn.com/Readme01-06-04/Readme.asp. Downloaded January 23, 2002.

M

Madison, James
(1751–1836) *president, secretary of state, representative, Revolutionary War leader*

James Madison served eight years each as the fourth president of the United States, as secretary of state under Thomas Jefferson, and as a member of the U.S. House of Representatives during its first years of operation. He served well in each of these offices, but it was his work from the summer of 1787 to the summer of 1789 in drafting, interpreting, and supporting the ratification of the U.S. Constitution that earned him the reputation as the "Father of the Constitution." Another great achievement was drafting the Bill of Rights, the first 10 amendments to the U.S. Constitution.

Madison was born at the home of his maternal grandparents in Port Conway, Virginia, on March 5, 1751 (or March 16, 1751, on the calendar used today). Soon after his birth, his mother took him to their house in Orange County, Virginia. This 5,000-acre tobacco and grain plantation was worked by about 100 slaves. As a child, Madison received most of his education from tutors until he entered Princeton University (then called the College of New Jersey). Graduating in 1771, he continued studying with the college president, John Witherspoon, for another six months. He thought about becoming either a clergyman or an attorney but did not enter either career.

In 1774, at age 23, Madison began his political career as a member of the Orange County Committee of Safety. By 1776, he was elected to the

Virginia revolutionary assembly that declared Virginia independent from Britain and drafted a new state constitution. Here he met THOMAS JEFFERSON and aided him in strengthening the usual promise of religious toleration with a pledge of a further "liberty of conscience." In 1777, Madison was defeated for reelection to the assembly but was elected to the governor's council where he worked for Virginia governors PATRICK HENRY and Thomas Jefferson.

In 1780, Madison was the youngest person ever elected to the Continental Congress, where he served until 1784, earning the reputation as the most effective representative in the assembly. Viewing the Continental Congress's weakness, Madison became a leader of "nationalists" who favored a stronger central government. In 1783, he returned to Virginia and served in the legislature, pushing for continued expansion of religious freedom and certain other reforms urged by then Governor Jefferson.

Although only 36 years of age, Madison represented Virginia in the 1787 Constitutional Convention. He drafted the Virginia (or Randolph) Plan, giving taxing and law-enforcement powers to the national government, strengthening the executive branch, providing a popularly elected House of Representatives, a longer term Senate, and an independent federal judiciary. This became the fundamental outline of the final document. Implicit in the Constitution was Madison's clear belief in the separation of powers and the system of checks and balances. He also kept a more complete copy of the debates than anyone else, and his notes, published posthumously, remain the standard source of the convention proceedings.

After the convention, he joined ALEXANDER HAMILTON and JOHN JAY in writing *The Federalist Papers*, a series of newspaper articles that supported the Constitution's ratification in the tough New York fight. These papers are still regarded as the best explanation of the U.S. constitutional system's theory. Madison's ratification efforts angered those Virginians who opposed a stronger central government, and they acted together in the Virginia legislature to block his election to the first U.S. Senate. Early in 1789, he managed to win election to the U.S. House of Representatives over JAMES MONROE, who joined Patrick Henry and GEORGE MASON in opposing ratification.

Madison's stature grew in the first Congress. He prepared the legislation for creating the Departments of State, Treasury, and War. He drafted most of the first tariff act and, most significantly, the Bill of Rights, which are the first 10 amendments to the Constitution. Madison was so close to President GEORGE WASHINGTON that he drafted most of his first inaugural address and fought for Washington's policies during the first two years. However, Madison sided with Jefferson in reaction to the pro-commercial bias they saw in the financial plans of Treasury Secretary Alexander Hamilton. As Washington increasingly favored Hamilton, Jefferson and Madison found themselves in opposition. Wanting to perpetuate the United States as an agrarian republic, they finally organized the opposition to Hamilton's policies that coalesced into the Democratic Republican Party, now known simply as the Democratic Party.

While in the first Congress that met in Philadelphia, Madison met and married Dolley Payne Todd, a young widow, in 1794. Increasingly, he was shut out of national politics. Hamilton had Washington's ear, and the two men jointly shifted U.S. foreign policy against revolutionary France and toward Great Britain. Hamilton's international policy was reflected in the instructions he sent with John Jay to London that came back as Jay's Treaty, which was ratified in the spring of 1796. While this may have been the best anyone could have done, it outraged the anti-British, pro-French sympathizers, such as Jefferson, Madison, and Monroe.

The Jefferson supporters attempted to reverse national policy by supporting Jefferson for president over JOHN ADAMS in 1796. They came close but failed by three votes, with Jefferson becoming vice president under the prevailing Electoral College system. Madison then returned to Virginia and began to make improvements on his estate. In 1798, the Federalists passed the Alien and Sedition Acts, which outraged Madison and the other anti-Federalists. Madison wrote the Virginia Resolutions of 1798, urging that the states take joint action in declaring these laws unconstitutional. He was elected to the Virginia legislature in 1799 and 1800, and he used this position as a forum to defend the states against the encroachments of Federalist policies. He worked especially hard for Jefferson's election as president in 1800.

Upon his election, Jefferson appointed Madison secretary of state. In this capacity, Madison urged Jefferson to consider the purchase of New Orleans. This set in motion the negotiations that led, under James Monroe's actions in Paris, to the acquisition of the entire Louisiana Purchase. Madison also supported the armed naval action against the Barbary pirates from 1801 and 1805. Although this action and the ensuing treaty with Tripoli were popular, the practical effect was short-lived, and the pirates remained a problem.

The major dilemma the United States faced during the administrations of Jefferson and Madison was the spillover from the Napoleonic Wars. Britain and France were locked in a deadly conflict so severe that they trampled on the neutral rights of sovereign nations, such as the United States, which lacked the military and economic might to defend themselves. Both countries abused U.S. shipping on the high seas, but the more powerful British naval power seemed to pose the greater threat. Jefferson and Secretary of State Madison attempted to cope with the abuses by economic power, such as supporting passage in 1807 of the Embargo Act, which prohibited trade with all European countries. This damaged the United States more than either Britain or France. After two years, that act was replaced by the Non-Intercourse Act, which opened trade with everyone except Britain and France. The United States hoped this law would force the British and French to recognize American neutral maritime rights, but U.S. merchants continued trading with both countries, and both countries continued to abuse American shipping.

The Democratic Republicans were still popular in the United States and the Federalists were disunited, so Jefferson was able to push successfully for Madison to follow him into the White House (overcoming a bid by James Monroe for the honor). Madison retained Jefferson's vice president from his second term (former New York governor GEORGE CLINTON), and this team defeated Federalist nominee CHARLES COTESWORTH PINCKNEY of South Carolina by 122 electoral votes to 47.

The Democratic Republican coalition was beginning to fray. Madison was forced to accept cabinet members in the State, War, and Navy Departments who proved to be unwise in the long run. Facing the continued problems from Britain and France, Madison tried a new tack in 1810. He supported a law that allowed him to reopen trade with either country if it would promise to honor U.S. neutral rights on the high seas. France publicly indicated that it would comply, and Madison reopened trade with France. However, Napoleon secretly ordered his navy to continue harassing U.S. shipping. Madison recognized that there was pressure for the United States to go to war, but he also knew that the nation was unprepared. He was unable to push through necessary defense measures and was reluctant to violate his republican principles by assuming emergency powers.

In November 1811, WILLIAM HENRY HARRISON and his troops engaged the Shawnee at Tippecanoe. The United States had grown impatient with the abuses of the British on the high seas and now felt threatened by the British action in stirring up the Indians in the western areas of the country. Madison worked with a newly elected group of congressmen that included HENRY CLAY and JOHN CALDWELL CALHOUN—known as the "War Hawks"—to somewhat strengthen the national defense. While still inadequate for full defense, Madison realized that a stronger stand with Britain was necessary, especially as he faced reelection. In June 1812, after another futile attempt to negotiate with the British, Madison asked for, and got, a declaration of war. The War of 1812 had begun.

James Madison, the fourth president of the United States, is so famous for his work creating the U.S. Constitution that he is known as the "Father of the Constitution." *(Library of Congress)*

Madison and the War Hawks hoped for an easy victory since the British were preoccupied with Napoleon, but the war went badly for U.S. forces in Canada. One army surrendered at Detroit, another was defeated on the Niagara River, and a third conducted a disgraceful retreat from Montreal. In 1813, the naval war went a bit better with the USS *Constitution* defeating the *Guerriere* at sea and Commodore Perry defeating the British on Lake Erie.

By 1814, the U.S. forces were greatly improved, but they then faced the more experienced, battle-hardened troops of the British, who were released from duty in Europe as the result of Napoleon's defeat. The British attacked and burned Washington, D.C., but were stopped at Fort McHenry in Baltimore. A British drive south from Canada was stopped on Lake Champlain. Neither side could claim any clear victory, but, unbeknownst to the United States, the British leadership was tired of war and thought the U.S. conflict was not worth the price. Negotiations went forward in late 1814 in Ghent, but the fighting continued in the United States. Even though the treaty had been signed, the United States finally won a major victory over the British on January 8, 1815, in New Orleans where ANDREW JACKSON's ragtag band routed the experienced British regulars, inflicting 2,000 casualties while receiving only a few dozen in return.

In February 1815, the news of the victory and the treaty arrived at about the same time in Washington and ushered in a period of rejoicing. It was not a moment too soon for Madison. He had won reelection (over the curious campaign of DEWITT CLINTON) in 1812 on the strength of his past accomplishments and the immature hopes for victory early in the war. Most of 1813 and 1814 had seen humiliation for the United States, including the burning of the Capitol and White House in Washington. Now came a great victory, and Madison basked in the glory of success. He also changed his mind on the issue of a weak national government, now coming out in favor of the Second National Bank, some federally financed internal improvements, and a moderate tariff to protect infant industries. The end of the war and these new measures led to an economic boom. Madison finished his term on a high note. Madison had appointed James Monroe his secretary of state and later secretary of war. After serving faithfully, Monroe was elected Madison's successor.

Madison retired to his estate at Montpelier, helped Jefferson found the University of Virginia, readied his papers for posthumous publication, and advised his successor on foreign policy. He died on June 28, 1836.

Further Reading

Banning, Lance. *The Sacred Fire of Liberty: James Madison and the Founding of the Federal Republic.* Ithaca, N.Y.: Cornell University Press, 1995.

Brant, Irving. *The Fourth President: A Life of James Madison.* Norwalk, Conn.: Easton Press, 1986.

Brugger, Robert J. "Madison, James." Available on-line. Discovery Channel School, original content provided by World Book Online. URL: http://www.discoveryschool.com/homeworkhelp/worldbook/atozhistory/m/337320.html. Downloaded November 11, 2001.

Donovan, Frank R. *Mr. Madison's Constitution: The Story behind the Constitutional Convention.* New York: Dodd, Mead, 1965.

Goldwin, Robert A. *From Parchment to Power: How James Madison Used the Bill of Rights to Save the Constitution.* Washington, D.C.: AEI Press, 1997.

Ketcham, Ralph. *James Madison: A Biography.* Charlottesville: University Press of Virginia, 1990.

Koch, Adrienne. *Jefferson and Madison: The Great Collaboration.* New York: Oxford University Press, 1970.

"Madison, James." Available online. URL: http://www.whitehouse.gov/history/presidents/jm4.html. Downloaded Oct 20, 2001.

Madison, James. *Writings.* New York: Literary Classics of the United States, 1999.

McCoy, Drew R. *The Last of the Fathers: James Madison and the Republican Legacy.* New York: Cambridge University Press, 1991.

Moore, Virginia. *The Madisons.* New York: McGraw-Hill, 1979.

Morris, Richard B. *Witnesses at the Creation: Hamilton, Madison, Jay, and the Constitution.* New York: New American Library, 1989.

Owsley, Frank L. *Filibusters and Expansionists: Jeffersonian Manifest Destiny, 1800–1821.* Tuscaloosa: University of Alabama Press, 1997.

Rakove, Jack N. *James Madison and the Creation of the American Republic.* New York: HarperCollins. 1990.

Rutland, Robert. *James Madison: The Founding Father.* Columbia: University of Missouri Press, 1997.

———. *The Presidency of James Madison.* Lawrence: University Press of Kansas, 1990.

Smith, Joseph Burkholder. *The Plot to Steal Florida: James Madison's Phony War.* New York: Arbor House, 1983.

Stagg, J. C. A. *Mr. Madison's War: Politics, Diplomacy, and Warfare in the Early American Republic, 1783–1830.* Princeton, N.J.: Princeton University Press, 1983.

Mansfield, Michael Joseph
(Mike Mansfield)
(1903–2001) *diplomat, senator, representative*

Michael Joseph "Mike" Mansfield served as Senate majority leader longer than anyone else. Retiring from the Senate at age 74, he was asked by Democratic president JAMES EARL CARTER to serve as U.S. ambassador to Japan. Republican RONALD WILSON REAGAN asked him to continue in that post until had he served longer in that post than any other individual. His chief opponent in the Senate, Republican minority leader Senator Hugh D. Scott, Jr., once said of him, "He's the most decent man I've ever met in public life."

Mansfield was born in New York City on March 16, 1903. His parents were Irish immigrants and worked as domestics in New York hotels. His mother died when he was a toddler, so he was sent to live with relatives in Great Falls, Montana, and there he started working at an early age in the store they owned. He was very unhappy and ran away several times.

At age 14, he lied about his age and enlisted in the U.S. Navy shortly before the United States entered World War I. After serving in the Atlantic during the war, he served in the army for another year immediately after the war. At age 17, he enlisted for two years in the Marine Corps. The Marines sent him to the Philippines, Japan, and China, stimulating a lifelong interest in the Orient. When he returned to Butte, Montana, in 1922, Mansfield worked as a copper mine "mucker," clearing away debris in underground shafts with a pick and shovel.

His future wife, Maureen Hayes, a schoolteacher he met in Butte, persuaded him to enroll in the Montana School of Mines. Since he had not finished the eighth grade, he registered as a special student and took high school and college courses simultaneously. After a brief period as a mining engineer, he entered the University of Montana in Missoula where he studied history, including Asian history. Graduating with a master's degree, he began teaching there. He was a popular professor of Far Eastern and Latin American affairs, and he built up a network of former students, who helped him in his political career.

Mansfield lost his first contest for the U.S. House of Representatives in 1940, but he bounced back in 1942, winning a close race for the First Congressional District seat vacated by JEANNETTE RANKIN, who could not win because she had voted against the declaration of war in World War II. In the House, Mansfield compiled a liberal voting record, supporting labor unions, price controls, a higher minimum wage, the Marshall Plan (for European reconstruction after World War II), and aid to Turkey and Greece. He opposed the House Un-American Activities Committee and the Twenty-second Amendment, which limited presidents to two terms in office.

In 1952, Mansfield ran against Republican Senator Zales N. Ecton, who sought to win reelection by enlisting the support of arch anti-Communist Senator JOSEPH RAYMOND McCARTHY. McCarthy accused Mansfield of being "either stupid or a dupe" on the domestic Communist issue, but in spite of this, Mansfield defeated Ecton, thereby bucking the national Republican trend as presidential candidate DWIGHT DAVID EISENHOWER won by a landslide.

In 1956, after Mansfield's four years in the Senate, Democratic majority leader LYNDON BAINES JOHNSON pressed him to become assistant majority leader because Johnson did not want an all-southern Democratic Senate leadership. Although he resisted the appointment, he eventually accepted.

When Johnson was elected vice president in 1961, Mansfield was elevated to Democratic majority leader. Mansfield's dislike of Johnson's strong-arm style leadership made him seem weak and ineffective, but he actually guided more effective liberal legislation through the Senate than Johnson did. After President JOHN FITZGERALD KENNEDY was assassinated and Vice President Johnson became president, Mansfield engineered the passage of a host of civil rights, health, education, and welfare legislation. His leadership was essential in the passage of the Civil Rights Act of 1964, which outlawed discrimination in all public accommodations, and the Voting Rights Act of 1965, which made possible the widespread participation of southern blacks in state and federal elections. Mansfield often said his greatest achievement was his role in winning the 1971 Senate approval of the proposed Twenty-sixth Amendment to give those 18 and older the right to vote.

Initially, he supported U.S. involvement in Southeast Asia, but he favored withdrawal after the assassination of President Ngo Dinh Diem of

South Vietnam in November 1963. From then on, he pushed for withdrawal of U.S. troops and cessation of the bombing. After RICHARD MILHOUS NIXON was elected president in 1968, Mansfield aided him when he could. For instance, he used his Asian contacts to facilitate Nixon's 1972 visit to China, the first step toward the restoration of normal relations between that country and the United States. However, Mansfield continued to criticize Nixon for prolonging the Vietnam War. When the Watergate scandal came to light in 1973, he became a firm opponent of the Nixon administration. In 1973, he was a principal architect of the War Powers Act, which was designed to check the president's ability to commit U.S. troops abroad without the consent of Congress.

Despite his strong liberal voting that included the advocacy of gun control (exceedingly unpopular in Montana), his generally conservative constituents reelected him to the Senate in 1958, 1964, and 1970, and each time he won with a margin that exceeded 60 percent. He undoubtedly would have been reelected in 1976 had he not retired.

His retirement from the Senate was short-lived. In 1977, President JAMES EARL CARTER pressed him to accept a diplomatic post. Initially, Carter wanted him to go to Mexico, but Mansfield felt the altitude in Mexico City would not help his wife's health. Carter then suggested Japan, and Mansfield accepted that post in which he was very well received and ably defended U.S. interests. In 1981, he expected to be removed from his position—either due to advanced age or political differences—by the incoming Republican president RONALD WILSON REAGAN. In fact, he had already packed his bags when Reagan telephoned him to ask him to stay on. He remained for an additional seven years, making his 10 years of service the longest tenure of any U.S. ambassador to Japan.

Even after his second retirement, Mansfield was still active and continued to go almost every weekday to his office at Goldman Sachs. The week after his 95th birthday, he inaugurated a leadership lecture series, which was sponsored by the Senate Republican leader, CHESTER TRENT LOTT of Mississippi.

He died on October 6, 2001, in Washington, D.C.

Further Reading

Andrew, John A. *Lyndon Johnson and the Great Society.* Chicago: I. R. Dee, 1998.

Bernstein, Irving. *Guns or Butter: The Presidency of Lyndon Johnson.* New York: Oxford University Press, 1996.

Brands, H. W. *The Foreign Policies of Lyndon Johnson: Beyond Vietnam.* College Station: Texas A&M University Press, 1999.

Caro, Robert A. *The Years of Lyndon Johnson: The Path to Power.* New York: Knopf, 1990.

Gardner, Lloyd C. *Pay Any Price: Lyndon Johnson and the Wars for Vietnam.* Chicago: Elephant Paperbacks, 1997.

Goldsmith, John A. *Colleagues: Richard B. Russell and His Apprentice, Lyndon B. Johnson.* Macon, Ga.: Mercer University Press, 1998.

"Mansfield, Mike" in *Congress A to Z: Third Edition,* edited by David R. Tarr and Ann O'Connor. Washington, DC.: Congressional Quarterly, 1999.

Valeo, Francis R. *Mike Mansfield, Majority Leader—A Different Kind of Senate 1961–1976.* Armonk, N.Y.: M. E. Sharpe, 1999.

Marcantonio, Vito Anthony
(1902–1954) *representative*

Vito Anthony Marcantonio was the most radical Republican ever to win a seat in the U.S. House of Representatives, the most electorally successful radical politician, and probably the most radical politician in the Congress in the 20th century.

Marcantonio was born on December 10, 1902, and lived his whole life in the same East Harlem neighborhood in New York City. He received his law degree from New York University in 1925 and was admitted to the bar in 1926. He practiced law in New York City and became an assistant U.S. district attorney in 1930.

Marcantonio began in politics as a protégé of FIORELLO HENRY LAGUARDIA. LaGuardia, whose daughter died in 1921, regarded Marcantonio almost as his son. LaGuardia appointed him his campaign organizer in 1922, and this gave him a 10-year apprenticeship under a master New York City politician. When LaGuardia was elected New York City mayor in 1933, Marcantonio inherited his district, his organization, and his party label.

Marcantonio was elected to Congress as a Republican in 1934 from an East Harlem district with a predominantly Italian, Puerto Rican, and African-American constituency. Despite his strong support of President FRANKLIN DELANO ROOSEVELT's New Deal policies, as a Republican he was defeated in the 1936 Democratic Party landslide that accompanied Roosevelt's reelection.

In 1938, Marcantonio was elected as an American Labor Party (ALP) member to his old seat in the U.S. House of Representatives. Until the end of his congressional career, he benefited from a New York law that permitted cross-filing as a candidate of more than one party. In many races, he won not only the ALP nomination, but also some or all of the Republican, Democratic, and Liberal Party nominations as well. As a member of a very small third party, however, he received no committee assignments, and this shut him out of much legislative activity and would have spelled the end of a career for a normal member of Congress. Marcantonio compensated for this disadvantage by mastering legislative procedure and, more important, by providing his constituents with a high level of social services. His precinct organization reregistered its voters every year, guaranteed that each of his constituents got an annual letter inviting them to a personal meeting with Marcantonio in his district office, and produced a 96% turnout rate—the highest in New York City if not in the United States as a whole.

Marcantonio honored the ethnic spirit of his district by standing up for Italians toward the end of World War II, pointing out that they overthrew Mussolini and not the Allied forces. He criticized the United States for what his constituents regarded as colonial control over Puerto Rico and supported civil rights legislation for African Americans a generation before it became a popular issue in the 1960s Civil Rights movement.

There was a price to be paid for this progressivism. The American Communist Party actively supported the ALP. Marcantonio not only never repudiated this Communist support but he also supported its right to exist, saying that the Communist Party was an "American political party operating in what it considers to be the best interests of the American working class and people."

Marcantonio was the lawyer for W. E. B. DuBois, a civil rights activist and well-known Communist. He also supported Paul Robeson, the famous left-wing African-American singer and actor who ultimately moved to the Soviet Union to escape what he perceived as persecution in the United States. Marcantonio cast the only vote in Congress against the Korean War, and he was an outspoken opponent of Senator JOSEPH RAYMOND MCCARTHY and the House Committee on Un-American Activities (HUAC).

All of Marcantonio's activities created a firestorm of press vilification unique in New York City history. In 1944, the New York legislature gerrymandered (or unfairly altered) his congressional district boundaries to include Yorkville, a predominantly Irish-American and German-American community south of East Harlem whose constituents were intensely hostile to left-wing politics. In spite of this new district, Marcantonio won the election. In 1947, the Wilson-Pakula Act stopped him from running in the Democratic and Republican Party nominations. This meant he had to run solely under the ALP party label at a time when the ALP was almost universally condemned as Communist controlled, but still Marcantonio won.

Finally, in 1950, the major parties decided to work together and named the same candidate as a Democratic, Republican, and Liberal Party nominee to run against Marcantonio. Only by combining all their votes behind one candidate could they overcome Marcantonio's strength in East Harlem and defeat him.

Marcantonio practiced law until he died of a heart attack on a city street as he emerged from a subway in New York City on August 9, 1954.

Further Reading

LaGumina, Salvatore J. *Vito Marcantonio: The People's Politician.* Dubuque, Iowa: Kendall/Hunt, 1969.

Meyer, Gerald. "Vito Marcantonio" in *The Encyclopedia of Third Parties in America,* edited by Immanuel Ness and James Ciment. Armonk, N.Y.: M. E. Sharpe, Inc., 2000.

———. *Vito Marcantonio: Radical Politician, 1902–1954.* Albany: State University of New York Press, 1989.

Schaffer, Alan. *Vito Marcantonio: Radical in Congress.* Syracuse, N.Y.: Syracuse University Press. 1966.

Marshall, John

(1755–1835) *chief justice of the United States, secretary of state, representative, Revolutionary War leader*

John Marshall served as the chief justice of the United States for more years and had more influence on the development of the U.S. Supreme Court than any other individual.

Marshall was born on September 24, 1755, near Germantown in Fauquier (then called Prince William) County, Virginia. While his father was a friend of GEORGE WASHINGTON and later moved up in state and local politics (John Marshall's mother was distantly related to THOMAS JEFFERSON), Marshall's birth as the first of 15 children was in a modest frontier setting. His father provided nearly all of his early education at home. He had no formal education until after his service in the Revolutionary War.

Marshall served three years as an officer in the Revolutionary War, participating in the cam-

John Marshall was the longest serving and greatest chief justice of the United States. *(Library of Congress)*

paigns and battles of Norfolk, Brandywine, Monmouth, Stony Point, and Valley Forge. Marshall returned to Williamsburg to study law for a few months with the renowned George Wythe at the College of William and Mary. He was admitted to the bar in 1780 and practiced law on the western frontier. He was elected a delegate to the Virginia assembly in 1782 (and elected two more nonconsecutive times in 1787 and 1795). A strong supporter of the new U.S. Constitution, he also served in the Virginia convention that ratified the U.S. Constitution.

From 1780 until about 1786, Marshall built a lucrative law practice and was very successful financially. However, he invested in land in the northern sector of Virginia, and financial obligations from that investment consumed his attention and much of his resources for over a decade. His financial trouble deterred him from accepting several significant governmental position at this time.

Marshall turned down President Washington's offer to make him U.S. attorney general in 1795 and minister to France in 1796. President JOHN ADAMS offered to name him secretary of war or associate justice on the Supreme Court. Reluctantly, Marshall agreed to go as one of the commissioners to France in the diplomatic dispute that ended in the XYZ Affair. In the XYZ affair, Marshall and the other two commissioners were to attempt to limit important disagreements between France and the United States. The infamous French foreign minister demanded $250,000 for himself and a $12 million loan for France before any discussions could begin. The U.S. commissioner refused and sent a report back to President Adams. Adams deleted the names of the offending Frenchmen and substituted the letters, "X", "Y", and "Z" when he submitted the report to Congress, thereby giving the incident its name.

Marshall's effectiveness in France made him a popular figure, particularly with Federalists. With Washington's urging and support, he was elected to the U.S. House of Representatives in 1799, but he stayed only briefly. President Adams was increasingly unpopular as his term went on, but Marshall continued to support him. Since Adams was undermined by a number of disloyal cabinet officers, he needed help and prevailed on Marshall to become his secretary of state in 1800.

When Oliver Ellsworth resigned as chief justice in 1800, Adams first asked the former chief justice, JOHN JAY, to take the post, but Jay declined. After considering others, Adams nominated Marshall to become chief justice of the United States. Despite some opposition, the Senate confirmed him on January 27, 1801, and he took office on February 4 of that year.

Marshall was still financially pressed and the pay of the Chief Justice of the Supreme Court was modest. By 1804, Marshall was so badly pressed that he began his five volume biography, *The Life of George Washington.* Written quickly, the biography does not possess the quality of Marshall's other writings. Worse for Marshall, sales were poor since President THOMAS JEFFERSON, by then angry with Marshall, refused to allow federal postmaster to take orders for it.

Marshall served for a record of more than 34 years, participated in more than 1,000 decisions, and authored more than 500 opinions. During his tenure, the Court began issuing single majority opinions, enabling it to speak with a more definitive, unified voice, which established the Court's authority in the national government. Rulings during this era, such as in *McCulloch v. Maryland,* bolstered federal power over the states. Marshall wrote the 1803 decision in *Marbury v. Madison,* which established judicial review of laws passed by Congress and established the Supreme Court as the final authority on the meaning of the Constitution. In the *Dartmouth College Case,* he interpreted the constitutional requirement of the inviolability of contract, another favorite subject of his. He interpreted the interstate commerce clause of the Constitution in *Gibbons v. Ogden,* expanding federal power at the expense of the states.

Marshall attempted to interpret the Constitution with great respect for the words actually used, and this became particularly important in the trial of AARON BURR for treason. Marshall, a friend of ALEXANDER HAMILTON, had no reason to like the man who had killed Hamilton in a duel in 1804, and he was under pressure from President Jefferson

and the Congress to aid in convicting him. To his credit, Marshall read the exact words of the U.S. Constitution in holding that there must be "the Testimony of two witnesses to the same overt act," and his adherence to principle meant that the Burr prosecution failed.

Marshall resigned as chief justice on July 6, 1835, the day he died, at the age of 79.

Further Reading

Beveridge, Albert J. *The Life of John Marshall.* Boston: Houghton Mifflin, reprint, 1970.

Corwin, Edward S. *John Marshall and the Constitution: A Chronicle of the Supreme Court.* New Haven, Conn.: Yale University Press, 1921.

Craigmyle, Thomas S. *John Marshall in Diplomacy and in Law.* New York: C. Scribner's Sons, 1989.

Faulkner, Robert Kenneth. *The Jurisprudence of John Marshall.* Princeton, N.J.: Princeton University Press, 1968.

Frankfurter, Felix. *The Commerce Clause under Marshall, Taney and Waite.* Gloucester, Mass.: Peter Smith, reprint 1978.

Gunther, Gerald. *John Marshall's Defense of McCulloch v. Maryland.* Stanford, Calif.: Stanford University Press, 1969.

Haskins, George L. *Foundations of Power: John Marshall, 1801–15.* New York: Macmillan, 1981.

Hobson, Charles F. *The Great Chief Justice: John Marshall and the Rule of Law.* Lawrence: University Press of Kansas, 1996.

Johnson, Herbert Alan. *The Chief Justiceship of John Marshall, 1801–1835.* Columbia: University of South Carolina Press, 1998.

Jones, William Melville. *Chief Justice John Marshall: A Reappraisal.* New York: Da Capo Press, 1971.

Kutler, Stanley I. *John Marshall.* Englewood Cliffs, N.J.: Prentice-Hall, 1972.

Newmyer, R. Kent. *The Supreme Court under Marshall and Taney.* Arlington Heights, Ill.: Harlan Davidson, 1986.

Rhodes, Irwin S. *The Papers of John Marshall.* Norman: University of Oklahoma Press, 1969.

Robarge, David Scott. *A Chief Justice's Progress: John Marshall.* Westport, Conn.: Greenwood, 2000.

Rudko, Frances Howell. *John Marshall and International Law: Statesman and Chief Justice.* New York: Greenwood, 1991.

Shevory, Thomas C. *John Marshall's Law: Interpretation, Ideology, and Interest.* Westport, Conn.: Greenwood, 1994.

Smith, Jean Edward. *John Marshall: Definer of a Nation.* New York: Holt, 1996.

White, G. Edward. *The Marshall Court and Cultural Change, 1815–35.* New York: Macmillan, 1988.

Marshall, Thurgood
(1908–1993) *associate justice of the Supreme Court, solicitor general*

Thurgood Marshall was the first African-American solicitor general of the United States and the first African-American associate justice of the U.S. Supreme Court. As the chief counsel for the National Association for the Advancement of Colored People (NAACP) for 30 years, he systematically challenged racial segregation, and ultimately in the landmark case of *Brown v. Board of Education*

Thurgood Marshall was the first African-American associate justice of the U.S. Supreme Court. *(Library of Congress)*

(1954), he persuaded the U.S. Supreme Court to overthrow the concept of "separate but equal," which had been its chief legal underpinning.

Marshall was born in Baltimore, Maryland, on July 2, 1908. He attended Lincoln University in Oxford, Pennsylvania, where he graduated with honors in 1930. After being refused admission to the University of Maryland's all-white law school (in 1936, he challenged and defeated that institution's segregation in *Murray v. Maryland*), he entered the Howard University Law School. Charles H. Houston, the school's vice dean and the NAACP's first chief counsel, deeply impressed Marshall since he was the first African American to win a case before the U.S. Supreme Court. Graduating magna cum laude from Howard in 1933, Marshall went to work for the NAACP legal department and became its chief counsel in 1938.

From then until appointed to the U.S. Court of Appeals in 1961 by President JOHN FITZGERALD KENNEDY, Marshall argued more than 30 cases before the U.S. Supreme Court and won 29 of them, successfully challenging racial segregation, especially in education. Finally, he persuaded the Court to overturn *Plessy v. Ferguson* (1896) and its doctrine of "separate but equal" in *Brown v. Board of Education.* On the U.S. Court of Appeals, he wrote 112 opinions, and none of them were overturned.

In 1965, President LYNDON BAINES JOHNSON named Marshall the first African-American solicitor general of the United States, the chief lawyer for the United States in proceedings before the U.S. Supreme Court. Two years later, Johnson appointed him the first African American to sit on the Supreme Court. On the Court, he consistently opposed discrimination based on race or sex, opposed the death penalty, and supported the rights of criminal defendants.

As more conservatives were named to the Court, Marshall found himself in the minority. After his retirement in 1991, he was outspoken in his criticism of the Court.

When Thurgood Marshall died on January 24, 1993, he was only the second justice to lie in state in the Supreme Court's chambers. Chief Justice EARL WARREN, who had written the unanimous opinion in *Brown*—Marshall's most famous case— was the other.

Further Reading

Ball, Howard. *A Defiant Life: Thurgood Marshall and the Persistence of Racism in America.* New York: Crown Publishers, 1998.

Bland, Randall Walton. *Private Pressure on Public Law: The Legal Career of Justice Thurgood Marshall, 1934–1991.* Lanham, Md.: University Press of America, 1993.

Davis, Michael D. *Thurgood Marshall: Warrior at the Bar, Rebel on the Bench.* Secaucus, N.J.: Carol Publishing Group, 1994.

Goldman, Roger. *Thurgood Marshall: Justice for All.* New York: Carroll & Graf, 1993.

Krug, Elisabeth. *Thurgood Marshall: Champion of Civil Rights.* New York: Fawcett Columbine, 1993.

Mello, Michael. *Against the Death Penalty: The Relentless Dissents of Justices Brennan and Marshall.* Boston: Northeastern University Press, 1996.

Prentzes, G. S. *Thurgood Marshall.* New York: Chelsea, 1993.

Rowan, Carl Thomas. *Dream Makers, Dream Breakers: The World of Justice Thurgood Marshall.* Boston: Little, Brown, 1993.

Tushnet, Mark V. *Making Civil Rights Law: Thurgood Marshall and the Supreme Court, 1936–1961.* New York: Oxford University Press, 1996.

———. *Making Constitutional Law: Thurgood Marshall and the Supreme Court, 1961–1991.* New York: Oxford University Press, 1997.

Williams, Juan. *Thurgood Marshall: American Revolutionary.* New York: Times Books, 1998.

Martin, Joseph William, Jr.
(1884–1968) *Speaker of the House, representative*

Joseph William Martin, Jr., served in the U.S. House of Representatives as a Republican from Massachusetts for 42 years. Not only was he one of the longest-serving Republicans in Congress, but he was also one of the longest-tenured Republican leaders in the House, serving from 1939 to 1959. He also served two stints as Speaker of the House.

Born on November 3, 1884, in North Attleboro, Bristol County, Massachusetts, Martin graduated from North Attleboro High School in 1902. He started out as a newspaper reporter in 1902, and he bought the North Attleboro *Evening Chronicle* in 1908 and later the Franklin (Massachusetts) *Sentinel.*

Martin was elected to the Massachusetts house of representatives in 1912 and the Massachusetts senate in 1917. He also served as chairman of the Massachusetts Street Railway Investigating Commission and as chairman of the Massachusetts Legislative Campaign Committee.

Named the executive secretary of the Republican State Committee in 1922, Martin parlayed that into election to the U.S. House of Representatives in 1924. He was reelected 20 more times and served a total of 42 years. He was named the Republican Party leader of the House in 1939 and served in that capacity for 20 years until 1959. He was Speaker of the House from 1947 to 1949 and from 1953 to 1955.

Martin was a delegate to six Republican National Conventions between 1916 and 1956, and he was the permanent chairman of the Republican National Conventions for five of those conventions in 1940, 1944, 1948, 1952, and 1956.

Martin was defeated in the Republican primary in 1966 and retired to North Attleboro, Massachusetts, in January 1967. He died in Hollywood, Florida, on March 6, 1968.

Further Reading

Loomis, Burdett A. *Esteemed Colleagues: Civility and Deliberation in the U.S. Senate.* Washington, D.C.: Brookings Institution, 2000.

Martin, Joseph W. *My First Fifty Years in Politics.* Westport, Conn.: Greenwood Press, 1975.

"Martin, Joseph W" in *Congress A to Z: Third Edition,* edited by David R. Tarr and Ann O'Connor. Washington, D.C.: Congressional Quarterly, 1999.

"Martin, Joseph William, Jr." Available online. Discovery Channel School, original content provided by World Book Online. URL: http://www.discoveryschool.com/homeworkhelp/worldbook/atozhistory/m/723345.html. Downloaded November 15, 2001.

Mason, George
(1725–1792) *Revolutionary War leader*

George Mason was a rare early colonial Virginia planter who opposed slavery. He was also an early opponent of British colonial policy, an early supporter of the Revolutionary War, and a participant in the drafting of the U.S. Constitution.

Mason was born in 1725 in Fairfax County, Virginia, into one of the most affluent colonial Virginia plantation families. As a trustee of Alexandria, Virginia, a Fairfax County court justice, and a Truro parish vestryman, Mason exercised great influence in local politics from 1754 to 1779. Overlapping with this service, he was a member (and often treasurer) of the Ohio Company, a prominent colonial land development company, from 1752 until 1773.

In 1759, he was elected to the Virginia House of Burgesses, where he was an early opponent of British colonial policy. He proposed the nonimportation resolutions adopted by the Burgesses in 1769. In 1774, he drafted the Fairfax Resolves, which set out the constitutional position of the colonial relationship to the British Crown. As a member of the 1776 Virginia Constitutional Convention, he wrote the influential Virginia Declaration of Rights, which was copied by other states and used as a basis for part of THOMAS JEFFERSON's draft of the Declaration of Independence.

Mason was an active member of the 1787 U.S. Constitutional Convention at Philadelphia, but his hatred of slavery was so strong that he opposed the final draft for not taking a stronger stand against slavery. He also feared the U.S. Constitution's centralization of power, particularly since it did not include a bill of rights. Mason refused to sign the Constitution and, with PATRICK HENRY and JAMES MONROE, led the fight in Virginia against its ratification. His proposed bill of rights became the basis for some of the first 10 amendments (or the Bill of Rights) to the U.S. Constitution.

Mason died on October 7, 1792.

Further Reading

Cohen, Martin B. *Federalism: The Legacy of George Mason.* Fairfax, Va.: George Mason University Press, 1988.

Davidow, Robert P. *Natural Rights and Natural Law: The Legacy of George Mason.* Fairfax, Va.: George Mason University Press, 1986.

Rutland, Robert A. *George Mason, Reluctant Statesman.* Baton Rouge: Louisiana State University Press, 1980.

Shumate, T. Daniel, ed. *The First Amendment: The Legacy of George Mason.* Fairfax, Va.: George Mason University Press, 1985.

McCain, John
(1936–   ) *candidate for president, senator, representative, author*

John McCain is the only major presidential candidate in U.S. history to have been a prisoner of war except for President ANDREW JACKSON, and Jackson was only held prisoner for about a month while McCain was held for five and one-half years during the Vietnam War. After the war, McCain was elected to the House of Representatives and later to the U.S. Senate, where he gained a reputation as a conservative willing to work across party lines on issues such as campaign finance reform. He ran a surprisingly strong campaign against GEORGE WALKER BUSH for the 2000 Republican nomination for president but could not overcome Bush's financial resources and formidable organization.

John McCain was born on August 29, 1936, in the Panama Canal Zone, where his father was serving in the U.S. Navy. His family moved frequently throughout his childhood years as his father had various naval assignments. McCain went to the U.S. Naval Academy where both his father and grandfather had attended, and he received a bachelor's degree in 1958.

Upon graduation, he became a navy fighter pilot and eventually served in the Vietnam War. In October 1967, on a bombing raid over North Vietnam, his plane was shot down, and he was captured. Since his father was a U.S. Navy admiral and commander in chief of Pacific forces, the North Vietnamese saw the propaganda value in offering the young McCain early release, but he refused unless all those captured before him were also released since that was the honorable requirement of the U.S. military code. The price he paid for this courageous decision was five hard years of beatings and torture during imprisonment in the infamous "Hanoi Hilton" prison.

McCain was a prisoner of war in Hanoi until 1973. The holder of the Bronze Star, Silver Star, and Purple Heart medals for his courageous service, McCain attended the National War College after he was returned to the United States. From 1977 to 1980, he served as director of the Navy Senate Liaison Office, but his injuries were so severe that a full return to the service was impossible. He retired from the navy in 1981 with the rank of captain.

Having divorced his first wife in 1980, he remarried and moved to Arizona, his second wife's home state. In 1982, McCain was elected to the U.S. House of Representatives and was reelected two years later. In 1986, he was elected to the U.S. Senate. Soon after becoming a senator, he became involved in the Lincoln Savings and Loan scandal. He was accused, along with five other senators, of allegedly applying improper pressure on federal bank regulators in return for receiving political campaign contributions from Charles Keating, the head of Lincoln Savings. Largely cleared of serious wrongdoing after a lengthy investigation, he was reelected to the Senate in 1992 and 1998.

In the U.S. Senate, McCain has chaired the Indian Affairs Committee and Commerce, Science, and Transportation Committee, and he has served on the Armed Services Committee. While generally conservative, he has been a maverick. He often refuses to toe the Republican Party line; for example, he is an aggressive opponent of the tobacco industry. McCain has also striven to reach across party lines on certain key issues. In 1995, McCain joined with Hawaii's Democratic Senator DANIEL KEN INOUYE to push through the Congress legislation to regulate casino gambling on Indian reservations. In 1996, McCain and Wisconsin's Democratic senator Russell Feingold cosponsored a bill to encourage limits on campaign spending by rewarding candidates who agreed to spending limits with free or lower-cost broadcasting time and discounted postage rates. Both senators have introduced the bill repeatedly since then, but the Republican Senate leadership prevented the bill from being voted on until 2001, when it was narrowly defeated.

In 1999, McCain published his best-selling autobiography, *Faith of My Fathers*, detailing much of his early life, family background, and experiences in Vietnam. This book helped launch his 2000 campaign for the Republican presidential nomination, a campaign he referred to as a fight "to take our government back from the power brokers and special interests."

This powerful message brought him early success in the influential New Hampshire primary and again in the Michigan primary. However, the massive financial resources and tightly controlled party support behind Texas governor George W. Bush forced McCain to withdraw after a poor showing in the Super Tuesday primaries in March 2001. Pointedly, he did not endorse Governor Bush as the Republican candidate until late in the campaign.

Since his presidential defeat, he has continued to push for his campaign reforms in the Senate.

Further Reading

McCain, John. *Faith of My Fathers*. New York: Random House, 1999.

Romano, Lois. "Out of the Fire, Politics Calls: Ex-POW Turns Washington Insider," *Washington Post* (March 2, 2000): A01.

Timberg, Robert. *John McCain: An American Odyssey*. New York: Simon & Schuster, 1999.

Walsh, Edward. "John McCain," *Washington Post* (January 21, 2000): A1.

Walsh, Edward, and Helen Dewar. "'Stirring the Pot' In an Elite Club," *Washington Post* (March 3, 2000): A01.

McCarthy, Eugene Joseph

(1916–) *candidate for president, senator, representative, author*

Eugene Joseph McCarthy was most famous as the Vietnam War opponent who challenged and nearly defeated the incumbent president, LYNDON BAINES JOHNSON, in the 1968 New Hampshire Democratic presidential primary. While McCarthy lost narrowly, he came so close that his success encouraged New York Senator ROBERT FRANCIS KENNEDY to enter the Democratic presidential race and helped persuade Johnson not to run for reelection.

McCarthy was born on March 29, 1916, in Watkins, Minnesota. He earned a B.A. degree from St. John's University in 1935 and an M.A. degree in sociology from the University of Minnesota in 1938. He was a professor of economic education at St. John's University from 1940 to 1942. After the United States entered World War II, he served as a technical assistant for military intelligence from 1942 to 1946. Following the war, he returned to the College of St. Thomas in St. Paul as an instructor in sociology and economics, and he served as acting head of the sociology department from 1946 to 1948.

McCarthy entered politics as the chairman of Ramsey County Democratic Farmer Labor Party (DFL) in 1947. He was elected to the U.S. House of Representatives from Minnesota's Fourth District in 1948 and served in the House from 1949 to 1959. He ran for and won a seat in the U.S. Senate in 1958 and was reelected in 1964.

As a college professor and a poet, McCarthy gained a reputation as an intellectual in politics. During the 1960s, he was increasingly critical of U.S. participation in the Vietnam War. By 1967, he decided to mount a campaign for the Democratic presidential nomination as a way to amplify his views. He attracted a great deal of student and intellectual support, but he was expected by political professionals to lose badly. When he came close to upsetting the incumbent President Johnson in the 1968 New Hampshire primary, his success led Robert Kennedy to enter the presidential race and persuaded Johnson not to run for reelection. McCarthy won primary elections in Wisconsin and Oregon, but he lost three states to Kennedy. When Robert Kennedy was assassinated, McCarthy became the sole remaining antiwar candidate, but he generated such hostility from President Johnson and the party regulars that they united behind Vice President HUBERT HORATIO HUMPHREY, who won the Democratic nomination even though he had not entered any primaries in 1968.

McCarthy retired from the Senate in 1970 and began an unsuccessful campaign for the Democratic presidential nomination in 1972. Losing the nomination to Senator GEORGE STANLEY MCGOVERN, he resumed teaching in 1973. He also became a senior editor at Simon and Schuster in New York City that same year and a syndicated columnist in 1977. In 1976 and 1988, he ran for

the presidency as an independent candidate but received less than 1 percent of the popular vote in each election. McCarthy was also an unsuccessful candidate for the 1992 Democratic presidential nomination. Over the years, he has authored several books and continued to be a nationally recognized commentator on political matters.

Further Reading

Larner, Jeremy. *Nobody Knows: Reflections on the McCarthy Campaign of 1968.* New York: Macmillan, 1970.

McCarthy, Abigail Q. *Private Faces/Public Places.* Garden City, N.Y.: Doubleday, 1972.

McCarthy, Eugene J. *The Hard Years: A Look at Contemporary America and American Institutions.* New York: Viking, 1975.

———. *The Ultimate Tyranny.* New York: Harcourt Brace Jovanovich, 1980.

———. *Up 'Til Now.* New York: Harcourt Brace Jovanovich, 1987.

Rising, George. *Clean for Gene: Eugene McCarthy's 1968 Presidential Campaign.* Westport, Conn.: Praeger, 1997.

McCarthy, Joseph Raymond
(1908–1957) *senator*

Joseph Raymond McCarthy, a Republican U.S. senator from Wisconsin, was one of the most controversial figures in American politics. Considered by some to be a patriot, eventually his indiscriminate charges brought about his censure in the U.S. Senate. His method of guilt by association and character assassination by use of unsubstantiated and sensationalist charges created a new highly derogatory word in the English language: McCarthyism.

McCarthy was born on November 14, 1908, in Grand Chute (near Appleton), Wisconsin. He graduated from Marquette University Law School in 1935. In 1939, he won his first election as a Wisconsin circuit judge by lying about his opponent's qualifications, including his opponent's age. While serving on the bench, he performed so poorly that the Wisconsin Supreme Court reprimanded him. When the United States entered World War II, he resigned as a judge and joined the U.S. Marine Corps. He was assigned as a tail gunner and rose to the rank of captain, but although he adopted the nickname "Tail Gunner Joe," he saw little action in combat. In 1946—running on the misleading slogan, "Wisconsin needs a tail gunner!"—he defeated incumbent Republican U.S. Senator Robert M. La Follette, Jr., in the Republican primary and went on to win the general election.

His Senate efforts were undistinguished, so by 1950 he was in serious danger of losing his 1952 reelection bid. He needed a new public relations gimmick and decided to tap into the anticommunist hysteria that was sweeping the country. On February 9, 1950, he went to Wheeling, West Virginia (far from Wisconsin in case his ploy failed), and made a speech in which he waved a piece of paper from the Federal Bureau of Investigation (FBI), which he claimed contained the names of 205 so-called card-carrying communists still working for the U.S. State Department. Challenged to produce proof, he failed to do so, but he would attack the questioner's motives and shift ground by changing the number of names on the list or by making new charges. His flair for the dramatic, his position as a senator, and the national insecurity over communism all gave his charges a massive public response that stunned even McCarthy himself. The onset of the Korean War, the announcement that the Soviet Union had exploded an atomic bomb, and the ongoing investigations of Alger Hiss as a spy by then congressman RICHARD MILHOUS NIXON all worked together to create a climate in which McCarthy's charges gained widespread support.

The Democrats tried to respond. When McCarthy charged that Owen Lattimore, a Johns Hopkins professor and State Department diplomat, was a top Russian spy in the State Department, Maryland's Democratic Senator Millard Tydings conducted an official Senate committee investigation and produced an FBI report that proved Lattimore had never been associated with communism or communist agencies. McCarthy then challenged Tydings's loyalty, fabricated a photograph showing Tydings talking with American Communist Party member Earl Browder, and said Tydings was defending Lattimore because Tydings was a communist sympathizer as well. McCarthy's charge was said to be responsible for

Joseph McCarthy was so notorious for smearing his opponents and using guilt by association that his name has been transformed into the negative word *McCarthyism. (Library of Congress)*

Tydings's defeat in 1950. After the Republicans took control of the Senate, McCarthy became the chairman of the Senate Government Operations Committee (the Senate version of the House Un-American Activities Committee) and used this committee chairmanship as a forum to slander and vilify many individuals whose careers were thereby ruined. Senator William Benton of Connecticut, who filed an early motion censuring McCarthy for slandering General George Marshall, was also defeated for reelection.

While many senators knew McCarthy's campaign was a sham, most were away aware of his widespread support and were afraid to challenge him. Those who did and survived, such as Republic Senator MARGARET CHASE SMITH and Democratic Senator ESTES COREY KEFAUVER, were subjected to vicious attacks for their courage. Eventually, McCarthy attacked the U.S. Army once too often, and it counterattacked through army counsel Joseph N. Welch. In televised hearings, Welch showed how McCarthy had faked photographs and falsified documents. This evidence damaged McCarthy's credibility to such a degree that the Democrats won control of the Senate in the 1954 elections. The Senate investigated McCarthy's financial irregularities and abuse of office, and by December 2, 1954, a Senate majority felt secure enough to censure McCarthy for attacking senators and Senate committees. Censured and without a committee chairmanship to grandstand with, McCarthy's influence was severely diminished, and he was broken in health. He died on May 2, 1957, when he was only 48 years old.

Further Reading

Buckley, William F. *McCarthy and His Enemies: The Record and Its Meaning*. Washington, D.C.: Regnery, 1995.

Fried, Albert. *McCarthyism: The Great American Red Scare*. New York: Oxford University Press, 1997.

Fried, Richard M. *Nightmare in Red: The McCarthy Era in Perspective*. New York: Oxford University Press, 1991.

Healer, M. J. *McCarthy's Americans: Red Scare Politics in State and Nation, 1935–1965*. Athens: University of Georgia Press, 1998.

Herman, Arthur. *Joseph McCarthy: Reexamining the Life and Legacy of America's Most Hated Senator*. New York: Free Press, 2000.

Reeves, Thomas C. *The Life and Times of Joe McCarthy*. Lanham, Md.: Madison Books, 1986.

Rovere, Richard H. *Senator Joe McCarthy*. Berkeley: University of California Press, 1995.

Schrecker, Ellen. *Many Are the Crimes: McCarthyism in America*. Boston: Little, Brown, 1998.

McClellan, George Brinton
(1826–1885) *candidate for president, governor*

George Brinton McClellan served for a time as the general in chief of the Union army during the U.S. Civil War. An able organizer and trainer of troops, some authorities rank McClellan as great general, but most agree with President ABRAHAM LINCOLN that he was too cautious on the battlefield. Lincoln fired him in November 1862. In 1864, Mc-

Clellan was the Democratic presidential candidate against Lincoln, but he lost badly.

McClellan was born on December 3, 1826, in Philadelphia, Pennsylvania. He graduated second in his class from West Point in 1846. He served ably in the Mexican War from 1846 to 1848. He then worked on various army engineering projects, notably on the survey for a Northern Pacific Railroad route across the Cascade Range in 1853 and 1854. He was sent to Europe to study the latest military tactics, but he resigned from the army in 1857 to become an Illinois Central Railroad official until the outbreak of the Civil War.

When the Civil War started, McClellan became a major general commanding Ohio volunteers and then quickly a regular army major general. In June and July 1861, he cleared the Confederates out of western Virginia. After the Union defeat in the First Battle of Bull Run in the summer of 1861, he was given command of the troops in and around Washington, known as the Army of the Potomac. In November of that year, he became general in chief of all armies. Lincoln, reflecting public opinion, pressed for an early offensive, but McClellan insisted on adequate training and equipment for his army. When no offensive was forthcoming, Lincoln relieved him as general in chief four months later but allowed him to retain an army command.

McClellan finally advanced in the spring of 1862, moving against Richmond from the east in the Peninsular Campaign. After McClellan fought his way close to Richmond, General Robert E. Lee's Confederates counterattacked him in the Battles of the Seven Days and drove him back, destroying his offensive. Many military scholars have blamed this loss on McClellan's overcautious behavior. The powers in Washington then gave most of his troops to General John Pope, but when Pope was defeated in the Second Battle of Bull Run in the summer of 1862, McClellan was given his troops back.

McClellan led his army to meet a Confederate invasion of Maryland, and the two armies butchered each other at Antietam on September 17, 1862. Nearly 12,000 troops on each side died in the bloodiest single battle of the war. McClellan forced the Confederates to retreat, but he did not follow them. This delay angered Lincoln, and he replaced McClellan with General Ambrose Burnside in November 1862, ending McClellan's military career. In 1864, McClellan was the Democratic candidate for president, but he rejected the party's peace platform. President Lincoln was very worried about McClellan's campaign early on, but General ULYSSES S. GRANT was then in charge of the U.S. Army. Grant won enough military victories to give Lincoln the boost he needed to be reelected by a substantial majority. McClellan was later chief engineer of the New York City department of docks and was elected New Jersey governor from 1878 to 1881.

He died on October 29, 1885. His defense of his military record, *McClellan's Own Story,* was published posthumously in 1887.

Further Reading

Catton, Bruce. *Mr. Lincoln's Army.* Garden City, N.Y.: Doubleday, 1962.

Hassler, Warren W. *General George B. McClellan: Shield of the Union.* Westport, Conn.: Greenwood, 1974.

Hensel, Howard M. *The Anatomy of Failure: The Case of Major General George B. McClellan and the Peninsular Campaign.* Montgomery, Ala.: Air Command and Staff College, Maxwell Air Force Base, 1985.

Newell, Clayton R. *Lee vs. McClellan: The First Campaign.* Washington, D.C.: Regnery, 1996.

Sears, Stephen W. *George B. McClellan: The Young Napoleon.* New York: Ticknor & Fields, 1988.

Webb, Alexander S. *The Peninsula: McClellan's Campaign of 1862.* New York: T. Yoseloff, 1963.

Wheeler, Richard. *Sword Over Richmond: An Eyewitness History of McClellan's Peninsula Campaign.* New York: Harper & Row, 1986.

Williams, T. Harry. *McClellan, Sherman, and Grant.* New Brunswick, N.J.: Rutgers University Press, 1962.

McCloy, John Jay
(1895–1989) *assistant secretary of war, diplomat*

John Jay McCloy served as an adviser for every American president from FRANKLIN DELANO ROOSEVELT through JAMES EARL CARTER. This alone would make him a major American political leader, but his most significant individual contribution was his successful effort to transform war-torn Germany into a strong bulwark against the Soviet Union.

Born on March 31, 1895, in Philadelphia, Pennsylvania, McCloy graduated from Amherst College in 1916 and went to Harvard Law School before he joined the army in May 1917. After two years' service as a captain in France and Germany, he returned to Harvard Law School and graduated in 1921. For the next 20 years, he concentrated on his corporate law practice in New York City, where he became acquainted with HENRY LEWIS STIMSON, a distinguished New York lawyer.

In October 1940, McCloy became a special expert consultant on counterespionage to Stimson, the secretary of war in Franklin D. Roosevelt's administration. By April 1941, McCloy had been appointed assistant secretary of war by President Roosevelt. While holding this post during World War II, McCloy helped secure passage of the Lend-Lease Act. He supported the top-secret intelligence effort that broke the Japanese war codes, supervised the evacuation of Japanese-Americans from the West Coast to internment camps farther inland, successfully argued for the creation of Japanese-Americans army units, and visited many of the operations in the various war theaters.

A key diplomatic figure, McCloy also participated in the Casablanca, Cairo, and Potsdam Conferences with Roosevelt. He was instrumental in developing the plans for the Nuremberg war crimes trials after the end of the war.

Following World War II, McCloy returned to New York to practice law; however, he kept being called back for advice on governmental affairs. In 1946 and 1947, McCloy served as a member of the committee on atomic energy for the State Department. From 1947 to 1949, he worked to establish the credibility of the International Bank for Reconstruction and Development and lent his prestige to the organization by serving as its president.

From 1949 to 1952, McCloy may have played his most important role in American history by working to create the Western-oriented Democratic German Federal Republic. Holding three offices simultaneously, McCloy was the chief economic cooperation administration representative, the U.S. military governor of the American zone in occupied West Germany, and the first U.S. high commissioner for Germany.

McCloy became chairman of the board of Chase Manhattan Bank in 1953 while he chaired the prestigious Council on Foreign Relations at the same time. In that role, he provided advice to DWIGHT DAVID EISENHOWER's administration.

In January 1961, President JOHN FITZGERALD KENNEDY appointed McCloy his chief adviser on disarmament. Nine months later, McCloy resigned in protest against the Kennedy administration's decision to restart its nuclear testing program in retaliation for the Soviet Union resuming above ground nuclear weapons testing. From 1963 to 1964, McCloy served on the Warren Commission, which investigated the causes of President Kennedy's assassination.

While maintaining his law practice in the 1960s and 1970s, McCloy frequently served as a special adviser on national security and foreign affairs matters to Presidents LYNDON BAINES JOHNSON, RICHARD MILHOUS NIXON, GERALD RUDOLPH FORD, and Jimmy Carter. He died on March 11, 1989, in Stamford, Connecticut.

Further Reading

Bird, Kai. *The Chairman: John J. McCloy: The Making of the American Establishment.* New York: Simon & Schuster, 1992.

Fischer, Erika J. *John J. McCloy: An American Architect of Postwar Germany: Profiles of a Trans-Atlantic Leader and Communicator.* New York: P. Lang, 1994.

McCormack, John William
(1891–1980) *Speaker of the House, representative*

One of the longest serving members of Congress, John William McCormack served as Speaker of the U.S. House of Representatives from 1962 to 1971. Before his election as Speaker, McCormack had been deputy to SAMUEL TALIAFERRO RAYBURN, the top House Democrat from 1940 until Rayburn's death in 1961.

McCormack was born on December 21, 1891, in Boston, Massachusetts, and attended public schools there. As a young man he entered politics as a delegate to the Massachusetts State Constitutional Convention in 1917 and 1918. He also served in the U.S. Army during World War I. He was elected to the Massachusetts state house of representatives in 1920 and served there until elected to the Massachusetts state senate, where he served from 1923 to 1926. McCormack was elected to the U.S. House of Representatives from his South Boston district in 1928 and served in the Congress from 1929 to 1971. McCormack gained a reputation in Congress as a strong supporter of his party's legislative programs.

McCormack indirectly influenced the proposal and adoption of the Twenty-fifth Amendment to the U. S. Constitution. When President JOHN FITZGERALD KENNEDY was assassinated and Vice President LYNDON BAINES JOHNSON became president, there was no vice president. The existing law of succession to the presidency called for the Speaker of the House of Representatives to succeed to the presidency when there was no vice president.

McCormack sat behind President Johnson whenever he made nationally televised appearances before both houses of Congress. Because of his age and a muscular condition that caused his mouth to drop open especially when sitting for long periods, he appeared particularly frail before the national television audience. Since McCormack was not regarded as a suitable president, this frequent visual reminder of the vulnerability of the U.S. system led to calls for revision of the U.S. Constitution to provide for the appointment of a new vice president whenever a vacancy occurred. A provision to this effect was included in the Twenty-fifth Amendment that Congress passed July 6, 1965, and that was ratified February 10, 1976.

McCormack was next in line for the presidency for 14 months, from November 1963 until the newly elected vice president, HUBERT HORATIO HUMPHREY, was sworn in on January 20, 1965. McCormack was in good health throughout this period, but his appearances went a long way toward influencing the adoption of the new amendment.

In 1969, a group of liberal House Democrats tried to replace McCormack as Speaker, but he was reelected by a wide margin. McCormack retired from the House in January 1971, after more than 42 consecutive years of service.

He died in Dedham, Massachusetts, on November 22, 1980.

Further Reading

Bartlett, Charles. "McCormack, John William." Available by World Book Online. URL: http://www.discoveryschool.com/homeworkhelp/worldbook/atozhistory/m/35098.html. Downloaded November 6, 2001.

Gordon, Lester I. *John McCormack and the Roosevelt Era.* Boston, Mass.: Boston University, 1976.

"McCormack, John W." in *Congress A to Z: Third Edition,* edited by David R. Tarr and Ann O'Connor. Washington, D.C.: Congressional Quarterly, 1999.

McGovern, George Stanley

(1922–) *candidate for president, senator, representative*

George Stanley McGovern was a U.S. senator and the 1972 Democratic presidential nominee. He was defeated in an election filled with irregularities, including the burglary of the Democratic National Headquarters, illegal campaign contributions, and numerous dirty tricks, which all led to the resignation of President RICHARD MILHOUS NIXON, who faced impeachment for wrongdoing in that campaign.

McGovern was born on July 19, 1922, in Avon, South Dakota, the son of a Methodist minister. An excellent debater in public high school, McGovern won a scholarship to Dakota Wesleyan University in 1940. In World War II, he served in the U.S. Army Air Force and flew 35 European missions in a B-24, for which he received the Distinguished Flying Cross. Initially beginning study at a seminary in 1946, he switched to history and earned a doctorate at Northwestern University in 1953.

After teaching at South Dakota Wesleyan for a year, he became the South Dakota Democratic Party's executive secretary. He used this role as a base to win a seat in the U.S. House of Representatives in 1956 and reelection in 1958. He lost a bid for the U.S. Senate in 1960, but he was rewarded with the directorship of the Food for Peace Program by President JOHN FITZGERALD KENNEDY. He was elected to the U.S. Senate in 1962 and served a total of three terms before losing in the 1980 election, which was a landslide for President RONALD WILSON REAGAN and other Republicans.

McGovern reluctantly supported the early military action in Vietnam, but he soon became a sharp critic of President LYNDON BAINES JOHNSON's escalation of the war. In 1969, McGovern was named chairman of the Democratic Party presidential nomination reform commission, whose new primary rules favored an "outsider" candidate such as himself. In 1972, he won in a series of presidential primary victories under the new rules and became the Democratic presidential nominee. Shortly after the convention, McGovern's vice presidential running mate, Missouri's Senator Thomas F. Eagleton, was exposed as having been hospitalized for depression three times in the 1960s. Initially, McGovern supported Eagleton but finally asked him to step aside as the controversy damaged the ticket horribly. McGovern then named Sargent Shriver, brother-in-law of former President Kennedy and director of the Peace Corps, his new running mate, but valuable campaign momentum was lost.

McGovern lost to incumbent President Richard Nixon in a landslide in which McGovern got only 38% of the popular vote and won the Electoral College votes of only Massachusetts and the District of Columbia. In the primaries, McGovern supported very advanced liberal policies, such as guaranteed annual income for every family in the United States whether they worked or not, and he had to abandon these in these general election campaign. Changing vice presidential running mates and public policies between the primary and the general election almost certainly damaged McGovern, but one can never know how well he might have done without the improper actions of the Nixon campaign and the Watergate scandal.

McGovern continued in the Senate after his presidential defeat and won reelection in 1974, but he was defeated in 1980. McGovern also ran for the 1984 Democratic presidential nomination, but he dropped out after losing every early primary election he entered. In 1998, President WILLIAM JEFFERSON CLINTON appointed him to be the U.S. representative to the United Nations Food and Agriculture Organization.

Further Reading

Anson, Robert S. *McGovern.* New York: Holt, Rinehart & Winston, 1972.

Broder, David S. "McGovern, George Stanley." Available online. Discovery Channel School, original content provided by World Book Online. URL: http://www.discoveryschool.com/homeworkhelp/worldbook/atozhistory/m/351375.html. Downloaded November 8, 2001.

Dougherty, Richard. *Goodbye, Mr. Christian: A Personal Account of McGovern's Rise and Fall.* Garden City, N.Y.: Doubleday, 1973.

Hart, Gary. *Right from the Start: A Chronicle of the McGovern Campaign.* New York: Quadrangle, 1973.

Hernon, Joseph Martin. *Profiles in Character: Hubris and Heroism in the U.S. Senate—1789–1990.* Armonk,N.Y.: M. E. Sharpe, 1997.

Mailer, Norman. *St. George and the Godfather.* New York: Arbor House, 1983.

"McGovern, George" in *The Presidency A to Z: Second Edition,* edited by Michael T. Nelson. Washington, D.C.: Congressional Quarterly Press, 1998.

McGovern, George S. *Grassroots: The Autobiography of George McGovern.* New York: Random House, 1977.

Weil, Gordon Lee. *The Long Shot: George McGovern Runs for President.* New York: Norton, 1973.

White, Theodore H. *The Making of the President, 1972.* New York: Athenaeum, 1973.

Witker, Kristi. *How to Lose Everything in Politics Except Massachusetts.* New York: Mason & Lipscomb, 1974.

McKinley, William

(1843–1901) *president, representative*

William McKinley shaped the modern presidency and the underlying strength of the United States in world leadership. Under his guidance, the United States won the Spanish-American War (1898) and captured, purchased, or otherwise gained possession of Guam, Hawaii, the Philippines, Puerto Rico, and American Samoa. Elected by a clear majority in 1896 and reelected by the largest margin to that time in 1900, McKinley was shot and killed about six months into his second term. He became the third U.S. president to be assassinated.

McKinley was born on January 29, 1843, in Niles, Ohio, where his father owned a small iron foundry. When he was nine years old, his family moved to Poland (near Youngstown), Ohio, where young McKinley could attend a private school known as the Poland Seminary. In 1860, he started attending Allegheny College but became ill and left. He began teaching school, but in 1861, he became the first man in the town of Poland to volunteer to fight in the Civil War. He joined the Ohio Infantry unit headed by future U.S. President RUTHERFORD BIRCHARD HAYES. He was promoted to the rank of second lieutenant for bravery at the Battle of Antietam in 1862, and he was promoted to brevet major by the time he left the army in 1865.

After working briefly for a local Ohio judge, he studied law in Albany, New York, before entering the Ohio bar and beginning his practice in Canton, Ohio, in 1867. He was elected Stark County, Ohio, prosecuting attorney in 1869, but he was defeated for reelection by a narrow margin in 1871. Five years later, McKinley won a seat in the U.S. House of Representatives where he served seven terms almost continuously from 1877 to 1891. In 1884, the U.S. House of Representatives decided that McKinley's opponent had received more votes and was given his seat for about nine months until McKinley won the seat back in the 1884 election.

McKinley was defeated for reelection in 1890 because the legislature redrew his congressional district's boundary lines unfairly. In fact, the Ohio legislative majority had been trying to eliminate McKinley for some time, and McKinley had never run in exactly the same congressional district in any of his races for Congress. This necessity of responding to repeated unfairness honed McKinley's political skills to a much higher degree than most of his contemporaries. In the end, the discipline McKinley acquired from this ordeal made him more successful both as presidential candidate and as president.

McKinley parlayed his 1890 defeat for Congress into a successful win for governor of Ohio. In Congress, McKinley had always favored civil service reforms and other progressive measures. Now he had an executive position in which to carry out some of his preferred policies. As governor, he created a state board to resolve labor conflicts and kept the support of many workers despite having called out the National Guard to quell violence in a coal miners' strike. He improved Ohio's roads, canals, and institutions and inaugurated tax reform, including *higher* rates on corporations without antagonizing business.

In 1892, he ran for the Republican presidential nomination but received 182 delegate votes compared to 535 for the winner, BENJAMIN HARRISON. This second-place finish meant McKinley was poised to win in 1896. His congressional career had emphasized higher tariffs, the hallmark of Republican orthodoxy. On currency McKinley had once voted for silver (or easy currency), but he had repudiated the vote and adopted a moderate "harder currency" stance on "bimetallism." With his other progressive reforms, he was positioned to win for president no matter whom the Democrats nominated. MARK ALONZO HANNA, an Ohio political operative, also aided him, and the two men cultivated a strong political friendship.

McKinley and Hanna needed each other and all the skill they could muster because they were up against the charismatic WILLIAM JENNINGS BRYAN, the 1896 Democratic presidential nominee. Bryan criss-crossed the country, stirring up his followers—a necessity to win the presidency in the pro-business climate of the 1890s. Unfortunately, Bryan's success in mobilizing his base led to mobilizing his opposition. The business community was terrified of Bryan, overlooked any antibusiness policies of McKinley, and poured unprecedented amounts of cash into Hanna's hands. Hanna admitted to accepting an unprecedented $3.5 million in donations from businesses and banks, and he doubtless received much more in undisclosed contributions.

McKinley had the discipline to run a front-porch campaign, in which more than 750,000 people were transported to Canton, Ohio, to hear him speak. McKinley had a relatively "safe" voting record and could make safe speeches to relatively controlled audiences. With the money to smooth the way, McKinley was able to win the presidency with a clear majority of all the popular votes cast—the first time this had happened since 1872. McKinley garnered 7.1 million popular votes to

6.5 million for Bryan. In the Electoral College, the vote was 271–176. This apparently wide gap in the final result should lead to the conclusion that the win was easy; however, Bryan was formidable and the McKinley-Hanna team pulled out all the stops. Their tactics included threatening workers in the northeast that their factories would be closed if Bryan won and arranging for the banking community to release extra gold to spur liquidity, make money easier to borrow, and undercut Bryan's appeal for silver and easy money.

As the new president, McKinley found the domestic issues to be relatively simple. Gold was discovered in Alaska, further increasing the amount of money in circulation, and the nation gradually lifted out of the depressed conditions with which his term started. He, in line with the prevailing Republican orthodoxy, signed the Dingley tariff law that again raised tariffs and supported

William McKinley, the third U.S. president to be assassinated, shaped the modern presidency and America's role in the world. *(Library of Congress)*

the 1900 Gold Standard Act, since enough gold was in circulation so as not to unduly restrict economic growth.

Given the furor of the 1896 campaign, it was surprising that international affairs dominated McKinley's first term. The Cubans, almost constantly in rebellion against Spain in the latter half of the 19th century, revolted again. McKinley genuinely wished to avoid war by pressuring Spain to make concessions and ultimately free Cuba, but realistically no Spanish government could give up Cuba and stay in power. McKinley was pressured to enter the war, but he had resisted such pressure before. In the end, he may have gone to war because he genuinely believed that the Spanish would never yield.

The impetus for U.S. intervention was the explosion of the USS *Maine*. Now widely believed to have been an accident, the explosion on the battleship was then widely regarded as a deliberate attack by Spain. In any case, the United States entered the Spanish-American war and won it in 113 days. Though the war was fought over Cuba, the United States did not take over Cuba, except for a brief occupation to establish the conditions for independence. However, the United States took all the rest of Spain's colonies, except for a few in North Africa. It also took Puerto Rico as a war indemnity and paid $20 million for the Philippines. In addition, the United States negotiated the control of American Samoa from Germany and Britain, and it annexed the Republic of Hawaii. These acquisitions made the United States very powerful in the Pacific and a world power overall.

The United States then found it necessary to quell a very bloody guerrilla war in the Philippines, by sending a massive repression campaign that killed thousands of Filipinos in the name of democracy. The United States also sent an expeditionary force of 5,000 men into China to stop the Boxers, an anti-Western group of rebels who had killed hundreds of Chinese Christians and some Western missionaries. The Boxers had laid siege to the diplomatic quarter in Tianjin for weeks as a young engineer and future president, HERBERT CLARK HOOVER, led the civilian resistance in China. The United States claimed to be acting under its internationally neutral "Open Door" pol-

icy, but its self-interest in offering this policy reduces the strength of its claim.

Foreign policy aggrandizement did not hurt McKinley for reelection. At the Republican National Convention, the only issue was who would replace Vice President Garrett Hobart, who had died. The convention settled on New York's reform governor, THEODORE ROOSEVELT. In the general election, prosperity at home and apparent success abroad led McKinley to widen his lead in the rematch with William Jennings Bryan. He received 7.2 million popular votes to 6.3 million for Bryan and 292 Electoral College votes to 155 for Bryan.

McKinley indicated to his aides that he wished to move in a progressive direction in his second term. He suggested replacing blind adherence to higher tariffs with a policy that called for reciprocal trade agreements and reforms aimed at limiting the concentrations of great wealth and power held by corporations and trusts. Unfortunately, he was not able to carry out these ideas. While making a speech in Buffalo, New York, on September 6, 1901, he was shot. Although there were early hopes for his recovery from a stomach wound, gangrene set in, and he died eight days later, on September 14.

Further Reading

Dobson, John. *Reticent Expansionism: The Foreign Policy of William McKinley.* Pittsburgh, Pa.: Duquesne University Press, 1988.

Glad, Paul W. *McKinley, Bryan, and the People.* Philadelphia: Lippincott, 1964; reprint Ivan R. Dee, 1991.

Gould, Lewis L. "McKinley, William." Available online. Discovery Channel School, original content provided by World Book Online. URL: http://www.discoveryschool.com/homeworkhelp/worldbook/atozhistory/m/351660.html. downloaded November 8, 2001.

———. *The Presidency of William McKinley.* Lawrence: Regents Press of Kansas, 1980.

———. *The Spanish-American War and President McKinley.* Lawrence: University of Kansas Press, 1982.

———. "William McKinley" in *The American Presidents*, edited by Frank N. Magill, John L. Loos, and Tracy Irons-Georges. Pasadena, Calif.: Salem Press, 2000.

Hernon, Joseph Martin. *Profiles in Character: Hubris and Heroism in the U.S. Senate—1789–1990.* Armonk, N.Y.: M. E. Sharpe, 1997.

Higgins, Eva E. *William McKinley—An Inspiring Biography.* New York: Daring Books, 1990.

Johns, A. Wesley. *The Man Who Shot McKinley.* South Brunswick, N.J.: A. S. Barnes, 1970.

Leech, Margaret. *In the Days of McKinley.* Norwalk, Conn.: Easton Press, 1986.

"McKinley, William." Available online. URL: http://www.whitehouse.gov/history/presidents/wm26.html. Downloaded January 23, 2002.

"McKinley, William." in *The American President,* by Philip B. Kunhardt, Jr., Philip B. Kunhardt III, and Peter W. Kunhardt. New York: Riverhead Books, 1999.

"McKinley, William" in *The Presidency A to Z: Second Edition,* edited by Michael T. Nelson. Washington, D.C.: Congressional Quarterly Press, 1998.

Olcott, Charles S. *William McKinley.* New York: AMS Press, 1972.

McNamara, Robert Strange

(1916–   ) *secretary of defense, president of the World Bank, author*

Robert Strange McNamara was U.S. secretary of defense under Presidents JOHN FITZGERALD KENNEDY and LYNDON BAINES JOHNSON from 1961 to 1968. In that role, he was helpful in the successful resolution of the Cuban Missile Crisis and instrumental in the escalation of U.S. involvement in the Vietnam War.

McNamara was born on June 9, 1916, in San Francisco. He graduated from the University of California at Berkeley in 1937 and the Harvard Business School in 1939. He taught business administration at Harvard from 1940 to 1943. In World War II, he served in the U.S. Army Air Force. After the war, he became an executive at the Ford Motor Company in 1946 and moved up the ranks until he was named Ford's president in November 1960.

McNamara served very little time as the chief executive at Ford because President Kennedy asked him to become U.S. secretary of defense in early 1961. McNamara introduced modern "systems management" techniques at the Department of Defense, and he adopted the concept of "flexible response," which moved the U.S. military strategy away from threatening nuclear weapons for nonnuclear communist conflicts and strengthened U.S. conventional fighting forces. Although he supported escalation of the Vietnam War for several years, he came to doubt its usefulness, and he ultimately resigned as secretary of defense in early 1968.

McNamara then became president of the World Bank where he remained until 1981. After his retirement, he wrote extensively, principally about the war in Vietnam, in two major books.

When McNamara was appointed secretary of defense, he was heralded as one of the "best and the brightest" of the officials brought into government by President Kennedy. Initially, he brought a new level of intellectual substance to military planning called cost-benefit analysis. This was particularly effective in providing a method for analyzing the factors relevant to fighting and preventing thermonuclear war. This same analysis was singularly inappropriate for the issues involved in the war in Vietnam. The challenge that faced McNamara during his tenure as secretary of defense, caused this very capable man, who had left a successful career as head of one of the nation's "Big Three" automakers, to be dragged down by the Vietnam conflict.

Further Reading

Hendrickson, Paul. *The Living and the Dead: Robert McNamara and Five Lives of a Lost War.* New York: Knopf, 1996.

Lengle, James I. "McNamara, Robert Strange." Available Online. Discovery Channel School, original content provided by World Book Online. URL: http://www.discoveryschool.com/homeworkhelp/worldbook/atozhistory/m/351880.html. Downloaded November 6, 2001.

McNamara, Robert Strange. *The Essence of Security.* New York: Harper & Row, 1968.

———. *In Retrospect: The Tragedy and Lessons of Vietnam.* New York: Times Books, 1995.

———. *Argument Without End.* New York: Public Affairs, 1999.

———. *One Hundred Countries, Two Billion People.* New York: Praeger, 1973.

Murdock, Clark A. *Defense Policy Formation: A Comparative Analysis of the McNamara Era.* Albany: State University of New York Press, 1974.

Shapley, Deborah. *Promise and Power: The Life and Times of Robert McNamara.* Boston: Little, Brown, 1993.

Monroe, James

(1758–1831) *president, secretary of state, secretary of war, diplomat, senator, Revolutionary War leader*

James Monroe has been best remembered for the 1823 Monroe Doctrine, which warned European countries not to establish colonies or otherwise interfere with the independent nations of the Western Hemisphere. But Monroe should also be remembered as the diplomat most responsible for the Louisiana Purchase and as the fifth president of the United States. In addition, he served as Virginia governor, U.S. senator, U.S. minister to France, Spain, and Britain, secretary of state, and secretary of war—and for a time, he held both secretary positions simultaneously during the War of 1812.

Monroe was born on April 28, 1758, in Westmoreland County, Virginia, into the family of a modest planter, Colonel Spence Monroe. Tutored at home until he was 12 years old, he attended nearby Parson Archibald Campbell's school for four years. When he was 16, James entered the College of William and Mary, but he did not graduate since he entered the Revolutionary War as a lieutenant when he was only 18 years of age.

In 1776, he fought with GEORGE WASHINGTON's army at Harlem Heights and White Plains in New York, at Brandywine and Germantown in Pennsylvania, and at Monmouth in New Jersey. This service placed him in Valley Forge during the winter of 1777–78. His most notable service was at the Battle of Trenton, New Jersey, where he was wounded in the shoulder and cited for bravery.

In 1778, Monroe, having been promoted to lieutenant colonel, went back to Virginia to raise more troops for Washington, but he did not succeed because troops were needed to defend Virginia. Monroe then met Virginia's governor, THOMAS JEFFERSON, who became his instructor in the law and lifelong friend. In 1782, Monroe was

elected to the Virginia Assembly. The next year, he was elected to the Congress of the Articles of Confederation, where he served until 1786. Monroe began practicing law in Fredericksburg, Virginia, and was soon elected again to the Virginia Assembly where he served for four years. In 1788, Monroe was elected to the Virginia convention called to ratify the U.S. Constitution. His opposition to a strong central government put him on the side of PATRICK HENRY and GEORGE MASON, who opposed the ratification. Monroe's opposition was only moderate, and he accepted ratification willingly. In 1789, he moved to Charlottesville, Virginia, to be closer to Jefferson's estate, Monticello.

In 1788, Monroe lost in a race against JAMES MADISON for the first U.S. House of Representatives, but two years later he was rewarded with the vacant seat in the U.S. Senate by the Virginia legislature. With Jefferson and Madison, he became one of the founders of the Democratic Republican Party. In 1794, President Washington needed a diplomat who could improve relations with the French, so he appointed Monroe—a well-known Francophile—even though he knew Monroe opposed many of his policies. Monroe misunderstood the purpose of his mission, thinking he was expected to preserve the Franco-American friendship even though Washington felt he had to adopt a pro-British policy. Monroe sounded too much like a Democratic Republican Party spokesman rather than a representative of Washington's Federalist administration government. Secretary of State TIMOTHY PICKERING, a secret close associate of ALEXANDER HAMILTON, pressured Washington to recall Monroe in 1796 after he criticized the pro-British Jay Treaty, prepared according to Hamilton's instructions.

After Monroe's recall, he defended himself by publishing a harsh attack on Washington's foreign policy and was soon embroiled in a bitter personal dispute with Hamilton. Monroe was blamed for publication of slanders against Hamilton, but Monroe denied responsibility and Hamilton eventually dropped his objections.

In 1799, Monroe was elected Virginia's governor, and in that role he opposed the Alien and Sedition Acts and aided Jefferson's election as president. In 1803, President Jefferson sent Monroe to Paris to help Robert R. Livingston negotiate the purchase of the city of New Orleans. By the time Monroe's ship reached France, Napoleon had presented Livingston and Monroe not just the city of New Orleans but the entire Louisiana Territory on a take-it-or-leave-it basis. Although the purchase of the whole territory exceeded their instructions, Monroe and Livingston accepted the offer without waiting to consult Jefferson. Although Jefferson was unsure the U.S. Constitution authorized the purchase, he eventually approved it. The purchase proved so popular that Monroe's prestige rose dramatically.

Jefferson appreciated Monroe's initiative and sent him to Spain to help CHARLES COTESWORTH PINCKNEY try to buy Florida. They failed, but Jefferson had so much confidence in Monroe that he appointed him the U.S. minister to Britain. By this time, the Napoleonic War between Britain and France had so poisoned the atmosphere that Monroe—asked to negotiate a trade pact—could only get a treaty with terms so unfavorable to the United States that Jefferson was afraid to send it to the Senate.

With this implicit rebuke, Monroe returned to Virginia and, blaming Secretary of State Madison for the failure to send the treaty to the Senate, became a protest candidate against Madison for president in 1808. When Madison won the nomination and the presidency, Monroe was elected to the Virginia Assembly until he was elevated to the governor's office for a second time in 1811. Monroe's disagreement with Madison was short-lived, and he served only about three months in the governor's office. Madison desperately needed Monroe to serve as his secretary of state after his first one proved disloyal. U.S. relations with both Britain and France were strained because of the reciprocal blockades both countries placed on neutral shipping, including that of the United States, during the Napoleonic Wars.

Monroe soon concluded that war was inevitable and asked to be placed in charge of the army when the War of 1812 was declared, but Madison convinced him to stay in his cabinet. In 1814, when Madison's secretary of war, John Armstrong, was forced to resign because of his incompetence during the burning of Washington, D.C., Madison turned to Monroe to take over as secretary of war while remaining secretary of state. Holding both offices for the war's duration, Monroe led the U.S. Army to several brilliant victories, further enhancing his prestige.

By 1816, Monroe was easily elected president over the Federalist candidate, Rufus King of New York, by 183-34 Electoral College votes. The Federalist Party fatally damaged itself with secession talk over the War of 1812 just as ANDREW JACKSON was defeating the British at New Orleans. The party's demise after the 1816 election led Monroe's administration to be referred to as "the era of good feelings."

Monroe promoted this positive atmosphere by adopting a conciliatory policy toward the Federalists after the election. Following his inauguration, he toured New England, allowing the Federalists to rush to demonstrate their loyalty. Monroe hoped that this new "era" would place free government on a solid footing by eliminating party strife, but the "good feelings" did not survive his second term. His first term was a success, however, and even the 1818–19 economic depression did not significantly damage Monroe's popularity. In the 1820 election, Monroe was unopposed. He was given every Electoral College vote except that of William Plumer, a New Hampshire elector. Plumer said that no president except Washington should be elected unanimously, so he cast his vote for JOHN QUINCY ADAMS.

In domestic policy, Monroe accepted the orthodox Jeffersonian strict interpretation of limited congressional power under the Constitution. He would not accept "The American System" proposed by HENRY CLAY to strengthen the nation with construction of new roads and canals to open the West unless a constitutional amendment was passed to give Congress this power specifically. (Monroe did however, give limited support for protective tariffs to encourage Northern manufacturers to develop home markets.)

In 1818, Missouri applied for admission to the Union as a slave state. The northern-dominated U.S. House of Representatives aroused southern anger by adding to the Missouri admission bill a proviso that no more slaves could be imported into the state. The Senate—evenly divided between North and South—defeated this provision and

James Monroe had a distinguished political career before being elected the fifth U.S. president. *(Library of Congress)*

forced concessions known as the Missouri Compromise. This agreement stated that (1) Maine entered the Union as a free state, (2) Missouri entered as a slave state, but (3) slavery was banned from the rest of the Louisiana Purchase north of the southern boundary of Missouri. Monroe did not interfere in the debates, except to say he would veto any bill placing any special limits on Missouri's admission to the Union.

Monroe's conduct of foreign policy was very successful. Since the War of 1812, Georgians had been harassed by Indians from Spanish Florida. When fighting broke out between the Seminole Indians and Georgia settlers in 1817, Monroe ordered Andrew Jackson to attack the Indians. Jackson chased them into the Florida Everglades, captured Pensacola, Spanish Florida's capital, and another Spanish post at St. Marks. Two of Monroe's cabinet officers, William Crawford and JOHN CALDWELL CALHOUN, wanted Jackson reprimanded for exceeding his instructions. But Secretary of State John Quincy Adams dissented from criticizing Jackson and pressed Monroe to negotiate the ceding of Florida to the United States in return for the cancellation of $5 million in American claims against Spain. Monroe wisely took the latter course.

Adams also helped Monroe give the nation one of the most impressive strings of diplomatic successes. Britain signed the 1817 Rush-Bagot Agreement, limiting naval forces on the Great Lakes, as well as the 1818 agreement to use the 49th parallel as the boundary between the United States and Canada from Lake of the Woods on the Minnesota-Ontario border as far west as the Rocky Mountains. The British also agreed to joint occupation of the Oregon territory. U.S. diplomats persuaded Spain to give up its claims to Oregon in 1819 and the Russians to do the same in 1824.

During the Napoleonic Wars, Spain was so embroiled in the European conflict that most of its South American colonies took the opportunity to declare their independence from Spain. As early as 1817, acting on U.S. sympathy with these Latin American revolutions, Henry Clay had begun a campaign for recognition of these new countries. After the United States had safely acquired Florida through negotiation, Monroe finally recognized these new nations during the period of 1822 to 1824.

With Napoleon gone, Spain began to talk about using the so-called Holy Alliance to put down South American revolutions as they had done in Europe. In 1823, Britain's Foreign Minister George Canning, recognizing the benefits to Britain of the newly opened Latin American trade, proposed that the United States and Britain jointly oppose any such Holy Alliance intervention. Monroe talked with Jefferson and Madison, who favored the British idea. Many in his cabinet agreed, but John Quincy Adams had a better idea. Instead of the United States in effect allying with the British, the United States could simply take advantage of the fact that the British fleet would block any European invasion of South America and unilaterally declare Latin America off limits to further European colonization. Monroe explained this plan, later known as the Monroe Doctrine, in his annual message to Congress in December 1823. While Monroe's statement received little European attention, Britain's opposition and its fleet blocked any intervention until France's abortive Mexican invasion during the U.S. Civil War.

Monroe retired to Virginia and served for five years as the head of the University of Virginia. In 1829, he became presiding officer of the Virginia Constitutional Convention. Long public service had left Monroe a poor man, and he was too old to resume his law practice. Late in 1830, his financial distress forced him to move to New York City to live with his daughter, and he died there on July 4, 1831.

Further Reading

Ammon, Harry. *James Monroe, The Quest for National Identity.* Charlottesville: University Press of Virginia, 1990.

Cresson, W. P. *James Monroe.* Norwalk, Conn.: The Easton Press, 1986.

Cunningham, Noble E. *The Presidency of James Monroe.* Lawrence: University Press of Kansas, 1996.

Gilman, Daniel Coit. *James Monroe.* New York: Chelsea House, 1981.

Hanser, Richard. *The Glorious Hour of Lt. Monroe.* New York: Athenaeum, 1976.

May, Ernest R., *The Making of the Monroe Doctrine.* Cambridge, Mass.: Belknap Press of Harvard University, 1992.

"Monroe, James." Available online. URL: http://www.whitehouse.gov/history/presidents/jm5.html. Downloaded October 20, 2001.

Morgan, George. *The Life of James Monroe.* New York: AMS Press, 1969.

Noonan, John T., Jr. *The Antelope: The Ordeal of the Recaptured Africans in the Administrations of John Quincy Adams and James Monroe.* Berkeley: University of California Press, 1990.

Owsley, Frank L. *Filibusters and Expansionists: Jeffersonian Manifest Destiny, 1800–1821.* Tuscaloosa: University of Alabama Press, 1997.

Wilmerding, Lucius. *James Monroe: Public Claimant.* New Brunswick, N.J.: Rutgers University Press, 1960.

Morse, Wayne Lyman
(1900–1974) *senator, federal mediator*

Wayne Lyman Morse was a U.S. senator so grounded in the independent progressive tradition that he ran and won his U.S. Senate elections first as a Republican and later as a Democrat while serving as an independent part of the time. Called the "conscience of the Senate," he cast one of only two votes against the 1964 Gulf of Tonkin Resolution, which signaled U.S. escalation of the Vietnam War.

Morse was born on October 20, 1900, into a rural farming family near Madison, Wisconsin. He graduated from the University of Wisconsin with a B.A. degree in speech and economics in 1923 and an M.A. degree in speech in 1924. He went to the University of Minnesota as a professor of speech and rhetoric, took law courses, and graduated with the LL.B. law degree in 1928.

Following that, Morse attended Columbia University Law School, received a J.D. degree in 1929, and took a professorship at the University of Oregon School of Law. In 1930, Morse became the dean of Oregon's law school, the youngest dean of any ABA-accredited law school in the country. Practicing labor arbitration law part-time while serving as dean, he successfully settled the 1935 Portland Ferryboatmen's Union case and became so well known that he was appointed as the U.S. Department of Labor Pacific Coast arbitrator in 1939. In that role, his record of fairness made him popular with both businesses and unions. During World War II, he served on the National War Labor Board.

In 1944, Morse successfully ran as a Republican representing Oregon for the U.S. Senate, and he was reelected in 1950. He took progressive stances on a wide range of issues, such as public power, education, civil rights, labor-management relations, Latin American affairs, and international law, and he was always at odds with the Republican Party's reactionary elements. By 1952, declaring himself an "independent Republican," he did not endorse DWIGHT DAVID EISENHOWER for president. After allowing the Republicans to organize the U.S. Senate—almost evenly divided between Democrats and Republicans—he left the Republican Party entirely and became so independent that he placed his chair in the middle of the center aisle of the Senate chamber, between the seats of the two major parties to emphasize his independence.

Morse joined the Democratic Party in 1955 and was successfully reelected in 1956 and 1962 as a Democrat. An outspoken critic of U.S. involve-ment in the Vietnam War, he attacked Democratic President LYNDON BAINES JOHNSON's 1964 Gulf of Tonkin Resolution and argued—correctly as it turned out—that the United States had provided the so-called North Vietnamese attack on the U.S. destroyers that led to the resolution. He then joined with Alaska's Senator Ernest Gruening to vote against it. Largely for this vote, Republican Bob Packwood defeated him for reelection in 1968. In 1972, Morse challenged Oregon's other Republican senator, Mark Hatfield, a moderate lib-eral, and was defeated.

In 1974, Wayne Morse won the Democratic primary to challenge Packwood for his old Senate seat, but he died on July 22, a few months before the election.

Further Reading

Drukman, Mason. *Wayne Morse: A Political Biography.* Portland: Oregon Historical Society Press, 1997.

Sabin, Cornelius Ayer. *The Speeches of Wayne L. Morse, 1944–51.* Ann Arbor, Michigan: University Micro-films, 1958.

Smith, A. Robert. *The Tiger in the Senate: The Biography of Wayne Morse.* Garden City, N.Y.: Doubleday, 1962.

Moseley-Braun, Carol

(1947–) *senator, ambassador*

Carol Moseley-Braun was the fourth African American and the first African-American woman to serve in the U.S. Senate.

Carol Moseley was born on August 16, 1947—the daughter of a law enforcement official and a medical technician—and raised on Chicago's South Side. In 1969, Moseley graduated from the University of Illinois at Chicago with a B.A. degree in political science. In 1972, she finished a J.D. at the University of Chicago Law School. After finish-ing law school, she married one of her classmates, Michael Braun, and became an assistant U.S. attor-ney from 1973 to 1977.

In 1978, she was elected to the Illinois House of Representatives and was the first African American to serve as that chamber's assistant ma-jority leader. In that position, she impressed many

with her high ethical standards and was widely known as the "Conscience of the House." In 1989, she became the recorder of deeds in Cook County, Illinois.

In 1992, she was angered because the two-term Republican incumbent Alan Dixon had voted to confirm Clarence Thomas's U.S. Supreme Court nomination to the Senate after hearings had aired allegations that he had sexually harassed a female African-American coworker. Dixon lost in the Republican primary, but Moseley-Braun went on to defeat Republican Richard S. Williamson in the general election. She was the first woman ever elected to the U.S. Senate by the voters in Illinois and one of only six women who served in the U.S. Senate during the 1993–94 session. As the sole African American in the Senate from 1992 to 1998, she was frequently asked to address the problems of African Americans who did not live in her district, and she sought to respond to issues on a national basis.

Her legislative concerns included minority rights, education, welfare, and other liberal social is-sues. Her most memorable speech was made in op-position to a proposal to grant a patent on the Confederate flag, which she not surprisingly regarded as a symbol of slavery in the antebellum South.

Among her accomplishments were her service as the only female ever to sit as a permanent mem-ber of the powerful Senate Finance Committee. She also was a member of the Judiciary Commit-tee, the Banking, Housing, and Urban Affairs Committees, the Small Business and Aging Com-mittees, and the bipartisan Commission on Entitle-ments and Tax Reform. She worked to assist the historic preservation of the Underground Railroad. She also supported measures aimed at equal pay for equal work for women and a variety of other tax and entitlement issues.

Unfortunately for her political career, she was dogged almost from the first by charges of financial irregularities, perhaps more shocking given her earlier designation as the conscience of the Illinois House of Representatives. She was accused of sharing her inheritance from her mother with her siblings instead of using it to repay the government for their support of her mother in a publicly funded facility for the elderly. Eyebrows were raised about her frequent overseas travel at public expense and the large financial contributions she received from someone designated by the media as a military dictator of an African country.

Moseley-Braun was not reelected in 1998, but in 1999, she was named the U.S. ambassador to New Zealand, where she served until 2001.

Further Reading

Jeter, Jon. "Moseley-Braun in Trouble," *Washington Post* (October 1, 1998): A16.

Miles, Johnnie H., Juanita J. Davis, Sharon E. Ferguson-Roberts, and Rita Giles. *Almanac of African-American History*. Paramus, N.J.: Prentice Hall, 2001.

"Moseley-Braun, Carol." Available online. URL: http://suburbanchicagonews.com/elections/polls/C17senpoll.htm. Downloaded September 17, 1998.

"Moseley-Braun, Carol," *New York Times* (March 19, 1992): A20.

"Moseley-Braun, Carol," *Washington Post* (April 28, 1992): C1.

Will, George. "Moseley-Braun May Find Defeat." Available online. URL: http://www.chicago-law.net/RealCases/will.html. Downloaded September 28, 1998.

Moynihan, Daniel Patrick

(1927–) *diplomat, senator, author*

Daniel Patrick Moynihan was a prominent bipartisan intellectual before he became a Democratic New York senator from 1977 to 2001.

Moynihan was born on March 16, 1927, in Tulsa, Oklahoma, but he grew up in a poor neighborhood in New York City. He graduated from Tufts University with a B.A. degree in 1948, an M.A. degree in 1949, and a Ph.D. degree in 1961. He was an assistant to Democratic New York Governor Averell Harriman in the 1950s. In 1963, he published (with Nathan Glazer) *Beyond the Melting Pot*, an influential study of American ethnicity.

From 1961 to 1965, Moynihan worked in the Department of Labor during the administrations of Presidents JOHN FITZGERALD KENNEDY and LYNDON BAINES JOHNSON. In 1965, his office issued a publication entitled *The Negro Family: The Case for National Action*, which was commonly known as the Moynihan Report. Its conclusion that black urban poverty could be traced in part to a breakdown of the black family caused an uproar, and Moynihan left government to teach at Harvard. From 1966 to 1969, he headed the Joint Center of Urban Studies at Harvard University and the Massachusetts Institute of Technology.

In 1969 and 1970, Moynihan returned to government as a special adviser to President RICHARD MILHOUS NIXON, who later named him U.S. ambassador to India from 1973 to 1975. President GERALD RUDOLPH FORD appointed him U.S. ambassador to the United Nations in 1975, and he served in that position until New York elected him as a Democrat to the U.S. Senate in 1976. He was reelected in 1982, 1988, and 1994. Although Moynihan's books and policy recommendations in the 1960s and 1970s were considered critical documents in the formulations of "neoconservatism," he became a vocal critic of Presidents RONALD WILSON REAGAN and GEORGE HERBERT WALKER BUSH, even though they were supported by many other "neoconservatives." He was a consistent supporter of Democratic Presidents JAMES EARL CARTER and WILLIAM JEFFERSON CLINTON. Moynihan retired from the Senate in 2001 and joined the faculty of the Maxwell School of Citizenship and Public Affairs of Syracuse University.

While Moynihan has acquired the status of an icon in some circles, his role as an intellectual gadfly has led him to take curious stands that would not normally be acceptable in the political world and particularly in the clublike atmosphere of the U.S. Senate. Moynihan has effectively switched back and forth between the Republican and Democratic parties. His policy recommendations have ranged from extremely liberal to neoconservative. At the end of his career, Moynihan was in the unusual posture of supporting President Clinton's wife, HILLARY RODHAM CLINTON, as his successor in the Senate, while opposing ALBERT GORE, President Clinton's own candidate for successor, for president of the United States. In the end, Gore carried New York in the Democratic primary and the general election by a wide margin, while Hillary Clinton was only modestly winning her own race. Moynihan's own recommendations seemingly did not affect the largest number of voters in his own home state. Moynihan's legacy contains many such unusual results.

Further Reading

Broder, David. "Moynihan, Daniel Patrick." Available online. Discovery Channel School, original content provided by World Book Online. URL: http://www.discoveryschool.com/homeworkhelp/worldbook/atozhistory/m/376350.html. Downloaded November 17, 2001.

Loomis, Burdett A. *Esteemed Colleagues: Civility and Deliberation in the U.S. Senate.* Washington, D.C.: Brookings Institution, 2000.

Moynihan, Daniel P. *Came The Revolution: Argument in the Reagan Era.* San Diego, Calif.: Harcourt Brace Jovanovich, 1988.

———. *Coping: Essays on the Practice of Government.* New York: Random House. 1973.

———. *Counting Our Blessings: Reflections on the Future of America.* Boston: Little, Brown, 1980.

———. *A Dangerous Place.* Boston: Little, Brown. 1978.

———, ed. *On Understanding Poverty: Perspectives from the Social Sciences.* New York: Basic Books, 1969.

———, ed. *Toward a National Urban Policy.* New York: Basic Books, 1970.

Schoen, Douglas E. *Pat: A Biography of Daniel Patrick Moynihan.* New York: Harper & Row, 1979.

Murphy, Frank

(1890–1949) *associate justice of the Supreme Court, governor, author*

Frank Murphy was the one of the strongest defenders of civil liberties, civil rights, and the underprivileged ever to serve as associate justice on the U.S. Supreme Court. He was also a prominent Michigan judge, Detroit's mayor, Michigan's governor, U.S. governor-general and high commissioner of the Philippines, and U.S. attorney general.

Murphy was born on April 13, 1890, into a poor Irish immigrant family in Harbor Beach, Michigan. As a child factory worker, he developed a strong hatred of the exploitation of workers and a genuine sympathy for the underprivileged. Through constant struggle, he finally managed to pay for a legal education at the University of Michigan. Graduating in 1914, he worked in De-

troit as a law clerk during the day and a teacher at night. In 1917, Murphy fought with U.S. Army in World War I in France. After the war, he remained in Europe under a special program that allowed him to study law in Trinity College in Ireland and in Lincoln's Inn in England.

Back in Michigan, he was chief assistant U.S. attorney of Michigan's Eastern District, where it was said he never lost a case. In 1923, after three years of private practice, he was appointed a recorder's court judge in Detroit. In 1930, Murphy was elected Detroit's Democratic mayor. From then until 1933, he received national recognition for his efforts to help the unemployed during the Great Depression.

A strong supporter of FRANKLIN DELANO ROOSEVELT's New Deal, Murphy was appointed by Roosevelt U.S. governor-general of the Philippines in 1933 and U.S. high commissioner for the Philippines in 1936. Roosevelt asked Murphy to run for governor of Michigan in 1936, and he was elected in the fall. The following year, although the courts authorized him to use troops to quell a Flint, Michigan, automobile workers strike, he used his office to negotiate a peaceful settlement instead. This earned him a national reputation as a defender of the workers as well as the undying enmity of the Michigan business community, which stopped at virtually nothing to make sure he was defeated in 1938.

Roosevelt then appointed Murphy U.S. attorney general in 1939 and associate justice of the U.S. Supreme Court in 1940. For a short time in 1942, he left the bench to serve again in the U.S. Army. Murphy served as an infantry officer at Ft. Bennett during the Supreme Court recesses, but his absence—although during a court recess—upset Chief Justice Harlan Fiske Stone. Murphy reluctantly did not repeat his military service. He returned to the Court where he consistently defended civil liberties and civil rights, including his most famous dissent in *Korematsu v. United States* (1944), declaring the wartime internment of Japanese Americans unconstitutional.

Murphy died unexpectedly on July 19, 1949, in Detroit.

President Harry S. Truman appointed U.S. Attorney General Tom C. Clark to replace Murphy.

This caused a domestic furor because Murphy was a Catholic and Clark was a Presbyterian, the first time a Catholic had not served on the Supreme Court in a half century. Murphy had such a strong record on civil liberties that many feared that Clark, who had prosecuted suspected Communists with great vigor as attorney general, would move the Supreme Court in a conservative direction. Perhaps mindful of the reputation of the justice he replaced, Clark moved in a generally liberal direction on the Court. However, there seems little doubt that civil libertarian issues suffered from the loss of Murphy on the Court.

Further Reading

Fine, Sidney. *Frank Murphy*. Ann Arbor: University of Michigan Press, 1975.

———. *Frank Murphy: A Michigan Life*. Ann Arbor: Historical Society of Michigan, 1985.

———. *Frank Murphy in World War I*. Ann Arbor: Michigan Historical Collections, University of Michigan, 1968.

Howard, J. Woodford, "Frank Murphy," in *The Oxford Companion to the Supreme Court*, edited by Kermit L. Hall. New York: Oxford University Press, 1992.

———. *Mr. Justice Murphy: A Political Biography*. Princeton, N.J.: Princeton University Press, 1968.

Lunt, Richard D. *The High Ministry of Government: The Political Career of Frank Murphy*. Detroit, Mich.: Wayne State University Press, 1965.

Murphy, Frank. *In Defense of Democracy*. Washington, D.C.: American Council on Public Affairs, 1940.

———. *Mr. Justice Murphy and the Bill of Rights*. Dobbs Ferry, N.Y.: Oceania Publications, 1965.

Muskie, Edmund Sixtus

(1914–1996) *senator, secretary of state, governor*

Edmund Sixtus Muskie was the first Democrat ever elected to the U.S. Senate by Maine voters, the first Democratic governor elected in Maine in two decades, as well as a vice presidential candidate, a presidential candidate, and secretary of state.

Muskie was born on March 28, 1914, in Rumford, Maine, the son and grandson of Polish immigrants. His father had changed the family name from Marciszewski. Muskie graduated as the class valedictorian from Stephens High School in Rumford in 1928. A member of Phi Beta Kappa, class president, and star debater, he graduated cum laude from Bates College in 1936. After graduating from Cornell University Law School in 1939, he began practicing law in Waterville, Maine. In World War II, he served in the U.S. Navy in both the Atlantic and Pacific theaters.

In 1946, Muskie was elected as a Democrat to the Maine House of Representatives and reelected in 1948 and 1950. Since Maine was an overwhelmingly Republican state, he rose to the highest rank ever achieved by a Democrat at that time when he was named the Democrats minority leader during his last two terms. He was named the Federal Office of Price Stabilization director for Maine in 1951. When he was elected Maine's governor in 1954, he was the first Democrat to hold that office in 20 years.

In 1958, after two gubernatorial terms, he was the first Democrat ever elected to the U.S. Senate by Maine voters. Reelected in 1964, 1970, and 1976, he served on the Foreign Relations, Governmental Affairs, and Environmental and Public Works Committees during his 21 years in the Senate. He was also the first chair of the Senate Committee on the Budget, a committee he worked hard to create.

Democratic presidential nominee HUBERT HORATIO HUMPHREY selected him to be his vice presidential running mate in 1968. Although Republican presidential nominee RICHARD MILHOUS NIXON narrowly defeated the Democratic ticket, Muskie became the leading contender for the Democratic nomination in 1972. But as the subject of many of the "dirty tricks" of the Nixon Presidential Reelection Committee, he was eventually forced out of the race.

In May 1980, President JAMES EARL CARTER named Muskie U.S. secretary of state, a position he held until the end of Carter's term. After leaving public office, he entered a Washington, D.C., law firm, but he continued to be active in the public realm, serving on the President's Special Review Board to investigate the Iran-Contra controversy. In 1972, he published his autobiographical book, *Journeys*.

Muskie died on March 26, 1996, in Washington, D.C.

Further Reading

Asbell, Bernard. *The Senate Nobody Knows.* Baltimore, Md.: Johns Hopkins University Press, 1981.

Lippman, Theo. *Muskie.* New York: Norton, 1971.

Lengle, James. "Muskie, Edmund Sixtus." Available online. Discovery Channel, original content provided by World Book Online. URL: http://www.discovery school.com/homeworkhelp/worldbook/atozhistory/ m/379060.html. Downloaded November 17, 2001.

Loomis, Burdett A. *Esteemed Colleagues: Civility and Deliberation in the U.S. Senate.* Washington, D.C.: Brookings Institution, 2000.

Nevin, David. *Muskie of Maine.* New York: Random House, 1972.

N

Nixon, Richard Milhous
(1913–1994) *president, vice president, senator, representative, author*

After a lifelong struggle to become president, Richard Nixon succeeded in 1968 only to fall victim to scandal after his 1972 landslide reelection. He became the first president ever to resign under the threat of impending impeachment and only one of three ever to be faced with impeachment proceedings.

Born on January 9, 1913, in Yorba Linda, California, Richard Milhous Nixon attended nearby Whittier College and later Duke University Law School. He practiced law in California and at the Office of Price Administration (OPA) in Washington, D.C., briefly before entering the U.S. Navy in World War II. After the war, he defeated Democrat Jerry Voorhis for Congress by using—his critics charged—unfounded innuendoes that Voorhis was a communist sympathizer.

Serving on the House Un-American Activities Committee, Nixon rose quickly to national prominence with his successful prosecution of Alger Hiss as a spy for the Soviet Union. This prominence aided in his defeat of Helen Gahagen Douglas in the 1950 U.S. Senate campaign, again accompanied by charges that Nixon used anticommunist smear tactics. The Hiss prosecution angered many liberals who cast Nixon in the role of a rigid ideologue determined to use anticommunism as a tool to repeal the New Deal programs. Nixon's popularity in conservative Republican circles was almost equaled by intense hatred in liberal Democratic circles.

Nominally committed to California's favorite son, Republican Governor EARL WARREN, Nixon surreptitiously aided DWIGHT DAVID EISENHOWER's presidential bid over that of Senator Robert Taft and Warren, and he parlayed that effort into winning the 1952 Republican vice presidential nomination. Almost undone at the campaign's outset by sudden revelations that he had received special funding from a group of California businessmen, he deftly answered the charge in a speech, including maudlin references to his pet dog, Checkers. He mollified public opinion enough to satisfy Eisenhower, but he simultaneously reinforced the liberal conception of his disreputability. Elected with Eisenhower to two vice presidential terms, Nixon was the odds-on favorite for the 1960 Republican nomination but lost a close race to President JOHN FITZGERALD KENNEDY. Two years later, he lost a premature comeback in the California gubernatorial race, but his career was far from over.

Conservative BARRY MORRIS GOLDWATER's failed 1964 presidential bid left the Republicans without a clear candidate to take advantage of the problems in the Democratic Party. But Richard Nixon announced his candidacy and received the Republican nomination. The political divisions over the Vietnam War and civil rights seriously weakened President LYNDON BAINES JOHNSON, and he chose not to run for reelection. So Vice President HUBERT HORATIO HUMPHREY took Johnson's place as the Democratic nominee of a badly split party.

The race was very close, and Nixon was elected with only 43 percent the popular vote while Humphrey received 42.7 percent and American Independent GEORGE CORLEY WALLACE received 13.5 percent. The political divisions over Vietnam and the struggle for black equality in the face of white (particularly southern) resistance led to this close result and dominated the Nixon years.

This division was manifest in Nixon's controversial Supreme Court appointments, arguably his longest-lasting impact. Nixon had the opportunity to appoint four Supreme Court justices during his relatively brief five and one-half years as president. Only three other presidents (BENJAMIN HARRISON, WILLIAM HOWARD TAFT, and WARREN GAMALIEL HARDING) appointed as many justices in such a short time. His early appointments of Minnesotan

Richard Nixon became the first president ever to resign under the threat of impending impeachment, and one of only three ever to be faced with impeachment proceedings. (*Library of Congress, Official White House photo*)

WARREN EARL BURGER for the retiring Chief Justice EARL WARREN and HARRY ANDREW BLACKMUN (another Minnesotan) to replace the scandal-plagued Abe Fortas engendered little controversy. But when Nixon attempted to fulfill a campaign promise made to southern supporters by appointing a southerner to the Court, he failed twice in a row. He finally succeeded when he chose Lewis Powell, a distinguished moderate Virginia Democrat. Later, Nixon successfully appointed conservative WILLIAM HUBBS REHNQUIST, who has remained on the Court more than a quarter of a century (and subsequently was appointed chief justice).

Nixon can be credited domestically with the creation of the Environmental Protection Agency (EPA) and general revenue sharing as an alternative to excessively restrictive categorical grants to states and cities. But it was in foreign affairs that he expected to have his greatest impact, because he believed that these were the president's most important duties. During the 1968 campaign, he had promised that he had a plan to end the war in Vietnam. To "hawks," or supporters of the Vietnam War, he implied that he planned to use stronger military action to win the war. To "doves," or supporters of U.S. disengagement, he implied that he planned peace negotiations to disengage from Vietnam even without a victory.

Nixon later publicly acknowledged he had no plan, but the general outline of his foreign and military policy seemed to follow these contradictory goals. With HENRY ALFRED KISSINGER as head of his National Security Council (and later secretary of state) Nixon devised a plan for lessened tensions (or détente) with the Soviet Union and rapprochement with the previously isolated People's Republic of China, two major allies of North Vietnam, to pressure the Vietnamese into a more favorable settlement.

While Nixon succeeded in improving relations with the Soviet Union and China, he did not achieve his principal goal of pressuring the Vietnamese into accepting a favorable settlement. His policy used a carrot-and-stick approach, offering North Vietnam the "carrot" of a negotiated eventual withdrawal of U.S. forces if they reduced their military effort and the "stick" of increased bombing of North Vietnam and a ground invasion of Cambodia to defeat the Vietnamese militarily. Neither materially shortened the war nor avoided ultimate North Vietnamese success. Such agreements served only as a cover for U.S. disengagement from a losing military effort.

As president of a badly divided nation and facing Democratic control in both houses of Congress, Nixon recognized that he would lose if the Democrats united in the 1972 election campaign. Demonstrations against his administration's Vietnam policy indicated his weakness. The depth of this division produced in him a kind of siege mentality, including a willingness to bend or break laws, if necessary, to divide the opposition. This led to the creation of the so-called Plumber's Unit responsible for the burglary and wiretapping of the Democratic headquarters in the Watergate complex.

Perhaps through Nixon's efforts at manipulation, Democrats nominated a weak GEORGE STANLEY MCGOVERN, whom Nixon easily defeated in a landslide. But the Nixon campaign's excesses included the fatefully destructive Watergate burglary, and his involvement in the cover-up of the burglary unraveled in his second term. A unanimous Supreme Court, including three of his appointees, ordered him to turn over damaging tape recordings that revealed his involvement and ultimately led to his resignation under the threat of impending impeachment.

In retirement, Richard Nixon attempted again to rebuild his reputation by writing extensively on foreign affairs, and he did achieve a measure of success. He died on April 22, 1994, in New York City.

Further Reading

Ehrlichman, John. *Witness to Power: The Nixon Years.* New York: Simon & Schuster, 1982.
Genovese, Michael A. *The Nixon Presidency.* New York: Greenwood, 1990.
"Nixon, Richard." Available online. URL: http://www.whitehouse.gov/history/presidents/rn37.html. Downloaded November 11, 2001.
Nixon, Richard M. *Beyond Peace.* New York: Random House, 1994.
———. *In the Arena.* New York: Simon & Schuster, 1990.
———. *Leaders.* New York: Warner Books, 1982.
———. *1999: Victory Without War.* New York: Simon & Schuster, 1988.
———. *No More Vietnams.* New York: Avon, 1986.
———. *Real Peace.* Boston: Little, Brown, 1983.
———. *RN: The Memoirs of Richard Nixon.* New York: Grosset & Dunlap, 1978.
———. *Six Crises.* Garden City, N.Y.: Doubleday, 1962.
Oudes, Bruce, ed. *From the President: Richard Nixon's Secret Files.* New York: Harper & Row, 1990.
Safire, William. *Before the Fall: An Inside View of the Pre-Watergate White House.* Garden City, N.Y.: Doubleday, 1975.
Sussman, Barry. *The Great Cover-up: Nixon and the Scandal of Watergate.* Arlington, Va.: Seven Locks Press, 1992.
White, Theodore H. *Breach of Faith: The Fall of Richard Nixon.* New York: Athenaeum, 1975.
Wicker, Tom. *One of Us: Richard Nixon and the American Dream.* New York: Random House, 1991.

Norris, George William
(1861–1944) *senator, representative*

In representing Nebraska in Congress for more than 40 years, George William Norris moved as his conscience dictated from Republicanism to independence. Except for the opposition of conservative Republicans in the Senate, Norris's outstanding record would have earned him the highest rank the Senate could vote for one of its members.

Norris was born on July 11, 1861, in Sandusky, Ohio. His father and older brother both died when Norris was only three years old, so his mother, then 46 years old and in her 12th pregnancy, raised and provided for George and his six sister on the family farm where they lived near poverty. Her strength of character and these circumstances colored Norris's decisions throughout his political career.

In 1883, Norris received his law degree from the law school at Northern Indiana Normal University at Valparaiso and entered the bar the same year. He taught school intermittently to pay for his education, and with his degree and life experiences, moved west in 1885. He traveled to Washington State before settling in Nebraska where he had relatives and a deed to an 80-acre farm near Tecumseh, Nebraska. After a brief stay there, he moved to Beaver City where he married, practiced law, and speculated in real estate.

By 1892, Norris was the elected prosecuting attorney for Furnas County, and in 1895, he was an elected Nebraska district judge. To be closer to the center of his circuit, Norris moved to Mc-Cook in 1899.

In 1902, he was elected to the U.S. House of Representatives and reelected four more times. In 1910, Norris launched a campaign to strip the House Speaker, then Republican "Boss" JOSEPH GURNEY CANNON, of the power over the House Rules Committee, which controlled the flow of all legislation. After skillful parliamentary maneuvering and a bitter fight, Norris led the bipartisan group to victory over Cannon.

Although he had broken ranks with his party over a vital issue, this did not hurt him in Nebraska, where he was nominated and elected to the Senate in 1912 and reelected for four additional terms. Over the next 30 years, Norris used his Senate forum to help farmers and workers.

Although he fought his fellow Republicans, Norris was not a Democrat. He opposed the internationalist foreign policy of Democratic President THOMAS WOODROW WILSON, voting against U.S. entry into World War I and believing that the banks and munitions makers had drummed up the pro-war hysteria. For this vote he was vilified nationally and in Nebraska, but his reputation for truth-telling and diligent campaigning persuaded Nebraskans to send him back to the Senate in 1918. Norris also opposed Wilson's Versailles Treaty, but he ceased to be an isolationist by the eve of World War II.

As a progressive Republican, he supported many nonpartisan reform measures. He authored the 1932 act that initiated the Twentieth Amendment to the Constitution, abolishing the "lame duck" session of Congress and changing the presidential inauguration date from March 4 to January 20. He successfully urged the concept of the nonpartisan, one-house (or unicameral) legislature, which he believed would curb abuses of the conference committees that allowed the ruling party to secretly rewrite legislation to favor its own positions (although this was not an issue before the U.S. Senate). In 1937, Nebraska became the only state with a single-chamber legislature.

Conservative Republican regulars could tolerate some of these reforms, but they parted company with Norris over many other issues, particularly as Norris pushed for federal aid to farmers and workers in the Great Depression. In 1932, Norris joined another maverick Republican, New York's FIORELLO HENRY LA GUARDIA, to pass the Norris-La Guardia Act, which forbade the courts from using injunctions in labor disputes to prevent strikes, boycotts, or picketing. In the 1932 presidential election, Norris did not endorse Republican president HERBERT CLARK HOOVER, and he actively campaigned for the Democratic presidential nominee, FRANKLIN DELANO ROOSEVELT.

Pro-business Republicans, such as Henry Ford, who called Norris a "socialist" for supporting public electric power through the 1933 Tennessee Valley Authority Act and the Rural Electrification Administration, forced Norris out of the Republican Party and compelled him to run as an independent in 1936. This action would have defeated most politicians, but Norris was returned to office in 1936.

In 1942, the pro-business conservatives finally were able to defeat Norris when he was 81 years of age. His autobiography, *Fighting Liberal*, was published posthumously in 1945 after his death on September 2, 1944.

After his death, the entire U.S. Senate was prepared to name George Norris one of the greatest U.S. senators of all time, but the conservative Republican senators from Nebraska blocked Norris from receiving this honor. Other Nebraskans felt differently. In 1961, Norris was the first person to have his bust placed in the Nebraska Hall of Fame at the Nebraska State Capitol.

Further Reading

Hernon, Joseph Martin. *Profiles in Character: Hubris and Heroism in the U.S. Senate—1789–1990*. Armonk, N.Y.: M. E. Sharpe, 1997.

Lief, Alfred. *Democracy's Norris: The Biography of a Lonely Crusade*. New York: Stackpole Sons, 1967.

Lowitt, Richard. *George W. Norris: The Triumph of a Progressive, 1933–1944.* Urbana: University of Illinois Press, 1978.

Neuberger, Richard Lewis. *Integrity: The Life of George W. Norris.* New York: The Vanguard Press, 1937.

Norris, George W. *Fighting Liberal: The Autobiography of George W. Norris.* Lincoln: University of Nebraska Press, 1992 (originally published in 1945).

"Norris, George W" in *Congress A to Z: Third Edition,* edited by David R. Tarr and Ann O'Connor. Washington, D.C.: Congressional Quarterly, 1999.

"Norris, George W." Available online. URL: http://www.nebraskahistory.org/sites/norris/moreinfo.htm. Last updated May 22, 2000.

Zucker, Norman L. *George W. Norris: Gentle Knight of American Democracy.* Urbana: University of Illinois Press, 1966.

Nye, Gerald Prentice
(1892–1971) *senator*

Best known as the rabid isolationist who coined the phrase "Merchants of Death" to describe the World War I–era munitions manufacturers, Gerald Nye was a devoted Progressive and an emotional speaker, who played an important role in the politics of the 1930s and 1940s.

Born on December 19, 1892, in Hortonville, Wisconsin, Gerald Prentice Nye went straight from high school into working and owning newspapers in Wisconsin, Iowa, and North Dakota. Having settled in North Dakota, he supported Wisconsin's Progressive candidate for president, ROBERT MARION LA FOLLETTE, in 1924.

In 1925, Nye was appointed to fill a vacancy in the U.S. Senate from North Dakota. As a Republican member of North Dakota's Nonpartisan League, Nye's politics cut across party lines. The Nonpartisan League attempted to prevent the domination of North Dakota's farm economy by the East Coasts banks and other special financial interests from either party. From this political perspective, Nye was elected to three consecutive six-year terms in United States Senate.

Nye's first loyalty was to the protection of the farmers of North Dakota, but he supported other progressive domestic policy measures. He served as a serious critic of the policies of President WARREN GAMALIEL HARDING while serving on the committee that investigated the Teapot Dome scandal in the 1920s. Initially, he supported President FRANKLIN DELANO ROOSEVELT's New Deal programs, but later he became so disillusioned with Roosevelt's foreign policy that he drifted into opposition to the president's domestic policies as well.

Since it was expected that Nye would support farmers as a senator from North Dakota, he attracted more attention as a result of his isolationism. During the 1920s, he led the fight to stop the United States from joining the World Court. In 1934, he sponsored a U.S. Senate resolution that led to an investigation of the munitions industry in World War I. As the chairman of the Senate probe that conducted that 1934–37 investigation, Nye revealed how much the business and financial community had been involved in manufacturing the weapons that were sold to Britain and France for use against Germany in World War I. Arguing that this practice led the United States unnecessarily to enter World War I on the side of the British and French so that, by winning, they would have the money to repay the banks and arms makers, Nye created his famous "Merchants of Death" line.

Nye toured the country making speeches and defending his isolationist policies. With the help of Senator WILLIAM EDGAR BORAH and others, Nye wrote, sponsored, and enacted a series of neutrality bills designed to keep the United States out of World War II. In 1940, he won a seat on the Senate Foreign Relations Committee and in that role tried in vain to prevent the passage of the Lend-Lease Act. However, after the Japanese attack on Pearl Harbor, Nye patriotically supported the war effort. Isolationism was clearly out of fashion in the middle of the war, and Nye lost has attempt to win a fourth term in the Senate in 1944.

Nye went into business as a management consultant in Washington, D.C., from 1946 until his retirement from business. He died on July 17, 1971.

Further Reading
Cole, Wayne S. *Senator Gerald P. Nye and American Foreign Relations.* Minneapolis: University of Minnesota Press, 1962.

Davis, Kenneth S. *FDR: Three Volumes.* New York: Random House, 1993.

McElvaine, Robert S. "Franklin Delano Roosevelt" in *The American Presidents,* edited by Frank N. Magill, John L. Loos, and Tracy Irons-Georges. Pasadena, Calif.: Salem Press, 2000.

McJimsey, George T. *The Presidency of Franklin Delano Roosevelt.* Lawrence: University Press of Kansas, 2000.

Morris, Jeffrey. *The FDR Way.* Minneapolis: Lerner Publications, 1996.

O'Connor, Sandra Day

(1930–) *associate justice of the Supreme Court, state judge, state legislator*

The first woman to serve as an associate justice on the U.S. Supreme Court, Sandra Day O'Connor was appointed by President RONALD WILSON REAGAN to fill the vacancy created by the retirement of Justice Potter Stewart in 1981. In 1972, she was also the first woman to hold the office of elected majority leader in a state senate anywhere in the United States.

Born on March 26, 1930, in El Paso, Texas, Sandra Day was raised on a family-owned Arizona ranch that her grandfather Henry C. Day established in the 1880s, when Arizona was still a territory. After age five, she spent the school months with her maternal grandmother in El Paso so she could attend Radford School, a private girls' school, but she returned each summer to the ranch. When she was 13, she decided to stay at the ranch and attend the nearest school in Duncan, Arizona. This meant traveling 22 miles each school day, leaving before daylight and returning after dark. The next year she was sent back to Radford. After a year, she transferred to El Paso's Austin High School where she graduated at age 16.

She graduated magna cum laude from Stanford University in 1950 with a B.A. degree in economics. In her senior year, she overlapped college with her first year at Stanford Law School. She served as one of the editors on the *Stanford Law Review* and won membership in the Order of the Coif, a legal honor society. She graduated in 1952, third in her law school class of 102 students and married a fellow student, John O'Connor, later that year. One of her fellow editors and the top-ranking student in the class was future U.S. chief justice WILLIAM HUBBS REHNQUIST.

After graduation, she practiced law intermittently in Arizona while raising her small children. In 1965, with her children in school, she began working full-time as assistant Arizona attorney general. In 1969, Arizona governor Jack Williams appointed her to fill an unexpired term created by a vacancy in the Arizona senate. She was elected in her own right in 1970 and reelected in 1972. When she entered her next senate term in 1973, she was elected the Republican majority leader, the first woman in such a post in the United States. The next year, O'Conner was elected a Maricopa County trial court judge. Five years later the Arizona governor—a Democrat—appointed her to the Arizona Court of Appeals, the second highest court in the state.

O'Connor had long been an active Republican and Reagan supporter, boosting him for president in his losing bid against incumbent President GERALD RUDOLPH FORD in 1976 at the Republican National Convention. With her bipartisan political appointment history, her generally conservative record, and her support of Reagan, she was a leading candidate to help Reagan fulfill his pledge to appoint a woman to the U.S. Supreme Court at his first opportunity. When Justice Stewart announced

Sandra Day O'Connor was the first woman to be appointed to the U.S. Supreme Court. *(Library of Congress)*

his retirement in June 1981, Reagan appointed O'Connor, who easily won confirmation.

Although it is difficult to categorize the views of Supreme Court justices, O'Connor has been regarded as a moderately conservative member and has been especially careful to defend conservative protections of federalism and the state judicial systems. She has not voted as conservatively as the three best-known conservatives: Chief Justice Rehnquist and Associate Justices ANTONIN SCALIA and Clarence Thomas. She has often voted with Associate Justice Anthony Kennedy to provide conservative votes in close five-to-four decisions.

O'Connor is often the fifth justice and writes her own concurring opinion, thereby limiting the effectiveness of the conservative majority decision. She often writes long, careful historical reviews of the issues (in contrast to Scalia, a textualist who seldom departs from the text and writes short opinions) and uses conservative principles. The harsh-est criticism leveled against O'Connor came as the result of her vote to join the five-to-four decision in the 2000 presidential election case, *Bush v. Gore.* That vote departed from her conservative principles, especially those protecting the decisions of state courts, since it overturned a Florida Supreme Court decision interpreting Florida state law.

Further Reading

Bentley, Judith. *Justice Sandra Day O'Connor.* New York: J. Messner, 1983.

Fiss, Owen M. "O'Connor, Sandra Day." Available online. Discovery Channel School, original content provided by World Book Online, http://www.discoveryschool.com/homeworkhelp/worldbook/atozhistory/o/399040.html. Downloaded November 19, 2001.

Fox, Mary Virginia. *Justice Sandra Day O'Connor.* Hillside, N.J.: Enslow, 1983.

Gherman, Beverly. *Sandra Day O'Connor: Justice for All.* New York: Viking, 1991

Henry, Christopher. *Sandra Day O'Connor.* New York: Franklin Watts, 1994.

Herda, D. J. *Sandra Day O'Connor.* Springfield, N.J.: Enslow, 1995.

Holland, Gini. *Sandra Day O'Connor.* Austin, Tex.: Raintree Steck-Vaughn, 1997.

Huber, Peter W. *Sandra Day O'Connor.* New York: Chelsea House, 1990.

Van Sickel, Robert W. *Not a Particularly Different Voice: The Jurisprudence of Sandra Day O'Connor.* New York: P. Lang, 1998.

Woods, Harold. *Equal Justice: A Biography of Sandra Day O'Connor.* Minneapolis, Minn.: Dillon Press, 1985.

O'Neill, Thomas Philip, Jr.
(Tip O'Neill)
(1912–1994) *Speaker of the House, representative, author*

Thomas Philip O'Neill, Jr., was one of the most colorful figures ever to serve as the Speaker of the U.S. House of Representatives. Always following his maxim, "all politics is local," he served as a Democratic representative from Massachusetts for 34 years from 1953 to 1987, and as Speaker for the last 10 years of them.

O'Neill was born on December 9, 1912, in Cambridge, Massachusetts. He was nicknamed "Tip" after James O'Neill, a major league baseball player who frequently hit foul balls off the tip of his bat. After graduation from Boston College in 1936, he was immediately elected as a Democrat to the Massachusetts House of Representatives where he served from 1937 to 1953. O'Neill became the Massachusetts House speaker in 1949.

In 1953, he was elected to fill the U.S. House of Representatives seat previously held by JOHN FITZGERALD KENNEDY, and he was consistently re-elected until he retired in 1987. So popular was he in his district that the Republicans never put a candidate up against him after 1966. O'Neill was an early supporter of the Vietnam War policy of the Democratic presidents until the 1968 Tet offensive, which caused him to turn against it. At that point, he became a critic. This endeared him to the students who lived in his district, but he had a great deal of trouble explaining his new position to the working-class voters who were the main basis of his support.

A loyal liberal Democrat and skillful parliamentary strategist, he became majority whip in 1971 and majority leader in 1973. After the retirement of fellow Democrat CARL BERT ALBERT, O'Neill became the Speaker of the House from 1977 to 1987. O'Neill predicted the resignation of President RICHARD MILHOUS NIXON following investigations into the Watergate Affair, but he fully supported impeachment if it became necessary

O'Neill also favored many programs in line with the liberal wing of the Democratic Party. He was for education, civil rights, antipoverty programs, Medicare, national health insurance, environmental protection, and he was against excessive defense spending. However, his name was not attached to many of the significant measures to achieve these policies, because of the long-standing tradition in the House that leaders would allow others to take credit for the work they did. Legislative leaders for the first two-thirds of the 20th century avoided appearing to "show off." Instead, they would allow others to take credit for work they did, in return for demanding loyalty from those they benefited. In this way, they gained lasting power. For O'Neill, being Speaker of the House was fame enough. An example of someone who held the opposite attitude was NEWTON LEROY GINGRICH, who basked in the glory of being called the most powerful man in America and who held the job for only four years. No scandal touched O'Neill, who could have held the office for much longer than the 10 years he was Speaker. He retired on his own terms in 1987, wrote his memoirs, and was respected as an elder statesman.

He died on January 5, 1994.

Further Reading

Clancy, Paul R. *Tip, A Biography of Thomas P. O'Neill, Speaker of the House.* New York: Macmillan, 1980.

Loomis, Burdett A. *Esteemed Colleagues: Civility and Deliberation in the U.S. Senate.* Washington, D.C.: Brookings Institution, 2000.

O'Neill, Tip. *All Politics Is Local, And Other Rules of the Game.* New York: Times Books, 1994.

———. *Man Of the House: The Life and Political Memoirs of Speaker Tip O'Neill.* New York: Random House, 1987.

"O'Neill, Thomas P., Jr." in *Congress A to Z: Third Edition,* edited by David R. Tarr and Ann O'Connor. Washington, D.C.: Congressional Quarterly, 1999.

P

Paine, Thomas

(1737–1809) secretary of the Continental Congress, Revolutionary War leader, author

Thomas Paine was a popular writer who did more to foster the Revolutionary War than any other publicist. He also, with much less success, tried to spread the principles of the American Revolutionary War in Europe.

Paine was born on January 29, 1737, at Thetford, Norfolk County, England, a son of a Quaker. After a brief formal education, he started working for his father. Later he was appointed an excise officer, but he was fired for organizing the other excise officers to fight for higher salaries in 1772.

In 1774, Paine made the acquaintance of Benjamin Franklin, who was visiting London. Franklin urged him to move to America and gave him letters of recommendation. By November of that year, Paine was in Philadelphia, and he first published an attack on slavery in the spring of 1775. He was caught up in the revolutionary fervor surrounding the Boston Tea Party and the skirmishes at Lexington and Concord. In January 1776, he published *Common Sense,* a small book in which he asserted that the colonies were too large for continued British domination and called for their independence. In short order, he sold a half million copies of this pamphlet, showing how widespread the agitation was for independence even before the adoption of the Declaration of Independence.

In December 1776, Paine started a series of pamphlets called *The Crisis* (also known as the *American Crisis Papers*), which he continued to publish until 1783, again encouraging the revolutionary cause and being widely read. Paine volunteered in the Continental Army, but he quickly returned to politics. In 1777, he became the secretary of the Continental Congress's Committee of Foreign Affairs, but he was forced to resign in 1779 because he gave out secret information. For the next several years, he worked in the Pennsylvania Assembly as a clerk and continued publishing his pamphlets.

In 1787, Paine returned to England and wrote *The Rights of Man* (the first part in 1791 and the second in 1792), in which he attacked Edmund Burke's *Reflections on the Revolution in France* and defended the French Revolution. This book also attacked English institutions, and he fled to Paris in 1792 to avoid prosecution for treason.

In France, Paine was elected a member of the French National Convention and jumped into French politics. He voted against the execution of the dethroned French King Louis XVI, and the radical Jacobins threw him into prison for almost a year from December 1793 to November 1794. While in prison he wrote the antireligious *The Age of Reason,* published in two parts in 1794 and 1795. In terms of U.S. public opinion, he made his situation worse in 1794 by writing a highly critical *Letter to Washington,* which spoke out against the first U.S. president.

In 1802, President THOMAS JEFFERSON invited Paine to the United States. When he returned later that year, he wrote more essays against the Federalist Party and religion, but he was virtually ostracized and he died in poverty on June 8, 1809.

Further Reading

Aldridge, Alfred Owen. *Man of Reason: The Life of Thomas Paine.* London: Cresset Press, 1990.

Ayer, A. J. *Thomas Paine.* Chicago: University of Chicago Press, 1990.

Conway, Moncure D. *The Life of Thomas Paine.* London: Routledge/Thoemmes, 1996.

Farley, Karin Clafford. *Thomas Paine: Revolutionary Author.* Austin, Tex.: Raintree Steck-Vaughn, 1994.

Foner, Eric. *Tom Paine and Revolutionary America.* New York: Oxford University Press, 1977.

Fruchtman, Jack. *Thomas Paine: Apostle of Freedom.* New York: Four Walls, Eight Windows, 1994.

Keane, John. *Tom Paine: A Political Life.* Boston: Little, Brown, 1995.

Paine, Thomas. *The Writings of Thomas Paine.* London: Routledge/Thoemmes, 1996 (reprint).

Philip, Mark. *Paine.* New York: Oxford University Press, 1989.

Wilson, Jerome D. *Thomas Paine.* Boston: Twayne, 1989.

Woll, Walter. *Thomas Paine: Motives for Rebellion.* Frankfort am Main and New York: P. Lang, 1992.

Pelosi, Nancy d'Alesandro

(1941–   ) *minority whip in the U.S. House of Representatives, representative*

Nancy Pelosi was the first woman elected as the Democratic minority whip in the U.S. House of Representatives and the first woman ever elected as a leader in either party in the Congress. Holding this position has made Pelosi the highest ranking female elected official in either party in the United States.

Nancy d'Alesandro was born on March 26, 1941, in Baltimore, Maryland, into a politically active Italian family. Her father, Thomas J. d'Alesandro, represented Baltimore for five terms in Congress and served as the mayor for a dozen years. She graduated from Trinity College in Washington, D.C., married Paul Pelosi, and moved to San Francisco, California.

Pelosi was selected as a Democratic National Committeewoman from California in 1976 and served in that capacity for 20 years. In 1984, she was selected as the chair for the Democratic National Convention Host Committee in San Francisco. As a party leader, she was the co-chair of the 1992 Democratic Platform Committee of the Democratic National Committee and vice-chair of the 1996 Democratic National Convention.

In 1987, Pelosi was elected to the U.S. House of Representatives from California's 8th Congressional District, representing the City of San Francisco. She was appointed to the powerful House Appropriations Committee and has served on the Appropriations Subcommittee on Foreign Operations and Export Financing. Her seniority is responsible for her being named the ranking Democrat on the Permanent Select Committee on Intelligence.

Pelosi has chaired the Congressional Working Group on China, a role in which she has long expressed concern about human rights issues in China and Tibet. She has been co-chair of the AIDS Task Force of the House Democratic Caucus and advocates increased funding for AIDS/HIV and breast cancer prevention and research. She has also worked to provide jobs, health, education, and pension security for American workers, international family planning, AIDS prevention, and environmental protection.

Before being elected minority whip on October 25, 2001, Pelosi held leadership responsibilities in Congress by serving on the influential House Democratic Steering Committee, as at-large whip for Congressional Democrats, and vice-chair of the Democratic Study Group. By being elected minority whip, Pelosi reversed the historic trend of women losing high-profile congressional positions to their male colleagues.

Further Reading

Earnshaw, Doris. *California Women Speak.* Davis Calif.: Alta Vista Press, 1994.

Jones, Mary Lynn F. "Pelosi Victory Inspires Women in Both Parties," *The Hill.* (October 25, 2001).

"Pelosi, Nancy." Available on-line. URL: http://www.tibet.ca/wtactive/2000/3/24_5.html. Downloaded November 11, 2001.

Pepper, Claude Denson

(1900–1989) *senator, representative*

Claude Denson Pepper was a unique political figure who was first elected to the U.S. Senate, was defeated, and came back to be elected to the U.S. House of Representatives. He was also a rare political liberal from a southern state.

Pepper was born on September 8, 1900, in Dudleyville, Chambers County, Alabama. Graduating from high school in Alabama in 1917, he entered the University of Alabama and graduated Phi Beta Kappa in 1921. He graduated from Harvard Law School in 1924 and taught law for a year at the University of Arkansas. He moved to Perry, Florida, and started practicing law in 1925.

In 1928, Pepper was elected to a single term in the Florida House of Representatives. In 1934, he ran for and lost the Democratic U.S. Senate nomination as an ardent supporter of FRANKLIN DELANO ROOSEVELT. Two years later, he ran unopposed in a special U.S. Senate election. Openly calling himself a "liberal" on domestic economic issues, Pepper fought to increase the federal appropriations in the South because of its economic deprivation.

In the Senate, Pepper became a member of the Foreign Relations Committee where his internationalist views allowed him to advance President Roosevelt's foreign policy initiatives in the crucial fights against the isolationists in 1940 and 1941. Pepper repeatedly attacked the conservative business interests, warned of the growing conservative strength, and tried to prevent the dismantling of the New Deal throughout his career. He was re-elected in 1938 and 1944.

After World War II, Pepper toured Europe and the Middle East, met with world leaders, including Stalin, and favored an open world based on cooperation among the great powers. He increasingly opposed HARRY S. TRUMAN's containment strategy against the Soviet Union. Although he never advocated an end to segregation, Pepper evolved slowly into a more liberal position on civil rights. These liberal positions shut him out of membership with the southerners in the Senate "club" and opened him to the charge that he neglected Florida by trying to be an international statesman.

In 1950, George Smathers openly exploited the communist issue and covertly used the racial issue to defeat Pepper in the Democratic primary. Pepper developed a more conservative stance in 1958 when he ran against incumbent Senator Spessard L. Holland in the Democratic primary, but the strategy did not work.

From 1950 through 1962, Pepper practiced law in Miami, Florida. When Florida gained three additional seats in the U.S. House as a result of the population growth shown in the 1960 census, Pepper easily won one of the new seats created in Miami. His work in the House of Representatives focused on aid to the elderly, banking and currency legislation, anticrime proposals, and Latin American trade. He was consistently reelected and served until his death on April 1, 1989.

Further Reading

Danese, Tracy E. *Claude Pepper and Ed Ball: Politics, Purpose, and Power.* Gainesville: University Press of Florida, 2000.

Pepper, Claude. *Pepper: Eyewitness to a Century.* San Diego, Calif.: Harcourt Brace Jovanovich, 1987.

Perkins, Frances
(Fannie Coralie Perkins)
(1882–1965) *secretary of labor, author*

Frances Perkins became the first woman to be a member of a presidential cabinet in the United States, serving as President FRANKLIN DELANO ROOSEVELT's secretary of labor from 1933 to 1945.

Fannie Coralie Perkins was born on April 10, 1882, in Boston, Massachusetts, and changed her given name to Frances in about 1905. She graduated from Mount Holyoke College in 1902 and earned a master's degree from Columbia University in 1910. She worked at Hull House, the progressive social welfare institution, and became executive secretary of the New York Consumers' League from 1910 to 1912, and of the New York Committee on Safety from 1912 to 1917. Perkins was clearly ahead of her times in many respects. She married Paul Caldwell Wilson in 1913 but retained her maiden name for professional purposes. In 1923, Governor ALFRED EMANUEL SMITH appointed her to the New York State Industrial Board, where she became the chair in 1926. In 1929, Governor Franklin Roosevelt appointed her New York's industrial commissioner in charge of enforcing factory and labor laws.

In some respects, Frances Perkins resembled ANNA ELEANOR ROOSEVELT. She came from an upper-class New England family with many wealthy connections, but she devoted her life to helping the poor and disadvantaged. She was an intensely private—even shy—person who nonetheless was a success in the rough and tumble of New York politics.

Perkins held her own in repeated clashes with both business and labor. After a lengthy strike, 4,400 Rome, New York, mill workers rioted. As a part of her duties to mediate labor disputes, Perkins was already on the train to Rome when news arrived that a knifing had occurred, gunshots had been fired, and the state police had been called. She resisted the train conductor's insistence that she not go in such a dangerous situation. Upon arriving, she ignored the danger posed by the armed workers at one end of the bridge and insisted on passing through the armed workers' barricade to make a speech in the middle of the bridge. The workers obliged, and her speech pacified the situation. In another instance in a courtroom, a witness lost control and began walking toward his opponent across the room. Perkins sensed the man had a gun, moved quickly behind him, and held his arm until a guard could disarm him.

Despite her courage, she was not initially a popular choice when Roosevelt put forth her name for secretary of labor. Unions opposed her because she was not a union member, and business disliked her because she was perceived as too close to labor. Since she was acceptable neither to businessmen nor labor, many political leaders regarded her as a liability. Despite these apparent liabilities, Roosevelt trusted her—perhaps precisely because she was not under anyone else's control or influence. In the end, she served with distinction.

As president, Roosevelt named Perkins U.S. secretary of labor over the bitter objections of business, labor, and political leaders. While in the cabinet, she became chairman of the President's Committee on Economic Security, which prepared a report forming the basis for the 1935 Social Security Act. As secretary of labor, she also pushed for higher wages as well as legislation to end industrial strife and standardize state industrial laws.

In 1946, President HARRY S. TRUMAN appointed her to the U.S. Civil Service Commission, where she served until 1953. Besides books on labor problems, she published *The Roosevelt I Knew* in 1946. After leaving government service, she taught at Cornell University until her death on May 14, 1965.

Further Reading

Anderson, James Russell. *The New Deal Career of Frances Perkins: Secretary of Labor, 1933–1939.* Ann Arbor, Mich.: University Microfilms, 1968.

Davis, Kenneth S. *FDR: Three Volumes.* New York: Random House, 1993.

Hamby, Alonzo L. "Perkins, Frances." Available online. Discovery Channel School, original content provided by World Book Online, http://www.discoveryschool.com/homeworkhelp/worldbook/atozhistory/p/423660.html. Downloaded November 19, 2001.

Martin, George Whitney. *Madam Secretary, Frances Perkins.* Boston: Houghton Mifflin, 1976.

McJimsey, George T. *The Presidency of Franklin Delano Roosevelt.* Lawrence: University Press of Kansas, 2000.

Mohr, Lillian Holmen. *Frances Perkins: That Woman in FDR's Cabinet!* Croton-on-Hudson, N.Y.: North River Press, 1979.

Morris, Jeffrey. *The FDR Way.* Minneapolis: Lerner Publications, 1996.

Perkins, Frances. *The Roosevelt I Knew.* New York: Viking, 1946.

Severn, Bill. *Frances Perkins: A Member of the Cabinet.* New York: Hawthorn Books, 1976.

Perot, Henry Ross
(Henry Ray Perot)
(1930–   ) *candidate for president*

Henry Ross Perot, a billionaire business entrepreneur, ran for U.S. president as an independent in 1992. He ran again in 1996 as the nominee of the Reform Party, an organization he founded. Although he lost both times, he received about 20 percent of the vote in 1992 and about 5 percent in 1996 while receiving no Electoral College votes either time.

Perot was born on June 27, 1930, in Texarkana, Texas. His parents initially named him Henry Ray but changed his name to Henry Ross when he was 12 years old. In 1953, Perot graduated from the U.S. Naval Academy and served in the navy for four years. In 1957, Perot became a computer salesman for International Business Machines (IBM), but he left IBM in 1962 to found Electronic Data Systems (EDS), a computer service company that designed, installed, and operated data processing for customers by contract. Entering the market with this service at just the right time, Perot succeeded by handling medical claims for Blue Cross and other giant insurance corporations. After only six short years, Perot took EDS public in a cleverly managed stock offering that ended up making Perot several hundred million dollars as the majority stockholder. With his newly acquired wealth, Perot turned to his first philanthropic effort—an ultimately futile gesture to free U.S. prisoners of war held by communist forces in North Vietnam. In 1979, he succeeded in a more modest effort to free two EDS employees who had been taken hostage in Iran. Because of his success in 1979 in freeing prisoners abroad, and even in spite of his failure in Vietnam, Perot became something of a populist folk hero despite his great wealth.

Not that he neglected his business interests. In the meantime, EDS still prospered to such a degree that he was able to sell the company to General Motors (GM) for $2.5 billion in specially issued stock and was given a place on the board of directors of General Motors. Defying convention, Perot then openly criticized GM's management so severely that GM proceeded to buy back his seat on their board for $700 million in 1986. Perot then founded another company in 1988. With billions of dollars at his disposal, Perot turned his attention to politics.

In February 1992, Perot said he would run for president if supporters would get his name on ballots in all 50 states. In July, he suddenly announced he would not run, but campaign workers placed his name on all state ballots anyway. In October, Perot reversed himself and announced he would run after all. Despite these changes, many people supported Perot because they considered him a political "outsider" with no commitments to special interest groups. He came in third and received slightly less than 20 percent of the popular vote in the election, won by Democrat WILLIAM JEFFERSON CLINTON over incumbent Republican President GEORGE HERBERT WALKER BUSH.

In 1996, Perot founded the Reform Party and became its presidential nominee, but he did far less well, finishing a poor third behind the winning incumbent Democratic President Clinton and the losing Republican nominee, ROBERT JOSEPH DOLE.

Further Reading

Barta, Carolyn. *Perot and His People: Disrupting the Balance of Political Power.* Fort Worth, Tex.: Summit Group, 1993.

Black, Gordon S. *The Politics of American Discontent: How a New Party Can Make Democracy Work Again.* New York: Wiley, 1994.

Crotty, William J. *America's Choice: The Election of 1992.* Guilford, Conn.: Dushkin Publishing Group, 1993.

Gross, Ken. *Ross Perot: The Man Behind the Myth.* New York: Random House, 1992.

Mason, Todd. *Perot: An Unauthorized Biography.* Homewood, Ill.: Dow Jones-Irwin, 1990.

Perot, H. Ross. *Ross Perot: My Life and the Principles for Success.* Arlington, Tex.: Summit, 1996.

Posner, Gerald L. *Citizen Perot: His Life and Times.* New York: Random House, 1996.

Tatum, Henry K. "Perot, Ross." Available online. Discovery Channel School, original content provided by World Book Online, http://www.discoveryschool.com/homeworkhelp/worldbook/atozhistory/p/423850.html. Downloaded November 19, 2001.

Westlind, Dennis. *The Politics of Popular Identity: Understanding Recent Populist Movements in Sweden and the United States.* Lund, Sweden: Lund University Press, 1996.

Pickering, Timothy

(1745–1829) *secretary of state, secretary of war, senator, representative, postmaster general, Revolutionary War leader*

Timothy Pickering was a leading figure in the Revolutionary War, in the U.S. Constitutional Convention, and in the administrations of both Presidents GEORGE WASHINGTON and JOHN ADAMS. But Pickering's scheming with ALEXANDER HAMILTON led to his being fired by President

Adams and his later scheming against President JAMES MADISON during the War of 1812 led to the destruction of his political career and the demise of the Federalist Party that he represented.

Pickering was born on July 17, 1745, in Salem, Massachusetts. He graduated from Harvard College in 1763. He then worked as a clerk in the office of register of deeds, studied law, was admitted to the bar in 1768, and opened a law practice in Salem. As a selectman and assessor in Salem from 1772 to 1777, he was an active revolutionary against the British and worked with the Committee on the State of Rights of Colonists in 1773 and the Massachusetts committee of correspondence in 1774 and 1775. He was elected to the Massachusetts state legislature in 1776.

A colonel in the Massachusetts militia, Pickering joined Washington's army in the American Revolution. Because of his distinguished service in the 1776–77 winter campaign and his knowledge of military strategy, Washington appointed him his adjutant general, a role in which he served until he was he was made a member of the Board of War and Ordinance in January 1778. Washington named Pickering the quartermaster general of the army in 1780, and he served there until 1783.

After the America Revolution, Pickering moved to Pennsylvania where he negotiated for the federal government in the dispute over Connecticut and Pennsylvania land claims and treaties with various Native American tribes. He was a member of the Pennsylvania state constitutional convention in 1789 and 1790. Pickering was a strong supporter of Washington and skillful at negotiation and administration, so it was natural for Washington to appoint him to various cabinet positions as the need arose.

Washington named him U.S. postmaster general in 1791 and moved him over to secretary of war briefly in 1795. When EDMUND RANDOLPH resigned, Washington appointed Pickering the U.S. secretary of state in 1795. When John Adams was elected president in 1796, he kept Pickering and other members of Washington's cabinet, not knowing that three of them were secret associates of Alexander Hamilton and would take orders from Hamilton aimed at destroying Adams. Ultimately, Adams fired Pickering and some others when he learned that they had been scheming with Hamilton to lead the United States into war with France.

Returning to Massachusetts, Pickering was an unsuccessful candidate for election in 1802 to the U.S. House of Representatives, but he was appointed chief justice of the Court of Common Pleas and General Sessions of the Peace. The Massachusetts legislature elected him as a Federalist to the U.S. Senate, filling the vacancy caused by the resignation of Dwight Foster in 1803. He was reelected in 1804 but was not reelected in 1810. In 1811, the Senate censured him for breach of confidence. He served as a member of the Massachusetts executive council in 1812 and 1813 until he was elected to the U.S. House of Representatives where he served two terms until March 3, 1817.

From the start of the War of 1812, Pickering denounced the war as "Mr. Madison's War" since he had long favored the British over the French in foreign policy. As early as 1804 he supported plans to have New England secede from the Union. By 1814, he felt he had sufficient support for his plans and was active in the Hartford Convention, which met in secret, denounced the war, and laid plans for the secession. After ANDREW JACKSON's stunning defeat of the British in New Orleans and after the simultaneous announcement of a treaty ending the War of 1812, Pickering and the other Federalists looked not only foolish but also almost treasonous. His career was over even in the Federalist stronghold of Massachusetts, and he declined to run in 1816. He returned to Salem and ran again for Congress one more time in 1820, but he was defeated. His own political decline paralleled the end of the Federalist Party in the United States.

He died in Salem, Massachusetts, on January 29, 1829.

Further Reading

Brown, Richard D. "Pickering, Timothy." Available online. Discovery Channel School, original content provided by World Book Online, http://www.discoveryschool.com/homeworkhelp/worldbook/atozhistory/p/429110.html. Downloaded November 19, 2001.

Clarfield, Gerard H. *Timothy Pickering and the American Republic.* Pittsburgh, Pa.: University of Pittsburgh Press, 1980.

McCulloch, David. *John Adams*. New York: Simon & Schuster, 2001.

McLean, David. *Timothy Pickering and the Age of the American Revolution*. New York: Arno Press, 1982.

Pickering, Octavius. *The Life of Timothy Pickering*. Boston: Little, Brown, 1970.

Prentiss, Hervey Putnam. *Timothy Pickering as the Leader of New England Federalism, 1800–1815*. New York: Da Capo, 1972.

Pierce, Franklin

(1804–1869) *president, senator, representative, governor*

The youngest man up to his time to be elected president, Franklin Pierce served during the tense period leading to the Civil War. Regarded as a "dark horse" candidate, he won the 1852 Democratic presidential nomination after four stronger candidates had fought to a stalemate. To win, he indicated his strong support for the Compromise of 1850, which sought to settle the slavery dispute. However, he endorsed the 1854 Kansas-Nebraska Act, which undid the 1850 compromise. That action reopened the slavery controversy in a particularly violent way, seriously divided his Democratic Party, destroyed the Whig Party, created the Republican Party, and paved the way for the Civil War. Pierce had some modest successes, but historians have generally concluded that his failure to deal with the slavery question wiped out any positive rating for his administration. An amiable man, he was unequal to the task he faced and is often rated one of the most ineffective presidents who served a full four-year term.

Franklin Pierce was born on November 23, 1804, in Hillsborough Lower Village, New Hampshire. His father had served heroically as a general in the Revolutionary War and was a strong follower of ANDREW JACKSON as the Democratic govenor of New Hampshire. Franklin was educated at a number of distinguished private college preparatory schools. He also attended Bowdoin College, where he befriended Nathaniel Hawthorne and graduated in 1824 after advancing from last place to near the top of his class. He then studied law and was admitted to the New Hampshire bar in 1827.

Entering politics as a Jacksonian Democrat, Pierce was elected to the New Hampshire General Court (legislature) in 1829, the year his father began his second term as governor. Young Pierce served as speaker in 1831 and 1832, and the following year he was elected to the House of Representatives. In 1837, the New Hampshire General Court named him a U.S. senator—the youngest in the Senate at 32 years of age. Pierce loyally supported the Jacksonian party line.

He was popular in Washington, but his wife's health suffered from the climate and she hated the social requirements. Ultimately, she persuaded him to resign from the Senate in 1842 before the end of his term, return to New Hampshire, and open a successful law firm. He was still active in politics and managed the New Hampshire Democratic campaigns so effectively that President JAMES KNOX POLK appointed him U.S. district attorney for New Hampshire in 1845 and urged him to become U.S. attorney general in 1846. Pierce was also offered reappointment to the U.S. Senate, but he declined to became either U.S. senator or U.S. attorney general because he wanted to fight in the Mexican War.

Pierce actually enlisted as a private, but he was soon promoted to colonel and later brigadier general. In May 1847, he departed for Veracruz, Mexico. By July, he marched his troops through Mexico, and although he suffered a serious leg wound at the Battle of Churubusco in August, he stayed with his command until the capture of Mexico City. Political opponents attempted to criticize Pierce for cowardice because the leg injury took him out of action briefly, but the charge did not hurt his political career.

Resuming his law practice in Concord in 1848 after the war, Pierce stayed active in politics. He vigorously supported the Compromise of 1850 and supported his former law instructor, Levi Woodbury, for the Democratic presidential nomination. When Woodbury died in 1851, the New Hampshire party leaders chose Pierce as their state's favorite son. In June 1852, the Democratic national nominating convention was unable to choose from among Illinois Senator STEPHEN ARNOLD DOUGLAS and three prominent former Cabinet members—JAMES BUCHANAN, William L. Marcy, and

Lewis Cass. The group nominated Pierce for president and Alabama's Senator William R. D. King for vice president.

The Whigs nominated General WINFIELD SCOTT, Pierce's commander in the Mexican War, for president. While no real issues appeared to divide the parties and the Compromise of 1850 had temporarily quieted the slavery issue, Scott indicated that he really opposed slavery, destroying his campaign in the South. As a New Englander, Pierce got some northern support, and the South trusted him because he had supported the Compromise of 1850 and endorsed strict enforcement of the Fugitive Slave Law. Always friendly, Pierce showed genuine pleasure in meeting people and had a terrific gift for remembering names and faces. The license with which he promised favors and the difficulty he had saying "no" bought him votes on Election Day but led to problems later, when he discovered he had promised more than he could deliver. Pierce won the election by 1.6 million popular votes to 1.3 million for Scott and carried all but four states, winning 254 of the 296 Electoral College votes.

After the election, a personal tragedy occurred. His family was in a train accident and saw their 11-year-old son burned by an exploding boiler. Mrs. Pierce had always hated her husband's candidacy and despised returning to Washington, so she now obsessed that Providence had exacted this terrible price for her husband's acceptance of the presidential nomination. Her reclusive mental illness distracted Pierce, himself grief-stricken and insecure, at the very time he needed to focus all his energy on the demanding political situation he faced.

Unfortunately, Pierce was also the first president to serve almost his entire term without a vice president since William R. D. King, ill for several months, died in April 1853 without ever performing any duties in his office. Pierce could have used King's help.

Nonetheless, Pierce brilliantly promoted harmony in his party by choosing men from all factions for his cabinet. Although its diversity forced Pierce to agonize over some tough divisions, his cabinet turned out to be the only one in U.S. history to remain unchanged throughout an entire administration. Pierce bravely appointed the first

Franklin Pierce was the youngest man elected president at the time, but his failure to abate the tensions over slavery has generally led to his being poorly regarded as president. *(Library of Congress)*

Catholic to a presidential cabinet, and this caused him criticism from the nativist, anti-Catholic Know-Nothing Party.

In international affairs, Pierce followed both of his heroic Democratic predecessors, Jackson and Polk, in a bold, partially successful, expansionistic foreign policy. Pierce negotiated a reciprocal tariff treaty with England, which gave U.S. fishermen rights in Canadian waters in return for Canadian trade privileges in the United States. He vigorously, but unsuccessfully, protested Britain's continued maintenance of colonies in Central America, asserting that the 1850 Clayton-Bulwer Treaty outlawed this. In 1853, he advocated annexing Hawaii, but this plan failed when the cooperative Hawaiian king died. However, the Gadsden Purchase in the same year gave the country a southern railroad route to the Pacific Coast and settled the boundary question with Mexico. After Commodore Matthew C. Perry's forceful entry into Japan, Pierce insisted that the Senate ratify a trade agreement treaty with Japan, opening it to U.S. commerce.

These expansionistic moves were generally popular, but Pierce's plans to acquire Cuba became controversial. Initially, Cuba's seizure of a U.S. merchant ship, *Black Warrior,* and an abortive antimonarchial revolution in Spain gave Pierce some hope. He ordered his diplomats to meet at Ostend, Belgium, in the fall of 1854, to separate Cuba from Spain. Their handiwork, a document known as the Ostend Manifesto, proposed to use European bankers to pressure Spain to sell Cuba to the United States, but it also made a veiled threat that the United States might seize Cuba under certain remote circumstances. This supposedly confidential document fell into the hands of the press, who garbled it so badly that abolitionists raged on about the extension of slavery and killed any hope of closing a deal. Pierce tried to disassociate himself from the Ostend Manifesto, but public skepticism was high.

If the slavery controversy complicated foreign affairs, it was deadly in domestic politics. Pierce desperately needed the Senate to complete the ratification of the Gadsden Purchase and of Canadian treaties and to confirm several crucial pending appointments, but these were blocked when Illinois Senator Stephen A. Douglas introduced the Kansas-Nebraska Bill in January 1854 in an effort to speed western settlement and enrich himself by opening a new railroad in which he had an interest. The bill created two new territories, Kansas and Nebraska, out of western Indian lands and provided that settlers in the new territories would decide for themselves whether to permit slavery. Douglas's bill threatened to upset the uneasy slavery truce established by the compromises of 1820 and 1850. The bill did not clearly define the status of slavery during the territorial period.

Pierce personally disliked the proposal, for he saw that it would ignite the slavery issue nationally. Still, the pressure from Douglas and his band of senators, who threatened to block approval of his appointments and treaties, led him to endorse the Kansas-Nebraska Bill. A furious debate devel-

oped, but the bill passed on May 30. Passage led to a wild rush of pro-slavery and antislavery radicals into Kansas, where a local civil war broke out.

Pierce attempted to administer the act impartially by appointing a balanced group of pro-slavery and antislavery officials. In Kansas, two governments emerged—a southern-dominated one at Lecompton, which Pierce declared legal, and a northern one at Topeka, which he ordered to disband. He sent troops to maintain order but did not succeed in dislodging the Topeka free-state government. Eventually, Pierce restored a measure of order, but the deaths were high and the damage was done.

Pierce hoped to be renominated in 1856, but the rising slavery agitation and his handling of the Kansas bloodbath eliminated him from serious consideration. This is tragic because, on other matters, Pierce was a success. The United States was living in one of its most prosperous eras as the California gold rush still moved people westward on railroads promoted by federal land grants and as new land was added by the Gadsden Purchase.

Although Pierce suffered, the Democrats were not yet dead, and their 1856 presidential nominee, James Buchanan, won easily. The Whigs disintegrated, the Know-Nothing Party and the Republican Party split the antislavery vote, and the Republicans' first presidential nominee, JOHN CHARLES FRÉMONT, although popular, proved unable to put together a majority. After he left office, Pierce took his wife abroad, visited Europe, spent two years on the island of Maderia (trying unsuccessfully to improve her health), and then returned home where she died on December 2, 1863. Pierce at first supported President ABRAHAM LINCOLN's attempts to save the Union, but he later bitterly criticized him for limiting civil liberties during the Civil War. Pierce became so unpopular for these attacks that he lived as a recluse until his death on October 8, 1869.

Further Reading

Gara, Larry. *The Presidency of Franklin Pierce.* Lawrence: University Press of Kansas, 1991.
Hawthorne, Nathaniel. *The Life of Franklin Pierce.* New York: Garrett Press, reprinted 1970.
Klein, Philip S. "Pierce, Franklin." Available online. Discovery Channel School, original content provided by

World Book Online. URL: http://www.discovery school.com/homeworkhelp/worldbook/atozhistory/p/429580.html. Downloaded November 19, 2001.

Nichols, Roy F. *Franklin Pierce: Young Hickory of the Granite Hills.* Newtown, Conn.: American Political Biography Press, 1993.

"Pierce, Franklin." Available online. URL: http://www.whitehouse.gov/history/presidents/fp14.html. Downloaded November 11, 2001.

Pinchback, Pinckney Benton Stewart

(1837–1921) *senator, representative*

Pinckney Benton Stewart Pinchback raised two companies of soldiers during the Civil War and still remained at the lowly rank of captain. The son of a white man and a former slave, he was the only person who was elected to the U.S. House of Representatives and yet was denied his seat, and he was the only person to be elected to the U.S. Senate and be denied admission.

Born on May 10, 1837, in Macon, Georgia, to a white Mississippi planter and a former slave, Pinchback was raised a freeman only because his father had emancipated his mother and she fled to Ohio after Pinchback's father died. Pinchback attended high school in Cincinnati and thereafter worked as a cabin boy and steward on riverboats on the Ohio River.

In 1862, Pinchback traveled down the Ohio and Mississippi Rivers to New Orleans, where he raised two companies of black soldiers, called the Corps d'Afrique, an effort that normally would have resulted in his being named the officer in charge with a high rank. Because he was only part white, he was denied the commission.

Despite the racism that still existed, Pinchback decided to remain in Louisiana after the Civil War, hoping there would be advantages for him under the military Reconstruction government. As a Republican, he won a seat in the state senate in 1868. He advanced to the position of president pro tem of that body. He then served briefly as lieutenant governor when the incumbent died in 1871. From December 9, 1872, to January 13, 1873, he was the acting governor of Louisiana while the elected governor underwent impeach-

ment proceedings. His five weeks as acting governor was the highest office he was allowed to hold.

In 1872, he won a race for the U.S. House of Representatives but he was denied his seat when his white Democratic opponent challenged the election returns and was upheld under questionable circumstances. In 1873, Pinchback was elected to the U.S. Senate by the state legislature, but he again was denied the seat because the election results were challenged. Although candidates in such positions would normally be allowed to take their seats in the U.S. Senate pending resolution of the election contest, this time the U.S. Senate denied Pinchback his seat. Eventually, Pinchback realized that he would never be allowed to hold a federal office and dropped his claim in return for the payment of the salary he would have earned if he had been allowed to serve.

By this time, Reconstruction had ended in Louisiana. Pinchback switched parties to become a Democrat in 1877. In 1882, he was allowed to hold his last public post, that of the surveyor of customs in New Orleans.

A decade later at the age of 50, Pinchback earned his law degree from Dillard University (then called Straight University) in New Orleans and passed the bar in 1887. He never practiced law in Louisiana because he moved to Washington, D.C., in 1890.

He died on December 21, 1921.

Further Reading

Haskins, James. *The First Black Governor: Pinckney Benton Stewart Pinchback.* Trenton, N.J.: Africa World Press, 1996.

———. *Pinckney Benton Stewart Pinchback.* New York: Macmillan, 1973.

Lonn, Ella. *Reconstruction in Louisiana.* New York: Russell & Russell, 1967.

Pinchot, Gifford

(1865–1946) *government agency director, governor, author*

Gifford Pinchot was one of the first conservationists to be a government leader in the United States. When President WILLIAM HOWARD TAFT fired him in 1910, it exacerbated a conflict between Taft and former President THEODORE ROOSEVELT. This argument led to a split in the Republican Party in the 1912 election that enabled President THOMAS WOODROW WILSON to win a three-way race.

Pinchot was born on August 11, 1865, in Simsbury, Connecticut. After graduating from Yale University in 1889, he traveled to Europe to study forestry in France and other European countries. When he returned to the United States, he began systematic forestry work at Biltmore, the Vanderbilt estate near Asheville, North Carolina, in 1892. He became a member of the National Forest Commission in 1896.

In 1898, President WILLIAM MCKINLEY named Pinchot to the Division of Forestry, which later was renamed the Bureau of Forestry and then the Forest Service. In 1903, he helped found the Yale school of forestry and remained a professor there until 1936, while also serving in various governmental capacities. President Roosevelt appointed him chief of the U.S. Forest Service in 1905. Following the advice of Pinchot, Roosevelt greatly expanded the nation's forest reserves. In 1908, Pinchot became chairman of the National Conservation Commission, which surveyed the nation's natural resources for the first time.

In 1910, President Taft fired Pinchot because he openly criticized Secretary of the Interior RICHARD ACHILLES BALLINGER for his administration of coal lands in Alaska. Taft's dismissal of Pinchot outraged large sections of the U.S. public. Since former President Roosevelt was a strong Pinchot supporter, Taft's action almost completely destroyed the already strained friendship between Taft and Roosevelt. In 1912, Pinchot helped form the Progressive Party and urged Roosevelt to accept their presidential nomination when he failed to take the Republican nomination away from Taft.

Pinchot remained active in conservation and politics. He was elected the governor of Pennsylvania in 1923 and reorganized Pennsylvania's state government, reducing 139 agencies into 15 departments and three commissions before voluntarily leaving office in 1927. He unsuccessfully sought the Republican nomination for the U.S. Senate but was again elected Pennsylvania's governor in 1931. He was a strong governor and urged relief during the Great Depression. Realizing that federal assistance was a necessity during the Depression, he supported Democrat FRANKLIN DELANO ROOSEVELT over the Republican incumbent HERBERT CLARK HOOVER in 1932.

Pinchot served until 1935, when he again sought unsuccessfully to win the Republican nomination for the U.S. Senate. Because he supported Roosevelt, he received little assistance from the leaders of the Republican Party. During the last three months of his term, Pinchot became extremely ill and was kept in a New York City hospital, so his wife became, in reality, the acting governor. By 1938, he recovered his health and again ran for the Republican nomination for governor. He was then 73 and Roosevelt was far less popular, so the Republican voters overwhelmingly defeated him.

He died on October 4, 1946. In 1947, his autobiography, *Breaking New Ground,* was published posthumously.

Further Reading

Bixler, Patricia E. *"Gifford Pinchot"* in Historic Pennsylvania Leaflet No. 39, edited by Harold L. Myers. Harrisburg: Pennsylvania Historical & Museum Commission, 1976.

Cherny, Robert W. "Pinchot, Gifford." Available online. Discovery Channel School, original content provided by World Book Online. URL: http://www.discovery school.com/homeworkhelp/worldbook/atozhistory/p/430860.html. Downloaded November 21, 2001.

Fausold, Martin L. *Gifford Pinchot: Bull Moose Progressive.* Westport, Conn.: Greenwood, 1973.

Hays, Samuel P. *Conservation and the Gospel of Efficiency: The Progressive Conservation Movement, 1890–1920.* Pittsburgh, Pa.: University of Pittsburgh Press, 1999.

Mason, Alpheus Thomas. *Bureaucracy Convicts Itself: The Ballinger-Pinchot Controversy of 1910.* New York: Viking, 1941.

McCulloch, Winifred. *The Glavis-Ballinger Dispute.* Syracuse, N.Y.: Inter-University Case Program, 1952.

Penick, James L. *Progressive Politics and Conservation: The Ballinger-Pinchot Affair.* Chicago: University of Chicago Press, 1968.

Pinchot, Gifford. *Breaking New Ground.* Washington, D.C.: Island Press, reprinted 1998.

Pinkett, Harold T. *Gifford Pinchot: Private and Public Forester.* Urbana: University of Illinois Press, 1970.

Pinckney, Charles Cotesworth
(1746–1825) diplomat, candidate for president, Revolutionary War leader

Charles Cotesworth Pinckney fought in the Revolutionary War, signed the U.S. Constitution, served as an important diplomat, ran once for the vice presidency, and ran twice for the presidency.

Pinckney was born on February 25, 1746, in Charleston, South Carolina, into a prominent family, which included his brother, THOMAS PINCKNEY, and his cousin, Charles Pinckney. His family sent him to England to be educated, where he attended the Westminster school and Oxford. He studied law at the Temple (a British court at which British students studied law) and also attended the military academy at Caen, France.

In 1769, Pinckney began to practice law in Charleston. In 1775, he was elected to the South Carolina provincial congress and joined the Continental Army. He was first appointed a captain but soon became the commander of the first regiment of Carolina infantry. After the British were pushed out of the South, Pinckney went to the North and became an aide-de-camp to GEORGE WASHINGTON, fighting in the battles at Brandywine and Germantown, Pennsylvania. When the British threatened the South again, he returned to Charleston and helped repulse a number of British attacks before being captured in 1780. He was freed at the end of the war.

Pinckney was elected a delegate to the 1787 U.S. Constitutional Convention and worked to obtain South Carolina's ratification of the Constitution. In 1796, Washington sent him to France, but he was not received by the French government. The following year, President JOHN ADAMS sent ELBRIDGE GERRY and JOHN MARSHALL to assist him in France, but the three refused to pay a bribe to French officials as a prerequisite for opening negotiations with them. Adams used this incident to arouse public opinion against the French in what became known as the XYZ Affair. Pinckney was an unsuccessful Federalist candidate for the vice presidency on the ticket with Adams in 1800.

Pinckney was nominated as the Federalist candidate for president in 1804 and 1808, but he lost both times. He died on August 16, 1825.

Further Reading
Hernon, Joseph Martin. *Profiles in Character: Hubris and Heroism in the U.S. Senate—1789–1990*. Armonk, N.Y.: M. E. Sharpe, 1997.

Williams, Frances Leigh. *A Founding Family: The Pinckneys of South Carolina*. New York: Harcourt Brace Jovanovich, 1978.

Zahniser, Marvin R. *Charles Cotesworth Pinckney: Founding Father*. Chapel Hill, N.C.: Published for the Institute of Early American History and Culture, Williamsburg, Va., 1967.

Pinckney, Thomas
(1750–1828) Revolutionary War leader, governor, diplomat, representative, candidate for vice president

Thomas Pinckney was a Revolutionary War soldier and the diplomat who arranged the Pinckney Treaty with Spain in 1795.

Pinckney was born October 23, 1750, in Charleston, South Carolina, into the prominent family that included his brother, Charles Cotesworth Pinckney, and his cousin, Charles Pinckney. As they had done for his older brother, his family sent him to Britain and France to be educated.

Returning from Europe, he joined the militia at the start of the Revolutionary War, fought in Florida, and helped repulse the British at Charleston, but he was wounded, captured at Camden, and released at the end of the war. In 1787, he was elected South Carolina's governor and served until 1789. President GEORGE WASHINGTON appointed him the U.S. minister to England in 1792. While he was in London, Washington sent him to Spain as an envoy extraordinary to negotiate a commercial treaty. The 1795 Pinckney Treaty, properly known as the Treaty of San Lorenzo, established trade relations with Spain, allowed joint unrestricted navigation of the Mississippi by the United States and Spain, provided for the right of deposit at New Orleans, and established the boundaries of Louisiana and Florida, at least for the time being.

When he returned to the United States in 1796, Pinckney became a Federalist candidate in the 1796 presidential election, intending to be elected vice president under JOHN ADAMS, but he was defeated by THOMAS JEFFERSON under the rules of the Electoral College that prevailed at the time. He was then elected to the U.S. House of Representatives in 1797 and served for four years. He supported most of the Federalist proposals but voted against the Sedition Act. The House of Representatives appointed him one of its managers to try the case against William Blount, a senator from Tennessee in 1798. He was one of the few Federalists who demonstrated no eagerness for war with France. In the War of 1812, Pinckney loyally supported the United States as a major general. After he retired from public life, he continued to work as an attorney. He wrote articles for the prominent southern journal *Southern Agriculturist* principally on the methods of importing and raising improved livestock.

Further Reading

Cross, Jack Lee. *London Mission: The First Critical Years.* East Lansing: Michigan State University Press, 1968.

Hernon, Joseph Martin. *Profiles in Character: Hubris and Heroism in the U.S. Senate—1789–1990.* Armonk, N.Y.: M. E. Sharpe, 1997.

Pinckney, Charles Cotesworth. *Life of General Thomas Pinckney.* Boston: Houghton, Mifflin, reprinted 1895.

Smith, W. Calvin. "Pinckney, Thomas." Available online. Discovery Channel School, original content provided by World Book Online. URL: http://www.discoveryschool.com/homeworkhelp/worldbook/atozhistory/p/430895.html. Downloaded November 21, 2001.

Williams, Frances Leigh. *A Founding Family: The Pinckneys of South Carolina.* New York: Harcourt Brace Jovanovich, 1978.

Polk, James Knox

(1795–1849) *president, Speaker of the House, representative*

James Knox Polk was the only Speaker of the U.S. House of Representatives to be elected president, the only president to fulfill all his campaign promises in a single term, the first president to decline to run for reelection, and the president who acquired clear title to more territory than any other. His wife, Sarah Childress Polk, was his full political partner and the first presidential spouse to fill such a role. Polk was such a hardworking president that he was exhausted by the end of his four-year term and died just three months after it ended.

Polk was born on November 2, 1795, on a farm near Pineville in Mecklenburg County, North Carolina. His family had moved to North Carolina from Pennsylvania about 30 years earlier, contributed distinguished patriots in the Revolutionary War, and benefited from the vast land speculation in the western section of North Carolina that ultimately became Tennessee. In 1806, Polk's immediate family moved to some of the most fertile of these Tennessee lands on the Duck River near Columbia in what was to became Maury County. James Polk was sick as a child until he had a rare but successful gallstone surgery at age 16.

After he recovered from the operation, he was in excellent health, studied at two different college preparatory schools for two successive years, and then began his sophomore year at the University of North Carolina. He graduated at the top of his class in 1818, returned to Tennessee, and studied law with the renowned criminal attorney Felix Grundy, who used his political connections to introduce Polk to ANDREW JACKSON and a life of politics.

In 1819, Grundy secured for Polk the clerkship of the state senate. Polk was admitted to the bar and elected to the Tennessee House of Representatives in 1823. In the legislature, Polk sided against his family's former political allies, but this move matched the sentiments of General Andrew Jackson (a family friend with a similar political background), with whose future Polk's career was now firmly tied. In 1824, Polk ran for and was elected to Congress at the same time Jackson ran for president. When Jackson received the largest number of popular and Electoral College votes—but not a majority—the U.S. House of Representatives chose JOHN QUINCY ADAMS over Jackson for president.

In Congress, Polk was one of its youngest members and aggressively attacked Adams to help pave the way for Jackson in 1828. After Jackson's election, Polk became the Jackson floor leader and spokesman. As chairman of the House Ways and Means Committee, Polk was in an excellent position to aid Jackson in his fight against the Second National Bank. For his excellent service, he was rewarded by being named Speaker of the House, a difficult job in those years but one in which he performed well and sharpened his political skills. After 14 years in the House, Jackson persuaded Polk to return to Tennessee to run for governor since the Democrats were feuding and Jackson thought only Polk could win. Polk won in 1839, but he lost in 1841 and 1843. Still, Polk had earned Jackson's support for a vice presidential nomination in 1840, although that was not sufficient. The Democrats chose Kentucky's Richard M. Johnson, who went down to defeat with incumbent Democratic President MARTIN VAN BUREN.

In 1844, Polk was again a candidate for the vice presidency as Van Buren sought the nomination for a second term. However, Van Buren felt antislavery pressure in the North and, in a letter, sought to backtrack on his earlier support for the immediate annexation of Texas. Democrats in the South and West were furious—no one more so than Andrew Jackson, who withdrew his support for Van Buren and began to work quietly for Polk. When Van Buren and Michigan's Lewis Cass deadlocked well below the necessary two-thirds then required for nomination, Polk's name was suddenly introduced and he swept to the nomination on the next ballot. The Democrats chose New York's Senator Silas Wright to run with Polk for vice president, but Wright admired Van Buren so much that he became the first person in U.S. history to refuse a vice presidency after it was formally offered to him. The delegates then chose Pennsylvania's George M. Dallas. Although often called the first "dark horse" candidate, Polk was much stronger than this phrase implied.

The 1844 Whig presidential nominee, HENRY CLAY—like Van Buren—sought to sidestep the Texas annexation question, but Polk's forthright call for immediate annexation and his own deft compromise on the tariff question allowed him to pull even with the much better known Clay. In New York, the antislavery Liberty Party candidate, JAMES GILLESPIE BIRNEY, pulled enough votes from Clay to give New York—and thereby the election in the Electoral College—to Polk. The popular vote gave Polk a narrow 40,000-vote margin.

In the campaign, Polk had cleverly advanced a very popular but misleading position. He asserted

that both Texas and the Oregon territory already belonged to the United States, and he favored "reannexing" Texas and "reoccupying" all of Oregon up to the line of 54 degrees 40 minutes—the famous "54–40 or fight." His actual goals, though still ambitious, were more modest. Polk wanted Texas annexed immediately, (but that would be achieved by JOHN TYLER before Polk was sworn in). On inauguration day, Polk summarized his campaign goals into four major items—all of which he achieved in four years.

First, Polk wanted the tariff reduced so it was essentially used for revenue and used for protection only incidentally. In the first tariff bill ever introduced by the executive branch, Polk's Treasury secretary, Robert Walker, pushed through Congress the "Walker Tariff," which eliminated coffee and tea duties, reduced rates generally, and had only a minor protective effect.

James Knox Polk, the only Speaker of the U.S. House of Representatives to be elected president, acquired clear title to more U.S. territory than any other president and was the only president to fulfill all his campaign promises in one term. *(Library of Congress)*

Second, Polk wanted to restore the independent Treasury that Democratic President Van Buren had created. The Whigs had repealed the independent Treasury plan during their four-year stay in the White House, but Polk's Independent Treasury Act of 1846 restored the original so that neither the state banks nor private business controlled U.S. deposits. This system lasted until the Federal Reserve System was established by THOMAS WOODROW WILSON.

Third, Polk wanted Oregon's northern boundary peacefully settled with Britain. Although Polk had called for 54-40 in the campaign, he actually was prepared to settle for the 49th parallel, and he offered this compromise to the British. They rejected this, then blundered, then offered Polk what he wanted all along. Polk thereby achieved his third major goal in the 1846 Oregon Treaty.

Fourth, Polk wanted California and had previously offered to buy it from Mexico, but Mexico was in no mood to sell while being threatened over Texas. Mexico foolishly rejected all attempts at negotiations and refused to settle the question of the southern boundary of Texas because they wanted the whole area back. They got nothing. When negotiations stalemated, U.S. general ZACHARY TAYLOR advanced his troops beyond the traditional Nueces River boundary down to the Rio Grande. There the Mexicans skirmished with the U.S. troops. Taylor and Polk asked for and got a declaration of war. Polk distrusted both Taylor and WINFIELD SCOTT, whom he thought might be Whig political rivals, so he attempted to manage the war himself. In the end, all three should probably be credited for the final victory. Polk, however, clearly gets the credit for winning the peace. He brushed off pressure to take all of Mexico and settled for all the territory he originally wanted to buy. Polk got California, and it must have given him great pleasure to announce, close to the end of his term, that gold had been discovered there.

It is possible that no other president ever worked so hard in four years. At the end of his term, he kept all his promises including the one about not running again. Nearing collapse, he returned to Tennessee, contracted cholera, and died on June 15, 1849.

Further Reading

Bergeron, Paul H. *The Presidency of James K. Polk.* Norwalk, Conn.: Easton Press, 1991.

Bowers, Claude G. *Making Democracy a Reality: Jefferson, Jackson, and Polk.* Memphis, Tenn.: Memphis State College Press, 1954.

Commager, Henry Steele. "Polk, James Knox." Available on-line. Discovery Channel School, original content provided by World Book online. URL: http://www.discoveryschool.com/homeworkhelp/worldbook/atozhistory/p/437440.html. Downloaded November 22, 2001.

Haynes, Sam W. *James K. Polk and the Expansionist Impulse.* New York: Longman, 1997.

Hoyt, Edwin Palmer. *James Knox Polk.* Chicago: Reilly & Lee, 1965.

Mahin, Dean B. *Olive Branch and Sword: The United States and Mexico, 1845–1848.* Jefferson, N.C.: McFarland & Company, 1997.

McCormac, Eugene. *James K. Polk.* New York: Russell & Russell, 1965.

McCoy, Charles A. *Polk and the Presidency.* New York: Haskell House, 1973.

Nelson, Anna Kasten. *Secret Agents: President Polk and the Search for Peace with Mexico.* New York: Garland, 1988.

"Polk, James K." Available online. URL: http://www.whitehouse.gov/history/presidents/jp11.html. Downloaded November 11, 2001.

Sellers, Charles Grier. *James K. Polk: Jacksonian, 1795–1843.* Norwalk, Conn.: Easton Press, 1987.

Williams, Frank B. *Tennessee's Presidents.* Knoxville: University of Tennessee Press, 1981.

Winders, Richard Bruce. *Mr. Polk's Army: The American Military Experience in the Mexican War.* College Station: Texas A&M University Press, 1997.

Powell, Adam Clayton, Jr.
(1908–1972) *representative*

Adam Clayton Powell, Jr., was one of the most militant civil rights leaders during the 1950s and early 1960s. He was the first African American elected to the U.S. House of Representatives from New York and the first to chair a standing House committee.

Powell was born on November 29, 1908, in New Haven, Connecticut, and grew up in Harlem,

New York, where his father was the minister of the Abyssinian Baptist Church, one of the largest African-American congregations in the United States. Powell dropped out of City College of New York before attending Colgate University, from which he graduated in 1930. While helping his father in the church, he studied at Union Theological Seminary and Columbia University, from which he received an M.A. degree in religious education in 1932.

In 1937, Powell took over from his father at Abyssinian and began his career as a militant African-American leader. In 1941, Powell was elected as an independent to a city council seat, an office he used as a forum to challenge discrimination. After the 1940 census, New York City became eligible for a new congressional district, and the New York legislature created one in Harlem, so heavily populated by African Americans that it was virtually certain to elect an African American—the first in New York and the second in the nation (after the seat held by Chicago's Big Bill Dawson). Powell ran and won a vigorous 1944 campaign, receiving support from Democrats (on whose ballot he ran), Republicans, Liberals, and Communists.

Although shut out of much routine legislative action, he successfully challenged racial discrimination where he could. He demanded that African-American journalists be permitted to sit in the House press gallery, and he stopped the segregation in congressional service facilities. Many House members stopped using the word n----- in Congress, because they knew Powell would publicly challenge them on the House floor. For years he forced many members who claimed to be for civil rights to vote on the Powell Amendment, which would have denied federal funds to institutions that discriminated racially. Repeatedly rebuffed by many Democrats, Powell retaliated by supporting incumbent Republican President DWIGHT DAVID EISENHOWER, whom he claimed was mildly progressive on civil rights.

In 1960, Powell pulled out all the stops while campaigning for the Democratic nominee JOHN FITZGERALD KENNEDY, carrying many African-American voters into the Kennedy camp—and providing Kennedy his narrow margin of victory in several close states. That year, Powell became chair of the House Committee on Education and Labor—the first time an African American chaired a standing House committee. Over the next six years, Powell helped pass progressive legislation on the minimum wage, Medicare, Medicaid, and Head Start. His notorious Powell Amendment finally became law as the landmark 1964 Civil Rights Act.

Unfortunately, his personal excesses were catching up with him. At one point, he survived an income tax evasion indictment over alleged kickbacks from staffers by drawing a hung jury. In 1960, however, Powell was not so lucky. A constituent won a libel judgment for a huge amount of money because Powell had called her a "bag lady"—someone who carried bribes from illegal gambling operations to the police. Powell refused to pay and was forced to stay out of New York or face arrest for contempt of court. This impasse dragged on for years until Powell settled the case.

In addition to the negative publicity Powell received about his heavy absenteeism from the House and for personal extravagances, a House committee finally determined in 1966 that Powell had improperly paid his wife out of House committee funds and had taken improper and costly vacations at government expense. After the November 1966 election, the House voted to prevent Powell from taking his seat. Powell challenged the vote in federal courts, and the U.S. Supreme Court ultimately found that the House could expel a member but not simply prohibit a duly elected member from taking his seat. In the meantime, Powell had won his seat back twice—once in a 1967 special election and again in the 1968 regular election. Powell was fined $25,000 and denied his seniority. He took his seat in 1969, but he was defeated in the 1970 Democratic primary by Charles Rangel.

He died on April 4, 1972.

Further Reading

Alexander, E. Curtis. *Adam Clayton Powell, Jr.: A Black Power Political Educator.* New York: ECA Associates, 1983.

Bardolph, Richard. "Powell, Adam Clayton, Jr." Available on-line. Discovery Channel School, original content provided by World Book Online. URL:

http://www.discoveryschool.com/homeworkhelp/ worldbook/atozhistory/p/442810.html. Downloaded November 22, 2001.

Hamilton, Charles V. *Adam Clayton Powell, Jr.* New York: Collier Books, 1992.

Hapgood, David. *The Purge That Failed: Tammany v. Powell.* New York: Holt, 1959.

Haskins, James. *Adam Clayton Powell.* Trenton, N.J.: Africa World Press, 1993.

Haygood, Wil. *King of the Cats: The Life and Times of Adam Clayton Powell, Jr.* Boston: Houghton Mifflin, 1993.

Hickey, Neil. *Adam Clayton Powell and the Politics of Race.* New York: Fleet, 1965.

Jacobs, Andy. *The Powell Affair: Freedom Minus One.* Indianapolis, Ind.: Bobbs-Merrill, 1973.

Lewis, Claude. *Adam Clayton Powell.* Greenwich, Conn.: Fawcett, 1963.

Powell, Adam Clayton. *Adam on Adam: The Autobiography of Adam Clayton Powell, Jr.* Secaucus, N.J.: Carol, 1994.

Weeks, Kent M. *Adam Clayton Powell and the Supreme Court.* New York: Dunellen, 1971.

Randolph, Edmund
(1753–1813) *secretary of state, attorney general*

Edmund Randolph was a distinguished patriot during the Revolutionary War, the first attorney general of the United States, and the second secretary of state (after THOMAS JEFFERSON). His famous Randolph Plan (or Virginia Plan) was presented at the 1787 Constitutional Convention and became a substantial part of the final version of the U.S. Constitution. Wrongly accused of taking bribes, but ultimately vindicated, he had the courage to defend AARON BURR against the false charge of treason leveled against him and to save Burr from hanging.

Randolph was born on August 10, 1753, in Williamsburg, Virginia, into one of the most distinguished Virginia families. He studied law both at William and Mary and under his father, John Randolph, until his father fled—as a Loyalist—to England when the Revolutionary War began. Randolph served briefly as aide-de-camp to GEORGE WASHINGTON early in the war, but at age 23 he was elected as Virginia's attorney general, a role he held for a decade. In 1776, he was also elected to the Virginia constitutional convention. From 1779 to 1782, he simultaneously served in the Continental Congress, and in 1786, he was elected governor of Virginia.

In 1787, Randolph was active in the U.S. Constitutional Convention where he presented the Randolph Plan (or Virginia Plan), drafted by JAMES MADISON and himself. At the end of the convention, he strenuously opposed the final draft of the constitution, but he finally supported its ratification as the best that could be accomplished at the 1788 Virginia ratifying convention. Washington asked him to become the first U.S. attorney general in 1789, and he stayed in that position until Washington appointed him to be the second U.S. secretary of state in 1794 when Thomas Jefferson resigned.

Randolph, a distant relative of Jefferson, also had difficulties because ALEXANDER HAMILTON had Washington's ear and was pressing for his foreign policy agenda that opposed France and sought the most favorable terms from England. Hamilton wrote a secret message to JOHN JAY, laying out the terms he wished to see incorporated in such a treaty, and Jay, ignoring the contrary wishes of Jefferson and Randolph, dutifully brought back the Jay Treaty. To discredit Randolph, the British captured dispatches of a French diplomat implying falsely that Randolph might take a French bribe. Asked by Washington whether this was true, Randolph was humiliated and resigned.

Randolph then practiced law in Virginia and ultimately cleared his name years later. No friend of Aaron Burr, he nonetheless successfully defended him when he was falsely charged with treason in 1807.

Randolph died on September 12, 1813.

Further Reading

Hernon, Joseph Martin. *Profiles in Character: Hubris and Heroism in the U.S. Senate—1789–1990.* Armonk, N.Y.: M. E. Sharpe, 1997.

Reardon, John J. *Edmund Randolph.* New York: Macmillan, 1975.

Rankin, Jeannette
(1880–1973) *representative*

Jeannette Rankin was the first woman to be elected to the U.S. House of Representatives and the only member of Congress to vote against the declarations of war before both World Wars I and II.

Born on June 11, 1880, on a ranch near Missoula, Montana, Jeannette Rankin was the eldest of seven children of a rancher, who also served as a

Jeannette Rankin was the first woman elected to the U.S. Congress and the only congressperson to vote against declaring war in both World Wars I and II. *(Library of Congress)*

Republican county commissioner. Her mother was a schoolteacher and provided most of her elementary and secondary education. In 1902, she graduated from the University of Montana in biology. Her family believed in education, and all the children attended the University of Montana. Three of the girls went on to Wellesley, and the only boy later attended Harvard Law School. After attempting careers as a seamstress, a schoolteacher, and a furniture designer and finding none satisfactory, Jeannette Rankin journeyed east to visit her brother at Harvard. Appalled by the housing conditions in the Boston slums, she decided on a career in social work. She moved to New York and attended the New York School of Philanthropy in 1908–09.

Moving back west to Seattle, Rankin began her life work as a social worker. She soon joined in the women's suffrage movement, campaigning extensively in Washington State in 1910. She campaigned for suffrage in California in 1911, just as Republican Governor HIRAM WARREN JOHNSON and the other progressives came to power. By pushing women's suffrage successfully in California, the suffrage movement made one of its biggest gains and developed momentum that carried suffrage through on the national level. Rankin then returned to Montana to labor for suffrage from 1912 to 1914. She crisscrossed the state many times and developed contacts in virtually every town and village. She became a field secretary for the National Association of Women's Suffrage in 1913 and saw suffrage granted in Montana.

In 1916, she was elected as a Republican congresswoman at large from Montana, one of the few states that allowed women to vote at that time. She sponsored the first bill that would have allowed women citizenship independent of their husbands. She also introduced legislation that would have provided government funded education for maternal and infant hygiene. These and other protective measures for women and children were popular and would have been consistent with a lengthy legislative career.

However, Rankin was a pacifist and voted against U.S. entry into World War I in the company of 49 other members of the House. Because of her vote against the war, she was denied the Republican nomination for the U.S. Senate in 1918. She then ran as an independent for the U.S. Senate but lost. Having given up her House seat to run for the U.S. Senate, she was now out of office. In 1919, with Jane Addams and Florence Kelley, she attended the Congress of the International Council of Women. In 1920, she became the secretary of Florence Kelley's National Consumer League where she continued to work until 1924. She also worked for the Women's International League for Peace and Freedom.

In 1928, she moved to Georgia and became an organizer for the National Council for the Prevention of War during 1929 through 1939. In 1940, she returned to Montana and ran on an explicitly antiwar platform. Again, she was elected to the House of Representatives from Montana's at large seat. Again, she had an opportunity to vote on a declaration of war after Pearl Harbor was bombed in December 1941. Again, she voted no. Again, she was not reelected, but she still ran unsuccessfully for the U.S. Senate in 1943.

A follower of Indian pacifist Mohandas Gandhi, she opposed U.S. participation in the Korean War and questioned the role of the United States in developing countries. Out of politics, she visited India several times and founded a women's "cooperative homestead" in Georgia. She returned to the national spotlight on January 15, 1968, as the head of the Jeannette Rankin Brigade. Even though she was 87 years old, she led more than 5,000 antiwar women to Washington, D.C., to demonstrate against U.S. involvement in Vietnam.

Rankin died on May 18, 1973, in Carmel, New York. In 1985, Montana placed a bronze statue of her in the U.S. Capitol in Washington, D.C., in the place of honor reserved for Montana's outstanding representative.

Further Reading

Giles, Kevin S. *Flight of the Dove: The Story of Jeannette Rankin.* Beaverton, Ore.: Touchstone Press, 1980.

Hernon, Joseph Martin. *Profiles in Character: Hubris and Heroism in the U.S. Senate—1789–1990.* Armonk, N.Y.: M. E. Sharpe, 1997.

Josephson, Hannah. *Jeannette Rankin: First Lady in Congress.* Indianapolis, Ind.: Bobbs-Merrill, 1974.

"Jeannette Rankin" in *Congress A to Z: Third Edition,* edited by David R. Tarr and Ann O'Connor. Washington, D.C.: Congressional Quarterly, 1999.

Olson, James. "Rankin, Jeannette." Available online. Discovery Channel School, original content provided by World Book Online. URL: http://www.discoveryschool.com/homeworkhelp/worldbook/atozhistory/r/459540.html. Downloaded November 22, 2001.

White, Florence Meiman. *First Woman in Congress: Jeannette Rankin.* New York: J. Messner, 1980.

Rayburn, Samuel Taliaferro
(1882–1961) *Speaker of the House, representative*

Samuel Taliaferro Rayburn served longer as Speaker of the U.S. House of Representatives than any other person. Rayburn also served 49 consecutive years as a member of the House of Representatives, the longest tenure of any representative.

Rayburn was born on January 6, 1882, near Clinch River in Roane County, Tennessee. In 1887, he and his family moved to a small cotton farm in Fannin County, Texas. In 1900, he attended East Texas Normal College, completed its three-year program in two years, and earned the B.S. degree, even though he had to teach school simultaneously to pay for college. He taught for two years and then began studying at the University of Texas Law School.

In 1906, he was elected to the Texas state legislature and continued in law school between legislative sessions until he graduated in 1908. In 1911, he was chosen Speaker of the Texas House of Representatives, but he left for Washington in 1913 after his successful election in 1912. After 1912, the Republicans never again offered a candidate against him.

A protégé of JOHN NANCE GARNER, Rayburn followed Garner's example, avoided making speeches, and quickly rose through the ranks. In 1937, he was elected the Democrat's majority leader. When Speaker WILLIAM BANKHEAD died in 1940, Rayburn became Speaker. For the next 21 years, he served as the House Speaker whenever the Democrats had a majority in the Congress, and this covered all the years from 1940 to 1961 except for 1947–49 and 1953–55. He followed a traditional pattern for a southern congressional leader by giving the "glory" of being identified with the passage of legislature to others, so that few specific pieces of legislation are even identified with him.

In 1932, Rayburn was Garner's presidential campaign manager and was a major negotiator in formulating the 1932 Roosevelt-Garner ticket. He presided over the 1952 and 1956 Democratic National Conventions.

Rayburn died of cancer on November 16, 1961.

Further Reading

Hairgrove, Kenneth Dewey. *Sam Rayburn: Congressional Leader, 1940–1952.* Ann Arbor, Mich.: University Microfilms International, 1975, 1980.

Hamby, Alonzo L. "Rayburn, Sam." Available online. Discovery Channel School, original content provided by World Book Online. URL: http://www.discoveryschool.com/homeworkhelp/worldbook/atozhistory/r/460500.html. Downloaded November 22, 2001.

Little, Dwayne Lee. *The Political Leadership of Speaker Sam Rayburn, 1940–1961.* Ann Arbor, Mich.: University Microfilms, 1972.

Mooney, Booth. *Roosevelt and Rayburn: A Political Partnership.* Philadelphia: Lippincott, 1971.

"Rayburn, Samuel Taliaferro." The Handbook of Texas Online. Available online. URL: http://www.tsha.utexas.edu/handbook/online/articles/view/RR/fra49.html. Downloaded November 22, 2001.

"Sam Rayburn" in *Congress A to Z: Third Edition,* edited by David R. Tarr and Ann O'Connor. Washington, D.C.: Congressional Quarterly, 1999.

Steinberg, Alfred. *Sam Rayburn.* New York: Hawthorn Books, 1975.

Reagan, Ronald Wilson
(1911–   ) *president, governor*

Ronald Reagan was the only president whose early career was primarily as a movie star, the only president who survived being shot by a would-be assassin while in office, and the only president in a contested election to win every state but one. His supporters have insisted he brought about a conservative revolution, but even skeptics on this point have acknowledged that his presidency ac-companied a decided conservative shift in national politics.

Ronald Wilson Reagan was born on February 6, 1911, in Tampico, Illinois, and his family moved to Dixon, Illinois, when he was nine years of age. He began his career in sports broadcasting after he graduated from Eureka College. While covering a sporting event in California in 1937, he signed a contract to appear as a radio announcer in a movie. He proved so successful in that movie that he subsequently appeared in 49 other films between 1937 and 1964. In World War II, he served three years in the U.S. Army by making training films.

In 1947, Reagan first became interested in politics when he was elected president of the Screen Actors Guild where he served until 1951 (and again in 1959). He was a New Deal Democrat and a FRANKLIN DELANO ROOSEVELT supporter in the 1930s and 1940s, but he was among those Democrats who supported Republicans such as DWIGHT DAVID EISENHOWER and RICHARD MILHOUS NIXON in the 1950s.

In 1962, Reagan joined the Republican Party and delivered a campaign speech for 1964 Republican presidential candidate BARRY MORRIS GOLDWATER so famous that it launched his campaign for governor of California. In 1966, he defeated the Democratic two-term incumbent governor, Edmund G. "Pat" Brown, and he served two terms. As governor, he initially raised taxes, because he said the state was bankrupt, but he later cut government spending for education, welfare, and medical services.

Using the governor's office as a base, he ran for the 1968 Republican presidential nomination, but he lost to Nixon. He made a full-fledged race for the 1976 Republican presidential nomination against the incumbent president, GERALD RUDOLPH FORD, who had been appointed as vice president and succeeded to the presidency upon the resignation of Nixon in 1974. Ford was weakened not only by his pardon of Nixon but also for his liberal choice of NELSON ALDRICH ROCKEFELLER for vice president. Reagan was favored by the increased use of primaries and by a new delegate allocation that increased Republican representation in his stronghold in the South and West. Reagan failed by a mere 60 delegate votes from winning the Republican presidential nomination and came closer than any other 20th-century challenger to taking his party's presidential nomination away from a sitting president. Ford then lost the general election to JAMES EARL CARTER.

By 1980, Reagan was unstoppable for the Republican nomination. Challenged by a number of others, only GEORGE HERBERT WALKER BUSH managed to stay in the race until April when Reagan had locked up the nomination. Reagan later named Bush his vice presidential running mate. Reagan began the race with a 15 percent lead in the opinion polls and was assisted by the campaign of independent JAMES BAYARD ANDERSON, who took votes away from Democratic incumbent Carter. Carter was hurt by the nation's economic performance during a period labeled "stagflation," which featured both high interest and high unemployment. He also was held responsible for the seizure of the U.S. embassy personnel as hostages in Iran and the failure to get them back. Although Carter waged a diligent campaign and closed the gap in the polls, it was not enough to overcome Reagan's long lead, and Reagan won the popular vote by 51% to Carter's 42% with 7% going to Anderson.

On March 30, 1981, a mentally disturbed John Hinckley wounded Reagan in an assassination attempt that left the president hospitalized for several weeks, but he recovered and used the public sympathy to push through Congress a major conservative retrenchment. This included urging a balanced budget to combat inflation and a simultaneous tax cut that he said would stimulate the economy and would collect more revenue than the older higher tax rates. Called "supply-side economics," the program was passed by a skeptical Congress. At the same time, Congress cut domestic spending while increasing military spending at the highest rate in peacetime U.S. history. Reagan also advocated building an expensive antiballistic system of uncertain workability, but Congress would only authorize research into the possibility. Assisted by tax cuts and deficit financing, the U.S. economy lifted out of the recession of the early 1980s, but with large budget deficits.

In October 1983, Reagan ordered the invasion of the Caribbean island of Grenada, saying it was a dangerous Cuban-Soviet military base and Americans there were in jeopardy. The successful

Ronald Wilson Reagan, the only president who survived being shot by a would-be assassin while in office, led a decidedly conservative shift in national politics. *(Library of Congress, Official White House photo)*

Grenada operation lasted just a few days and distracted attention from other international events, such as a terrorist bombing of a U.S. Marine barracks in Lebanon that killed 241 servicemen. With economic improvement, the successful Grenada invasion, and his status as an incumbent, Reagan defeated 1984 Democratic nominee Walter Mondale by a landslide, carrying every state except Mondale's home state of Minnesota and the District of Columbia. This gave Reagan 525 electoral votes, the most received by a presidential candidate in U.S. history and the highest percentage of any contested race.

After the election, Reagan began to ease his opposition to the Soviet Union as the new Soviet leader Mikhail Gorbachev seemed willing to negotiate in an atmosphere of openness. The two leaders agreed to an Intermediate-Range Nuclear-Force Missile Treaty (INF treaty), which substantially reduced intermediate nuclear forces.

Reagan was generally successful until the 1986 off-year elections, when the Democrats gained a few more seats in the House of Representatives and regained control of the Senate by a 55–45 margin. After 1986, his problems increased, starting with his attempt to name a strong conservative to the Supreme Court. He first nominated Robert Bork, who had written extensively about what he saw as the excessively liberal trend on the U.S. Supreme Court. These writings gave his opponents many issues to raise against him in the Senate confirmation hearings, and he was defeated by a 58–42 margin.

Reagan then nominated a conservative Harvard Law professor, Douglas Ginsburg, but it was discovered that he had smoked marijuana even during his Harvard teaching years just a short time before his nomination. Ginsburg then withdrew his name from consideration. Reagan finally named a moderate conservative, Anthony M. Kennedy, and he was approved. After the 1986 congressional elections, the Iran-contra Affair revealed the White House's complicity in the illegal diversion of profits from secret arms-for-hostage deals with Iran for the use of the Contra guerrillas fighting the Sandinista government in Nicaragua.

When it became apparent that Reagan's real goal was to overthrow the Sandinistas, Congress had prohibited the use of U.S. funds for this purpose, and the Reagan administration had ignored the law. Reagan claimed that national security adviser Vice Admiral John Poindexter or his aide, Lieutenant Colonel Oliver North, had not informed him of the Iran-contra connection. Both the selling of arms to Iran in exchange for the release of hostages (something Reagan said he would never do) and the use of this money to aid the Contras (contrary to congressional enactments) set off a series of embarrassing investigations that resulted in indictments of both Poindexter and North. While no one ever proved Reagan knew about the illegal acts, Reagan appeared to be negligent in his duty to enforce the law.

At the end of Reagan's term, the international situation with the Soviet Union had improved. Economic growth, however, remained relatively modest, although the rate of inflation dropped below 6% during his tenure, but the deficits almost tripled the size of the national debt.

Reagan left office after his two term's and saw Vice President Bush elected as president. In 1994, Reagan disclosed that he had Alzheimer's disease in hopes of increasing public awareness of the illness.

Further Reading

Blumenthal, Sidney, and Thomas Byrne Edsall, eds. *The Reagan Legacy*. New York: Pantheon Books, 1988.

Cannon, Lou. *President Reagan: The Role of a Lifetime*. New York: Simon & Schuster, 1991.

Combs, James. *The Reagan Range: The Nostalgic Myth in American Politics*. Bowling Green Ky.: Bowling Green State University Popular Press, 1993.

Dallek, Rober. *Ronald Reagan*. Cambridge, Mass.: Harvard University Press, 1999.

D'Souza, Dinesh. *Ronald Reagan: How an Ordinary Man Became an Extraordinary Leader*. New York: Simon & Schuster, 1999.

Fischer, Beth A. *The Reagan Reversal: Foreign Policy and the End of the Cold War*. Columbia: University of Missouri Press, 1997.

Fitzgerald, Frances. *Way Out There in the Blue: Reagan, Star Wars, and the End of the Cold War*. New York: Simon & Schuster, 2000.

Jentleson, Bruce W. *With Friends Like These: Reagan, Bush And Saddam, 1982–1990*. New York: Neston. 1994.

Karaagac, John. *Between Promise and Policy: Ronald Reagan and Conservative Reformism*. Lanham, Md.: Lexington Books, 2000.

Laham, Nicholas. *The Reagan Presidency and the Politics of Race: In Pursuit of Colorblind Justice and Limited Government*. Westport, Conn.: Praeger, 1998.

Noonan, Peggy. *What I Saw at the Revolution: A Political Life in the Reagan Era*. New York: Random House, 1990.

Reagan, Nancy. *My Turn: The Memoirs of Nancy Reagan*. New York: Random, 1989.

Reagan, Ronald. *A Shining City: The Legacy Of Ronald Reagan*. New York: Simon & Schuster, 1998.

"Reagan, Ronald." Available online. URL: http://www.whitehouse.gov/history/presidents/rr40.html. Downloaded November 11, 2001.

Reeves, Richard. *The Reagan Detour*. New York: Simon & Schuster, 1985.

Round, Michael A. *Grounded: Reagan and the PATCO Crash*. New York: Garland Pub. 1999.

Schieffer, Bob. *The Acting President*. New York: Dutton, 1989.

Sick, Gary. *October Surprise: America's Hostages in Iran and the Election of Ronald Reagan.* New York: Times Books, 1991.

Sloan, John W. *The Reagan Effect: Economics And Presidential Leadership.* Lawrence: University Press of Kansas, 1999.

Strober, Deborah H. *Reagan: The Man and His Presidency.* Boston: Houghton Mifflin, 1998.

Walsh, Kenneth T. *Ronald Reagan.* New York: Park Lane Press, 1997.

Wills, Garry. *Reagan's America: Innocents at Home.* New York: Penguin Books, 1987.

Winik, Jay. *On the Brink: The Dramatic, Behind-the-Scenes Saga of the Reagan Era.* New York: Simon & Schuster, 1996.

Woodward, Bob. *Shadow.* New York. Simon & Schuster, 1999.

Reed, Thomas Brackett

(1839–1902) *Speaker of the House, representative*

Thomas Brackett Reed, Speaker of the U.S. House of Representatives during the 1890s, was responsible for reforming the rules of the House so that it could succeed as an effective legislative body, although this also led to the charge that he was a czar who exercised autocratic power over the Congress.

Reed was born on October 18, 1839, in Portland, Maine. Graduating from Bowdoin College in 1860, he migrated to California where he studied the law while teaching school. Although he was admitted to the California bar, he went back to Maine. In 1868, he was elected to the Maine state assembly. Two years later, he moved up to the state senate and also became state attorney general. In 1876, he was elected as a Republican to the U.S. House of Representatives. He rose quickly in the House Republican hierarchy and became Speaker from 1889 to 1891 and again from 1895 to 1899.

Until Reed became Speaker, the House had operated under a rule promoted successfully by Representative (and former president) JOHN QUINCY ADAMS that allowed members to attend sessions of Congress but refrain from voting on quorum calls to stop all legislative action. Adams justified this procedure as a part of his antislavery campaign

earlier in the century. However, by the 1890s, the rule had outlived its usefulness, and the House was threatened with such gross inefficiency that little work could be done. Reed changed this situation by pushing through a rule that allowed him to count as present all who were actually present in the chamber.

In turn, "Reed's Rules" outlived their usefulness and were changed in 1910 in a revolt against the autocratic Speaker Joseph G. Cannon. Although Reed was called a czar, he was hardly a dictator. He opposed—and lost—several major issues of his day, including U.S. involvement in the 1898 Spanish American War, the annexation of Hawaii, and other features of President WILLIAM MCKINLEY's foreign policy. Although reelected to Congress in 1898, Reed was so disturbed by McKinley's policies that he retired in protest and practiced law until his death on December 7, 1902.

Further Reading

Hernon, Joseph Martin. *Profiles in Character: Hubris and Heroism in the U.S. Senate—1789–1990.* Armonk, N.Y.: M. E. Sharpe, 1997.

Lukes-Lukaszewski, Edward A. "Reed, Thomas Brackett." Available on line. Discovery Channel School, original content provided by World Book Online. URL: http://www.discoveryschool.com/homeworkhelp/worldbook/atozhistory/r/462740.html. Downloaded November 22, 2001.

McCall, Samuel W. *Thomas B. Reed.* New York: AMS Press, 1972.

Offenberg, Richard S. *The Political Career of Thomas Brackett Reed.* New York: New York University, 1963.

Robinson, William A. *Thomas B. Reed: Parliamentarian.* New York: Dodd, Mead, 1930.

"Thomas B. Reed." in *Congress A to Z: Third Edition,* edited by David R. Tarr and Ann O'Connor. Washington, D.C.: Congressional Quarterly, 1999.

Rehnquist, William Hubbs

(1924–) *chief justice of the United States, associate justice of the Supreme Court, assistant attorney general*

William Hubbs Rehnquist is one of only three sitting associate justices of the Supreme Court ever elevated to the post of chief justice. Although some expected he would lead a major conservative retrenchment on the Court, his leadership has made only minor changes in the existing constitutional law.

Rehnquist was born on October 1, 1924, in Milwaukee, Wisconsin. After high school, he joined the U.S. Air Force weather service in World War II and served three years. After the war, he attended Stanford University where he received both B.A. and M.A. degrees in 1948 before transferring to Harvard where he earned an M.A. degree in political science in 1950. Returning to Stanford, he graduated at the top of his 1952 law school class—a class in which SANDRA DAY O'CONNOR graduated third. He then served as law clerk to Supreme Court Justice Robert H. Jackson for the 1952–53 term.

While working for Jackson, he wrote a memorandum upholding the constitutionality of the "separate but equal" legal doctrine established in the 1896 Plessy v. Ferguson case. At his confirmation hearings for the Supreme Court, he claimed the views in the memorandum were those of Justice Jackson, but this answer did not persuade everyone since Jackson voted against the "separate but equal" doctrine in the Brown v. Board of Education case in 1954.

Following his clerkship, Rehnquist began practicing law in Phoenix, Arizona, where he became involved in conservative Republican politics. In Arizona, he met Richard Kleindienst, later deputy attorney general under President RICHARD MILHOUS NIXON, who appointed Rehnquist as assistant U.S. attorney general in charge of the legal counsel division in the U.S. Department of Justice in 1968. Rehnquist was frequently a Nixon administration spokesman before Congress.

Because of his service there, Nixon appointed Rehnquist to the Supreme Court in 1971. As an associate justice, Rehnquist almost always took the most extreme conservative positions and showed a willingness to dissent alone, if necessary, to articulate his conservative views. In 1986, President RONALD WILSON REAGAN named him the successor to retiring Chief Justice WARREN EARL BURGER. While the Court under Rehnquist has been more conservative than its predecessors, it has mainly made fairly small modifications in the existing trend of constitutional law. The harshest criticism of Rehnquist came as the result of his vote in the 2000 presidential election case, Bush v. Gore. That decision departed from conservative principle by overturning a Florida Supreme Court decision that interpreted the state's own law.

Further Reading

Boles, Donald E. Mr. Justice Rehnquist: Judicial Activist: The Early Years. Ames: Iowa State University Press, 1987.

Davis, Derek. Original Intent: Chief Justice Rehnquist and the Course of American Church-State Relations. Buffalo, N.Y.: Prometheus Books, 1991.

Davis, Sue. Justice Rehnquist and the Constitution. Princeton, N.J.: Princeton University Press, 1989.

Irons, Peter H. Brennan vs. Rehnquist: The Battle for the Constitution. New York: Knopf, 1994.

Rehnquist, William H. Grand Inquests: The Historic Impeachments of Justice Samuel Chase and President Andrew Johnson. New York: Morrow, 1992.

Savage, David G. Turning Right: The Making of the Rehnquist Supreme Court. New York: Wiley, 1993.

Tucker, D. F. B. The Rehnquist Court and Civil Rights. Brookfield, N.H.: Dartmouth, 1995.

Yarbrough, Tinsley. The Rehnquist Court and the Constitution. New York: Oxford University Press, 2000.

Revels, Hiram Rhoades
(1822–1901) senator

Hiram Rhodes Revels was the first African American elected by a state legislature to serve in the U.S. Senate.

Revels was born in September 1822 in Fayetteville, North Carolina, not as a slave but a free man whose parents, of African and Native American descent, were also free. He was apprenticed to a barber (his brother) who died before the end of the apprenticeship, and Revels decided to abandon barbering to further his education.

In 1844, he went to a Quaker school in Liberty, Indiana, and to a seminary in Ohio before attending Knox College. Revels was ordained an African Methodist Church minister in 1845 and traveled throughout the Midwest and border states establishing schools and churches.

By the time the Civil War broke out, he was the principal of a school and pastor of a church in Baltimore. Since Maryland was a slave state on the border between the North and South, it was vital to the Union that Maryland not secede as some in the state wished it would. Revels devoted himself to the Union cause by organizing two African-American Union regiments in Maryland. He then went to organize a school for African Americans in St. Louis, Missouri, another border state. He again recruited African Americans into a Missouri regiment in 1863 and then became a Union chaplain, serving with a Mississippi regiment of free blacks.

At the conclusion of the war, Revels settled in Natchez, Mississippi, where he was elected an alderman in 1868 and elected a state senator from Adams County, Mississippi, that same year. In 1870, the Reconstruction era state legislature elected Revels to be the first African-American U.S. Senator, filling the vacancy created when JEFFERSON DAVIS resigned the U.S. Senate to become president of the Confederacy. Revels served from February 25, 1870, until March 4, 1871.

After completing his term in the U.S. Senate, he was named president of Alcorn State University (then called simply Alcorn University), the state's first African-American college. In 1873, he was secretary of state ad interim for Mississippi. The next year, the Mississippi Republican Reconstruction governor Ames decided that Revels had deferred too much to the white Democrats, and he fired Revels as Alcorn's president. Revels fought back by calling Ames a "carpetbagger" and joining the Democrats to oust Ames and his associates. The new Democratic governor immediately reappointed Revels as Alcorn's president, and he stayed there until his retirement in 1882.

He remained active in religious work after his retirement and died on January 16, 1901, while attending a church conference.

Further Reading

Buckmaster, Henrietta. *The Fighting Congressmen: Thaddeus Stephens, Hiram Revels, James Rapier, Blanche K. Bruce.* New York: Scholastic Book Services, 1971.

Lawson, Elizabeth. *The Gentleman from Mississippi: Our First Negro Congressman: Hiram R. Revels.* New York: International Publishers, 1960.

Litvin, Martin. *Hiram Revels in Illinois: A Biographical Novel.* Galesburg, Ill.: Log City Books, 1974.

Swain, Carol M. *Black Faces, Black Interests: Representation of African Americans in Congress.* Cambridge, Mass.: Harvard University Press, 1995.

Weiss, Nancy J. "Revels, Hiram Rhodes" Available online. Discovery Channel School, original content provided by World Book Online. URL: http://www.discoveryschool.com/homeworkhelp/worldbook/atozhistory/r/466550.html. Downloaded November 23, 2001.

Rockefeller, Nelson Aldrich

(1908–1979) *candidate for president, vice president, governor*

Nelson Aldrich Rockefeller was only the second person ever to be appointed the vice president of the United States under the Twenty-fifth Amendment of the U.S. Constitution. The first was GERALD RUDOLPH FORD, who served as president while Rockefeller was vice president. Ford was elevated to the presidency upon the resignation of President RICHARD MILHOUS NIXON in the face of impending impeachment. While Rockefeller served as vice president, both the president and vice president were appointed (and not elected) to their respective offices. Rockefeller also served four successful terms as governor of New York and ran for president three times.

Rockefeller, the second son of John D. Rockefeller, Jr., and grandson of oil tycoon John D. Rockefeller, Sr., was born on July 8, 1908, in Bar Harbor, Maine. Educated in distinguished private schools, he graduated from Dartmouth College in 1930.

In 1931, he began his business career by investing in a Venezuelan Standard Oil subsidiary, became interested in Latin America, and started to serve either intermittently or part-time in a variety of governmental posts. By 1940, President FRANKLIN DELANO ROOSEVELT had appointed Rockefeller the coordinator of inter-American affairs and assistant secretary of state for American republic affairs. Although Rockefeller stayed only for a year, President HARRY S. TRUMAN asked him to chair the International Development Advisory Board in 1950. In 1953, President DWIGHT DAVID

EISENHOWER appointed Rockefeller the head of a presidential advisory committee on government organization, whose plans resulted in creation of both the Department of Health, Education and Welfare and the U. S. Information Agency, as well as major changes in the Departments of Agriculture, Defense, and Justice.

In 1958, Rockefeller was elected New York's governor and then was reelected three times. He began a dramatic growth in state spending on education, transportation, health, welfare, housing, and environmental protection, which required substantial tax increases. This record created Rockefeller's reputation as a liberal Republican. Although he tried to develop a more conservative image to win conservative votes in primaries needed to win the Republican presidential nomination, Rockefeller was always regarded as the leader of the liberal Republican wing of the party.

By 1960, although he denied he was interested in running for president, he intimated that he would be open to the idea of a draft for president at the 1960 Republican convention. The Republicans nominated Richard Nixon instead, who then lost the presidency to JOHN FITZGERALD KENNEDY. In 1964, it seemed Rockefeller would have a good chance, but he had divorced, remarried, and become a new father during the campaign, and these changes led to a decline in the polls. Senator BARRY MORRIS GOLDWATER, the Republican conservative leader, defeated Rockefeller on the first ballot but was in turn defeated in the 1964 Democratic landslide.

In 1968, Rockefeller again seemed to be a likely nominee, and he called a press conference to announce he was going to run. However, marital difficulties—including the threat of another divorce—led him to vacillate at the press conference. Later, when he finally resolved his marital problems, he entered the race late in the campaign, but by then Nixon had largely captured the nomination. Rockefeller was reelected New York's governor for a fourth time in 1970. But he resigned in 1973 before completing his term to run the Commission on Critical Choices for America, a private organization he created that was supposed to develop national policy alternatives.

In August 1974, President Nixon resigned while facing impending impeachment and the newly elevated President Ford nominated Rockefeller for vice president. After extended congressional investigation into his financial resources, he was confirmed by both houses of Congress and sworn in on December 19, 1974. While Rockefeller was a loyal subordinate, Ford faced a serious challenge for the presidential nomination from conservative Republican RONALD WILSON REAGAN. Rockefeller's identification as a liberal threatened to derail Ford's nomination, so Rockefeller withdrew as a candidate for vice president, probably under pressure.

After retiring, Rockefeller returned to his private pursuits in New York and died of a heart attack on January 26, 1979.

Further Reading

Bleecker, Samuel E. *The Politics of Architecture: A Perspective on Nelson A. Rockefeller.* New York: Rutledge Press, 1981.

Cobbs, Elizabeth Anne. *The Rich Neighbor Policy: Rockefeller and Kaiser in Brazil.* New Haven: Yale University Press, 1992.

Colby, Gerard. *Thy Will Be Done: The Conquest of the Amazon: Nelson Rockefeller and Evangelism in the Age of Oil.* New York: HarperCollins, 1995.

Donovan, Robert J. *Confidential Secretary: Ann Whitman's 20 Years with Eisenhower and Rockefeller.* New York: Dutton, 1988.

Morrow, Lance. *The Chief: A Memoir of Fathers and Sons.* New York: Random House, 1984.

Persico, Joseph E. *The Imperial Rockefeller: A Biography of Nelson A. Rockefeller.* New York: Simon & Schuster, 1982.

Reich, Cary. *The Life of Nelson A. Rockefeller: Worlds to Conquer.* New York: Doubleday, 1996.

Rodgers, William H. *Rockefeller's Follies: An Unauthorized View of Nelson A. Rockefeller.* New York: Stein & Day, 1966.

Turner, Michael. *The Vice President as Policy Maker: Rockefeller in the Ford White House.* Westport, Conn.: Greenwood Press, 1982.

Underwood, James E. *Governor Rockefeller in New York: The Apex of Pragmatic Liberalism in the United States.* Westport, Conn.: Greenwood Press, 1982.

Rogers, William Pierce
(1913–2001) *secretary of state, attorney general*

William Pierce Rogers served as U.S. attorney general under President DWIGHT DAVID EISENHOWER from 1957 to 1961 and also served as secretary of state under President RICHARD MILHOUS NIXON from 1969 to 1973.

Rogers was born on June 23, 1913, in Norfolk, New York, and he graduated from Colgate University in 1934 and Cornell University Law School in 1937. After a short period practicing law on Wall Street, he joined THOMAS EDMUND DEWEY's task force against crime as an assistant district attorney in New York County. He served in the navy during World War II.

After the war, Rogers served as counsel for two Senate investigating committees, and he later was an assistant attorney general under Eisenhower before he was appointed U.S. attorney general. In that post, he organized the first civil rights division of the attorney general's office.

In 1965, President LYNDON BAINES JOHNSON appointed him a delegate to the United Nations General Assembly and, in 1967, to the 14-nation committee on the future of Southwest Africa.

A longtime friend and political associate of Nixon, Rogers played a critical role in persuading Nixon to defend himself in the 1953 presidential campaign with the famous Checkers speech, and he advised Nixon repeatedly over the years. It was not surprising when Nixon appointed Rogers the U.S. secretary of state. However, Nixon decided he wanted to centralize foreign policy developments in the White House, and he gave increasingly greater authority to his National Security Advisor, HENRY ALFRED KISSINGER. Rogers yielded to his diminution of the normal prominence given to the secretary of state, making it easy for Kissinger to persuade Nixon to replace Rogers with Kissinger as secretary of state during Nixon's second term.

After Rogers left government service, he practiced law until his death on January 1, 2001.

Further Reading
Genovese, Michael A. *The Nixon Presidency.* New York: Greenwood, 1990.
"Rogers, William Pierce." Available online. Discovery Channel School, original content provided by World Book Online. URL: http://www.discoveryschool.com/homeworkhelp/worldbook/atozhistory/r/722983.html. Downloaded November 23, 2001.
Wicker, Tom. *One of Us: Richard Nixon and the American Dream.* New York: Random House, 1991.

Roosevelt, Anna Eleanor
(1884–1962) *first lady, diplomat, author*

Eleanor Roosevelt was the most effective female political leader in U.S. history through the end of the 20th century and one of the most effective leaders of either gender. Anyone tempted to attribute her prominence solely to her marriage to President FRANKLIN DELANO ROOSEVELT would make the mistake of overlooking her many accomplishments prior to her husband's election as president. Such a view would also overlook her 17-year career after leaving the White House. As a dominant leader of the Democratic Party, she was asked by the male leaders to repair situations they could not mend.

Anna Eleanor Roosevelt was born on October 11, 1884, in New York City into a prominent New York family. As a favorite niece of President THEODORE ROOSEVELT, she was born with many advantages, but her childhood was so unhappy that it might have crippled someone lacking her indomitable will. Her mother was a cold, unfeeling person who belittled her personal appearance. She adored and sought warmth from her father, but he was an alcoholic. Both of her parents died when she was very young, and she was then under the custody of a very strict grandmother.

She was first tutored privately but, at age 15, was sent to England to attend Allenswood, a finishing school near London. Encouraged by Headmistress Marie Souvestre, Eleanor developed a social conscience and emerged as a student leader in the school. In 1902, when she returned to New York to emerge as a debutante, she broke out of

Eleanor Roosevelt is considered by many to be the most effective female political leader in American history and one of the most effective leaders of either gender. *(Library of Congress)*

New York's high society rituals by working with the poor at a New York settlement house.

On March 17, 1905, her uncle, President Theodore Roosevelt, gave her away in marriage to a distant cousin, Franklin Roosevelt. Over the next 11 years, she gave birth to six children, five of whom grew to maturity. In the bringing up of her children, she submitted to the domination of her formidable mother-in-law. After Franklin Roosevelt was elected to the New York state senate in 1910, she assisted his career by playing the appropriate social role. After he was appointed the assistant secretary of the navy during World War I, she pitched in by working with the Red Cross, helping in the navy knitting rooms, and visiting veterans' hospitals. She also supported St. Elizabeth's Hospital for the criminally insane.

When Franklin contracted polio in 1921, she really began a career of her own, acting in the ca-

pacity of her husband's political representative. She was active in the Women's Trade Union League and the League of Women Voters. She then organized the women in nearly all the counties in New York for the Democratic Party. In 1926, she helped found a furniture factory in Hyde Park to aid the unemployed. The next year she became vice principal and part owner of New York's Todhunter School, also teaching history and government there. By 1928, when Franklin openly reentered politics as New York's governor, she had become a public figure in her own right as the head of the national women's campaign for the Democratic Party.

If one contrasted her career accomplishments with her husband's as of 1928, they would have seemed much more equal. Franklin had been a New York state legislator briefly, an assistant secretary of the navy, and an unsuccessful vice presidential candidate. Eleanor edited a national party newspaper, spoke out nationally on political issues, and was the head of a major element in the 1928 Democratic presidential campaign. She played that role again in the 1932 campaign, enlarged her role in her husband's subsequent reelections, and continued at the center of Democratic presidential campaigns until 1960.

After Franklin was elected president, she did more than simply inherit a "megaphone" to amplify her views; she created a whole new way of projecting women in politics. She initiated weekly press conferences with women reporters, lectured throughout the country, and had her own radio program. Her newspaper column, *My Day*, was syndicated throughout the country. Her activities for labor unions, women's rights, civil rights, the needy, the elderly, and the unfortunate were so intensely political that she was said to be "a cabinet minister without portfolio."

Although liberal, she was not a part of the far left. She openly criticized her former friend Henry A. Wallace when he gave blind support to the Soviet Union as the aggrieved party in the cold war. Eleanor was not fooled, and she was the ramrod behind the creation of the Americans for Democratic Action (ADA), a liberal anticommunist organization. Without the ADA, liberals would have had a much harder time battling against Senator JOSEPH

RAYMOND MCCARTHY's vicious attempts to label all liberals as communists or "fellow travelers."

On many occasions when the male leaders of the Democratic Party got into situations from which they could not extricate themselves, they had to call on Eleanor Roosevelt to resolve the difficulty. In 1948, when the Democratic Party was so split that JOHN STROM THURMOND led the Dixiecrats out of the convention and Henry A. Wallace (FDR's vice president in the third term) bolted to the Progressive Party, Eleanor went to the Democratic Convention and spoke for President HARRY S. TRUMAN. Throughout his presidency, she wrote many long letters to Truman advising him on policy.

In the 1950s, she campaigned hard for ADLAI EWING STEVENSON in both 1952 and 1956, and she supported him in 1960, but everyone realized that a two-time loser could not be nominated again. She distrusted JOSEPH PATRICK KENNEDY, SR., and did not initially support his son JOHN FITZGERALD KENNEDY. When John Kennedy was nominated, important liberal segments of the Democratic Party preferred Stevenson or HUBERT HORATIO HUMPHREY, and they threatened to sit on their hands in this close election. Kennedy needed a way to energize this faction, and he called on Roosevelt. Whatever her personal misgivings, she appeared in one of the most effective of the Kennedy commercials late in the 1960 campaign, even though she was in her late 70s. Upon election, Kennedy appointed her chair of the national Commission on the Status of Women.

Eleanor Roosevelt was in the central leadership councils of the Democratic Party for the nine presidential elections from 1928 to 1960, making her a core leader of her political party longer than almost any other person can claim to have held such a role. Eleanor Roosevelt's influence started in 1928 before her husband had even been elected governor of New York and lasted 17 years after he died. Other first ladies have had influence while their husbands were president, but only Roosevelt had influence as a political leader long after she ceased being first lady.

She was centrally bound up with elections, election campaigns, holding public office, or being close to those who did hold public office for a third of a century. She wrote and spoke about social issues, but the aim was to win elections and shape the political idiom and political dialogue of her age and beyond. Her work on civil rights was political, not merely social. Later political women who have impact in the economic, social, and political realm stand on the shoulders of Eleanor Roosevelt.

Eleanor Roosevelt played an important diplomatic role in international politics. In 1945, when she was no longer first lady, President Truman tapped her to be one of the five initial delegates to the international conference to write the United Nations (UN) Charter. More than any other person, male or female, she fought a hard, three-year-long battle to include the Universal Declaration of Human Rights. This was not a popular proposition in the United States, since the South was still wedded to racial segregation, to say nothing of the colonial powers of Britain, France, or the Soviet Union. Roosevelt was up against colonialist defenders, such as Winston Churchill and Charles de Gaulle as well as Stalin through his agent, Molotov. Against tremendous odds, Eleanor Roosevelt prevailed where male political leaders might well have failed, resulting in the UN General Assembly passing the declaration in December 1948. She remained the U.S. delegate to the UN until the end of the Truman administration in 1952. Even the conservative Republican JOHN FOSTER DULLES, later DWIGHT DAVID EISENHOWER's secretary of state, acknowledged that he was initially skeptical of her ability but came to admire her skill at the UN.

President Kennedy appointed her a delegate to a special session of the UN in 1961. She is the only American ever to be appointed to the UN twice.

She died on November 7, 1962, in New York City.

Further Reading
Caroli, Betty Boyd. *The Roosevelt Women.* New York: Basic Books, 1998.
Cook, Blanche Wiesen. *Eleanor Roosevelt,* 2 volumes. New York: Viking, 1999.
Faber, Doris. *The Life of Lorena Hickok: E. R.'s Friend.* New York: W. Morrow, 1980.
Goodwin, Doris Kearns. *No Ordinary Time: Franklin and Eleanor Roosevelt: The Home Front in World War II.* New York: Simon & Schuster, 1995.

Hickok, Lorena A. *Eleanor Roosevelt: Reluctant First Lady.* New York: Dodd, Mead, 1980.

Lash, Joseph P. *Eleanor: The Years Alone.* New York: Norton, 1972.

———. *Eleanor and Franklin: The Story of Their Relationship.* New York: New American Library, 1973.

———. *Love, Eleanor: Eleanor Roosevelt and Her Friends.* New York: McGraw-Hill, 1985.

Levy, William Turner. *The Extraordinary Mrs. R: A Friend Remembers Eleanor Roosevelt.* New York: John Wiley, 1999.

Roosevelt, Eleanor. *The Autobiography of Eleanor Roosevelt.* New York: Da Capo Press, 1992.

Sandak, Cass R. *The Franklin Roosevelts.* New York: Crestwood House; Toronto: Maxwell Macmillan Canada; New York: Maxwell Macmillan, 1992.

Scharf, Lois, *Eleanor Roosevelt: First Lady of American Liberalism.* Boston: Twayne, 1987.

Youngs, J. William T. *Eleanor Roosevelt.* New York: Longman, 2000.

Roosevelt, Franklin Delano
(1882–1945) *president, governor, assistant secretary of the navy*

Franklin Delano Roosevelt was the only president to serve more than 12 years in office, to win four presidential elections, and to serve during a major economic disaster (the Great Depression) and a major war (World War II). When one realizes that he is also the only president who accomplished all this while never taking a single unaided step (because his legs were paralyzed as the result of polio), one understands why he is consistently ranked with GEORGE WASHINGTON and ABRAHAM LINCOLN as one of the greatest presidents of the United States.

Roosevelt was born on January 30, 1882, at the family estate in Hyde Park, New York, into a wealthy, prominent family. President THEODORE ROOSEVELT was his fifth cousin, and his wife, ANNA ELEANOR ROOSEVELT, was his fifth cousin, once removed. His family's great wealth allowed him to be educated by private tutors until he was 14 and to attend Groton, an elite private college preparatory school from which he graduated in 1900.

His preparation at Groton allowed him to complete all the essential requirements for gradua-

tion from Harvard in three years, but he stayed the fourth year because he had been selected as the editor of the *Harvard Crimson.* His grades were mediocre, but the Harvard curriculum at that time was so sterile—it is now widely agreed—that high grades might have been a sign of poor judgment. Roosevelt judged himself most harshly for not being socially acceptable enough to be admitted to Porcellian, Harvard's most prestigious social club.

Although he had known his distant cousin Eleanor since childhood, it was only while at Harvard that he began to show a romantic interest in her. Despite opposition from his domineering mother, Franklin and Eleanor were married in 1905. Eleanor's favorite uncle, President Theodore Roosevelt, gave the bride away. The marriage was successful as far as the public knew at the time. Later revelations indicate that Franklin had an affair with Lucy Mercer some time before World War I.

Despite whatever personal pain this may have caused Eleanor, she and Franklin were reconciled, and she played a remarkable role in supporting him during his illness and making his political success possible. Not one presidential election win, let alone four, would have been possible for Franklin without Eleanor's help. When Franklin contracted polio in 1921, both his indomitable willpower and her unending support were necessary for the recovery that made his later political career possible. Further, Eleanor clearly possessed a deep sympathy for the underprivileged, and she nudged his social conscience while his incredible political sense restrained some of her impulsiveness.

Roosevelt attended Columbia University Law School until he passed the New York state bar examination in 1907, and then he quit, without taking the degree, to work for a Wall Street law firm. He was bored with the law and jumped at the chance to enter politics in 1910. The local (Dutchess County) Democratic Party asked him to be a candidate for the state senate in a district that had not elected a Democrat in 50 years. Although he had no political experience, he could finance his own campaign and had a well-known political name. Benefiting in part from a trend away from the Republican Party due to growing political splits, he campaigned diligently, listened attentively to advisers and voters, and won handily.

Roosevelt gained national attention for his fight to oppose the regular New York City Tammany Hall choice for U.S. senator (Senate elections were still conducted in the state legislatures in 1911). His efforts defeated Tammany's first choice, and Roosevelt counted it a success that Tammany was forced to compromise, although the final choice was a Tammany figure. Coupled with his progressive record on a wide range of issues, he was easily reelected despite suffering from typhoid fever during the campaign.

Roosevelt had also defied Tammany by supporting THOMAS WOODROW WILSON for the 1912 Democratic presidential nomination. After Wilson's nomination and election, Roosevelt was rewarded with appointment as assistant secretary of the navy, a post his cousin Theodore Roosevelt had held during his rise to power. It was no accident, then, that people thought that Franklin Roosevelt reminded them of Theodore during this period. This was even more obvious during World War I when Assistant Secretary Roosevelt toured Europe, visited the front lines, and met many important European leaders.

His wealth, his name, his own accomplishments, and the need to balance the ticket headed by Ohio's Governor JAMES MIDDLETON COX, led to Roosevelt's selection as the 1920 Democratic vice presidential running mate. Both Cox and Roosevelt were enthusiastic optimists who campaigned vigorously, but they could not overcome the dismal last year and a half of the Wilson presidency. They lost to the Republican ticket of WARREN GAMALIEL HARDING and CALVIN COOLIDGE.

With the Republicans in control, Roosevelt returned to his law practice and became vice president of Fidelity and Deposit Company of Maryland, a surety bonding firm, for a few months before he contracted polio in August 1921. Roosevelt fought back under the care of Eleanor and his trusted aide, Louis Howe. In 1924, he found out about Warm Springs, Georgia, where the medicinal waters proved somewhat helpful to his condition. Discovering that other patients could barely pay for the cost of the treatment, he founded the Warm Springs Foundation for other polio victims and offered financial help where possible. His recovery was noteworthy throughout the nation, and it was

Franklin Delano Roosevelt served longer as president than anyone else (12 years), won four presidential elections, and led the nation during a major economic disaster and a major war. *(Library of Congress)*

shown most dramatically in his memorable (though futile) speech nominating New York Governor ALFRED EMANUEL SMITH for the presidency.

While Smith did not get the nomination in 1924, with Roosevelt's help he was unstoppable for the Democratic presidential nomination in 1928. Roosevelt had intended to spend the rest of the year in Warm Springs, but Smith pressed Roosevelt to run for New York's governor's office. While Smith lost the presidency to the Republican nominee, HERBERT CLARK HOOVER, and even lost New York by 100,000 votes, Roosevelt carried the state by a close but respectable 25,000 votes. As governor, Roosevelt fought a Republican-controlled legislature for many progressive measures, such as conservation, state-supported pensions, unemployment insurance, laws limiting female and child working hours, and public power. He attracted some first-class talent to his administration—many of whom became the nucleus of his presidential staff. In 1930, he was reelected by a record 750,000-vote margin. With the nation in the grip of the Great Depression, Roosevelt became the first governor of any state to establish effective relief for the poor and unemployed.

By June 1932, when the Democratic National Convention began, Roosevelt was a clear leader as the most dynamic and imaginative governor in the country. However, his lead was not long enough to overcome the then required rule that the Democratic nominee obtain two-thirds of the delegates. Only when House Speaker JOHN NANCE GARNER ordered his delegates to vote for Roosevelt in return for the vice presidential nomination did Roosevelt have enough to win on the fourth ballot. The Roosevelt-Garner ticket bridged the gap between the urban eastern and rural southern-western wings of the party and, given the dismal Hoover record, the Roosevelt-Garner ticket won by 22,821,857 votes to 15,761,841. The ticket also won all but six states and the Electoral College vote by 472–59. The Democrats captured large majorities in both houses of Congress.

When Roosevelt was inaugurated at the age of 51 on March 4, 1933, the economy was so bad that almost 15 million U.S. citizens were unemployed. Well more than a million of these were homeless, wandering around the country looking for work, squatting in tents or ramshackle huts in makeshift villages called "Hoovervilles" on the outskirts of cities. Many others had panicked and attempted to rescue their savings from failing banks, forcing banks to close in 38 of the 48 states. Yet Roosevelt substantially dampened those fears with his immediate declaration of a national bank holiday and his upbeat inaugural phrase, "The only thing we have to fear, is fear itself—nameless, unreasoning, unjustified terror."

Within two days, he had summoned Congress into a special session and started pushing through legislation in the famous "one hundred days," the single most remarkable 100 days of legislating in the nation's history. His approach was essentially pragmatic. He shunned the nationalization of the banks in favor of a banking bill that investigated all banks, lent money to those that were certified as solvent, and left the others closed. He then used the magic of radio to convince a sufficiently large number of U.S. citizens that it was safer to keep their money in the newly certified banks than to put it under a mattress. He cut federal salaries and the size of individual pensions for veterans, but he got a half billion dollars spent for relief. He pushed for the legalization of 3.2% beer (the alcoholic content by weight) and obtained congressional approval of the Twenty-first Amendment repealing Prohibition, which was ratified by the end of 1933.

These were all conservative measures that did not really represent the New Deal, which had three aims: relief, reform, and recovery. The relief program was the most successful. Roosevelt took the nation off the gold standard and devalued the currency by 40 percent. This alienated the creditors but gave a measure of relief to the far more numerous debtors. He pushed Congress to appropriate federal relief grants to states and local agencies through the newly created Federal Emergency Relief Administration and ordered HARRY LLOYD HOPKINS, its new head, to spend the money quickly. Direct work relief was pushed through under the 1933 Civil Works Administration (CWA), which spent another $1.5 billion by 1935. Other 1933 relief measures authorized were the Civilian Conservation Corps (CCC), which employed more than 2 million young men on conservation work; the Home Owners Loan Corporation, which offered assistance to mortgagors and homeowners; and the Public Works Administration (PWA), which put billions of dollars into construction of large-scale projects. These programs gave some assistance, offered hope to the seriously disadvantaged, and restored some confidence in the government.

For reform measures, the New Deal claimed the Federal Deposit Insurance Corporation (FDIC) as its own, although the extremely successful measure that prevented ruinous runs on banks originated in Congress (and was opposed by Roosevelt until Vice President Garner talked him into it). The 1934 Securities and Exchange Commission (SEC) made a timid, symbolic start at regulating the stock exchanges. The most important reform may well have been the 1933 Tennessee Valley Authority (TVA), the nucleus of which had been kept alive by Senator GEORGE WILLIAM NORRIS for a decade. This public corporation built dams that generated cheap hydroelectric power while controlling floods, but it also manufactured fertilizer, conserved the soil, and fostered local social experiments.

Roosevelt's most far-reaching programs, the National Recovery Administration (NRA) and the Agricultural Adjustment Administration (AAA), aimed at recovery, but they were essentially failures. The NRA followed a philosophy known as corporatism that encouraged management and labor to establish codes of fair competition within each industry by creating codes for pricing, production, and guaranteed rights of collective bargaining, minimum wages, and maximum hours for labor. After a seemingly bright beginning, the NRA failed. Unions complained that the courts threw out the protections for labor. Small businessmen protested that the agreed rules were biased toward the large corporations. Astute observers noticed that monopolies were exempted from antitrust prosecution. Worst of all, some large employers were slow to accept the codes, and still others evaded them entirely.

The AAA aimed at raising farm prices by setting production quotas that were to be approved by farmers in referenda. Once the production quotas were established, cooperating farmers would receive subsidies. While the AAA appeared to increase farm income by 50 percent, it was really the record-breaking droughts in the "dust bowl" of the lower Great Plains that were responsible for most of the production cuts. Income went up because of disaster-induced scarcity. The rich farmers benefited—sometimes by running tenant farmers off the land and into the roaming homeless throngs—and the poor consumers in the cities paid higher prices.

Both the NRA and AAA were failures before the Supreme Court declared them unconstitutional. Both programs were unconstitutional for very sound reasons, and even progressive justices, such as BENJAMIN NATHAN CARDOZO, voted against them. Roosevelt deflected the blame for these programs to the Court, but this may perhaps be justified since Roosevelt was blamed for being against big business when the only real beneficiaries of the programs were large corporations and commercial farmers.

By 1935, with only about 18 months before the next election, Roosevelt had little to show for his efforts besides a slow-moving relief effort and a few conservative reforms. Roosevelt had helped

big business in hopes that such government cooperation would work, but big business responded with attack. They were tied to Hoover and, thus, politically weakened. The growing strength of the left was a bigger threat. The communists, socialists, and others were noisy, but not really electoral threats. Louisiana's Democratic Senator HUEY PIERCE LONG was both noisy and an electoral threat. For these reasons, Roosevelt moved to the left. He tried to abolish public-utility holding companies, raise taxes on the wealthy, and move monetary control from Wall Street bankers to Washington. Congress balked and Roosevelt compromised, but at least these steps helped undercut the more extreme demagogues.

While these steps did not succeed, Roosevelt successfully passed three important laws in 1935. The 1935 Works Progress Administration (WPA) spent about $11 billion in relief for work projects to as many as 3.2 million Americans a month between 1935 and 1942. The National Labor Relations (or the Wagner) Act set up the National Labor Relations Board (NLRB) and provided the first effective guarantee of the right for labor to bargain collectively on equal terms with management. The industrial unionism movement then used these protections to swell union membership in the 1930s and 1940s. The 1935 Social Security Act provided for federal old age pensions and for cooperation with the states for unemployment compensation and for assistance to needy blind and disabled persons, as well as dependent children. The act, though far from perfect, became the basis of a limited welfare state that later politicians have not dared dismantle.

In 1936, these limited achievements were enough to propel Roosevelt to reelection over his Republican opponent, Kansas Governor ALFRED MOSSMAN LANDON. Roosevelt got 27,751,841 popular votes and carried 46 states with 523 electoral votes; Landon got 16,679,491 votes and carried only two states with eight electoral votes. This landslide exceeded any other contested national election.

As often happens, the landslide generated overconfidence and contained the seeds of more trouble. Roosevelt's most serious error occurred when he took the voter's confidence as a mandate to pack the Supreme Court. This proposal would have permitted him to add up to six judges to the conservative U.S. Supreme Court—one for each justice over 70 years of age who did not retire. The proposal caused such an outcry that the Congress, including staunch Roosevelt supporters, simply would not go along. At the same time, funding for relief was cut back and a sharp economic downturn occurred. In 1938, Roosevelt finally asked for more relief funding but was turned down. In the 1938 elections, the conservatives made such strong gains that Roosevelt lost his effective majority in Congress. Further progress toward the New Deal was over.

Foreign affairs was only a minor part of the earlier Roosevelt agenda. Tennessee Senator CORDELL HULL was the U.S. secretary of state from 1933 to 1944, but Roosevelt wanted to be his own secretary of state, and Hull was never a powerful insider. Hull did work out reciprocal trade agreements and took some steps toward making the United States a "good neighbor"of Latin America.

Hull's role became more evident as the European war became more likely. Roosevelt correctly perceived the danger from Hitler, Mussolini, and the Japanese militarists, but he was limited by the widespread isolation sentiment in the country and in the Congress. Neutrality legislation on the books seriously limited Roosevelt's room to maneuver, and much of this legislation had to be overcome before effective resistance was possible. As this threat grew, Roosevelt had fewer political resources to expend on domestic reform and a greater need to husband those resources for foreign policy concerns.

Roosevelt tried to use German aggressiveness to obtain a revision of a neutrality act that provided for an embargo on armaments to all belligerents, whether attacked or attacker. Only after Hitler conquered Poland in September 1939 and war broke out in Europe did Roosevelt succeed in gaining repeal of the embargo. However, the repeal still required the Allies to pay cash for any arms supplied by the United States. In 1940, as Britain ran out of money, Roosevelt came up with a thoroughly pro-Ally arrangement for Britain under which the British leased their bases in the Western Hemisphere (which they could not defend in any case) to the United States in return for 50 reputedly "overaged" but still useful U.S. destroyers.

Roosevelt also secured vastly increased defense expenditures, which brought about domestic economic recovery at last. In September 1940, Roosevelt managed to push through the Congress the first peacetime draft in U.S. history.

In the 1940 election, the Republicans nominated Wendell Willkie, a relatively progressive corporate executive who agreed with Roosevelt's internationalism and even with some New Deal policies. The thrust of Willkie's attack was that no president should be given a third term and that some New Deal programs contained excessive regulation. When France, widely believed to have the most powerful army in the world, collapsed in only six weeks and the Germans began bombing Britain, concerns about having a familiar figure in charge helped Roosevelt. Fears of giving the president an unprecedented third term were enough to reduce Roosevelt's popular vote considerably from his previous elections, but he still won by a popular vote of 27,243,466–22,334,413 and an Electoral College vote of 449–82.

Once reelected, Roosevelt pushed for "lend-lease" aid to Britain and, after Germany's June 1941 attack on Russia, aid to the Soviet Union as well. Roosevelt also secretly ordered U.S. destroyers to escort Allied convoys part of the way across the Atlantic to protect the supplies against German submarines. This allowed U.S. destroyers to help locate German submarines for the British to attack. When a German submarine fired a torpedo at the U.S. destroyer *Greer* in September 1941, Roosevelt pretended to be surprised and indignantly ordered U.S. warships to begin shooting at German warships if they were spotted.

Hoping to slow Japanese aggression, Roosevelt gradually imposed an embargo of goods to Japan, because they refused to honor his demand to stop their encroaching activities in China and Indochina. The Japanese militarists then decided to attack Pearl Harbor in Hawaii on December 7, 1941, and the Philippines the following day. They also moved quickly into Southeast Asia. The United States then declared war on Japan, and Germany cooperated by declaring war on the United States.

The war had a logic of its own. First, concerns about the Great Depression faded, not just because the war was a greater threat, but also because full employment was now inevitable as the nation moved to a war footing. Strategically, Roosevelt had little choice but to focus on Germany first, because no effective action could be taken against the Japanese until the U.S. Pacific Ocean fleet could be rebuilt. Another major strategic consideration was when to attempt to invade the European continent. Without the necessary military buildup in England and the construction of landing craft, such an attack would have been futile if attempted in 1943, as the Russians and others wished. Roosevelt rightly decided not to resist this inherent logic, and the war was effectively won as the United States mobilized its formidable industrial strength. Needless to say, New Deal programs were stalled or abandoned as the cooperation of the business community was necessary for the war effort. Above all, Roosevelt pragmatically held together the wartime alliance among such disparate parties as Britain and the Soviet Union.

The harshest criticisms of Roosevelt were leveled at him for what was perceived to be a softness toward the Soviet Union in allowing them to occupy Eastern Europe. Yet Roosevelt was also wise in recognizing that the Russian occupation of Eastern Europe occurred as the inevitable result of the flow of military operations, which no amount of diplomatic maneuvering could have avoided.

Roosevelt also had to consider running for reelection under the U.S. constitutional system, the existence of the war notwithstanding. His doctors knew he was ill and at risk for serious or fatal illness, but they could not know for sure. They could not have spoken out publicly or they would have been regarded as giving the enemies of the United States valuable information. Roosevelt held off a long time in announcing his intentions about seeking a fourth term. Finally, he said he would seek reelection so as to avoid a wartime change of leadership, even though he expressed a strong desire to retire. The conservative Democrats disliked Vice President Henry Wallace intensely and a revolt was possible, so Roosevelt bowed to pressure and took a border-state Democrat, Missouri's Senator HARRY S. TRUMAN, as his new vice presidential running mate.

In the 1944 general election, Roosevelt defeated the Republican nominee, New York's Governor THOMAS EDMUND DEWEY, by 25,612,474 popular votes to 22,017,570. This was the closest of his popular vote margins. The Electoral College vote was also closer but still a substantial 432 for Roosevelt to 99 for Dewey.

Roosevelt was 63 years old when he died suddenly at Warm Springs, Georgia, on April 12, 1945.

Further Reading

Blum, John Morton. *The Progressive Presidents: Roosevelt, Wilson, Roosevelt, Johnson*. New York: Norton, 1982.

Burns, James MacGregor. *Roosevelt: The Soldier of Freedom*. New York: Harcourt Brace Jovanovich, 1970.

Davis, Kenneth S. *FDR: Three Volumes*. New York: Random House, 1993.

Freidel, Frank B. *Franklin D. Roosevelt: Four Volumes*. Boston: Little, Brown, 1952.

Gallagher, Hugh. *FDR's Splendid Deception: The Moving Story of Roosevelt's Massive Disability*. Arlington, Va.: Vandamere Press, 1999.

Goodwin, Doris Kearns. *No Ordinary Time: Franklin and Eleanor Roosevelt: The Home Front in World War II*. New York: Simon & Schuster, 1995.

Hickok, Lorena A. *The Story of Franklin D. Roosevelt*. New York: Grosset & Dunlap, 1956.

Lash, Joseph P. *Eleanor and Franklin: The Story of Their Relationship*. New York: New American Library, 1973.

Link, Arthur Stanley. *The Age of Franklin D. Roosevelt, 1921–1945*. New York: Knopf, 1973.

McJimsey, George T. *The Presidency of Franklin Delano Roosevelt*. Lawrence: University Press of Kansas, 2000.

Morris, Jeffrey. *The FDR Way*. Minneapolis: Lerner Publications, 1996.

"Roosevelt, Franklin." Available online. URL: http://www.whitehouse.gov/history/presidents/fr32.html. Downloaded November 11, 2001.

Sandak, Cass R. *The Franklin Roosevelts*. New York: Crestwood House; Toronto: Maxwell Macmillan Canada; New York: Maxwell Macmillan, 1992.

Schlesinger, Arthur M. *The Age of Roosevelt: Three Volumes*. Boston: Houghton Mifflin, 1964.

Schuman, Michael. *Franklin D. Roosevelt: The Four-Term President*. Springfield, N.J.: Enslow Publishers, 1996.

Sherwood, Robert E. *Roosevelt and Hopkins*. New York: Harper, 1950.

Ward, Geoffrey C. *A First-Class Temperament: The Emergence of Franklin Roosevelt*. New York: Harper & Row, 1989.

Roosevelt, Theodore

(1858–1919) *president, vice president, governor, assistant secretary of the navy, police commissioner, author*

Theodore Roosevelt was the youngest person to serve as president of the United States. He expanded the use of presidential power within the country and the power of the country within the international system. For his efforts to settle the Russo-Japanese War, he became the first American to win the Nobel Peace Prize. An outdoorsman and naturalist, he made the first significant increases in the protection of natural resources by creating national parks and forests. As president, he was responsible for taking the steps necessary to construct the Panama Canal. He was also the first president to fly in an airplane, the first president to visit a foreign country while in office, and the first president to use

At age 42 when he was sworn in after McKinley's death, Theodore Roosevelt was the youngest person ever to serve as the American president. He was also the first American to win the Nobel Peace Prize and expanded the use of presidential power. *(Library of Congress)*

the White House to arbitrate a labor dispute, using the government on the side of labor.

Roosevelt was born in New York City on October 27, 1858, into a wealthy, prominent New York family. ANNA ELEANOR ROOSEVELT was his niece and FRANKLIN DELANO ROOSEVELT was his fifth cousin. As a child, he suffered from nearsightedness and asthma. As a youth, he participated in a strenuous bodybuilding program to overcome his asthma and general weakness. He studied with tutors until he went to college at Harvard, where he earned good grades, wrote a book, *The Naval War of 1812* (published in 1880), and graduated Phi Beta Kappa in 1880.

After college, he married Ann Hathaway Lee and began studying at Columbia University Law School. In 1881 at the age of 23, he was elected to the New York state assembly and reelected to two more annual terms in 1882 and 1883. In 1882, Roosevelt served briefly as leader of the Republican minority in the assembly, but he refused to take orders and was removed by the bosses. However, he worked with Democratic Governor STEPHEN GROVER CLEVELAND and became involved in civil service reform.

In 1884, he left politics because he suffered political reverses and a double personal tragedy: his wife died two days after giving birth and his mother died the same day of typhoid fever. Roosevelt did not run for reelection but was still active in politics. He supported a reform candidate for the Republican nomination against JAMES GILLESPIE BLAINE, whose personal character he did not trust. However, when Blaine won the nomination, Roosevelt supported him in the general election against the Democratic nominee, Grover Cleveland.

When Blaine lost, Roosevelt had no prospects for a presidential appointment, and he went to South Dakota, bought a ranch, raised cattle, wrote two books, helped arrest a band of outlaws, and lost about half of his net worth when his cattle died in severe winter weather. In 1886, he returned to New York City, lost a race for mayor, married Edith Kermit Carow, and settled in New York, where he wrote two biographies and a book on the West.

In 1888, he worked hard for Republican presidential nominee BENJAMIN HARRISON and was rewarded with an appointment to the Civil Service

Commission, where he used publicity to call attention to abuses and raised the public consciousness of the commission even though many of the reforms he recommended were not adopted. President Cleveland, who defeated Harrison in 1892, extended his appointment on the commission.

Roosevelt was appointed police commissioner in New York City in 1895 and again fought the corruption in the police department, which angered Democrats and Republicans alike. He even walked the streets at night to catch policemen sleeping on the job. In 1896, he supported Republican presidential nominee WILLIAM MCKINLEY and applied for a position in Washington. McKinley was disinclined to bring such an upstart into his administration, but Roosevelt's political support was too strong, and McKinley finally appointed him the assistant secretary of the navy.

In this position, Roosevelt pressed for strong naval preparedness for war with Spain over Cuba, sometimes exceeding his authority. Even before war was declared, Roosevelt began recruiting for a special volunteer unit to fight in the war. When war was declared, Roosevelt immediately resigned his navy post, became lieutenant colonel in the First Regiment of the U.S. Cavalry Volunteers (the Rough Riders), organized a group of Ivy League college graduates and cowboy friends from his ranching days, and went to Cuba where he was soon promoted to colonel. Finding Kettle Hill, which flanked a Spanish stronghold on San Juan Hill, he charged up it and gained national fame.

After the war, he returned to New York, where several powerful groups urged him to run for various public offices. U.S. Senator Thomas C. Platt, New York's Republican boss, did not like Roosevelt, but he needed a candidate who could win the governor's race. Roosevelt accepted Platt's offer and won the election, but he refused to follow orders and even pushed through the legislature a bill to require taxes from public utility franchises. This hurt Platt directly since he had taken money from these utilities to prevent them from having to pay taxes. More than any of the other reforms that Roosevelt initiated, this tax irritated Platt so much that he pressed President McKinley to take Roosevelt as his vice presidential running mate. Finding a new vice president was

necessary since Garret Hobart, McKinley's first vice president, had died in 1899.

McKinley, perhaps remembering Roosevelt's virtual insubordination as assistant secretary of the Navy, resisted, and Roosevelt himself was not really interested in giving up the New York governor's office. However, the pressure was intense, and eventually both McKinley and Roosevelt gave in. The McKinley-Roosevelt ticket easily defeated the Democratic nominee, WILLIAM JENNINGS BRYAN.

On September 6, 1901, McKinley was shot by an anarchist, Leon Czolgosz. Initially, McKinley was expected to recover, but an infection set in, and McKinley died a week later. On September 14, 1901, Roosevelt—"that damn cowboy" as McKinley's friend Senator MARK ALONZO HANNA called him—was president of the United States. He was only 42 years old. Promising to keep McKinley's promises "absolutely unbroken," Roosevelt returned the outstanding members of McKinley's cabinet—John Hay, ELIHU ROOT, and Philander Knox—but otherwise he did not hew closely to the McKinley line.

Early on, Roosevelt tried to convince businessmen that he would not interfere with them, but he never quite succeeded. In December 1901, in his first address to Congress, he praised industrial leaders but pointed out that some of them had done "real and grave evils." By 1902, inflation was high, and the citizenry blamed the trusts for high prices. Roosevelt responded by ordering his Justice Department to file an antitrust action against the Northern Securities Company, a holding company run by the richest men in the United States to control railroad rates. When the U.S. Supreme Court upheld the government's prosecution, Northern Securities was broken up. Roosevelt was nicknamed "trustbuster" for the Northern Securities case and the additional 40-plus prosecutions (including John D. Rockefeller's oil trust and James B. Duke's tobacco trust) that his administration pursued.

From the point of view of big business, worse was yet to come. Roosevelt was about to become the first U.S. president to use the power of the federal government to broker a deal between labor and capital that was not stacked against labor. In the spring of 1902, the Pennsylvania hard coal miners went on strike, asking for relief from 12-hour, six-day-a-week shifts for an average wage of $560 per year (or pennies per hour). The mine owners rejected this request and carried the strike through to the fall.

With the prospect of facing a winter without heat, people began to panic. Roosevelt invited the leaders of both parties to meet him in Washington and proposed an arbitration that the union accepted, but the mine owners stonewalled Roosevelt. Irritated by their attitude, Roosevelt threatened to seize the mines and have federal troops run them. The owners finally caved in, agreed to arbitration, and gave the miners a nine-hour day with a 10% wage hike and the right to supervise the weighing of the coal (which was the basis on which they kept their jobs). On the surface, Roosevelt was even-handed, but labor knew that they had achieved much just by having a level playing field.

Roosevelt sponsored the 1903 Elkins Act to prohibit railroads from rebates (or kicking back money) to favored shippers, which put rivals out of business, but such practices had not stopped. Roosevelt then pushed Congress to pass the 1906 Hepburn Railway Rate Act to reduce the evil rebates, although they still were not stopped entirely.

After publication of The Jungle, Upton Sinclair's novel that detailed unsanitary conditions in the meatpacking industry, Roosevelt ordered an investigation, producing what he called a "sickening report." Threatening to publish the report if Congress did not correct the situation, Congress obliged with the Meat Inspection Act and the Food and Drugs Act.

Roosevelt is well known as the first president to make a significant effort at conservation. He elevated the protection of the forests by creating the U.S. Forest Service in 1905 and appointing professional forester GIFFORD PINCHOT its head. He also created 18 national monuments and added about 150 million acres to the national forests, three times as much land as all three of his presidential predecessors combined. In 1902, he supported the Newlands Act, a Democratic Party proposal that created 30 irrigation project, including the Roosevelt Dam. Significantly, he vetoed a proposed law that would have opened the Muscle Shoals area of the Tennessee River in Alabama to private development, thereby saving it (with the help of Senator GEORGE WILLIAM NORRIS) for his cousin FRANKLIN DELANO ROOSEVELT to turn into the Tennessee Valley Authority.

Since Roosevelt is often accused of treating Latin America unfairly, it is worth noting that he withdrew U.S. troops from Cuba in 1902. He did fear that unstable governments in Latin America would undermine the independence of countries there and therefore violate the Monroe Doctrine. When Venezuela did not pay its debts to Britain and Germany, and those two countries blockaded its ports, Roosevelt successfully persuaded the British—and threatened the Germans—into withdrawing. He then required Venezuela to pay a settlement that he negotiated. Similarly, when the Dominican Republic verged on bankruptcy through corruption, he had the United States take over Dominican customs and used the proceeds from the reformed customs system to pay off the European creditors. This was done with at least tacit Dominican consent. These actions were in line with his Roosevelt Corollary to the Monroe Doctrine, which said the United States might be required to intervene in Latin American countries to stop irresponsible actions to forestall European intervention.

Roosevelt took the forceful steps necessary for the building of the Panama Canal. He wanted the United States to be the only nation in control since the project was financed with U.S. money. He negotiated with the British for an end to the Clayton Bulwer Treaty, which had tied the United States to a joint U.S.-British canal. Roosevelt bought out the French interest and was prepared to buy the rights from Colombia. In 1902, the corrupt Colombian Senate balked, presumably trying to up the price. At this point, Roosevelt persuaded the Panamanians to revolt, recognized their government, paid them $10 million, and obtained the right to a 10-mile-wide strip. By later standards, Roosevelt's actions appear high-handed, but all his actions were known before the Nobel committee awarded Roosevelt the Nobel Peace Prize in 1906, and this award is an indication of the acceptance of Roosevelt's actions at the time.

In Asia, Roosevelt acted in accordance with what he understood to be U.S. interests in promoting the "open door." In 1905, he helped settle the Russo-Japanese War, for which he received the

Nobel Prize. He quietly recognized Japanese influence in Korea and Manchuria (seeing Japan as a counterbalance to European powers). He also feared Japanese actions against what he perceived to be the badly exposed Philippine Islands. When the city of San Francisco interfered with the conduct of his foreign policy by segregating its schools against the Japanese, he forced San Francisco to change its mind and also negotiated the so-called gentleman's agreement under which the Japanese voluntarily restrained the immigration of their citizens to the United States.

Roosevelt was destined to win a full term easily in 1904. His most serious threat would have been a challenge for the Republican nomination from Senator Mark Hanna, who would have had the money and business support, but he died early in 1904. The Democrats virtually conceded the election by running a lackluster conservative, New York's Judge Alton B. Parker. Roosevelt teamed up with Indiana Senator Charles W. Fairbanks, his vice presidential running mate, and won 7,628,831 votes to 5,084,533, the greatest popular vote margin to that time, and won 336–140 in the Electoral College. Perhaps too exuberant in victory, Roosevelt declared he would not run for president again and thereby made himself a lame duck. This lame duck status reduced his effectiveness in his battles with Congress thereafter.

Roosevelt had pushed for major increases in U.S. naval strength, built 16 new battleships and cruisers, and moved the United States from having the fifth largest navy at the beginning of his term to being the second only to the British by the end of his term. In a show of strength, he then sent his navy—painted white—around the world as the Great White Fleet.

Roosevelt honored his pledge not to run again in 1908, but he named his successor, WILLIAM HOWARD TAFT, whom he pushed into running and then pushed everyone else to accept. Taft won easily over William Jennings Bryan. Roosevelt misread Taft as a Progressive in the same sense that he was. He left Taft alone for two years while he went on a safari in Africa and traveled to Europe to pick up his Nobel Peace Prize. While abroad, he had been alerted that Taft was not following his ideals. He tried to reconcile Taft with the Progressives, but

Taft was psychologically unprepared to fight the conservative business interests as Roosevelt had. The breach was inevitable.

One cause of the break was Taft's firing of Gifford Pinchot, but the real cause was the threat that the Progressives would create a new party and run Wisconsin Senator ROBERT MARION LA FOLLETTE, with whom Roosevelt had a long-running feud. Roosevelt tried for the Republican nomination and won the majority of the primaries and a majority of the delegates at the convention but found Taft's control of the machinery was so strong that many of his delegates were unfairly excluded by the credentials committee. Roosevelt then felt he had the justification to leave the party for the Progressive Party where he easily displaced La Follette. If the Democrats had not shrewdly nominated a progressive candidate in THOMAS WOODROW WILSON, Roosevelt might have won. He campaigned vigorously and courageously. At one point, he was shot by a would-be assassin, whose bullet hit his glasses case, which saved his life. With the bullet lodged in his chest, he finished his long speech (slowing the bleeding with a handkerchief) before going to the hospital.

Woodrow Wilson won only 42 percent of the popular vote but won the Electoral College vote decisively. Roosevelt and his running mate, California's progressive governor HIRAM WARREN JOHNSON, carried California, Michigan, Minnesota, Pennsylvania, South Dakota, and Washington, but they garnered only 27% of the popular vote. Taft won only 23% and carried only two states, Utah and Vermont. The remainder was scattered among other small parties—most notably the Socialist Party's Eugene V. Debs, who got almost a million votes, or about 7% of the total.

After this loss, Roosevelt "retired" to an exhausting and nearly fatal South America journey, and he continued to write. While he complained about President Wilson's foreign policy, he supported Wilson on the war. In fact, he tried to persuade Wilson to let him organize another volunteer division as he had during the Spanish American War. Wilson declined to let Roosevelt do so, saying that Roosevelt was too old. Wilson's action, however, created the suspicion that he really feared Roosevelt was not too old but still young enough to do so. Wilson did not want to be upstaged by the man who led troops up San Juan Hill.

Roosevelt was clearly planning to run for the Republican nomination in 1920 when he would have been only 62 years old. Most observers believe he might have won, but he had many serious medical conditions, and he died on January 6, 1919.

Further Reading

Beale, Howard K. *Theodore Roosevelt and the Rise of America to World Power.* Baltimore, Md.: Johns Hopkins, 1984.

Blum, John Morton. *The Progressive Presidents: Roosevelt, Wilson, Roosevelt, Johnson.* New York: Norton, 1982.

———. *The Republican Roosevelt.* Cambridge, Mass.: Harvard University Press, 1977.

Brands, H. W. *T.R.: The Last Romantic.* New York: Basic Books, 1997.

Burton, David H. *Theodore Roosevelt: An American Politician: An Assessment.* Madison, N.J.: Fairleigh Dickinson University Press, 1997.

Cooper, John Milton. *The Warrior and the Priest: Woodrow Wilson and Theodore Roosevelt.* Cambridge, Mass.: Belknap Press of Harvard University Press, 1983.

Gould, Lewis L. *The Presidency of Theodore Roosevelt.* Lawrence: University Press of Kansas, 1991.

Jeffers, H. Paul. *Commissioner Roosevelt: The Story of Theodore Roosevelt and the New York City Police, 1895–1897.* New York: J. Wiley & Sons, 1994.

Manners, William. *TR and Will: A Friendship that Split the Republican Party.* New York: Harcourt, Brace & World, 1969.

Markham, Lois. *Theodore Roosevelt.* New York: Chelsea House, 1985.

Meltzer, Milton. *Theodore Roosevelt and His America.* New York: Franklin Watts, 1994.

———. *Theodore Roosevelt: A Life.* New York: Morrow, 1992.

Morris, Edmund. *The Rise of Theodore Roosevelt.* New York: Ballantine Books, 1980.

Morris, Sylvia Jukes. *Edith Kermit Roosevelt: Portrait of a First Lady.* New York: Coward, McCann & Geoghegan, 1980.

Reckner, James R. *Teddy Roosevelt's Great White Fleet.* Annapolis, Md.: Naval Institute Press, 1988.

Renehan, Edward. *The Lion's Pride: Theodore Roosevelt and his Family in Peace and War.* New York: Oxford University Press, 1999.

Rhodes, James Ford. *The McKinley and Roosevelt Administrations, 1897–1909.* Port Washington, N.Y.: Kennikat Press, 1965.

"Roosevelt, Theodore." Available online. URL: http://www.whitehouse.gov/history/presidents/tr27.html. Downloaded November 11, 2001.

Roosevelt, Theodore. *Theodore Roosevelt: An Autobiography.* Norwalk, Conn.: Easton Press, 1996.

———. *The Works of Theodore Roosevelt: Twenty Volumes.* New York: C. Scribner's Sons, 1926.

Tilchin, William N. *Theodore Roosevelt and the British Empire: A Study in Presidential Statecraft.* New York: St. Martin's Press, 1997.

Wimmel, Kenneth. *Theodore Roosevelt and the Great White Fleet: American Sea Power Comes of Age.* Washington, D.C.: Brassey's, 1998.

Root, Elihu

(1845–1937) *secretary of state, secretary of war, senator*

Elihu Root was one of the most brilliant and innovative administrators in U.S. history, serving as secretary of war for WILLIAM MCKINLEY and secretary of state for THEODORE ROOSEVELT. He won the 1912 Nobel Peace Prize for his numerous contributions to world peace, and he also served as a U.S. senator.

Root was born on February 15, 1845, in Clinton, New York, son of a Hamilton College mathematics professor. He graduated first in his class at Hamilton College in 1864, taught school for a year, then entered New York University Law School, where he graduated in 1867. In 1868, he founded a law firm and by 1875 had established himself as a prominent New York corporate attorney. As a young lawyer, he defended New York Mayor William Marcy Tweed (Boss Tweed) in his corruption trial. Although there was nothing improper in this, Root afterward avoided elective public office for fear of being smeared as a Tweed supporter.

Wealthy by the age of 30, he represented banks, railroads, and some of the greatest financiers of the day. He had such a solid grasp of the law, a formidable analytic power, a creative genius for solving problems, and a gift for both oral and written expression that he was recognized as the leader of the U.S. bar by his colleagues.

Although he had participated in local New York Republican politics, he did not have a national reputation when President William McKinley appointed him secretary of war in 1899. Since the nation had just concluded the Spanish-American War, the decision to appoint a nonmilitary man seemed inappropriate, but McKinley realized he needed a lawyer, not a military man, to cope with the postwar management of the new U.S. acquisitions abroad. Theodore Roosevelt kept Root in the post after he became president upon McKinley's assassination.

From then until 1904, Root restored departmental discipline, reorganized the War Department administration, established new merit system promotion procedures, founded the Army War College, expanded West Point, opened special schools for the various subbranches of the Army, created a general staff, and increased central control over the National Guard.

As McKinley foresaw, Root spent most of his time deciding what to do with the three major dependencies the United States had acquired during the war. In 1901, Root devised a plan for returning Cuba to the Cubans, but this plan contained the Platt Amendment to the Cuban constitution, which gave the United States the right to intervene in Cuban affairs. Root drafted a democratic charter for Philippine governance, providing for free government, protection of local customs, and eventual self-determination. For Puerto Rico, he pushed through the elimination of tariffs on their goods imported into the United States.

Having accomplished so much, he thought his job was done, so he returned to his private law practice in 1904. A year later President Roosevelt urged him to become secretary of state, a position in which his innovative administrative and diplomatic records are equally impressive. Root ended the spoils system in the consular service by putting it under the civil service and followed through on implementation of the open-door policy in China he had helped to formulate as secretary of war.

In 1906, Root made an unprecedented diplomatic tour through Latin America, strengthening friendly relations with South America and sponsoring the 1907 Central American Peace Conference. This conference created the Central American Court of Justice, an international tribunal for the ju-

dicial settlement of disputes. After reaching a "gentlemen's agreement" to limit Japanese immigration into the United States, he concluded the 1908 Root-Takahira agreement, by which both nations agreed to maintain the status quo in the Pacific and to uphold the open-door policy in China. Altogether, he negotiated some 40 reciprocal arbitration treaties, including the Permanent American-Canadian Joint High Commission for the settlement of future problems, after ironing out the current American-Canadian problems with the British Lord Bryce.

The New York legislature elected Root to the U.S. Senate in 1909, and he used this position to play an active role in settling the North Atlantic fisheries dispute. He also opposed a bill that would have exempted U.S. shipping transiting the Panama Canal from paying the tolls other countries were required to pay, but he promoted the cause of international arbitration.

Root became the first president of the Carnegie Endowment for International Peace in 1910 and remained in that post until 1925. In 1912, he received the Nobel Peace Prize for his contributions to world peace.

By 1914, the Seventeenth Amendment to the U.S. Constitution, providing for the direct election of U.S. senators, had been ratified. Root refused to run for the Senate that fall because he continued to fear being smeared for having represented Boss Tweed in 1873. He apparently did explore the possibility of pursuing the 1916 Republican presidential nomination but deferred to the draft for CHARLES EVANS HUGHES.

After THOMAS WOODROW WILSON's 1916 reelection, Root opposed Wilson's neutrality policy but supported him on World War I. Root accepted Wilson's appointment as ambassador extraordinary to Russia in 1917. Root attempted to forge a compromise between Wilson's 1919 Versailles Treaty and its League of Nations and the conservative Senate Republicans and other isolationists, but he failed. President WARREN GAMALIEL HARDING appointed him a delegate to the Washington Naval Conference of 1921–22, and he largely drafted its Five-Power Treaty, which limited naval armament.

Having once instructed the U.S. delegates to the 1907 Hague Conference to support creation of a World Court, he then devoted the rest of his life to the cause of international arbitration. In 1920, the Council of the League of Nations requested that he serve on a committee to create the Permanent Court of International Justice, which was set up in 1921. He continued to try to negotiate a compromise that would persuade the U.S. Senate to allow the United States to join the World Court. In 1929, on his 84th birthday, Root traveled to Geneva where he succeeded in convincing the delegates from 55 nations to accept a revised protocol for U.S. participation in the court. The U.S. Senate had demanded the revision in 1926 as the basis for joining the court but then delayed and finally declined to live up to its word.

Elihu Root died on February 7, 1937, about a week shy of his 93rd birthday.

Further Reading

Cherny, Robert W. "Root, Elihu." Available online. Discovery Channel School, original content provided by World Book Online. URL: http://www.discovery school.com/homeworkhelp/worldbook/atozhistory/r/475020.html. Downloaded November 24, 2001.

Cummins, Lejeune. *The Origin and Development of Elihu Root's Latin American Diplomacy.* Berkeley: University of California, 1964.

Jessup, Philip Caryl. *Elihu Root.* Hamden, Conn.: Archon Books, 1964; reprinted, New York: Dodd, Mead, 1991.

Leopold, Richard William. *Elihu Root and the Conservative Tradition.* Boston: Little, Brown, 1954.

Schambra, William A. *Elihu Root, the Constitution, and the Election of 1912.* Ann Arbor, Mich.: University Microfilms International, 1990.

Ros-Lehtinen, Ileana

(1952–) *representative, state legislator*

Ileana Ros-Lehtinen was the first Hispanic woman elected to Florida's state legislature and the first Hispanic woman elected to the U.S. House of Representatives.

Ileana Ros was born on July 15, 1952, in Havana, Cuba. In 1959, she moved with her family to Miami, Florida, to escape from Castro's regime in Cuba. Educated in the United States, she studied at Miami-Dade Community College, where she received an associate's degree in 1972. Later she studied at Florida International University, where she earned a B.A. in 1975 and an M.S. in 1987. She has continued her work for a doctorate in education at the University of Miami. She was a teacher and administrator at the Eastern Academy, a private elementary school that she helped to establish.

In 1982, Ros was the first Hispanic woman elected to the Florida House of Representatives where she served until 1986, when she moved up to being the state senator. As a state legislator, she pushed through the Pre-Paid College Tuition Program, a college tuition assistance program for Floridians. While in the legislature, she met and later married Dexter Lehtinen, a state legislator and former U.S. attorney for the southern district of Florida. Upon the death of longtime Democratic congressman CLAUDE DENSON PEPPER in 1989, Ros-Lehtinen defeated 10 other candidates in an election to fill the vacancy in the U.S. House of Representatives. According to the 1990 census, her district is 67 percent Hispanic, and she has been consistently reelected, sometimes without opposition.

In the House of Representatives she serves on the Government Operations and Foreign Affairs Committees. The latter has helped her achieve some foreign policy goals particularly important to her Cuban-American constituents, such as the Cuban Democracy Law and the Helms-Burton Act. By the 104th Congress, she was elevated to the chair of the Africa Subcommittee, which made her the first Hispanic woman to chair a U.S. House of Representatives subcommittee. She was also designated vice chair of the Western Hemisphere Subcommittee.

The true significance of Ros-Lehtinen is not that she is the first Hispanic woman to achieve national prominence. Generally, the Hispanic political community has remained somewhat fluid in its political loyalties, shifting support from Democratic to Republican candidates based on their perception of which party would aid them the most. Most frequently, the Hispanic community has leaned toward the Democratic Party. The Cuban-American community in Florida has been much more staunchly aligned with the Republican Party than have the Mexican-American or Puerto

Rican–American communities. Composed of a large number of exiles from Castro's communist regime in Cuba, they have been staunchly anticommunist conservatives, who have been more comfortable in the Republican Party. Ros-Lehtinen is one of the most prominent Hispanic American elected officials and the most prominent Republican Cuban-American official.

Further Reading

Fernandez, Mayra. *Ileana Ros-Lehtinen: Lawmaker.* Cleveland, Ohio: Modern Curriculum Press, 1994.
Telgen, Diane, and Jim Kamp, eds. *Notable Hispanic American Women.* Detroit, Mich.: Gale Research, 1993.

Rush, Benjamin
(1746–1813) *Revolutionary War leader, treasurer of the U.S. Mint*

Benjamin Rush, the most famous medical teacher of his generation in the United States, was a signer of the Declaration of Independence, a physician with the Continental army, a supporter of ratification of the U.S. Constitution, and the treasurer of the U.S. Mint in Philadelphia for more than 15 years.

Rush was born on December 24, 1745, in Byberry Township, Pennsylvania, an area so near 18-century Philadelphia that it is now incorporated in the city. In 1751, his father died, and he was raised by his mother and stepfather. He was educated by Reverend Samuel Finley, an uncle, who later became the president of Princeton University (then known as the College of New Jersey). Rush graduated from Princeton in 1760, changed his mind about a career in law, started studying medicine in Philadelphia, and finished his medical education in Edinburgh, London, and Paris. Part of his education was paid for from funds advanced by Benjamin Franklin, whom he met while abroad.

In 1769, Rush returned to Philadelphia, practiced medicine, and was active in politics. In 1773, he wrote a pamphlet against slavery and the following year helped organize the first antislavery organization in the United States, known as the Pennsylvania Society for Promoting the Abolition of Slavery. Strongly in favor of independence, he became a member of the provincial conference of

Pennsylvania and chaired the committee that produced a report calling on the Continental Congress to declare independence. During this period, he began a lifelong friendship with JOHN ADAMS.

In late July 1776, he was elected to the Continental Congress. Although the Declaration of Independence had already been approved when he joined the Congress, Rush signed it anyway and with enthusiasm. After less than a year in the Continental Congress, he was named the surgeon general of the Middle Department of the Continental Army. An impatient man, Rush encountered the stolid gravity of GEORGE WASHINGTON, who could be unforgiving of disloyalty. Rush was so strongly antimonarchial that he suspected Washington of harboring authoritarian goals as commander in chief and supported a secret movement, known as the Conway Cabal, to replace Washington with General Horatio Gates. Rush then left the army and held no other federal post until John Adams became president.

In 1786, Rush founded in Philadelphia the first free medical clinic in the United States. He supported the ratification of the U.S. Constitution as a member of the Pennsylvania Ratification Convention in 1787. In 1791, he became a professor of medicine at the College of Philadelphia, lectured at the University of Pennsylvania, and helped found Dickinson College. He was a believer in "blood-letting" for many illnesses and was criticized strongly for this belief. He attacked slavery, the use of alcohol or tobacco, and excessive attention to classical education. In 1793, and again in 1798, Dr. Rush was credited with curing the epidemic of yellow fever in Philadelphia, at great risk to his own health, by seeing often more than a hundred patients a day.

In 1797, John Adams appointed Rush the treasurer of the U.S. Mint in Philadelphia, Pennsylvania. Rush was at the height of his national reputation when he died in Philadelphia on April 19, 1813.

Further Reading

Binger, Carl A. L. *Revolutionary Doctor: Benjamin Rush.* New York: Norton, 1966.
D'Elia, Donald J. *Benjamin Rush: Philosopher of the American Revolution.* Philadelphia: American Philosophical Society, 1974.

Goodman, Nathan G. *Benjamin Rush, Physician and Citizen.* Philadelphia: University of Pennsylvania Press, 1934.

Hawke, David Freeman. *Benjamin Rush: Revolutionary Gadfly.* Indianapolis, Ind.: Bobbs-Merrill, 1971.

King, Lester S. *Transformations In American Medicine: From Benjamin Rush To William Osler.* Baltimore Md.: Johns Hopkins University Press, 1991.

Neilson, Winthrop. *Verdict for the Doctor: The Case of Benjamin Rush.* New York: Hastings House, 1958.

Rusk, David Dean

(1909–1994) *secretary of state, diplomat*

David Dean Rusk served as U.S. secretary of state from 1961 to 1969 under Presidents JOHN FITZGERALD KENNEDY and LYNDON BAINES JOHNSON. As secretary of state, he became a leading spokesman for the Johnson administration's Vietnam War policy.

Rusk was born on February 9, 1909, in Cherokee County, Georgia, into a poor family of tenant farmers. He graduated from Davidson College in North Carolina in 1931. He then went to England where he was a Rhodes Scholar at Oxford University and received a master's degree in 1934. Moving to Oakland, California, Rusk became a political science professor at Mills College in 1934 and the college dean in 1938.

During World War II, he served as the deputy chief of staff for the China-Burma-India theater. In that capacity, he was responsible for making decisions on the disposition of forces after the sudden surrender of the Japanese in August 1945. Rusk has acknowledged that—by accepting the 38th parallel as the line of demarcation between Russian and American troops in Korea in 1945 because it was close to the existing positions of both countries' troops—he unintentionally signaled to the Russians that the United States was willing to accept the division of Korea into spheres of interest that had existed previously.

After the war, Rusk worked in the War Department until he joined the State Department in 1946. He worked for both departments until he became assistant secretary of state in 1950, where he remained during the Korean War. In this capacity, he assisted in the development of the Marshall Plan and the North Atlantic Treaty Organization (NATO).

Rusk left government service in 1952 to become president of the Rockefeller Foundation, where he worked until Kennedy asked him to become his secretary of state. Since Kennedy wished to act as his own secretary of state, Rusk dutifully kept a low profile, but he was much more important during the Johnson administration when he defended Johnson's foreign and military policy in Southeast Asia.

Rusk was named a distinguished fellow at the Rockefeller Foundation in 1969 and professor of international law at the University of Georgia in 1970. He died on December 20, 1994.

Further Reading

Cohen, Warren I. *Dean Rusk.* Totowa, N.J.: Cooper Square Publishers, 1980.

Rusk, Dean. *As I Saw It.* New York: Penguin, 1991.

Schoenbaum, Thomas J. *Waging Peace and War: Dean Rusk in the Truman, Kennedy, and Johnson Years.* New York: Simon & Schuster, 1988.

Zeiler, Thomas W. *Dean Rusk: Defending the American Mission Abroad.* Wilmington, Del.: SR Books, 2000.

S

Scalia, Antonin
(1936–) *associate justice of the Supreme Court, Justice Department official*

Antonin Scalia is the first American of Italian heritage appointed to the U.S. Supreme Court. He has been generally regarded as the most consistently conservative member of the Court because of his adherence to a textualist approach to constitutional interpretation.

Scalia was born March 11, 1936, in Trenton, New Jersey. Both his father and his maternal grandparents were immigrants to the United States. Always an excellent student, he graduated first in his class at St. Francis Xavier, a Manhattan military prep school. His bachelor's degree in history was granted summa cum laude, and he was the class valedictorian when he graduated from Georgetown University in 1957. He also received his degree from Harvard Law School magna cum laude and served as note editor of the *Harvard Law Review.*

Starting out in private practice in 1961 in Cleveland, Ohio, Scalia decided to become a law professor at the University of Virginia in 1967. In 1971, he was appointed the general counsel in the Office of Telecommunications Policy in the administration of President RICHARD MILHOUS NIXON, a role in which he helped develop the framework for cable television. From 1972 to 1974, he chaired the Administrative Conference of the United States, an independent agency aimed at improving the efficiency of the administrative process.

In 1974, President GERALD RUDOLPH FORD appointed him the assistant attorney general for the Office of Legal Counsel in the Department of Justice. At the end of the Ford administration, Scalia again taught law at the Georgetown University Law Center (briefly), then at the University of Chicago from 1977 to 1982, with a year's leave to teach at Stanford University.

In 1982, President RONALD WILSON REAGAN appointed Scalia to the U.S. Court of Appeals for the District of Columbia Circuit, the federal court considered to be second in importance only to the Supreme Court. Most of the opinions Scalia wrote on the Court of Appeals were affirmed by the Supreme Court (if they were appealed). In 1986, Reagan nominated Scalia to the Supreme Court, and the Senate confirmed him unanimously.

On the Court, Scalia has consistently argued—in lone dissents if necessary—that the proper mode of constitutional interpretation is to adhere as closely as is reasonable to the actual text of the document. In 1988, the Court upheld the congressional creation of the independent counsel law, but Scalia forcefully dissented, maintaining that Congress had impermissibly given at least some traditional executive power to someone not fully within presidential control—an arrangement without any support in the Constitution. Scalia then asked, "Once we depart from the text of the Constitution, just where short of that do we stop?" This question remains a good summary of the textualist approach to interpreting the Constitution.

By adhering to the text, Scalia has been unwilling to find constitutional rights unless they are clearly set forth in the text of the Constitution, and therefore he has rejected any constitutional basis for a right to an abortion or a right to refuse life-sustaining treatment. Scalia's consistent textual interpretation does not always produce a result endorsed by conservative politicians. For example, although he abhors flag burners, he joined the more liberal members of the Court in defending flag burning as a constitutionally protected form of political expression. In 1990, he similarly dissented when the Court's majority permitted children testifying in abuse cases to do so by closed-circuit television because that practice was inconsistent with the Sixth Amendment, which protects the right of the accused to confront his or her accuser. Scalia has demonstrated that he believes that the U.S. Supreme Court must set forth clear, decisive rules, not subjective balancing tests.

The harshest criticism of Scalia has come as the result of his vote in the 2000 presidential election case, *Bush v. Gore*. That decision departed from his own conservative textualist principle when he used a breathtakingly broad interpretation of the Fourteenth Amendment's equal protection clause to overturn a Florida Supreme Court decision that exercised a traditional power to interpret its own state's law.

Further Reading

Brisbin, Richard A. *Justice Antonin Scalia and the Conservative Revival.* Baltimore, Md.: Johns Hopkins University Press, 1997.

Schultz, David A. *The Jurisprudential Vision of Justice Antonin Scalia.* Lanham, Md.: Rowman & Littlefield Publishers, 1996.

Smith, Christopher E. *Justice Antonin Scalia and the Supreme Court's Conservative Moment.* Westport, Conn.: Praeger, 1993.

Schurz, Carl

(1829–1906) *senator, secretary of the interior, diplomat*

Carl Schurz, one of the most famous U.S. citizens of German birth, became a radical reformer in U.S. politics.

Schurz was born on March 2, 1829, at Liblar (near Cologne), Germany, and studied at the University of Bonn until he was forced to flee Germany after having fought against autocracy in the Revolution of 1848. After his escape to Switzerland, Schurz immigrated to the United States in 1852 and eventually to Wisconsin.

Schurz and his wife were both ardent reformers. While he became active in the abolitionist fight in 1856, she founded in Watertown, Wisconsin, the first kindergarten in the United States. With his fluent command of both German and English and a knack for oratory, Schurz was nominated by the Republicans for lieutenant governor in 1857. He lost the election but studied law and was admitted to the Wisconsin bar.

Schurz campaigned for ABRAHAM LINCOLN in 1860, and Lincoln appointed him U.S. minister to Spain in 1861. Early in the Civil War, Schurz was in Madrid, but he resigned his post to join in the fighting. By 1863, he was promoted to major general and fought at Chancellorsville, Gettysburg, and Chattanooga. In 1865, he was stationed under General William T. Sherman in North Carolina.

After the Civil War, Schurz was a correspondent of the New York *Tribune*, as well as joint editor and owner of the St. Louis *Westliche Post*, a German-language newspaper in St. Louis, Missouri. This paper became such a powerful influence in the West that it helped Schurz be elected as a Republican to the U.S. Senate from Missouri in 1869.

Schurz was appalled by both the Radical Republicans and the corruption of ULYSSES S. GRANT's administration. He helped form the 1872 Liberal Republican Party and supported publisher HORACE GREELEY against Grant. In 1876, Schurz supported RUTHERFORD BIRCHARD HAYES, an anti-corruption, hard-money candidate, for president and was rewarded with appointment to the cabinet as secretary of the interior.

After his term as secretary of the interior ended in 1881, Schurz became an editor of the New York *Evening Post*, where he remained until he resigned in a policy dispute in 1883. He then moved over to Harper's *Weekly* in 1892 and stayed there for six years. In 1884, believing Republican presidential candidate, JAMES GILLESPIE BLAINE, was corrupt, Schurz convinced many *mugwumps* (as the former Liberal Republicans were called) to oppose Blaine and support the Democratic presidential nominee, STEPHEN GROVER CLEVELAND (another hard-currency man and dedicated reformer), in 1884, 1888 and 1892.

By 1896, Schurz was again a Republican supporting WILLIAM MCKINLEY because he opposed the pro-silver, soft-currency views of the Democratic presidential nominee, WILLIAM JENNINGS BRYAN. However, the currency question became less important in 1900, so Schurz switched over to Bryan because of his anti-imperialist views.

He died on May 14, 1906.

Further Reading

Fuess, Claude Moore. *Carl Schurz, Reformer.* New York: Dodd, Mead, 1932.

Schurz, Carl. *Abraham Lincoln.* Boston: Houghton, Mifflin, 1899.

———. *Autobiography of Carl Schurz.* New York: Scribner, reprinted 1961.

Seip, Terry. "Rutherford B. Hayes" in *The American Presidents,* edited by Frank N. Magill, John L. Loos, and Tracy Irons-Georges. Pasadena, Calif.: Salem Press, 2000.

Terzian, James P. *Defender of Human Rights: Carl Schurz.* New York: J. Messener, 1965.

Trefousse, Hans Louis. *Carl Schurz.* Knoxville: University of Tennessee Press, 1982.

Scott, Winfield
(1786–1866) *candidate for president*

Winfield Scott, who lost the race for president against FRANKLIN PIERCE in 1844, was a U.S. Army officer for more than 50 years, spanning all the wars between the War of 1812 and the start of the Civil War. His most distinguished service came during the Mexican War from 1846 to 1848. He was affectionately nicknamed "Old Fuss and Feathers" because of his careful dress and demeanor.

Scott was born on June 13, 1786, near Petersburg, Virginia. He attended the College of William and Mary briefly, then studied law, but dropped law to join the U.S. Army in 1808. In the War of 1812, Scott was a lieutenant colonel on the Canadian border when he was captured near Niagara

Falls at the Battle of Queenstown Heights. Released a month later and then a colonel, Scott successfully attacked Fort George.

In March 1814, he was promoted to brigadier general and fought the British to a standstill at Chippewa and Lundy's Lane on the Canadian border. At Lundy's Lane, Scott battled so tenaciously that even after two horses were shot from under him and he was seriously wounded, he fought on and had to be carried from the field. A national hero, he was awarded medals by both the federal government and Virginia, and he was promoted to major general. Scott remained in the Army, wrote a manual of battle tactics, and eventually was named general in chief of the army in 1841.

In 1847, during the Mexican War, Scott led the army into Mexico, winning at Vera Cruz, Cerro Gordo, Contreras, Churubusco, Molino del Rey, and Chapultepec, and then capturing Mexico City. He was passed over by the Whigs for the 1848 presidential nomination in favor of ZACHARY TAYLOR, another Mexican War hero. The Whigs then picked Scott as their 1852 nominee, but he lost to Democrat FRANKLIN PIERCE.

In April 1861, Scott went to Washington, where he recruited men to defend the capital, but, at 73 years of age, he was too old for active duty and retired. He died on May 29, 1866.

Further Reading

Eisenhower, John S.D. *Agent of Destiny: The Life and Times of General Winfield Scott.* New York: Free Press, 1997.

Elliott, Charles W. *Winfield Scott: The Soldier and the Man.* New York: Arno Press, 1979.

Johnson, Timothy D. *Winfield Scott: The Quest for Military Glory.* Lawrence: University Press of Kansas, 1998.

Long, Laura. *Fuss 'N' Feathers: A Life of Winfield T. Scott.* New York and Toronto, Canada: Longmans, Green, 1944.

Seward, William Henry
(1801–1872) *secretary of state, senator, governor*

William Henry Seward was a major political influence in the United States for more than four decades, from the presidency of JOHN QUINCY ADAMS through that of ANDREW JOHNSON. A moderate who favored a conciliatory Reconstruction policy, he remained loyal to Johnson even at a cost to his own popularity.

Seward was born on May 16, 1801, in the town of Florida in Orange County, New York. He graduated from Union College in 1820, studied law, and was admitted to the bar in 1822. He began practicing law in Auburn, New York, where he became politically active, initially in the Anti-Masonic Party. He supported John Quincy Adams for president in 1824, although this was risky given the strength of the ANDREW JACKSON forces.

Elected as an Anti-Mason to the state senate in 1830, he was defeated for reelection in 1833. With his close personal and political friend Thurlow Weed, Seward became one of the two most influential Whigs in New York State. He ran as the Whig candidate for governor in 1834 but lost; however, he won the governor's office in 1838 and was reelected in 1840.

As governor, Seward worked for progressive reforms in education, internal improvements, and protections for immigrants and fugitive slaves. Defeated for reelection in 1842, he practiced law until the antislavery cause made possible his election to the U.S. Senate in 1849 and his reelection in 1855.

When the Whig Party disintegrated, Seward and Weed joined the new Republican Party in 1855. Although he had an excellent record, many Republicans distrusted Thurlow Weed's political machine, and the Republicans never gave him their party's presidential nomination. Seward was disappointed to have been defeated by Lincoln for the presidential nomination, but he worked for Lincoln's election and accepted the new president's offer to make him the secretary of state.

Seward apparently thought he would be powerful in the government and wrote a memo to Lincoln, pompously suggesting that the country could avoid a civil war by starting a war against some countries in Europe. Lincoln rebuffed those suggestions and made it clear that he would exercise the critical executive power. Seward then served

faithfully, although Lincoln had a difficult time keeping both Seward and his archrival, Treasury Secretary SALMON PORTLAND CHASE, in the same cabinet. With the help of CHARLES FRANCIS ADAMS, Seward handled the British relations well. He objected to French interference in Mexico and stopped it after the Civil War was over.

Seward was also a target of the same assassination plot that killed Lincoln. Recovering from a carriage accident, Seward was in a body cast when an accomplice of John Wilkes Booth stabbed him. His cast actually deflected some of the more serious blows until Seward's cries for help brought him aid. Seward recovered and kept his cabinet position under President Andrew Johnson.

Seward was a moderate on Reconstruction, supported Johnson's Reconstruction policy, and was excoriated by the Radicals for standing by Johnson during the impeachment trial. Those who tried to threaten him into deserting Johnson were greeted with an emphatic, "I will see you damned first." Seward's most enduring achievement was the purchase of Alaska from Russia in 1867, but his enemies called the purchase "Seward's folly," mainly because he stood by Johnson. He also tried to purchase most of the Virgin Islands, but the Senate was too stubborn to approve the plan. His wisdom—and their folly—was appreciated only decades later.

Although crippled, he traveled around the world after the end of the Johnson term. On returning home, his condition worsened, and he died on October 10, 1872.

Further Reading

Bancroft, Frederic. *The Life of William H. Seward.* Gloucester, Mass.: P. Smith, 1967.

Lothrop, Thornton K. *William Henry Seward.* New York: AMS Press, 1972.

Paolino, Ernest N. *The Foundations of the American Empire: William Henry Seward and U.S. Foreign Policy.* Ithaca, N.Y.: Cornell University Press, 1973.

Taylor, John M. *William Henry Seward: Lincoln's Right Hand.* New York: HarperCollins, 1991.

Van Deusen, Glyndon G. *William Henry Seward.* New York: Oxford University Press, 1967.

Shultz, George Pratt

(1920–) *secretary of state, secretary of the Treasury, secretary of labor, author*

George Pratt Shultz served as secretary of labor, director of the Office of Management and Budget, and secretary of the Treasury under President RICHARD MILHOUS NIXON as well as secretary of state in the administration of President RONALD WILSON REAGAN.

Shultz was born on December 13, 1920, in New York City. He graduated from Princeton University in 1942 and received a Ph.D. from the Massachusetts Institute of Technology (MIT) in 1949. Shultz taught economics at MIT from 1948 to 1957 (with some short leaves of absence). He became a professor of industrial relations at the University of Chicago in 1957 and dean of the graduate school of business in 1962, a position he held until he entered Nixon's administration in 1969. He began his government service as Nixon's secretary of labor in 1969 and 1970. In 1970, Nixon appointed Shultz director of the newly created Office of Management and Budget. In 1972, he was named secretary of the Treasury, but he had a serious disagreement with Nixon over policy and resigned in 1974.

Before joining the Reagan administration, Shultz served seven years as president of the Bechtel Group, Inc., a large international engineering company. Shultz also served in the United States and abroad as an adviser to governments and to management and labor groups. As an arbitrator in labor disputes, he became noted for his fairness and his ability to bring about settlements. Shultz was named secretary of state after ALEXANDER MEIGS HAIG resigned in 1982 as the result of a number of disagreements with others in the Reagan administration. Shultz served the remainder of the term. His experience as an economist and as a former secretary of the Treasury meant that he focused more on international economic questions than did other secretaries of state. He was deliberately kept out of the plans to trade arms for hostages and the illegal plans to use the proceeds from that sale to fund the Contra rebels in Nicaragua. When this scandal developed, he persuasively demonstrated that he was not involved. Unfortunately, this also indicated the degree to which important foreign policy issues were resolved by circumventing the regular State Department hierarchy. After he retired from government, he became a part-time professor of business at Stanford University.

Further Reading

Friedman, Thomas L. *From Beirut to Jerusalem*. New York: Farrar, Straus, Giroux, 1989.

Neff, Donald. *Fallen Pillars: U.S. Policy Towards Palestine and Israel since 1945*. Washington, D.C.: Institute for Palestine Studies, 1995.

Rees, Albert, and George P. Shultz. *Workers and Wages in an Urban Labor Market*. Chicago: University of Chicago Press, 1970.

Shultz, George P. *Leaders and Followers in an Age of Ambiguity*. New York: New York University Press. 1975.

———. *Turmoil and Triumph: My Years as Secretary of State*. New York: Scribner's, 1993.

Shultz, George P., and Kenneth W. Dam. *Economic Policy Beyond the Headlines*. Chicago: University of Chicago Press, 1998.

Shultz, George P., and Arnold R. Weber. *Strategies for the Displaced Worker: Confronting Economic Change*. New York: Harper & Row, 1966.

Smith, Alfred Emanuel

(1873–1944) *candidate for president, governor*

Alfred Emanuel Smith was a successful reform governor of New York State and the first Roman Catholic to be nominated for president by a major party.

Smith was born in poverty on December 30, 1873, in New York City. When his father died, he was forced to quit school after the eighth grade to earn money selling newspapers or working in the Fulton Fish Market. In 1894, he attended a political meeting and became involved in a local race in which he supported an anti-Tammany Hall candidate. His candidate lost, but another anti-Tammany candidate was elected mayor, and Smith was appointed a process server in the Commissioner of Jurors' office.

Over the years, he softened his opposition to Tammany and accepted their help in becoming a state assemblyman in 1903. Once reelected, he became speaker of the assembly in 1913 with a reputation for progressive politics. He was elected New York County sheriff in 1915 and then was elected president of the New York City board of aldermen in 1917. In 1918, Smith was elected New York's governor. Despite his successful record, he was not reelected during the 1920 Republican landslide that elected President WARREN GAMALIEL HARDING. He regained the office in 1922 and was reelected in 1924 and 1926.

In 1924, FRANKLIN DELANO ROOSEVELT, dubbing Smith with his enduring nickname—the "happy warrior"—placed Smith's name before the Democratic National Convention as a candidate for the presidential nomination. Blocked by William G. McAdoo, the bitter contest resulted in a deadlock, giving the 1924 nomination to John W. Davis in the end. Smith ran again in 1928, this time easily gaining the Democratic presidential nomination, the first Roman Catholic so nominated. Smith's Catholicism and his anti-Prohibition stance hurt him badly in the South, and he lost to Republican HERBERT CLARK HOOVER. Retiring to private life, he became president of the firm that erected and operated the Empire State Building in New York City in 1929.

Although he rather belatedly endorsed Roosevelt for president in 1932, he had a bitter break with him after the 1932 election. The underlying basis for the break probably rested on jealousy at Roosevelt's success, but the official reasons were Smith's newfound supporters in the business community. Smith strongly opposed Roosevelt in 1936 and 1940. Smith died in New York City on October 4, 1944.

Further Reading

"Alfred E. Smith" in *The Presidency A to Z: Second Edition*, edited by Michael T. Nelson. Washington, D.C.: Congressional Quarterly Press, 1998.

Allen, William H. *Al Smith's Tammany Hall: Champion Political Vampire*. New York: Institute for Public Service, 1928.

Davis, Kenneth S. *FDR: Three Volumes*. New York: Random House, 1993.

Graham, Frank. *Al Smith: American*. New York: G. P. Putnam's Sons, 1945.

Josephson, Matthew. *Al Smith: Hero of the Cities; A Political Portrait Drawing on the Papers of Frances Perkins*. Boston: Houghton Mifflin, 1969.

McElvaine, Robert S. "Franklin Delano Roosevelt" in *The American Presidents* edited by Frank N. Magill, John L. Loos, and Tracy Irons-Georges. Pasadena, Calif.: Salem Press, 2000.

McJimsey, George T. *The Presidency of Franklin Delano Roosevelt*. Lawrence: University Press of Kansas, 2000.

Morris, Jeffrey. *The FDR Way*. Minneapolis: Lerner Publications, 1996.

Moses, Robert. *A Tribute to Governor Smith*. New York: Simon & Schuster, 1962.

Neal, Donn C. *The World Beyond the Hudson: Alfred E. Smith and National Politics, 1918–1928*. New York: Garland Publishing, 1983.

O'Connor, Richard. *The First Hurrah: A Biography of Alfred E. Smith*. New York: Putnam, 1970.

Smith, Alfred E. *Up to Now: An Autobiography*. New York: The Viking Press, 1929.

Smith, Margaret Chase
(1897–1995) *senator, representative*

Margaret Chase Smith was the only woman elected to the U.S. Senate for four consecutive terms. She had a distinguished career, supporting many progressive ideas. With an outstanding attendance record over her entire career, she did not miss a single roll call vote from June 1955 to July 1968. One of her most courageous and memorable actions was her early condemnation of the tactics of her fellow Republican senator JOSEPH RAYMOND MCCARTHY.

Born on December 14, 1897, in Skowhegan, Maine, Margaret Chase was too poor to afford to go to college. She worked as a teacher, secretary, and successful businesswoman before she married Maine state senator Clyde Harold Smith in 1930. After he was elected as a Republican to the U.S. House of Representatives in 1936, she became his office manager. When he died in 1940, she ran for his seat and won. She was reelected to three more terms. Although a Republican, she had a very independent voting record, supporting some New Deal legislation, the defense buildup before World

Margaret Chase Smith was the first woman elected to the U.S. Senate. *(Library of Congress)*

War II, and opposing permanent status for the House Un-American Activities Committee.

Smith demonstrated calm under stress. She was returning from a House committee fact-finding tour of military and industrial conditions in Central Europe after World War II when the transoceanic plane on which she was traveling lost one engine and was damaged in its second engine. The emergency was so severe that lifejackets were given out to the passengers. Smith had the presence of mind to open a package of harmonicas she had purchased in Switzerland, passed them out, and led the passengers in playing and singing on their way back to a safe landing in the Azores.

In 1948, she was elected to the U.S. Senate where she continued to vote independently and won five consecutive terms nonetheless. One of her most courageous actions came in 1950 when she joined six other Republican senators to denounce Wisconsin's Republican senator Joe McCarthy for his guilt-by-association smear tactics. Her statement, coming in the famous Declaration of Conscience speech in 1950, brought her to national attention. Speaking later of this stirring defense of basic American principles of democracy and fair play, she said, "I didn't do it for approval or disapproval. I just thought it had to be done." During her Senate career, she worked hard and long at her job, compiling a record of 2,941 consecutive roll calls in her 24-year stint in the Senate. She was defeated in her attempt to win a fifth consecutive term in 1972.

Although seriously considered as a possible Republican vice presidential nominee in both 1952 and 1968, she was never given that honor. She remained active with speeches and writing during her retirement. She died on May 29, 1995, at the age of 97.

Further Reading

Fleming, Alice M. *The Senator from Maine: Margaret Chase Smith.* New York: Crowell, 1969.

Graham, Frank. *Margaret Chase Smith: Woman of Courage.* New York: John Day Co., 1964.

Sherman, Janann. *No Place for a Woman: A Life of Senator Margaret Chase Smith.* New Brunswick, N.J.: Rutgers University Press, 2000.

Vallin, Marlene Boyd. *Margaret Chase Smith: Model Public Servant.* Westport, Conn.: Greenwood, 1998.

Wallace, Patricia W. *Politics of Conscience: A Biography of Margaret Chase Smith.* Westport, Conn.: Praeger, 1995.

Stanton, Edwin McMasters
(1814–1869) *secretary of war, attorney general*

Edwin McMasters Stanton served in the cabinet of three presidents during the decade of the 1860s. He served as JAMES BUCHANAN's attorney general, but his most significant service was as President ABRAHAM LINCOLN's secretary of war. He was the holdover secretary of war in ANDREW JOHNSON's cabinet, and his dismissal triggered Johnson's impeachment.

Stanton was born on December 19, 1814, in Steubenville, Ohio. He started Kenyon College in 1831 but dropped out three years later because of a lack of funds. He then studied law in his guardian's office until admitted to the bar in 1836. He began practicing law in Ohio, moved to Pittsburgh, Pennsylvania, in 1847, and finally settled in Washington, D.C., in 1856.

He held only minor judicial offices before 1858 when, as acting U.S. counsel handling fraudulent Californian land cases, he did a masterful job and came to the attention of President Buchanan, who named him U.S. attorney general in 1860. Stanton was a Democrat, devoted to the Union, and he supported JOHN CABELL BRECKENRIDGE for president in 1860. But Stanton had already earned the respect of Lincoln for his handling of a patent case in 1856.

When Simon Cameron, Lincoln's first secretary of war, proved corrupt, Lincoln appointed Stanton to the post in 1862. Stanton was outspoken, made many enemies, and even quarreled with Lincoln, but his honest, vigorous management of the War Department earned him respect. After Lincoln's assassination, President Johnson made the mistake of keeping Stanton even when it became clear that Stanton was sabotaging Johnson's Reconstruction plans to aid Johnson's enemies in the Congress.

Had Johnson fired Stanton sooner, he could have avoided having the dismissal become grounds for impeachment. In the end, Congress passed the Tenure of Office Act—which was later determined to be unconstitutional—to prevent a president from removing a cabinet officer whom he had appointed without the consent of Congress. Since Lincoln had appointed Stanton and not Johnson, the law technically did not apply when Johnson finally fired Stanton. Stanton refused to leave the office and barricaded the door. Johnson's enemies in Congress then attempted to remove Johnson for violating the Tenure of Office Act, among other things. They impeached Johnson in the U.S. House of Representatives, but he was acquitted of the impeachment in the U.S. Senate by one vote. Stanton finally departed the office in May 1868.

In 1869, President ULYSSES S. GRANT appointed Stanton to the Supreme Court, but he died just a short time later on December 24, 1869, before he could take his seat on the Court.

Further Reading

Boritt, Gabor. "Stanton, Edwin McMasters," Available online. Discovery Channel School, original content provided by World Book Online. URL: http://www.discoveryschool.com/homeworkhelp/worldbook/atozhistory/s/529420.html. Downloaded November 25, 2001.

Flower, Frank A. *Edwin McMasters Stanton: The Autocrat of Rebellion, Emancipation, and Reconstruction.* New York: AMS Press, 1973.

Hearn, Chester G. *Ellet's Brigade: The Strangest Outfit of All.* Baton Rouge: Louisiana State University Press, 2000.

Kelley, William D. *Lincoln and Stanton: A Study of the War Administration of 1861 and 1862.* New York: G. P. Putnam's Sons, 1885.

Pratt, Fletcher. *Stanton: Lincoln's Secretary of War.* Westport, Conn.: Greenwood, 1970.

Thomas, Benjamin. *Stanton: The Life and Times of Lincoln's Secretary of War.* New York: Knopf, 1962.

Williams, Ben A. "Mr. Secretary." New York: Macmillan, 1940.

Stevens, Thaddeus
(1792–1868) *representative*

Often called the most egalitarian of all the Radical Republicans after the Civil War, Thaddeus Stevens was one of the prime instigators of the impeachment of President ANDREW JOHNSON.

Stevens was born on April 4, 1782, in Danville, Vermont. He was crippled by a clubfoot, and his childhood was hard, particularly since his alcoholic father could not hold a job and abandoned his family before dying in the War of 1812. Stevens's mother worked as a domestic to support her children. Stevens still managed to graduate from Dartmouth College in 1814, then teach school and study law until he passed the bar. He was successful at practicing law both in Gettysburg and later Lancaster, Pennsylvania.

Elected to the Pennsylvania state legislature as a Federalist in 1833, he served until 1841 (part of the later years as an Anti-Mason). He practiced law until he was elected as an antislavery Whig to the U.S. House of Representatives in 1848. He opposed both the Fugitive Slave Law and the Compromise of 1850, and he quit the Whig Party in 1853 in disgust over their moderate slavery stand.

In 1858, Stevens was reelected to Congress as a member of the new antislavery Republican Party, and he soon became chair of the powerful House Ways and Means Committee. He opposed ABRAHAM LINCOLN's moderate Reconstruction plans and became even more vehemently opposed to President ANDREW JOHNSON's Reconstruction policy.

The Radicals made major gains in the 1866 congressional elections and overturned Johnson's Reconstruction program, occupied the South militarily, proscribed most former Confederates, and gave African Americans the right to vote. Stevens himself proposed the Fourteenth Amendment and made ratification of it mandatory for readmission to the Union by former Confederate states. Stevens became a member of the congressional committee on Reconstruction, but he was often disappointed because moderates were in control.

Stevens dominated the committee that drew up the impeachment charges against Johnson. He was one of the House managers in the subsequent trial before the Senate, but he was so ill that he had to be carried into the Senate chamber during Johnson's impeachment trial. Stevens died on August 11, 1868, less than three months after Johnson's acquittal by a single vote in the Senate. Stevens requested that he be interred in a cemetery with African Americans rather than in a white cemetery closed to them.

Further Reading
Buckmaster, Henrietta. *The Fighting Congressmen: Thaddeus Stephens, Hiram Revels, James Rapier, Blanche K. Bruce.* New York: Scholastic Book Services, 1971.
Callender, Edward B. *Thaddeus Stevens: Commoner.* New York: AMS Press, 1972.
Current, Richard N. *Old Thad Stevens: A Story of Ambition.* Westport, Conn.: Greenwood, 1980.
Meltzer, Milton. *Thaddeus Stevens and the Fight for Negro Rights.* New York: Crowell, 1967.
Rehnquist, William H. *Grand Inquests: The Historic Impeachments of Justice Samuel Chase and President Andrew Johnson.* New York: Morrow, 1992.
Smith, Gene. *High Crimes and Misdemeanors: The Impeachment and Trial of Andrew Johnson.* New York: Morrow, 1977.
Trefousse, Hans L. *Thaddeus Stevens: Nineteenth-Century Egalitarian.* Chapel Hill: University of North Carolina Press, 1997.

Stevenson, Adlai Ewing
(1900–1965) *candidate for president, governor, diplomat*

Adlai Ewing Stevenson was the reform governor of Illinois, three times a candidate for president, and twice the presidential nominee of the Democratic Party. He had his largest impact in altering the political idiom and raising the level of public debate in the United States.

Stevenson was born on February 5, 1900, in Los Angeles, California, into a politically active family. He was the grandson of Adlai E. Stevenson (the first) who was one of STEPHEN GROVER CLEVELAND's vice presidents. Raised in Bloomington, Illinois, Stevenson was educated at the Choate School. He graduated with a B.A. from Princeton in 1922, studied at Harvard Law School, but completed his legal studies and received his law degree from Northwestern University in 1926.

After practicing law briefly, he went to Washington to work for the Agricultural Adjustment Administration in 1933 and moved over to be the chief counsel to the Federal Alcohol Control Administration in 1934. He returned to Chicago to practice law but continued to be interested in foreign affairs. In 1935, he was elected president of the Chicago Council on Foreign Relations. His eloquent speeches against isolationism resulted in his being named to head up the Committee to Defend America by Aiding the Allies in 1940.

In 1941, Stevenson became principal attorney for the U.S. secretary of the navy, where his duties also included speech writing. In 1945, he moved to the State Department, where he helped prepare for the creation of the United Nations and was sent as a UN delegate in 1946 and 1947.

Elected the Democratic governor of Illinois in 1948, he was a progressive governor and attracted attention as a prospective 1952 Democratic presidential candidate. He wanted to run for a second gubernatorial term but finally accepted a draft to run against DWIGHT DAVID EISENHOWER in the presidential election. Stevenson succeeded in reaching out to a new generation of Democrats, but he lost the election, carrying only nine states with an Electoral College vote total of 89. Eisenhower won 39 states with a total of 442 Electoral College votes.

After the election, Stevenson continued to speak out as titular leader of the Democratic Party, attracted more Democratic support, and actively sought the 1956 nomination. He won the nomination on the first ballot, but he lost again to Eisenhower by an even wider margin.

In 1960, his supporters again pressed him to run, but his reluctant posture was easily outpaced by the vigorous campaign of JOHN FITZGERALD KENNEDY. Stevenson worked hard for the ticket and hoped to be named the U.S. secretary of state, but Kennedy did not want a political rival in such a prominent post, so Stevenson had to settle for U.S. ambassador to the United Nations. While he performed well and spoke eloquently, he was not happy defending policies with which he did not fully agree—especially after LYNDON BAINES JOHNSON became president upon Kennedy's assassination.

Stevenson had decided to retire when he suffered a heart attack while in London. He died on July 14, 1965.

Further Reading

Broadwater, Jeff. *Adlai Stevenson and American Politics: The Odyssey of a Cold War Liberal.* New York: Twayne, 1994.

Harris, Patricia Milligan. *Adlai: The Springfield Years.* Nashville, Tenn.: Aurora Publishers, 1975.

Martin, John Bartlow. *Adlai Stevenson and the World: The Life of Adlai E. Stevenson.* Garden City, N.Y.: Doubleday, 1977.

McKeever, Porter. *Adlai Stevenson: His Life and Legacy.* New York: Morrow, 1989.

Rowse, Arthur E. *Slanted News: A Case Study of the Nixon and Stevenson Fund Stories.* Westport, Conn.: Greenwood Press, 1973.

Sievers, Rodney M. *The Last Puritan? Adlai Stevenson in American Politics.* Port Washington, N.Y.: Associated Faculty Press, 1983.

Walton, Richard J. *The Remnants of Power: The Tragic Last Years of Adlai Stevenson.* New York: Coward-McCann, 1968.

Stimson, Henry Lewis

(1867–1950) *secretary of state, secretary of war, diplomat, author*

Henry Lewis Stimson was an exceptional bipartisan figure in U.S. politics. He served the country under six presidents, holding cabinet posts under four presidents from both major parties.

Stimson was born on September 21, 1867, in New York City. Graduating from Yale in 1888, he took his legal education at Harvard. After graduating in 1890, he joined ELIHU ROOT in his New York law firm. THEODORE ROOSEVELT appointed Stimson the U.S. attorney for the southern district of New York. He remained in that post until he ran unsuccessfully as a Republican for governor of New York in 1910.

President WILLIAM HOWARD TAFT named Stimson the U.S. secretary of war in 1911, and he served in that role for the remainder of Taft's administration. During World War I, he was a colonel of the 31st Field Artillery. In 1927, President CALVIN COOLIDGE sent Stimson to Nicaragua to mediate a civil disorder there. At the successful conclusion to that mission, Coolidge named him governor-general of the Philippines. Although he opposed Philippine independence, he eased the harsh rule of General Leonard Wood, his predecessor.

In 1929, HERBERT CLARK HOOVER designated him the U.S. secretary of state. Stimson chaired the U.S. delegation to the London Naval Conference in 1930 and 1931 and the Geneva Disarmament Conference in 1932. After the Japanese invasion of Manchuria in 1932, he issued a declaration, now known as the Stimson Doctrine, holding that the United States would not recognize any seizure of territory or other situation brought about by aggression. Stimson called for an economic boycott of Japan, but Hoover declined to agree with him.

Returning to his law practice in 1933, Stimson continued to urge economic measures against Japan and support FRANKLIN DELANO ROOSEVELT's preparedness for war. When President Roosevelt appointed him secretary of war in 1940, many Republicans read Stimson out of the party.

Despite his age, he served with energy throughout World War II, reorganizing the military and supervising the creation of the atomic bomb. Stimson acted as a significant adviser on atomic policy to President Roosevelt and, to a lesser degree, to President HARRY S. TRUMAN, under whom he continued to serve. Stimson tried to end the war sooner by recommending that the Allies offer terms of surrender, allowing for Japan to keep its emperor. Failing at that, he finally recommended to Truman that atomic bombs be used on Japanese cities, although he was responsible for keeping the historically significant Kyoto, the original Japanese capital, off the target list.

Stimson later justified the use of nuclear weapons, arguing that they hastened Japan's surrender and thus saved lives. After leaving the War Department, Stimson set out this defense of the atomic bombings in an article entitled "The Decision to Use the Atomic Bomb." This piece was published in *Harper's* magazine in February 1947 and repeated in his memoirs.

He died on October 20, 1950.

Further Reading

Current, Richard N. *Secretary Stimson: A Study in Statecraft.* Hamden, Conn.: Archon Books, 1970.

Ferrell, Robert H. *The American Secretaries of State and their Diplomacy: Volume Eleven: Frank B. Kellogg, Henry L. Stimson.* New York: Cooper Square, 1963.

Hodgson, Godfrey. *The Colonel: The Life and Wars of Henry Stimson, 1867–1950.* New York: Knopf, 1990.

Morison, Elting Elmore. *Turmoil and Tradition: A Study of the Life and Times of Henry L. Stimson.* New York: Athenaeum, 1964.

Rappaport, Armin. *Henry L. Stimson and Japan, 1931–33.* Chicago: University of Chicago Press, 1963.

Stimson, Henry L. *Democracy and Nationalism in Europe.* Princeton, N.J.: Princeton University Press, 1934.

———. *The Far Eastern Crisis.* New York: Harper, 1936.

———. *On Active Service in Peace and War.* New York: Harper, 1948.

"Stimson, Henry Lewis." Available online. Discovery Channel School, original content provided by World Book Online. URL: http://www.discovery school.com/homeworkhelp/worldbook/atozhistory/ s/723236.html. Downloaded November 26, 2001.

Sumner, Charles
(1811–1874) *senator*

Charles Sumner, a strong abolitionist, was a leader of the Radical Republicans after the Civil War and active proponent of the impeachment of ANDREW JOHNSON. Before the war, he was so severely beaten for delivering an antislavery speech in the U.S. Senate that it took him three years to recover.

Sumner was born on January 6, 1811, in Boston, Massachusetts. He graduated from Harvard University in 1833 and was admitted to the bar in 1834. He traveled from 1837 to 1840 and developed a strong—even radical—reform point of view. He favored prison reform, improved education, and, above all, an end to slavery. Sumner started out as a Whig, but he rejected their moderate stance on slavery and helped found the Free Soil Party in 1848. In 1849, Sumner filed a legal challenge to the segregated schools of Boston.

In 1851, Sumner's Free Soilers and the Democrats combined to take control of the Massachusetts legislature. Sumner then was elected to the U.S. Senate, where he was soon the premier opponent of slavery, attempting to repeal the Fugitive Slave Act and opposing the 1854 Kansas-Nebraska Act. He was active in the creation of the Republican Party in 1854.

In May 1856, he delivered an antislavery speech entitled "The Crime Against Kansas." In the speech he made vicious remarks against South Carolina's Senator Andrew P. Butler, saying he had taken vows to "the harlot, Slavery." Butler was not present to defend himself, but two days later his nephew, U.S. Representative Preston Brooks, charged into the Senate chamber and beat Sumner senseless with a heavy walking stick. Sumner was disabled for the next three years but was reelected to the Senate despite his infirmity.

Returning to the Senate in 1859, Sumner was a major leader of the Radical Republicans. Before and during the Civil War, Sumner was against any compromise with the Confederates and for the immediate abolition of slavery. He was so extreme that he even quarreled with ABRAHAM LINCOLN, for whom he at least had a degree of respect. Sumner wanted immediate emancipation, the full right to vote for all former slaves, and the use of black troops, but Lincoln would not move as fast as Sumner wanted.

After Lincoln's assassination, Sumner had no respect at all for Andrew Johnson, who had been elevated to the presidency, even though Johnson followed Lincoln's policy quite closely. By 1866, the Radical Republicans had won enough seats in the congressional elections to control the Congress. They overturned Johnson's moderate Reconstruction policy and passed the 1866 Civil Rights Bill, protecting freed slaves from southern Black Codes (or laws severely restricting freed slaves).

The division between Johnson and the Radical Republicans was so severe that it was only a matter of time before the U.S. House of Representatives impeached Johnson. Sumner was the most radical leader of the attacks against Johnson, and he was horrified when several Republicans refused to vote to convict and Johnson was acquitted by a single vote. Sumner was increasingly on the outs with members of his own party.

During the administration of ULYSSES S. GRANT, Sumner attacked Grant for not doing enough to help African Americans in the South. Grant proposed to annex Santo Domingo, consulted Sumner (as chair of the Senate Foreign Rela-

tions Committee), and thought he had Sumner's concurrence. After Grant's efforts became public, Sumner denounced the plan in harsh terms. Grant and his Senate supporters felt betrayed and stripped Sumner of his chairmanship of the Senate Foreign Relations Committee. Sumner responded by severing ties with Grant, helping form a new Liberal Republican Party, and supporting HORACE GREELEY in his futile campaign for president in 1872.

Sumner, increasingly discouraged and suffering from a heart condition, died on March 11, 1874.

Further Reading

Donald, David H. *Charles Sumner.* New York: Da Capo Press, 1996.

———. *Charles Sumner and the Coming of the Civil War.* New York: Fawcett Columbine, 1989.

Pierce, Edward L. *Memoir and Letters of Charles Sumner.* New York: Arno Press, 1969.

Sefton, James E. "Sumner, Charles." Available online. Discovery Channel School, original content provided by World Book Online. URL: http://www. discoveryschool.com/homeworkhelp/worldbook/ atozhistory/s/539300.html. Downloaded November 26, 2001.

Smith, Gene. *High Crimes and Misdemeanors: The Impeachment and Trial of Andrew Johnson.* New York: McGraw-Hill, 1985.

Storey, Moorfield. *Charles Sumner.* New York: Chelsea House, 1983.

T

Taft, William Howard
(1857–1930) *president, secretary of war, chief justice of the United States*

William Howard Taft was the only president of the United States to serve as chief justice of the United States. He might well have been remembered for many of his other very considerable accomplishments but shares the misfortune of JOHN ADAMS, JAMES MADISON, MARTIN VAN BUREN, ANDREW JOHNSON, and LYNDON BAINES JOHNSON of following immediately after a great, charismatic president. The historical memories of Taft's accomplishments have been diminished as a result. Nothing diminished his physical size, however; at 300 pounds, he was the heaviest of all presidents.

Taft was born on September 15, 1857, in Cincinnati, Ohio, into a prominent, politically active family. His father served as the U.S. secretary of war and U.S. attorney general under ULYSSES S. GRANT as well as a diplomat abroad.

Taft graduated with distinction at Yale in 1878, but he returned to the family base in Cincinnati to study law at the University of Cincinnati Law School. He graduated and was admitted to the bar in 1880. In 1881, he was appointed the assistant prosecuting attorney of Hamilton County. In 1882, he was appointed the collector of internal revenue for Cincinnati, but he quit because he could not tolerate the spoils system that required him to appoint unqualified people to jobs just because they had powerful political backers. He practiced law in Cincinnati from 1883 to 1887. He finally achieved his fondest goal—a judicial appointment—when he was named to an Ohio state court vacancy in 1887. The following year he was elected judge on his own, the only office to which he was ever elected other than president.

President BENJAMIN HARRISON named Taft the U.S. solicitor general in 1890 and two years later appointed him to the federal bench, where he established himself as a competent, impartial judge. In some cases, he even seemed sympathetic to the problems of the working man, which was progressively ahead of his time. In 1900, President WILLIAM MCKINLEY called him to chair a commission to find a way to end U.S. military rule in the Philippine Islands. Taft's excellent work led McKinley to name him the first civil governor of the Philippines in 1901. Staying until 1904, Taft's administration was an example of sound colonial administration, since he had no trace of racial prejudice. Regrettably, the U.S. military—much of it southern-dominated—had so much bigotry that the troops often could not tell the difference between African Americans and Filipinos.

Taft appreciated Filipinos, problems and granted them the widest possible degree of self-government without being foolishly blind to the extremists among the Filipino leaders. Taft also recognized that two essential steps toward independence were education and an equitable distribution of the agricultural land in the country. Since Roman Catholic friars and their orders owned nearly all the land and provided nearly all the education, neither equitable land distribution

William Howard Taft was the only president who also served as chief justice of the United States. *(Library of Congress)*

nor quality education was possible. Taft negotiated a 1903 agreement with the Vatican whereby the church lands were sold in small parcels to Filipinos, using loan funds provided by the United States, and education was improved.

After THEODORE ROOSEVELT was elevated to the presidency following McKinley's death, he wanted Taft, whom he had known as solicitor general under Harrison, back in Washington. He twice offered Taft a seat on the U.S. Supreme Court, but both times Taft declined, pleading that his work in the Philippines was not finished. When Roosevelt became desperate for a new secretary of war, he demanded Taft come to Washington with the understanding that Taft could continue to manage Philippine affairs from the United States. Although Roosevelt was impulsive and energetic and Taft was judicial and restrained, they were close personal friends and political allies. Roosevelt now saw Taft as his presidential successor and wanted

him in the cabinet. While Taft did not have military experience, he was an excellent administrator and international problem solver, acting successfully in building the Panama Canal, calming disorder in Cuba, and dampening conflicts with Japan.

This record as a number-two man made it appear that Taft would be a good president, but Taft did not really want to be president. Urged on by his wife, his family, and his presidential friend, Taft accepted the 1908 Republican nomination. Given Roosevelt's popularity and blessing, Taft easily won over the Democratic nominee, WILLIAM JENNINGS BRYAN, by a 1.2 million popular vote margin (7,600,000 to 6,400,000) and an Electoral College vote of 321–162.

Almost immediately, Taft's troubles with the Progressives began. It was not that Taft did not follow Roosevelt's polices; it was that he did not pursue those policies with Roosevelt's publicity and flair. Taft was wrongly accused of abandoning Roosevelt's legacy when, in reality, he fulfilled and exceeded it. Taft's administration prosecuted twice as many antitrust suits against big monopolies as Roosevelt's had. Taft was devoted to conservation and preserved a very responsible amount of U.S. forest land and on better legal ground than Roosevelt had. Taft did, however, fire Roosevelt's forester friend, GIFFORD PINCHOT, but Taft had grounds for doing so, since Pinchot had publicly used exaggerated or unsubstantiated charges to attack his superior, Secretary of the Interior RICHARD ACHILLES BALLINGER. Even if Taft should have found another way to resolve this personnel problem, Taft's actual record on conservation should not be judged by the Pinchot controversy alone.

Taft also angered Progressives by refusing to openly attack House Speaker JOSEPH GURNEY CANNON. But if a president attacked a congressional officer, other congressmen would have found it necessary to defend Cannon as a part of their defense of institutional integrity. Taft would have helped Cannon more by attacking him than by avoiding public comment. Taft was actually following Roosevelt's policy, because Roosevelt had not attacked Cannon either. Progressives also criticized Taft because the Payne-Aldrich Tariff Act he accepted did not lower tariff rates enough to suit them, but the same act lowered tariff rates too much to suit business conservatives. Taft actually showed the courage to tackle a problem that Roosevelt ducked. Taft, it seemed, could not solve the tariff problem better than any other president had, going back to the days of GEORGE WASHINGTON.

Taft was not recognized, one way or the other, for many other good things he did. His administration saw the creation of a separate Department of Labor, the parcel post, the postal savings system, two new states (New Mexico and Arizona), and congressional approval of the constitutional amendments making possible a federal income tax and popular election of senators. All this was accomplished even though Taft's party lost control of the House of Representatives in 1910.

After the Democrats took the House in 1910, the Progressive Republicans anticipated losing the presidency in 1912 and pressured Roosevelt to run. Apparently, ROBERT MARION LA FOLLETTE's threat to run as the nominee of a new Progressive Party was a major inducement for Roosevelt. Taft was hurt by Roosevelt's decision to run and, feeling aggrieved, fought back. He used the power he had over the party machinery to make sure Roosevelt did not take the Republican nomination away from him. Roosevelt claimed to be robbed, accepted the Progressive Party's presidential nomination, ran a vigorous campaign, and split the normal Republican vote. In the end, the people elected the Democrat THOMAS WOODROW WILSON, whom Roosevelt also despised. Wilson received only 42% of the popular vote but captured the Electoral College vote handily. Roosevelt garnered 27% of the popular vote but carried only six states. Taft won only 23% of the popular votes and carried only Utah and Vermont. The remaining popular vote went to candidates from other parties, including about 7% for the Socialist Eugene V. Debs.

Taft taught law at Yale until 1921 when President WARREN GAMALIEL HARDING nominated him as chief justice of the United States after the death of Chief Justice Edward D. White. Taft finally received the office he had long wanted and immediately served to promote harmony and efficiency on what had been a badly divided Court. Taft was an active lobbyist who fought for a new Supreme Court building, greater Court discretion over the cases that it was required to hear, and accelerating

the work of the Court. Taft suffered from a serious heart condition and retired on February 3, 1930. He died in Washington, D.C., about a month later on March 8, 1930.

Further Reading

Anderson, Donald F. *William Howard Taft: A Conservative's Conception of the Presidency.* Ithaca, N.Y.: Cornell University Press, 1973.

Anderson, Judith Icke. *William Howard Taft.* New York: Norton, 1981.

Burton, David Henry. *Taft, Holmes, and the 1920s Court: An Appraisal.* Madison, N.J.: Fairleigh Dickinson University Press, 1998.

Coletta, Paolo Enrico. *The Presidency of William Howard Taft.* Lawrence: University Press of Kansas, 1973.

Duffy, Herbert S. *William Howard Taft.* New York: Minton, Balch & Company, 1930.

Haley, P. Edward. *Revolution and Intervention: The Diplomacy of Taft and Wilson with Mexico, 1910–1917.* Cambridge, M.I.T. Press, 1970.

Kelly, Frank K. *The Fight for the White House: The Story of 1912.* New York: Crowell, 1961.

Manners, William. *TR and Will: A Friendship That Split the Republican Party.* New York: Harcourt, Brace & World, 1969.

Mason, Alpheus Thomas. *William Howard Taft: Chief Justice.* New York: Simon & Schuster, 1965.

Minger, Ralph Eldin. *William Howard Taft and United States Foreign Policy: The Apprenticeship Years, 1900–1908.* Urbana: University of Illinois Press, 1975.

Scholes, Walter V. *The Foreign Policies of the Taft Administration.* Columbia: University of Missouri Press, 1970.

"Taft, William Howard." Available online. URL: http://www.whitehouse.gov/history/presidents/wt28.html. Downloaded November 11, 2001

Wilensky, Norman M. *Conservatives in the Progressive Era: The Taft Republicans of 1912.* Gainesville: University of Florida Press, 1965.

Taney, Roger Brooke
(1777–1864) *chief justice of the United States, attorney general, secretary of the Treasury*

Roger Taney was the fifth chief justice of the United States and had a distinguished record on the Supreme Court until he wrote his opinion in the *Dred Scott* case, unleashing tremendous criticism of the Court and aggravating the slavery issue on the eve of the Civil War.

Taney was born on March 17, 1777, on his family's tobacco plantation in Calvert County, Maryland. He graduated from Dickinson College in 1795 and studied law in Annapolis, Maryland, before being admitted to the bar in 1799. Almost immediately, he was elected as a Federalist to the Maryland House of Delegates, but he served only one term before resuming his law practice. He was furious with the leadership of the Federalist Party over its opposition to the War of 1812, withdrew briefly, and then gained control of the Maryland Party and was elected to a five-year term in the state senate in 1816.

Having finished his state senate term and established a large practice, Taney moved to Baltimore in 1823. The next year he came out strongly for ANDREW JACKSON for president, abandoning the Federalists and JOHN QUINCY ADAMS. When Jackson was elected four years later, Taney became a major figure in the Democratic Party.

In 1831, Jackson decided he needed someone trustworthy and of Taney's caliber to fight the Second Bank of the United States, so he appointed Taney the attorney general of the United States. Taney, for his part, wrote much of the Jackson message that vetoed the 1832 rechartering of the bank. Jackson ordered his Treasury secretaries, first, Louis McLane and later William J. Duane, to begin withdrawing U.S. funds from the bank, but the national bank law was written so that the discretion to withdraw federal funds from the bank was solely in the hands of the Treasury secretary. In 1833, when McLane and Duane both refused to withdraw the federal funds, Jackson fired them and appointed Taney in succession, who made the withdrawals.

In 1835, Jackson then appointed Taney an associate justice of the Supreme Court. The Senate, angry with both Jackson and Taney, refused to confirm him. However, when Chief Justice JOHN MARSHALL died, the Senate's new leadership confirmed Taney as chief justice.

Over the next 20 years, Taney modified some of the Marshall Court decisions, but he essentially followed the sound direction that Marshall had set.

Had Taney died of yellow fever when his wife and daughter did some nine years before the *Dred Scott* decision, his reputation would have been that of a distinguished follower of the Marshall Court, but that did not happen. Taney was personally opposed to slavery, but his view of the U.S. Constitution was that slavery was included as a property in the text. His forlorn hope that the Court could solve a problem that neither the presidents nor Congress could solve led him down a disastrous path. The Court could easily have resolved the *Dred Scott* case without making a broad ruling on slavery since there were narrow grounds for dismissing the case. The Court could also have used the political questions doctrine to duck the issue.

Instead, the curiously divided Court issued five different opinions, but Taney's is regarded as the majority opinion. Taney reached the very broad conclusion that, among other things, no African American—born slave or born free—could become a U.S. citizen or sue in federal court. To this conclusion, Taney added that Congress had no right to restrict slavery in the territories, although states could ban slavery if they wished. This latter conclusion declared unconstitutional the Compromise of 1820. This was only the second time in the Court's history that it had invalidated a congressional enactment (the first was the minor provision invalidated in the famous *Marbury v. Madison* case) and the first time a major law was thrown out.

By throwing out the Compromise of 1820, Taney had repudiated a core belief of the Republican Party (the descendant of the Free Soilers) and should have known that a significant political force like the Republican Party would fight back. The Republicans' fight against *Dred Scott* did not destroy the party. Instead, both its membership and one of its key leaders, a hitherto unknown ABRAHAM LINCOLN, were given a tremendous boost. During the Civil War, Taney ruled against Lincoln's suspension of the writ of habeas corpus in *Ex parte Merryman* (1861), but Taney was very unpopular, and the decision did little to restrain Lincoln's conduct of the war.

Taney died on October 12, 1864.

Further Reading

Ehrlich, Walter. "Roger B. Taney" in *The Oxford Companion to the Supreme Court,* edited by Kermit L. Hall. New York: Oxford University Press, 1992.

Feller, Daniel. "Andrew Jackson" in *The American Presidents,* edited by Frank N. Magill, John L. Loos, and Tracy Irons-Georges. Pasadena, Calif.: Salem Press, 2000.

Frankfurter, Felix. *The Commerce Clause under Marshall, Taney and Waite.* Gloucester, Mass.: Peter Smith, 1978.

Hernon, Joseph Martin. *Profiles in Character: Hubris and Heroism in the U.S. Senate—1789–1990.* Armonk, N.Y.: M. E. Sharpe, 1997.

Horowitz, Morton. *The Transformation of American Law 1780–1860.* New York: Oxford University Press, 1992.

Lewis, Walker. *Without Fear or Favor: A Biography of Chief Justice Roger Brooke Taney.* Boston: Houghton Mifflin, 1965.

Newmyer, R. Kent. *The Supreme Court under Marshall and Taney.* Arlington Heights, Ill.: Harlan Davidson, 1986.

Siegel, Martin. *The Taney Court, 1837–1864.* Millwood, N.Y.: Associated Faculty Press, 1987.

Smith, Charles William. *Roger B. Taney: Jacksonian Jurist.* New York: Da Capo Press, 1973.

Swisher, Carl Brent. *Roger B. Taney.* New York: Macmillan, 1935.

Taylor, Zachary
(1784–1850) *president*

Zachary Taylor was a great nonpolitical U.S. soldier for more than 40 years. He was so nonpolitical that he had never even voted in an election before he ran for president. He was the second Whig president elected and the second president to die before the end of his term. The nation was already seriously divided by the tensions that ultimately led to the Civil War. During his 16 months as president, he was unable to demonstrate whether he could have done much to solve the situation.

Zachary Taylor was born on November 24, 1784, near Barboursville, in Orange County, Virginia, into a prominent slave-owning family with a distinguished background. One ancestor was William Brewster, who came to America on the *Mayflower.* Taylor was JAMES MADISON's second cousin, and Robert E. Lee was a distant relative.

His father had been a lieutenant in the Revolutionary War and received a war bonus of 6,000 acres near Louisville, Kentucky, where he took his family in 1785. At that time, there were no schools in Kentucky, and Taylor was tutored briefly. He essentially had only a practical education as a farmer before 1808 when at age 23 he entered the U.S. Army as a first lieutenant. In 1810, he was promoted to captain, and in 1812, he won promotion to major for his defense of Fort Harrison against an Indian attack in the War of 1812.

In 1814, although outnumbered three to one, he fought a British and Indian force to a stalemate on Credit Island in Illinois territory before retreat-

Zachary Taylor, a heroic general, resisted the Compromise of 1850 and was prepared to lead the Union forces against any states if they carried out their threat to secede, but he died, opening the way for compromise. *(Library of Congress)*

ing. In 1819, he became a lieutenant colonel. Serving in Wisconsin during the Black Hawk War, he received Chief Black Hawk's surrender in 1832. He earned his nickname, "Old Rough and Ready," and was promoted to brigadier general during his Florida campaign against the Seminole Indians, whom he defeated at Lake Okeechobee on December 25, 1837. In 1841, headquartered at Fort Smith, Arkansas, Taylor was commander of the second department of the western division of the U.S. Army.

By August 1845, he was already at the mouth of the Nueces River near Corpus Christi, Texas, with a small force of regulars while awaiting the widely expected war with Mexico. As Mexican threats grew more ominous, President JAMES KNOX POLK ordered him to advance into the disputed territory between the Nueces and Rio Grande Rivers. Taylor moved to a new supply base at Fort Texas (later Fort Brown at Brownsville, Texas).

Mexico regarded this as an invasion, crossed the Rio Grande, killed or captured all members of a small detachment, and the war was on. Taylor defeated the Mexicans in battles at Palo Alto and Resaca de la Palma. Although Taylor's forces were outnumbered, he inflicted three times as many casualties as he took. After the United States declared war on May 13, 1846, Taylor invaded Mexico and captured Matamoros and Monterrey.

With such a record of success, Taylor was the logical choice to move down Mexico's central valley and capture Mexico City. However, President Polk was worried that Taylor, believed to be a potential Whig rival, would be too successful. So Polk took most of the seasoned regular troops away from Taylor and gave them to General WINFIELD SCOTT. This exposed Taylor to a Mexican army (led by Santa Anna) of close to 20,000 troops when he was down to only 4,760 troops—only about 10% of whom were regulars. Outnumbered four or five to one, Taylor used every advantage of the rugged terrain to beat back assault after assault until he won the Battle of Buena Vista. By winning against such bad odds, Taylor became a national hero. Polk created the dangerous result he feared most when he took Taylor's best troops away from him in the first place.

The Whigs were anxious to have such a military hero as their presidential candidate. (Their only other victory had come from running WILLIAM HENRY HARRISON in 1840.) The southern Whigs were particularly keen on having a slaveholding Mississippi plantation owner as president, but all Whigs recognized Taylor's appeal. Taylor, who had never voted in any election, was reluctant to get into politics, but he finally relented. With New York's MILLARD FILLMORE as the vice presidential running mate, he defeated the Democratic nominee, Michigan's Lewis Cass, for president. Both Taylor and Cass waffled on slavery, and Taylor would not have won except that former Democratic President MARTIN VAN BUREN, taking a clear stand against the extension of slavery into the territories as the Free Soil Party nominee, took enough votes from Cass to give Taylor the victory. Van Buren did not carry any states but split the votes in enough states to make the difference. The popular vote was 1,362,101 for Taylor and 1,222,674 for Cass, with Van Buren receiving 291,616. Taylor bested Cass in the Electoral College vote of 163–127.

A religious man, Taylor refused to take the oath of office on Sunday, March 4, 1849, and this has led some scholars to assert that technically the president pro tempore of the Senate, DAVID RICE ATCHISON, was acting president on March 4, 1849, because there was no president that day.

Since Taylor served only about 16 months, his only tangible accomplishment was the 1850 Clayton-Bulwer Treaty, in which Britain and the United States agreed that any canal built across Nicaragua would be joint and have its neutrality guaranteed. But 52 years later, Republican President THEODORE ROOSEVELT found it necessary to successfully persuade the British to give up their rights under this treaty so he could arrange to build the Panama Canal.

As president, Taylor supported the Wilmot Proviso, which excluded slavery from all the territory acquired as a result of the Mexican War. He favored rapid admission of both California and New Mexico as states to the Union, so there would be no debate over the status of slavery while they were territories. This position made Taylor a "doughface" in reverse—a southern man with northern principles. ("Doughface" was a highly derogatory word used by abolitionists against northerners who were sympathetic to slavery and the South.) In fact, Taylor essentially followed the principles of his second cousin James Madison or his ideological ancestor ANDREW JACKSON, both of whom owned slaves but strongly supported the Union over slavery.

Taylor was remarkably cross-pressured on the slavery question. He owned upward of 200 slaves by the time of his death. Taylor's daughter, Sarah, married JEFFERSON DAVIS, the future president of the Confederacy, against her father's wishes. Then Sarah died just three months after the wedding, but Taylor still reconciled with Davis. And Taylor's son, Richard, served as a general in the Confederate Army.

In these troubled times, some congressmen carried firearms, and fistfights broke out among politicians. Responding to fear of civil war, Taylor, a slave owner but a Jacksonian Unionist, believed he would use force, if necessary, to stop any rebellion. Any southerner who might have been inclined to take Taylor lightly (since he was a quiet man who walked around Washington dressed so unobtrusively that he was often unrecognized) needed to remember that he never lost a battle and was not called "Old Rough and Ready" for nothing. He was the only president until ABRAHAM LINCOLN with a clear position on slavery. His death deprived the nation of an opportunity to see what a southern slave-owning president might have persuaded the South to do on the free soil issue if truly pressed.

Before the Compromise of 1850 issue could be resolved, Taylor became ill apparently from drinking tainted milk and died on July 9, 1850. Enough suspicion existed about a possible assassination by poisoning that a 1991 team of experts exhumed President Taylor's body and ran tests, but those tests indicated he died of natural causes.

Further Reading

Austerman, Wayne R. "Zachary Taylor" in *The American Presidents*, edited by Frank N. Magill, John L. Loos, and Tracy Irons-Georges. Pasadena, Calif.: Salem Press, 2000.

Bauer, K. Jack. *Zachary Taylor: Soldier, Planter, Statesman of the Old Southwest*. Baton Rouge: Louisiana State University Press, 1985.

Dyer, Brainerd. *Zachary Taylor*. New York: Barnes & Noble, 1967.

Hamilton, Holman. *Zachary Taylor*. Norwalk, Conn.: Easton Press, 1989.

Hernon, Joseph Martin. *Profiles in Character: Hubris and Heroism in the U.S. Senate—1789–1990*. Armonk, N.Y.: M. E. Sharpe, 1997.

Holt, Michael F. "Taylor, Zachary." Available online. Discovery Channel School, original content provided by World Book Online. URL: http://www.discoveryschool.com/homeworkhelp/worldbook/atozhistory/t/548740.html. Downloaded December 1, 2001.

McKinley, Silas Bent. *Old Rough and Ready: The Life and Times of Zachary Taylor*. New York: Vanguard Press, 1946.

Nichols, Edward Jay. *Zach Taylor's Little Army*. Garden City, N.Y.: Doubleday, 1963.

Smith, Elbert B. *The Presidencies of Zachary Taylor and Millard Fillmore*. Lawrence: University Press of Kansas, 1988.

"Taylor, Zachary." Available online. URL: http://www.whitehouse.gov/history/presidents/zt12.html. Downloaded November 11, 2001.

"Zachary Taylor," in *The American President*, by Philip B. Kunhardt, Jr., Philip B. Kunhardt III, and Peter W. Kunhardt. New York: Riverhead Books, 1999.

"Zachary Taylor" in *The Presidency A to Z: Second Edition*, edited by Michael T. Nelson. Washington, D.C.: Congressional Quarterly Press, 1998.

Thurmond, John Strom
(1902–) *candidate for president, senator, governor*

On May 25, 1997, Strom Thurmond became the longest serving member of the U.S. Senate and the only person to win eight consecutive senate elections—seven of them for a full term.

Born on December 5, 1902, in Edgefield, South Carolina, John Strom Thurmond graduated from Clemson in 1923. He taught school from then until 1929 when he became a superintendent of schools. He studied law and was admitted to the bar in 1930. By 1933, he had moved up to both city and county attorney, and he held these posts until he became circuit court judge and a member of the state senate.

Thurmond was awarded several medals for his service in the 82nd Airborne Division during his World War II service. He parlayed an outstanding war record into election as South Carolina's Democratic governor in 1946. In 1948, he led his state's delegation to the Democratic National Convention and was outraged by the civil rights plank HUBERT HORATIO HUMPHREY succeeded in including in the 1948 Democratic Party platform. He stormed out of the convention with several southern delegates in tow and founded the Dixiecrat Party (or States' Right Party), became their presidential nominee, and carried four southern states with a total of 39 Electoral College votes.

Out of office from 1951 to 1954, he practiced law but made a startling comeback, winning the first-ever successful campaign for the U.S. Senate as a write-in candidate. He set another record as the senator who gave the longest single Senate filibuster speech in opposition to the 1957 Civil Rights Act.

In 1964, Thurmond joined the Republican Party and carried the state for that party's presidential candidate, Senator BARRY MORRIS GOLDWATER. Thurmond was also instrumental in securing the 1968 Republican presidential nomination for RICHARD MILHOUS NIXON and supporting several conservative Republican presidential candidates.

Thurmond's long service in the Senate meant that when the Republicans retained control of the Senate in 1996, he became the chairman of the Senate Armed Services Committee and the president pro tempore of the Senate—the third in succession to the presidency. His advanced age did attract concern within the ranks of Senate Republicans. When the Republicans took control of the Senate from the Democrats in 1994, there was some talk about whether Thurmond was up to the task of managing a major committee, but Thurmond responded to this challenge so quickly and vigorously that the Republicans felt compelled to follow the seniority system strictly and allow him to take the chairmanship.

As chair, he showed his continued vigor by criticizing President WILLIAM JEFFERSON CLINTON's defense budget and his willingness to send U.S. troops on unnecessary peacekeeping missions around the world without adequate preparation. By

1999, Thurmond recognized his increasing frailty and yielded his chairmanship to Republican Senator John Warner of Virginia. He retained the largely honorary post of president pro tempore of the Senate (although he rarely took the chair) until the Democrats retook control of the Senate in 2001. Although Thurmond was not working for a ninth consecutive Senate election in 2002, he had one more landmark ahead of him. In 2002, he was hospitalized frequently and is often escorted carefully to the Senate chamber and his office, but he still attends Senate business. If he lives to the end of his current term, he will be the only sitting senator to ever be 100 years old.

Further Reading

Bass, Jack. *Ol' Strom: An Unauthorized Biography of Strom Thurmond.* Atlanta, Ga.: Longstreet, 1998.

Cohodas, Nadine. *Strom Thurmond and the Politics of Southern Change.* Macon, Ga.: Mercer University Press, 1994.

Ellers, Joseph C. *Strom Thurmond: The Public Man.* Orangeburg, S.C.: Sandlapper Publishing, 1993.

Lachicotte, Alberta Morel. *Rebel Senator: Strom Thurmond of South Carolina.* New York: Devin-Adair, 1967.

Tilden, Samuel Jones
(1814–1886) *candidate for president, governor*

Samuel Jones Tilden lost one of the most controversial presidential elections in U.S. history when RUTHERFORD BIRCHARD HAYES defeated him in 1876. He was also one of the leading reformers of the Democratic Party in the second half of the 19th century and an outstanding New York governor.

Tilden was born on February 9, 1814, in New Lebanon, New York. Frequently ill while a student, he studied at Yale briefly but attended New York University from which he graduated. He became a very successful corporate lawyer after being admitted to the bar in 1841. As a strong ANDREW JACKSON supporter, he backed JAMES KNOX POLK in 1844. Known as a "barnburner" because of his opposition to the expansion of slavery, he was a delegate to the 1848 Free Soil Convention, but he did not abandon the Democratic Party for the Republican Party as it became popular in the 1850s.

He was not active politically during the Civil War but opposed ABRAHAM LINCOLN and rallied to ANDREW JOHNSON's moderate Reconstruction program. By 1866, he had become active in New York state politics, chairing the state Democratic committee from 1866 to 1874. His credentials as a reformer were cemented by his successful campaign to destroy the influence of the infamously corrupt Tweed Ring (headed by William Marcy Tweed) and reforming state government. Elected as a reform Democrat in 1874, he further improved state government and destroyed the corrupt Canal Ring that misappropriated funds intended for canal construction.

The success of these reforms led to his nomination as the Democratic candidate to oppose Rutherford B. Hayes in 1876. Hayes had a reputation for personal honesty, but he passively allowed others to campaign for him, and this was particularly vicious in the South where charges of irregularities dogged both Republican and Democratic campaigns. The Democrats charged that the U.S. military still stationed at various places in southern states under military Reconstruction were improperly helping African Americans to vote. Republicans retorted that this was necessary to stop the Ku Klux Klan and other white supremacy groups from using force to stop African Americans from voting. The officially reported popular vote results favored Tilden over Hayes by 4,288,000 to 4,034,000, but the results from four southern states were contested.

If the electoral votes from those four states were thrown out entirely on grounds that they were irredeemably tainted by one side or the other or both, Tilden led Hayes 184–165 and would have won the presidency in both the popular and Electoral College votes. However, if none of the contested state votes were thrown out, then Tilden only needed to win one of the four states to be elected president. Hayes could only win in the unlikely event that all of the contested state votes were given to him, and then he would win the presidency by only one Electoral College vote—185–184.

However unlikely that it might seem that the Republican Party leaders would try to reverse the outcome in all four states so that Hayes could win

by one Electoral College vote, that is exactly what they set out to do—and they succeeded. The three major states, Louisiana, Florida, and South Carolina, were sure to vote Democratic if the clear majority white voters had their way, even if all the African Americans were allowed to vote unimpeded, because African Americans were in a minority. However, the existing counting or "returns" boards were still controlled by Reconstruction Republicans. Believing that these Republicans would follow their partisan advantage, the Republican Party's national chairman, Zack Chandler, audaciously announced that Hayes won by a single Electoral College vote and then made his wish come true.

Republican party operatives sought out affidavits charging Democrats with fraud in several counties (or parishes in the case of Louisiana), and the Republican-controlled counting boards accepted these affidavits at face value and threw out the votes in counties that voted Democratic until enough Democratic votes had been discarded so that Hayes was the winner. Alleging fraud, the minority Democrats on the counting boards sent in returns showing that Tilden was the winner.

Congress then was forced to decide which set of "official" returns should be accepted. The Democrats controlled the House and the Republicans controlled the Senate. The two houses deadlocked on which set of returns should be accepted. Thus, if the Democrats stood firm, all the returns from the contested states would have to be eliminated and Tilden would have won 184–165 in the Electoral College. He was, of course, the popular vote winner by a wide margin.

Touting the "virtues" of compromise, some Democrats joined the Republicans in voting for a "bipartisan" electoral commission to conduct an "impartial" investigation. Five members were chosen from each house and five more from the Supreme Court. The Republican Senate picked three Republicans and two Democrats; the Democratic House picked three Democrats and two Republicans. The Supreme Court picked two Democrats and two Republicans and a final crucial member, David Davis—the only Supreme Court justice thought to be an independent.

This commission might have produced an impartial result, except that the Illinois legislature elected Davis to the U.S. Senate, and he resigned from the Court and withdrew from the commission. Seeking a replacement, the Supreme Court picked Joseph P. Bradley, a Republican but the member thought to be the most fair-minded. Bradley may indeed have been the most impartial Republican that could be found, but he was a Republican. The issue dragged on until just a few days before the inauguration in March 1877 when Bradley received a late night visit from an important Republican. This meeting apparently helped Bradley make up his mind, and he ended up voting a straight party line. All contested cases, no matter what the diverse facts may have been, were decided in favor of Hayes.

The matter still required the confirmation of Congress, and the Democrats still controlled the House and could use the filibuster in the Senate. Again, had the Democrats stood firm, Tilden would have won. The Democrats delayed for a long time, but eventually the pressure was on many Democrats to accept the commission's findings because they had voted for the commission in the beginning. Believing that they would lose if the issue dragged out past the scheduled inauguration, they finally yielded and accepted a face-saving compromise. The Democrats would drop their objections to the commission's findings for Hayes if Hayes would agree to end military Reconstruction in the South, appoint a Democrat to his cabinet, and agree to subsidies for a southern transcontinental railway. Representatives for Hayes agreed to these terms as long as the southerners promised not to punish the southern Republicans unduly and to treat African Americans fairly. Several parts of this compromise were clearly not enforceable. The only real certainty was that Hayes would be president.

Having won the popular vote and arguably the Electoral College vote in the 1876 presidential campaign but still denied the presidency because of the actions of members of both parties, Tilden had reason to be unhappy with many members of his own party as well as the Republicans. He declined to run for president again in either 1880 or 1884.

A wealthy man, he lived comfortably in retirement. He left more than $3 million dollars for the construction of the New York Public Library upon his death on August 4, 1886.

Further Reading

Flick, Alexander Clarence. *Samuel Jones Tilden: A Study in Political Sagacity.* Westport, Conn.: Greenwood, 1973.

Hernon, Joseph Martin. *Profiles in Character: Hubris and Heroism in the U.S. Senate—1789–1990.* Armonk, N.Y.: M. E. Sharpe, 1997.

"Rutherford B. Hayes" in *The American President,* by Philip B. Kunhardt, Jr., Philip B. Kunhardt III, and Peter W. Kunhardt. New York: Riverhead Books, 1999.

"Samuel J. Tilden" in *The Presidency A to Z: Second Edition,* edited by Michael T. Nelson. Washington, D.C.: Congressional Quarterly Press, 1998.

Seip, Terry. "Rutherford B. Hayes" in *The American Presidents,* edited by Frank N. Magill, John L. Loos, and Tracy Irons-Georges. Pasadena, Calif.: Salem Press, 2000.

Severn, Bill. *Samuel J. Tilden and the Stolen Election.* New York: I. Washburn, 1968.

Tilden, Samuel J. *Letters and Literary Memorials of Samuel J. Tilden.* New York: Harper, 1908.

———. *The Writings and Speeches of Samuel J. Tilden.* New York: Harper & Brothers, 1885.

Truman, Harry S.

(1884–1972) *president, vice president, senator, county judge, author*

Harry S. Truman served as president at a critical period in U.S. history. He was elevated to the presidency upon the death of FRANKLIN DELANO ROOSEVELT and suffered in the popularity polls by comparison with his illustrious predecessor. Often unpopular while in office (only 25% of the people thought he was doing a good job in 1952), his reputation as a great president developed after he left office as people came to appreciate his responses to the crises of the times.

Truman was born on May 8, 1884, in Lamar, Missouri, into a modest farm family. He was never given a middle name because his parents could not decide which of his two grandfathers he should have been named after. The initial "S" was intended to give each an opportunity to claim Truman was his namesake. Six years after his birth, his family moved to Independence, Missouri. His nearsightedness necessitated thick glasses that kept him out of many normal boyhood activities but made him an avid reader and a good student in high school.

Although he did go to a business school briefly after high school, his family was too poor to permit him going to college, and his eyesight was too poor to allow him to go to West Point. Before World War I, Truman worked in the mailroom of a newspaper, as a clerk and bookkeeper at two different banks, as a timekeeper for a construction crew on a railroad, and as a farmer. He also became active in the Masons and the local Democratic Party.

Truman, working through the Missouri National Guard, helped organize Battery D of the 129th Field Artillery, 35th Division, American Expeditionary Force, and became its captain in France. His unit not only fought in some of the most bitter fighting, but he also showed heroic leadership in battle. Returning home, he joined the army reserve and eventually rose to the level of colonel. He also married his childhood sweetheart and opened a business with a friend. The business failed, and Truman spent the next 15 years paying off those debts, but he finally did so.

"Big Tom" Pendergast, Democratic Party boss of Kansas City, had a nephew who had met and admired Truman during the war and who recommended Truman to his uncle. In 1922, Pendergast supported Truman in his election as county judge of the Jackson County (Missouri) Court. While Truman failed to win reelection in 1924, he was returned to office in 1926 and stayed in the office until 1934, when Pendergast successfully supported Truman, who ran as a New Deal Democrat for election to the U.S. Senate. Truman worked hard in the Senate on the Interstate Commerce Committee and helped enact the 1938 Civil Aeronautics Act and the 1940 Transportation Act.

In spite of his own success, Truman was almost defeated because Pendergast had been convicted and imprisoned for income tax evasion. Truman was blamed for his ties with Pendergast even though he had not participated in anything illegal. In his second term, Truman sponsored a number of Senate investigations and chaired the Special Committee to Investigate the National Defense Program. He promoted economy and effi-

Harry S. Truman served as president at a critical period in U.S. history and formulated the essential foreign policy principles for the United States during the cold war. *(Library of Congress)*

ciency among defense contractors, saved the taxpayers billions of dollars, and brought himself national attention.

As a strong supporter of Roosevelt, as a friend to all Democratic Party factions, and as a border state Democrat, Truman became a compromise candidate for vice president when the party leadership forced Roosevelt to drop Henry A. Wallace in 1944. The Roosevelt-Truman ticket comfortably defeated the Republican presidential nominee, THOMAS EDMUND DEWEY, in the 1940 general election. With a scant 83 days from the inauguration until Roosevelt's death on April 12, 1945, Truman had little preparation for the presidency. He had to learn as the problems of the office pressed in upon him, and events moved swiftly.

Less than two weeks after Truman took office, the first United Nations conference met in San

Francisco. About three weeks later, Germany surrendered. Less than three months later, in July, Truman went to Potsdam, Germany, to confer with the British leader, Winston Churchill, and the Russian leader, Joseph Stalin. While in Potsdam, the president received the secret message that U.S. scientists had successfully tested the first atomic bomb. Truman informed Stalin, but only very indirectly. Without waiting to return to Washington for any further consultation on the matter, he ordered its use against Japan. Less than four months after taking office, Truman's most momentous decision to drop the first two atomic bombs in a conflict had been completed. On August 14, four months and two days after he had taken office, Japan agreed to end the war.

Critics of Truman for authorizing the use of the atomic bomb on Japan often fail to consider the very compressed time frame in which he operated in making the decision. Truman was apparently much influenced by his old Senate friend JAMES FRANCIS BYRNES, who quite clearly thought that dropping the bomb would not only end the war with Japan but would allow the United States to threaten the Soviet Union into a more cooperative posture on a whole range of issues. On the hopes for influencing the Russians, Byrnes was mistaken, for the Soviets hardened their attitude under the threat. Tensions in U.S.-Soviet relations were likely in any case, and the threat made them a reality. Given the shortness of time, the rapidity with which events unfolded, and Truman's lack of preparedness for the presidency, it was unlikely that he would turn his back on a trusted Senate colleague like Byrnes in favor of any other advisers he inherited from Roosevelt—many of whom he did not know well. In time, Truman came to see serious flaws in Byrnes and replaced him as secretary of state, but the bomb had been dropped long before then.

The flow of military operations brought the Russians deep into Central Europe where their interests sharply clashed with those of the United States and Great Britain. Some conservatives argued that Roosevelt and Truman "gave" Central and Eastern Europe away. But, in fact, the Soviets were probably so entrenched that Central European countries could not resist Russian penetration no matter how creative the U.S. diplomacy

was or how kindhearted it appeared to be. Many liberals argued that Truman's diplomacy failed because any U.S. diplomacy was likely to fail.

Time was short, events moved fast, and Truman did what he could. In essence, he formulated the containment policy that undergirded U.S. foreign policy for the next 45 years. The rigid boundaries in Europe meant Truman could do little there, although he successfully resisted Soviet pressure with the Berlin Airlift when the Soviets sought to force the Western powers out of the divided city of Berlin. Truman enunciated the 1947 Truman Doctrine, which set out a containment policy against Soviet advances, and he sponsored the Marshall Plan for rebuilding Western Europe to limit the ability of the Soviets to undermine governments in areas their armies did not occupy.

By the spring of 1949, Truman had pushed for the development of the North Atlantic Treaty Organization (NATO), a regional organization so successful it survived the end of the cold war and the destruction of the communist Soviet Union that motivated its creation. In 1950, Truman pushed through the Four Point program and the Mutual Security Administration in 1951. Taken together, these policies sponsored by Truman and his secretary of state, DEAN GOODERHAM ACHESON, were the basis of post–World War II foreign policy. The changes made by subsequent administrations were comparatively minor modifications to the essential structure devised by the Truman administration. The Truman policies made a difference in the diplomatic outcomes in Southern Europe (Greece and Turkey) and Western Europe (France, Germany, and Italy). The Russians essentially gained nothing in Europe that they had not acquired by the flow of World War II military operations.

Truman is also criticized for excessive partisanship, but he played a significant role, as did Michigan's Republican Senator ARTHUR HENDRICK VANDENBERG, in developing a bipartisan foreign policy. Though far from perfect, that policy replaced the disastrous isolationist-internationalist debate of the pre–World War II era.

Truman was far less successful in domestic policy, both because international issues were so paramount and because the reformist impetus of the Great Depression was absent. Truman did set a reform agenda that lasted for years, and some parts of it were still on the table at the end of the 20th century. Truman could not pass much of this agenda simply because the votes were not there. To be sure, Roosevelt might have done better, but even Roosevelt had made very little progress after 1936.

Nowhere was Truman's courage in setting the national agenda clearer than in the case of the rights of African Americans. Truman had to rely chiefly on executive action in desegregating the armed forces and using the White House as a "bully pulpit" on the issue. Truman failed to pass laws assuring equal employment opportunities, ending poll taxes, stopping lynchings, and desegregating public transportation. Nearly all southerners opposed him, and southern senators filibustered effectively against his legislative proposals. Nonetheless, Truman tried when Roosevelt had been afraid even to present the key questions for debate.

The best evidence that Truman accomplished all that was reasonable came from the result of the 1948 election. The Republicans were due to win that election after 16 years out of the White House. They would have been equally likely to win even if Roosevelt had lived to the end of his fourth term, for then there would have been no incumbent in the White House. The early 1948 polls showed the Republican prospective nominee winning by a landslide, and a Republican lead continued until the major pollsters stopped polling in early October.

The reasonably progressive New York Governor Thomas E. Dewey and the outstanding California Governor EARL WARREN led the confident, united Republicans. Worse, both the left and right wings of his own Democratic party had deserted Truman. The left wing, under the banner of the Progressive Party, had nominated the former Roosevelt vice president, Henry A. Wallace, and left the party before the Democrats even met in convention. Truman, courageously standing for the civil rights plank introduced by HUBERT HORATIO HUMPHREY, had provoked JOHN STROM THURMOND to lead most of the southern delegates out the door.

Truman did not quit. He traveled 31,000 miles and made 350 speeches, often off the cuff, trying simply to persuade the members of the Roosevelt coalition to stick with him to protect the programs that had helped them. Although the support for Truman apparently did not develop until late October or early November, after the pollsters stopped polling, it did come. He upset Dewey by 24,105,000 to 21,970,000 popular votes and gained 303 Electoral College votes to Dewey's 189.

Truman's second term was dominated by foreign policy concerns arising principally in Asia, an area that the United States had usually considered secondary to Europe. Truman first tried to settle peacefully the Chinese civil war between Chiang Kai-shek's Nationalists and Mao Zedong's Communists, but the situation was so favorable for Mao Zedong that he pushed Chiang's forces onto the Chinese island of Formosa (later referred to as Taiwan). In the momentum of the Chinese Communist victory, the North Koreans, with Russian approval, sought to unify the divided Korean peninsula under their control. The members of Congress, as well as President Truman, bear responsibility for believing that the atomic bomb could be used to threaten Communists in Asia into cooperating and that an adequate conventional army was unnecessary. Clearly, North Korea saw the U.S. weakness and invaded the South on June 25, 1950. Truman reacted decisively, obtained United Nations (UN) support (because the Soviet Union was temporarily boycotting the UN Security Council), resisted North Korean advances, retook the South Korean areas, and pushed on so that UN forces controlled most of the peninsula.

At this point, overly aggressive statements by the U.S. (and UN) commander, General Douglas MacArthur, led to Chinese fears of invasion and a Chinese counterattack that forced the U.S.-led forces back to the middle of the peninsula. Truman had acted with tacit congressional support but without specific congressional authorization, so he sought to carry the war on his own authority as commander in chief. When MacArthur continued to press for a wider war, publicly in defiance of Truman's orders, Truman fired him, unleashing tremendous criticism. All this controversy obscured the real accomplishment that the Communists had been contained without unleashing a nuclear war.

Other policies in Asia fell in line with Korean policy. The United States extended its protection to the Nationalist forces on Formosa, increased aid to the French fighting their colonial war in Southeast Asia, and signed a Japanese peace treaty and an alliance with Japan. Conventional military forces were now dramatically increased in size, cost, and sophistication.

Domestically, not only were new progressive steps now on hold, but also the Truman administration faced the attacks from Wisconsin Republican Senator JOSEPH RAYMOND MCCARTHY, who began a campaign of unsubstantiated charges of Communist spies and supporters in high places in the Democratic administration. Truman tried, but failed, to put much of a damper on the discontent these attacks caused.

Although constitutionally able to run for another term (since the recently passed Twenty-second Amendment's two-term limit did not apply to the current White House occupant), Truman decided he could not win and endorsed Illinois Governor ADLAI EWING STEVENSON as his successor. Stevenson lost to the Republican presidential nominee, DWIGHT DAVID EISENHOWER, in 1952.

Truman retired to Missouri, where he published his memoirs in 1956 and 1957. He lived in reasonably good health for nearly 20 years until shortly before his death on December 26, 1972.

Further Reading

De Luna, Phyllis Komarek. *Public versus Private Power during the Truman Administration*. New York: Peter Lang, 1997.

Donaldson, Gary. *Truman Defeats Dewey*. Lexington: University Press of Kentucky, 1999.

Donovan, Robert J. *Conflict and Crisis: The Presidency of Harry S. Truman, 1945–1948*. New York: Norton, 1977. Reprint Columbia: University of Missouri Press, 1996.

———. *Tumultuous Years: The Presidency of Harry S. Truman, 1949–1953*. Columbia: University of Missouri Press, 1996.

Feinberg, Barbara S. *Harry S. Truman*. New York: Franklin Watts, 1994.

Ferrell, Robert H. *Choosing Truman: The Democratic Convention of 1944*. Columbia: University of Missouri Press, 1994.

———. *Truman and Pendergast*. Columbia: University of Missouri Press, 1999.

Gullan, Harold I. *The Upset That Wasn't: Harry S. Truman and the Crucial Election of 1948*. Chicago: Ivan R. Dee, 1998.

Hamby, Alonzo L. *Man of the People: A Life of Harry S. Truman*. New York: Oxford University Press, 1995.

Hogan, Michael J. *A Cross of Iron: Harry S. Truman and the Origins of the National Security State, 1945–1954*. New York: Cambridge University Press, 1998.

Karabell, Zachary. *The Last Campaign: How Harry Truman Won the 1948 Election*. New York: Knopf, 2000.

Kelly, Frank K. *Harry Truman and the Human Family*. Santa Barbara, Calif.: Capra Press, 1998.

McCullough, David G. *Truman*. Norwalk, Conn.: Easton Press, 1994.

Moskin, J. Robert. *Mr. Truman's War: The Final Victories of World War II and the Birth of the Postwar World*. New York: Random House, 1996.

Pierpaoli, Paul G. *Truman and Korea: The Political Culture of the Early Cold War*. Columbia: University of Missouri Press, 1999.

Savage, Sean J. *Truman and the Democratic Party*. Lexington: University Press of Kentucky, 1997.

"Truman, Harry S." Available online. URL: http://www.whitehouse.gov/history/presidents/ht33.html. Downloaded November 11, 2001.

Truman, Harry S. *Memoirs: Two Volumes*. Garden City, N.Y.: Doubleday, 1955–1956.

Underhill, Robert. *FDR and Harry: Unparalleled Lives*. Westport, Conn.: Praeger, 1996.

Wainstock, Dennis. *The Decision to Drop the Atomic Bomb*. Westport, Conn.: Praeger, 1996.

———. *Truman, Macarthur, and the Korean War*. Westport, Conn.: Greenwood Press, 1999.

Walker, J. Samuel. *Prompt and Utter Destruction: Truman and the Use of Atomic Bombs against Japan*. Chapel Hill: University of North Carolina Press, 1997.

Tyler, John

(1790–1862) *president, vice president, senator, representative, Confederate leader*

John Tyler was the first vice president to succeed to the presidency upon the death of a president (WILLIAM HENRY HARRISON), and his decisive actions created the precedents that governed such transfers until the passage of the Twenty-fifth Amendment in the 1960s. He was the only president to be expelled from the party that elected him while he was still in office and the first president against whom members of his own party began impeachment proceedings. In all this partisan turmoil, he vetoed nearly all important legislation passed during his term and was the first president to have a veto overridden by a two-thirds vote in both houses of Congress. A widower, he was the first president to be married in the White House. Tyler was the only U.S. president to support the secession of the South during the Civil War and be elected to the legislature of a Confederate state.

John Tyler was born on March 29, 1790, at his family's tidewater tobacco plantation, Greenway estate, in Charles City County, Virginia. He was part of a politically prominent family, as his father served intermittently as a judge, as Speaker of the Virginia House of Delegates, and as governor. At age 12, Tyler entered the College of William and Mary where he graduated at the age of 17 in 1807. He studied law under his father's direction and was admitted to the bar in 1809. In 1811, he was elected to the Virginia House of Delegates when he was only 21, but he left the legislature to enter the army as a captain in the War of 1812. He saw no action in the war and went back to the legislature after about a month.

In 1816, Tyler was elected to a vacant seat in the U.S. House of Representatives and then won a full term. As a Virginian follower of THOMAS JEFFERSON, Tyler fought for a strict interpretation of the U.S. Constitution. He opposed Kentucky Representative HENRY CLAY's "American System" because it spent federal money and established a national bank without specific constitutional authorization and, worse, required high tariffs to generate the money to disperse. In 1821, Tyler resigned from the Congress because he was ill. As he recovered, he served as chancellor of the College of William and Mary for a short time and then was elected governor of Virginia in 1825. He served in that role until the legislature elected him to the U.S. Senate in 1827.

Although he opposed nullification, his strict constructionist views led him to oppose Democratic President ANDREW JACKSON, who acted against South Carolina's attempt to nullify acts of Congress. Tyler, more a Jeffersonian than a Jacksonian, be-

came increasingly opposed to Jackson. When the Virginia legislature ordered Tyler to vote for the removal of a vote that formally condemned Jackson in 1836, Tyler resigned from the Senate rather than comply. This raised Tyler's prestige in the eyes of Jackson's diverse opponents, now increasingly called Whigs. At that time, the Whig Party was only a loose coalition of groups with no common policy and many contradictory points of view.

In 1836, the Whigs experimented with a strategy of encouraging a number of sectional leaders to run for president and vice president, hoping no one would received a majority and the election—in keeping with the rules of time—would be decided in the House of Representatives (for president) and in the Senate (for vice president). This unlikely ploy failed in the presidential race, and MARTIN VAN BUREN won a clear victory in the Electoral College for president. But the vice presidential contest did not produce an Electoral College vote majority, and the contest was decided by the Senate—for the first and only time in U.S. history. Kentucky's Richard M. Johnson won, but Tyler, one of the Whig vice presidential candidates, carried four Southern states, although not his home state of Virginia.

In 1840, to balance the ticket with a southerner, the Whigs chose Tyler as the vice presidential running mate of Indiana's William Henry Harrison. Tyler accepted the nomination only because he apparently believed that the Whigs had dropped their fight for a national bank, protective tariffs, and the "American Plan," and Tyler was still strongly opposed to these measures. The Whigs, shouting their slogan "Tippecanoe and Tyler too!" elected the Harrison-Tyler ticket by a huge Electoral College majority. The oldest man ever elected president, Harrison died one month after his inauguration.

The Whig cabinet members apparently thought they would continue to run the government after Harrison's death and that Tyler would be only an "acting" president. However, Tyler insisted on taking the same oath of office that the president took and then assumed the office in full. While some initially sought to belittle him, the cabinet agreed in the end, and both houses of Congress passed resolutions saying that Tyler was president.

This agreement did not end the conflict. When Congress sent Tyler a bill creating a new national bank, he vetoed it. During the commotion that followed, Clay argued that Tyler, although president, should follow the wishes of his cabinet and congressional majorities or resign. Clay would not have made this appeal to any duly elected president, and it was obviously an attempt to keep Tyler in a diminutive "acting" president posture.

Clay used words, but the Whigs inspired armed mobs who surrounded the White House and threatened to do much worse. Hurling both insults and stones at the windows, they raged on until Tyler gave out guns to the servants to protect the White House. When the mob recognized Tyler would stand firm, they left. The Whigs in Congress responded with another banking bill that Tyler also vetoed, saying it was as abusive as a private banking monopoly.

John Tyler was the first vice president to become president upon the death of an elected president. *(Library of Congress)*

Thinking they could force him out, Tyler's entire cabinet resigned except for DANIEL WEBSTER, who was negotiating with the British over the northern boundary of Maine. Clay also resigned from the Senate. Tyler apparently anticipated such an action because he was ready with new cabinet appointments within two days. When the Senate approved Tyler's cabinet choices, the Whigs also declared that Tyler was no longer a Whig, since they said he was trying to create a new party. The Whigs then began to send Tyler bills that they knew he would veto in an effort to make him look bad. Tyler vetoed them anyway, giving him a larger number of vetoes than those cast by President Andrew Jackson. Along the way, Tyler maneuvered the Senate into splitting a bill that contained both a mildly protective tariff and the distribution bill. Tyler accepted the tariff but pocket vetoed the distribution bill.

In March 1842, the House adopted a resolution condemning him for offenses they thought justified impeachment, and Tyler responded, as Jackson had, with a protest message. In January 1843, the House introduced a formal impeachment bill, but the charges were so exaggerated that some Whigs even joined the Democrats to defeat the move by a vote of 127–83.

In the 1842 congressional elections, the Whigs had lost control of the legislature. Tyler took this as a sign that the people were with him and persevered with his actions. In international affairs, he was quite successful. In 1842, Tyler ended the Seminole Indian War in Florida. That same year, Tyler superintended the resolution with the United Kingdom of the Maine-Canada boundary, which was settled by the Webster-Ashburton Treaty, essentially on terms negotiated by Webster, who had remained secretary of state for this purpose. The United States also signed an 1844 agreement with China, opening China to American commerce for the first time.

In 1836, Texas had declared its independence from Mexico and had petitioned to join the Union, but the issue was still unresolved by the second half of Tyler's term. Tyler, like most southerners, favored annexation, but northern congressmen opposed annexation because Texas would have added another slave state to the Union. Tyler sent the

Senate a treaty admitting Texas, but the Senate, needing two-thirds affirmative votes, rejected it. Tyler then proposed admitting Texas by joint congressional resolution. Congress did not approve this joint resolution until after JAMES KNOX POLK's 1844 election, but before his inauguration, thinking that Polk would sign it. However, Tyler signed it on March 1, 1845, taking this honor from Polk. Two days later, on Tyler's last full day in office, he signed a bill admitting Florida to the Union. Texas, however, formally joined the Union on December 29, 1845, several months after Tyler had left office.

Tyler's first wife was ill at the time of his elevation to the presidency, and she died during his term. In 1844, Tyler was on board the USS *Princeton* to review the firing of a new naval cannon. The gun exploded, killing eight people, including David Gardiner, a former New York state senator, whose daughter Julia was among the guests in the presidential party. The tragedy apparently brought Tyler and Julia closer together, and they were married quietly in New York City on June 26, 1844, the first time a president was married while in office.

Tyler wanted to run for president again, but he knew a Whig nomination was out of the question and the Democratic nomination was remote. He had maneuvered both the leading Whig and Democrat candidates, Clay and Van Buren, respectively, into an unfavorable position on the Texas annexation. He recognized that a candidate forthrightly for immediate Texas annexation would win. Tyler even toyed with the idea of running as an independent and trying to throw the election into the House of Representatives, but he dropped this idea when Polk, a strong proponent of Texas annexation, won the Democratic nomination. As Tyler predicted, Polk defeated Clay.

On the outs with both Whigs and Democrats, Tyler retired to his Virginia estate and lived quietly until just before the Civil War. In February 1861, he headed a Southern peace mission to Washington, seeking a compromise in the secession crisis, but Congress rejected the southerners' proposals. Tyler then went to the Virginia secession convention, voted in favor of Virginia leaving the Union,

and won election to the Confederate House of Representatives in November 1861. Tyler was the only U.S. president to join the Confederacy. He died on January 18, 1862, before joining the Confederate legislature.

Further Reading

Chidsey, Donald Barr. *And Tyler Too.* Nashville, Tenn.: T. Nelson, 1978.

Chitwood, Oliver P. *John Tyler: Champion of the Old South.* New York: Russell & Russell, 1964.

Fickle, James C. "John Tyler" in *The American Presidents,* edited by Frank N. Magill, John L. Loos, and Tracy Irons-Georges. Pasadena, Calif.: Salem Press, 2000.

Fraser, Hugh Russell. *Democracy in the Making: The Jackson-Tyler Era.* New York: Bobbs-Merrill, 1969.

Hernon, Joseph Martin. *Profiles in Character: Hubris and Heroism in the U.S. Senate—1789–1990.* Armonk, N.Y.: M. E. Sharpe, 1997.

"John Tyler" in *The Presidency A to Z: Second Edition,* edited by Michael T. Nelson. Washington, D.C.: Congressional Quarterly Press, 1998.

Merk, Frederick. *Fruits of Propaganda in the Tyler Administration.* Cambridge, Mass.: Harvard University Press, 1971.

Morgan, Robert J. *A Whig Embattled: The Presidency under John Tyler.* Hamden, Conn.: Archon Books, 1974.

Peterson, Norma Lois. *The Presidencies of William Henry Harrison and John Tyler.* Lawrence: University Press of Kansas, 1989.

Seager, Robert. *And Tyler Too: A Biography of John and Julia Gardiner Tyler.* Norwalk, Conn.: Easton Press, 1989.

"Tyler, John." Available online. URL: http://www.whitehouse.gov/history/presidents/jt10.html. Downloaded November 2001.

"Tyler, John" in *The American President,* by Philip B. Kunhardt, Jr., Philip B. Kunhardt III, and Peter W. Kunhardt. New York: Riverhead Books, 1999.

Tyler, Lyon Gardiner. *John Tyler and Abraham Lincoln: Who Was the Dwarf?* Richmond, Va.: Richmond Press, Inc., Printers, 1929.

———. *The Letters and Times of the Tylers.* New York: Da Capo Press, 1970.

Van Buren, Martin

(1782–1862) *president, vice president, secretary of state, senator, governor, author*

Martin Van Buren, ANDREW JACKSON's first secretary of state and second vice president, was Jackson's key adviser and an early creator of the modern political machine. Elected in his own right in 1836, he was the first president to face a major economic depression, and his failure to solve it led to his defeat in 1840.

Martin Van Buren was born on December 5, 1782, in Kinderhook, New York, a Dutch settlement. He attended the local school and began to study law with a local attorney when he was 14 years of age. In 1801, Van Buren continued his studies in New York City, was admitted to the bar in 1803, and went into practice with his half brother.

Politically, he was a Jeffersonian and won election to the New York Senate in 1812. Reelected in 1816, Van Buren was shortly thereafter appointed New York's attorney general and began to create the first modern political machine known as the Albany Regency. However, New York Democrats were divided into the supporters of DEWITT CLINTON and his opponents, known as the Bucktails. As a Bucktail leader, Van Buren was removed as attorney general in 1819. Van Buren fought back, successfully supporting an independent Federalist for the U.S. Senate in 1820 against a Clinton nominee.

Van Buren then became the front-runner for the next vacancy, which occurred in 1821. Taking office in December 5, 1821, Van Buren led the fight against imprisonment for debt and finally succeeded in outlawing such penalties in 1828. He also opposed slavery but did not succeed in his early bills to block the further spread of slavery. Reelected in 1827, he supported the joining of the Albany Regency with the Richmond Junto, a typical Democratic Party alliance. The alliance backed Andrew Jackson, who won the presidency in 1828, while Van Buren became the successful Democratic nominee for New York's governor.

Resigning the Senate to be inaugurated governor, Van Buren served only two months before President Jackson named him U.S. secretary of state. Van Buren successfully sought damages for American shippers from French and Danish naval ships during the Napoleonic Wars, and he reopened trade with the British West Indies. More important, Van Buren, despite very great differences in personality, became Jackson's closest political adviser.

Van Buren shrewdly displaced JOHN CALDWELL CALHOUN in Jackson's favor, in part because, as a widower, he could easily avoid the domestic problems other married politicians (including Calhoun) had over the Peggy Eaton affair (when Jackson defended Peggy Eaton, the wife of his secretary of war). Eventually, Jackson, to get rid of those he did not want, was forced to replace his entire cabinet including Van Buren, but he promised to appoint Van Buren the U.S. minister to Britain.

The Senate tied on confirming Van Buren's appointment to Great Britain, and Vice President Calhoun cast the tiebreaking vote against Van

Buren. Jackson took Calhoun and the Senate vote as a personal insult, supported Van Buren's nomination to the vice presidency, and made it clear that Van Buren was to be the next president. Van Buren's opponents thought they had destroyed his career. In reality, by making him a victim, they guaranteed his appointment as vice president and ultimate election as president.

Jackson and Van Buren won the 1832 election easily and even increased their party's congressional majority in 1834 (the only time that a party in the White House increased its congressional majority in the sixth year of a presidency until WILLIAM JEFFERSON CLINTON repeated the feat in 1998). After the election, Vice President Van Buren opposed the Bank of the United States but only reluctantly backed Jackson's decision to withdraw federal deposits from the national bank. He feared this action would split the party and cause an economic downturn, as it eventually did in Van Buren's presidency. Van Buren was also worried about Jackson's strong actions to enforce national authority during the nullification crisis. To avoid disaster, Van Buren engineered a compromise tariff that mitigated South Carolina's grievance and eased the controversy for the time being.

In spite of these apparent disagreements with Jackson, Van Buren kept Jackson's support, possibly because Jackson recognized the value of an adviser who would not always tell him only what he wanted to hear. With Jackson's support, Van Buren won the 1836 Democratic nomination easily. He also won the general election against a cluster of Whig candidates including WILLIAM HENRY HARRISON, the main Whig candidate, with a small plurality over all Whig candidates and by 170–73 Electoral College votes. In the vice presidential race, the Whig strategy worked, and no candidate won a majority of the Electoral Votes. The U.S. Senate then chose Kentucky Representative Richard M. Johnson, marking the only time that the Senate has ever chosen a vice president.

While Jackson's support was critical for Van Buren's victory, the fallout from Jackson's policies doomed Van Buren's reelection bid four years later. Over Jackson's objections in 1835, Congress had allowed the sales of public lands to nonresident land speculators. Everyone, including clerks and

Martin Van Buren, considered by many to be one of the best trained men ever elected president, was hampered by serving during the first major depression in U.S. history. *(Library of Congress)*

shoeshine boys, started speculating in public lands. All the state banks and even branches of the national bank speculated by making loans without security in gold or silver. Unable to limit the speculation any other way, Jackson had issued his *Specie Circular* of July 11, 1836, requiring public land payments to be made only in gold and silver. Since banks could no longer make unsecured loans, the speculation stopped, but the banking crisis and financial crash were inevitable.

About two months after Van Buren took office, the financial crash hit on May 10, 1837, with Philadelphia and New York City banks leading all the nation's banks to close. The first real U.S. economic depression started. Van Buren responded cautiously by calling Congress into special session to pass the independent treasury bill to protect federal deposits in the banks. Defeated twice, the independent treasury bill finally passed in 1840. Bankers were angry, and the Whigs also appealed to businessmen and the unemployed, saying Van

Buren should adopt HENRY CLAY's "American Plan" to aid business and the unemployed. The growing national conflict over slavery led Van Buren to be attacked by both sides.

The antislavery forces said Van Buren was trying to create a new slave state in Florida by prosecuting the costly war against the Seminole Indians there. The pro-slavery forces attacked Van Buren for not immediately annexing Texas as a slave state, believing—with some justice—that Van Buren did not want to admit a new slave state. Van Buren temporarily resolved the dispute with the British over the boundary between Maine and Canada, but he got little credit for the good work he did there.

Although the Democrats nominated the unpopular Van Buren for reelection in 1840, they refused to nominate the even more unpopular Vice President Johnson. They could agree on no other, so Van Buren was the only presidential candidate in U.S. history to seek election without a running mate. The Whigs nominated William Henry Harrison for president and chose former Senator JOHN TYLER of Virginia as his vice presidential running mate. Harrison took campaigning to a new level with campaign slogans, such as "Tippecanoe and Tyler too," and "Keep the Ball Rolling." Harrison falsely charged that Van Buren was an aristocrat who had no interest in helping businesses or the unemployed in the depression. Although Van Buren lost the Electoral College vote by 234–60, he lost the popular vote only by about 150,000 votes out of 2,400,000 votes cast.

The Democrats intended to renominate Martin Van Buren in 1844, thinking he would win because of the vicious—but somewhat laughable—fight that developed between John Tyler and the Whig congressional establishment. But the Texas annexation issue doomed Van Buren. Van Buren had arranged a "gentleman's agreement" with Henry Clay to neutralize the Texas issue by agreeing jointly not to push the issue and say so publicly. However, President John Tyler was not a party to this agreement, and he—along with nearly all southerners and most westerners—wanted Texas annexed immediately. By pushing the issue into the open public debate, Tyler forced both Clay and Van Buren into an unpopular foot-dragging posture. Clay survived initially and got the Whig presidential nomination, but southern

Democrats—particularly Andrew Jackson—were furious with Van Buren. Jackson switched from supporting his old, close friend, Van Buren, to supporting his even older and closer friend, JAMES KNOX POLK, who was forthrightly for immediate annexation. Curiously, Van Buren mainly blamed Lewis Cass for deserting him in 1844, and this affected the later 1848 presidential campaign. Polk won the nomination and then turned the same Texas annexation issue against Clay to win the presidency in 1844.

In 1848, Van Buren took the basic Democratic platform, added the Wilmot Proviso to it, and carried antislavery Democrats into the antislavery Free-Soil Party, who had nominated him for president. Van Buren lost the election but took so many New York votes from Democratic presidential nominee Lewis Cass that the Whig candidate, ZACHARY TAYLOR, was elected. As the slavery disputes grew more intense, Van Buren was clearly opposed to slavery, but he loyally supported fellow Democrats FRANKLIN PIERCE in 1852 and JAMES BUCHANAN in 1856. Van Buren died at his estate, Lindenwald, near Kinderhook, New York, on July 24, 1862.

Further Reading

Bancroft, George. *Martin Van Buren to the End of his Public Career.* New York: Harper, 1889.

Cole, Donald B. *Martin Van Buren and the American Political System.* Princeton, N.J.: Princeton University Press, 1984.

Curtis, James C. *The Fox at Bay: Martin Van Buren and the Presidency, 1837–1841.* Lexington: University Press of Kentucky, 1970.

Hoyt, Edwin Palmer. *Martin Van Buren.* Chicago: Reilly & Lee, 1964

Lynch, Denis Tilden. *An Epoch and a Man: Martin Van Buren and his Times.* Port Washington, N.Y.: Kennikat Press, 1971.

Marszalek, John F. *The Petticoat Affair: Manners, Mutiny, and Sex in Andrew Jackson's White House.* New York: Free Press, 1997.

Mushkat, Jerome. *Martin Van Buren: Law, Politics, and the Shaping of Republican Ideology.* DeKalb: Northern Illinois University Press, 1997.

Niven, John. *Martin Van Buren: The Romantic Age of American Politics.* Norwalk, Conn.: The Easton Press, 1986.

Rayback, Joseph G. *Martin Van Buren.* New York: Eastern Acorn Press, 1982.

Remini, Robert V. *Martin Van Buren and the Making of the Democratic Party.* New York: Norton, 1970.

Shepard, Edward Morse. *Martin Van Buren.* New York: Chelsea House, 1983.

"Van Buren, Martin." Available online. URL: http://www.whitehouse.gov/history/presidents/mv8.html. Downloaded November 11, 2001.

Van Buren, Martin. *The Autobiography of Martin Van Buren.* New York: Da Capo Press, reprint 1973.

Wilson, Major L. *The Presidency of Martin Van Buren.* Lawrence: University Press of Kansas, 1984.

Vance, Cyrus Roberts
(1917–2002) *secretary of state, secretary of the army, deputy secretary of defense, diplomat*

Cyrus Roberts Vance served in important administrative and cabinet level positions under three Democratic presidents, was an important figure in the escalation of the Vietnam War, and attempted unsuccessfully to negotiate an end to the Vietnam War. He was the chief negotiator who ended the Greek and Turkish fighting over the island of Cyprus. After being a successful secretary of state, he resigned in 1980 on grounds of principle—the first secretary of state to do so in 65 years.

Vance was born on March 27, 1917, in Clarksburg, Virginia. He received his bachelor's degree from Yale in 1939 and his law degree from there in 1942. After serving in the navy during World War II, he practiced law in New York City. A Democrat, he became the special counsel to Senate investigating committees in 1957 and, briefly, general counsel to the Defense Department in 1960. In 1962, President JOHN FITZGERALD KENNEDY appointed him secretary of the army, where he served until President LYNDON BAINES JOHNSON named him deputy secretary of defense in 1964.

Vance supported the escalation of the Vietnam War until 1968 when he concluded that the domestic turmoil in the United States was not worth any prospective victory in Southeast Asia. Johnson then sent Vance to the Paris Peace Talks to try to obtain a negotiated settlement. He failed there but succeeded in his negotiations with the Greeks and Turks over Cyprus. In 1969, he went back to his law practice.

President JAMES EARL CARTER appointed Vance secretary of state in 1977, and he successfully supported several of Carter's foreign policy initiatives until the fall of Iran in 1979 and the seizure of the U.S. embassy staff. Vance counseled patience and nonviolence, but Carter secretly authorized a helicopter mission to try to rescue the hostages. When one of the helicopters crashed and the mission was aborted, Vance felt he was no longer a trusted member of the Carter cabinet and resigned—the first secretary of state to do so since WILLIAM JENNINGS BRYAN resigned from THOMAS WOODROW WILSON's cabinet in 1915. Vance continued to advise on foreign policy issues after he left the government, and he served the United Nations as a mediator. He died on January 12, 2002.

Further Reading
Loveland, Anne. "Jimmy Carter" in *The American Presidents,* edited by Frank N. Magill, John L. Loos, and Tracy Irons-Georges. Pasadena, Calif.: Salem Press, 2000.

McLellan, David S. *Cyrus Vance.* Totowa, N.J.: Rowman & Allanheld, 1985.

Vance, Cyrus R. *Hard Choices: Four Critical Years in Managing America's Foreign Policy.* New York: Simon & Schuster, 1983.

Vandenberg, Arthur Hendrick
(1884–1951) *senator*

During more than 20 years in the U.S. Senate, Arthur Hendrick Vandenberg made one of the most dramatic changes from being an isolationist to a supporter of President HARRY S. TRUMAN's bipartisan foreign policy of international intervention and containment of the Soviet Union and other communist countries.

Vandenberg was born on March 22, 1884, in Grand Rapids, Michigan. He studied law at the University of Michigan Law School but did not finish because of ill health. Instead, he became editor of the *Grand Rapids Herald,* an influential daily newspaper in Michigan politics. Eventually he parlayed his political influence into an appointment to fill a vacancy in the U.S. Senate in 1928. Elected to full terms in 1934, 1940, and 1946, he was still serving in the Senate at the time of his death.

He was a conventionally conservative Republican and followed the isolationist view until Pearl Harbor produced U.S. entry into World War II. He had, for example, opposed the Lend-Lease proposal of the Roosevelt administration. During World War II, he began to change gradually in response first to Axis threats and later to Communist threats to the United States.

In 1945, Vandenberg was named a delegate to the United Nations because he was a Republican now open to internationalist appeals. In 1946, he was sent to the Paris foreign ministers conference and, a year later, to the Pan-American conference. Although Vandenberg often exacted political favors for his internationalist support, his influence in carrying Midwestern Republican isolationists into support of internationalism was valuable. This was particularly true when he introduced the resolution that became the basis for U.S. participation in the North Atlantic Treaty Organization (NATO) and when he supported the Marshall Plan. He was the U.S. Senate president pro tempore from 1947 to 1949.

He died on April 18, 1951.

Further Reading

Eldersveld, A. Martin. *A Review and Thematic Analysis of Arthur H. Vandenberg's Senate Addresses on Foreign Policy.* Ann Arbor: University of Michigan, 1962.

Hernon, Joseph Martin. *Profiles in Character: Hubris and Heroism in the U.S. Senate—1789–1990.* Armonk, N.Y.: M. E. Sharpe, 1997.

Tompkins, C. David. *Senator Arthur H. Vandenberg, The Evolution of a Modern Republican, 1884–1945.* Lansing: Michigan State University Press, 1970.

"Vandenberg, Arthur H." in *Congress A to Z: Third Edition,* edited by David R. Tarr and Ann O'Connor. Washington, D.C.: Congressional Quarterly, 1999.

Vandenberg, Arthur H., and Joe Alex Morris, eds. *The Private Papers of Senator Vandenberg.* Boston: Houghton Mifflin, 1952.

Wade, Benjamin Franklin
(1800–1878) *senator*

Benjamin Franklin Wade was a lifelong opponent of slavery and, after the Civil War, a Radical Republican determined to see that the freed slaves and Unionists in the South were protected. In deep disagreement with President ANDREW JOHNSON, he favored Johnson's impeachment and removal from office. As president pro tempore of the Senate at that time, he would have become president if the Senate had convicted Johnson. Ironically, Wade's radical, domineering nature was one of Johnson's greatest assets in the impeachment fight, since many senators were more afraid of Wade than they were of Johnson and voted to acquit rather than convict. Johnson survived by one vote, and some who voted for him were Republican.

Wade was born on October 27, 1800, near Springfield, Massachusetts. In 1821, his parents took the family to Andover, Ohio. Wade lacked formal schooling and tried several jobs before deciding to study law. Admitted to the Ohio bar in 1827, he started a successful practice in Jefferson, Ohio. He was the prosecuting attorney for Ashtabula County for two years before being elected to the Ohio senate in 1837 as an antislavery Whig. He strongly opposed a tough new fugitive slave law and was defeated for reelection in 1839, but he made a comeback in 1841. Appointed a third judicial district justice, he avoided all antislavery activities while serving as judge.

The Whig-dominated Ohio legislature sent Wade to the U.S. Senate in 1851 and reelected him in 1857 and 1863. Wade was a devoted abolitionist, opposing the Fugitive Slave Act, the Kansas-Nebraska Act, and even, on the eve of the Civil War, the Crittenden plan to save the Union.

During the Civil War, he led the Radical Republicans and often criticized Lincoln for moving too slow on emancipation and in the protection of the Unionists and freed slaves in the South. He cosponsored the Wade-Davis Bill that required all southern states to make a list of all their white male residents. Only after 50 percent of the males on the list had taken an oath to support the U.S. Constitution could the state hold an election for delegates to write a new constitution. Such delegates would have to state they had never held office in the Confederacy or fought in its army as well as swear an oath to uphold the U.S. Constitution.

Lincoln did not sign the Wade-Davis bill, but he used it as leverage to force southern states that wanted to rejoin the Union to choose either the Wade-Davis plan or the more moderate Lincoln plan. When Andrew Johnson became president after Lincoln's death, he continued Lincoln's plan. This infuriated Wade, and he led the Republicans—who gained control of the Congress after the 1866 elections—to take over the Reconstruction policy. In 1867, Wade was elected president pro tempore of the Senate and became next in line to succeed to the presidency. His domineering nature actually drove Senate votes away from the conviction of Johnson out of fear of what Wade might do, and Johnson avoided conviction by just one vote. Wade failed to be named the vice presidential running mate with Grant in 1868 and also lost his reelection bid that year.

He retired from politics, practiced law for the next decade, and died on March 2, 1878.

Further Reading

"Ben Wade" in *The American President,* by Philip B. Kunhardt, Jr., Philip B. Kunhardt III, and Peter W. Kunhardt. New York: Riverhead Books, 1999.

"Ben Wade" in *The Presidency A to Z: Second Edition,* edited by Michael T. Nelson. Washington, D.C.: Congressional Quarterly Press, 1998.

Hernon, Joseph Martin. *Profiles in Character: Hubris and Heroism in the U.S. Senate—1789–1990.* Armonk, N.Y.: M. E. Sharpe, 1997.

Rabel, George. "Andrew Johnson" in *The American Presidents,* edited by Frank N. Magill, John L. Loos, and Tracy Irons-Georges. Pasadena, Calif.: Salem Press, 2000.

Riddle, Albert Gallatin. *The Life of Benjamin F. Wade.* Cleveland, Ohio: Williams, 1888.

Trefousse, Hans L. *Benjamin Franklin Wade: Radical Republican from Ohio.* New York: Twayne, 1963.

"Wade, Benjamin F." in *Congress A to Z: Third Edition,* edited by David R. Tarr and Ann O'Connor. Washington, D.C.: Congressional Quarterly, 1999.

Wagner, Robert Ferdinand
(1877–1953) *senator*

Robert Ferdinand Wagner was one of the most successful of all progressive reformers and New Deal supporters to serve in the U.S. Senate during the second quarter of the 20th century. For this reason, he was often called "the legislative pilot of the New Deal."

Wagner was born on June 8, 1877, in Nastatten, Germany. When he was eight years old, his family moved to New York City. He earned a bachelor's degree from City College of New York in 1898 and a law degree from New York University in 1900.

While developing his successful law practice, he became a part of the Tammany Hall machine, but he cleverly used Tammany to advance his reform agenda. He met their minimum requirements, using their strength to pass 50 out of 60 advanced welfare and worker benefit bills through the New York legislature while working with his colleague, ALFRED EMANUEL SMITH.

Wagner was elected to a 14-year term on the New York Supreme Court (despite its name, the New York Supreme Court is an entry level court, not the highest appellate court in New York). He broke new ground by using an injunction, not against a labor union, but against management in forcing them to abide by an agreement they made with the workers.

After eight years on the bench, Wagner ran as a Democrat for the first of his four consecutive terms in the U.S. Senate. Even before the Great Depression, Wagner supported federal aid to relieve unemployment. In 1932, he finally managed to convince Republican President HERBERT CLARK HOOVER to support Wagner's 1932 Relief and Construction Act, which had an avowed goal of federal responsibility for a suitable level of nationwide employment.

After Democratic President FRANKLIN DELANO ROOSEVELT's 1932 election, Wagner pushed through nearly the entire New Deal program, including his most famous National Labor Relations (or Wagner) Act in 1935. Wagner did not support Roosevelt's 1937 "Court-packing" plan nor his 1938 executive branch reorganization. Even with ANNA ELEANOR ROOSEVELT's help, Wagner was never able to get President Roosevelt to support an antilynching law or a full employment bill. He became ill and resigned from the Senate in 1949, but not before he pushed through the 1949 Public Housing Act.

He died on May 4, 1953.

Further Reading

Davis, Kenneth S. *FDR: Three Volumes.* New York: Random House, 1993.

Hernon, Joseph Martin. *Profiles in Character: Hubris and Heroism in the U.S. Senate—1789–1990.* Armonk, N.Y.: M. E. Sharpe, 1997.

Huthmacher, J. Joseph. *Senator Robert F. Wagner and the Rise of Urban Liberalism.* New York: Athenaeum, 1971.

McJimsey, George T. *The Presidency of Franklin Delano Roosevelt.* Lawrence: University Press of Kansas, 2000.

Morris, Jeffrey. *The FDR Way.* Minneapolis, Minn.: Lerner Publications, 1996.

"New Deal" in *Congress A to Z: Third Edition,* edited by David R. Tarr and Ann O'Connor. Washington, D.C.: Congressional Quarterly, 1999.

Wallace, George Corley
(1919–1998) *candidate for president, governor*

George Corley Wallace was the southern segregationist governor who said, "Segregation now, segregation tomorrow, and segregation forever!" He made this infamous statement in defiance of the federal government's growing involvement in support of the integration of African Americans into the mainstream of U.S. politics. In 1968, he carried his defiance into one of the most successful third-party bids for the presidency. Paralyzed as the result of an assassination attempt in 1972, his presidential career was over, but his gubernatorial career lasted long enough for him to be transformed into a supporter of civil rights for African Americans—to such a degree that he was elected governor on the strength of their votes.

Wallace was born on August 25, 1919, in the tiny hamlet of Clio, Alabama. While in high school he won the 1936 Alabama Golden Gloves bantamweight boxing championship and boxed professionally to pay for his education at the University of Alabama, up through his law degree in 1942. During World War II, he served in the air force in the Pacific theater. Wallace was elected to the state legislature in 1947 and served two terms. In 1948, he led the fight against the inclusion of HUBERT HORATIO HUMPHREY's civil rights plank in the Democratic National Convention, but he did not join JOHN STROM THURMOND's walkout from the convention.

In 1953, Wallace became a state circuit court judge. He gained statewide attention when he defied a federal court order that demanded the 1956 voting records for the U.S. Civil Rights Commission, which was investigating charges of discrimination. He used the publicity from this action to make himself known so he could run for governor in 1958. He lost to a candidate who used racial

politics even more viciously than Wallace did. Wallace drew the conclusion that one could never stress segregation enough and promised that he would never be "outsegregationed" again. Using his famous "segregation forever" slogan, he was elected governor in 1962. Fulfilling his pledge, he stood in the schoolhouse door at the University of Alabama to stop two African-American students from registering. This was truly for show, since President JOHN FITZGERALD KENNEDY simply federalized the Alabama National Guard, and Governor Wallace stood aside to let the students register just a few hours later.

Alabama at that time operated under a constitutional provision (frequently found in southern states) that did not allow a governor to serve two terms in a row (although anyone could serve as many terms as the voters would allow simply by staying out of office for four years between terms). To circumvent this provision, Wallace ran his wife in the 1966 gubernatorial election with the understanding that he would be her "assistant"—and actually run the state. Alabama's voters went along with this, and Wallace was then free to launch his third-party presidential campaign on the American Independent Party ticket.

Wallace did not believe he could win the presidency outright, but he thought he could win enough Electoral College votes to deny either Republican RICHARD MILHOUS NIXON or Democrat Hubert Humphrey a majority of the Electoral College votes, which would throw the election into the U.S. House of Representatives. This would allow southern members of Congress to exact favors from one of the two major party candidates in return for allowing that person to become president.

Wallace almost succeeded in his objective. He won 10 million popular votes (or 13% of the three-party vote) and 46 Electoral College votes. Had either Wallace or Humphrey won two more states, the Electoral College deadlock would have occurred and the U.S. House of Representatives would have been forced to decide the issue. Humphrey was actually within 10,000 votes in two major states, almost denying their Electoral College votes to Nixon and throwing the election into the House where Wallace would have been able to bargain to achieve his objectives. He was a hero in

Alabama, and the legislature repealed the ban on consecutive terms in 1969 (although repeal was not necessary for Wallace in 1970, it would have been an obstacle in 1974). Wallace was elected to his second term in 1970.

Wallace's near success led to his grander visions of winning the Democratic nomination in 1972, and he abandoned the American Independent Party in favor of a Democratic primary campaign. His hopes were dashed by a would-be assassin who wounded him so severely that he was paralyzed from the waist down for the rest of his life. In 1974, he was easily reelected as governor, served his third four-year term, then laid out a single term (1979–83). He ran successfully for his fourth and final term in 1982 and served from 1983 to 1987. Wallace was often ill due to complications from the gunshot wound, and he died on September 13, 1998.

Further Reading

Canfield, James L. A Case of Third Party Activism: The George Wallace Campaign Worker and the American Independent Party. Lanham, Md.: University Press of America, 1984.

Carlson, Jody. George C. Wallace and the Politics of Powerlessness: The Wallace Campaigns for The Presidency. New Brunswick: Transaction Books, 1981.

Carter, Dan T. George Wallace, Richard Nixon, and the Transformation of American Politics. Waco, Tex.: Markham Press Fund, 1992.

———. The Politics of Rage: George Wallace, the Origins of the New Conservatism, and the Transformation of American Politics. Baton Rouge: Louisiana State University Press, 2000.

Crass, Philip. The Wallace Factor. New York: Mason/Charter, 1976.

Frady, Marshall. Wallace. New York: Random House, 1996.

Greenhaw, Wayne. Watch Out for George Wallace. Englewood Cliffs, N.J.: Prentice-Hall, 1976.

Jones, William Grover. The Wallace Story. Northport, Ala.: American Southern Publishing Company, 1966.

Lesher, Stephan. George Wallace: American Populist. Reading, Mass.: Addison-Wesley, 1993.

Wallace, Cornelia. C'nelia. Philadelphia: A. J. Holman Company, 1976.

Wallace, George. The Wallaces of Alabama: My Family. Chicago: Follett, 1975.

Warren, Earl

(1891–1974) *chief justice of the United States, candidate for vice president, governor, state attorney general*

Widely regarded as the Supreme Court's most influential chief justice since JOHN MARSHALL, Earl Warren led the Court from 1953 to 1969, its most active period of constitutional revision. His profound impact on the political discourse of his day is indicated by the intense hatred he inspired among conservatives, particularly in the South, where billboards calling for his impeachment dotted the landscape.

Born in Los Angeles, California, on March 19, 1891, Warren received both his undergraduate degree and law preparation at the University of California at Berkeley. After service in World War I, Warren began his California political career under the aegis of the progressive politics of the state's Republican Governor HIRAM WARREN JOHNSON (1910–17). Warren moved up from Alameda County district attorney to state attorney general in 1938. A strong record as an anticrime prosecutor propelled him into the California governor's office in 1942. Running as a Republican but cross-filing as a Democrat, he won three terms—one time with both party nominations—while becoming more progressive in his political views. In 1948, he was THOMAS EDMUND DEWEY's vice presidential running mate, but their campaign was not well coordinated. The Dewey and Warren families were not close, and one rumor even has it that Warren's wife voted for President HARRY S. TRUMAN in the election.

Four years later, Warren was himself a candidate for the Republican presidential nomination, mainly as a California favorite son. At an appropriate moment, he withdrew in favor of DWIGHT DAVID EISENHOWER. Strategically aiding Eisenhower's 1952 Republican presidential nomination, he was rewarded with the chief justice appointment in 1953, after which he is credited with molding the fractious justices behind the unanimous landmark 1954 *Brown v. Board of Education* school desegregation decision.

On free expression and civil liberties, Warren was a strong supporter of Justices WILLIAM JOSEPH BRENNAN JR., HUGO LAFAYETTE BLACK, and

WILLIAM ORVILLE DOUGLAS, but he did not take some of their more liberal stands. A progressive on a still conservatively dominated Court, he remained in the minority with Justices Black, Brennan, and Douglas throughout the 1950s. With liberal ARTHUR JOSEPH GOLDBERG replacing conservative FELIX FRANKFURTER in 1962, Warren found himself in command of solid five-vote majorities on virtually every issue. In 1965, another liberal, Abe Fortas, replaced Goldberg, and the liberals were further strengthened with liberal THURGOOD MARSHALL's replacement of moderate Tom Clark in 1967.

The Warren Court transformed American law, providing the greatest single period of constitutional change in the nation's history. While single cases, such as *Marbury v. Madison* (1803) or *Dred Scott v. Sandford* (1857), were often individually significant, no court ever overturned so many federal statutes or transformed so many areas of the law. In no decade besides the 1960s were so many highly controversial decisions handed down. To cite only some of the issue areas involved—desegregation, civil rights, civil liberties, obscenity, school prayer, legislative reapportionment, incorporation of the Bill of Rights to the states by way of the Fourteenth Amendment, protection of those accused of crimes, and issues of the Vietnam War—is to recognize how significant this decade was for the Court and for American society.

Far less successful was Warren's role in the investigation into the assassination of President JOHN FITZGERALD KENNEDY on the commission that bore his name. President LYNDON BAINES JOHNSON pressured Warren to take the lead on the assassination inquiry after the killing of the putative assassin, Lee Harvey Oswald, by nightclub owner Jack Ruby. Warren was reluctant to undertake the stress, responsibility, and distraction from Court duties, but he relented when Johnson insisted that only someone of the stature of the chief justice could lay to rest concerns of a conspiracy reaching beyond Oswald. The Warren Commission did find that Kennedy was killed by Oswald as a lone assassin, but its conclusion—although never overturned—has been repeatedly assailed by a wide variety of critics ever since.

Not generally credited as a great legal scholar, he is still considered the driving force behind the

Earl Warren is often referred to as the Supreme Court's most influential chief justice since John Marshall, because he led the Court during one of its most active eras of constitutional revision. *(Library of Congress)*

Court era that carries his name. Since he left the Court, the long-lasting legacy of the decisions made in his era has transformed U.S. constitutional law and society. While some of the decisions have been modified, the vast bulk of the rulings remain intact.

Estranged from RICHARD MILHOUS NIXON, Warren attempted to resign so a Democratic president could appoint his successor. Events delayed his retirement until after the Republican Nixon was inaugurated president so Nixon could appoint conservative WARREN EARL BURGER as his replacement. Warren continued to be active in retirement, often speaking and writing, until his death in Washington, D.C., on July 9, 1974.

Further Reading

Cox, Archibald S. *Warren Court: Constitutional Decision as an Instrument of Reform.* Cambridge, Mass.: Harvard University Press, 1968.

Christman, Henry M., ed. *The Public Papers of Chief Justice Earl Warren.* Westport, Conn.: Greenwood, 1974.

Kluger, Richard. *Simple Justice: The History of Brown v. Board of Education and Black America's Struggle for Equality.* New York: Random House, 1977.

Schwartz, Bernard. *Super Chief: Earl Warren and His Supreme Court.* New York: New York University Press, 1984.

Tushnet, Mark, ed. *The Warren Court in Historical and Political Perspective.* Charlottesville: University Press of Virginia, 1993.

White, G. Edward. *Earl Warren: A Public Life.* New York: Oxford University Press, 1982.

Washington, George
(1732–1799) *president, Revolutionary War leader*

George Washington was the first president of the United States, consistently ranked as one of the greatest U.S. presidents, and not infrequently ranked as one of the greatest men in world history. He held three vitally important offices: commander in chief

George Washington was the first president of the United States and is consistently ranked as one of the greatest U.S. presidents. *(Library of Congress)*

of the Continental forces during the Revolutionary War; president and presiding officer of the 1787 Convention that drew up the U.S. Constitution; and the first president of the United States. This simple list belies his unique contribution because, without his military leadership, the Revolutionary War might well have been lost. Without his unique personality leading the nation during the drafting of the U.S. Constitution and initiating the government, the new nation might well have dissolved in warring factions.

Washington was born on February 11, 1732 (or on February 22, 1732, under the calendar currently in use), at Pope's Creek Plantation in Westmoreland County, Virginia. When George was about three years old, his family moved to Mount Vernon, a large, still undeveloped plantation. He received very little formal education except from tutors. However, his older half-brother, Lawrence, who had been educated in England and who served as George's guardian and father figure after their father's death in 1743, undoubtedly contributed much to his education.

Lawrence's fortuitous marriage into the Fairfax family gave young Washington important advantages. In 1747, at about 15 years of age, Washington accompanied George Fairfax on a journey to survey the Shenandoah Valley. From then on, Washington was a strong supporter of the development of America west of the Appalachian Mountains and became a land speculator himself. When Lawrence Washington died in 1752, young Washington moved to Mount Vernon (which he rented from his niece until he inherited it in 1761). In 1753, although he was only 21 years of age, Washington was appointed a major in the Virginia militia through his connection to the Fairfax family, and he later briefly became a colonel.

Washington's first battle was momentous, although the outcome was not very impressive. Sent to repel French and Indian fighters in the Ohio Valley, Washington's men stumbled on a small French detachment, killed 10, wounded one, and captured 21 while losing only a single soldier from their unit. Unknown to him at the time, those shots were the first in the French and Indian War.

In the next engagement of the war, Washington's men, deep in the frontier, built a makeshift fort, called *Necessity*, but without food or dry powder they were forced to surrender. After Washington signed a humiliating statement, the French let him and his men return to Williamsburg, Virginia, where they were hailed as heroes for their courage even though they were defeated. Washington learned he could not retain the rank of colonel because a British rule allowed colonials to rise no higher than captain. Rather than take a cut in rank, Washington resigned.

A year later, he was sent as a civilian to guide the British regular troops under General Braddock to fight the French. Washington advised Braddock to learn to fight as the French and Indians would, but Braddock did not listen. When the fighting began, Braddock was killed, and Washington had to organize the retreat. Upon returning home, Washington became a hero and was appointed colonel and commander in chief of the Virginia militia.

With too few men and supplies, Washington still soldiered on for the next few years, fighting sporadically and trying to defend the Virginia settlers from Indian raids. When the French and Indians finally were driven from the Ohio Valley, Washington retired from the military and returned to his plantation at Mount Vernon.

In 1759, he married a rich widow, Martha Custis, and adopted her two children by her first marriage. By 1761, when he inherited Mount Vernon, his combined property made him a very wealthy planter. Elected to the Virginia House of Burgesses in 1759 and remaining there until 1774, Washington was an early opponent of colonial rule, a critic of the 1765 Stamp Act, and a supporter of the Bostonians at a time when most Virginians felt Boston's cause was not their own.

Washington adopted a national viewpoint, which he carried with him after his election in 1774 to the First Continental Congress. In 1775, in his second year of service to the Continental Congress, he was unanimously chosen as commander in chief of the Continental forces. Washington believed he was not sufficiently experienced to manage the war effort, but he knew there was no one else to do it. He made many mistakes but learned as he went along. Above all, he never gave up.

Envisioning Washington as an early master of guerrilla warfare helps to explain his success. He fought as a guerrilla because he lacked the resources to do otherwise. He husbanded his resources and avoided set-piece battles unless he knew he could win. If he calculated he would lose, he retreated so as not to lose what small forces he possessed. His risky, but brilliantly timed, Christmas Eve raid on Trenton, New Jersey, and his second successful surprise raid at Princeton a week later were both classic guerrilla maneuvers that saved the war effort after a dismal year of losses and retreats. His refusal to quit even during the impossibly hard 1777–78 winter at Valley Forge was essential for success.

It is noteworthy that Washington had a couple of rivals for the post of commander in chief in JOHN HANCOCK and Horatio Gates (pushed by BENJAMIN RUSH), but they both failed when they met lesser challenges than those faced by Washington. In the end, Washington lost more battles than he won, but he won the battles that counted. Guerrilla leader Washington knew he was fighting a political war. Only after the colonials won at Saratoga was the hope for French assistance received. And only with French assistance was Washington's success at Yorktown achieved.

With the exception of Washington's Farewell Address, his speech at Newburgh, New York, to disgruntled officers, who had been denied their years of back pay and threatened armed revolt, was perhaps his most important and certainly critical for establishing trust among virtually all parties. Washington convinced the officers not to revolt and then persuaded the Continental Congress (sometimes referred to as the Congress of the Confederation) to pay the troops their full five years of back pay.

Washington returned to private life at Mount Vernon, but it soon became clear that the existing government of the wartime Articles of Confederation was inadequate for the new nation. After a few preliminary meetings, Washington agreed to preside at a 1787 convention to draft a new government. As the group met in secret to prevent the entire process from breaking down at the outset, Washington's immense prestige was essential to giving the product of the convention a fair hearing. Since the new government was to be stronger, it was critical that features such as the single executive would be accepted. For that purpose, the common knowledge that Washington would be elected as the first president was critical to ratification—a process that was a close call in a number of states.

Upon his election, Washington was keenly aware of the importance of setting a good example, because virtually every action he took could be taken as a precedent for later actions. Given the diverse fears in the country and the propensity for sectionalism to rear its head as it had under the Articles of Confederation, Washington carefully selected his first vice president and cabinet.

His choices represented all sections of the country and a wide variety of opinions about the new government. Vice President JOHN ADAMS, from Boston and a known conservative, had been abroad for the drafting of the new document. Secretary of State THOMAS JEFFERSON, a Virginian, was a known devotee of republican principle as the author of the Declaration of Independence. He also had been abroad and could not be accused of blindly supporting a document he had created. Secretary of the Treasury ALEXANDER HAMILTON was simply the best financial mind available, and he represented the mercantile class from New York. He had, of course, helped draft the U.S. Constitution and assisted its ratification through his authorship of part of the *Federalist Papers*, but some representation from the convention delegates was prudent. Attorney General EDMUND RANDOLPH was another drafter of the U.S. Constitution, but he had reservations about the document and supported the effort only because it was the best available alternative. Secretary of War HENRY KNOX, another Bostonian, was a trusted military comrade from the war, whose skill in this capacity was recognized by his having served in a similar capacity under the Articles of Confederation. A second New Yorker, JOHN JAY, was named the first chief justice of the United States. Geographic and political diversity abounded in the first cabinet and other critical appointments.

Washington needed the broadest representation in the cabinet because the initial decisions of the government were bound to be divisive. Washington and a majority of the members of the early Congress accepted Hamilton's economic plans, but they drew fire from the Virginia agrarians, such as Jefferson, JAMES MADISON, JAMES MONROE, and Randolph. Still, Hamilton was correct, as even his critics were forced to agree in the end. (Jefferson, Madison, and Monroe would not have been able to purchase Louisiana in 1803 if Hamilton had not straightened out U.S. finances starting in 1789.)

Hamilton's financial plans included an excise tax on whiskey that led to the Whiskey Rebellion. Washington and Hamilton then led an army into the field to defeat the malcontents by a show of force, fortunately sufficient to quell the disturbance. More important, public confidence that order could be restored was established by the action.

Washington may not have been brilliant in formulating financial plans or drafting documents, but he was absolutely sound in recognizing the United States was too weak to start fighting with European powers, which would have been the consequence of following Jefferson's conception of the requirements of the U.S.–French treaty of assistance. Washington tried hard to keep both Hamilton and Jefferson in the cabinet; he succeeded for a time but ultimately failed. His ability to bridge the gap still served to hold the government together in the first critical four years.

Washington also supported Anthony Wayne in quelling the Indians in 1794 and reducing—although not eliminating—the British mischief-making in the young country. The British finally departed from the forts they promised to give up in 1783, but they did not actually abandon them until 1795. U.S. diplomacy was not robust, but it was perhaps as good as could be hoped for from such a weak nation. In 1795 THOMAS PINCKNEY secured the opening of the Mississippi River to trade through New Orleans, and he negotiated a temporary border between the United States and Spanish possessions in Florida.

Washington accomplished a great deal during his first two terms. Even more was accomplished by establishing the principle (though not yet a law) that a president should serve for only two terms. As the one man who could have been king, Washington took a long step toward reassuring everyone that there would be no king when he decided to quit after eight years.

Washington agreed to go back to the army two years later when war fever against Britain seemed to threaten a new conflict. His sage advice to his successor, John Adams, not to yield to the popular hysteria may have hurt Adams's chances for election, but it certainly saved the country from needless war and possible destruction.

Washington died on December 14, 1799, but the reverence for what he had accomplished had already begun.

Further Reading

Alden, John R. *George Washington*. Baton Rouge: Louisiana State University Press, 1996.

Brochures, Richard. *Founding Father: Rediscovering George Washington*. New York: Free Press, 1996.

Callahan, North. *Thanks, Mr. President: The Trail-Blazing Second Term of George Washington*. New York: Cornwall Books, 1991.

———. *George Washington, Soldier and Man*. New York: Morrow, 1972.

Clark, E. Harrison. *All Cloudless Glory: The Life of George Washington*. Washington, D.C.: Regnery, 1995.

Ferling, John E. *The First of Men: A Life of George Washington*. Knoxville: University of Tennessee Press, 1988.

Flexner, James T. *Washington, The Indispensable Man*. Boston: Little, Brown, 1994.

Freeman, Douglas Southall. *Washington*. Norwalk, Conn.: Easton Press, 1985.

Irving, Washington. *George Washington*. New York: Da Capo, 1994.

Marshall, John. *George Washington*. New York: Chelsea House, 1983.

McDonald, Forrest. *The Presidency of George Washington*. New York: Norton, 1975.

Morgan, Edmund Sears. *The Genius of George Washington*. New York: Norton, 1981.

Nordham, George Washington. *The Age of Washington: George Washington's Presidency, 1789–1797*. Chicago: Adams Press, 1989.

Randall, Willard Sterne. *George Washington*. New York: Henry Holt, 1997.

Smith, James Morton. *George Washington*. New York: Hill & Wang, 1969.

Smith, Richard Norton. *Patriarch: George Washington and the New American Nation*. Boston: Houghton Mifflin, 1993.

Wall, Charles Cecil. *George Washington, Citizen-Soldier*. Charlottesville: University Press of Virginia, 1980.

"Washington, George." Available online. URL: http://www.whitehouse.gov/history/presidents/gw1.html. Downloaded November 11, 2001.

Wills, Garry. *Cincinnatus: George Washington and the Enlightenment*. Garden City, N.Y.: Doubleday, 1984.

Wilson, Woodrow. *George Washington*. New York: Schocken Books, 1969.

Webster, Daniel
(1782–1852) *secretary of state, senator, representative*

Daniel Webster was the most famous orator in the United States and one of the best lawyers of his age. Although he started as a states' rights advocate, he gained his greatest fame as the champion of a strong national government. For years after his death, even up to the Civil War, students memorized quotable lines from his orations.

Webster was born on January 18, 1782, in Franklin (then called Salisbury), New Hampshire, and he graduated from Dartmouth College in 1801. He taught school briefly, studied law in Boston, was admitted to the bar in 1805, and began a successful law practice in Portsmouth, New Hampshire. Portsmouth was a thriving seaport until President THOMAS JEFFERSON's embargo and the War of 1812 destroyed most of its overseas trade. Webster naturally supported the local shippers while opposing trade restrictions and war. Elected as a Federalist to the U.S. House of Representatives in 1813 and serving to 1817, he objected to war taxes and drafting soldiers for the War of 1812, but he did not participate in or support the Hartford Convention.

In 1816, he moved to Boston where his constituency changed from shippers to industrialists. Accordingly, he dropped his free trade and states' rights stance in favor of protective tariffs and a strong national government to aid business. This is reflected in his defense of strong government in the famous 1819 Supreme Court case *McCulloch v. Maryland*, where he defended the congressional authorization of the Bank of the United States even though the creation of such a bank is not specifically authorized under the congressional powers granted in the U.S. Constitution. Webster gained even more fame when he defended his alma mater before the Supreme Court in the 1819 *Dartmouth College* case.

Elected again to the House in 1823, he became the greatest orator of his time both for his eloquent speeches in the House and his brilliant public addresses. In 1827, the Massachusetts state legislature elected him to the U.S. Senate, where he became a national political figure of the United States. As a thoroughgoing nationalist, he defended the pro-Union side in the famous Webster-Hayne Debate with Robert Y. Hayne in 1830. Although Webster supported President ANDREW JACKSON at this time in the nullification crisis, he strongly opposed him on virtually all other issues, especially the bank and financial policy.

In 1836, when the Whigs adopted the unsuccessful policy of running different Whig presidential candidates in different parts of the country and hoping to throw elections into the U.S. House of Representatives, Webster was supported in New England, but he carried only Massachusetts (and Democrat MARTIN VAN BUREN won). He was mentioned as a presidential candidate at other times, but he never reached that lofty goal.

In 1840, the Whig candidate, WILLIAM HENRY HARRISON, was elected president and appointed Webster the U.S. secretary of state. When Harrison died, all the other Whig cabinet officers quit because of the fight with Harrison's successor, JOHN TYLER. But Webster stayed on to complete the 1843 Webster-Ashburton Treaty, which settled the northern boundary of Maine on favorable terms for the United States. He quit the Tyler cabinet over the issue of the immediate annexation of Texas, which was a Tyler policy that the antislavery Webster opposed. He returned to the Senate in 1845 and hoped to be nominated for president in 1848, but he lost out to Mexican War hero ZACHARY TAYLOR. Webster worked for the Compromise of 1850, which may have avoided a civil war at that time, but the antislavery Whigs criticized him for making any concessions to the slave forces. Webster then served as the secretary of state for MILLARD FILLMORE from 1850 to 1852, where he is remembered mainly for his endorse-

ment of Hungarian independence from the Austro-Hungarian Empire.

Webster was denied the 1852 Whig presidential nomination because both the North and South punished him for his role in the Compromise of 1850. Again he was passed over for a Mexican War hero—this time WINFIELD SCOTT. Webster correctly predicted his party's defeat and died shortly after the general election on October 24, 1852.

Further Reading

Bartlett, Irving H. *Daniel Webster.* New York: Norton, 1978.

Baxter, Maurice G. *One and Inseparable: Daniel Webster and the Union.* Cambridge, Mass.: Harvard University Press, 1984.

Carey, Robert L. *Daniel Webster as an Economist.* New York: AMS Press, 1966.

Current, Richard N. *Daniel Webster and the Rise of National Conservatism.* Prospect Heights, Ill.: Waveland Press, 1992.

Dalzell, Robert F. *Daniel Webster and the Trial of American Nationalism.* Boston: Houghton Mifflin, 1973.

Fisher, Sydney G. *The True Daniel Webster.* Philadelphia: J.B. Lippincott, 1991.

Lodge, Henry Cabot. *Daniel Webster.* New York: Chelsea House, 1983.

McMaster, John B. *Daniel Webster.* New York: Century, 1991.

Peterson, Merrill D. *The Great Triumvirate: Webster, Clay, and Calhoun.* New York: Oxford University Press, 1987.

Remini, Robert V. *Daniel Webster: The Man and His Time.* New York: Norton, 1997.

Wiltse, Charles M., ed. *The Papers of Daniel Webster: Four Volumes.* Hanover, N.H.: Published for Dartmouth College by the University Press of New England, 1974–89.

Wheeler, Burton Kendell
(1882–1975) *candidate for vice president, senator, author*

Burton Kendall Wheeler was a leading progressive member of the U.S. Senate for four terms and a well-known isolationist in the years leading up to World War II.

Wheeler was born on February 27, 1882, in Hudson, Massachusetts, but he moved west to attend school at the University of Michigan, from which he graduated with a law degree in 1905. In the following year he was admitted to the bar, moved to Montana, and opened a law practice in Butte.

In 1911, Wheeler was elected to the Montana House of Representatives and in 1913 became the U.S. attorney for Montana. In this post, he became known as a radical for refusing to prosecute pacifists on the grounds of their First Amendment rights under the U.S. Constitution.

In 1922, he ran as a Democrat for the U.S. Senate in a vicious campaign in which he was smeared for his constitutional beliefs, but he won. Two years later he left the Democratic Party temporarily to run for the vice presidency on a Progressive Party ticket with Wisconsin's Republican Senator ROBERT MARION LA FOLLETTE.

When the ticket lost, Wheeler returned to the Democratic Party and supported ALFRED EMANUEL SMITH in 1928 and FRANKLIN DELANO ROOSEVELT in 1932. While he supported Roosevelt's progressive New Deal legislation, he was one of the first senators to oppose his Supreme Court "Court-packing" bill, and as an isolationist, he was a consistent opponent of Roosevelt's military preparedness and aid to the Allies prior to U.S. entry into World War II. Although he made a brief try for the Democratic presidential nomination on a peace platform, he gave that up in favor of running for his fourth consecutive senatorial bid.

Wheeler died on January 7, 1975.

Further Reading

Cameron, Donald J. *Burton K. Wheeler as Public Campaigner.* Evanston, Ill.: Northwestern University, 1966.

Colman, Elizabeth Wheeler. *Mrs. Wheeler Goes to Washington: Mrs. Burton Kendall Wheeler, Wife of the Senator from Montana.* Stockton, Calif.: Colman, 1989.

Davis, Kenneth S. *FDR: Three Volumes.* New York: Random House, 1993.

Hernon, Joseph Martin. *Profiles in Character: Hubris and Heroism in the U.S. Senate—1789–1990.* Armonk, N.Y.: M. E. Sharpe, 1997.

"Wheeler, Burton K." in *Congress A to Z: Third Edition,* edited by David R. Tarr and Ann O'Connor. Washington, D.C.: Congressional Quarterly, 1999.

Wheeler, Burton K. *Yankee from the West: The Candid, Turbulent Life Story of the Yankee-Born U.S. Senator from Montana.* Garden City, N.Y.: Doubleday, 1962.

Wilson, Edith Bolling Galt
(1872–1961) *first lady, presidential adviser*

Edith Bolling Galt Wilson has been called—perhaps unfairly—the "first woman to run the U.S. government" or "the secret president" because of the role she played when her husband, President THOMAS WOODROW WILSON, suffered a stroke that left him a disabled invalid during the last 18 months of his presidency.

Edith Bolling was born in Wytheville, Virginia, on October 15, 1872, into a large, socially prominent aristocratic family which had lost much of their wealth during the Civil War. She studied at home and never left her hometown until she was 12 years of age. At age 15, she studied music at Martha Washington College for a year and then transferred to a smaller school in Richmond, Virginia. In 1896, her married sister introduced her to Norman Galt, a well-to-do jeweler, and they were soon married. Although they had no children, this was a successful marriage until Galt died suddenly in 1908. Fortunately, Edith Galt chose a good manager to continue to make the family's jewelry business a financial success.

Through friends, but apparently largely by accident, she met President Wilson in March 1915 as he was still in mourning over the loss of his first wife. However, he was struck by her beauty, charm, and intelligence. After a courtship of only a few months, they married before the end of the year. They honeymooned only briefly before moving into the White House.

Even prior to the wedding, Edith Wilson had begun to act as her husband's confidential adviser on many official matters. After the sinking of the *Lusitania,* it is alleged that she even rewrote some of his official messages to Germany. Never far from each other's side, they performed nearly all daily activities together. She stayed in the room when his stenographer took dictation, met appointments, and attended public affairs. She screened his appointments to keep out anyone who might irritate him. During World War I, she was given secret information and even was allowed to decode secret messages from Wilson's diplomats abroad.

Once the United States declared war on Germany, the White House was closed to the public, and almost anyone wanting to talk the president had to go through the first lady. She played an active role in public relations activities after the war began, leading the campaign for women to sew clothes for the troops and spearheading the sale of war bonds by using Hollywood celebrities. In all these activities, her secretarial and political help resembles that given by JAMES KNOX POLK's wife, Sarah. However, Sarah Polk was involved in Polk's career for decades, not just the last few years of his presidency, and Polk was not disabled during his term of office.

In 1918, when the war ended, Edith Wilson urged the president to head up the peace delegation to Paris and allow her to attend. In Europe, she was constantly at the president's side during his daily briefings, and she arranged his public appearances. She was the only woman allowed to attend the president's famous League of Nations speech to the closed session of the conference. Foreign leaders objected that it was impossible to have a close conversation with President Wilson, even if they sat next to him at formal dinners, because he always sat next to her and spoke to almost no one else.

When Wilson returned from Paris to discover the opposition that had arisen to the Versailles Peace Treaty he had negotiated, he launched his nearly 10,000-mile speaking tour to try to persuade the nation to ratify the new treaty. Edith Wilson was at his side all along the way. When Wilson collapsed on September 25 outside of Pueblo, Colorado, she ordered the train to speed back to Washington. When a group of physicians tried to examine the president at the time, she sent most of them out of the room, claiming that Wilson's mind was unaffected by the stroke.

She made an immediate decision to restrict access to the president to only his doctor and herself. For the rest of his term, no one saw Wilson except those two. She justified her actions to Wilson's cabinet by insisting that she was following Wilson's orders. She reminded his advisers that Wilson had made her his close partner much earlier in his presidency to be sure she would be ready if necessary to help him in an emergency. No one dared cross her or they risked dismissal, as Secretary of State Robert Lansing discovered. Only a few trusted associates were allowed to visit Wilson even briefly, and she refused to allow any public discussion of the stroke. Eventually, she began signing his name to official documents, carefully initialing them so she was not forging his signature. As cabinet members resigned or were fired, she personally offered appointments to Wilson loyalists, sometimes over tea it is alleged.

It is impossible to know the extent of her influence during Wilson's disability. She published her own memoirs in 1939, and in that book she insisted she was following the doctor's orders in all her actions and that the president was clear, lucid, and precise in his understanding throughout the last few months of his presidency. She claimed that he often disagreed with her advice, as when she suggested he accept some of the proposed Republican amendments to the League of Nations and he refused.

After Wilson left the White House, she cared for him until his death in 1924. After Wilson's death, she served as the director of the Woodrow Wilson Foundation. In January 1961 she attended the inauguration of President JOHN FITZGERALD KENNEDY. Edith Wilson died at 89 years of age on December 28, 1961, on the 105th anniversary of Woodrow Wilson's birth.

Further Reading

Goblin, James. *Edith Wilson: The Woman Who Ran the United States.* New York: Viking, 1992.

Hatch, Alden. *Edith Bolling Wilson, First Lady Extraordinary.* New York: Dodd, Mead, 1961.

Ross, Ishbel. *Power with Grace: The Life Story of Mrs. Woodrow Wilson.* New York: Putnam, 1975.

Shachtman, Tom. *Edith and Woodrow: A Presidential Romance.* New York: Putnam, 1980.

Smith, Gene. *When the Cheering Stopped.* New York: Morrow, 1964.

Tribble, Edwin, ed. *A President in Love: The Courtship Letters of Woodrow Wilson and Edith Bolling Galt.* Boston: Houghton Mifflin, 1981.

Wilson, Edith Bolling Galt. *My Memoir.* Indianapolis, New York: Bobbs-Merrill, 1939.

Wilson, Thomas Woodrow

(1856–1924) *president, governor, author*

If Woodrow Wilson had never been elected governor of New Jersey or president of the United States, he would still remain a significant figure in American history. One of the first in this country to earn a doctorate in political science, he went on to publish more than a dozen scholarly books in his career. He was in the forefront of the creation of a new discipline in higher education known as public administration. He founded the American Political Science Association and served for eight significant years as an innovative president of Princeton University. Although a stroke left him debilitated in the last 18 months of his presidency, an objective evaluation of his presidency would reveal that he had one of the most outstanding records of innovation in domestic legislation, one of the most successful wartime administrations, and a leading role in promoting international peace and security.

Thomas Woodrow Wilson was born on December 28, 1856, in Staunton, Virginia, but raised in Augusta, Georgia, and Columbia, South Carolina, where his father was a minister and a college teacher. In 1873, Wilson enrolled at Davidson College but dropped out because he was ill. Recovering sufficiently two years later, he then went to Princeton University and graduated in 1879. He was briefly enrolled at the University of Virginia law school, but he became ill again and went home. After studying privately, he was admitted to the Georgia bar in 1882.

Wilson was not successful as a lawyer and did not like the work, so he decided to become a college teacher. For that purpose, he went to Johns Hopkins University, which had recently started a graduate school modeled on new professional disciplinary principles derived from European, particularly German, universities. In 1886, he earned his doctorate in political science and proceeded to publish his dissertation entitled *Congressional Government* in 1887.

Given the critical acclaim his dissertation received, it is no surprise that he was accepted for teaching jobs at some of the most prestigious colleges in the country. He was employed at Bryn Mawr College from 1885 to 1888 and then Wesleyan University from 1888 to 1890. During this time, he also wrote a second book entitled *The State.*

In 1890, Wilson was accepted for a position at Princeton, which began his two decades–long service at that institution. While there he published nine major books, including his *History of the American People,* as well as a number of journal articles. His accomplishments were so great that he became Princeton's president in 1902. Over the next eight years, Wilson was a stunning innovator,

Woodrow Wilson led the United States during one of the most intense periods of domestic political reform, led America successfully during the First World War, and had a major role in promoting international peace and security. *(Library of Congress)*

reorganizing Princeton's curriculum, revising its academic departments, and introducing the preceptorial concept of education. Given the near impossibility of reforming any university, Wilson's accomplishments were outstanding and may be more remarkable than his later accomplishments: transforming New Jersey state government, reforming the U.S. government, or creating the League of Nations. As Princeton's president he could not do everything. He was not able to eliminate Princeton's class-based eating clubs or gain control of the newly created graduate school, despite a bitter fight. Apparently realizing that university reform really is difficult, Wilson began thinking about running for governor.

In 1906, Colonel George Harvey, the editor of *Harper's Weekly,* first raised the possibility of Wilson's running for governor of New Jersey. With Harvey's help, Wilson began making speeches around New Jersey and addressing important political topics, such as lowering tariffs, controlling monopolies, and adopting various progressive political reforms.

In 1910, the New Jersey Democratic Party political bosses offered Wilson the Democratic gubernatorial nomination, expecting they could control him after the election. Wilson won, but he insisted on a vigorous, independent, and progressive administration. Well before the Democratic National Convention in 1912, Wilson had rammed the following programs through the New Jersey Legislature: election reform, direct party primaries, new public utility regulations, improved workers' compensation, municipal reform, and a complete reorganization of the public school system.

Wilson ran for president in 1912—only two years after becoming governor—and vigorously contested the new presidential preference primaries across the nation. By convention time, Wilson was still trailing Speaker of the House JAMES BEAUCHAMP CLARK, who appeared well on his way to securing a nomination with a long lead on the first ballot. However, Clark needed to win two-thirds of the delegates under the Democratic Party rules to win the presidential nomination. At this point, Wilson's southern background and his progressive accomplishments as governor combined to give him a boost. He also received support from the beloved WILLIAM JENNINGS BRYAN, long-term titular head of the Democratic Party. In the end, the convention deadlocked and finally turned to Wilson. Wilson's quest for the presidency still required an uphill fight against the Republicans, who had won the last four presidential campaigns and all, except two, during the previous 50 years. Worse, the Republicans were running an incumbent president for reelection.

However, the incumbent Republican President, WILLIAM HOWARD TAFT, was in a bitter fight with his Republican predecessor, his former close friend and the former president, THEODORE ROOSEVELT. Roosevelt challenged Taft for the 1912 Republican presidential nomination, won most of the primaries, controlled most of the delegates, but was easily defeated by Taft, who controlled the party machinery. Roosevelt then bolted the Republican Party and accepted the presidential nomination of the Progressive, or Bull Moose, Party. This effectively split the Republican vote and made it possible for Wilson to win.

Wilson received only 42 percent of the popular vote, but he won 40 states and captured the Electoral College vote handily. Roosevelt garnered 27 percent of the popular vote but carried only six states. Taft won only 23 percent of the popular votes and carried only two states. The remaining popular vote went to the Socialist Eugene V. Debs and other candidates.

On being inaugurated, Wilson acted quickly, calling Congress into a special session to underscore the need for tariff reform. Although the fight was difficult, six months later Wilson sponsored the Underwood Tariff Act, which not only reduced the tariff rates generally from 40 percent to 26 percent but also increased the number of duty-free items. Since the Sixteenth Amendment to the U.S. Constitution had recently been ratified, Wilson also managed to add the first constitutional income tax in U.S. history as a rider to the bill. Undeterred by the thought of fighting more than one massive fight in a single session, Wilson also pushed for passage of legislation to create a new national banking system. Although partly responsive to the earlier proposals from former conservative Republican Senator NELSON WILMARTH ALDRICH, Wilson's Federal Reserve

System offered protections not available in the more conservative proposals. At the conclusion of Wilson's second major legislative campaign of the year, he was able to sign into law the Federal Reserve Act, creating a central bank and 12 regional banks that were all managed and regulated by a presidentially appointed Federal Reserve Board. This system also authorized the issuance of a new national currency, called Federal Reserve notes, not directly tied to gold or silver. In the following year, Wilson pushed through his third major reform: the establishment of the Federal Trade Commission, an independent regulatory agency designed to prevent unfair business competition by trusts and other monopolies.

Foreign relations proved more difficult. The spillover of raids from the Mexican revolution into the U.S. Southwest led Wilson to send the U.S. Marines to Vera Cruz in 1914. After the raids continued, Wilson sent the U.S. Army under General John J. Pershing across the Mexican border in a frustrating, unsuccessful attempt to capture the Mexican rebel leader, Pancho Villa. Later, Wilson decided to send the Marines into Haiti in 1915 and into the Dominican Republic in 1916.

In 1914, war broke out among all the major European powers. Wilson sought to avoid involvement with a policy of strict neutrality, but this proved increasingly difficult. The Germans needed to stop the British from buying needed war material from the United States, since the British blockade of Germany had shut off their own imports. Moreover, the Germans had a new powerful, surreptitious weapon: the submarine.

In May 1915, the Germans torpedoed the *Lusitania*, a British passenger ship. Many lives were lost, including those of 100 Americans. Wilson ordered Secretary of State Bryan to deliver a stern warning to the Germans that the continuation of submarine attacks on ships carrying Americans would lead to U.S. retaliation. Although Bryan had supported Wilson for president, he was essentially a pacifist, and he balked at delivering a message likely to lead to war. Bryan resigned and Wilson chose ROBERT LANSING to replace him. When German submarines sank another passenger ship, the *Arabic*, Wilson sent another stern warning, and the Germans promised they would no

longer attack passenger ships. Still later, the Germans sank the merchant ship the *Sussex*, and this time Wilson forced the Germans to promise to obey all international laws governing merchant ships on the high seas. Although Wilson's policy had not been a complete success, his partial success formed the basis of his 1916 campaign pledge: "He Kept Us Out of War."

Wilson's 1916 Republican presidential opponent was CHARLES EVANS HUGHES, who ran a formidable campaign and almost won. But the Progressive Party's HIRAM WARREN JOHNSON controlled the California governor's office, and he opposed Hughes. Given this split, the California vote was extremely close and was decided by only a handful of votes delivered by wagon train through a snowstorm to the nearest county balloting station. Wilson carried that little town of Wilsonia (later named after the president) and thereby the state of California, earning him enough Electoral College votes to be reelected.

The war in Europe continued. The Germans were being starved by the British blockade and decided they had to renew unrestricted submarine warfare, even if it meant provoking the United States to enter the war. After the Germans renewed unrestricted submarine warfare, more U.S. citizens were killed as German submarines torpedoed more merchant ships. Wilson then asked Congress for a declaration of war and got it.

Wilson chose General Pershing to lead the U.S. forces, which were not subordinated to either British or French command. Wilson pushed an army draft through Congress by a very narrow margin. He also persuaded the Congress to allow him to seize and run the railroads. He named Bernard Baruch the head of a special office to manage U.S. wartime economic mobilization and placed HERBERT CLARK HOOVER in charge of U.S. food production.

When U.S. strength was added to that of Britain and France, Germany was defeated. Having provided the critical military strength needed for victory, Wilson then thought he could dictate a peace treaty based on his famous Fourteen Points. Under the Fourteen Points, future international law was to be governed by "open covenants openly arrived at," freedom of the seas, equal trade arrangements, removal of economic barriers, arms reduction, impartial resolution of colonial disputes, and a variety of territorial adjustments based on the notion of national self-determination. Above all, international peace was to be achieved through the establishment of a new international organization called the League of Nations.

To make sure his plans were adopted, Wilson decided to attend the Paris peace conference in person—the first time a sitting U.S. president had traveled to Europe. Apparently, his second wife, EDITH BOLLING GALT WILSON, also pushed him to go as long as he took her along. Wilson also decided he could negotiate a peace treaty based on his Fourteen Points only if he conducted the negotiations without interference from his domestic political opponents in the U.S. Senate. This meant giving up the opportunity to co-opt the senators into supporting the peace treaty he negotiated and risked making then angry. Excluding senators, particularly for the opposite political party, proved to be a fatal mistake.

In Paris, Wilson was overwhelmed by the outpouring of affection and the cheers of the crowds, but that did not mean the leaders of the victorious nations were prepared to accept Wilson dictating a peace treaty based on his Fourteen Points. Despite his strong bargaining position, he was forced to back down on point after point in the context of the rival European factions. Winning even part of what he wanted was exhausting.

When Wilson returned home, he discovered that many Republican and Democratic political opponents had united to oppose his peace plan. They feared that joining the League of Nations would mean the United States would then be frequently involved in bloody European wars. A U.S. treaty may be adopted only with the affirmative advice and consent of two-thirds of the U.S. Senate, so any significant opposition is dangerous because it takes only one-third plus one (or 33 of the 96 senators in 1919) to block a treaty.

Undeterred by the opposition, Wilson began a whirlwind cross-country speaking tour by train to build popular support for his peace treaty and to force the Senate to adopt it. Wilson's political opponents had already begun attacking the treaty and sent their supporters to give speeches opposing

the president's plan. Despite all this opposition, Wilson's tour seemed to pay off. Wilson started out facing extremely hostile crowds, but he found that the longer he traveled and the more he spoke the greater enthusiasm he engendered. In fact, he had probably turned the corner on public opinion when he reached the West Coast.

However, the strain was growing. In his first term, he brilliantly fought and won exhausting domestic political battles. During the second, he fought a major war—second only to the Civil War in its impact on the county. He wore himself down further in difficult peace negotiations in Paris. Finally, he traveled by train across the entire United States, making dozens of speeches, preparing a new speech for every stop, and typing them all himself. Ultimately, his health gave way.

On the second leg of the trip back to Washington, he continued to make speaking stops along the way. Outside of Pueblo, Colorado, the president felt ill, and his aides stopped the train so he could get off to get some fresh air. His condition was far more serious than a need for fresh air; he had suffered a paralyzing stroke. Wilson's wife, Edith Wilson, then took charge, canceling all future speaking engagements and ordering the train back to Washington. Allowing only Dr. Grayson, the president's personal physician, real access to the president, Edith Wilson took charge of his health and the public announcements concerning it. She ordered Wilson's most immediate aides to cover up the seriousness of the president's illness by suggesting the president had the flu, and she forced them to keep up this pretense for months, until the notion of such a lengthy battle with the flu became unbelievable.

Had she candidly admitted what happened to Wilson, his program for the League of Nations might have been carried on a wave of sympathy for the heroic, fallen president. Alternatively, if Wilson had, through Mrs. Wilson, compromised some of the treaty terms most offensive to the Senate, Wilson could still have gained the senatorial agreement without losing any significant international support. Indeed, both the British and French governments indicated their willingness to modify the treaty's terms to achieve Senate approval. Wilson, paralyzed and rigidly clinging to his own formula, refused to the end. The treaty that included the league proposal was deadlocked and finally killed. The treaty without America's involvement in the League of Nations was ultimately approved.

For his efforts for world peace, Wilson was awarded the 1919 Nobel Peace Prize. He hoped to run for reelection to a third term in 1920, but his health ruled that out. In his place, the Democrats nominated Ohio's progressive governor, JAMES MIDDLETON COX, for president and Wilson's assistant secretary of the navy, FRANKLIN DELANO ROOSEVELT, for vice president. These two carried the Wilson plan courageously but futilely into the presidential general election against future President WARREN GAMALIEL HARDING. Wilson left the White House and moved into a small home in Washington where he remained an invalid. He died on February 3, 1924.

In Wilson's first term, he was an innovative domestic reformer, whose changes in U.S. politics affected a generation. In his second term, he was also an outstanding wartime president who produced a victory in about 18 months. He also crafted a peace treaty containing many of the principles of international organization currently used in the United Nations. As a southerner at heart, he reintroduced segregation into the armed forces and took no steps to end segregation anywhere in the nation. Despite his clear understanding of the importance of freedom of expression and civil liberties, he allowed Attorney General A. Mitchell Palmer and his young aide, JOHN EDGAR HOOVER, to prosecute left-wing political figures, including nationally recognized socialist leader Eugene V. Debs, for their political ideas. The Supreme Court ultimately overturned some of these convictions. But why Wilson's administration allowed the prosecutions in the first place is unclear, although perhaps his illness and diminished capabilities offer part of the answer. Nonetheless, Wilson's accomplishments normally result in his being ranked fairly high among all American presidents.

Further Reading

Ambrosius, Lloyd E. *Wilsonian Statecraft: Theory and Practice of Liberal Internationalism During World War I*. Wilmington, Del.: SR Books, 1991.

Auchincloss, Louis. *Woodrow Wilson: A Penguin Life*. New York: Viking Penguin, 2000.

Blum, John Morton. *The Progressive Presidents: Roosevelt, Wilson, Roosevelt, Johnson*. New York: Norton, 1982.

———. *Woodrow Wilson and the Politics of Morality*. New York: HarperCollins, 1990.

Calhoun, Frederick S. *Power and Principle: Armed Intervention in Wilsonian Foreign Policy*. Kent, Ohio: Kent State University Press, 1986.

Clements, Kendrick A. *Woodrow Wilson: World Statesman*. Chicago: Ivan R. Dee, 1999.

Cooper, John Milton. *The Warrior and the Priest: Woodrow Wilson and Theodore Roosevelt*. Cambridge, Mass.: Belknap Press of Harvard University Press, 1983.

Esposito, David M. *The Legacy of Woodrow Wilson: American War Aims in World War I*. Westport, Conn.: Praeger, 1996.

Ferrell, Robert H. *Woodrow Wilson and World War I, 1917–1921*. New York: Harper & Row, 1985.

Gardner, Lloyd C. *Safe for Democracy: Anglo-American Response to Revolution, 1913–1923*. New York: Oxford University Press, 1984.

Hoover, Herbert. *The Ordeal of Woodrow Wilson*. New York: Mcgraw-Hill, 1958; Baltimore: Johns Hopkins University Press, reprint 1992.

Knock, Thomas J. *To End All Wars: Woodrow Wilson and the Quest for a New World Order*. Princeton, N.J.: Princeton University Press, 1995.

Link, Arthur Stanley, ed. *The Papers of Woodrow Wilson*. Princeton, N.J.: Princeton University Press, 1966.

———. *The Diplomacy of World Power: The United States, 1889–1920*. London: Edward Arnold, 1970.

———. *The Higher Realism of Woodrow Wilson*. Nashville, Tenn.: Vanderbilt University Press, 1971.

———. *The Impact of World War I*. New York, Harper, 1969.

———. *Woodrow Wilson and the Progressive Era, 1910–1917*. New York: Harper & Row, 1963.

———. *Wilson*. Princeton, N.J.: Princeton University Press, 1968.

———. *Woodrow Wilson: Revolution, War, and Peace*. Arlington Heights, Ill.: AHM Publishing Corporation, 1979.

———. *Wilson: The Diplomatist*. Chicago: Quadrangle, 1965.

Mulder, John M. *Woodrow Wilson: The Years of Preparation*. Princeton, N.J.: Princeton University Press, 1978.

Ninkovich, Frank A. *The Wilsonian Century: U.S. Foreign Policy Since 1900.* Chicago: University of Chicago Press, 1999.

Randolph, Sallie G. *Woodrow Wilson: President.* New York: Walker, 1992.

Schild, Georg. *Between Ideology and Realpolitik: Woodrow Wilson and the Russian Revolution, 1917–1921.* Westport, Conn.: Greenwood Press, 1995.

Schulte Nordholt, J. W. *Woodrow Wilson: A Life for World Peace.* Berkeley: University of California Press, 1991.

Smith, Gene. *When the Cheering Stopped.* New York: Morrow, 1964.

Steigerwald, David. *Wilsonian Idealism in America.* Ithaca, N.Y.: Cornell University Press, 1994.

Walworth, Arthur. *Woodrow Wilson.* Norwalk, Conn.: Easton Press, 1985.

"Wilson, Woodrow." Available online. URL: http://www.whitehouse.gov/history/presidents/ww29.html. Downloaded November 11, 2001.

Bibliography and Recommended Sources

Asbell, Bernard. *The Senate Nobody Knows.* Baltimore, Md.: Johns Hopkins University Press, 1981.

Baker, Richard A., and Roger Davidson, eds. *First Among Equals: Senate Leaders of the 20th Century.* Washington, D.C.: Congressional Quarterly, 1991.

Baker, Ross K. *House and Senate: Second Edition.* New York: Norton, 1995.

Bennett, Anthony J. *The American President's Cabinet.* New York: St. Martin's Press, 1995.

Blum, John Morton. *The Progressive Presidents: Roosevelt, Wilson, Roosevelt, Johnson.* New York: Norton, 1982.

Bowman, John S. *The Cambridge Dictionary of American Biography.* New York: Cambridge University Press, 1995.

Browne, Ray B. *Contemporary Heroes and Heroines.* Detroit, Mich: Gale Research, 1990.

Catton, Bruce. *The American Heritage New History of the Civil War.* New York: Viking, 1996.

Chafe, William H. *The Paradox of Change: American Women in the Twentieth Century.* New York: Oxford University Press, 1991.

Concise Dictionary of American Biography. New York: Scribner's, 1997.

Contemporary Black Dictionary: Profiles from the International Black Community. Detroit, Mich.: Gale Group, 2001.

Cronin, Thomas E., and Michael A. Genovese. *The Paradoxes of the American Presidency.* New York: Oxford University Press, 1998.

Current Biography. New York: H. W. Wilson, 1940 to present.

Cushman, Clare, ed. *The Supreme Court Justices: Illustrated Biographies: Second Edition.* Washington, D.C.: Congressional Quarterly, 1991.

Davidson, Roger. *Congress and Its Members: Seventh Edition.* Washington, D.C.: Congressional Quarterly, 1991.

Degregorio, William A. *The Complete Book of the U.S. Presidents.* New York: Wing Books, 1984.

Dictionary of American Biography. New York: Charles Scribner's Sons, 1996.

Friedman, Leon, and Fred L. Israel, eds. *Justices of the United States Supreme Court, 1789 to 1991: Their Lives and Major Opinions,* 5 vols. New York: Chelsea House, revised edition, 1969–1995.

Gaddis, John Lewis. *The United States and the Origins of the Cold War, 1941–1947.* New York: Columbia University Press, 1972.

Garcia, Mario T. *Mexican Americans: Leadership, Ideology, and Identity, 1930–1960.* New Haven, Conn.: Yale University Press.

Garraty, John A., and Mark C. Carnes. *American National Biography.* New York: Oxford University Press, 1999.

Goldstein, Leslie F. *In Defense of the Text: Democracy and Constitutional Theory.* Lanham, Md: Rowman & Littlefield, 1991.

Gosnell, Harold Foote. *Negro Politicians: The Rise of Negro Politics in Chicago.* Chicago: University of Chicago Press, 1967.

Graff, Henry F., ed. *The Presidents: A Reference History: Second Edition.* New York: Scribner's, 1996.

Hall, Kermit L., ed. *The Oxford Companion to the Supreme Court.* New York: Oxford University Press, 1992.

Hernon, Joseph Martin. *Profiles in Character: Hubris and Heroism in the U.S. Senate—1789–1990.* Armonk, N.Y.: M. E. Sharpe, 1997.

Hess, Stephen. *Presidents and the Presidency.* Washington, D.C.: Brookings Institution, 1996.

Hofstadter, Richard. *The Age of Reform: From Bryan to F.D.R.* New York: Knopf, 1955.

———. *The American Political Tradition and the Men Who Made It.* New York: Vintage, reprint, 1989.

Horowitz, Morton. *The Transformation of American Law 1780 to 1860.* New York: Oxford University Press, 1992.

James, Edward T., and Janet Wilson James. *Notable American Women, 1607 to 1950: A Biographical Dictionary.* Cambridge, Mass.: Belknap Press, 1971.

Kane, Joseph N. *Facts about the Presidents: A Compilation of Biographical and Historical Information from George Washington to Bill Clinton: Sixth Edition.* New York: H. W. Wilson, 1993.

Kaptur, Marcy. *Women of Congress.* Washington, D.C.: Congressional Quarterly, 1996.

Kennedy, John Fitzgerald. *Profiles in Courage.* New York: Pocket Books, 1957.

Kluger, Richard. *Simple Justice: The History of Brown v. Board of Education and Black America's Struggle for Equality.* New York: Random House, 1977.

Kunhardt, Philip B., Jr., Philip B. Kunhardt III, and Peter W. Kunhardt. *The American President.* New York: Riverhead Books, 1999.

Levy, Leonard W., and Louis Fisher, ed. *Encyclopedia of the American Presidency.* New York: Simon & Schuster, 1994.

Lewis, Thomas T., and Richard L. Wilson. *Encyclopedia of the Supreme Court,* 3 vols. Pasadena, Calif.: Salem Press, 2001.

Logan, Rayford W., and Michael R. Winston. *Biographical Dictionary of American Negro Biography.* New York: Norton, 1982.

Loomis, Burdett A., ed. *Esteemed Colleagues: Civility and Deliberation in the U.S. Senate.* Washington, D.C.: Brookings Institution, 2000.

Lorant, Stefan. *The Glorious Burden: The American Presidency.* Lenox, Mass.: Author's Editions, 1976.

Magill, Frank N., John L. Loos, and Tracy Irons-Georges, eds. *The American Presidents.* Pasadena, Calif.: Salem Press, 2000.

Martin, Fenton S., and Robert Goehlert. *How to Research the Presidency.* Washington, D.C.: Congressional Quarterly, 1996.

Michaels, Judith E. *The President's Call: Executive Leadership from FDR to George Bush.* Pittsburgh: University of Pittsburgh Press, 1997.

Miles, Johnnie H., Juanita J. Davis, Sharon E. Ferguson-Roberts, and Rita Giles. *Almanac of African-American History.* Paramus, N.J.: Prentice Hall, 2001.

National Cyclopedia of American Biography. Clifton, N.J.: James T. White, 1984.

Nelson, Michael T., ed. *The Presidency A to Z: Second Edition.* Washington, D.C.: Congressional Quarterly Press, 1998.

Ness, Immanuel, and James Ciment, eds. *The Encyclopedia of Third Parties in America.* Armonk, N.Y.: M. E. Sharpe, 2000.

Neustadt, Richard E. *Presidential Power and the Modern Presidents: The Politics of Leadership from Roosevelt and Reagan: Fourth Edition.* New York: Free Press, 1990.

Peters, Ronald M., Jr., ed. *The Speaker: Leadership in the U.S. House of Representatives.* Washington, D.C.: Congressional Quarterly Press, 1995.

Ragsdale, Bruce A. *Black Americans in Congress, 1870 to 1989.* Washington, D.C.: U.S. Government Printing Office, 1996.

Ragsdale, Lyn. *Vital Statistics on the Presidency: Washington to Clinton.* Washington, D.C.: Congressional Quarterly Press, 1996.

Rehnquist, William H. *Grand Inquests: The Historic Impeachments of Justice Samuel Chase and President Andrew Johnson.* New York: Morrow, 1992.

Rennert, Richard Scott, ed. *Female Leaders.* New York: Chelsea House, 1993.

Salmore, Stephen A., and Barbara G. Salmore. *Candidate, Parties, and Campaigns: Electoral Politics in America.* Washington, D.C.: Congressional Quarterly, 1989.

Schlesinger, Arthur M., Jr., ed. *History of U.S. Political Parties: Four Volumes.* New York: Chelsea House, 1981.

Schwartz, Bernard. *A History of the Supreme Court.* New York: Oxford University Press, 1993.

Sicherman, Barbara, and Carol Hurd Green. *Notable American Women: The Modern Period: A Biographical Dictionary.* Cambridge, Mass.: Belknap Press, 1980.

Smith, Gene. *When the Cheering Stopped.* New York: Morrow, 1964.

Smith, Jessie Carney. *Notable Black American Women.* Detroit, Mich.: Gale Research, 1992.

Smith, Steven S. *The American Congress.* Boston: Houghton Mifflin, 1995.

Swain, Carol M. *Black Faces, Black Interests: Representation of African Americans in Congress.* Cambridge, Mass.: Harvard University Press, 1995.

Tarr, David R., and Ann O'Connor, eds. *Congress A to Z: Third Edition.* Washington, D.C.: Congressional Quarterly, 1999.

Telgen, Diane, and Jim Kamp, eds. *Notable Hispanic American Women.* Detroit, Mich.: Gale Research, 1993.

Thomas, Norman C., Joseph A. Pitka, and Richard Watson. *The Politics of the Presidency: Fourth Edition.* Washington, D.C.: Congressional Quarterly Press, 1997.

Witt, Linda, Karen M. Paget, and Glenna Matthews. *Running as a Woman: Gender and Power in American Politics.* New York: Free Press, 1993.

Entries by Offices Held or Sought

PRESIDENT
Adams, John
Adams, John Quincy
Arthur, Chester Alan
Buchanan, James
Bush, George Herbert Walker
Bush, George Walker
Carter, James Earl
Cleveland, Stephen Grover
Clinton, William Jefferson
Coolidge, Calvin
Eisenhower, Dwight David
Fillmore, Millard
Ford, Gerald Rudolph
Garfield, James Abram
Grant, Ulysses S.
Harding, Warren Gamaliel
Harrison, Benjamin
Harrison, William Henry
Hayes, Rutherford Birchard
Hoover, Herbert Clark
Jackson, Andrew
Jefferson, Thomas
Johnson, Andrew
Johnson, Lyndon Baines
Kennedy, John Fitzgerald
Lincoln, Abraham
Madison, James
McKinley, William
Monroe, James
Nixon, Richard Milhous
Pierce, Franklin
Polk, James Knox

Reagan, Ronald Wilson
Roosevelt, Franklin Delano
Roosevelt, Theodore
Taft, William Howard
Taylor, Zachary
Truman, Harry S.
Tyler, John
Van Buren, Martin
Washington, George
Wilson, Thomas Woodrow

VICE PRESIDENT
Adams, John
Agnew, Spiro Theodore
Arthur, Chester Alan
Barkley, Alben William
Breckinridge, John Cabell
Burr, Aaron
Bush, George Herbert Walker
Calhoun, John Caldwell
Clinton, George
Colfax, Schuyler
Coolidge, Calvin
Curtis, Charles
Fillmore, Millard
Ford, Gerald Rudolph
Garner, John Nance
Gerry, Elbridge
Gore, Albert Arnold, Jr.
Humphrey, Hubert Horatio
Jefferson, Thomas
Johnson, Andrew
Johnson, Lyndon Baines

Nixon, Richard Milhous
Rockefeller, Nelson Aldrich
Roosevelt, Theodore
Truman, Harry S.
Tyler, John
Van Buren, Martin

UNSUCCESSFUL CANDIDATE FOR PRESIDENT OR VICE PRESIDENT
Anderson, John Bayard
Bell, John
Birney, James Gillespie
Blaine, James Gillespie
Bland, Richard Parks
Breckinridge, John Cabell
Bryan, William Jennings
Butler, Benjamin Franklin
Clark, James Beauchamp
Clay, Henry
Clinton, DeWitt
Cox, James Middleton
Dewey, Thomas Edmund
Dole, Elizabeth Hanford
Dole, Robert Joseph
Douglas, Stephen Arnold
Frémont, John Charles
Goldwater, Barry Morris
Gore, Albert Arnold, Jr.
Greeley, Horace
Hughes, Charles Evans
Humphrey, Hubert Horatio
Kennedy, Edward Moore

London, Meyer
Longworth, Nicholas
Lott, Chester Trent
Madison, James
Mansfield, Michael Joseph
Marcantonio, Vito Anthony
Marshall, John
Martin, Joseph William, Jr.
McCain, John
McCarthy, Eugene Joseph
McCormack, John William
McGovern, George Stanley
McKinley, William
Nixon, Richard Milhous
Norris, George William
O'Neill, Thomas Philip, Jr.
Pelosi, Nancy d'Alesandro
Pepper, Claude Denson
Pickering, Timothy
Pierce, Franklin
Pinchback, Pinckney Benton
    Stewart
Pinckney, Thomas
Polk, James Knox
Powell, Adam Clayton, Jr.
Rankin, Jeannette
Rayburn, Samuel Taliaferro
Reed, Thomas Brackett
Ros-Lehtinen, Ileana
Smith, Margaret Chase
Stevens, Thaddeus
Tyler, John
Webster, Daniel

SECRETARY OF A MAJOR PRESIDENTIAL CABINET DEPARTMENT

Acheson, Dean Gooderham
Adams, John Quincy
Albright, Madeleine Korbell
Baker, James Addison III
Baker, Newton Diehl
Ballinger, Richard Achilles
Belknap, William Worth
Bell, John
Blaine, James Gillespie
Bryan, William Jennings

Buchanan, James
Byrnes, James Francis
Calhoun, John Caldwell
Cameron, Simon
Chase, Salmon Portland
Cisneros, Henry
Clay, Henry
Clifford, Clark McAdams
Daugherty, Harry Micajah
Davis, Jefferson
Denby, Edwin
Dole, Elizabeth Hanford
Dulles, John Foster
Fall, Albert Bacon
Farley, James Aloysius
Haig, Alexander Mcigs
Hamilton, Alexander
Hoover, Herbert Clark
Hopkins, Harry Lloyd
Hughes, Charles Evans
Hull, Cordell
Jefferson, Thomas
Kellogg, Frank Billings
Kennedy, Robert Francis
Kissinger, Henry Alfred
Knox, Henry
Lansing, Robert
Madison, James
Marshall, John
McNamara, Robert Strange
Monroe, James
Muskie, Edmund Sixtus
Perkins, Frances
Pickering, Timothy
Randolph, Edmund
Rogers, William Pierce
Root, Elihu
Rusk, David Dean
Schurz, Carl
Seward, William Henry
Shultz, George Pratt
Stanton, Edwin McMasters
Stimson, Henry Lewis
Taft, William Howard
Taney, Roger Brooke
Van Buren, Martin
Vance, Cyrus Roberts
Webster, Daniel

SENATOR

Aldrich, Nelson Wilmarth
Atchison, David Rice
Baker, Howard Henry, Jr.
Barkley, Alben William
Bell, John
Benjamin, Judah Philip
Benton, Thomas Hart
Beveridge, Albert Jeremiah
Black, Hugo LaFayette
Blaine, James Gillespie
Borah, William Edgar
Breckinridge, John Cabell
Brooke, Edward William
Bruce, Blanche Kelso
Buchanan, James
Burr, Aaron
Byrnes, James Francis
Calhoun, John Caldwell
Cameron, Simon
Campbell, Ben Nighthorse
Carmack, Edward Ward
Chase, Salmon Portland
Clay, Henry
Clinton, DeWitt
Clinton, Hillary Rodham
Conkling, Roscoe
Curtis, Charles
Daschle, Thomas
Davis, Jefferson
Dirksen, Everett McKinley
Dole, Robert Joseph
Douglas, Stephen Arnold
Dulles, John Foster
Ellsworth, Oliver
Ervin, Samuel James, Jr.
Fall, Albert Bacon
Frémont, John Charles
Fulbright, James William
Goldwater, Barry Morris
Gore, Albert Arnold, Jr.
Hanna, Mark Alonzo
Harding, Warren Gamaliel
Harrison, Benjamin
Harrison, William Henry
Hull, Cordell
Humphrey, Hubert Horatio

Inouye, Daniel Ken
Jackson, Andrew
Johnson, Andrew
Johnson, Hiram Warren
Johnson, Lyndon Baines
Kassebaum, Nancy Landon
Kefauver, Estes Corey
Kellogg, Frank Billings
Kennedy, Edward Moore
Kennedy, John Fitzgerald
Kennedy, Robert Francis
La Follette, Robert Marion
Lee, Richard Henry
Lodge, Henry Cabot, Jr.
Long, Huey Pierce
Lott, Chester Trent
Mansfield, Michael Joseph
McCain, John
McCarthy, Eugene Joseph
McCarthy, Joseph Raymond
McGovern, George Stanley
Monroe, James
Morse, Wayne Lyman
Moseley-Braun, Carol
Moynihan, Daniel Patrick
Muskie, Edmund Sixtus
Nixon, Richard Milhous
Norris, George William
Nye, Gerald Prentice
Pepper, Claude Denson
Pickering, Timothy
Pierce, Franklin
Pinchback, Pinckney Benton
    Stewart
Revels, Hiram Rhoades
Root, Elihu
Schurz, Carl
Seward, William Henry
Smith, Margaret Chase
Sumner, Charles
Thurmond, John Strom
Truman, Harry S.
Tyler, John
Van Buren, Martin
Vandenberg, Arthur Hendrick
Wade, Benjamin Franklin
Wagner, Robert Ferdinand

Webster, Daniel
Wheeler, Burton Kendell

GOVERNOR
Adams, Samuel
Adams, Sherman
Agnew, Spiro Theodore
Bush, George Walker
Byrnes, James Francis
Carter, James Earl
Cleveland, Stephen Grover
Clinton, George
Clinton, William Jefferson
Coolidge, Calvin
Cox, James Middleton
Dewey, Thomas Edmund
Dickinson, John
Gerry, Elbridge
Hancock, John
Hayes, Rutherford Birchard
Henry, Patrick
Hughes, Charles Evans
Jay, John
Jefferson, Thomas
Johnson, Andrew
Johnson, Hiram Warren
La Follette, Robert Marion
Landon, Alfred Mossman
Long, Huey Pierce
McClellan, George Brinton
Murphy, Frank
Muskie, Edmund Sixtus
Pierce, Franklin
Pinchot, Gifford
Pinckney, Thomas
Reagan, Ronald Wilson
Rockefeller, Nelson Aldrich
Roosevelt, Franklin Delano
Roosevelt, Theodore
Seward, William Henry
Smith, Alfred Emanuel
Stevenson, Adlai Ewing
Thurmond, John Strom
Tilden, Samuel Jones
Van Buren, Martin
Wallace, George Corley
Warren, Earl
Wilson, Thomas Woodrow

SUBCABINET OFFICIAL INCLUDING AGENCY, DEPARTMENT, BUREAU, OR COMMISSION HEAD, NATIONAL SECURITY ADVISOR, AND PRESIDENTIAL ADVISER
Arnold, Thurman
Baker, James Addison III
Biddle, Nicholas
Brzezinski, Zbigniew Kazimierz
Bush, George Herbert Walker
Casey, William Joseph
Douglas, William Orville
Dulles, Allen Welsh
Ehrlichman, John
Greenspan, Alan
Haldeman, Harry Robbins
Hoover, John Edgar
Kennedy, Joseph P.
Kissinger, Henry Alfred
McGovern, George Stanley
McNamara, Robert Strange
Morse, Wayne Lyman
Pinchot, Gifford
Rehnquist, William Hubbs
Roosevelt, Franklin Delano
Roosevelt, Theodore
Scalia, Antonin

DIPLOMAT
Adams, Charles Francis
Adams, John
Adams, John Quincy
Albright, Madeleine Korbell
Biddle, Nicholas
Buchanan, James
Bush, George Herbert Walker
Cameron, Simon
Dulles, Allen Welsh
Dulles, John Foster
Ellsworth, Oliver
Gadsden, James
Gerry, Elbridge
Goldberg, Arthur Joseph
Hoover, Herbert Clark
Hopkins, Harry Lloyd
House, Edward Mandell

Jay, John
Jefferson, Thomas
Kellogg, Frank Billings
Kennedy, Joseph Patrick, Sr.
Kirkpatrick, Jeane Duane Jordan
Lansing, Robert
Lodge, Henry Cabot, Jr.
Mansfield, Michael Joseph
McCloy, John Jay
Monroe, James
Moynihan, Daniel Patrick
Pinckney, Charles Cotesworth
Pinckney, Thomas
Roosevelt, Anna Eleanor
Rusk, David Dean
Schurz, Carl
Stevenson, Adlai Ewing
Stimson, Henry Lewis
Vance, Cyrus Roberts

FIRST LADY
Clinton, Hillary Rodham

Roosevelt, Anna Eleanor
Wilson, Edith Bolling Galt

REVOLUTIONARY WAR LEADER AND/OR COLONIAL LEADER
Adams, John
Adams, Samuel
Bradford, William
Burr, Aaron
Chase, Samuel
Clinton, George
Dickinson, John
Gerry, Elbridge
Hamilton, Alexander
Hancock, John
Henry, Patrick
Jackson, Andrew
Jay, John
Jefferson, Thomas
Knox, Henry
Lee, Richard Henry
Madison, James

Marshall, John
Mason, George
Monroe, James
Paine, Thomas
Pickering, Timothy
Pinckney, Charles Cotesworth
Pinckney, Thomas
Rush, Benjamin
Washington, George

OFFICIALS OF THE CONFEDERATE STATES OF AMERICA
Atchison, David Rice
Benjamin, Judah Philip
Breckinridge, John Cabell
Davis, Jefferson
Tyler, John

ENTRIES BY YEAR OF BIRTH

1590–1719
Bradford, William

1720–1729
Adams, Samuel
Mason, George

1730–1739
Adams, John
Clinton, George
Dickinson, John
Hancock, John
Henry, Patrick
Lee, Richard Henry
Paine, Thomas
Washington, George

1740–1749
Chase, Samuel
Ellsworth, Oliver
Gerry, Elbridge
Jay, John
Jefferson, Thomas
Pickering, Timothy
Pinckney, Charles Cotesworth
Rush, Benjamin

1750–1759
Burr, Aaron
Hamilton, Alexander
Knox, Henry
Madison, James
Marshall, John

Monroe, James
Pinckney, Thomas
Randolph, Edmund

1760–1769
Adams, John Quincy
Clinton, DeWitt
Jackson, Andrew

1770–1779
Clay, Henry
Harrison, William Henry
Taney, Roger Brooke

1780–1789
Benton, Thomas Hart
Biddle, Nicholas
Calhoun, John Caldwell
Gadsden, James
Scott, Winfield
Taylor, Zachary
Van Buren, Martin
Webster, Daniel

1790–1799
Bell, John
Birney, James Gillespie
Buchanan, James
Cameron, Simon
Polk, James Knox
Stevens, Thaddeus
Tyler, John

1800–1809
Adams, Charles Francis
Atchison, David Rice
Chase, Salmon Portland
Davis, Jefferson
Fillmore, Millard
Johnson, Andrew
Lincoln, Abraham
Pierce, Franklin
Seward, William Henry
Wade, Benjamin Franklin

1810–1819
Banks, Nathaniel Prentiss
Benjamin, Judah Philip
Butler, Benjamin Franklin
Douglas, Stephen Arnold
Frémont, John Charles
Greeley, Horace
Stanton, Edwin McMasters
Sumner, Charles
Tiden, Samuel Jones

1820–1829
Belknap, William Worth
Breckinridge, John Cabell
Colfax, Schuyler
Conkling, Roscoe
Grant, Ulysses S.
Hayes, Rutherford Birchard
McClellan, George Brinton
Revels, Hiram Rhoades
Schurz, Carl

1830–1839
Arthur, Chester Alan
Blaine, James Gillespie
Bland, Richard Parks
Cannon, Joseph Gurney
Cleveland, Stephen Grover
Fuller, Melville Weston
Garfield, James Abram
Hanna, Mark Alonzo
Harlan, John Marshall
Harrison, Benjamin
Pinchback, Pinckney Benton
    Stewart
Reed, Thomas Brackett

1840–1849
Aldrich, Nelson Wilmarth
Bruce, Blanche Kelso
Holmes, Oliver Wendell, Jr.
McKinley, William
Root, Elihu

1850–1859
Ballinger, Richard Achilles
Brandeis, Louis Dembitz
Carmack, Edward Ward
Clark, James Beauchamp
House, Edward Mandell
Kellogg, Frank Billings
La Follette, Robert Marion
Roosevelt, Theodore
Taft, William Howard
Wilson, Thomas Woodrow

1860–1869
Berger, Victor Luitpold
Beveridge, Albert Jeremiah
Borah, William Edgar
Bryan, William Jennings
Byrns, Joseph Wellington
Curtis, Charles
Daugherty, Harry Micajah
Fall, Albert Bacon
Garner, John Nance
Harding, Warren Gamaliel
Hughes, Charles Evans
Johnson, Hiram Warren

Lansing, Robert
Longworth, Nicholas
Norris, George William
Pinchot, Gifford
Stimson, Henry Lewis

1870–1879
Baker, Newton Diehl
Bankhead, William
Barkley, Alben William
Byrnes, James Francis
Cardozo, Benjamin Nathan
Coolidge, Calvin
Cox, James Middleton
Denby, Edwin
De Priest, Oscar Stanton
Hoover, Herbert Clark
Hull, Cordell
London, Meyer
Smith, Alfred Emanuel
Wagner, Robert Ferdinand
Wilson, Edith Bolling Galt

1880–1889
Black, Hugo LaFayette
Dulles, John Foster
Farley, James Aloysius
Frankfurter, Felix
Kennedy, Joseph Patrick, Sr.
La Guardia, Fiorello Henry
Landon, Alfred Mossman
Martin, Joseph William, Jr.
Perkins, Frances
Rankin, Jeannette
Rayburn, Samuel Taliaferro
Roosevelt, Anna Eleanor
Roosevelt, Franklin Delano
Truman, Harry S.
Vandenberg, Arthur
Wheeler, Burton Kendell

1890–1899
Acheson, Dean Gooderham
Adams, Sherman
Arnold, Thurman Wesley
Dirksen, Everett McKinley
Douglas, William Orville

Dulles, Allen Welsh
Eisenhower, Dwight David
Ervin, Samuel James, Jr.
Hoover, John Edgar
Hopkins, Harry Lloyd
Long, Huey Pierce
McCloy, John Jay
McCormack, John William
Murphy, Frank
Nye, Gerald Prentice
Smith, Margaret Chase
Warren, Earl

1900–1909
Albert, Carl Bert
Blackmun, Harry Andrew
Brennan, William Joseph, Jr.
Burger, Warren
Clifford, Clark McAdams
Dewey, Thomas Edmund
Fulbright, James William
Goldberg, Arthur Joseph
Goldwater, Barry Morris
Johnson, Lyndon Baines
Kefauver, Estes Corey
Lodge, Henry Cabot, Jr.
Mansfield, Michael Joseph
Marcantonio, Vito Anthony
Marshall, Thurgood
McCarthy, Joseph Raymond
Morse, Wayne Lyman
Pepper, Claude Denson
Powell, Adam Clayton, Jr.
Rockefeller, Nelson Aldrich
Rusk, David Dean
Stevenson, Adlai Ewing
Thurmond, John Strom

1910–1919
Agnew, Spiro Theodore
Brooke, Edward William
Casey, William Joseph
Ford, Gerald Rudolph
Humphrey, Hubert Horatio
Kennedy, John Fitzgerald
McCarthy, Eugene Joseph
McNamara, Robert Strange

Muskie, Edmund Sixtus
Nixon, Richard Milhous
O'Neill, Thomas Philip, Jr.
Reagan, Ronald Wilson
Rogers, William Pierce
Vance, Cyrus Roberts
Wallace, George Corley

1920–1929
Abzug, Bella Savitsky
Anderson, John Bayard
Baker, Howard Henry, Jr.
Brzezinski, Zbigniew Kazimierz
Bush, George Herbert Walker
Carter, James Earl
Chisholm, Shirley Anita St. Hill
Dole, Robert Joseph
Ehrlichman, John
Greenspan, Alan
Haig, Alexander Meigs

Haldeman, Harry Robbins
Inouye, Daniel Ken
Kennedy, Robert Francis
Kirkpatrick, Jeane Duane Jordan
Kissinger, Henry Alfred
McGovern, George Stanley
Moynihan, Daniel Patrick
Rehnquist, William Hubbs
Shultz, George Pratt

1930–1939
Albright, Madeleine Korbell
Baker, James Addison III
Campbell, Ben Nighthorse
Dole, Elizabeth Hanford
Ferraro, Geraldine Anne
Jordan, Barbara Charline
Kassebaum, Nancy Landon
Kennedy, Edward Moore
McCain, John

O'Connor, Sandra Day
Perot, Henry Ross
Scalia, Antonin

1940–1949
Bush, George Walker
Cisneros, Henry
Clinton, Hillary Rodham
Clinton, William Jefferson
Daschle, Thomas
Gephardt, Richard Andrew
Gingrich, Newton Leroy
Gore, Albert Arnold, Jr.
Hastert, Dennis
Lott, Chester Trent
Moseley-Braun, Carol
Pelosi, Nancy d'Alesandro

1950–1959
Ros-Lehtinen, Ileana

INDEX

Boldface locators indicate main entries. *Italic* locators indicate photographs.